Basic Skills Curriculum

Reading • Writing • Math
and more basic skills for successful learning

Grade 8

YOU decide when to practice and what to practice!

Advantages of the Basic Skills Curriculum

Quality . . . as the nation's #1 educational publisher, the skills you practice are the skills taught in most classrooms.

Flexibility . . . you decide what skills to practice and when to practice, allowing you to follow the curriculum used in the classroom.

Price . . . more pages and more practice for fewer dollars than any other book of its' kind.

Test Taking Lessons . . . score better on achievement tests! No other book of this kind teaches children how to take standardized tests.

Published by McGraw-Hill Learning Materials, 1997

Contents

READING

by Anne Marie Mueser
John Alan Mueser

Project Editor: Sandra Kelley

Text: Design and Production by Harry Chester Associates

Illustrated by John W. Frost
Leonard B. Cole

THINGS TO REMEMBER ABOUT READING

Use these skills as you read.

DETAILS
Find and remember the important details.

SEQUENCE
Understand and remember the order in which things happens.

CONTEXT
To help you find the meaning of a word, use the words and sentences nearby.

MAIN IDEA
Put the details together and find the main idea.

INFERENCE
Find the meanings that are not stated, and draw conclusions.

CAUSE AND EFFECT
Understand what makes things happen and why.

PREDICTING OUTCOMES
Based on what you have read, tell what will happen next.

UNDERSTANDING CHARACTER
Find out about people through their words and actions.

Published by McGraw-Hill Learning Materials, 1997

DIRECTIONS

Do each step with a number. If you are working on speed of reading, do the steps with ★ too.

1. Find the right page.

★ Get a watch or timer. Start timing as soon as you begin to read.

2. Read the selection carefully. Be sure to read all of it.

3. Read the first item after the selection. Look at all the choices and then pick the best one. Mark your answer in the right space on your answer sheet.

	1	2	3	
1	a b c d	a b c d	a b c d	a
2	a b c d	a b c d	a b c d	a
3	a b c d	a b c d	a b c d	a

4. Do the rest of the items the same way you did the first one. Be sure to read all the choices before you pick and mark one.

★ Check your watch and stop timing. Write down the time it took you to complete the page.

5. Check your answers with the Answer Key. Write the number you got correct at the bottom of the page.

Answer Key

6. Mark the number you got right in the correct place on your Progress Plotter.

Progress Plotter

★ Mark your time in minutes on the Progress Plotter.

7. Find the correct place on the Skills Tracker for the page you have just finished. Circle the item number for any one you got wrong.

Skills Tracker

	1	2
Details	4	1, 2
Sequence	4	—
Context	2	4
Main Idea	1	—
Inference	3, 5, 6	3, 6
Cause & Effect	3	2
Pred. Outcomes	6	5
Underst. Char.	6	5, 6

8. If you got any items wrong, go back and try them again. Make sure you know how to do them. Ask your teacher if you still need help.

1

Have you ever seen a marmoset? This small monkey with enormous eyes and long white tufts of hair protruding from its ears is an appealing creature with soft fur of dark gray or brown.

The native home of the marmoset is the rain forests of South America, but since these animals are friendly and inexpensive to buy and feed, they are shipped world wide. Marmosets are excellent residents of zoos because they are easy to keep and their antics are entertaining to visitors.

Many medical laboratories throughout the world have discovered the usefulness of the marmoset as a laboratory subject. The marmoset is gradually taking the place of rats and mice in these laboratories because this little monkey is physically so much more like humans than the rodents are.

Marmosets usually have twins or triplets rather than single babies. The father marmoset carries his offspring about as they cling to his back. The mother only holds them at feeding time. Because humans didn't know about this unusual division of labor in the marmoset family, the first time marmosets were bred in captivity resulted in tragedy. Laboratory workers decided to move the father to another cage to make sure that he didn't injure the young ones. The adult marmoset who was not carrying the babies was moved. It wasn't long before the babies starved to death.

1. Marmosets are originally from
   (a) research labs.
   (b) experimentation.
   (c) rain forests.
   (d) North America.

2. This selection is mainly about
   (a) how to train monkeys.
   (b) doing experiments.
   (c) research scientists.
   (d) a small, useful monkey.

3. Examples of rodents are
   (a) cockroaches.
   (b) marmosets.
   (c) laboratory workers.
   (d) rats and mice.

4. Marmosets can now be found
   (a) in many doctor's offices.
   (b) in trees in city parks.
   (c) in many parts of the world.
   (d) only in rain forests.

5. The first caged marmoset babies starved because workers
   (a) fed them the wrong food.
   (b) frightened them.
   (c) forgot to feed them.
   (d) moved the mother by mistake.

6. A pair of marmosets
   (a) usually fight a lot.
   (b) run in opposite directions.
   (c) usually have twins or triplets.
   (d) go out with other monkeys.

7. Marmosets are used for research to
   (a) keep the workers entertained.
   (b) save the lives of rats.
   (c) test things for human use.
   (d) study ways of traveling.

8. You can guess that a marmoset would
   (a) eat its young alive.
   (b) be dangerous to small dogs.
   (c) make an interesting pet.
   (d) run away from any zoo.

Time __________ # Correct ______

2

One of the most unusual graduation speakers of the 1983 commencement season was not a person at all. The speaker was Robot Redford, a robot who delivered the commencement address at a community college in suburban Maryland.

The speaker, carefully programmed, arrived on the stage under its own power and proceeded to tell the audience of 685 graduates, their families, and friends that they would have to learn to work with robots and technology to solve society's problems. The robot described itself as an extension of a person to help humans increase the workload. Although this particular robot can be programmed to speak, the voice heard wasn't that of the robot, because it was feared that the robot's voice was not loud enough to carry throughout the hall. An amplified voice of a human was used instead, while the listeners watched the robot.

Robot Redford was followed by a person, William Bakaleinikoff, who spoke about the need for cooperation between people and technology. Mr. Bakaleinikoff's experience with his topic included the fact that he had created Robot Redford and had provided the voice for the robot's words to the graduates.

There was quite a bit of controversy over the choice of a robot as a commencement speaker. Some students thought it was insensitive and degrading to use a robot. Others thought the idea was clever and innovative.

"I'll never forget this speech," said one graduate. "You forget a political leader, but you won't forget a robot."

1. Robot Redford was a
   (a) handsome movie actor.
   (b) student at a college.
   (c) talking robot.
   (d) homework machine.

2. A robot is designed to
   (a) make humans unnecessary.
   (b) let humans do more work.
   (c) make graduation speeches.
   (d) cause lots of trouble.

3. Technology is
   (a) always done by robots.
   (b) too difficult for students.
   (c) applied science.
   (d) the study of human feelings.

4. The selection suggests that people
   (a) always dislike technology.
   (b) should cooperate with technology.
   (c) will be replaced by robots.
   (d) enjoy commencement speeches.

5. You can infer from this selection that
   (a) everyone understands technology.
   (b) many people own their own robots.
   (c) some people distrust technology.
   (d) every college needs a robot.

6. Something innovative is
   (a) unusually noisy.
   (b) new and different.
   (c) too expensive to buy.
   (d) often in the way.

7. Controversy is
   (a) talking together.
   (b) disagreement.
   (c) explanation.
   (d) modern poetry.

8. Robot Redford's speech was
   (a) the best ever given.
   (b) too long for most graduates.
   (c) unlikely to be forgotten.
   (d) too difficult to understand.

Time ________ # Correct ______

3

Imagine for a moment what it would be like if all the supermarkets, clothing stores, schools, doctors, and other things we take for granted just disappeared. Imagine that there were no established neighborhoods or towns. What would life be like? The early settlers of this country didn't know the luxury of having all these things available.

The Spanish women who came with their families from Mexico to the New Mexico territory long ago faced a life that was especially hard. They found no conveniences in their new land. They found nothing but empty country.

The Spanish settlers formed towns and set up ranches. Women had key roles in this society. They served as doctors and teachers and were responsible for the education of the children. They made many of the things they needed, including all their clothing. It was the wife of the patrón, or head of the ranch, to whom the workers came with news both good and bad. The patrón's wife was the first to learn of births and deaths, sicknesses or other misfortunes.

The ranches and towns were far from any medical doctors. The women used their knowledge of plant medicine, passed down from mother to daughter, to gather and use healing herbs and plants from the mountains. Some women were midwives and delivered babies born in the area.

Some of the women added new discoveries to their knowledge of healing remedies of old. For example, when smallpox broke out in the village of La Liendre, the wife of the patrón tried to convince the villagers to be vaccinated with the newly discovered serum. She managed to get the vaccine from her cousin, a doctor in El Paso. The people were very superstitious and didn't want to try this new mysterious medicine. So she became godmother to many of the village children, and in this role was able to have them vaccinated. Her value to the health and safety of the village was literally a matter of life and death.

1. The wife of the patrón was
   (a) married to the head of the ranch.
   (b) usually found in the kitchen.
   (c) one who had an easy life.
   (d) unable to make her own clothes.

2. The main idea of this selection is that women in early Spanish settlements
   (a) had to treat smallpox.
   (b) were confined to the home.
   (c) feared the men in their lives.
   (d) had important, lifesaving roles.

3. People first refused smallpox vaccinations
   (a) because smallpox wasn't serious.
   (b) in fear of something new.
   (c) because they cost too much.
   (d) as unnecessary medication.

4. Life in New Mexico's early days
   (a) had no modern conveniences.
   (b) was easy for most people.
   (c) required lots of cash.
   (d) centered around the school.

5. The women practiced medicine because
   (a) the men were unable to.
   (b) they couldn't afford doctors.
   (c) villages had too many babies.
   (d) doctors were far away.

6. A superstitious person
   (a) fears the mysterious or unknown.
   (b) is stronger than anyone else.
   (c) cooperates with everyone.
   (d) laughs out loud at things.

7. Midwives are people who
   (a) have husbands.
   (b) work on a ranch.
   (c) distrust doctors.
   (d) deliver babies.

8. Which came first?
   (a) The patron's wife got vaccine.
   (b) Smallpox hit La Liendre.
   (c) Children were vaccinated.
   (d) People refused vaccination.

Time ________ # Correct ______

4

A person, whom we'll call Mr. O, once stole a driver's license from another young man. The thief then had the misfortune to be critically injured in an automobile accident.

Unconscious and unable to communicate, Mr. O was transported to the nearest hospital, where doctors fought to save his life. The police, not realizing the identification had been stolen, notified the family of the youth whose license Mr. O was using.

For five months Mr. O remained in a hospital bed. He was virtually unidentifiable under the layers and layers of bandages. During this time, the other youth's parents visited the hospital often. They were glad to see that the person they thought was their son was alive and recovering. They brought many gifts to the mummylike young man. Mr. O, his head concealed by the layers of gauze, accepted the gifts without a word.

Mr. O would definitely have been better off if he had avoided all three of these things—stealing the license, having the accident, and accepting the gifts. When the bandages came off and the truth became apparent, Mr. O, on top of all his other troubles, was arrested and charged with fraud.

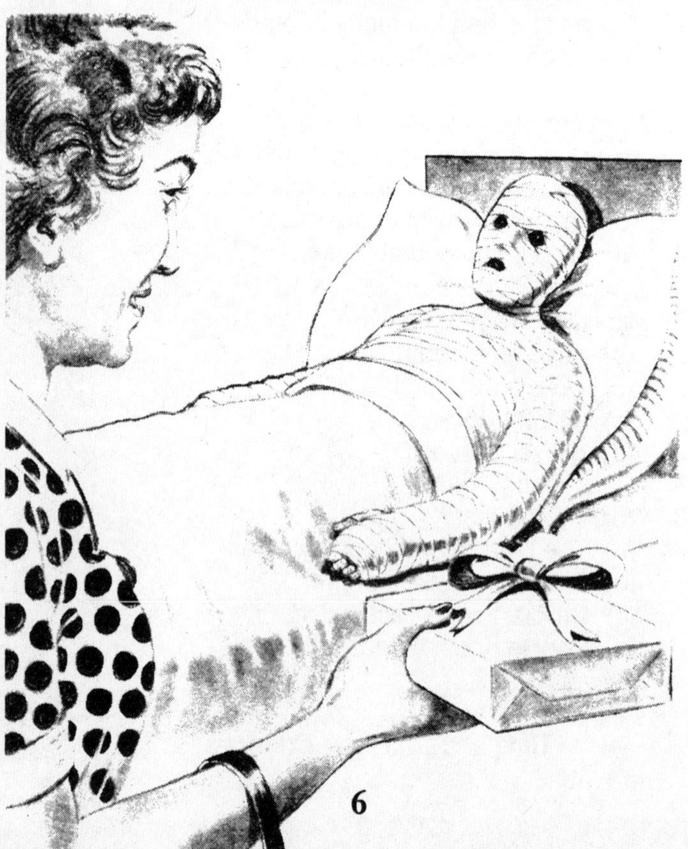

1. First, Mr. O
   (a) stole an automobile.
   (b) accepted gifts.
   (c) was charged with fraud.
   (d) stole a driver's license.

2. After the accident, the police called
   (a) the owners of the car.
   (b) the victim of the crash.
   (c) those they thought were family.
   (d) the nearest funeral home.

3. Mr. O was really
   (a) well-liked.
   (b) a dishonest person.
   (c) wealthy.
   (d) an excellent driver.

4. Another word for apparent is
   (a) relative.
   (b) obvious.
   (c) concealed.
   (d) entertaining.

5. The parents in this story
   (a) cared about their son.
   (b) were difficult to fool.
   (c) couldn't drive a car.
   (d) worked for the police.

6. Without the bandages, Mr. O
   (a) would have died immediately.
   (b) might have been caught sooner.
   (c) would have seen his family.
   (d) might have lost his sight.

7. To be charged with fraud is to
   (a) be sent directly to jail.
   (b) be accused of cheating.
   (c) injure one's parents.
   (d) steal an automobile.

8. After his recovery, Mr. O
   (a) was sent to his own mother.
   (b) probably went to jail.
   (c) bought a new car.
   (d) couldn't see his friends.

Time ________ # Correct _____

5

Over a period of several months, the police in Florida City, Florida, made numerous arrests of people charged with the unlawful possession and sale of marijuana. In each case, the marijuana had been confiscated by the police and held as evidence that a crime indeed had been committed. The marijuana was placed in a carefully locked room in the police station where the exact quantity for each case was carefully measured and noted. The marijuana was stored in this locked property room along with many other items needed for future court cases. At one point, the Florida City police were storing more than half a ton of marijuana leaves along with other stolen and confiscated property.

Someone noticed that the sizable quantity of marijuana was beginning to diminish. Then the supply vanished entirely. At first the police chief alleged that the culprits in the great marijuana disappearance were rats who were known to inhabit portions of the police station and the surrounding area. Rats are known to consume a wide variety of food items and not to be especially choosy about what they eat. So the loss of a half a ton of marijuana to ravenous rodents was not considered too far-fetched to be believed.

Some investigators, however, found the rat story more than they could swallow, so they pursued the matter further. Eventually, the rats in question were found to be human. A father and son who both worked in the police property office pleaded guilty to the theft of the marijuana. The two were sentenced to 15 years in the penitentiary.

1. This story tells that
   (a) marijuana is stored in bales.
   (b) Florida has a warm climate.
   (c) most police officers are honest.
   (d) marijuana is illegal in Florida.

2. To diminish means to
   (a) become smaller.
   (b) come to an end.
   (c) grow stale.
   (d) vanish completely.

3. Investigators are people who
   (a) cover up the entire truth.
   (b) ask questions and find evidence.
   (c) sell marijuana on the side.
   (d) work for the Chamber of Commerce.

4. A ravenous rodent is a
   (a) small mouse.
   (b) hungry rat.
   (c) dark furry creature.
   (d) small animal that smokes.

5. Which happened last?
   (a) The marijuana was confiscated.
   (b) Two men pleaded guilty.
   (c) Two people were sentenced.
   (d) The marijuana disappeared.

6. The main message of this story is
   (a) rats can get stoned.
   (b) keep your doors locked.
   (c) going to jail is tough.
   (d) crime does not pay.

7. The explanation that rats ate the pot
   (a) satisfied everyone.
   (b) was hard to believe.
   (c) explained the rats' behavior.
   (d) was found to be the truth.

8. The marijuana vanished because
   (a) the rats ate it.
   (b) the rodents carried it away.
   (c) it decayed and disappeared.
   (d) it was stolen.

Time ________ # Correct _____

6

Robin and Roger Van are the devoted owners of a pet basset hound named George. One day they decided to give George a bath. For the task they selected a cake of the most elegant, expensive, and fragrant bath soap they could find. Nothing was too good for their pet, not even a piece of their mother's most costly French toilet soap. George was the best lathered and most fragrantly perfumed hound in the neighborhood that day. No other canine creature smelled quite like George did.

The morning after the bath, the basset hound could be seen frantically digging a hole in the backyard lawn. His excavation apparently completed to his satisfaction, the dog dashed off and retrieved something. He returned to the hole, deposited the object, and methodically began to cover it up. When he had completely refilled the hole and buried the object safely below the ground's surface, George ceased his labors.

Never before had anyone in the Van family observed George digging and burying. He was usually too lazy even to bury a bone, and his atypical behavior really intrigued everyone. The family members, their curiosity aroused, did their own digging at the site of the canine excavation. What do you think they found there? Would you believe the bar of soap?

1. George was a
   (a) friend of the family.
   (b) very fragrant cat.
   (c) young bathgiver.
   (d) basset hound.

2. The soap used on George was made
   (a) to kill fleas.
   (b) especially for people.
   (c) by digging.
   (d) for bathing animals.

3. Which happened last?
   (a) George got a lovely bath.
   (b) The dog buried the soap.
   (c) George smelled like perfume.
   (d) The family dug up soap.

4. The "canine excavation" was a
   (a) place for bathing a dog.
   (b) remedy for a toothache.
   (c) site to bury George.
   (d) hole dug by the dog.

5. Something atypical is
   (a) unusual or rare.
   (b) done by machine.
   (c) common to dogs.
   (d) difficult to finish.

6. George buried the soap because he
   (a) needed digging practice.
   (b) knew his owners were watching.
   (c) wanted to keep it for next time.
   (d) disliked his bath so much.

7. The people dug up the soap to
   (a) repair the hole in the lawn.
   (b) find out what George had buried.
   (c) save buying another bar.
   (d) use it for their own baths.

8. A good title for this story would be
   (a) If You Can't Beat It, Bury It
   (b) Bathing Pet Dogs Quickly
   (c) Robin, Roger, George, and Alice
   (d) Let Sleeping Dogs Lie

Time ________ # Correct ______

7

Faith Materowski, born February 23, 1983, was the smallest newborn ever to survive birth at Hackensack Medical Center in New Jersey. In July she was able to go home with her family, and although she was not yet five months old, she had already become somewhat of a celebrity. News reporters and television cameras were on hand to record the happy event, and the little girl rewarded the attentive observers with a tiny glimmer of a smile.

Faith was born three months early, which is about as premature as an infant can be and still develop normally. Many babies that premature do not live much beyond birth or are severely handicapped. Faith weighed as little as one pound shortly after she arrived. She was so tiny that nurses made her comfortable on a miniature water bed which was constructed from a plastic sandwich bag. For the first three months after she was born, Faith required help to maintain respiration. On May 26, she was able to breathe on her own.

A few years ago, it would have been unheard of for a premature infant like Faith to live very long, if at all, after birth. Advances in the field of neonatology (care of the newborn), combined with baby Faith's incredibly strong constitution and supportive family, made the difference in this case.

Faith's parents chose the baby's name as a special symbol of their strong religious beliefs. They believed from the start that their faith would give them the strength to cope with the sometimes difficult demands of their premature daughter's early weeks. They knew that "Faith" was a perfect name for the little girl.

Faith has one older sister, Marina, age 11. Marina didn't seem to mind that the newborn was getting so much attention. She was delighted to have a little sister. Marina told reporters that she expected to be the baby-sitter.

1. Faith achieved early fame because
   (a) her parents are very wealthy.
   (b) she stars in a television show.
   (c) she survived against great odds.
   (d) people knew her sister.

2. A premature baby is one who
   (a) weighs less than six pounds.
   (b) is born before being ready.
   (c) cries through the night.
   (d) refuses to drink formula.

3. Babies as small as Faith
   (a) require extra blankets.
   (b) often die at birth.
   (c) cry very loudly.
   (d) sleep without breathing.

4. The Materowskis named the child
   (a) after her grandmother.
   (b) to show their faith.
   (c) for her sister.
   (d) as the doctors requested.

5. Which came first? Faith
   (a) went home for the first time.
   (b) met her sister Marina.
   (c) was born three months early.
   (d) took her first breath on her own.

6. This story is mainly about
   (a) feeding premature babies.
   (b) studying neonatology.
   (c) Hackensack General Hospital.
   (d) a premature baby who made it.

7. Nurses used a sandwich bag to
   (a) make Faith more comfortable.
   (b) wrap the diapers in.
   (c) hold the child's drinking water.
   (d) play water games.

8. You can tell that the Materowskis
   (a) enjoyed staying in the hospital.
   (b) love their daughter very much.
   (c) intend to have many children.
   (d) are good friends of a doctor.

Time ________ # Correct ______

8

Every day, people carrying animals and plants are stopped at American borders and ports of entry on the chance that exotic pests might be part of what they are trying to bring into the country. This action is taken by U.S. government officials in an effort to prevent the introduction of foreign species that could cause serious environmental disturbances. Every visitor or citizen reentering the country must submit to a U.S. Department of Agriculture inspection if he or she has been on a farm or ranch outside the U.S. or is carrying any plants, animals, or animal products. Strict quarantine laws are necessary to insure that health problems for our livestock and plants will not be imported accidentally or willfully.

We have learned the necessity for drastic controls the hard way. After a new pest arrives on the scene, corrective measures may be too late. The gypsy moth is an excellent example of this. This devastating insect, which now is eating its way through the forests of the northeastern United States, was deliberately imported to Massachusetts in 1869. The French naturalist who was responsible for bringing in the moths and who should have known better, was breeding silkworms and wanted to use the moths to strengthen his breeding stock. His experiment was worse than a total failure. Some of the moths escaped from the laboratory and reproduced. Their offspring have been defoliating our trees ever since.

1. Which happened first?
   (a) A Frenchman bred silkworms.
   (b) The need for quarantine was seen.
   (c) Moths escaped from a lab.
   (d) Gypsy moths were imported.

2. Willfully means
   (a) after death.
   (b) in a hurry.
   (c) defoliated.
   (d) on purpose.

3. Certain plants and animals are barred from entering the U.S. because
   (a) we have enough already.
   (b) they come from poor countries.
   (c) they could cause harm.
   (d) government agents need work.

4. Quarantine laws attempt to
   (a) raise funds for agriculture.
   (b) keep problems isolated.
   (c) prevent trafficking in drugs.
   (d) provide legal assistance.

5. The gypsy moth came to the U.S.
   (a) quite by accident.
   (b) to get out of France.
   (c) as food for small birds.
   (d) as part of an experiment.

6. This selection discusses the gypsy moth
   (a) to explain ailing silkworms.
   (b) as a reason to have quarantine laws.
   (c) because it has become popular.
   (d) in relation to industry.

7. Defoliating means
   (a) removing the wrapping.
   (b) melting the ice off.
   (c) taking all the leaves off.
   (d) curing diseased trees.

8. This selection suggests that
   (a) agricultural markets are many.
   (b) prevention of problems is best.
   (c) quarantine cures illness.
   (d) gypsy moths are good company.

Time ________ # Correct ______

9

For 75 years, Louise Morman had lived in the same house in Knox County, Tennessee. Mrs. Morman, a 93-year-old widow, was very poor, but despite her age and poverty she managed quite well. She had a fiercely independent spirit and wouldn't tolerate strangers minding her business.

In many places, an old person with low income can be exempt from paying property taxes. Unfortunately, the tax authorities in Knox County didn't know that Mrs. Morman was old and poor. All they knew was that the taxes on her house were overdue. So, they sold her house at public auction to pay the back taxes. A Tennessee businessman purchased the property for $690.

Mrs. Morman apparently knew nothing about the tax sale of her home. She continued to maintain residence there. The new buyer wanted her to move, but she refused to communicate with the people he sent to talk to her. Finally the buyer turned to the courts for assistance in moving Mrs. Morman out of the house which she no longer legally owned. The court ordered Mrs. Morman to move, and when she didn't, the sheriff evicted her. The old woman's furniture and personal effects were removed from the house and dumped in a weed-filled vacant lot across the street.

Newspapers all over the country told the story of the 93-year-old widow who had been put out of the only home she had known for three quarters of a century. Two days later, the buyer of the house decided to give it back to Mrs. Morman.

Why did the buyer have a sudden change of heart? No one knows for sure. County records at that time indicated that this same businessman owed back taxes on as many as 40 properties of his own in the county. In the city of Knoxville, records showed more than $15,000 overdue on some 38 properties. The glare of publicity certainly did not show the person in a favorable light. Mrs. Morman, however, cared little about the man's motives. She had her home again.

1. Louise Morman was a
   (a) very religious person.
   (b) friend of a businessman.
   (c) secure homeowner.
   (d) poor old widow.

2. The house was auctioned because
   (a) its owner didn't want it.
   (b) the taxes weren't paid.
   (c) it earned too much money.
   (d) the authorities liked it.

3. To be evicted means to
   (a) come out a winner.
   (b) be cheated.
   (c) be put out.
   (d) require covering.

4. Mrs. Morman was evicted because
   (a) the sheriff didn't like her.
   (b) she had sold her home.
   (c) she kept too many animals.
   (d) the court ordered it.

5. To tolerate is to
   (a) put up with.
   (b) fight with.
   (c) be independent.
   (d) stir up.

6. The buyer bought the house
   (a) as his personal residence.
   (b) to upset Mrs. Morman.
   (c) as an act of kindness.
   (d) as an investment.

7. The buyer of the house
   (a) knew Mrs. Morman personally.
   (b) worked for the government.
   (c) didn't always do what he should.
   (d) followed every law exactly.

8. Mrs. Morman didn't talk to the buyer's representatives because
   (a) they wouldn't talk to her.
   (b) the taxes were already paid.
   (c) the court told her not to.
   (d) she didn't know she had to.

Time ________ # Correct ______

10

Chances are, you have met dragons in books, but not in real life. The Komodo dragon is a large lizard—up to ten feet long—native to an island in the Indian Ocean. There are small lizards called flying dragons because they have winglike folds of skin which function as little parachutes. These, however, are not the dragons we're referring to. The ones we mean are those you'll find in stories and art.

In mythology, the dragon was a monster reptile somewhat similar to a crocodile. Dragons were usually described as fire-breathing creatures with wings and huge claws. In mythology, literature, and art, the dragon was usually a significant symbol. The exact meaning of the symbol varied with the culture. In the sacred writings of the ancient Hebrews, for example, the dragon usually represented evil and death. In contrast, the ancient Greeks and Romans understood the dragon to be a wise and protective influence capable of communicating to humans the secrets of the universe.

In Christian art, the dragon often is the symbol of sin. The dragon is frequently portrayed as crushed under the feet of martyrs and saints to symbolize the triumph of good over evil. A popular legend about St. George, patron saint of England, tells how he saved a town in Libya by killing the dragon (driving out evil) just before the king's daughter was to be sacrificed to the evil creature.

The dragon appears as an important force in the mythology of Oriental countries. Among the Chinese people, for example, the dragon is traditionally regarded as a symbol of good fortune.

1. This selection is mainly about
   (a) St. George of England.
   (b) the Komodo dragon.
   (c) Oriental art and mythology.
   (d) dragons in art and literature.

2. The Komodo dragon is
   (a) only found in storybooks.
   (b) a real lizard.
   (c) similar to an eagle.
   (d) one with winglike folds.

3. The ancient Greeks and Romans
   (a) disliked and feared dragons.
   (b) stamped out evil.
   (c) thought dragons to be wise.
   (d) used small dragons to fly.

4. Christian art depicts dragons
   (a) as symbols of sin.
   (b) along with most churches.
   (c) to show wisdom and strength.
   (d) as a means of transportation.

5. A painting of a dragon carrying off a person might mean
   (a) yielding to sin or temptation.
   (b) entertaining the masses.
   (c) controlling one's destiny.
   (d) overcoming evil thoughts.

6. In which culture were the dragons the most favored creatures?
   (a) ancient Hebrew
   (b) British
   (c) early Christian
   (d) ancient Greek or Roman

7. To symbolize means to
   (a) make a clanging noise.
   (b) paint a colored picture.
   (c) stand for something.
   (d) understand the words.

8. To understand what a dragon means,
   (a) one must see them in a zoo.
   (b) it's necessary to take a picture.
   (c) only an expert can help you.
   (d) you must know the cultural context.

Time ________ # Correct ______

11

Mary Leakey was digging one afternoon and she found some footprints in the ground. These were not ordinary footprints, and the discovery caused great excitement. The tracks she found had been made in Africa three-and-a-half million years earlier. Layers and layers of volcanic ash and lava 450 feet thick had preserved these prints. They were made by a human creature.

Dr. Leakey, a British anthropologist, said that scientists now have the techniques to verify the age of the prints by testing the soil. By examining the footprints directly, Dr. Leakey and her colleagues should be able to tell the approximate height of the creature. Their initial guess is that the hominid, or humanlike creature, was probably about four feet tall.

In addition to finding the prints of what she is quite certain was a hominid, Dr. Leakey discovered other animal and bird prints. These included evidence of a creature that apparently walked on its knuckles, and an animal that can be described as a monster elephant.

Dr. Leakey's discoveries indicate that human creatures very probably lived three-and-one-half million years ago, two million years earlier than scientists had thought up until now. That's a long time when you stop to think that records of the earliest human civilization date back only five thousand years. Columbus traveled to North America about five hundred years ago. The United States is only a little more than two hundred years old. The telephone has been around for slightly more than one hundred years. Movies, TV, cars, planes, and rockets are all inventions made within the last century. Three-and-a-half million years seems like a long time indeed.

1. The discovery was valuable because
   (a) Leakey worked too hard.
   (b) no one saw it happen.
   (c) the footprints were so large.
   (d) the footprints were so old.

2. The humanlike creature was probably
   (a) quite a monster.
   (b) about four feet tall.
   (c) born with four feet.
   (d) friendly to giraffes.

3. The footprints Dr. Leakey found are
   (a) three-and-a-half million years old.
   (b) two-and-a-half million years old.
   (c) four-and-a-half million years old.
   (d) three thousand years old.

4. An anthropologist studies
   (a) human civilizations.
   (b) animals in nature parks.
   (c) rocks in the mountains.
   (d) recent inventions.

5. Television, computers, and telephones
   (a) are necessary for all people.
   (b) are relatively recent inventions.
   (c) must be carried on the back.
   (d) are made by anthropologists.

6. Scientists tell the age of footprints
   (a) by measuring the shoes.
   (b) from the books they read.
   (c) by counting on their fingers.
   (d) by studying the soil.

7. Which happened last?
   (a) Columbus came to North America.
   (b) The first hominid made footprints.
   (c) The telephone was invented.
   (d) Television was invented.

8. Mary Leakey will probably
   (a) never find another track.
   (b) keep on digging and studying.
   (c) sell her television set.
   (d) buy a new computer.

Time ________ # Correct ______

12

Many people have had the problem of having no money when payment of an important debt is due. This type of financial embarrassment has been known to hit wealthy and prominent people as well as others.

One Civil Court judge in New York City, despite a generous annual income, was plagued with debt. His monthly mortgage payment was due and his checking account was empty. So the judge, who prefers that his name not be divulged, sold hot dogs one weekend at Yankee Stadium to make money.

Judge X put on the outfit of the stadium hawkers and added dark glasses in an effort to preserve his anonymity. The judge, who as a boy had sold hot dogs at the stadium, made $150 that weekend. However, he was not as anonymous as he had hoped.

Unfortunately, the judge was not assigned to the bleachers where he might have avoided his colleagues. He had to work in the expensive infield box seats where the chances of running into his friends were great. On his first pass through the aisles, the judge saw several attorneys who had practiced law in his courtroom. He hastily retreated, only to end up selling a frank to a high government official who knew him well.

Ever since that weekend, Judge X has been the subject of much teasing from his colleagues. Now, to supplement his income, he teaches one night a week at a law school. Although it's considered a much more respectable thing for a judge to do, it probably isn't as lucrative or even as much fun!

1. The judge took an extra job
   (a) to keep busy.
   (b) because he liked baseball.
   (c) to make money.
   (d) to get some hot dogs.

2. Judge X wore dark glasses
   (a) to protect his eyes.
   (b) because they looked handsome.
   (c) so he could see better.
   (d) so he wouldn't be recognized.

3. The judge knew he could sell because
   (a) anyone can sell hot dogs.
   (b) his wife told him he could.
   (c) he had done it as a boy.
   (d) he was a very smart man.

4. If he had worked in the bleachers, Judge X probably would not have
   (a) made as much money.
   (b) seen as many lawyers.
   (c) had as much fun.
   (d) wanted to go home.

5. An anonymous person
   (a) is generally overweight.
   (b) sends nasty letters.
   (c) is always prominent.
   (d) doesn't want to be named.

6. If something is divulged, it is
   (a) made public.
   (b) not very popular.
   (c) taken in vain.
   (d) sold at auction.

7. Something lucrative is
   (a) basically dishonest.
   (b) enlightening.
   (c) money-making.
   (d) delicious to eat.

8. This story suggests that
   (a) anyone can have money troubles.
   (b) being a judge is lots of fun.
   (c) selling hot dogs is easy.
   (d) judges have it made.

Time ________ # Correct ______

13

Kevin Sullivan and Joe Kramer were fishing one evening in July, 1983, near Jones Beach. They were standing on the end of a 900-foot jetty, a narrow strip of land extending out into the sea. The tide was coming in and the boys were enjoying their fishing very much. They completely ignored everything but the task at hand. They were unaware that an anxious crowd was gathering at the other end of the jetty where it joined the main part of the beach.

As the tide came in, the water submerged most of the jetty. The boys paid no attention to the rising water. They were too busy fishing. A Coast Guard boat came along and an officer used a loudspeaker to offer the boys assistance. They refused the offer and continued to fish.

Next a police helicopter came along, and the officers in the chopper assured the boys that they would save them. "We don't want to be saved," Kevin and Joe yelled to their would-be benefactors. The helicopter returned a few minutes later, and this time the boys were ordered to get on. The boys began to walk back toward the mainland. They didn't mind getting their sneakers wet. The officers in the helicopter had other ideas, however, and the boys were pulled aboard.

The boys couldn't understand what all the fuss was about. They returned to the jetty later that night to retrieve their fishing gear. "It was stupid," Joe said. Both boys laughed.

A police officer wasn't amused by the situation. "The tide was extremely high and the boys do not seem to realize what danger they were in."

"Don't they know the best fishing's at high tide?" retorted Kevin.

1. This story is mainly about
   (a) techniques of fishing.
   (b) two boys and an unwanted rescue.
   (c) duties of the Coast Guard.
   (d) disobeying the shore patrol.

2. Throughout the incident, Kevin and Joe
   (a) were extremely frightened.
   (b) believed they were in no danger.
   (c) nearly died in the ocean.
   (d) taunted the spectators.

3. The Coast Guard tried to help because
   (a) the boys requested assistance.
   (b) the crowd on the beach ordered it.
   (c) they believed the boys were in danger.
   (d) they had nothing else to do.

4. Someone who retorted
   (a) gave a sharp answer.
   (b) nearly drowned.
   (c) snickered quietly.
   (d) told the entire story.

5. Which happened first?
   (a) The boys retrieved their gear.
   (b) The Coast Guard came along.
   (c) The boys began to fish.
   (d) A helicopter took the boys.

6. Benefactors are people who
   (a) collect money.
   (b) provide assistance.
   (c) spoil everyone's fun.
   (d) manufacture fishing gear.

7. The jetty became submerged because
   (a) the Coast Guard flooded it.
   (b) it began to rain heavily.
   (c) the boys opened a dam.
   (d) the tide came in.

8. People in the crowd were anxious because
   (a) they thought the boys were in danger.
   (b) they were all getting sunburned.
   (c) the police were in a helicopter.
   (d) the Coast Guard issued a warning.

Time ________ # Correct ______

14

Have you ever stopped to think of where the hot water for your shower comes from? Do you know the source of hot water in the radiators that heat many homes? In most buildings in the United States, it's likely that the water has been heated by boilers run by fossil fuels—that is, coal, oil, or natural gas. The energy produced by burning fuel can also power generators that produce electricity to light homes and offices and operate the many appliances we often take for granted.

Today many Americans are looking for other sources of energy to provide light and heat. The search for alternate sources of energy is spurred by the fact that the supplies of these fuels are becoming scarce, which, in turn, leads to increased prices.

Not every country uses fossil fuels to the extent that the United States does. In Iceland, people have been heating their homes for many years by using geothermal energy. This means that they literally are using heat from within the earth. Underground water is heated by molten lava and it bubbles up in the form of hot springs. Icelanders harness this heat and use it. In some parts of the world people use the power of wind or water to produce heat and light. Scientists have even learned how to get energy from garbage as it decomposes.

Probably the two most talked about energy sources are nuclear and solar power. Although there is much controversy about the safety of nuclear power, a number of power plants around the world are producing energy by splitting atoms in nuclear reactors. Solar power involves using the sun's heat to provide warmth and to provide the energy needed to run machinery or appliances.

Which will be your energy source of the future? Will you depend on fossil fuels? Will you use solar or nuclear power? Will you use wind or water? Would geothermal or garbage power meet your needs? Think about it as you take your next hot shower.

1. This story is mainly about
   (a) using garbage for heat.
   (b) different sources of energy.
   (c) the gasoline shortage.
   (d) hot springs in Iceland.

2. Geothermal refers to
   (a) the study of the earth's crust.
   (b) heat used in automobiles.
   (c) heat from inside the earth.
   (d) preparation of foods.

3. Fossil fuels are
   (a) made by grinding rocks.
   (b) oil, natural gas, or coal.
   (c) cheaper than solar heat.
   (d) an unlimited supply.

4. Icelanders use geothermal power
   (a) as a form of entertainment.
   (b) to conserve their natural gas.
   (c) because it's nicer than solar.
   (d) because they have hot springs.

5. Hot water for your shower
   (a) will last for a long time.
   (b) requires energy to heat it.
   (c) uses up the drinking water.
   (d) is best heated with atoms.

6. When garbage decomposes, it
   (a) rots and gives off energy.
   (b) fills up the garbage can.
   (c) is no use to anyone.
   (d) develops wind and water.

7. Nuclear power is controversial because
   (a) it costs more than oil.
   (b) the sun helps to spread it.
   (c) bombs have killed people.
   (d) it may not be completely safe.

8. When something becomes scarce, it
   (a) is available in great amounts.
   (b) tends to cost more.
   (c) can never be used at all.
   (d) should be used on weekends.

Time __________ # Correct ______

Many consider Roger Bacon to be the father of modern science. It was this man, back in the thirteenth century, who declared that the answers to many of the questions that had been puzzling scientists were not buried deep in the writings of ancient Greek and Roman authors. He suggested that these answers would have to be sought out through study and experimentation with real things. With the adoption of Bacon's truly scientific method, many new discoveries took place.

The scientific method has specific, carefully planned steps. It does not rely on imagination, hearsay, or flights of fancy. First, a problem is identified. Then data are gathered about the problem and one or more hypotheses (hunches that can be tested) are formulated. Each hypothesis is tested by an experiment or observation, and conclusions are drawn.

In addition to developing the scientific method, Roger Bacon demonstrated remarkable ability to foresee future human accomplishments. He accurately predicted some things which others of his day thought to be impossible. He said that human beings would one day be able to fly through the air. He envisioned horseless carriages to transport people from place to place, and ships that would move under their own power and not depend on sails and wind.

Roger Bacon's thoughts were many years ahead of his time. In those days it was often unwise or imprudent to talk about or demonstrate radical ideas. Public showing of a new discovery often led to imprisonment for "dealing with the evil spirits." Roger Bacon was a very productive scientist. And, as you might well have guessed, he spent many years in English prisons.

1. Roger Bacon's method was
   (a) inconsiderate.
   (b) unrealistic.
   (c) scientific.
   (d) foolish.

2. The selection is mainly about
   (a) scientific laboratories.
   (b) how to fly a plane.
   (c) Roger Bacon.
   (d) time in prisons.

3. Envisioned means
   (a) imagined or predicted.
   (b) had an afterthought.
   (c) transported.
   (d) discovered.

4. To be imprudent is to
   (a) act unwisely.
   (b) be very intelligent.
   (c) behave in a rude way.
   (d) understand things.

5. Bacon spent years in prison because
   (a) he dreamed foolishly.
   (b) he built and sold model planes.
   (c) people feared his ideas.
   (d) he stole things for his work.

6. Bacon predicted that people would
   (a) run out of things to do.
   (b) need to improve prison life.
   (c) never learn how to live.
   (d) someday have cars and planes.

7.
   (a) Conclusions are drawn.
   (b) Data are gathered.
   (c) Hypotheses are formulated.
   (d) Observations are made.

8. Hypotheses are
   (a) straight lines.
   (b) testable notions.
   (c) firm conclusions.
   (d) foolish dreams.

Time ________ # Correct ______

16

Anyone daring enough to swim in rivers and streams of Central and South America might not survive long enough to tell about it. It is in many of these waters that the lethal piranha abound and consume their meals of flesh from whatever creatures are foolhardy enough to invade their territory. There are many legendary tales about fierce piranha attacks which have quickly killed and consumed their victims. Although some of these tales may be somewhat overstated, it's likely that most of them do have some basis in fact.

Piranha are relatively small. They measure from four inches to nearly two feet in length, with the average being about eight inches long. Their viciousness far exceeds their size. There are numerous different varieties of piranha, of which four types are believed to present a peril to humans. These fish are attractively colored, with bluish-gray, yellow, or green scales spotted with red or gold.

The teeth of the piranha are pointed, razor sharp, and designed to be extremely efficient. The points of the upper teeth fit exactly into the spaces between the points of the lower teeth when the piranha's mouth is closed. This enables the fish to sever chunks of meat neatly and quickly.

Piranha do not travel alone, which is why they can cause so much destruction to a large animal in such a short time. They often hunt in schools of several thousand. The horror stories of piranha reducing a person on horseback to a pile of bones may not be fiction. Whether or not these stories are exaggerations, perhaps the most suitable garb for venturing into piranha-infested waters would be a suit of armor.

1. Something lethal
   (a) chews its food well.
   (b) causes death.
   (c) is within the law.
   (d) is difficult to see.

2. The length of the piranha is
   (a) always eight inches.
   (b) not more than two feet.
   (c) the size of a razor.
   (d) four or more feet.

3. This story is mainly about
   (a) swimming in a river.
   (b) a school of pretty fish.
   (c) the small but deadly piranha.
   (d) how the piranha swims.

4. Someone's first dip in a river might be the last because
   (a) river water is very cold.
   (b) piranha fish eat people.
   (c) there are deadly snakes.
   (d) it's so easy to drown.

5. Something that's extremely efficient
   (a) requires frequent sharpening.
   (b) works very well.
   (c) prevents poisoning.
   (d) costs quite a bit.

6. The word schools refers to
   (a) training for the kill.
   (b) places for humans to learn.
   (c) learning to swim well.
   (d) groups of fish.

7. When done with an animal, piranha
   (a) leave only the bones.
   (b) permit the animal to leave.
   (c) rest at the river bottom.
   (d) share what's left.

8. An aquarium with piranha would be
   (a) ugly to look at.
   (b) impossible to see.
   (c) interesting for a cat.
   (d) a bad place for hands.

Time __________ # Correct ______

17

One of the weirdest disasters ever to befall an American city struck Boston one midwinter day just after the end of World War I. At exactly half past twelve on January 15, 1919, a giant tank containing 2.5 million gallons of molasses ruptured and poured out its contents into the street below.

The sticky mixture cascaded into Commercial Street in Boston's North End. Reaching a depth of fifteen feet and a width of 100 yards, this unrelenting river rolled on, covering everything in its path. Six school children on their way home for lunch were swallowed up and killed. A horse and wagon were engulfed and mired in their tracks. Half a dozen city workers eating their noon meal out in the yard also fell victims to the molasses flood. So quickly did the disaster occur that people were unable to budge before being struck down. All in all, twenty-one lives were known to have been lost.

Now, many years later, most memories of the Great Molasses Flood of 1919 have faded. A few old Bostonians, however, claim that on hot summer nights one can still detect a faint sweet smell of molasses in the cobblestone streets of the North End.

1. A good title for this story would be
   - (a) Making More Molasses
   - (b) The Great Molasses Massacre
   - (c) Destruction in American Streets
   - (d) Life in Boston's North End

2. The molasses struck
   - (a) carefully chosen victims.
   - (b) suddenly and without warning.
   - (c) because the workers loafed.
   - (d) everyone in Boston that day.

3. The number of deaths was said to be
   - (a) 100 or more.
   - (b) 6 children and 6 adults.
   - (c) 21 humans and one horse.
   - (d) fewer than 20.

4. The school children wouldn't have died if they had
   - (a) run the other way.
   - (b) been somewhat bigger.
   - (c) not been leaders.
   - (d) eaten lunch in school.

5. Ruptured means
   - (a) soured.
   - (b) burst open.
   - (c) repaired.
   - (d) enjoyed.

6. Something unrelenting
   - (a) will not borrow.
   - (b) won't give up or stop.
   - (c) tastes delicious.
   - (d) will make you sick.

7. People caught in the molasses
   - (a) tried to taste it.
   - (b) swam to safety.
   - (c) washed themselves off.
   - (d) were unable to move.

8. The molasses escaped because
   - (a) the tank burst.
   - (b) it was lunch hour.
   - (c) no one watched it.
   - (d) a worker let it out.

Time ________ # Correct ______

18

The invention of the cotton gin in 1793 had great impact on America's economic growth. Before the cotton gin, one worker required an entire day to remove by hand the seeds from one pound of cotton. With the invention of the cotton gin, that same worker became capable of processing fifty pounds of cotton a day. Cotton production in the southern United States increased from 1.5 million pounds in 1790 to an annual yield of 85 million pounds just twenty years later.

Who invented the cotton gin? Eli Whitney is generally credited with the development of this machine that so significantly altered life in the southern United States. Whitney was awarded a U.S. patent for the cotton gin in 1794.

There is evidence, however, that Eli Whitney was not the originator of the cotton gin after all. The idea for the device came from Catherine Greene, widow of General Nathanial Greene, and it was she who gave Whitney the plans for the cotton gin and arranged for him to build one. Mrs. Greene provided the financial backing for the venture, and it is fairly certain that she was responsible for suggesting the use of wire rather than wooden teeth to comb the cotton.

Mrs. Greene did not receive recognition for her contribution because women in the eighteenth century were not encouraged to accomplish such things. She would not have dared to take out a patent in her own name, even for so significant an invention. So, Eli Whitney has, to this day, gotten virtually all the credit for inventing the cotton gin, even though the brains and money behind the invention belonged to Catherine Greene.

It was more than fifteen years after Catherine Greene's invention that a female inventor was granted the first U.S. patent ever issued to a woman. On May 5, 1809, Mary Kies of Connecticut received a patent for a device to weave straw with silk or thread.

1. This selection tells you a cotton gin
   (a) creates liquid cotton.
   (b) removes seeds from cotton.
   (c) was very easy to invent.
   (d) was useful in battles.

2. The main idea of this selection is that the cotton gin
   (a) was not invented by Eli Whitney.
   (b) changed the southern economy.
   (c) uses wire instead of wooden teeth.
   (d) was patented in 1794.

3. You can be sure that Catherine Greene
   (a) knew George Washington.
   (b) knew Eli Whitney.
   (c) didn't use cotton.
   (d) applied for a patent.

4. Mrs. Greene didn't seek a patent because
   (a) she didn't deserve one.
   (b) she loved Eli Whitney.
   (c) women didn't do such things then.
   (d) the invention wasn't completed.

5. To comb cotton, the cotton gin used
   (a) fingers.
   (b) wire.
   (c) straw and thread.
   (d) wooden teeth.

6. Mary Kies was the first woman to
   (a) receive a U.S. patent.
   (b) use the cotton gin.
   (c) weave cloth for dresses.
   (d) invent anything useful.

7. The originator of something
   (a) pays for it.
   (b) always gets the patent.
   (c) invents or creates it.
   (d) markets it.

8. This selection suggests that
   (a) history books are perfect records.
   (b) women were poorer inventors than men.
   (c) history may not tell the whole truth.
   (d) Catherine Greene was a poor woman.

Time ________ # Correct ______

19

The Whitechapel Bell Foundry is located in the old Artichoke Inn and carriage yard on the outskirts of London's financial district. It has occupied this site since 1738 and can trace its heritage back through the centuries to 1425. Nothing much has changed at Whitechapel from one century to another.

Tradition at Whitechapel is an important part of what keeps the employees going. The work is hard, and it doesn't pay well. Nevertheless, workers take much pride in being a part of an industry that has such a long and impressive history.

It was from the courtyard of the Artichoke Inn that the Liberty Bell was shipped, without any cracks, to America in 1752. The bell was hung in Philadelphia, but it cracked soon after. It was recast and rehung, but it cracked irreparably in 1835 while being rung for the funeral of Chief Justice John Marshall.

Church bells are the main business for Whitechapel. During hard economic times, congregations are unlikely to place orders for items as expensive as a church bell.

The increased popularity of handbells rung by teams has accounted for the ability of Whitechapel to survive despite the fact that relatively few churches are buying new bells. Team handbell ringing, always popular in Britain, has spread to the United States, and many churches have bell choirs which play for the congregations and in competitions.

If you order a set of handbells, you may have to wait a while for delivery. Bells are still made in the old-fashioned way, and this process takes time.

1. The history of Whitechapel dates back
   (a) to prehistoric times.
   (b) more than five centuries.
   (c) to the first church bells.
   (d) to the American Revolution.

2. Employees of the bell foundry
   (a) have good salary and benefits.
   (b) are often injured on the job.
   (c) value tradition and history.
   (d) belong to a strong union.

3. In modern times, bells are made
   (a) using new materials and methods.
   (b) the same way they always were.
   (c) to compete with plastic chimes.
   (d) better than in the early days.

4. Which happened first?
   (a) The Liberty Bell was rehung.
   (b) The Liberty Bell was cast.
   (c) The bell cracked.
   (d) The Liberty Bell was shipped.

5. Something cracked irreparably is
   (a) beyond repair.
   (b) costly to fix.
   (c) pretty to look at.
   (d) noisy if used.

6. Whitechapel's present success involves
   (a) bells for new cathedrals.
   (b) the popularity of handbells.
   (c) repairing many church bells.
   (d) selling bells to schools.

7. In this story, congregations are
   (a) large uprisings.
   (b) groups of church members.
   (c) bell makers.
   (d) people who work with metal.

8. The Liberty Bell isn't used because
   (a) it's too noisy.
   (b) no one knows how to ring it.
   (c) there isn't liberty to celebrate.
   (d) it broke.

Time ________ # Correct ______

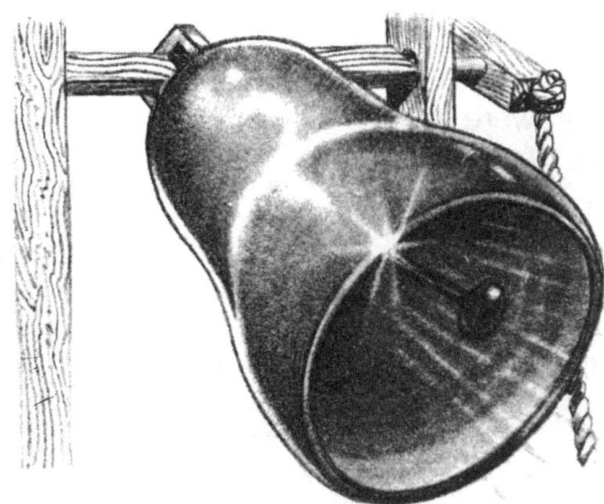

20

Trial by jury may not be a perfect system of administering criminal justice, but it is a great improvement over some earlier methods. The United States Constitution prohibits the use of cruel or unusual punishments. In old England, under Saxon rule, cruel and barbaric methods were used not only as punishments but to determine the guilt or innocence of the accused. These procedures were known as "ordeal by fire" and "ordeal by water." Fire was customarily used for nobility. Ordinary people were tried by water.

In one variety of "ordeal by fire," the accused was forced to take three steps while grasping a red-hot piece of iron in his or her bare hands. The hands were then bandaged, and the defendant was judged on the degree of healing that took place in three days. A variation on this technique involved walking barefoot and blindfolded on irregularly spaced red-hot irons. God supposedly guided the feet of the innocent.

For "ordeal by water" the accused was bound with ropes and tossed into a deep body of water. Those who floated were guilty. A person who sank was presumed innocent and, hopefully, pulled from the water before drowning. This quaint practice was based on the notion that the water would reject the guilty and accept the innocent.

Our judicial system may have flaws, but it's certainly preferable to the Saxon system!

1. Ordeal by fire is
   (a) a kind of card game.
   (b) a method of cooking.
   (c) an army shooting drill.
   (d) a kind of trial.

2. The Saxons were people who
   (a) were usually guilty.
   (b) lived long ago.
   (c) invented fire.
   (d) were innocent.

3. A person who sank in the water
   (a) always drowned.
   (b) was thought to be innocent.
   (c) couldn't swim to shore.
   (d) was judged to be guilty.

4. People of noble birth were usually
   (a) tried by fire.
   (b) thrown in the water.
   (c) tried by jury.
   (d) permitted to go free.

5. Something barbaric
   (a) strengthens a fence.
   (b) is gentle and kind.
   (c) is uncivilized.
   (d) resembles a doll.

6. In ordeal by fire, God was said to
   (a) punish the innocent.
   (b) keep the coals hot.
   (c) guide the feet of the innocent.
   (d) hold a person's hand.

7. This selection suggests that
   (a) trial by jury is impossible.
   (b) innocent people should be hurt.
   (c) trial by jury isn't so bad.
   (d) too much water causes crime.

8. The word flaws means
   (a) things that are not quite right.
   (b) places to walk.
   (c) our system of government and rules.
   (d) things done in a civilized manner.

Time ________ # Correct ______

21

Who invented the game of baseball? Would you answer "Abner Doubleday"? Most people would. Most other people would agree. Doubleday is commonly credited with the invention of the game of baseball. He is supposed to have set up the first game in a cow pasture in Cooperstown, New York, in 1839.

However, Doubleday may not truly be the originator of the game. Harold Peterson, a baseball historian, has cast some doubt on the authenticity of the Doubleday legend. It seems that the documentation for Doubleday's alleged role rests solely upon the reminiscences of a Mr. Graver, who at the age of eighty told about an event that had taken place when he was only fifteen years old.

Available records indicate that during the crucial period involved, Doubleday was a cadet enrolled at West Point. Records do not indicate that he took a leave or vacation long enough to travel to Cooperstown and invent the game of baseball. Quite possibly it was someone else who created the game now known as our "national pastime."

No matter what additional facts about baseball's beginnings may be presented to us by historical researchers, many American people are likely to go on believing that Abner Doubleday really did invent the game in that cow pasture in Cooperstown. It's a nice story, and people have been telling it for years. The people involved in professional baseball have done much to promote the Doubleday story. That cow pasture in Cooperstown is called Abner Doubleday Field. The Baseball Hall of Fame is located in Cooperstown. It is unlikely that mere facts will be enough to change the notions that so many people have about how baseball began. Old legends die hard.

1. Most people believe that baseball
   (a) is the world's oldest game.
   (b) began in the Middle Ages.
   (c) was invented by Peterson.
   (d) began at Cooperstown, N.Y.

2. Harold Peterson is a
   (a) friend of Abner Doubleday.
   (b) man hired by team owners.
   (c) baseball historian.
   (d) West Point cadet.

3. Doubleday was probably not baseball's inventor because he
   (a) didn't like team sports.
   (b) lived in Cooperstown.
   (c) was busy at West Point.
   (d) wanted someone else to.

4. Mr. Graver might have been wrong because
   (a) so many years had gone by.
   (b) he understood football better.
   (c) Cooperstown wasn't his home.
   (d) he liked to make up stories.

5. Who really invented baseball?
   (a) Abner Doubleday
   (b) The selection doesn't say.
   (c) a major league umpire
   (d) Mr. Graver's neighbor

6. Something with authenticity is
   (a) written well.
   (b) real or genuine.
   (c) stretched out.
   (d) difficult to believe.

7. Which came first?
   (a) Baseball was invented.
   (b) Doubleday entered West Point.
   (c) Mr. Graver saw a game.
   (d) Peterson studied baseball.

8. No matter what the facts about baseball's beginning, people seem to believe the legend because they
   (a) don't know any better.
   (b) are stupid about sports history.
   (c) never read the truth.
   (d) want to believe the story.

Time __________ # Correct ______

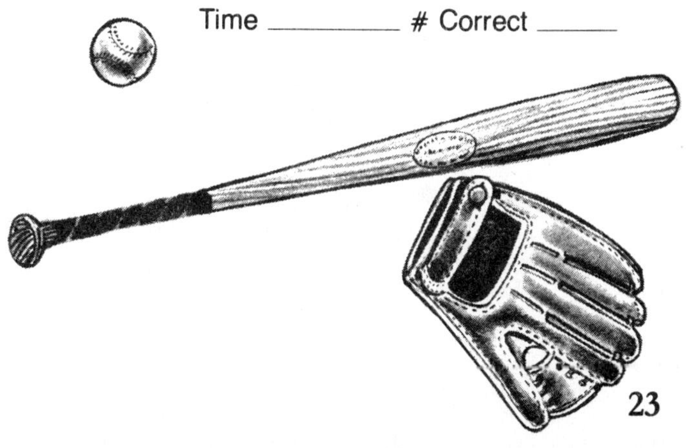

22

Porter Diggs, a private in the United States Army, found himself in more than a little bit of trouble after a drinking spree. Diggs borrowed a howitzer, which is a vehicle similar to a tank, from Fort Sill, Oklahoma, and drove it through a 10-foot-high fence to reach the street. He skipped the usual formalities with the security guards at the gates and turned the heavy-duty piece of equipment in the direction of town.

After leaving the military base, Pvt. Diggs drove the howitzer through the city streets shouting, "The Russians are coming. The Russians are coming." Unable to control the vehicle precisely, Diggs destroyed numerous street lamps and signs in his travels. Soon he wasn't traveling alone, but in a caravan. He was followed by an escort of police and privately owned vehicles.

At first, no one dared to intercept him directly because the howitzer appeared to be a very formidable and unfriendly object. When military officials assured everyone that the enormous cannon-like gun mounted on the tank was not loaded, some of the followers became more courageous. Three police officers managed to leap onto the device as it lumbered along and slowed down for a turn. After opening the hatch and climbing into the howitzer, the officers wrested the controls from Diggs, and then stopped the machine long enough to drag the soldier out.

Pvt. P. E. Diggs was quickly transported to jail in a more traditional street vehicle. He was charged with DWI (driving while intoxicated) and destruction of public property.

1. Mr. Diggs was a
   (a) driving instructor.
   (b) seasoned criminal.
   (c) private in the army.
   (d) Russian spy.

2. A formidable object is
   (a) painted army green.
   (b) pleasant to behold.
   (c) feared or dreaded.
   (d) small but sneaky.

3. At first, people thought that
   (a) Diggs might shoot them.
   (b) the tank was being serviced.
   (c) the Russians were coming.
   (d) officials ordered the move.

4. The police boarded the tank when
   (a) it speeded through the gate.
   (b) they knew it wasn't loaded.
   (c) army personnel ordered them to.
   (d) Diggs invited them to join him.

5. Which happened last?
   (a) Diggs went to jail.
   (b) The howitzer broke the fence.
   (c) Diggs had too much to drink.
   (d) Officials followed Diggs.

6. You can tell that a howitzer
   (a) handles well in traffic.
   (b) is similar to a sports car.
   (c) reaches extreme speeds.
   (d) is rather unwieldy.

7. A person convicted of DWI
   (a) is always sent to prison.
   (b) must write the letters often.
   (c) has had too much to drink.
   (d) fights with the police.

8. Pvt. Diggs probably wishes he had
   (a) been promoted to general.
   (b) stayed sober that day.
   (c) joined the Navy or Air Force.
   (d) taken friends for the ride.

Time __________ # Correct ______

Synchronized swimming is the most recent addition to the roster of official Olympic sports. Synchronized swimming involves performing and being judged on movements in the water according to very specific rules. Then the swimmers perform these movements in combinations and patterns set to music. Swimming in this way relates to swimming races in much the same way as figure skating compares to speed skating.

The hopes of the United States for success in the new swimming events depend heavily on the duet of Candy Costie and Tracie Ruiz, who have been swimming together since they were eleven years old. They work hard at their sport, and then spend 40 hours a week or more practicing their routines.

Although Candy and Tracie look very much alike, they are not related. They are often taken for sisters or even twins. Part of the success in synchronized swimming involves looking lovely and graceful while performing. In the duet events, the two performers must look like they belong together. Candy and Tracie certainly do. Before an event, the girls slick back their hair and adorn it with a decorative ornament. To hold the hair in place, the girls use a globby mixture of unflavored gelatin and water to keep every hair stuck firmly and neatly where it belongs throughout the performance. After their hair is done, they apply generous quantities of waterproof make-up to highlight their eyes.

When Tracie and Candy are in the water performing their routines, they are so graceful that they make it look easy. Few people really understand the hours and years of hard work that have gone into such a performance. It hasn't been easy at all.

1. Synchronized swimming is
   (a) lots of fun and games.
   (b) an official Olympic sport.
   (c) usually done alone.
   (d) easiest in the ocean.

2. Candy and Tracie are
   (a) twin sisters who swim.
   (b) young women who swim together.
   (c) television film stars.
   (d) small decorative ornaments.

3. The girls hold their hair back
   (a) so they can float better.
   (b) to look just like men.
   (c) to see the spectators.
   (d) so they look and swim better.

4. Candy and Tracie
   (a) swim once a week.
   (b) prefer swimming in summer.
   (c) have recently learned to swim.
   (d) swim 40 hours or more weekly.

5. This selection is mainly about
   (a) playing music underwater.
   (b) winning in the Olympic Games.
   (c) a synchronized swimming duet.
   (d) instruction in swimming.

6. First Candy and Tracie
   (a) dive into the water.
   (b) apply their eye makeup.
   (c) put gelatin on their hair.
   (d) perform their swimming routines.

7. Candy and Tracie first met
   (a) on the Olympic swimming team.
   (b) when they went to college.
   (c) when they were young girls.
   (d) at their neighbor's pool.

8. The routines in synchronized swimming look graceful and easy because
   (a) they aren't very complicated.
   (b) no one else understands them.
   (c) anything in water is graceful.
   (d) the performers have worked hard.

Time _________ # Correct ______

24

Stephen Gaines, a resident of San Francisco, decided to dine out one summer evening instead of preparing his own dinner. He had had a long, difficult day at the office, and he wanted someone else to do the cooking so he could relax. He chose an attractive seafood restaurant with <u>nautical</u> decor and what he felt sure would be a pleasant atmosphere. Mr. Gaines settled back in a captain's chair and ordered a complete dinner, from appetizer to dessert.

For a starter, Mr. Gaines had an excellent shrimp cocktail with spicy sauce. His soup was Manhattan clam chowder, which was followed by a bowl of crisp salad greens. As Mr. Gaines was pouring oil and vinegar on the salad, he noticed something extra in the bowl. At first he thought it might be an olive pit or perhaps an unground peppercorn. A closer look indicated that it was a fly. Mr. Gaines called the waiter and pointed out the <u>intruder</u>. The waiter removed the fly and threw it on the floor. He turned to Mr. Gaines and told him he could keep on eating the salad because the fly wasn't there anymore. Mr. Gaines was so angered by the waiter's behavior that he left without waiting for his main course of steamed abalone, or his dessert and coffee. He walked out without paying.

Mr. Gaines was later arrested and charged with "<u>defrauding</u> an innkeeper." He then sued the restaurant and won. The court ordered the restaurant to pay the diner nearly $1,000 in damages.

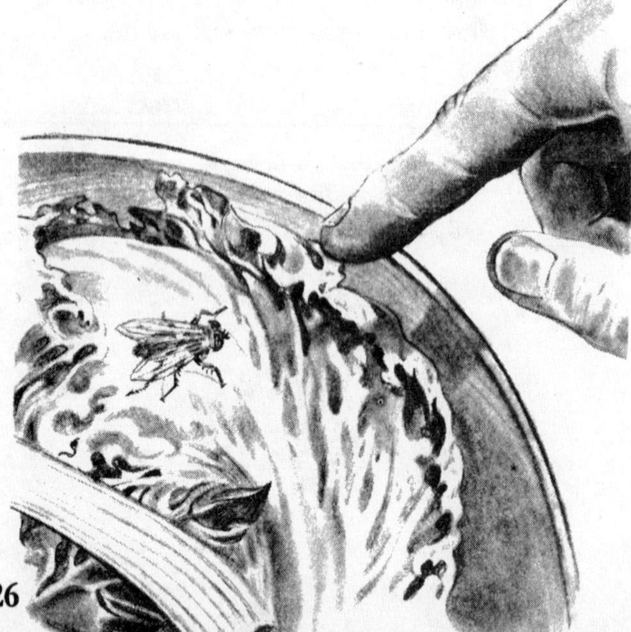

1. Mr. Gaines went out to eat
   (a) because he had no food.
   (b) for enjoyment and relaxation.
   (c) to pick a fight with someone.
   (d) to meet interesting people.

2. The main course he ordered was
   (a) steak and potatoes.
   (b) steamed clams and shrimp.
   (c) salad with oil and vinegar.
   (d) steamed abalone.

3. The word <u>nautical</u> refers to
   (a) ships and the sea.
   (b) small animals with claws.
   (c) casual and homey.
   (d) the appearance of a kitchen.

4. The waiter should have
   (a) called the police.
   (b) made Mr. Gaines wash dishes.
   (c) ordered the man to leave.
   (d) brought a new salad.

5. An <u>intruder</u> is
   (a) always welcome.
   (b) an uninvited guest.
   (c) usually very fierce.
   (d) sticky to the touch.

6. The waiter is best described as
   (a) efficient.
   (b) courteous.
   (c) stupid and rude.
   (d) entertaining.

7. <u>Defrauding</u> someone involves
   (a) preparing the dinner.
   (b) cheating them in some way.
   (c) stealing from a bank.
   (d) undressing very quickly.

8. Which happened last? Mr. Gaines
   (a) left without paying.
   (b) won money in court.
   (c) found a fly in the salad.
   (d) ordered dessert and coffee.

Time ________ # Correct _____

25

A Japanese woman and her daughter were finally reunited in May, 1983, after 38 years of separation caused by a tragic wartime incident. Tome Ohata, age 64, thought that her three children had perished long ago in that incident. Unknown to the mother, however, one daughter survived. Here is her story.

In 1945, near the end of World War II, Ohata and her family were living in a Japanese settlement in Manchuria, a part of China near the border of the Soviet Union. When Russian tanks invaded the village, Ohata and her three daughters, then ages 2, 4, and 5, tried to seek refuge in the bushes to conceal themselves from the oncoming invaders. The Japanese children were taken and bayonetted by troops on their own side to prevent the children's cries from revealing their presence to the enemy.

Although left for dead, five-year-old Wang miraculously survived the bayonet stabbing and walked back to the village. She was taken in and sheltered by a Chinese family who raised her as their own. Now, nearly 40 years later, Wang still bears a three-inch scar from the bayonet that almost killed her. She has dim memories of the incident which almost cost her her life. She has nothing but praise for her adoptive parents.

In 1983, the Japanese and Chinese governments worked together to assist a number of people in finding relatives who had been left behind in China when the Soviet troops invaded during World War II. Tome Ohata was one of the people who received this assistance, and that's how she and her long-lost daughter were able to find each other. Ohata, who speaks Japanese, used an interpreter to converse with her Chinese-speaking daughter. Their tears of joy needed no one to translate.

1. This story tells of children killed
   (a) as ritual sacrifice.
   (b) as punishment.
   (c) by their own people.
   (d) by serious disease.

2. Ohata didn't find Wang sooner because
   (a) she didn't want to.
   (b) government officials interfered.
   (c) she thought the girl had died.
   (d) others hid the child from her.

3. Adoptive parents
   (a) are the same as any others.
   (b) choose to raise a child.
   (c) can't afford a home.
   (d) capture children in wartime.

4. This story is mainly about
   (a) using a bayonet.
   (b) speaking Chinese and Japanese.
   (c) a Russian invasion.
   (d) a joyful reunion.

5. Which happened first?
   (a) Ohata's daughters were stabbed.
   (b) Russian troops invaded Manchuria.
   (c) World War II began.
   (d) Ohata was reunited with her child.

6. You can tell from this story that
   (a) the war was Russia's fault.
   (b) wars solve international problems.
   (c) children distrust their parents.
   (d) people do savage things in wartime.

7. The children were stabbed
   (a) because they were naughty.
   (b) to keep them quiet.
   (c) because the soldiers were angry.
   (d) so they wouldn't need food.

8. Ohata and her daughter cried because
   (a) they were so happy.
   (b) it was better than laughing.
   (c) their injuries still hurt.
   (d) they didn't like each other.

Time ________ # Correct _____

26

Caligula, the emperor of Rome from A.D. 37 to 41, owned what may have been history's most pampered horse. Caligula loved and cared for this special horse, whose name was Incitatus, in a most unusual way.

Incitatus lived in a palace surrounded by the splendor and riches of royalty. His marble stall had an ivory manger and a golden water bowl. An average citizen of Rome had far fewer comforts than Incitatus enjoyed. The horse ate better quality food than most of the people of his day. Slaves, whose sole duty was to satisfy the horse's every need, attended Incitatus constantly, while musicians entertained him with gentle melodies.

Each evening Incitatus had dinner in a large banquet hall with senators and other important guests. The perfumed horse wore elegant jeweled collars to these feasts. What happened if an invited guest did not care to dine with a horse? Such an uncooperative person could face exile or even death.

Caligula gave his horse virtually every luxury he could bestow. He even tried to appoint the horse to the office of Consul, an important political post that had once been held by Julius Caesar. The horse did not, however, assume political office. Two palace guards, feeling that Caligula had carried his bizarre affection for an equine companion to excess, murdered the emperor to end his mad rule.

1. Caligula was
   (a) an ancient Roman city.
   (b) a pampered horse.
   (c) a marble stall.
   (d) an emperor of Rome.

2. A pampered horse
   (a) has to wear diapers.
   (b) is well taken care of.
   (c) entertains others.
   (d) prepares the dinner.

3. Guests who didn't like horses
   (a) refused to dine with one.
   (b) stayed away from Caligula.
   (c) probably didn't admit it.
   (d) were sent to the doghouse.

4. Something bizarre is
   (a) sold in the market.
   (b) very costly.
   (c) equestrian in nature.
   (d) unusual or weird.

5. This story is mainly about
   (a) a horse that lived like a king.
   (b) killing uncooperative guests.
   (c) the emperor Caligula.
   (d) a jeweled collar for a horse.

6. Which happened first?
   (a) Caligula was killed.
   (b) Incitatus attended feasts.
   (c) Caligula became emperor.
   (d) Incitatus lived in a palace.

7. You can guess that Caligula
   (a) was a very popular man.
   (b) disliked dogs and cats.
   (c) was not of sound mind.
   (d) often drank bad wine.

8. Caligula was killed because he
   (a) got tired of Incitatus.
   (b) attacked the palace guards.
   (c) imitated Julius Caesar.
   (d) angered people with his crazy ways.

Time ________ # Correct _____

The explorer Ponce de Leon spent considerable time and effort nearly 500 years ago in his unsuccessful search for the "fountain of youth." He believed that when he located this elusive fountain its waters would keep him eternally young. Throughout history, people have tried in various ways to retard the aging process. Now a doctor in California thinks that we may actually have moved a step closer to doing so.

Dr. Jaime Miquel, whose research is conducted in conjunction with the National Aeronautics and Space Administration, says that weightlessness, such as that experienced by the astronauts in a gravity-free environment, could enable a person to live longer. In the absence of gravity, a person can survive with smaller supplies of food and oxygen. In a normal environment, about one-third of the body's energy is used to combat the effects of gravity. In a weightless environment, a person's organs don't have to work as hard and may last longer. Dr. Miquel's research indicates that a person could slow the aging process by as much as 10 to 15 percent while in space.

These findings do not, however, indicate that the key to a long life is to rush out and buy a ticket on the next space shuttle. While living in a weightless environment does appear to slow the aging process, it causes other problems. There is evidence that bones and muscles lose the ability to function normally when they adapt to a lack of gravity. In the case of every astronaut so far, this loss of muscle function has been reversed after the return to Earth. No humans have remained long enough in a weightless environment to show whether or not permanent damage might occur. Your best chance for a long life is to eat and drink sensibly, get enough rest, and avoid smoking.

1. For Ponce de Leon, eternal youth
   (a) was found in a fountain.
   (b) became easy to find.
   (c) was located in Florida.
   (d) was an impossible dream.

2. Something elusive is
   (a) brightly lit.
   (b) hard to find.
   (c) sticky.
   (d) confined to the rich.

3. Weightlessness occurs
   (a) when you don't eat.
   (b) on alternate Sundays.
   (c) in a gravity-free environment.
   (d) after a trip in space.

4. Weightlessness slows aging because
   (a) lighter people live longer.
   (b) the body's organs work less.
   (c) doctors want it to do so.
   (d) planets have no birthdays.

5. Life in outer space could cause
   (a) muscles to become stronger.
   (b) bone and muscle problems.
   (c) people to gain weight.
   (d) a shorter life span.

6. Your best chance of a long life
   (a) comes from taking a rocket.
   (b) involves taking care of yourself.
   (c) can't be controlled in any way.
   (d) depends on your marks in school.

7. Without gravity, a person requires
   (a) extra clothes for warmth.
   (b) objects for entertainment.
   (c) less food and oxygen.
   (d) additional food and water.

8. Staying eternally young means
   (a) never growing old.
   (b) wearing childish clothes.
   (c) having a good time.
   (d) celebrating birthdays.

Time ________ # Correct ______

28

"In company with the first woman ever to qualify for the Indianapolis 500, gentlemen start your engines." These historic words introduced the 1977 Indianapolis 500 race. The gentlemen were in the company of Janet Guthrie, who had qualified for the race with a speed of over 188 miles an hour. Until 1977, the race always began, "Gentlemen, start your engines."

Mechanical difficulties forced Ms. Guthrie to drop out of the 1977 race early, but she was pleased to have started at all. She qualified for the Indy 500 in 1978, and this time finished ninth. The 1978 race wasn't an easy one for her. She had to reach over and shift gears with her left hand, because she had broken her right wrist two days before the race. The car she drove had been built for someone else, and it was too short for her. The cramped conditions in the car caused discomfort and reduced circulation in her legs. Considering these handicaps, her finish in the top ten was quite remarkable. After her performance in the 1978 Indy 500, Guthrie was expected to continue her climb to the top of her sport.

Ms. Guthrie has not, however, enjoyed the success she and her fans had hoped for. This is not for lack of talent or determination. What she lacks, quite simply, is money. To reach the top in the highly competitive field of Indy-car racing requires abundant financial resources. Those who are independently wealthy or sponsored by a company willing to spend a lot of money have a chance to make it. Others don't.

At this time, no person or corporation has been willing to back Janet Guthrie, or any other woman, with enough money and the equipment necessary to win the major races. Ms. Guthrie feels that she has, in effect, been forced out of racing because of her inability to find a sponsor. This saddens her, because she finds racing an experience that has no equal. She would like to be able to participate in this experience again.

1. In 1977, the Indy 500 used a new announcement to start the race because
   (a) the starter forgot the old one.
   (b) a woman was racing that day.
   (c) Janet Guthrie didn't like it.
   (d) people were tired of listening.

2. To qualify, Ms. Guthrie had to
   (a) drive more than 200 m.p.h.
   (b) buy two extra cars.
   (c) prove she could drive fast.
   (d) complete 500 miles.

3. Guthrie dropped out of the 1977 race
   (a) to find another sponsor.
   (b) as soon as she became scared.
   (c) because her car broke down.
   (d) when she knew it was over.

4. A sponsor in car racing
   (a) helps pay for the sport.
   (b) never watches the races.
   (c) must own at least three cars.
   (d) writes advertisements.

5. This selection is mainly about
   (a) Janet Guthrie's first race.
   (b) the cost of fixing a car.
   (c) going to the Indy 500.
   (d) a woman in auto racing.

6. If Janet Guthrie were wealthy, she
   (a) would buy an airplane.
   (b) could continue racing.
   (c) would give it all away.
   (d) would never work or race again.

7. Something that's remarkable is
   (a) easy to do.
   (b) worth talking about.
   (c) unpleasant.
   (d) impossible.

8. Janet Guthrie raced because she
   (a) hated to drive slowly.
   (b) made a lot of money at it.
   (c) wanted to prove a point.
   (d) really loved doing it.

Time ________ # Correct ______

29

One increasing nuisance, made possible by advances in technology, is the "junk" telephone call. These calls are dispensed by a machine that can be programmed to dial numbers automatically without further human assistance. When a number is reached, the machine delivers a prepared sales pitch and even records the recipient's response.

The machine, which can call many hundreds of numbers during a regular business day, does present some problems. Certain of the devices, particularly the cheaper ones, do not disconnect if the person called chooses not to listen and hangs up. This has the potential to cause tragedy, as well as irritation and inconvenience. A woman in the Midwest, for example, attempted to call a doctor for her mother, who had just collapsed with what appeared to be a heart attack. The phone did not present a dial tone but a recorded sales pitch, which would not stop even after the woman hung up the phone. Fortunately, a neighbor's phone was usable, and help was summoned in time.

Certain models of the dialing devices can record orders for the product being sold. This has resulted in some odd situations. The parents of a Texas youngster, for example, found that a machine had sold their child a new roof for the house. Another family discovered that their three-year-old, who didn't know how to read, had subscribed to a dozen different adult magazines for which the parents were then being billed.

Many people regard the junk telephone call as even more offensive than junk mail. They point out that it's usually possible to recognize and discard junk mail without opening or reading it. A phone call, however, can't be recognized as junk until it has been answered and at least a portion of the message heard. Some people have resorted to the continuous use of answering machines on their home telephones! These devices can record messages if no one is home, and help screen the calls if someone is there. Other people, however, find the answering machines to be as objectionable as the junk calls. Some kind of regulation of the junk call nuisance may be required.

1. Many people think junk calls are
   (a) entertaining.
   (b) expensive.
   (c) bothersome.
   (d) necessary for life.

2. A junk telephone call is one
   (a) you can easily throw away.
   (b) dialed by a machine.
   (c) that comes in the mail.
   (d) usually very welcome.

3. Certain dialing machines
   (a) dial numerous wrong numbers.
   (b) only disconnect when the message ends.
   (c) are used to reach doctors.
   (d) control unnecessary conversation.

4. This selection is mainly about
   (a) the nuisance of junk phone calls.
   (b) buying a new roof by telephone.
   (c) fighting back with another device.
   (d) calling a doctor when in need.

5. Something offensive
   (a) usually plays a good game.
   (b) requires an answer.
   (c) is often disconnected.
   (d) irritates or offends you.

6. A telephone answering machine can
   (a) screen calls and take messages.
   (b) dial desired calls.
   (c) please everyone.
   (d) sell more magazines.

7. The article suggests that perhaps
   (a) junk calls should be controlled.
   (b) children shouldn't use phones.
   (c) doctors should make house calls.
   (d) magazines are the answer.

8. Unwanted calls are worse than junk mail because
   (a) they cost the consumer more.
   (b) they must be returned.
   (c) junk mail can be discarded.
   (d) phones don't ring very loudly.

Time ________ # Correct _____

30

Raymond Camacho celebrated his 18th birthday on Saturday, June 4, 1983, with a large party at his parents' home in Miami, Florida. When this party was over, early Sunday morning, Ray drove his girlfriend home. On the way back, his car crashed into a tree. Police and ambulance attendants who came to the scene found Ray to be unconscious with serious head injuries. The youth was taken to a hospital, where he was placed on a respirator to keep him breathing. Little hope was held out for his survival. He never regained consciousness.

Because Ray had been an exceptionally healthy boy, he was an excellent potential donor of organs and tissue to help save other lives. Ray's family thought very carefully about what to do. They sought religious guidance as well as medical advice. They decided that donating Ray's organs would help bring some good out of his tragic, untimely death. They didn't want their son's well-cared-for body to go to waste.

The organs and other tissue from Ray's body have helped 16 or more people, many of whom would not live otherwise. Ray's heart was transplanted to the chest of a middle-aged man whose own heart was failing. His kidneys went to other recipients who, without kidney transplants, faced frequent stays on a kidney dialysis machine or certain death. Ray's bones aided young people with bone cancer, while his skin was used for grafting onto burn victims.

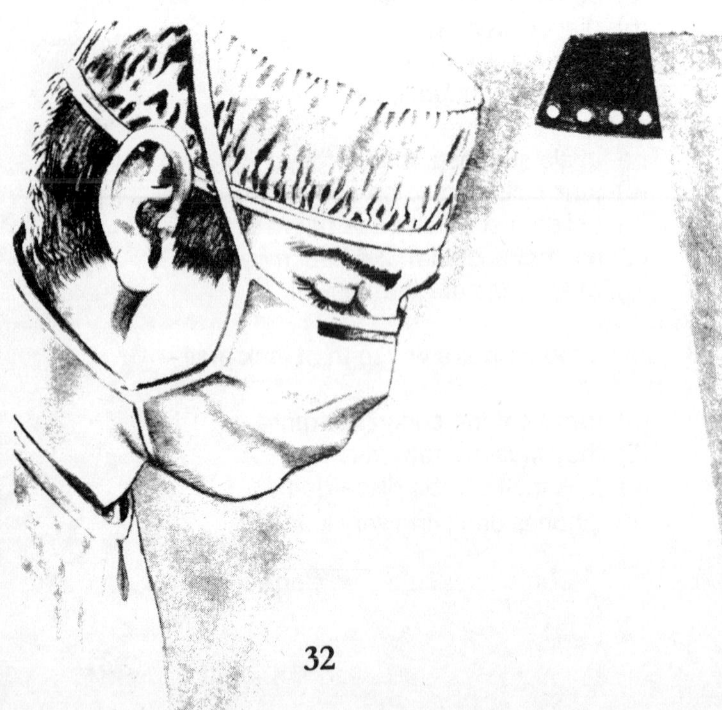

1. When Ray died, he was
   (a) just 18 years old.
   (b) too tired to care.
   (c) almost 18 years old.
   (d) not old enough to vote.

2. A respirator is a device to
   (a) keep people cool.
   (b) make someone sleep.
   (c) assist in breathing.
   (d) make sick people happy.

3. An unconscious person is
   (a) not awake or alert.
   (b) already dead.
   (c) able to speak clearly.
   (d) in need of food.

4. This story is mainly about
   (a) a death that saved other lives.
   (b) a birthday party for friends.
   (c) crashing into a tree.
   (d) Raymond Camacho's parents.

5. Which happened last?
   (a) Ray had a birthday party.
   (b) The car crashed into a tree.
   (c) Ray's organs were donated.

6. Ray's condition before the crash
   (a) involved being very drunk.
   (b) is not mentioned in the story.
   (c) was hard to describe.
   (d) should have kept him from driving.

7. The cause of Ray's death was
   (a) kidney failure.
   (b) a heart attack.
   (c) several broken bones.
   (d) head injuries and brain damage.

8. Ray's family can be described as
   (a) generous even while grieving.
   (b) careless about their son.
   (c) uncaring and selfish.
   (d) difficult to please.

Time ________ # Correct ______

31

Is the man a genius and an artist as some would claim? Or is he simply an attention-getter and what one major newspaper sarcastically described as the world's "largest exterior decorator"? The man is Christo, whose projects are unusual, enormous, controversial, and definitely not dull.

In May, 1983, after more than two years of legal battles to obtain permission to engage in his latest artistic endeavor, Christo completed a project called "Surrounded Islands" in Biscayne Bay near Miami, Florida. This venture involved surrounding eleven small islands with masses of shiny pink fabric. The "skirt" on each island billowed from the island's beaches two hundred feet out into the surrounding sea. Approximately 6.5 million square yards of fabric made up the skirts for "Surrounded Islands." Christo financed his project with money from the sale of some of his previous works and from a very large bank loan.

"Surrounded Islands" was not Christo's first work of mammoth size. In 1972, he suspended a huge cloth curtain between two mountain peaks in Colorado. In 1976, he created a cloth fence that ran for 24 miles in California. Christo plans these works to be ephemeral. He doesn't intend them to last very long. Within two weeks of creating these huge outdoor displays, he usually has them dismantled. He records them on film before destroying them.

Even though Christo does not install his works permanently, his creations are not always welcomed or encouraged. He once proposed using saffron-colored drapes to cover the paths in New York's Central Park. City officials prevented him from doing this, and sent him on his way to adorn the environment elsewhere. Christo vowed he would return after dressing the islands in Florida. Do you think New York will be ready for Christo when Christo is ready for New York?

1. Christo is the creator of
   (a) numerous small oil paintings.
   (b) draperies for dance floors.
   (c) large-scale artistic projects.
   (d) clothes for redwood trees.

2. "Surrounded Islands" involved
   (a) an enormous fence.
   (b) bright yellow curtains.
   (c) billowing pink skirts.
   (d) drapes for the paths.

3. A controversial person
   (a) hangs large curtains.
   (b) always makes noise.
   (c) causes disagreement.
   (d) makes too much money.

4. Christo pays for his work
   (a) by charging admission to it.
   (b) with inherited wealth.
   (c) with his wife's income.
   (d) with loans and sales of art.

5. An "exterior decorator" would
   (a) paint walls of a room.
   (b) adorn the window shades.
   (c) work on small paintings.
   (d) create things outside.

6. Christo's work seems to
   (a) make too much money.
   (b) stir up disagreements.
   (c) last for many months.
   (d) create good relations.

7. Something ephemeral
   (a) lasts a long time.
   (b) exists only in the mind.
   (c) has a strange odor.
   (d) has a very short life.

8. This selection is mainly about
   (a) how to hang large curtains.
   (b) fighting New York City.
   (c) an unusual man named Christo.
   (d) building a cloth fence.

Time ________ # Correct ______

32

Transfusion is the process by which blood from another source is transferred into a vein or artery of a person or animal. For someone who is seriously injured and bleeding profusely, an immediate transfusion may be the difference between life and death. Keeping blood fresh for use in transfusions used to be a problem. It spoiled quickly and then could not be used.

Charles Drew, a young black doctor, became an expert in the field of blood and blood transfusions. After much experimentation, Dr. Drew discovered a method of isolating the liquid part of the blood, called plasma, from whole blood. Plasma could then be changed into powder and stored for an indefinite period of time. The horrors of World War II created an immediate and urgent need for blood plasma. Drew's discovery had been most timely, and many thousands of lives were saved on battlefields all over the world.

One evening, after the war, Dr. Drew lost control of his car on a highway somewhere in the southern United States. The car crashed and Drew was injured seriously. Although he was taken to a hospital, the facility was a segregated one which did not offer Drew the care he needed. He lay there unattended and he died from loss of blood. Ironically, Dr. Drew's own discovery—blood plasma—could have saved his life.

1. The liquid part of blood
   (a) is called plasma.
   (b) was invented by Drew.
   (c) resembles chicken soup.
   (d) contains larger cells.

2. Before Drew's discovery,
   (a) stored blood often spoiled.
   (b) plasma was very expensive.
   (c) powdered blood was used.
   (d) few died from loss of blood.

3. Plasma is stored
   (a) by boiling it in kettles.
   (b) hidden in pockets.
   (c) in powder form.
   (d) with bandages.

4. Drew's discovery was timely because
   (a) the soldiers were very hungry.
   (b) prizes were offered for it.
   (c) many transfusions were needed in war.
   (d) he needed the money.

5. Dr. Drew died because
   (a) the hospital had no blood.
   (b) he received no care.
   (c) his age was against him.
   (d) his legs were broken.

6. At a different time or hospital,
   (a) Drew might have died sooner.
   (b) blood would have been lost.
   (c) there would have been nurses.
   (d) Drew might have been cared for.

7. Someone bleeding profusely is
   (a) already dead.
   (b) likely to leave the room.
   (c) bleeding from a small cut.
   (d) bleeding heavily.

8. Drew's death was especially tragic
   (a) for those who didn't know him.
   (b) as it happened at night.
   (c) because he was a doctor.
   (d) because it was unnecessary.

Time ________ # Correct ______

33

Paul Jacob Steinman is the son of Ron and Josephine Steinman, of New York. As expected in a Jewish family, Paul celebrated his bar mitzvah at age 13. A bar mitzvah is a special religious event in which a boy takes on certain of the spiritual responsibilities of being a man. There is a similar rite for girls called a bat mitzvah. Following the traditional religious ceremony for a bar mitzvah or bat mitzvah, it is customary for friends and relatives of the young person to gather together for feasting and celebrating.

The religious ceremony at Paul Steinman's bar mitzvah was true to tradition. After that, however, the event was not like the bar mitzvah feasts of any of his friends. For example, in addition to the regular silverware at each place setting, there were chopsticks inscribed "Paul's Bar Mitzvah, June 25, 1983." The food served was Vietnamese.

Paul's father, now producer of the news portion of NBC-TV's "Today" show, had covered the Vietnamese war on location for the television network back in the 1960s. In Saigon, he met a woman named Ngoc-Suong Tu, who was an orchestra leader there. She is now Mrs. Steinman. After the war, the Steinmans were able to bring a number of other relatives to the United States. One of these was Mrs. Steinman's mother, who had owned a restaurant in Saigon.

Mrs. Steinman converted to Judaism after her marriage. When it came time to plan her oldest son's bar mitzvah, she decided that the typical catered meal was not what she wanted. She and her mother planned, prepared, and served a feast that none of their new friends had ever experienced before. To comply with Jewish dietary laws, certain of the ingredients such as pork and shellfish had to be omitted and replaced with other items. Except for this necessary change, the menu was authentically Vietnamese.

The occasion of Paul Steinman's bar mitzvah reflected the blending of the two ancient cultures which had combined to make up his family's heritage. The people who attended found it to be a meaningful and moving experience.

1. This selection is mainly about
   (a) Ron Steinman in Saigon.
   (b) cooking and serving Vietnamese food.
   (c) avoiding pork and shellfish.
   (d) Paul Steinman's bar mitzvah.

2. Which came first?
   (a) Mrs. Steinman moved to America.
   (b) Mr. Steinman worked in Saigon.
   (c) Paul celebrated his bar mitzvah.
   (d) The Steinmans served Vietnamese food.

3. Chopsticks are used
   (a) as eating utensils.
   (b) for cooking rice.
   (c) as souvenirs of travel.
   (d) to dice and cut meat.

4. A boy has a bar mitzvah
   (a) as often as necessary.
   (b) on a Thursday evening.
   (c) once in a lifetime.
   (d) to learn to be a chef.

5. Paul's bar mitzvah was unusual because
   (a) it was held in Saigon.
   (b) there were television cameras there.
   (c) no one spoke English.
   (d) Vietnamese food was served.

6. Before her marriage, Mrs. Steinman
   (a) worked in a restaurant.
   (b) led an orchestra.
   (c) wrote songs for dancing.
   (d) traveled in Europe.

7. Something traditional is
   (a) new and different.
   (b) very expensive.
   (c) sold at the market.
   (d) according to custom.

8. The story suggests that Paul
   (a) dislikes his relatives.
   (b) speaks English very poorly.
   (c) has a close-knit family.
   (d) wants to live in Saigon.

Time __________ # Correct ______

34

The cockroach is a creature with considerable ability to evoke feelings of disgust among the humans with whom it often shares living quarters. Each generation of humans seems to make efforts to exterminate the cockroach, with little or no success. Somehow roaches manage to become immune to whatever insecticide is currently in vogue.

Cockroaches seem to be able to adapt to a wide variety of conditions. They have been known to go for weeks without food or water. They will, if necessary, consume just about anything in order to survive. Although they prefer to dine on starches, cockroaches are not usually very discriminating. Among the more offbeat cockroach meals are paper, glue or paste, books, and dirty laundry. Roaches are night creatures. They search for their meals in the dark, and hide by daylight.

A California man named Bob Brown found, quite by accident, what he considers to be a safe and effective means of dealing with roaches and rodents. Brown, a polio-crippled guitar player, tangled some strings on his electric guitar and noticed some rats running for shelter. He decided that there was probably something about the sound that the animals didn't like.

Brown continued to experiment, and he has now patented an ultrasonic device that he claims chases away rodents such as rats and mice, and cockroaches. Some people are quick to say that this is not really a new idea. Others laugh and say it won't work.

Will an ultrasonic device such as the one Brown developed really rid the world of cockroaches? While the device may make the creatures move out of a place temporarily, no one can be sure how long such a remedy will last. Cockroaches have been around for hundreds of millions of years. They survived the Ice Age, and they are likely to adapt to this ultrasonic irritation as well.

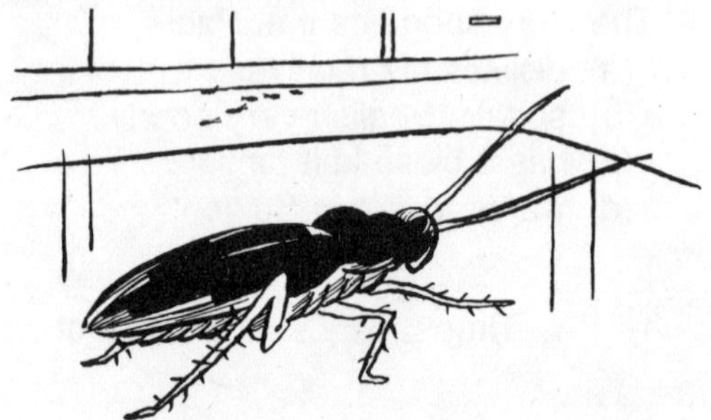

1. Cockroaches are
   (a) very ancient creatures.
   (b) a recently developed pest.
   (c) well liked.
   (d) larger than rats.

2. Which happened first?
   (a) The rats ran away.
   (b) Brown tangled his guitar strings.
   (c) Brown patented his device.
   (d) Brown's company made money.

3. Brown got started on his invention
   (a) because he had polio.
   (b) cleaning the house.
   (c) after an operation.
   (d) by accident.

4. This selection is mainly about
   (a) what to feed cockroaches.
   (b) a musician from California.
   (c) surviving the Ice Age.
   (d) cockroaches and people.

5. Cockroaches might invade a library
   (a) to learn to read.
   (b) in search of warmth.
   (c) in search of people.
   (d) to eat the books.

6. According to this story, people
   (a) can learn to like roaches.
   (b) are the cause of cockroaches.
   (c) disagree about Brown's invention.
   (d) have eliminated roaches.

7. When a new pest control is invented,
   (a) all the roaches will be gone.
   (b) roaches will probably adapt.
   (c) domestic animals will die.
   (d) it will be too costly to use.

8. An insecticide is used to
   (a) kill bugs.
   (b) feed roaches.
   (c) clean the house.
   (d) attract rats.

Time ________ # Correct ______

35

Numerous sports utilize the services of one or more referees. You will find, for example, referees in gymnastics, baseball, swimming and diving competition, football, figure skating, basketball, boxing, and tennis, among others. The referee's functions may vary from one sport to another, but all sports have one factor in common. The referee's judgment, no matter what the sport, can make the difference between winning or losing.

When a decision is announced, one can often hear loud cheering from the spectators. Sometimes there is booing because the people don't agree with the decision. Usually, however, no matter what the people think, the decision of the judge is final. With the instant replay, television viewers often get a second chance to watch a great catch, a slide into home plate, a knockout punch, a horse crossing the finish line, or some other special sports moment. Should the camera help the referees in making their decisions? Some people think so. The Japanese have been using the television instant replay in one of their sports for some time.

In Japan, where sumo wrestling is thought by many to be the national sport, a wrestler named Taiho was trying to break Futabayama's record of 69 consecutive victories. In the 46th match, Taiho's opponent was declared the winner by mistake because the judges had not seen the wrestler's foot leave the circle.

Soon after this mistake, the Japanese officials decided that they did not want champions to lose titles unfairly. Since some people pay as much as $375 for a ringside seat, the spectators have a right to see the match end with the correct winner. Now videotape cameras record the actions of the wrestlers. The camera is the most important referee of all. If a man or a woman makes a mistake in judgment, the camera will record it, and the instant replay will reveal it to all. The right winner will win.

1. This selection is mainly about
   (a) how to wrestle in Japan.
   (b) use of a camera as referee.
   (c) watching boxing on television.
   (d) why sumo wrestling is fun.

2. In most sports, the referee
   (a) doesn't count much.
   (b) gets paid too much.
   (c) can't see all the action.
   (d) has the final word.

3. A poor decision
   (a) can cause the wrong winner.
   (b) is usually reversed twice.
   (c) almost never happens.
   (d) shouldn't matter very much.

4. Sumo wrestling is said to be
   (a) very popular in China.
   (b) the Japanese national sport.
   (c) easy to judge correctly.
   (d) rarely watched by people.

5. Taiho was trying to
   (a) lose the match quickly.
   (b) murder Futabayama.
   (c) strangle the referee.
   (d) break a record.

6. Instant replay can
   (a) never reveal the truth.
   (b) show whether a decision was right.
   (c) break the television cameras.
   (d) change wrestling to baseball.

7. Which happened first?
   (a) The opponent's foot left the circle.
   (b) Taiho wanted to break a record.
   (c) The referee missed something.
   (d) The wrong person won the match.

8. You can tell that sumo wrestling
   (a) is played on a race track.
   (b) involves teams of nine.
   (c) is a contest between two.
   (d) is very unpopular in Japan.

Time ________ # Correct _____

36

In the evenings immediately following the full moon, a curious phenomenon transpires on the moonlit beaches of Southern California during the months from March to August. At this time, when the highest tide has begun to ebb, thousands of small silvery fish called grunion come up on the beach and cause entire sections of the shore to appear as shimmering silvery masses.

The fish first appear on the crests of waves. Each female is accompanied by several males. The female digs in the sand and deposits her eggs, which are then fertilized by the males. Then the fish all swim off on the next wave. This entire process takes only about thirty seconds for each little group of fish, yet there are so many fish that the event may have a duration of more than an hour on a given night.

The fertilized eggs develop in the sand and are hatched in approximately two weeks. Another high tide sweeps the baby grunion back out into the ocean, where they will remain until the "grunion run" the following year.

1. The grunion come to the beach
   (a) to sunbathe.
   (b) to mate.
   (c) one at a time.
   (d) for a vacation.

2. The selection describes grunion as
   (a) small silvery fish.
   (b) large silvery fish.
   (c) onion-colored fish.
   (d) small slippery fish.

3. A curious phenomenon is
   (a) always a moonlit beach.
   (b) the smell of small fish.
   (c) an unusual happening.
   (d) interested people.

4. It takes about two weeks for
   (a) grunion eggs to hatch.
   (b) female grunion to come back.
   (c) the entire grunion run.
   (d) grunion and their habits.

5. Which happens last in the year?
   (a) Grunion come up on the beach.
   (b) The high tide begins to ebb.
   (c) Baby grunion go back to the ocean.
   (d) The fertilized eggs hatch.

6. The beaches shimmer because
   (a) the sun shines on the waves.
   (b) the people like them that way.
   (c) evenings are cool in California.
   (d) the sand is full of silvery fish.

7. Something that transpires
   (a) occurs.
   (b) becomes very warm.
   (c) is moist.
   (d) disappears.

8. Without the grunion run,
   (a) the beaches would be clean.
   (b) people would be bored.
   (c) there would be no baby grunion.
   (d) the grunion would be bigger.

Time ________ # Correct ______

37

There's a high school in New York City that has one of the most successful Frisbee teams in the country. Competition for making the team is very tough, and many students at the school try out for it. Their game is what is known as "ultimate Frisbee," a contest in which the Frisbee is thrown from player to player until it is caught in the end zone. In strategy, the game resembles soccer, but it is played with a tossed disk rather than with a booted ball.

This particular high school team is so competent at Frisbee that its major opponents include some of the best colleges, and it regularly enjoys victories over these higher-level institutions. The high school players are at a disadvantage because their average height is less than that of their college opponents. They compensate for this with speed and cunning.

Perhaps one of the most unusual pieces of information about this outstanding high school Frisbee team is the identity of the school itself. These Frisbee players are from the Bronx High School of Science, well known for its high academic standards. This school has achieved considerable fame for its large number of winners in the annual Westinghouse Talent Search, and it includes among its graduates students who went on to win the coveted Nobel Prize.

Why would a high school so famous for its high level of scholarship have such a good Frisbee team? For some of the players, scientific explanation of the Frisbee's performance adds to the attractiveness of the game. One student wrote an essay on the physics of Frisbees and submitted it as part of his college application. He was accepted at the school.

For other students, the intellectual aspects of the game are less important than the physical excitement of engaging in the fast-paced sport, which can serve as an excellent outlet for tensions created by too much studying. "You enjoy running, going fast, diving and eating mud, and throwing Frisbees 30 miles an hour and catching them." That's how one of the players described the Frisbee's appeal.

1. The school in this story
   (a) provides Frisbees for everyone.
   (b) is located on the West Coast.
   (c) is best known for academics.
   (d) has many students in low tracks.

2. A subject related to Frisbees is
   (a) botany.
   (b) archaeology.
   (c) chemistry.
   (d) physics.

3. The students compete with college teams
   (a) because they are so good.
   (b) to travel farther.
   (c) to upset other high schools.
   (d) to save money.

4. Strategy in Frisbee is similar to
   (a) horse racing.
   (b) building sand castles.
   (c) ice hockey.
   (d) soccer.

5. To compensate is to
   (a) make up for.
   (b) run very rapidly.
   (c) think deep thoughts.
   (d) excel at everything.

6. Students seem to like Frisbee
   (a) because it's a fast sport.
   (b) as a way to cut classes.
   (c) to study its effects.
   (d) for a variety of reasons.

7. Something coveted is
   (a) kept nice and warm.
   (b) highly desirable.
   (c) easy to obtain.
   (d) difficult to see.

8. Ultimate Frisbee is a game
   (a) played with a larger disk.
   (b) played standing still.
   (c) using a stick and a Frisbee.
   (d) involving much running.

Time ________ # Correct _____

38

The scene was a courtroom in the state of New Mexico. A man was standing in front of the judge. The man had been accused of traveling 33 miles an hour in a 25-mile-per-hour zone. The man pleaded not guilty to the charge. The police officer who had issued the ticket swore under oath that his radar screen indicated 33 miles per hour as the exact speed of the man's car. The officer said he believed the radar to be perfectly precise.

The accused driver argued that the radar screen was wrong. He pointed out that a thunderstorm had hit the area shortly after he received the speeding ticket. He said that the blame for the high radar reading should have been placed on the thunderstorm, not on the driver of the car. He pointed out that the ionized air that precedes a thunderstorm can affect the accuracy of a speed radar unit. The judge agreed that the man's argument made sense and that static electricity in the air could have resulted in a false radar reading.

The driver was found not guilty of speeding, and the charges were dismissed. Luckily, he was trained as a physicist and was able to use a principle of advanced physics to prove the inaccuracy of the radar unit. Fortunately, the judge also knew physics and was able to understand what the driver was talking about.

1. This story takes place
   (a) on a road in New Mexico.
   (b) in a police station.
   (c) during a thunderstorm.
   (d) in a courtroom.

2. The driver and the judge were
   (a) old-time friends.
   (b) physicists.
   (c) arch enemies.
   (d) judges.

3. An inaccuracy is something which
   (a) travels too fast.
   (b) creates static electricity.
   (c) is incorrect.
   (d) stops an automobile.

4. The radar was wrong because
   (a) it needed a new part.
   (b) the rainstorm made it wet.
   (c) the officer read it too fast.
   (d) static electricity changed it.

5. Which came first?
   (a) A storm was brewing.
   (b) The driver got a ticket.
   (c) The judge dismissed the charge.
   (d) The officer testified.

6. Without the storm, the man
   (a) would have lost.
   (b) might have gone faster.
   (c) would not have been stopped.
   (d) would have fought the judge.

7. Something that precedes
   (a) causes a storm.
   (b) follows quickly after.
   (c) affects radar units.
   (d) comes before.

8. If the judge hadn't known physics,
   (a) the courtroom would have closed.
   (b) no one would have cared.
   (c) the officer would have lost.
   (d) the driver might have lost.

Time ________ # Correct ______

39

Margaret Wheeler and Blanche Rylatt each gave birth to an infant daughter at approximately the same time, in Nottingham, England, in 1936. Mrs. Wheeler's child was full term at birth. Mrs. Rylatt's daughter, on the other hand, was several weeks premature.

When Mrs. Wheeler was ready to leave the hospital, nurses handed her a tiny baby wrapped in a blanket. Right from the start, the mother suspected that an error had been made. She recalled her infant as somewhat plump with smooth, clear skin. The child she was given to take home, however, seemed small and scrawny. Its skin was covered with the fine downy little hairs often found on premature infants.

Mrs. Rylatt wasn't convinced that there had been any mistake, but she agreed to keep in touch with the Wheelers. Seven years later, after much negotiation and legal maneuvering, the women were able to ascertain that their daughters had indeed been switched in the hospital. The hospital records had each been signed by the wrong physician, and the wrong child presented to the parents for the trip home. The hospital finally admitted there had been an error.

At that point, however, both mothers decided that it would be too traumatic for the girls to be uprooted and switched back, so each child remained in the only home she knew. The families maintained close contact so each mother could observe her own daughter growing up. The girls were finally told the truth when they were grown.

Such a mistake would be just about impossible in today's modern maternity hospitals. Immediately after birth, a baby is labeled with the correct identification. Most hospitals put a bracelet on the newborn's wrist and another one on the ankle, just in case one comes off. The mother is given a matching bracelet. Each time the infant is brought to the mother, the bracelets are checked. Many places record the child's footprints as well. Before a baby leaves the hospital, the bracelets are again matched with the mother's bracelet.

1. This story began in a
   (a) hospital in England.
   (b) small-town courtroom.
   (c) baby's bedroom.
   (d) modern hospital.

2. The Rylatt child was born
   (a) on a Sunday.
   (b) several weeks premature.
   (c) in the room with baby Wheeler.
   (d) at full term.

3. A scrawny person is
   (a) pleasingly plump.
   (b) beautiful to look at.
   (c) thin and gaunt.
   (d) easy to hold.

4. Each mother was given the wrong baby
   (a) to make her happy.
   (b) by mistake at the hospital.
   (c) in an effort to upset people.
   (d) as a foolish joke.

5. Which happened first?
   (a) The babies were mixed up.
   (b) Each child was taken home.
   (c) The girls were told.
   (d) The mothers found out for sure.

6. Something traumatic is
   (a) easy to manipulate.
   (b) very expensive.
   (c) extremely upsetting.
   (d) small and very frail.

7. This story wouldn't happen today
   (a) because people would sue.
   (b) unless the parents wanted it to.
   (c) because hospitals are more careful.
   (d) because babies don't look alike.

8. The mothers in this story
   (a) abandoned their real children.
   (b) did what they thought was best.
   (c) should have been doctors.
   (d) were heartless and thoughtless.

Time ________ # Correct ______

40

Bighorn sheep, which once roamed North America in great numbers, now have only a small fraction of their former population. There once were more than three million bighorns. Now it is estimated that only 35,000 remain. Although the bighorns do not yet appear to be in danger of becoming extinct, people have become quite concerned that the herds have become so much smaller than they once were.

The bighorn sheep gets its name from the magnificent curling horns found on the male sheep. On older rams, the horns are massive, and they curve around so that they are pointing forward at eye level. The ewes have short horns which curve only slightly.

The marked decrease in the numbers of bighorn sheep is a result of disease and unfavorable changes in the habitat of these animals. For the sheep to thrive, they must be able to migrate freely. They need open grazing areas near the rocky cliffs they like to climb. Bighorns need open grazing areas so they can see any enemies approaching. These sheep do not have especially sensitive ears, and they must depend on the sense of sight to know when an enemy is near. In places where the underbrush has become dense, the sheep are more vulnerable because they have more difficulty seeing predators in time.

The development of the bighorn sheep can be traced back to the last Ice Age. In today's warmer climates, the sheep are not as resistant to disease as they would be if it were colder. Private groups and government agencies have taken an interest in the bighorn. Many people are working to improve the bighorns' grazing areas and to treat disease in these animals while there is still time to do so.

1. This selection is mainly about
   (a) animals of the Ice Age.
   (b) defending by hearing.
   (c) the appearance of bighorn ewes.
   (d) the bighorn sheep today.

2. The name of the bighorn
   (a) describes its appearance.
   (b) was assigned by the government.
   (c) applies just as well to goats.
   (d) is only used for rams.

3. An animal's habitat is its
   (a) predators.
   (b) offspring.
   (c) living space.
   (d) diet.

4. In places with lots of bushes,
   (a) bighorns have enough to eat.
   (b) there are good places to hide.
   (c) bighorns can't see enemies.
   (d) it's easy to get lost.

5. Bighorns developed
   (a) during the last Ice Age.
   (b) by climbing trees.
   (c) to cross with goats.
   (d) in warm climates.

6. Which came last?
   (a) There were 3 million bighorns.
   (b) The Ice Age ended.
   (c) Many bighorns died.
   (d) People are helping bighorns.

7. To be vulnerable means to
   (a) need new sources of food.
   (b) climb on steep cliffs.
   (c) be in some danger.
   (d) be sensitive to heat.

8. Bighorns are fewer in number because
   (a) people use them for food.
   (b) they make lovely fur coats.
   (c) the Ice Age is coming.
   (d) disease and enemies kill them.

Time ________ # Correct ______

	1	2	3	4	5	6	7	8
1	a b c d	a b c d	a b c d	a b c d	a b c d	a b c d	a b c d	a b c d
2	a b c d	a b c d	a b c d	a b c d	a b c d	a b c d	a b c d	a b c d
3	a b c d	a b c d	a b c d	a b c d	a b c d	a b c d	a b c d	a b c d
4	a b c d	a b c d	a b c d	a b c d	a b c d	a b c d	a b c d	a b c d
5	a b c d	a b c d	a b c d	a b c d	a b c d	a b c d	a b c d	a b c d
6	a b c d	a b c d	a b c d	a b c d	a b c d	a b c d	a b c d	a b c d
7	a b c d	a b c d	a b c d	a b c d	a b c d	a b c d	a b c d	a b c d
8	a b c d	a b c d	a b c d	a b c d	a b c d	a b c d	a b c d	a b c d
9	a b c d	a b c d	a b c d	a b c d	a b c d	a b c d	a b c d	a b c d
10	a b c d	a b c d	a b c d	a b c d	a b c d	a b c d	a b c d	a b c d

	1	2	3	4	5	6	7	8
11	a b c d	a b c d	a b c d	a b c d	a b c d	a b c d	a b c d	a b c d
12	a b c d	a b c d	a b c d	a b c d	a b c d	a b c d	a b c d	a b c d
13	a b c d	a b c d	a b c d	a b c d	a b c d	a b c d	a b c d	a b c d
14	a b c d	a b c d	a b c d	a b c d	a b c d	a b c d	a b c d	a b c d
15	a b c d	a b c d	a b c d	a b c d	a b c d	a b c d	a b c d	a b c d
16	a b c d	a b c d	a b c d	a b c d	a b c d	a b c d	a b c d	a b c d
17	a b c d	a b c d	a b c d	a b c d	a b c d	a b c d	a b c d	a b c d
18	a b c d	a b c d	a b c d	a b c d	a b c d	a b c d	a b c d	a b c d
19	a b c d	a b c d	a b c d	a b c d	a b c d	a b c d	a b c d	a b c d
20	a b c d	a b c d	a b c d	a b c d	a b c d	a b c d	a b c d	a b c d

	1	2	3	4	5	6	7	8
21	a b c d	a b c d	a b c d	a b c d	a b c d	a b c d	a b c d	a b c d
22	a b c d	a b c d	a b c d	a b c d	a b c d	a b c d	a b c d	a b c d
23	a b c d	a b c d	a b c d	a b c d	a b c d	a b c d	a b c d	a b c d
24	a b c d	a b c d	a b c d	a b c d	a b c d	a b c d	a b c d	a b c d
25	a b c d	a b c d	a b c d	a b c d	a b c d	a b c d	a b c d	a b c d
26	a b c d	a b c d	a b c d	a b c d	a b c d	a b c d	a b c d	a b c d
27	a b c d	a b c d	a b c d	a b c d	a b c d	a b c d	a b c d	a b c d
28	a b c d	a b c d	a b c d	a b c d	a b c d	a b c d	a b c d	a b c d
29	a b c d	a b c d	a b c d	a b c d	a b c d	a b c d	a b c d	a b c d
30	a b c d	a b c d	a b c d	a b c d	a b c d	a b c d	a b c d	a b c d

	1	2	3	4	5	6	7	8
31	a b c d	a b c d	a b c d	a b c d	a b c d	a b c d	a b c d	a b c d
32	a b c d	a b c d	a b c d	a b c d	a b c d	a b c d	a b c d	a b c d
33	a b c d	a b c d	a b c d	a b c d	a b c d	a b c d	a b c d	a b c d
34	a b c d	a b c d	a b c d	a b c d	a b c d	a b c d	a b c d	a b c d
35	a b c d	a b c d	a b c d	a b c d	a b c d	a b c d	a b c d	a b c d
36	a b c d	a b c d	a b c d	a b c d	a b c d	a b c d	a b c d	a b c d
37	a b c d	a b c d	a b c d	a b c d	a b c d	a b c d	a b c d	a b c d
38	a b c d	a b c d	a b c d	a b c d	a b c d	a b c d	a b c d	a b c d
39	a b c d	a b c d	a b c d	a b c d	a b c d	a b c d	a b c d	a b c d
40	a b c d	a b c d	a b c d	a b c d	a b c d	a b c d	a b c d	a b c d

Answer Key

	1	2	3	4	5	6	7	8
1	c	d	d	c	d	c	c	c
2	c	b	c	b	c	b	b	c
3	a	d	b	a	d	a	d	b
4	d	c	b	b	a	b	b	b
5	d	a	b	b	c	d	b	d
6	d	b	d	d	a	d	b	a
7	c	b	b	b	c	d	a	b
8	a	d	c	b	d	b	c	b
9	d	b	c	d	a	d	c	d
10	d	b	c	a	a	d	c	d

	1	2	3	4	5	6	7	8
11	d	b	a	a	b	d	d	b
12	c	d	c	b	d	a	c	a
13	b	b	c	a	c	b	d	a
14	b	c	b	d	b	a	d	b
15	c	c	a	a	c	d	a	b
16	b	b	c	b	b	d	a	d
17	b	b	c	d	b	b	d	a
18	b	a	b	c	b	a	c	c
19	b	c	b	b	a	b	b	d
20	d	b	b	a	c	c	c	a

Answer Key

	1	2	3	4	5	6	7	8
21	d	c	c	a	b	b	b	d
22	c	c	a	b	a	d	c	b
23	b	b	d	d	c	c	c	d
24	b	d	a	d	b	c	b	b
25	c	c	b	d	c	d	b	a
26	d	b	c	d	a	c	c	d
27	d	b	c	b	b	b	c	a
28	b	c	c	a	d	b	b	d
29	c	b	b	a	d	a	a	c
30	a	c	a	a	c	b	d	a

	1	2	3	4	5	6	7	8
31	c	c	c	d	d	b	d	c
32	a	a	c	c	b	d	d	d
33	d	b	a	c	d	b	d	c
34	a	b	d	d	d	c	b	a
35	b	d	a	b	d	b	b	c
36	b	a	c	a	c	d	a	c
37	c	d	a	d	a	d	b	d
38	d	b	c	d	a	c	d	d
39	a	b	c	b	a	c	c	b
40	d	a	c	c	a	d	c	d

Progress Plotter

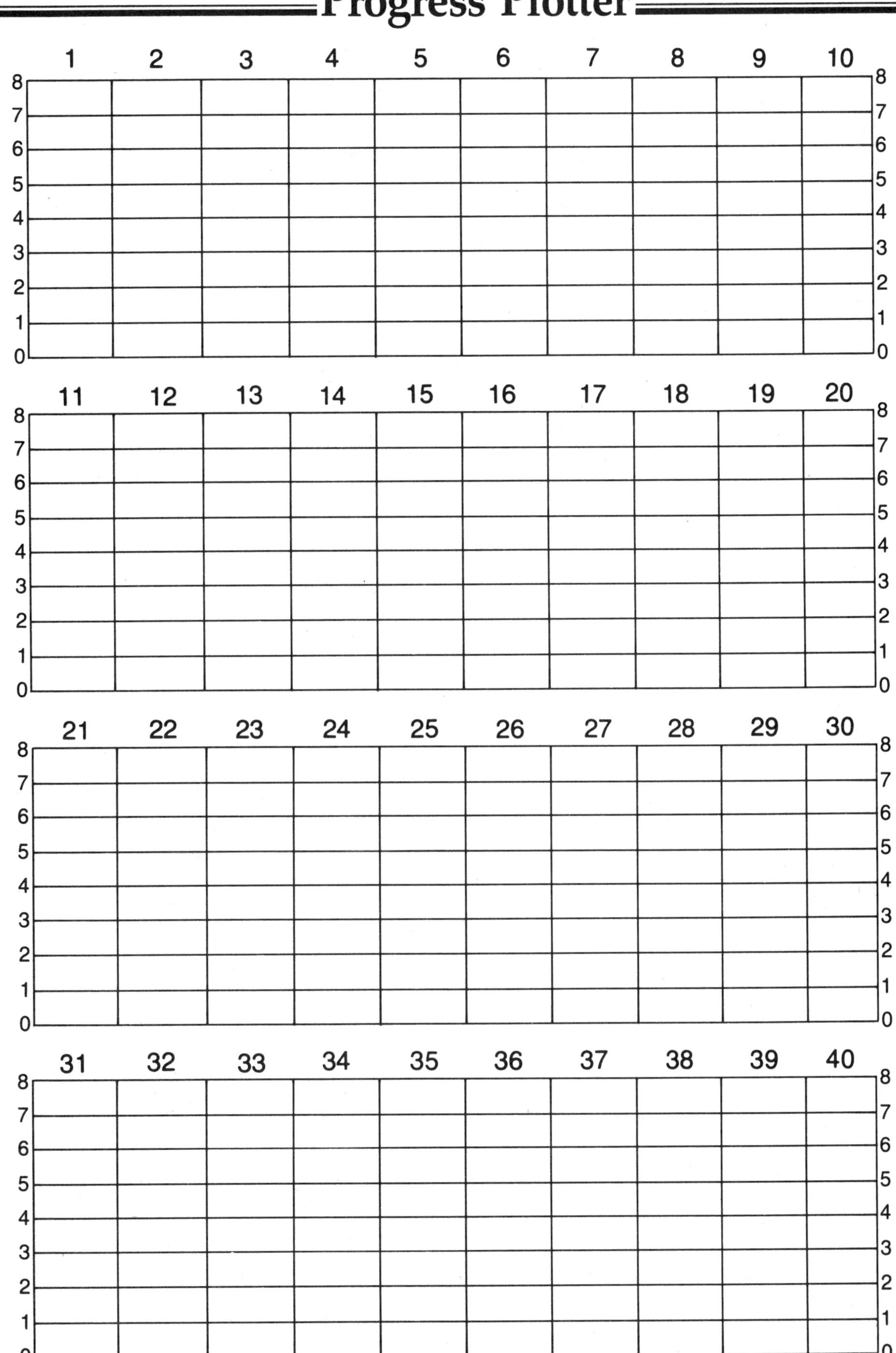

Skills Tracker

	1	2	3	4	5	6	7	8	9	10
Detail	1, 3, 6	1, 2	1, 4	1	1	1	7	5	1	2, 3, 4
Sequence	—	—	8	1, 2, 8	5	3	5	1	—	—
Context	3	3, 6, 7	6, 7	4, 7	2, 3, 4	4, 5	2	2, 7	3, 5	7
Main Idea	2	4	2	—	6	8	6	—	—	3
Inference	4, 5, 7, 8	4, 5, 8	3	5, 6	7	2, 4	1, 8	4, 6, 8	5, 6, 7	5, 6, 8
Cause & Effect	5, 7	—	3, 5	6	8	6, 7	1, 7	3, 4, 6	2, 4, 6, 8	5
Pred. Outcomes	—	—	8	6, 8	5	3	3, 7	3	—	—
Underst. Char.	5, 8	4	3	3, 5	—	6, 7	4, 7, 8	—	1, 5, 7, 8	3, 5, 8

	11	12	13	14	15	16	17	18	19	20
Detail	3	1	—	3	1, 6	2	2, 3	1, 5, 6	1, 2, 3, 6	1, 3, 4, 6
Sequence	7	—	5	—	7	7	—	—	4	—
Context	4	5, 6, 7	4, 6	2, 8	3, 4, 8	1, 5, 6	5, 7	7	5, 7	5, 8
Main Idea	—	—	1	1	2	3	1	2	—	—
Inference	5, 8	3, 4, 8	2, 3, 8	4, 5, 6	5	4, 8	1, 4	3, 8	—	2, 7
Cause & Effect	1	1, 2	3, 7	4, 6, 7	5	4, 8	4, 6	4	6, 8	3
Pred. Outcomes	7	4	—	6	6	4, 7	4, 6	—	—	—
Underst. Char.	2, 8	1, 2, 3	2, 3, 8	—	1, 5	7, 8	—	3, 4, 8	2	2

	21	22	23	24	25	26	27	28	29	30
Detail	1, 2	1	1, 2, 4, 7	1, 2	1	1	3, 4, 5	2, 3	1, 2, 3, 6	1
Sequence	7	3, 5	6	8	5	6	—	—	—	5
Context	6	2	—	3, 5, 7	3	2, 4	2, 3	4, 7	3, 5	2, 3
Main Idea	—	—	5	—	4	5	—	5	4	4
Inference	3, 4, 5, 8	4, 6, 7, 8	3, 8	4	6, 8	3, 7, 8	6	6, 8	7	6, 8
Cause & Effect	3, 4	7	3, 8	1	2, 7	8	4, 5, 7	1, 3	8	6, 7
Pred. Outcomes	—	3, 5	—	8	—	3	6	6	—	5
Underst. Char.	3, 8	4, 7, 8	3	1, 4, 6	2, 8	3, 7, 8	1	6, 8	—	6, 8

	31	32	33	34	35	36	37	38	39	40
Detail	1, 2, 4	1, 2, 3	6	1, 3	2, 3, 4, 5	2, 4	1, 2, 4	1, 2, 4	1, 2	2, 5
Sequence	—	2	2, 6	2	7	5	—	5, 7	1, 5	6
Context	3, 5, 7	7	3, 7	8	—	3, 7	5, 7	3, 7	3, 6	3, 7
Main Idea	8	—	1	4	1	—	—	—	—	1
Inference	5, 6	4, 5, 6, 8	4, 8	5, 6	6, 8	1, 8	3, 6, 8	6, 8	7, 8	4, 8
Cause & Effect	6	5, 6, 8	5	3, 5, 7	—	1, 6	3, 6	4	4	4, 8
Pred. Outcomes	—	6	2	5,7	7	8	—	6	7	6
Underst. Char.	1, 4, 6	6, 8	8	6, 7	5	1	3, 6	2, 8	8	—

Comprehension Puzzle–Enrichment

Complete each of these sentences. Put one letter in each box. Then follow the directions at the bottom of this page. (Reviewing the skills on page 1 or the outside back cover will help you find the right words.)

1. You can use the ______ to help you find the meaning of an unknown word.
2. Details in a story add up to the ______.
3. To ______ an outcome is to tell how you think a story will end.
4. A ______ is a person in a story.
5. A cause leads to an ______.
6. When the meaning is not stated directly, you must make an ______.
7. The order in which events occur is their ______.
8. To draw a ______ is to figure something out.

Write the circled letters in order here. If you did the page correctly, you'll end up with the word for what you've been practicing as you read the selections in this book.

Answers on page 719

SPOTLIGHT ON VOCABULARY

Contents

Project Manager: Sandra Kelley

Text: Development and Production by Educational Challenges, Inc.
Alexandria, Virginia

Illustrated by: Marcia Bergquist, Leslie Dunlap, Nancy Beatty Gleeson,
Ann W. Hawkins, Bobbi Tull

How to Use These Lessons

You use words every day of your life, to communicate with others and to learn about the world. A good vocabulary helps you to understand and enjoy reading more. It also helps you say and write exactly what you mean.

Each lesson will teach you skills you need to develop your vocabulary independently. You will practice these skills as you do the exercises. However, you should also use the skills on your own, whenever you read or write.

Boldface type is heavier or darker than the rest of the type. ▶

Many lessons also begin with a column of words in boldface in the left margin. These are the **key words.** Learn the ones you don't already know. You will find all the key words listed in the dictionary beginning on page 122.

In the left-hand margins of each lesson, you will also find clues and notes. Some will help you to complete the exercises correctly. Others give information about word etymologies. Read the sidenotes and think about them as you choose your answers.

Etymology (et′ə mol′ ə jē). means **the origin and history of a word.** ▶

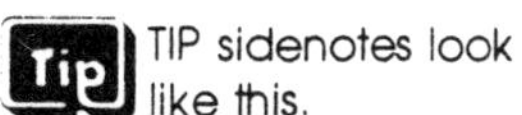

TIP sidenotes look like this. ▶

Some sidenotes are preceded by the word TIP. These sidenotes highlight important facts and rules you should remember. Pay special attention to these sidenotes. They will help you expand your vocabulary. The TIPS will be reviewed in the last lesson.

Unit 1

Suppose you are asked to help select a series of nature films to be shown during lunch hours. You start reading through film catalogues and find descriptions like these:

> *Owls* (22 min.) —Shows the elf owl in its habitat of the southwestern desert; **cavity**-nesting **barred** owls hatching eggs and rearing young; a great horned owl's **nocturnal** hunting, photographed with special nighttime film.
> *The Flightless Ostrich* (14 min.) —Records the **bizarre**, fantastically strange, appearance of the world's largest bird; captures the ostrich's unusual social behavior while **disproving** that the **wary** ostrich buries its head in the sand.

Some words will probably be unfamiliar to you. Look at the words in boldface. How can you figure out their meanings?

You know that a **cavity** in your tooth is a **hole**, so you can guess that **cavity**-nesting birds live in holes instead of building an outside nest. One of the meanings of **bar** is **a band or strip**, so you might guess that a **barred** owl has some kind of striped coloring.

Vocabulary for Reading

Since pictures of **nocturnal** hunting had to be made with special nighttime film, you have a clue that **nocturnal** means **something that occurs at night**.

Remember that **synonyms** are words that are similar in meaning.

Notice that the word **disproving** contains the prefix **dis**-. If you remember that **dis**- means **the opposite of**, you can figure out that **disproving** means **proving to be false**.

Sometimes a synonym for a word comes in the same sentence as the word. Can you find a clue to the meaning of **bizarre** in the same sentence? The words **fantastically strange** that come after **bizarre** give its meaning. The word **wary** is harder to guess about and you might need to look it up in the dictionary.

Knowing how to figure out the meanings of unfamiliar words allows you to read more easily and to expand your vocabulary. In Unit 1, you will be concentrating on developing vocabulary skills for reading. Here are some of the topics covered in this unit:

- how prefixes and suffixes change a word's meaning
- words that come from other languages, and how the dictionary indicates a word's origin
- how our language is constantly changed by the addition of new, modern words
- words that are spelled alike and words with multiple meanings
- how to use context clues to figure out new words

lesson 1 Prefixes

abdicate · **abduct**
abnormal · **abolish**
absence · **abstain**
coexist · **cohesion**
collaborate
compound · **concur**
converge

A **prefix** is a word part placed at the beginning of a word. Usually a prefix changes the meaning of the word. You can often figure out the meanings of new words you come across in your reading if you know the meanings of prefixes in the words.

Two common families of prefixes are **ab-** or **abs-** and **co-**, **col-**, **com-**, or **con-**. Study the definitions of the key words below. Try to figure out the meanings of the **ab-** and **co-** families of prefixes from the definitions.

abdicate (ab′ di kāt′), *v.* to resign from or give up (a throne or any high position of leadership).
abduct (ab dukt′), *v.* to carry off or kidnap by force or trickery.
abnormal (ab nôr′ məl), *adj.* not typical; different from what is normal.
abolish (ə bol′ ish), *v.* to do away with completely; put an end to.
absence (ab′ səns), *n.* 1. the state of being away. 2. a lack; state of being without something.
abstain (ab stān′), *v.* to refrain from; deny oneself.
coexist (kō′ ig zist′), *v.* to live together or at the same time.
cohesion (kō hē′ zhən), *n.* a sticking together.
collaborate (kə lab′ ə rāt′), *v.* to work together with others.
compound (kom′ pound), *adj.* made of two or more parts put together.
concur (kən kûr′), *v.* to agree with.
converge (kən vûrj′), *v.* to come together at a point.

The bound base **cur** in **concur** is from a Latin word meaning **to run**. It is also found in **recur** and **current**. ▶

A. Look at the meanings of the prefixes **ab-** and **co-**. Write the correct prefix on the line next to its definition.

1. ____________, with; together.
2. ____________, from; off; away; not.

B. Underline the correct key word to complete each sentence.

1. Ernesto had to (abstain, concur) from soccer practice until his poison ivy healed.

Tip Look at the prefix **inter-** in this sentence. Do you know its meaning? Look for prefixes, suffixes, and roots you know to help you figure out the meaning of an unfamiliar word. ▶

2. Five streets (abolish, converge) at that intersection.
3. The police uncovered a plot to (abduct, collaborate) the mayor.
4. The cast canceled today's rehearsal because of the (absence, cohesion) of the drama coach.
5. The new city law (abdicates, abolishes) the use of automobiles in the park on Sundays.

Look for the word whose root is a synonym for **live**. ▶

6. Our dog and cat usually (abstain, coexist) peacefully.
7. Jake had an (abnormal, compound) amount of homework to do over the past weekend.

C. In each group of sentences below, the first sentence contains a boldface key word. Circle the letter of the sentence that could logically follow the first sentence.

1. Less than a year after he became king, Edward VIII of England announced his decision to **abdicate**.
   a. His reign continued another twelve years.
   b. His brother immediately replaced him as king.

Did Tina and Rachel do their work together or separately? ▶

2. Tina and Rachel decided they would **collaborate** on their math homework.
   a. Tina went home with Rachel after school.
   b. They compared answers when they got to class the next day.
3. People at the picnic ate an **abnormal** amount of food.
   a. The committee members were pleased that they had planned so well.
   b. The food ran out before 2:00 P.M.
4. Norma's parents **concurred** with her ideas for a big slumber party next weekend.
   a. They told her to go right ahead with her plans.
   b. They told her she would have to cut the guest list in half.
5. The horse chestnut tree's leaf is an example of a **compound** leaf.
   a. It has only one part.
   b. It is made up of several parts.
6. There is little **cohesion** among the members of Max's family.
   a. They are always loyal to each other.
   b. They quarrel a lot and talk behind each others' backs.
7. In this historic play, the queen is **abducted** by rivals of the ruling family.
   a. The king offers a ransom for her return.
   b. She rewards them by giving them positions at court.

D. In each blank write the key word that makes the most sense.

Before you make each choice, think about what part of speech you need. ▶

Wolves are social animals. They (1.) ____________________ in a family group of up to 30 individuals with one male as the leader. If challenged by a stronger male within the group, the leader may (2.) ____________________ his position. There is a great deal of (3.) ____________________ among the members of a wolf pack. They all (4.) ____________________ in caring for the cubs. If the parents go off to hunt, in their (5.) ____________________ other wolves watch over the cubs. To kill a large animal, such as a moose, several wolves trail it and then (6.) ____________________ upon it in a joint attack.

Knowing the meanings of prefixes will help you to understand the meanings of many unfamiliar words in your reading.

lesson 2 Suffixes

characterize · **facial**
familiarize
fractional
functional · **medicinal**
rationalize · **theorize**

A **suffix** is a word part that is added to the end of a word. Suffixes are used for many purposes. Often a suffix changes a word to a different part of speech.

The suffix **-ize** changes an adjective or a noun to a verb. For example, when the suffix **-ize** is added to the adjective **real**, the verb **realize** is formed.

A. The key words defined below are verbs that contain the suffix **-ize**. Write a key word on the line next to its definition. Think of the adjective or noun form of the word to help you with its meaning. Use the dictionary if you need more help.

Sometimes the last letter of a word is changed or dropped before the suffix is added. ▶

1. ______________________, *v.* to form a theory or explanation.
2. ______________________, *v.* to make well-acquainted with something.

The word **reason** is related to this key word. ▶

3. ______________________, *v.* to explain (an act) in a seemingly reasonable way.
4. ______________________, *v.* to be typical of or peculiar to.

The suffix **-al** changes nouns and verbs to adjectives. For example, when **-al** is added to the noun **triumph**, the adjective **triumphal** is formed.

B. The key words defined below are adjectives that contain the suffix **-al**. Write the correct key word on the line next to each definition. Think of the noun or verb form of the word to help you.

1. ______________________, *adj.* of or located on the face.
2. ______________________, *adj.* referring to or containing a drug.
3. ______________________, *adj.* in working order; capable of performing.

The word you are looking for comes from the Latin word **fractus**, meaning **broken**. ▶

4. ______________________, *adj.* small or insignificant.

C. In each blank in the passage, write the key word that best completes the sentence. Use each key word only once.

Which key word has to do with what is typical or peculiar? ▶

We are all aware of our physical appearance. In a mirror or a photograph we can see how we look to others. Our actions and behavior (1.) ______________________ us as clearly as our height, build, and (2.) ______________________ features. Yet most of us are aware of only a (3.) ______________________ part of the causes of our behavior. Much of what we do is the result of ideas and feelings that are unconscious. We often (4.) ______________________ what we do and why, explaining it in some acceptable and reasonable way without understanding the real cause.

Freud (froid) lived from 1856 to 1939. ▶

Until recent times, doctors and scientists had not studied the workings of the human mind. Sigmund Freud, an Austrian physician, was one of the first people to (5.) ______________________ about the effect of the unconscious mind on everyday behavior. He developed methods to help people (6.) ______________________ themselves with hidden feelings and memories in order to gain insight into their behavior.

Which key word has to do with becoming acquainted with something? ▶

A clue to this key word is found earlier in this sentence. ▶

Although he had been trained in the science of medicine and the use of (7.) ______________________ remedies for illness, Freud came to believe that some illnesses were really caused by the mind and not the body. He believed that in such cases people could be helped to become (8.) ______________________ again if they could discover and talk about their problems.

Psychological means **having to do with the mind or emotions**. ▶

Profound means **deep** or **far-reaching**. ▶

Freud's ideas were at first doubted and criticized. Since he did his pioneering work, many other psychological theories have been developed that differ greatly from his. Nevertheless, his thinking has had a profound influence upon modern methods of treatment and upon new explanations of human personality development.

Understanding how suffixes change words will help you figure out the meanings of many new words in your reading.

---

lesson 3 More Suffixes

capitalism

conservatism

faddist · **feminism**

feudalism

liberalism

militarism

pacifist · **racism**

realist · **socialist**

Words that end in the suffixes -**ism** and -**ist** are nouns. Words ending in -**ist** are names for people. Words ending in -**ism** are most often names for abstract ideas, theories, qualities, or practices.

A. Study the definitions of the key words. Each has been formed by adding the suffix -**ism** or -**ist** to a noun, a verb, or an adjective. On the line after each definition write the noun, verb, or adjective from which the key word was made.

1. **capitalism** (kap′ i tə liz′ əm), *n.* an economic system in which most land and businesses are owned by individuals or companies rather than by the government.

____

2. **conservatism** (kən sûr′ və tiz′ əm), *n.* the quality of being opposed to social or political change.

____

The word may be shortened, or the last letter changed or doubled, before adding the suffix. ▶

3. **faddist** (fad′ ist), *n.* one who enthusiastically follows a fashion or a kind of behavior for a brief time.

____

4. **feminism** (fem′ ə niz′ əm), *n.* a belief in granting women the same rights as men, as in political or economic status.

____

The medieval period lasted from about the 9th to the 15th century. ▶

5. **feudalism** (fyo͞od′ ə liz′ əm), *n.* the social and economic system in medieval Europe in which a person held land from a lord in return for military service and other obligations.

____

You would think that someone who believes in **liberalism** would be a **liberalist**, but the correct term is **liberal**. ▶

6. **liberalism** (lib′ ər ə liz′ əm), *n.* the quality of favoring social or political change.

____

Militarism comes from the Latin word **miles** (pronounced mē′ les), meaning **a soldier**. ▶

7. **militarism** (mil′ i tə riz′ əm), *n.* 1. the policy of maintaining a powerful military force. 2. a tendency to regard military ideas as most important.

____

The Latin origin of this word is **pax** (peace) + **facere** (to make). ▶

8. **pacifist** (pas′ ə fist), *n.* one who opposes war and violence.

____

Ethnic means **national**, **cultural**, or **racial**. ▶

9. **racism** (rā′ siz əm), *n.* the belief that one's own race or ethnic group is superior.

____

10. **realist** (rē′ ə list), *n.* a person who faces facts as they are and avoids the imagined or impractical.

____

11. **socialist** (sō′ shə list), *n.* one who favors an economic system in which the community as a whole rather than private interests controls land, production, etc.

____

B. In each set of parentheses in the passage, underline the key word that makes sense.

People who run for public office or who actively support political candidates represent a wide variety of beliefs and causes. A candidate who favors (1. liberalism, conservatism) is likely to run a campaign centered upon social and political change. An individual who supports (2. feudalism, feminism) might promise to work for equal pay and employment opportunities for women if elected.

Which word comes from the Latin word for **peace**? ▶

A person who advocates (3. militarism, racism) may support a candidate who wants to increase defense spending, while a (4. realist, pacifist) campaigns for a candidate who favors greater contributions to world peace organizations.

Which belief has to do with racial superiority? ▶

A believer in (5. capitalism, feminism) talks about the need to have less government regulation of business. A (6. pacifist, socialist), on the other hand, argues for laws that favor public ownership over private control. A (7. realist, faddist), full of enthusiasm for a new notion, may pressure a candidate to promote it. However, a supporter of (8. liberalism, conservatism) may urge a candidate to keep things as they are. (9. Militarism, Racism) is often present in a campaign when one group of people thinks it has something to fear from a different ethnic group. To be successful, a candidate must be enough of a (10. faddist, realist) to present ideas in a way that will appeal to a large range of voters.

A VOTE FOR CHIERI?
A VOTE FOR CHANGE!
★ ★ ★ ★ ★ ★ ★ ★ ★ ★ ★ ★ ★

C. For many words both the **-ism** and the **-ist** suffix can be added.

To complete each sentence, change the suffix of the key word to form the other noun. ▶

If the theory or belief is called **capitalism**, the person who practices it is a (1.) ______________. A believer in **feminism** is a (2.) ______________. A **socialist** is a person who believes in the economic theory of (3.) ______________. The person who advocates **militarism** is a (4.) ______________.

The suffixes **-ism** and **-ist** can be added to some nouns, verbs, and adjectives to form new nouns.

lesson **4**

Bound Bases

chronicle

chronology

evoke · **manuscript**

scribe · **vocation**

Some root words cannot stand alone but must be combined with a prefix or suffix. These root words are called **bound bases**. Three bound bases and their meanings are listed in the box below.

> **chron**, time
> **scrib** or **scrip**, writing or written
> **voc**, calling or voice

A. In the passage, key words that are built on these bound bases are in boldface. Read the passage; then write each key word next to its definition following the passage.

The American novelist Willa Cather believed that the years most important in forming a writer are those between the ages of 8 and 15. During that time, without realizing it, the young person stores up much of the basic material that will later be used in the **manuscripts** of the adult writer.

The word **manu** in Latin means **by hand**. ▶

The **chronology** of Willa's life proved to be vital to her writing. For her, most of those important early years were spent in Red Cloud, Nebraska, in the late 1800s. She was born in Virginia, but when she was nine her father decided to move the family west. Willa hated to leave her home and friends, but she grew to love Nebraska. The land was very different from her native Virginia. It was open, rolling prairie, dry and with few trees, under a wide sky. Many of the neighbors were recent immigrants from Europe. When Willa grew up and writing became her **vocation**, she realized the powerful influence of her prairie years. Many of her novels and short stories are about Nebraska. They **evoke** a strong sense of the place, and of the spirit and strength of the people who settled there.

In some words the bound base **voc** changes to **vok**. ▶

Willa attended the University of Nebraska. Her first efforts as a **scribe** were articles for a newspaper and for the college magazine. After college, she moved to Pittsburgh and later to New York, but she always felt the need to go back to visit in Red Cloud. For many years, she was a successful editor for a magazine. Eventually she decided that writing was the most important thing to her, and she gave up her other work. Devoting all her time to writing fiction, she **chronicled** the people, scenes, and events that she knew best.

Which bound base are you looking for? Look for a clue in each definition.

1. to call forth, suggest, or produce ____________________
2. a writer or author, especially a news reporter

____

3. the order of events in time, from earliest to latest

____

4. one's profession, business, or calling ____________________
5. the written text of an author's work, prepared for publication

____

6. to record the events of a certain time ____________________

Look back at the definitions in part A if you need help.

B. Write the correct key word in each blank.

1. Stories about the South by Eudora Welty and about New York City by Edith Wharton are other examples of American fiction that ____________________ a strong sense of place.
2. When scientist Rachel Carson became concerned about the danger to the environment from the use of too many chemicals to kill pests, she wrote the ____________________ for her book *Silent Spring.*
3. The letters of Abigail Adams to her husband, John Adams, provide a fascinating, detailed ____________________ of the early years of America's independence.

Which key word means **the order of events in time**?

4. Two women ____________________ for major American newspapers were Anne O'Hare McCormick, for 30 years a reporter for the *New York Times*, and Marguerite Higgins, a reporter and war correspondent for the New York *Herald Tribune.*
5. The American photographer Margaret Bourke-White was first famous for her photographs of industry, and later her pictures helped to ____________________ the events of World War II.

Which key word means **to record**?

6. The ____________________ of journalism was expanded when the new field of radio and television broadcasting made possible careers such as that of Pauline Frederick, who became a news analyst for a major broadcasting system.

C. Think of some of the words that you already know that are built on the bound bases in this lesson. Write one or more on each line.

Think about prefixes and suffixes you know and use your dictionary to help you.

1. **chron** ____________________
2. **scrib** or **scrip** ____________________
3. **voc** ____________________

Some **voc** words are from the Latin word **vocare, to call**. Others come from the Latin **voc, voice**.

Bound bases are root words that cannot stand alone but need to have prefixes or suffixes added to them.

lesson **5**

Borrowed Words for Foods

coleslaw • curry
goulash • ketchup
marmalade • soy
succotash • tortilla
yogurt • zucchini

Many words in our language have been borrowed from other countries around the world. The key words in this lesson are the names of foods that have come from other languages.

A. The dictionary entries below give in brackets the origins of the words they define. Write the correct key word on the line at the beginning of each entry. Use your classroom dictionary if you need help with some of the words.

1. ____________________, *n.* a highly seasoned tomato sauce used on meat, fish, and such. [from the Chinese dialect word *ke-tsiap*, "pickled fish brine"]

Tip: Knowing a word's origin can often help you figure out its meaning.

2. ____________________, *n.* a salad of finely sliced or chopped raw cabbage. [from the Dutch word *koolsla*, which comes from *kool*, "cabbage" + *sla*, short for *salade*, "salad"]

A **rind** is the thick outer covering or skin of some fruits or cheeses.

3. ____________________, *n.* a jellylike preserve of fruit, especially of oranges, that contains bits of rind. [French]

4. ____________________, *n.* a stew of beef or veal and vegetables, with paprika or other seasonings. [from the Hungarian phrase *gulyas hus*, "herdsman's meat"]

Fermenting is a chemical process that makes something become sour.

5. ____________________, *n.* a salty brown liquid sauce made by fermenting soybeans in brine. [from Japanese, *sho-yu*]

6. ____________________, *n.* a summer squash shaped like a cucumber and having a smooth, dark-green skin. [from the Italian *zucca*, "gourd"]

Tamil is a language of India.

7. ____________________, *n.* 1. a yellowish powder made with several spices, used especially in the cookery of India. 2. food cooked and flavored with this powder. [from the Tamil word *kari*, "sauce"]

Another Spanish food word that has come into English is **tamale**, a mixed dish of meat, peppers, and cornmeal.

8. ____________________, *n.* a round, flat bread made from coarse cornmeal, characteristic of Mexican cookery. [American Spanish, from Spanish *torta*, "a round cake"]

9. ____________________, *n.* a custard-like food, prepared from milk curdled by bacteria. [from Turkish, *yōghurt*]

The Narragansett tribe formerly lived in what is now Rhode Island.

10. ____________________, *n.* a dish of corn kernels and lima beans cooked together. [from American Indian, the Narragansett word *msickquatash*, "boiled whole-grain corn (off the cob)"]

B. Underline the key word in parentheses that makes sense in each sentence.

1. Mrs. Antonelli sliced several small (ketchup, zucchini) to add to the salad.

2. Instead of salt, Toshio adds some (goulash, soy) sauce to the vegetables he cooks.
3. Jan picked a fresh cabbage to use for the (coleslaw, marmalade).
4. Every summer when fresh tomatoes are in season, Paula's mother makes a batch of homemade (ketchup, succotash).
5. On a cold night, a hearty hot dish of (goulash, marmalade) makes a perfect dinner.

Which key word is the name of a dairy product? ▶

6. Most (soy, yogurt) in America is made from cow's milk, but in the countries where it originated it was usually made from the milk of sheep or goats.
7. Fernando and Carlotta helped to grind the cornmeal to make the (curry, tortillas).

Which key word comes from an American Indian word? ▶

8. Early settlers in America learned from the Indians how to make (yogurt, succotash),
9. Pierre asked for some (coleslaw, marmalade) to go with his toast at breakfast.
10. The menu in the Indian restaurant listed fourteen different varieties of (curry, ketchup) dishes.

C. The words in the box are ones you already know that are borrowed from other languages. Write the correct word in the blank in each sentence.

banana	omelet	pizza	chow mein	bagel	taco

1. A Portuguese and Spanish word for fruit with a thick, peelable skin is ______________________.
2. A Mexican Spanish word for a tortilla wrapped around a filling such as meat or cheese is ______________________.

Another Chinese word that has come into English is **tea**, from the Chinese **ch'a**. ▶

3. A Chinese word for a dish made of cooked meat and vegetables, usually served over fried noodles, is ______________________.
4. A French word for eggs beaten, cooked, and folded over, often with a filling added, is ______________________.

Yiddish is a language developed from German that contains Hebrew and Slavic words written in Hebrew letters. ▶

5. A Yiddish word for a glazed, hard, doughnut-shaped roll is ______________________.
6. An Italian word for a thin crust covered with a spicy tomato and cheese mixture and baked is ______________________.

Many of our names for food come from other languages.

lesson 6 More Borrowed Words

beret • bouquet

camouflage • clique

collage • coupe

crochet • levee

sabotage • suite

All of the key words below have come into our language from French. Study their definitions.

beret (bə rā′), *n.* a soft, round cap that has no brim or visor, and fits snugly on the head.

bouquet (bō kā′), *n.* a bunch of flowers.

camouflage (kam′ ə fläzh′), *n.* 1. a disguise that blends into the background or looks like something else. 2. the act or technique of disguising military equipment or uniforms so they cannot be easily seen. —*v.* 3. to conceal or disguise by changing the appearance or covering up.

clique (klēk), *n.* a small group of people who are friendly with each other or work closely together and usually do not let outsiders join their activities.

collage (kə läzh′), *n.* a work of art composed by pasting materials and objects on a surface.

coupe (ko͞op), *n.* a closed, two-door automobile.

Note that in each of the words ending in **-et**, the **t** is silent. ▶

crochet (krō shā′), *v.* to make needlework by looping thread or yarn with a needle having a hook on the end.

levee (lev′ ē), *n.* an embankment designed to prevent a river from overflowing.

The French word **sabot** means **shoe**. The word **sabotage** was used after the French railway strike of 1912 when the strikers cut the shoes holding the railway lines. ▶

sabotage (sab′ ə täzh), *n.* 1. intentional interference with production or work in a factory, such as by enemy agents during a war. 2. any deliberate effort to defeat or do harm to an undertaking. —*v.* 3. to injure or attack by sabotage.

suite (swēt), *n.* 1. a number of related things forming a series or set: *a suite of rooms.* 2. a musical composition consisting of several short movements.

A. Underline the key word that makes sense in each sentence.

1. Claude inherited a green (coupe, levee) from his uncle.
2. Although the club has a large membership, one small (bouquet, clique) controls all the activities.

Either choice is possible, but which makes more sense? ▶

3. Edith says she is too clumsy to learn to (crochet, sabotage) well; she finds knitting easier.

Which word is the name of an art technique? ▶

4. Georges Braque was a French artist who was a master of the technique of (collage, levee).
5. The Millers have just bought a new (beret, suite) of oak dining room furniture.
6. Because of the heavy rains, several layers of sandbags have been added to the top of the (coupe, levee) north of town.

Another clothing loan-word from French is **blouse**. ▶

7. Nicole was wearing a stylish woolen (beret, clique).
8. The white fur of the polar bear is good (bouquet, camouflage) against the snow and ice.

If this was her first public performance it would be called her **debut** (dā byo͞o′), another French word. ▶

9. At the end of her performance, the ballerina was given a huge (bouquet, suite) of roses.
10. The explosion at the railroad station appeared to be an accident, not (camouflage, sabotage).

B. Read the movie review. In each blank write the key word that best completes the sentence.

A **chateau** (sha tō′) is a French castle or large country house.

Which key word names an article of clothing?

Unique, which means **one of a kind**, is another French word that has been added to our language.

In the new French movie at the Ritz, a group of art thieves plans to steal an oil painting and a valuable (1.) ____________________ from a chateau not far from Paris. By chance, a former member of the (2.) ____________________, who is now out of favor, learns of their underhanded scheme. Seeing his chance for revenge, he decides to (3.) ____________________ the thieves' plan. Disguised as a messenger, he delivers a (4.) ____________________ containing a hidden microphone to their (5.) ____________________ of rooms in the hotel. Wearing a peasant smock, a (6.) ____________________, and wooden shoes as his (7.) ____________________, he gains entrance to the chateau grounds. When he is discovered, he escapes in a dilapidated (8.) ____________________. Pursued by the enraged thieves, he drives wildly through Paris, over the bridges and along the (9.) ____________________ by the river. The movie is not unique, but it is good entertainment. I won't spoil the surprise ending for you, but I do suggest that you watch throughout the movie for a small woman who appears every now and then and who seems to do nothing but sit and (10.) ____________________.

Many words in our language are borrowed from French.

lesson **7**

Names of People and Places

boycott · **calico**

camellia · **cashmere**

limerick · **lynch**

marathon · **sequoia**

Words have come into our language in many ways. Some are borrowed from other languages. Others have been made from the names of people and places.

A. The dictionary entries below give the origins of the words they define. Write the correct key word on the line at the beginning of each dictionary entry.

1. ________________, *n.* a light, humorous verse of five lines. [named for Limerick, a county of Ireland]

Another kind of wool named for a place is **angora**, named for Ankara, Turkey. ▶

2. ________________, *n.* fine, downy wool from the Kashmir goats of India, or fabric or yarn made from this wool. [named for Kashmir, a region of northern India and West Pakistan]

A **justice of the peace** is a local public officer with some legal authority. ▶

3. ________________, *v.* to hang or otherwise kill a person by mob action and without legal authority. [perhaps named after Charles Lynch, an 18th-century Virginia planter and justice of the peace]

4. ________________, *n.* cotton cloth, usually printed on one side with a colored pattern. [named after Calicut, the former name of a seaport of India]

Sequoya, a Cherokee Indian, developed the first written alphabet for a North American Indian language. ▶

5. ________________, *n.* a large evergreen tree of California. [named after Sequoya, an American Indian leader and scholar]

6. ________________, *v.* to refuse to buy, use, or deal with as a form of protest or pressure. [named after Charles C. Boycott, a land agent in County Mayo, Ireland, who refused to lower rents]

Tip Knowing a word's origin can often help you figure out its meaning. ▶

7. ________________, *n.* 1. a long-distance foot race, especially one of 26 miles 385 yards. 2. any long contest of endurance. [so called after the 26-mile run of a Greek messenger from Marathon to Athens to bring news of the Greek victory over the Persians]

A **Jesuit** (jezh′ o͞o it) is a member of a Roman Catholic order, the Society of Jesus, founded in 1534. ▶

8. ________________, *n.* an Asian shrub or tree with shiny evergreen leaves and large white, pink, or red flowers. [named after Georg Josef Kamel, a 17th-century Jesuit missionary, who first described it.]

B. Underline the word that completes each sentence correctly. Then write **N** on the line next to the sentence if the correct word comes from a person's name. Write **P** on the line if the correct word comes from the name of a place.

________ 1. Kim planted the (camellia, cashmere) in the flower bed near the front door.

Both of these key words refer to cloth. Which is likely to be warmer? ▶

________ 2. A coat of (calico, cashmere) is warm and soft.

________ 3. The police worried that the angry crowd might attempt to (boycott, lynch) the prisoner.

Another plant named for a person is the **begonia**, named after the Frenchman Michel Bégon.

Which fabric has a printed design on it?

_________ 4. Alex, Sheila, and Charlie have been in training to qualify for the (limerick, marathon).

▶ _________ 5. The (camellia, sequoia) is a plant native to the western part of North America.

_________ 6. The commuters are threatening to (boycott, lynch) the bus company if fares are raised again.

▶ _________ 7. A spotted cat having several colors is sometimes called a (calico, cashmere) cat.

_________ 8. Marvin can make up a good (limerick, marathon) faster than anyone else.

C. The words in the box are ones you already know that come from names of people or places. Write the correct word in the blank in each sentence below the word box.

graham	Gypsy	magnolia	sandwich

The earl had this kind of food brought to him while he was gambling so he would not have to stop to eat.

They came originally from even farther east, near the border of India and Iran.

▶ 1. Slices of bread with a filling between, named for an English earl, are called a ____________________.

2. A North American evergreen tree or shrub with large, sweet-smelling flowers, named after French botanist Pierre Magnol, is a ____________________.

▶ 3. One of a nomadic people of Eastern Europe, whose name came from a form of the word **Egyptian**, is a ____________________.

4. A whole-wheat cracker named for an American vegetarian is a ____________________ cracker.

Many of our English words have come from the names of people and places.

lesson 8 Modern Words

helipad · **hot line**

meltdown

moonscape

moped · **ombudsman**

paramedic · **printout**

skyjacker

superpower

wetland

Our language constantly adds new words. Some result from scientific and technical developments, some from social and political change. Many new words are formed by combining or blending other words. Sometimes a new meaning is given to an old word. And sometimes an entirely new word must be invented. You already know the meanings of many modern words, even though they may be too new to be in the dictionary, because you see and hear them frequently.

Study the definitions of the key words below.

helipad (hel′ ə pad′), *n.* a small area for helicopters to land on or take off from.

hot line (hot′ līn′), *n.* 1. a direct Teletype or telephone line between two heads of state for instant communication in case of crisis. 2. any direct phone line for instant counseling or conferring.

meltdown (melt′ doun), *n.* the melting of the core of a nuclear reactor.

moonscape (mo͞on′ skāp), *n.* the surface of the moon or a picture of it.

Moped has a homograph, the past form of **mope**. ▶

moped (mō′ ped), *n.* a heavily built motorized bicycle. [from *mo(tor) ped(al)*]

The position originated in Scandinavia, and our word for it comes from Norwegian. ▶

ombudsman (ôm′ bo͝odz man′), *n.* a public official who investigates citizens' complaints against government officials or agencies.

paramedic (par′ ə med′ ik), *n.* a person trained to assist a physician and able to perform some kinds of medical tasks.

printout (print′ out′), *n.* the printed output of a computer.

What earlier word suggested this one? ▶

skyjacker (skī′ jak ər), *n.* one who forcibly takes over an airplane in flight.

superpower (so͞o′ pər pou′ ər), *n.* an extremely powerful nation; a nation capable of influencing the acts and policies of other nations.

wetland (wet′ land′), *n.* Usually **wetlands**. an area such as a swamp or tidal flat containing much soil moisture.

A. Underline the correct key word in the sentences.

1. A (helipad, paramedic) receives special technical training.
2. Safeguards must be used at nuclear plants to avoid the danger of a (hot line, meltdown).
3. The naturalist studied a variety of plant and animal life in the (moonscape, wetlands).
4. That complicated (moped, printout) needs to be read by a computer expert.
5. The city has appointed a special (paramedic, ombudsman) to deal with consumer problems.
6. The plans for the new convention center include putting a (helipad, superpower) on the roof.

7. Electronic devices at airports that scan luggage and people's clothing are intended to help spot a potential (ombudsman, skyjacker).
8. After the eruption of Mount St. Helens the area near the volcano looked like a (moonscape, printout).
9. A (hot line, meltdown) was set up in the mayor's office during the days of the rioting.

Neutral means **not taking sides.**

▶ 10. Some small countries try to remain neutral in the conflicts among the (superpowers, wetlands).

Which word names a vehicle?

▶ 11. A (moped, skyjacker) is a convenient way for people to travel short distances.

B. Write the key word that makes sense in each blank in the following passage.

It is vital for radio and television newscasters to keep up with modern language. A single broadcast can include topics as varied as these: a summit meeting attended by the heads of state of several

You need the plural form of the key word here.

▶ (1.) ____________________; the overpowering of an armed (2.) ____________________ by the crew of an airliner over the Atlantic; the danger of a (3.) ____________________ at a nuclear power plant; a crisis in the Near East serious enough to cause the

Which key word is a means of communication?

▶ President to talk on the (4.) ____________________ to leaders of several other governments; publication of new photographs of the (5.) ____________________ by the space agency; and the announcement of the first commercial production of a solar-powered

Which key word is something powered by an engine?

▶ (6.) ____________________.

Items of local interest might include an interview with the (7.) ____________________ who investigates complaints against the city housing authority; a report of the life-saving work of a team

You need a plural noun here.

▶ of (8.) ____________________ following a crash at a downtown (9.) ____________________; and a real estate developer's plan to drain the (10.) ____________________ and build a luxury hotel.

Regardless of the subject matter, broadcasters must be able to read smoothly and pronounce words accurately.

Our language is constantly being changed and enriched by the addition of new words created by current events.

lesson **9**

Multiple Meanings

define • determine
impression • margin
regard • slick

Many words have more than one meaning. The dictionary entry for a word gives all of its meanings. Context clues in your reading will often help you choose the correct meaning for the word as it is used. Sometimes you can tell the meaning of the word by the part of speech it is used as in the sentence.

Study the dictionary definitions of the words below.

Define comes from the Latin word **finis**, meaning **boundary**. It is thus related to the word **finish**. ▶

define (di fīn′), *v.* 1. to state or set forth the meaning of (a word or phrase). 2. to explain clearly. 3. to make clear the outline or form of: *a tower defined against the sky.*

determine (di tûr′ min), *v.* 1. to settle or decide (as in a dispute). 2. to come to a conclusion; resolve. 3. to find out by observation or investigation. 4. to cause, affect, or control.

Note that **impression** can mean a strong feeling or a vague one. ▶

impression (im presh′ən), *n.* 1. a strong effect produced on the mind or feelings. 2. a vague or indistinct notion or belief. 3. a mark produced by pressure.

margin (mär′ jin), *n.* 1. a border or edge. 2. the space around the printed matter on a page. 3. an extra amount, as of time or money, beyond what is actually needed.

regard (ri gärd), *v.* 1. to think of in a certain way. 2. to show respect or consideration for. 3. to look at; observe. —*n.* 4. thought, attention, or consideration.

Slick comes from an old English word meaning **to make smooth by hammering**. ▶

slick (slik), *adj.* 1. smooth and glossy; sleek. 2. slippery, especially from being covered with oil, ice, or water. 3. clever or tricky. —*n.* 4. a smooth or slippery place or spot.

A. Find the correct meaning of the boldface key word in each sentence. On the line after the sentence write the number of the meaning and the part of speech the word has in the sentence.

Tip Is **regard** used as a noun or a verb here? If a word has more than one meaning, be sure you understand which meaning it has in a given sentence. ▶

1. Although cleaning up the cafeteria is an unpleasant job, try to **regard** it as good experience. ______________________
2. The sidewalk outside the movie theater was **slick** after the freezing rain. ______________________

Is the teacher giving the meaning of a word or explaining something clearly? ▶

3. The science teacher **defined** the requirements for the regional science fair projects. ______________________
4. The referee **determined** that the receiver was out of bounds when he caught the ball. ______________________
5. When you go into the city, allow yourselves a **margin** of an hour in case the buses are slow. ______________________

The first part of the sentence is a clue to the right meaning. ▶

6. Toni wasn't sure, but she got the **impression** that the store manager was not eager to hire teenagers. ______________________
7. Some words are almost impossible to **define**. ______________________

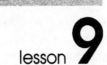

8. The new candidate for mayor made a very good **impression** on everyone when he gave his first speech. ____________

The **-ed** ending shows that a word is
- ☐ a noun.
- ☐ a verb.

9. Mr. O'Malley frowned as he **regarded** the kicking, screaming child. ____________
10. Leakage from the tank truck left a dangerous oil **slick** on the highway. ____________
11. Engineers have finally **determined** the source of the pollution in the stream. ____________
12. A row of trees has been planted around the **margin** of the field as a windbreak. ____________

B. In each blank in the passage, write the number of the meaning of the boldface key word as it is used in the sentence.

Intaglio is pronounced in tal′ yō.

Engraving uses a process of printing called intaglio. Instead of making the **impression** (1) ________ by inking the raised part of the plate, the ink is held in grooves cut into the printing surface. The artist cuts the design into a flat metal plate, usually of copper or zinc, using a sharp metal tool called a burin. The width, depth, and angle of the cuts help **determine** (2) ________ the look of the finished picture. Because fine lines can be made, an engraving can successfully **define** (3) ________ even tiny details.

Burin is pronounced byo͝or′ ən.

Which meaning of **define** has to do with shapes and outlines?

Ink is applied to the finished plate with a roller, rubbed evenly into the indentations, and the excess wiped away. The plate and paper are then put on the press. Paper for the print is chosen with **regard** (4) ________ to the size of the desired **margin** (5) ________. Absorbent, rather than **slick** (6) ________, paper is used. It is dampened to help it hold the ink better and produce a clear print.

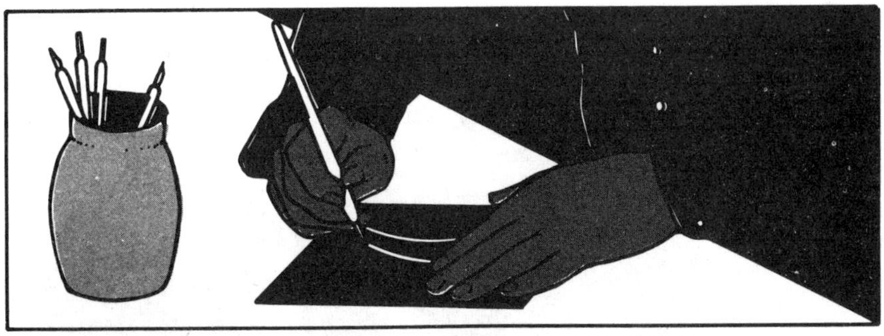

Absorbent means **able to soak up a liquid**.

The dictionary entry will help you to understand the precise use of a word that has more than one meaning.

lesson **10** # Homographs

converse · **drone**

hail · **peaked**

rank · **sheer**

steep

Two or more words that are spelled alike but have different meanings and histories are called **homographs**. Sometimes they are also pronounced differently. Because of their different origins, homographs have separate entries in the dictionary. Look at these entries for the homograph **stem**.

stem¹ (stem), *n.* the main stalk of a plant.
stem² (stem), *v.* to stop or check.

Now read these sentences using **stem**.

The sunflower **stem** was nine feet tall.
The guards could not **stem** the flow of the crowd onto the field at the end of the game.

The raised number after an entry word indicates that it is a homograph. Notice that homographs are sometimes different parts of speech.

Converse² is pronounced differently when it is a noun.

Tip Which **converse** is a verb? If a word has more than one meaning, be sure you understand which meaning it has in a given sentence.

A. Read each pair of homographs and the sentences in which they are used. Then write the number of the correct homograph next to each sentence.

converse¹ (kən vûrs′), *v.* to talk together; have a conversation.

converse² (kən vûrs′), *adj.* 1. opposite or contrary; turned around. —*n.* (kon′ vûrs). 2. something that is the opposite or reverse of another.

_______ 1. Lola and her grandmother found it hard to **converse** in such a noisy place.

_______ 2. Ted's mother's instructions were the **converse** of what his father had told him to do.

drone¹ (drōn), *n.* 1. a male bee. 2. a person who lives on the labor of others; loafer; idler.

drone² (drōn), *n.* 1. a low humming sound. —*v.* 2. to make a humming sound. 3. to speak in a monotonous tone.

_______ 3. There is not a single **drone** among all the members of that hard-working family.

_______ 4. The only sound Jean could hear was the distant **drone** of a small airplane.

Hail[1] comes from an old Norse word meaning **healthy**. It was a greeting that wished a friend good health. **Hail**[2] comes from a very old word meaning **a small pebble**.

hail[1] (hāl), *v.* 1. to greet or welcome, especially by calling out. 2. to call out to in order to attract attention.
hail[2] (hāl), *n.* 1. rounded pieces of ice that fall from the sky like rain. —*v.* 2. to pour down hail.

_________ 5. Yesterday's **hail** did great damage to the crops.

_________ 6. Greta shouted from the window to **hail** the letter carrier.

These homographs have different pronunciations.

peaked[1] (pēkt), *adj.* having a peak or point.
peaked[2] (pē′ kid), *adj.* pale, sickly, or thin.

_________ 7. Theirs is the green house with the **peaked** roof.

_________ 8. Carlos looked **peaked** for a long time after he had the flu.

Rank[1] and **rung** are related. Can you see how similar the ideas are?

rank[1] (rangk), *n.* social standing, class, or position.
rank[2] (rangk), *adj.* 1. growing quickly and coarsely: *rank weeds.* 2. having an unpleasantly strong smell or taste.

_________ 9. Is earl a higher **rank** than duke?

_________ 10. Mildew has given this basement storage room a **rank** odor.

Sheer also has a homophone, **shear**, which means **to cut**.

sheer[1] (shēr), *adj.* 1. extremely thin and fine; transparent or almost transparent. 2. utter or absolute: *sheer nonsense.*
sheer[2] (shēr), *v.* to turn from a course; swerve.

_________ 11. Karim had to **sheer** his bike suddenly when the child ran out into the street in front of him.

Sheer here is
- ☐ an adjective.
- ☐ a verb.

_________ 12. Such **sheer** curtains don't provide any insulation against the heat or the cold.

Another meaning of **steep** is **to involve deeply**. Can you tell which homograph entry it should go under?

steep[1] (stēp), *adj.* having a sharp slant up and down.
steep[2] (stēp), *v.* to soak or be soaked in water or another liquid below the boiling point.

_________ 13. At low tide, the gangplank to the old houseboat was very **steep**.

_________ 14. Don't **steep** the tea leaves in a metal pan because they will leave a stain.

B. Use one pair of homographs in a sentence or sentences of your own. Write a separate sentence for each homograph, or use both in the same sentence.

For homographs that are verbs, use **-s**, **-ed**, or **-ing** endings for variety.

____

____

____

____

Homographs are spelled alike but have different meanings and origins. They have separate entries in the dictionary.

lesson **11**

Context Clues

abrasive · **adorn**
deposit · **diatom**
intricate
microscopic
pigment · **porous**
propel · **reproduce**

Context clues can often help you understand the meaning of unfamiliar words when you are reading. Think about the meaning of the boldface word as you read the sentences below.

> Dorothy's father stopped the car at the **quarry** entrance, and the entire family took a tour of the large open pit. Big machines were cutting chunks of stone away from the rock walls.

If you did not know the meaning of **quarry**, the words **large open pit** would suggest part of the meaning. The next sentence would also help you to figure out that a quarry is a large open pit from which stone is obtained.

A. Read the passage, paying special attention to the key words in boldface. Look for context clues that will help you figure out their meanings. At the end of the passage, write each key word on the line next to its meaning.

Tip Does the context help you know what **diatoms** are? Look for context clues to help you figure out the meaning of a word you do not know.

Chlorophyll is the green coloring matter in plants.

Nearly all water animals are dependent in some way on the ► **microscopic** plants called **diatoms** found in almost every body of water. There are more than 10,000 known species of these tiny one-celled plants.

The cell walls of diatoms are composed mostly of silica, a stony substance that forms a shell. The shells are of many different shapes and are **adorned**, or decorated, with **intricate** patterns. These complex designs are beautiful when seen under a microscope. Although ► diatoms contain chlorophyll, the green color is masked by a brown **pigment** which makes them appear golden brown in color.

If there were no diatoms, most of the world's fish would die. Diatoms are the main food for tiny fish, which are, in turn, the food for larger fish. Fortunately, diatoms **reproduce** quickly by splitting in two. They do not produce young by growing seeds as many plants do. In just a few days, a single diatom is able multiply into several million tiny plants. Some diatoms can **propel** themselves from place to place. It is not completely understood how they are able to push themselves forward through the water.

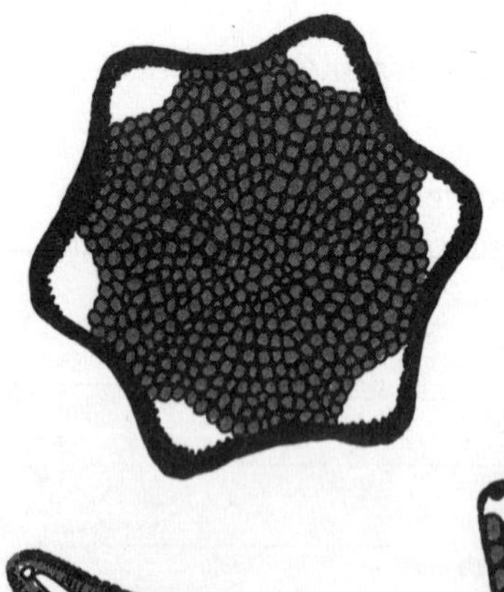

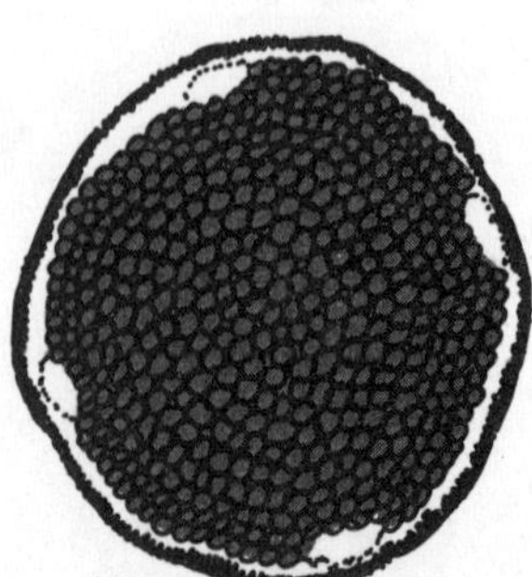

The hard cell walls of dead diatoms form a thick **deposit** on the bottom of oceans and lakes. After a long time this accumulation of old cell walls turns into a **porous** mineral called diatomite. Because diatomite is full of tiny holes, and liquids or gases can pass through it, it is used for making filters. Diatomite is also used as an **abrasive** for grinding or smoothing other materials.

The suffix -**ite** changes the name of the plant (diatom) to the name of the mineral (diatomite) which is formed from the remains of the tiny plants.

1. ______________________, complex; having many interrelated parts.
2. ______________________, a substance that gives color to living things.
3. ______________________, extremely small or fine; tiny.
4. ______________________, to decorate or add ornaments to.
5. ______________________, to produce offspring or young.
6. ______________________, a tiny one-celled water plant having a hard outer covering.
7. ______________________, a natural accumulation.
8. ______________________, a material or substance used for grinding or polishing.
9. ______________________, full of pores; capable of allowing the passage of liquids or gases.
10. ______________________, to cause to move forward or onward.

The clue word is related to the name of the instrument you would have to look through to see something this small. (3)

The word **pores** is a clue to the key word. (9)

B. Write the correct key word in each blank.

1. Birds and fish ______________________ by laying eggs.
2. The flower frog can sit on a white lily without being seen because of the ivory ______________________ in its skin.
3. Sam used an ______________________ to remove all the rust.
4. The ______________________ skin of a sponge allows water to pass through its body.
5. Bees build ______________________ hives that have many connected cells.
6. Most diatoms cannot be seen by the human eye because they are ______________________.
7. The wings of some butterflies are ______________________ with beautiful designs.
8. Many small fish depend on ______________________ for most of their food needs.
9. The up-and-down movement of a bottlenose dolphin's tail ______________________ it through the water.
10. ______________________ of frogs' eggs can be found in the shallow water of ponds and spring pools.

Which key word means **to produce young**? (1)

What key word means **having many interrelated parts**? (5)

Add -**ed** to the key word here. (7)

A **bottlenose dolphin** is also called a **porpoise**. (9)

Use a plural form. (10)

As you read, look for context clues that will help you to understand the meanings of new words.

lesson **12**

Context Clues with Commas

controversy

customary

dimension

distinct · **logical**

matchless

paramount

relish · **renowned**

situated · **sway**

Tip The word **or** is often a clue that the meaning of a key word follows. Look for context clues to help you figure out the meaning of a word you do not know.

The key word here is rephrased in the next sentence.

Sway comes from the Old Norse word **sveigja**, to bend. Can you see how it could have both a physical and a nonphysical meaning?

Synonyms are words that are nearly alike in meaning. Recognizing synonyms when you are reading will help you to learn the meanings of new words. Sometimes a synonym for an unfamiliar word is given in the same sentence, following a comma after the new word. Read the sentence below.

The painting was done in a **primitive**, or crude, style.

Notice the words following **primitive**, set off by commas. The word **crude** is a synonym for **primitive** in this sentence.

A. Read the passage below. Find the synonym for each boldface word. Some of the synonyms come after a comma; others do not. Underline the synonym for each boldface word.

The **renowned** American architect Frank Lloyd Wright first became famous in the early years of the 20th century. His designs did not follow the **customary**, or usual, styles of the time. Even his earliest work was a **distinct** departure from the old style, a clear break with the past.

Wright believed that function and location were the **paramount**, or supreme, considerations in designing any building. Both his use of space and the materials he chose were related to the building's purpose and to its surroundings. Because his theories were so different, they aroused great **controversy**. Every new Wright structure caused heated debate. When he designed the Imperial Hotel in Tokyo, many people criticized the plan as not being based on **logical** principles of construction. The design was proved reasonable indeed when, after the city's 1923 earthquake, this hotel was one of the few structures left standing. Wright was one of the first people to use new materials such as plate glass and acoustical walls, and modern technology such as air conditioning, all used in a 1905 office building.

Wright designed buildings of every **dimension**, from public buildings of great size, like the Guggenheim Museum in New York City, to private homes. A **matchless**, or incomparable, example of his architecture is a house named Falling Water that he built in western Pennsylvania. It is **situated** over a waterfall and stream, placed so that the water is seen and heard from everywhere in the house, and built to blend into the hillside and rocks of the landscape. The owners **relished** living in the house for many years. Now it can be enjoyed by many others as well; since the death of the owners, the house has been open part of the time to the public.

Wright's own winter home in Arizona was designed very differently. He built it to suit its desert surroundings, to take advantage of the bright light, and to give shelter from the heat.

Frank Lloyd Wright was a pioneer of modern architecture. In addition to his designing, he lectured and wrote. His new approaches to thinking about buildings have **swayed**, or influenced, architects all over the world and changed the looks of our cities.

B. Write a synonym for each key word on the line next to the word. Use the words you have underlined in the paragraphs on page 26.

1. dimension ______
2. logical ______
3. relish ______
4. distinct ______
5. controversy ______
6. matchless ______
7. situated ______
8. renowned ______
9. customary ______
10. paramount ______
11. sway ______

Tip Notice the suffix **-less**. Look for prefixes, suffixes, and roots you know to help you figure out the meaning of an unfamiliar word. ▶

C. Underline the key word that makes sense in each sentence.

1. There are (distinct, situated) architectural differences between the temples and palaces built by the ancient Greeks and those built by the ancient Romans.
2. Cathedrals of great (sway, dimension) constructed during the Middle Ages had high, pointed arches and many-colored stained glass windows.
3. The Taj Mahal in India, an elaborate white marble tomb, is (relished, situated) in a garden facing a reflecting pool.
4. Sir Christopher Wren is (customary, renowned) for planning the rebuilding of London after the Great Fire in 1666.
5. In the mid-1880s, it became (customary, distinct) to use iron and glass to build large structures such as railroad stations.
6. The Eiffel Tower, considered a marvel of engineering design when it was built in 1889, is a (paramount, logical) example of iron-and-steel construction.
7. One of the landmarks most (relished, swayed) by visitors to Washington, D.C., is the Lincoln Memorial, based on ancient Greek architecture.
8. On a clear day there is a (matchless, logical) view from the top of the Empire State Building.
9. A common (controversy, dimension) in many American cities is whether it is more (distinct, logical) to restore or to tear down old buildings.
10. The planning of buildings by present-day architects is greatly (relished, swayed) by the need to conserve energy.

Is this sentence about enjoyment or location? ▶ (item 3)

Would it make sense to say that visitors today influence the Lincoln Memorial? ▶ (item 7)

Notice that you need to find two key words in this sentence. ▶ (item 9)

A synonym for a word sometimes follows a comma after the word. Remember to look for synonyms of unfamiliar words when you are reading.

lesson **13**

Key Word Puzzles

Remember that the key words are listed at the beginning of each lesson.

The words needed to complete these puzzles are all key words from the lessons in Unit 1.

A. The key words in the box contain prefixes and suffixes. Use the clues to discover where each key word fits in the puzzle. Write the letters of the words in the puzzle blanks. The letters in the squares will form another key word with a prefix or suffix.

functional	feudalism	fractional	pacifist	coexist
abnormal	faddist	facial	realist	

1. Add a suffix to a noun meaning **a small part**.
2. Add a suffix to an adjective meaning **actual or true**.
3. Add a suffix to a verb meaning **to bring to a state of peace or calm**.
4. Add a prefix to an adjective meaning **usual or typical**.
5. Add a suffix to a verb meaning **to perform or operate**.
6. Add a suffix to a noun meaning **a fashion or craze popular for a brief time**.
7. Add a suffix to an adjective that refers to the social and economic system in medieval Europe.
8. Add a suffix to a noun meaning **the front part of the head**.
9. Add a prefix to a verb meaning **to live**.

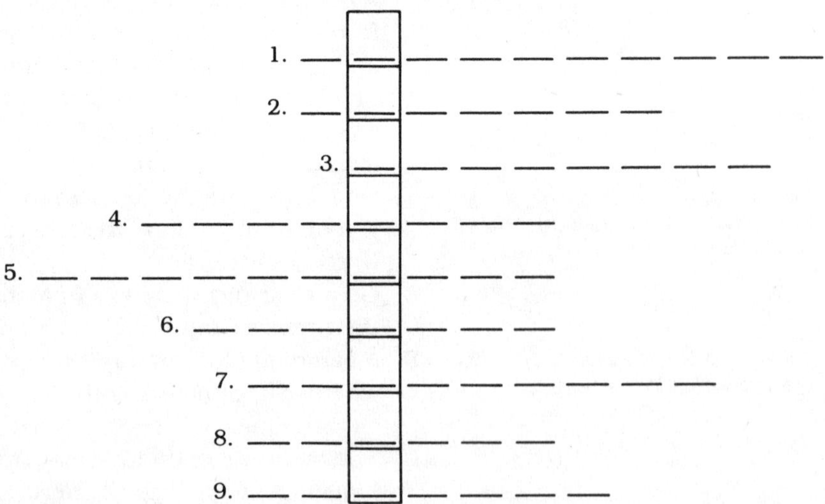

This key word contains a
☐ prefix.
☐ suffix.

Write the definition of the key word spelled by the letters in the squares of the puzzle. ____________________

____

B. Find the Unit 1 key words to fill in the crossword puzzle.

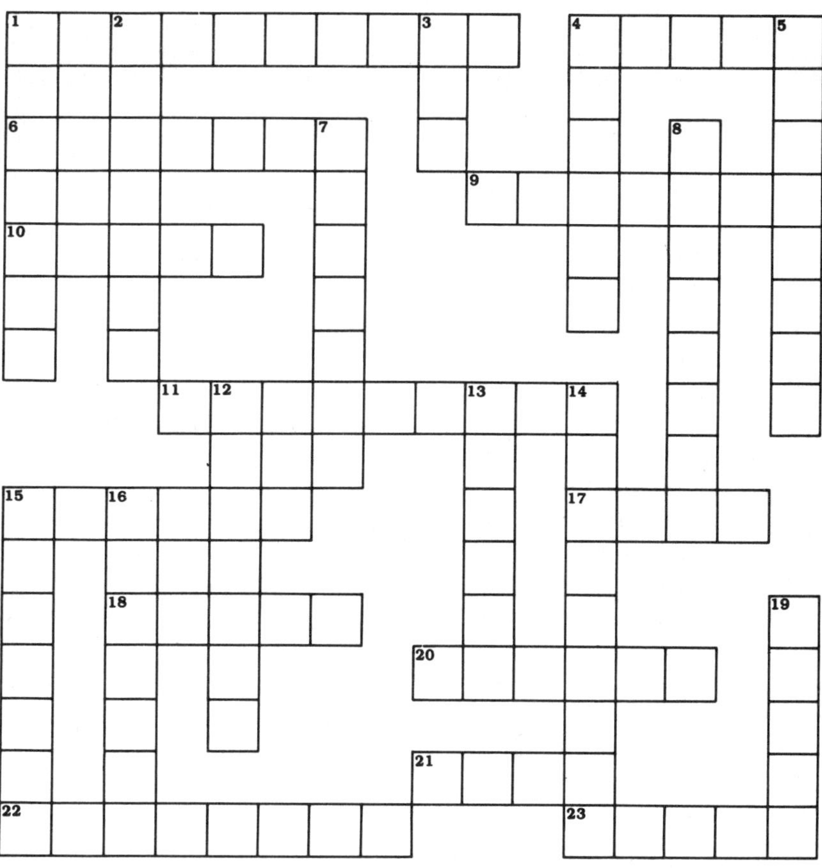

ACROSS

1. the quality of favoring social or political change
4. a heavily built, motorized bicycle
6. a stew of meat and vegetables, seasoned with paprika
9. a substance that gives color to living things
10. a closed, two-door automobile
11. a person trained to do some medical tasks and to assist a doctor
15. a tiny one-celled water plant with a hard outer covering
17. social standing or class
18. a series or set of things, such as a _________ of rooms
20. to enjoy something
21. to call out in order to attract attention
22. to form a theory or explanation
23. to call forth or suggest

DOWN

1. reasonable
2. a bunch of flowers
3. a salty brown liquid sauce
4. an edge or border
5. clear; unmistakable
7. a small landing or take-off area for helicopters
8. the melting of the core of a nuclear reactor
12. to eliminate, or put an end to
13. to state the meaning of
14. to record or write down events
15. a natural accumulation
16. a lack; the state of being without something
19. to make a dull humming or buzzing sound

Knowing the meanings of an increasing number of words will help you to work word puzzles.

Post-Test

A. Underline the correct word to complete each sentence.

1. Alex was disgusted to find (sabotage, succotash) for dinner again.
2. Traffic is always bad at that corner because several streets (collaborate, converge) there.
3. Because Jason is a (pacifist, realist), he does not spend time wishing things were different.
4. The planning committee is able to work well even during a crisis because there is such (cohesion, controversy) among the members.
5. Amy (regarded, relished) the oddly wrapped package with suspicion.
6. Before leaving on their two-day canoe trip, the Cassidys studied the map to (familiarize, rationalize) themselves with the river.
7. Only a (fractional, functional) part of the audience bothered to fill out the comment sheets after the meeting.
8. The route of the (marmalade, marathon) passed through the park and by the museum.
9. The (abrasive, abnormal) amount of snowfall last year affected business at all the ski resorts in this area.
10. The press conference was attended by (manuscripts, scribes) from all the local papers.
11. Everyone had counted on Ms. Fowler's leadership for the success of the fund-raising drive, and they were shocked when she (abdicated, converged).
12. When she returned from her trip, Michelle made a (collage, chronology) for her wall from the tickets, postcards, and other pieces of paper she had collected.

B. Match each word in Column A with its meaning in Column B. Write the letter of the correct meaning on the line next to each word in Column A.

	Column A	Column B
______	1. goulash	a. to refrain from; deny oneself
______	2. concur	b. cotton cloth with a bright colored pattern
______	3. paramedic	c. capable of allowing the passage of liquids or gases
______	4. beret	d. a stew of meat and vegetables
______	5. abduct	e. to agree with
______	6. paramount	f. a person trained to assist a physician
______	7. calico	g. supreme
______	8. diatom	h. to carry off by force or trickery
______	9. abstain	i. a tiny one-celled water plant
______	10. coupe	j. a soft, round, brimless cap
______	11. porous	k. to live together or at the same time
______	12. coexist	l. a closed, two-door automobile

C. Each group of sentences contains a homograph in boldface. Read the first sentence. Then put a check (✔) next to the sentence in the pair below it that contains the same homograph.

1. Terry jumped off the school bus and **hailed** her friends across the street.

   _________ a. The weather forecast predicted a thunderstorm, but it **hailed** instead.

   _________ b. Mr. and Mrs. Lobel **hailed** a taxi at the hotel entrance.

2. Mr. Schell is clearing a lot of trees and his power saw **drones** all day long.

   _________ a. Everyone fidgets when Merv **drones** on and on about his problems.

   _________ b. The beekeeper checked to be sure that all the **drones** had left the hive.

3. The baby's snowsuit had a **peaked** hood.

   _________ a. Jack is always so healthy that it was a shock to see him looking **peaked**.

   _________ b. The sharply **peaked** mountain was completely bare of snow.

4. It would be **sheer** foolishness for Marshall to paint the kitchen walls before all the cracks are patched.

   _________ a. The **sheer** beauty of the sunset left Nora speechless.

   _________ b. Mrs. Hurst was able to **sheer** the car and avoid hitting the dog.

5. Fred was out of breath after he climbed the **steep** flight of stairs.

   _________ a. At the workshop, Brian and Janet learned how to **steep** onion skins to obtain a natural dye.

   _________ b. Meg was the first to scramble up the **steep** ladder to the bell tower of the historic church.

D. Write the word from the box that makes sense in each blank.

suite	propel	impression	clique	camellia	controversy
adorn	boycott	customary	intricate	rationalize	

1. Mrs. Hardy's prize _________________ bush was badly damaged by the ice storm.
2. Swimming with fins lets you _________________ yourself quickly through the water.
3. Because of the highway construction, the bus didn't follow its _________________ route into the city.
4. Manuel tries to _________________ his behavior every time he gets into a fight.
5. The Washingtons had a huge family reunion in a _________________ at the hotel in Springfield last week.
6. Miranda is knitting a sweater with a very _________________ design.
7. The last city council meeting was entirely taken up by the _________________ over closing Anderson Junior High School.
8. Mrs. Kovacs used a feather and some ribbon to _________________ her old hat.
9. No two people seem to have the same _________________ of the new minister.
10. The local supermarket reports a definite drop in sales since the _________________ began a month ago.
11. Maryann was deliberately left out of the party planned by the _________________.

Unit 2

Whether or not you plan to earn your living as a writer, you will find it a great advantage to be able to express yourself clearly on paper. When your writing is vivid and precise, you are likely to hold the attention of your reader and get your point across.

Suppose the drama club is giving a play to raise money. You need good publicity to attract a large audience. Someone might write an item like the one below for the local paper. Do you see how it could be improved by changing the boldface words?

What are the main kinds of information that should be included in any news item?

Who

W ____________________

W ____________________

W ____________________

H ____________________

> The drama club of Lincoln School is putting on a **play** called "The Jade Tree." Rick Galinsky and Ann Sugiyama play the **main parts**. Performances will be on March 4, 5, 6, and 7. All shows are at 8 P.M. **accept** the one on March 7, which starts at 7 P.M. Tickets are $3.00. The **money** will be used to help **by** new lighting equipment. This is a **good** play that the whole family will **like**. Get your tickets early, before they are all sold out!

The word **play** in the first line gives the reader no clue. Is it a mystery? comedy? romance? Cross out **play** and write a more precise word above it. What **main parts** do Rick and Ann play? hero? empress? villain? tycoon? Cross out **main parts** and substitute more interesting words. The writer confused the word **accept** with the word **except**. Correct the error. **Money** is a general term. Substitute **profits**

Vocabulary for Writing

or **proceeds** to give the precise meaning of **money** as it is used here. In that same sentence the writer has chosen the wrong homophone, using **by** instead of **buy**. Correct the mistake. The words **good** and **like** are overused. Replace them with more vivid words that will ▶ galvanize the reader into rushing out to buy tickets.

Galvanize means **to stimulate** (as if by electric current); **to startle into sudden activity**.

The lessons in Unit 2 will help you discover how to make your writing more exact and interesting. You will learn about choosing correct homophones, look-alikes, and other confusing words. You will also learn how to

- select precise nouns and verbs.
- choose adjectives and adverbs to create a certain mood.
- use fresh and imaginative similes and metaphors.
- use a thesaurus to find new words.
- write for your audience.

lesson 1

Homophones

clause · claws

council · counsel

hoard · horde

manner · manor

miner · minor

taught · taut

Words that sound alike but have different spellings and different meanings are called **homophones**. **Stare** and **stair** are homophones. In your writing, it is important to be aware of homophones and to use them correctly.

Read these pairs of homophones and their definitions.

clause (klôz), *n.* 1. a group of words containing a subject and a verb. 2. a part of a law, contract, treaty, or the like. **claws** (klôz), *n.* sharp, curved nails on an animal's foot.
council (koun′ səl), *n.* 1. a group of persons called together to decide on or discuss something of importance. 2. a group of persons having the power to make laws or govern. **counsel** (koun′ səl), *n.* 1. advice or opinion. —*v.* 2. to give advice to; advise.
hoard (hôrd), *n.* 1. a supply of money, food, etc., that is hidden or carefully guarded for future use. —*v.* 2. to gather and save, often secretly and greedily. **horde** (hôrd), *n.* a large group; multitude; crowd.
manner (man′ ər), *n.* 1. a way in which something happens or is done. 2. a way of acting or behaving. **manor** (man′ ər), *n.* 1. an estate belonging to a lord in the Middle Ages. 2. any large, imposing house; mansion.
miner (mī′ nər), *n.* a person who works in a mine. **minor** (mī′ nər), *adj.* 1. smaller or less important. —*n.* 2. a person under legal age.
taught (tôt), *v.* the past tense of **teach**. **taut** (tôt), *adj.* tightly drawn; tense.

Horde comes from the Tartar (central Asian) word **urdu**, meaning **a military camp**. ▶

Notice that both **miner** and **minor** can function as nouns, but only **minor** can also be used as an adjective. ▶

Tip Be careful to use homophones and other easily confused words correctly in your writing. ▶

A. Write the correct homophone in each blank in the sentences.

Which of these homophones is a group of people? ▶

1. The city ________________ met to decide on the location of the new parking garage. (council, counsel)
2. Pack rats are known for their ability to ________________ anything that catches their fancy. (horde, hoard)
3. A ________________ rope fastened the motorboat to the pier. (taught, taut)
4. Sandy will have to sell her collie before her family moves to the new apartment because a ________________ in their lease says that no pets are allowed. (claws, clause)

Don't be fooled! One of the key words has to do with pets, but the clue here is **lease**—a legal rent agreement. ▶

Which word here is the best clue?
- ☐ leads
- ☐ house

5. Mr. Tunik has been a ________________ with Constant Coal Company for 30 years. (miner, minor)
6. Evergreen trees line the winding driveway that leads to the large house on the hill, March ________________. (Manner, Manor)
7. You can sometimes identify an animal by the marks its ________________ have made in the dirt. (clause, claws)

B. Read the passage and underline the correct homophone in each set in parentheses.

Industrial countries manufacture a large number of products.

Nimble means **quick-moving** or **agile**.

Which word means **advice**?

Which key word has to do with legal agreements?

A **migrant** worker travels from one region to another in search of work.

Imagine what your life would be like if you had begun working in a factory at the age of six or seven. In the 1700s and early 1800s, (1. hordes, hoards) of young children in industrial countries worked 12 to 15 hours a day.

Many parents sent their young children to work in textile factories. The factory owners preferred to hire children rather than their parents because the children would work for lower wages and their nimble hands were better able to operate the machines. At that time, (2. minors, miners) had no rights whatsoever. Some children were even chained to their machines. The factory owners knew that children would never be able to seek the (3. council, counsel) of lawyers to protect themselves, and many children had to work such long hours in filthy, lint-filled factories that they died at an early age.

Eventually, most industrial countries introduced laws to protect their child workers. A law passed in 1813 in Connecticut had a (4. clause, claws) requiring that all factory children be (5. taught, taut) reading, writing, and arithmetic at the factory every day. By 1860, a few states had set a minimum age, usually 10 or 12, at which children could be hired as factory workers.

Although children in our country are no longer forced to work in factories, many people feel that the (6. manor, manner) in which young children are hired as migrant farm laborers is also very unfair. Many of these children work long hours and miss out on part of their schooling as they move around the country harvesting crops.

Homophones are words that sound alike but have different spellings and different meanings. Learn to use them correctly in your writing.

lesson 2 Confusing Words

affect · effect

continual

continuous

disinterested

uninterested

imply · infer

personal · personnel

precede · proceed

The pairs of words shown below can be confusing unless you understand the differences in their meanings and when to use each word. That is why dictionaries sometimes include a paragraph explaining the correct usage of these word pairs.

affect, effect

—Usage. *Affect* is often confused with *effect*. *Affect* is a verb that means "to cause a change in a person or thing": *Dampness may affect a person's health. Dirt had affected the machine's operation.* The verb *effect* means "to bring about or accomplish": *The medicine effected a cure.* Used as a noun, *effect* means "something produced by a cause": *The ice storm had a bad effect on the pine trees.*

continuous, continual

—Usage. *Continuous* means "without stop or interruption." It should not be confused with *continual*, which means "happening at regular intervals; frequent or repeated": *a continuous flow of water; continual demands for payment of the bill.*

Unbiased is another synonym for **disinterested**.

disinterested, uninterested

—Usage. *Disinterested* should not be used as a synonym for *uninterested*. *Disinterested* means "impartial or without prejudice": *The committee gave a disinterested report.* *Uninterested* means "indifferent or without interest": *Some liked the story, but others remained uninterested.*

infer, imply

—Usage. *Infer*, which means "to understand or conclude," should not be used as a synonym of *imply*, which means "to hint or suggest": *He implied that I was cheating. I inferred that she was only a child.*

Tip If you know the meaning of the prefix **pre-**, you should remember the meaning of **precede**. Look for prefixes, suffixes, and roots you know to help you figure out the meaning of a word.

personal, personnel

—Usage. Although *personal* is often confused with *personnel*, their meanings are completely different. *Personal* is an adjective that means "belonging to or concerning a particular person": *a personal letter.* *Personnel* is a noun that is defined as "all the employees of a company or organization": *Some of the personnel of the insurance company are on vacation this month.*

precede, proceed

—Usage. *Precede* is sometimes confused with *proceed*. *Precede* means "to go or come before": *The rain preceded the flood.* *Proceed* means "to go forward or onward, especially after stopping," or "to continue": *The director signaled for the marching band to proceed down the field.*

A. Write the correct key word in the blank in each sentence.

Is Ms. Rodriguez unbiased, or does she want a certain team to win?

1. a. When Ms. Rodriguez umpires our games, she always tries to make __________________ decisions.

   b. After their exciting field trip this morning, the class was __________________ in settling down to work. (disinterested, uninterested)

Imply means **to hint**. In which sentence does **hint** make the best sense?

2. a. Gordon __________________ from the lack of hot water that the water heater was broken.

   b. Sue was angry when Mr. Berg __________________ that he thought she had purposely let the dog into the school building. (implied, inferred)

Notice that only one of the choices can be used as a noun.

In which sentence does something keep flowing without interruption?

The word **break** is a clue. Which adjective means **without a break**?

3. a. The 90° heat will probably ________________ the speed of the Burke High School track team.
   b. "Does listening to loud music on the stereo have any ________________ on how well you do your homework?" Yvette asked. (affect, effect)
4. a. At the first hint of warm weather, there is always a ________________ line of cars crossing the long bridge on the way to the beach.
   b. Marty made ________________ visits to the dentist for two years when he wore braces. (continual, continuous)
5. a. After picking up passengers at the terminal, the bus driver ________________ along the route.
   b. A band concert ________________ the school play. (preceded, proceeded)
7. a. When Nicholas went to apply for a job, he stopped at the ________________ department.
   b. "When the mail arrives, please open my business letters, and put my ________________ letters on my desk," Ms. Roberts told Nicholas. (personnel, personal)

B. Read the passage and underline the correct word from each pair in parentheses.

It may not be long before you will be looking for a job. If the job is with a big company, you will go to the (1. personnel, personal) office and fill out an application form. Be sure to read the form carefully and think before you write. Make your application form as neat as possible. If the people doing the hiring can (2. imply, infer) from your form that you are a careless, messy person, they probably will be (3. uninterested, disinterested) in having you work for them now or in the future.

When the company has a job opening that seems to fit your talents, they will (4. proceed, precede) to call you in for an interview. Many things can (5. affect, effect) the outcome of an interview. It's always a good idea to dress neatly and to think through your answers before speaking. Also, you might want to break the (6. continuous, continual) flow of the interviewer's questions and your answers by asking some questions about the company. The interviewer will be pleased that you have an interest in the company. Many companies will also want to have you take some tests, either (7. preceding, proceeding) or following the interview.

Be sure to use confusing word pairs correctly when you write. Dictionaries often have a paragraph to explain the correct usage of confusing pairs.

lesson 3 Word Look-Alikes

adapt • **adopt**
casual • **causal**
desert • **dessert**
inhabit • **inhibit**
later • **latter**
mishap • **misshape**

Many sets of words look very much alike. Sometimes only one letter is different in the two words. Sometimes two letters are reversed, as in **dairy** and **diary**. It is important to recognize these words when you read, and to spell them accurately when you write, because the meanings are usually quite different.

Read these sets of look-alikes and their meanings.

adapt (ə dapt′), *v.* 1. to make suitable to special requirements or new conditions; adjust. 2. to adjust oneself to different conditions, new surroundings, etc.
adopt (ə dopt′), *v.* 1. to choose or take as one's own. 2. to become the legal parent of. 3. to accept or formally approve.

casual (kazh′ o͞o əl), *adj.* 1. happening by chance. 2. without serious intention; offhand.
causal (kô′ zəl), *adj.* involving or expressing a cause.

Desert[1] and **desert**[2] are homographs. Which one is pronounced the same as **dessert**?

desert[1] (dez′ ərt), *n.* a very dry region with little or no vegetation.
desert[2] (di zûrt′), *v.* to leave or abandon.
dessert (di zûrt′), *n.* sweet food served as a last course.

inhabit (in hab′ it), *v.* to live or dwell in (a place).
inhibit (in hib′ it), *v.* to hold back, check, or restrain.

Later and **latter** both come from the Anglo-Saxon (old English) word **læt**, meaning **slow**.

later (la′ tər), *adv.* at a more advanced time.
latter (lat′ ər), *adj.* 1. the second mentioned of two (opposite of **former**). 2. more advanced in time: *the latter part of the month.*

Notice that, although **mishap** has the letters **s** and **h** together, they do not make the **sh** sound.

mishap (mis′ hap), *n.* an unfortunate accident.
misshape (mis shāp′), *v.* to shape badly; deform.

A. Choose the correct look-alike word to complete each sentence in the sets of sentences. Write the word in the blank.

Tip Be careful to use homophones and other easily confused words correctly in your writing.

1. a. Now that we have a new driver, the bus seems to arrive ________________ every day.
   b. Williamson and Hendricks both ran extremely well, and the ________________ won by only a fraction of a second.

2. a. Woodson School will ________________ a new lunch plan next fall.
   b. It may take time for Darra to ________________ to a new country and language.

3. a. There is a ________________ relationship between the amount of sunlight a tree receives and its rate of growth.

b. Several people started a ________________ game of volleyball after lunch.

Which sentence needs a verb? ▶

4. a. What happened to that cherry tree to ________________ it so badly?

b. The vacation went splendidly, without a ________________.

5. a. People sometimes ________________ a pet when they move.

b. The choices for ________________ were all terrible.

Irrigation is the use of artificial methods of water supply for crops. ▶

c. Irrigation makes farming possible in the ________________.

6. a. The same pair of bluebirds comes back every spring to ________________ our birdhouse.

b. Poor diet can ________________ normal growth.

B. In each set of parentheses underline the look-alike word that completes the sentence correctly.

Arid means **without moisture**. ▶

The arid climate of the American southwest (1. desert, dessert) is natural for the varied plants, animals, and birds that live there. All that (2. inhabit, inhibit) this area have learned one lesson well: water is precious. It is not for (3. casual, causal) consumption. Every living thing has (4. adapted, adopted) to the dry environment in its own way. Each has mastered the art of gathering what little water there is here, conserving or storing it, and getting along without it when necessary.

Conserving means **not losing or wasting**. ▶

Many of the animals lessen their exposure to the drying sun and air by living under rocks and in underground burrows. Most drink little water; some drink none at all. The (5. later, latter) get moisture only from the food they eat. The thick skin of the cactus (6. inhabits, inhibits) evaporation and allows the plant to store moisture. Sharp thorns ward off animals that would bite into the flesh. Plant growth is slow in this dry land, so damage from a (7. mishap, misshape) is not quickly repaired.

Do you need a noun or a verb here? ▶

In your writing, take care to use look-alike words correctly.

lesson **4**

Using Precise Verbs

affirm • **blurt**
disclose • **jest**
lament • **proclaim**
ramble • **sneer**
stammer • **storm**

You can make your writing more vivid and interesting if you use precise verbs instead of general ones. For example, **say** is a general verb. More precise verbs can replace **say**, such as **shout**, **groan**, **whisper**, or **whine**. Each of these verbs gives a clearer picture than **say** does.

You can show the feeling or attitude of a person in your writing, and use direct quotes more effectively, by using precise verbs in place of **say**. Read the following sentences.

"There's an inchworm on my hamburger," **shrieked** Sarah.
"There's an inchworm on my hamburger," **drawled** Sarah.

In the first sentence, **shrieked** shows that Sarah is excited and speaking shrilly. The use of the verb **drawled** in the second sentence indicates that Sarah is observing the inchworm rather lazily, and maybe with some amusement.

The key words listed below are precise verbs. Each of them can take the place of **say** in certain situations.

affirm (ə fûrm′), *v.* to state positively; maintain as true.
blurt (blûrt), *v.* to say suddenly, often without thinking.
disclose (di sklōz′), *v.* to make known or reveal.
jest (jest), *v.* to speak in a playful way; joke; tease.
lament (lə ment′), *v.* 1. to feel sorrow over; mourn for. 2. to wail; complain.
proclaim (prō clām′), *v.* to announce formally or publicly; declare.
ramble (ram′ bəl), *v.* to talk in an aimless way.
sneer (snēr), *v.* to speak with scorn or contempt.
stammer (stam′ ər), *v.* to speak with breaks or pauses, or with repetition of syllables; falter.
storm (stôrm), *v.* to show great anger; rant and rage.

Sneer is related to the Old Danish **snœre, to grin like a dog**. The word **snarl** is probably also related. ▶

Storm has several other meanings, mostly having to do with the weather or a military attack. Can you see the relationship among all these meanings? ▶

A. Underline the key word that best completes each sentence.

1. "Nobody in this family understands the problem!" (rambled, stormed) Emilio.

Which indicates a public announcement? ▶

2. The principal (blurted, proclaimed) that school would be closed because of the hurricane warning.
3. The boys keep trying to get Joan to (disclose, stammer) how she does her best magic tricks.

The key words can sometimes be substituted for **speak** or **talk** as well as for **say**. ▶

4. Sally (rambled, sneered) on about her trip to the mountains and (lamented, affirmed) it was the best vacation she had ever had.
5. Stan still (discloses, laments) that he wasn't chosen for the part in the operetta.
6. Before she could stop herself, Molly (blurted, stormed) out the answer to the riddle.

The words **villain** and **revenge** should serve as clues. ▶

7. "I'll get my revenge," (jested, sneered) the villain as the audience hissed at him.

How might his embarrassment cause him to speak?

8. The clown (blurted, jested) with the people in the front row.
9. Mr. Huntley, embarrassed by so much attention, (proclaimed, stammered) that he was pleased to accept the honor.

Tip Use precise words to make your writing clear and interesting.

You may use a key word more than once .

B. Each pair of incomplete sentences below is identical. Fill in the blank in the first sentence with a key word to show a certain attitude in the speaker. Then add a sentence that the speaker might say next that would reflect that attitude. Fill in the blank in the second sentence with another key word to show a different attitude of the speaker, and write another sentence that logically follows. Use as many key words as you can. The first sentence is done.

1. a. "I haven't done my homework," proclaimed David.
"What's more, I'm not going to do it."

Fill in a different key word. If you use **lamented**, what might David say next?

b. "I haven't done my homework," __________ David.
"__________."

2. a. "Lou's trying out for the talent show," __________
her sister. "__________."

Try saying the sentence out loud in the manner of the different key words to get an idea of what to say next.

b. "Lou's trying out for the talent show," __________
her sister. "__________."

3. a. "This soup is too hot," Betty __________.
"__________."

b. "This soup is too hot," Betty __________.
"__________."

4. a. "My uncle once owned a racehorse," __________
Mr. Ross. "__________."

b. "My uncle once owned a racehorse," __________
Mr. Ross. "__________."

Make up two sentences of your own.

5. __________

Use precise verbs in place of **say** to add interest to your writing and to show particular attitudes and feelings.

lesson 5

Using Precise Nouns

cruelty • **dignity**
hostility • **humanity**
integrity • **negligence**
optimism • **patience**
pessimism
sociability

Using precise nouns in place of general nouns when you write helps you to present your ideas clearly and makes your writing more vivid and interesting.

The key words are precise nouns that name character traits that people might possess. Study their meanings.

cruelty (kro͞o′ əl tē), *n.* behavior that causes pain or distress to others.

dignity (dig′ ni tē), *n.* proud, noble, or honorable character.

hostility (ho stil′ i tē), *n.* unfriendliness; a hostile attitude.

humanity (hyo͞o man′ i tē), *n.* kindness or sympathy.

integrity (in teg′ ri tē), *n.* honesty; holding to ethical or moral principles.

negligence (neg′ li jəns), *n.* carelessness; irresponsibility.

Tip: **Optimism** comes from the Latin word **optimus**, meaning **best**. Knowing a word's origin can often help you figure out its meaning.

optimism (op′ tə miz′ əm), *n.* a tendency to look on the hopeful side of things.

patience (pā′ shəns), *n.* the ability to put up with pain, delay, annoyance, or misfortune, without complaint or loss of temper.

Pessimism is the opposite of **optimism**. What do you think its Latin root, **pessimus**, probably means?

pessimism (pes′ ə miz′ əm), *n.* a tendency to see the gloomy side of things.

sociability (sō′ shə bil′ i tē), *n.* friendliness or agreeableness in company.

A. Underline the key word in parentheses that best completes each sentence below.

1. The (pessimism, sociability) of golden retrievers makes them delightful pets.
2. The painters' (negligence, patience) infuriated Mrs. Berger, and she insisted that they repair the damage.
3. At basketball practice, Doug's (humanity, pessimism) dampens everyone's enthusiasm.
4. The (cruelty, integrity) of the girl's teasing finally caused the dog to bite her.
5. Jan doesn't have the (dignity, patience) to wait in line for the season tickets.
6. The crowd's (hostility, sociability) became increasingly unpleasant during the candidate's speech.
7. The defendant hoped his case would be tried by a judge with a reputation for (humanity, negligence.)
8. Since he has encountered so many problems, Phil's continued (hostility, optimism) is amazing.

What character trait would be hardest to maintain if you felt foolish or ashamed?

9. Even though she felt foolish, Lynne managed to maintain her (dignity, cruelty).
10. The city council president has too much (integrity, optimism) to take a bribe.

B. In each blank in the passage, write a key word that makes sense. More than one word will fit in some blanks.

Inouye is pronounced in nō′ wā.

He is a **Nisei** (nē′ sā), which means a child born in America of Japanese parents who immigrated here.

Senator Daniel Inouye of Hawaii was the first Congressman elected by the new state of Hawaii in 1959 and the first American of Japanese descent ever to serve in Congress.

When he was born in 1924, Hawaii was a United States territory. For Hawaiians of Asian descent, the opportunities for good education and jobs were limited. The Inouye family was poor. Despite these disadvantages, Dan's approach to life as he was growing up was one of hope and (1.) ____________________. He had a strong sense of

The rest of the sentence is a clue.

(2.) ____________________ and wanted to use his life to help people; he intended to become a surgeon.

But when Dan was 17, World War II began. Because the United States was at war with Japan, some people regarded Japanese-Americans with (3.) ____________________. Despite the fact that they were loyal citizens, Japanese-Americans were often treated with

Some people wrongly assumed that all Japanese-Americans would sympathize with Japan.

(4.) ____________________, and many had property taken away. Since their loyalty was doubted, they were not at first allowed to enlist in the military service. Later, however, a special Nisei unit, the 442nd Combat Team, was formed and Dan signed up. While fighting in Europe, he was wounded and his right arm was amputated.

Dan spent the next 20 months in hospitals. It took time and (5.) ____________________ to learn to do everything left-handed, but he never allowed (6.) ____________________ to overwhelm him.

What trait relates most closely to making friends?

His (7.) ____________________ brought him many new friendships. Dan also spent a great deal of time reading and studying. By the time he returned home, he had decided to study law and go into politics. During his successful career in the decades since then, Dan has been

Which key words name admirable qualities?

admired by many people for his (8.) ____________________ and (9.) ____________________.

Use precise nouns instead of general ones in your writing.

lesson 6

Vivid Adjectives and Adverbs

clamorous

harmonious

impulsive • insipid

instantaneous • lucid

modest • monotonous

resilient

You can create certain moods in your writing by using precise adjectives and adverbs. Adjectives describe nouns and pronouns. Adverbs often describe verbs; they can also modify an adjective or another adverb.

In the following sentences, the use of different adjectives and adverbs creates two different moods.

An **elegant** waiter **grandly** served the **magnificent** meal.
A **disagreeable** waiter **sloppily** served the **unappetizing** meal.

The adjectives and adverbs used in the first sentence create a mood of pleasure and luxury. Those in the second sentence create a mood of carelessness and distaste.

Adverbs may tell how, when, or where. ▶

Study the definitions of the key words. Notice the adverb that is given at the end of the definition of each adjective.

clamorous (klam′ ər əs), *adj.* noisy or loudly demanding. **—clamorously**, *adv.*

The word **harmony** is the root of this adjective. ▶

harmonious (här mō′ nē əs), *adj.* 1. forming an agreeable combination or blend. 2. pleasant in sound. 3. sharing the same feelings; friendly. **—harmoniously**, *adv.*

impulsive (im pul′ siv), *adj.* acting on impulse; moved by sudden inclination or emotion. **—impulsively**, *adv.*

Insipid comes from the Latin word **sapere, to taste**. Note the negative meaning of the prefix **in-**. ▶

insipid (in sip′ id), *adj.* 1. without interesting or attractive qualities. 2. having little flavor. **—insipidly**, *adv.*

instantaneous (in′ stən tā′ nē əs), *adj.* occurring or completed in an instant. **—instantaneously**, *adv.*

lucid (lo͞o′ sid) *adj.* 1. clear; transparent. 2. easily understood. 3. thinking clearly; rational. **—lucidly**, *adv.*

modest (mod′ ist), *adj.* 1. not vain or boastful. 2. simple in form or appearance. 3. not excessive. **—modestly**, *adv.*

The prefix **mono-** means **one**. ▶

monotonous (mə not′ ᵊnəs), *adj.* 1. lacking in variety; dull. 2. continuing on the same tone. **—monotonously**, *adv.*

Resilient comes from the Latin **re**, meaning **back**, and **salire**, meaning **to jump**. ▶

resilient (ri zil′ yənt), *adj.* 1. having the power to return to the original shape or position after being bent or squeezed. 2. recovering readily (from illness, sorrow, etc.). **—resiliently**, *adv.*

A. Underline the correct adjective or adverb in each sentence.

1. The speaker's (resilient, monotonous) voice put about half of the audience to sleep.

Which describes something pleasant? ▶

2. Everyone enjoys spending time at Charlene's house because the atmosphere there is so (clamorous, harmonious).
3. The firefighters' response to the alarm was (instantaneous, monotonous).

Raved means **spoke about with enthusiasm**. Which word shows that Peg felt the opposite about Marta's cousins? ▶

4. Jody raved about Marta's visiting cousins, but Peg thought they were (insipid, resilient).
5. The crowd in the stadium grew (clamorous, modest) when the game failed to start on time.

Resolve means **to solve** or **to make clear**. Does this give you a clue to the right word?

6. Andrea's (impulsive, lucid) thinking frequently resolves knotty problems for us.
7. It seems impossible for Maria to behave (harmoniously, modestly) about winning the gymnastics competition.

8. Seth (impulsively, resiliently) threw his arms around his brother.
9. Mr. McClintock was less (lucid, resilient) than the doctor had predicted in recovering from the accident.

Tip Use precise words to make your writing clear and interesting.

B. Use each key word in a sentence of your own to create a mood. You may use either the adjective or the adverb.

1. **insipid** ______________________________

____

What else can you describe as **modest** besides a person?

2. **modest** ______________________________

____

3. **instantaneous** ______________________________

____

What things are **resilient**?

4. **resilient** ______________________________

____

5. **clamorous** ______________________________

____

6. **lucid** ______________________________

____

7. **monotonous** ______________________________

____

Remember that colors and sounds, as well as people's relationships, can be **harmonious**.

8. **harmonious** ______________________________

____

9. **impulsive** ______________________________

____

You can create certain moods in your writing by making use of exact adjectives and adverbs.

lesson **7**

Using a Thesaurus

accelerate · agitate
animate · immobile
indolent · invigorate
leisurely · mobilize
passive · sluggish

A **thesaurus** is a dictionary that lists synonyms and antonyms. Using a thesaurus can help you locate precise words to use in place of more general words in your writing.

Suppose you want to find a more exact word to use in place of **light**. If you look up **light** in a thesaurus, you will find synonyms such as **gleam**, **flash**, **shimmer**, **blaze**, **flicker**, and **sparkle**. Each word has a slightly different meaning. You can select the one that fits best in the sentence you are writing.

A. The following key words are all adjectives that mean **slow** or **not active**. Study their definitions. In the sentences that follow, write the key word that makes sense in each blank.

immobile (i mō′ bil), *adj.* 1. not moving; motionless. 2. not movable.

Indolent comes from the Latin **in** (not) and **dolere** (to feel pain). Thus an indolent person is someone who doesn't react strongly to anything. ▶

indolent (in′ də lənt), *adj.* having a disposition to avoid work or exertion; lazy.

leisurely (lē′ zhər lē), *adj.* without haste; unhurried.

passive (pas′ iv), *adj.* not reacting; acted upon rather than acting or causing action.

sluggish (slug′ ish), *adj.* 1. lacking in energy. 2. moving slowly; having little motion.

1. If we don't leave too early on our trip, we can have a relaxed, ____________________ breakfast before we start out.

Tip Which word means **unhurried**? Use precise words to make your writing clear and interesting. ▶

2. Walter is always helpful, but his ____________________ sister is an expert at disappearing when there is work to be done.
3. Mr. Trice is unhappy about working conditions in his office, but he is too ____________________ to speak out and try to have things changed.

Which word means **slow-moving**? ▶

4. The current in the river is too ____________________ to keep the waterwheel turning steadily.

Is Faye moving at all? Which word conveys that? ▶

5. Faye stood ____________________, waiting for the next sound from beyond the door.

B. The following key words are all verbs that mean **to activate** in a certain way. Study their meanings and think about the differences in them. In the sentences that follow, write the key word that makes sense in each blank.

accelerate (ak sel′ ə rāt′), *v.* 1. to cause to move, develop, or happen more quickly. 2. to move faster.

This word can convey an unpleasant meaning. ▶

agitate (aj′ i tāt′), *v.* 1. to move, stir up, or shake. 2. to disturb or excite.

animate (an′ ə māt′), *v.* 1. to give life to. 2. to make spirited and lively.

This word has a positive meaning.

invigorate (in vig′ ə rāt′), *v.* to give strength and vigor to; fill with energy.

Mobilize and **immobile** both come from the same Latin root **mobilis**, meaning **movable**.

mobilize (mō′ bə līz′), *v.* to assemble and organize in readiness for action.

You may need to add **-s**, **-ed**, or **-ing** endings to the key words.

1. Eduardo's face was ______________________ by the pleasure of seeing his friends again after so long.
2. When the hikers realized how late it was, they knew they must ______________________ their pace so they could reach camp before dark.

Might a trick be unpleasant to the people it is played on?

3. Ralph likes to think up little tricks to ______________________ his brother and sister.
4. A brisk walk or a swim will ______________________ you when you feel tired.

Which word conveys the idea of preparation before action is to be taken?

5. Ms. Suraci ______________________ the whole family to get the house painted over the weekend.

C. In each set of parentheses in the passage, underline the key word that makes sense.

Which means **inactive**?

Sitting around in an (1. immobile, animated) state all the time is not healthy. Some amount of regular exercise is recommended for everyone. Exercise helps keep your body fit. It builds strength and muscle tone. Even when you feel tired and (2. sluggish, accelerated), getting some exercise usually (3. agitates, invigorates) you and makes you feel better.

Which word means **to organize and prepare for action**?

It isn't necessary for you to (4. mobilize, animate) yourself to plan some complicated program, or to spend a lot of money. Walking, biking, playing ball, swimming, and skating are all good for you. Some people enjoy exercising in a (5. leisurely, immobile) way and are content to proceed at their own pace. They would rather not be

Are you looking for a word with a pleasant or unpleasant meaning?

(6. invigorated, agitated) by the pressures of team and competitive sports that others enjoy. Some people like to compete with themselves. If you run, for example, you may start out slowly and then, as your strength and endurance build up, gradually (7. mobilize, accelerate) your pace and try to beat your own record.

Which means **lazy**?

Even the most (8. sluggish, indolent) person should be able to find some enjoyable activity. People who are physically fit usually feel and look better. Their families and friends benefit, too, from having a

The word **lively** is a clue.

lively, (indolent, animated) person around the house instead of a (10. passive, mobilized) creature parked in front of the TV set.

Use a thesaurus to help you find precise words to use in place of more general words in your writing.

lesson **8**

Similes and Metaphors

Simile (sim′ ə lē) comes from the Latin word **similis**, which means **similar**.

A **simile** is a figure of speech comparing one thing to another that is quite different from it. A simile is introduced by the word **like** or the word **as**. The following sentences contain similes.

After she had hiked all day, Mona's legs felt **like lead**.
That book is **as dull as dishwater**.

Metaphor is pronounced met′ ə fôr′.

Another form of comparison called a **metaphor** does not use the words **like** or **as**. Instead, a metaphor states that one thing **is** another. The comparison in the following sentence is a metaphor.

The floor of Henry's closet **is a rat's nest**.

The use of interesting comparisons can make your writing more colorful. Many similes and metaphors have been used so often that they are no longer very effective. Try to use fresh, unexpected comparisons in your writing in place of more common ones.

A. Each of the sentences below contains an overused simile. Rewrite each simile using some fresh comparison.

1. People were crowded into the small room **like sardines in a can**.

What else is close together? Kernels in an ear of corn? Sticks of gum in a pack?

____

2. The hamster felt **as light as a feather** in Leon's hands. __________

What else is nearly weightless?

____

3. Mrs. Richter moved **like lightning** to catch the falling platter of hamburgers. __________________________________

What quality does your simile have to show?

4. Hoping the deer would come nearer, Andy stood **as still as a statue**. __________________________________

Use **as still** or **as quietly** for your new simile.

5. Tanya says that beating her brother at checkers is **as easy as rolling off a log**. __________________________________

What else can you think of that takes no effort at all?

6. The one-year-old twins who live down the street look **like two peas in a pod**. __________________________________

B. Fill in the blanks in the passage with similes and metaphors of your own. Try to make your comparisons unusual and colorful.

Fred left the Post Office and walked along the downtown street. It was the hottest day of the summer. The sun's glare was like (1.) ______________________, making his head hurt. His new striped shirt and maroon pants, which had been as crisp and clean as (2.) ______________________ when he left home, now felt as limp and soggy as (3.) ______________________.

Remember that **glare** means **brightness**. What similes can convey extreme brightness?

The package he was carrying seemed to get heavier and heavier, until

Use a metaphor here. ▶ it was a(n) (4.) ______________________ pulling at his arm.

The cement pavement was so hot that the soles of his feet felt like (5.) ______________________.

Reaching the bus stop, Fred put the package down and sat on it. A fat gray pigeon strutted around him, clucking, its toes as pink as (6.) ______________________. Finally, the bus came, lumbering up the street like (7.) ______________________. Fred climbed aboard and sat very still, trying not to think of the heat, until the bus reached his corner. He got off and headed home, where the cool shower and cold drink that were waiting for him seemed as

What things might be precious or valuable? ▶ precious as (8.) ______________________.

C. Choose a metaphor for each of the things below. Remember that the two things compared must resemble each other in some important way. Write your choice on the lines.

Shape and color may be important in these metaphors. ▶

1. a delicate flowering tree ______________________

   ____

2. a fat bush with glossy green leaves ______________________

   ____

Sound is an important part of this metaphor. ▶

3. a yowling, hissing cat ______________________

   ____

Use fresh similes and metaphors to add vitality to your writing.

lesson 9

Writing for Your Audience

When you write, it is important to have your audience clearly in mind. Think about who is going to read what you write, because it often makes a difference in your choice of words and phrases and in the general style of your writing.

A. Suppose you are writing to someone from another country who has studied English in school but is not familiar with our informal language and with figures of speech. Put an **X** next to the phrase in each pair that would be most easily understood.

Boondocks, a World War II slang word, came from the Tagalog (native Filipino) word **bunduk**, meaning **mountain**.

1. ________ a. go in for ________ b. have an interest in
2. ________ a. got sick ________ b. caught a bug
3. ________ a. to improve ________ b. to shape up
4. ________ a. outside of town ________ b. in the boondocks
5. ________ a. hang loose ________ b. relax
6. ________ a. a real letdown ________ b. a terrible disappointment

B. Suppose you are writing clues for a treasure hunt for a group of seven-year-olds. Underline the word in each pair that would allow the children to read and understand the clues most easily.

Which word from each pair is simpler?

1. crimson	red	6. quickly	immediately
2. round	circular	7. hidden	disguised
3. proceed	go	8. clockwise	to the right
4. stone	boulder	9. indicator	marker
5. bushes	shrubbery	10. large	immense

C. The sentence below is written in a style that would be suitable for a composition for school.

1. a. Our six-year-old German shepherd is tremendously strong, well-trained, obedient, and intensely loyal to the family.

Now write another sentence about a dog as you might write to a young brother or sister.

What information about a dog might interest a young child?

b. ____

____

Write another sentence in the style you would use in an informal piece for a class newsletter.

c. ____

____

Using the same procedure, rewrite the sentences below.

2. a. My least favorite family chore is to clean up the dishes and the kitchen after a Sunday dinner.

How would you write to a younger person? ▶ b. ______________________________

____

This is informal. ▶ c. ______________________________

____

This sentence is written to be read by your younger brother or sister. ▶ 3. a. Dad took us to see a good show about Eskimos and arctic animals at the museum.

What would you tell other 8th graders? ▶ b. ______________________________

____

How would you begin a school report about the museum trip? ▶ c. ______________________________

____

D. Write two sentences about something you have done recently—a sports event, a trip, a hobby—as you would describe it to your grandparents. Then rewrite the sentences describing what you have done as you would write to your best friend.

Who would be more likely to understand the special figures of speech used by people your age? ▶ ______________________________

____

____

____

Keep your audience clearly in mind whenever you write.

Post-Test

A. Choose the key word that completes each sentence correctly. Write it in the blank.

1. Although she seems to have a very ______________________ attitude, Doreen always turns in excellent work. (casual, causal)
2. The post office was unusually busy, with ______________________ lines of people at the windows all day. (continual, continuous)
3. Mr. Kirk put a special ______________________ in the contract when he sold his house so that he could take away his favorite azalea bushes. (clause, claws)
4. Lynnette was very ______________________ when the snowstorm threatened to ruin her plans for the Valentine party. (agitated, animated)
5. The bagpipe band ______________________ the clog dancers on the program at the folk festival. (preceded, proceeded)
6. The aisles in the supermarket are arranged in a ______________________ that makes it hard to find things. (manner, manor)
7. The math class usually goes over homework first and takes up new work during the ______________________ part of the hour. (later, latter)
8. When the tent was put up, the ropes were not pulled ______________________ enough, and it collapsed during the night. (taught, taut)
9. Jennie ______________________ from her mother's letter that her parents were enjoying their trip to Chicago. (implied, inferred)
10. The emergency power source in the hospital operating room is always hooked up so that it is ready for ______________________ use. (instantaneous, monotonous)
11. A potter will often purposely ______________________ a bowl or plate in order to get a certain artistic effect. (mishap, misshape)

B. Match each word in Column A with its meaning in Column B. Write the letter of the correct meaning on the line next to each word in Column A.

	Column A	Column B
________	1. indolent	a. to state positively; maintain as true
________	2. dignity	b. honesty; holding to ethical principles
________	3. affirm	c. lacking in energy; moving slowly
________	4. accelerate	d. to make known or reveal
________	5. sluggish	e. to organize in readiness for action
________	6. integrity	f. proud, honorable, or noble character
________	7. disclose	g. lazy; having a disposition to avoid work
________	8. mobilize	h. to cause to happen more quickly

C. Write a word from the box that makes sense in each blank.

insipid	adapt	resilient	lamented	leisurely
impulsive	adopt	negligence	proclaimed	pessimism

1. Robert's optimism about everything is a pleasant change from Art's constant gloominess and ____________________.
2. A stray kitten hung around the neighborhood for several days and then decided to ____________________ the Nagle family.
3. I thought the roast beef sandwiches at lunch were delicious, but the vegetable soup was ____________________.
4. A lot of damage was caused at the lake by the ____________________ of several people who didn't tie up their boats securely.
5. Dona has a tendency to make ____________________ decisions that she later regrets.
6. The lamp base wasn't the right kind to clamp onto the desk properly, but Jon was able to ____________________ it so it would fit.
7. The governor has ____________________ the second week in May as State History Week.
8. Charlie and his uncle go on a long, ____________________ fishing and camping trip together every summer.
9. Everyone ____________________ the town council's decision to cut funds for the summer recreation programs.
10. The new bows for archery class are much more ____________________ than the ones we used last year.

D. Underline the correct word in parentheses to complete each sentence.

1. What (affect, effect) will Bob's injury have on the team's chances for beating Madison School next week?
2. Every (desert, dessert) on the restaurant's long menu sounded wonderful and mouthwatering.
3. Instead of buying the big house they were looking at, the Tanakas decided to buy a (lucid, modest) house that has a huge back yard.
4. Rosa's friends often get her to help settle disagreements because she is able to take the (disinterested, uninterested) point of view.
5. Kathleen and Denis are both campaigning to be president of the student (council, counsel) for next year.
6. The new aquarium on the waterfront has been attracting (hoards, hordes) of visitors every weekend since it opened.
7. Ms. Larimer had to write a (personal, personnel) letter to send along with her application for the vacant apartment.
8. Ned (blurted, jested) with his little sister's friends and kept them entertained while they waited for the school bus.
9. Everybody is pleased with the (clamorous, harmonious) color scheme that the committee chose to decorate the club meeting room.
10. The (hostility, humanity) between the Mitchell children and their parents made their weekend guests feel uncomfortable.
11. A family of squirrels (inhabits, inhibits) the hole under the attic roof.

Unit 3

A. Can you answer the following test questions? In each row, circle the word that has the same or nearly the same meaning as the boldface word.

1. **pacific**	regular	noisy	peaceful
2. **dispute**	conduct	quarrel	decision
3. **initiated**	began	requested	completed
4. **miserly**	generous	stingy	helpful
5. **accessible**	alike	familiar	available

In each row, circle the word that has a meaning opposite to that of the boldface word.

6. **inept**	expert	ordinary	ungracious
7. **sufficient**	ample	inadequate	gigantic
8. **intricate**	delicate	simple	rapid
9. **agitate**	charm	irritate	calm
10. **erroneous**	approximate	absolute	accurate

B. Each of the words in the puzzle can be found somewhere in Part A. Write the letters of the correct words in the blanks. When you are done, the letters in the boxes will spell a word that sounds as if it means **encountered a quartet**.

1. antonym for **meager**
2. antonym for **different**
3. antonym for **soothe**
4. antonym for **finished**
5. antonym for **unhurried**
6. antonym for **displease**
7. antonym for **silent**
8. antonym for **selfish**

Vocabulary for Test-Taking

Notice that the blanks for each word go down, not across.

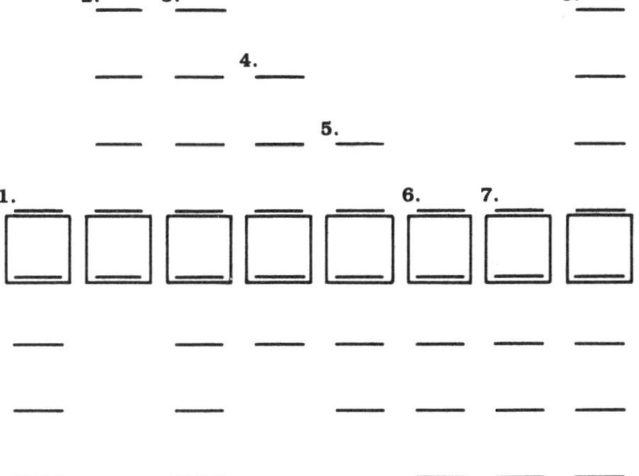

In order to do well on most tests and to solve many puzzles, you need to know words and their meanings. If you enjoy learning new words and working with words, it can be fun to take a test or solve a word puzzle.

In this unit, you will learn things about words that will help you on tests. You will learn that

- synonyms have similar meanings.
- antonyms have opposite meanings.
- context clues can help you learn the meanings of unfamiliar words in your reading.
- you can often figure out the meaning of an idiom by seeing how it is used in a sentence.

lesson 1

Synonyms

agonizing · **aptness**

aspire · **calculation**

endeavor · **essential**

fatigue · **formerly**

initial · **intrigue**

surmount

Words that have nearly the same meaning are **synonyms**. On tests you are often asked to find synonyms.

A. In each pair of sentences below, underline the word in the second sentence that is a synonym for the boldface word in the first sentence.

1. The polar regions of the world have long **intrigued** explorers. Through the 1800s, explorers who sailed to the Arctic and the Antarctic were fascinated by the beauty of the frozen landscape.
2. The **initial** exploration of these remote areas was done on foot or with the help of dog sleds. Those first expeditions were badly handicapped by the terrible weather and extreme cold.

The prefix **sur**- has a meaning similar to **super**-. ▶

3. In the far north, where there is no land under the ice, explorers had to **surmount** the problem of constantly shifting ice. In the south, they had to overcome the problems of high altitude.
4. People from many countries **aspired** to be the first to reach the North Pole. President Theodore Roosevelt aimed for an American triumph, choosing Robert E. Peary to lead an expedition.

Formerly is an adverb. Look for another adverb in the second sentence. ▶

5. Peary **formerly** had spent 20 years in the Arctic and understood its conditions. In planning the expedition, he used knowledge gained earlier from the Eskimos about survival methods.
6. He knew it was **essential** to set up a series of advance camps for supplies. He also knew it was necessary that the final push to the Pole be made by a small, well-rested group.

It took five months for word of their success to reach the United States. ▶

7. In April 1909, despite **fatigue** from a journey of more than 400 miles, Peary reached the North Pole with his aide, Matthew Henson, and four Eskimos. Their weariness did not spoil the excitement of the victory for them.
8. Following Peary's success, the **endeavor** to reach the South Pole became an urgent race. Two teams, one led by the Norwegian explorer Roald Amundsen and the other by the Englishman Robert Scott, both began the attempt at the same time.

Apt is from a Latin word meaning **fastened** or **fitted**. The suffix -**ness** makes the adjective into a
☐ noun.
☐ verb. ▶

9. Amundsen's team dressed warmly and lightly; his sleds were especially light in weight, pulled by excellent huskies with a special **aptness** for the conditions of the expedition. Scott used Siberian ponies instead of dogs to pull his heavy sleds, but the ponies proved to have no fitness for such a journey.
10. Amundsen's **calculations** for his expedition were based on traveling quickly. With his superb figuring aided by good weather, his team reached the South Pole on December 14, 1911, and returned safely to their base camp, making the 1,860-mile round trip in only 99 days.

In ancient Greece, an **agon** was a contest in which prizes were awarded. The verb **agonize** meant **to struggle for a prize**. ▶

11. Scott and his party reached the Pole a month later and had the **agonizing** disappointment of finding the Norwegian flag, Amundsen's tent, and a letter from him to Scott. Exhausted, they began the painful journey back, but their health was poor, they met bad weather, and all five died on the return trip.

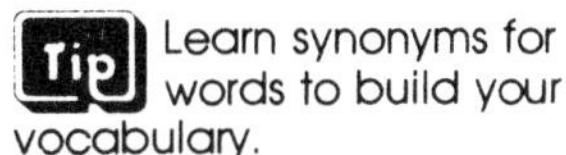
Learn synonyms for words to build your vocabulary.

B. Read the passage. In the blank after each boldface word, write the key word that is its synonym.

You may have to add **-s**, **-ed**, or **-ing** to the key word.

In our time, scientists and others continue to be **fascinated** (1. ________________) by the polar regions. But exploration of the North and South Poles has entered the age of technology. **Earlier** (2. ________________), members of expeditions had to expect isolation, **weariness** (3. ________________), and frostbite. Expeditions now can keep in touch with the outside world by radio. In addition, the use of motorized equipment, such as heavy tractors, makes travel less **painful** (4. ________________). The planners of a present-day expedition no longer need to base their **figuring** (5. ________________) on what a few people can carry with them. They can plan to have airplanes or helicopters transport **necessary** (6. ________________) supplies even to the most remote camp.

Both flights were made by U.S. Navy Commander Richard Byrd.

The **first** (7. ________________) airplane flights over both the North and South Poles were made during the 1920s. A 1931 **attempt** (8. ________________) to cross the North Pole by submarine under the ice failed. Finally, nearly 30 years later, an American nuclear-powered submarine, named the *Nautilus*, proved its **fitness** (9. ________________) for the task and made the historic crossing.

In Antarctica, scientific investigation is the main emphasis. Many nations, **overcoming** (10. ________________) their political differences for the sake of research, have worked together there in a truly international effort. But in the Arctic, the focus of exploration has shifted to economic interests. Especially since the discovery of oil, there is intense competition among nations who **aim** (11. ________________) to control the wealth of the region.

Learning synonyms for words will help you in taking tests.

lesson **2** # More Synonyms

abrupt · **advent**
comprehensible
convert · **convey**
global · **impact**
infinite · **probability**
tedious

Sometimes on tests you will be asked to find synonyms for words used in a paragraph.

A. Read the passage that was taken from a magazine article. For each boldface word in the passage, find a synonym in the list that follows it. Write the correct boldface word next to its synonym.

A generation ago, computers were almost unknown except to advanced mathematicians. The rapid development of computers in recent years has caused an **abrupt** change in society and the effect is **global**. In all **probability**, computers affect your daily life in countless ways that you are not even aware of. They have had an **impact** on the way information is stored, the way money is handled, and the way groceries are checked out at the supermarket. Computers can now do quickly many tasks that used to take hours or days of **tedious** human effort. They help to handle and organize the constant flow of new knowledge in many fields.

Look for a word in the list that can replace **infinite** and make sense in the sentence. ▶

Remember that synonyms must be the same part of speech. The -**ible** ending tells you that **comprehensible** is ▶
☐ an adjective.
☐ a noun.

The uses of computers seem to be **infinite**. We have become accustomed to the idea of computers storing and producing numbers, letters, and words. Some ideas are too complicated, or contain too much data, to be **conveyed** easily by numbers or words. But they may be quickly **comprehensible** if they can be shown as a moving image. The **advent** of new computer technology now makes it possible to **convert** data into three-dimensional, colored motion pictures. Seen in such a form, ideas may be easily grasped that would otherwise require great time and effort to absorb.

1. tiresome ______________________
2. sudden ______________________
3. coming ______________________
4. world-wide ______________________
5. change ______________________

6. understandable ______

7. effect ______

8. likelihood ______

9. limitless ______

10. communicated ______

Tip Learn synonyms for words to build your vocabulary.

B. Underline the word after each sentence that is a synonym for the boldface word in the sentence.

1. Theo hit her head on the windshield when the car made an **abrupt** stop at the corner.
   sudden   uneven   unexpected

The Latin root **vert**, **vers**, meaning **to turn**, is also found in **reverse**, **invert**, and **perverse**.

2. The energy crisis caused many people to **convert** their home heating from oil to natural gas.
   increase   change   supply
3. Jeff's directions for finding his house were not **comprehensible** to some people.
   readable   understandable   realistic
4. Protecting water supplies from pollution is a **global** problem.
   circular   national   world-wide
5. The swimming teacher has **infinite** patience with people who are afraid of the water.
   limitless   limited   varied

The Latin root **ven**, **vent**, meaning **to come**, is also found in **convene**, **invent**, and **prevent**.

6. With the **advent** of warm weather, stores may sell more fans and garden hoses.
   changing   enjoyment   coming
7. Ms. Johnson **conveyed** our message to her family.
   communicated   forgot   accepted
8. There is a high **probability** of a flu epidemic this winter.
   likelihood   problem   reaction
9. Julio spent a **tedious** afternoon at home, waiting for the rain-storm to stop.
   restful   tiresome   worried
10. The new zoning laws will have an enormous **impact** on the neighborhood near the high school.
   error   effect   allowance

C. Write two sentences about something you have recently seen in a magazine, newspaper, or book. Use at least one key word in each of your sentences.

1. ______

______

2. ______

______

On a test you are sometimes asked to find synonyms for words in a paragraph or sentence.

lesson **3**

Antonyms

adroit • dawdle
deteriorate
flexible • fragile
humility • illusion
ridicule • stability

Antonyms are words with opposite meanings, such as **loss** and **gain**. On tests you are often asked to find antonyms.

Study the key words and their meanings.

adroit (ə droit′), *adj.* expert or nimble in using the hands.
dawdle (dôd′ ᵊl), *v.* to waste time; idle.
deteriorate (di tēr′ ē ə rāt′), *v.* to become worse.
flexible (flek′ sə bəl), *adj.* 1. capable of being bent. 2. capable of being changed or rearranged.
fragile (fraj′ əl), *adj.* delicate or easily broken; frail.
humility (hyo͞o mil′ i tē), *n.* modesty; lack of self-importance.

Erroneous means **in error**. ▶

illusion (i lo͞o′ zhən), *n.* a false or erroneous idea or perception.

Ridicule comes from the Latin **ridere, to laugh**. ▶

ridicule (rid′ ə kyo͞ol), *n.* 1. speech or action that mocks or makes fun of. —*v.* 2. to mock.

This noun is formed from the adjective **stable**. ▶

stability (stə bil′ i tē), *n.* steadiness; permanence; reliability.

A. Note the boldface word in each group. Circle the letter next to the group of words that contains its antonym.

Which is the opposite of **dawdle**? ▶

1. to **dawdle**
   a. to hurry
   b. to waste time

Fragile is related to **fracture**. What does **fracture** mean? Does this give you a clue? ▶

2. a **fragile** plate
   a. a delicate plate
   b. an unbreakable plate

Illusion comes from the Latin word **ludere, to play**. Does that give you a clue? ▶

3. the **illusion**
   a. the reality
   b. the appearance
4. to **ridicule**
   a. to respect
   b. to mock
5. his **humility**
   a. his modesty
   b. his pride
6. a **flexible** schedule
   a. a rigid schedule
   b. a changeable schedule
7. to **deteriorate**
   a. to improve
   b. to worsen
8. the chair's **stability**
   a. the chair's reliability
   b. the chair's unsteadiness
9. an **adroit** carpenter
   a. a skillful carpenter
   b. a clumsy carpenter

Tip Remember that antonyms are words that have opposite meanings. ▶

B. Circle the antonym of the boldface word in each row.

1. **pride**	stability	humility	necessity	respect
2. **hurry**	respect	deteriorate	mock	dawdle
3. **clumsy**	wasteful	fragile	adroit	flexible
4. **improve**	deteriorate	mock	increase	dawdle
5. **rigid**	flexible	fragile	unbending	rugged
6. **reality**	stability	illusion	ridicule	certainty
7. **tough**	adroit	strong	rigid	fragile
8. **respect**	ridicule	modesty	pride	humility

C. The passage below is incorrect as it is written. On each line write a key word that is the antonym of the boldface word. Then the story will be correct.

In 1974 when Hank Aaron of the Atlanta Braves broke Babe Ruth's record for career home runs, he behaved with **pride** (1.) ____________________ and lack of pretension. He had always known that he and the game of baseball were good for each other.

He was born in Mobile, Alabama, in 1934. ▶

As a boy, Hank was always eager to play ball. He was **clumsy** (2.) ____________________ with a baseball and bat from the start, and although he was quite short and slim, he was certainly not **tough** (3.) ____________________. He wanted to be a professional baseball player. His father warned him that his dream might be just that, a(n) **reality** (4.) ____________________; the major leagues then had no black players. But this changed in 1947, when the Brooklyn Dodgers signed Jackie Robinson.

At the age of 17, Hank got his chance to play professional ball. With his parents' reluctant consent and with two dollars in his pocket, he left on the train for Indianapolis to play for a black team.

Which word conveys the same negative idea as **teasing**? ▶

Hank got a lot of teasing and **respect** (5.) ____________________ from his teammates at first because of his odd batting style, his tendency to **hurry** (6.) ____________________ too long before throwing the ball, and his amazing ability to fall asleep any time, any place. However, they quickly discovered that they could count on the

The words **count on** should be a clue. ▶

unsteadiness (7.) ____________________ of both his hitting and his fielding. The teasing stopped, and Hank Aaron's illustrious major league career of more than 20 years was about to begin.

Knowing antonyms for words will help you to do well on tests.

lesson **4**

Multiple Meanings

apply · **concern**
cycle · **major**
plant · **range**

For many entry words the dictionary lists more than one meaning. Context clues can often help you decide which meaning a word has in a sentence. Knowing which part of speech the word is in the sentence will also help you to understand its precise meaning. Read the entry words and their meanings.

apply (ə plī′), *v.* 1. to make practical or active use of. 2. to lay or spread on. 3. to be suitable or related. 4. to make a request or application.

concern (kən sûrn′), *v.* 1. to be of interest or importance to; relate to; affect. 2. to worry or trouble. —*n.* 3. something that relates to or affects a person. 4. anxiety or worry.

Cycle is from the Greek **kyklos**, **circle** or **wheel**. ▶

cycle (sī′ kəl), *n.* 1. a period of time in which certain things repeat themselves in a certain way. 2. any complete series of occurrences that repeats itself. 3. a bicycle, tricycle, or similar wheeled vehicle.

Notice which parts of speech the different meanings are. ▶

major (mā′jər), *adj.* 1. great in importance, rank, or stature. 2. serious or dangerous; requiring attention. —*n.* 3. an officer's rank in the U.S. Army, Air Force, or Marines. 4. the subject field in which a college student specializes.

plant (plant), *n.* 1. any member of the vegetable group of living things. 2. the buildings and equipment of a factory or other business. 3. a person placed in an audience to encourage applause or contribute to the action of the play. —*v.* 4. to put in the ground to grow. 5. to set firmly; put; place. 6. to place for the purpose of observing, spying, or informing.

Range is from an Old French word **renc**, which means **line**. If you look in a large dictionary, you will find at least forty different meanings for **range**. ▶

range (rānj), *n.* 1. the limits within which something varies, operates, or can be done. 2. a chain of mountains. 3. a large, open region for grazing livestock. 4. a large stove with burners and an oven.

Tip If a word has more than one meaning, be sure you understand which meaning it has in a given sentence. ▶

A. Read the sentences in which the key words are used. Decide which meaning the boldface key word has in each sentence and write the number of the correct meaning on the line next to the sentence.

________ 1. The parking restrictions on Broad Street do not **apply** on Sundays and holidays.

________ 2. The paint is available in a wide **range** of colors.

________ 3. Clean-up chores at summer camp were rotated in a weekly **cycle**.

________ 4. An undercover agent was **planted** at the meeting.

________ 5. Joellen's father is a retired **major**.

In this sentence **concern** is a
☐ noun.
☐ verb. ▶

________ 6. What they do with their money is none of his **concern**.

________ 7. Jill **planted** herself in the doorway and refused to budge.

_________ 8. Luis is going to **apply** for an after-school job at the shopping center.

_________ 9. The kitchen at Robinson School has a huge stainless steel **range**.

_________ 10. There was a **major** accident at the tunnel entrance.

B. In each blank in the passage, write the key word that best completes the sentence.

You may need to add **-s**, **-ed**, or **-ing** to the key words.

The difficulty of maintaining a pure water supply is a growing (1.) _______________ for every part of the country. In industrial areas, manufacturing (2.) _______________ use great quantities of water and discharge toxic wastes into the water supply. Another (3.) _______________ source of pollution is the chemical fertilizers and pesticides that are (4.) _______________ to fields and orchards and then are washed into streams and rivers and the underground water supply.

Another form of water pollution has recently been discovered. Water evaporates into the atmosphere and falls again as rain, snow, or other precipitation, in a constant (5.) _______________. If it falls back through badly polluted air, it may cause something called acid rain. Masses of moist air moving from west to east across the country often carry pollutants. When an air mass reaches the Adirondack Mountain (6.) _______________ in upstate New York, the moisture condenses and falls. The amount of acid in some mountain lakes has become so great that it has killed the fish and almost doubled the normal rate of erosion of the rocks around the lakes.

Circle the number of the correct meaning of the word you filled in.

1 2 3 4

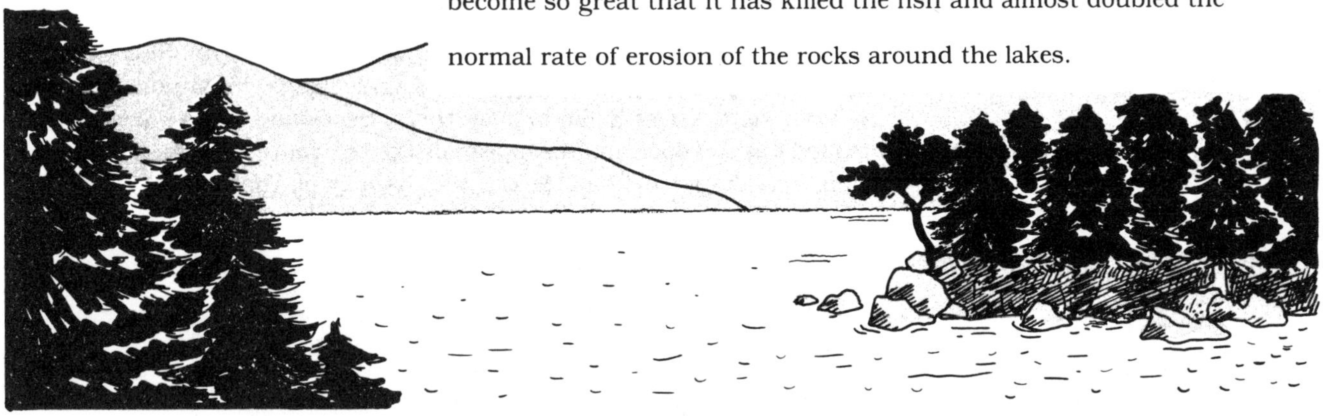

When a word has multiple meanings, context clues and the word's part of speech in the sentence will help you understand the correct meaning.

lesson **5**

Understanding Idioms

An expression or phrase called an **idiom** is a group of words that must be learned as a whole. It has a special meaning different from the meanings of the separate words.

Read the following passage, paying special attention to the idioms in boldface.

Moving day for the Meyers began just about as badly as Erika had expected. Her mother got everybody up before dawn so they would be ready by the time the movers came at 9 o'clock. Over a strange breakfast of leftovers, Erika observed her family.

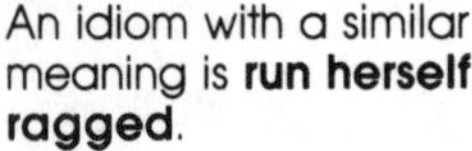
An idiom with a similar meaning is **run herself ragged**.

Her grandmother, who had **spread herself thin** for the past month, was exhausted. She had absolutely lost her sense of humor. Erika's mother was giving directions and advice. She was speaking quietly, trying to sound like a calm and reasonable person, but Erika could **read between the lines**. Her little brother Adam could hardly **keep his shirt on**. He would be in trouble within the hour, she was quite sure.

"I'll have some more coffee." The pot had boiled dry.

"Adam, get the cat's carrying case out of the closet." He knocked over a lamp and the ironing board.

"Erika, where did you put the keys to the new apartment?" Erika **drew a blank**.

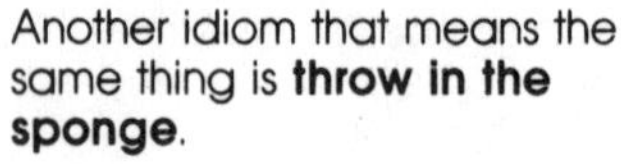
Another idiom that means the same thing is **throw in the sponge**.

"Well, that **takes the cake**!" said her mother. She was ready to **throw in the towel**.

Just then the movers arrived. The dog barked and jumped and ran around as if he **had a screw loose**.

But the movers **knew the ropes**. Things started to improve right away. They **took everything in their stride**. They gave Adam useful things to do. They had a box for packing Erika's drum that would just **fill the bill**. They **bent over backwards** to reassure Erika's grandmother that they would be careful with her furniture. She began to **snap out of** her bad mood and smile again. They found the lost keys, right where Erika had left them. Boxes and furniture were whisked out the door and disappeared into the van. By noon the rooms were empty and the Meyers were happily on their way to their new apartment.

A. The idioms from the passage are listed below. Circle the letter of the correct meaning for each idiom.

Which phrase can you substitute in the story in place of the idiom? ▶

1. spread herself thin
   a. attempted to do too many things at one time
   b. lost weight by exercising
2. read between the lines
   a. find additional meanings in what she said
   b. read over her shoulder

Are you looking for a literal, word-for-word meaning? ▶

3. keep his shirt on
   a. stay dressed
   b. remain patient or calm
4. drew a blank
   a. wrote in the air with her finger
   b. failed to remember
5. takes the cake
   a. removes the dessert
   b. exceeds or surpasses anything
6. throw in the towel
   a. do the laundry
   b. admit defeat; give up
7. had a screw loose
   a. was crazy
   b. needed repair
8. knew the ropes

Which phrase makes sense in the story? ▶

   a. were completely familiar with the operation
   b. had studied knot-tying
9. took everything in their stride
   a. walked with very large steps
   b. dealt with things calmly and easily
10. fill the bill
    a. write out the check
    b. be exactly what was needed
11. bent over backwards
    a. made every effort
    b. did acrobatics
12. snap out of
    a. undo the fastenings
    b. recover from

B. Many idioms are listed in the dictionary. They are included at the end of the entry for one of the main words in the expression. Try to find the meanings of the idioms below in your dictionary.

It might be listed under **skin** or under **teeth**. ▶

1. by the skin of one's teeth ______________________
2. go to the dogs ______________________
3. with a grain of salt ______________________

An idiom is a group of words whose meaning must be learned as a whole.

lesson 6

Context Clues in a Passage

anticipation

dedicated

disciplinarian

engage · **establish**

evident · **fortitude**

obscure · **ovation**

preserve

Paragraphs or stories followed by questions to answer are often part of a test. You have already learned how context clues can help you to discover the meanings of unfamiliar words in your reading. Read this passage and think about the meanings of the key words.

The American ballerina Maria Tallchief grew up in Fairfax, Oklahoma. Her father was an Osage Indian; her mother was of Scotch-Irish descent. Maria began piano and dance lessons before she was five, and her talent was **evident**. Because her ability was obvious to her parents, they wanted her to have the best training, and when she was about eight years old they moved to Los Angeles.

Maria was to prepare for a future as a concert pianist. She studied piano in **anticipation** of making it her career. At the same time, she and her sister Marjorie both studied dance. There was no doubt about Maria's talent in both areas; the question was which was most important to her. During all her school years, practicing **engaged** Maria's time before and after school. Ballet lessons occupied the early evening. She soon knew that dancing would be her career. Her ballet teachers were strict **disciplinarians**, but she didn't mind. It was right that they demand her obedience to the rules and standards of the ballet routine so that she would master every step and movement. She was so **dedicated**, so devoted to her art, that she was willing to strive for perfection.

> Marjorie also became a well-known ballet dancer.

> What do you think the root of this key word is? Write it here.

After high school, Maria joined the company of the Ballet Russe for a Canadian tour and a season in New York. It was a demanding year that tested her **fortitude**. The schedule was exhausting, there were many disappointments, and she was intensely lonely. But she knew she had the endurance to put up with any kind of hardship in order to dance.

> The Ballet Russe Company was formed by Russian dancers.

> **Fortitude** is related to **fortify** (to strengthen) and **fort** (an area that has been strengthened for military defense).

Whenever Maria danced, even in small parts, people realized that she had the makings of a great ballerina. Very soon she was no longer an **obscure** member of the corps but a well-known soloist. Her performances brought applause from the critics and her fellow dancers as well as the thundering **ovations** of her audiences.

> The **corps de ballet** is the group that dances together with no solo parts. **Corps**, pronounced kôr, is a French word.

When she was securely settled in her position as a major star, people suggested that she change her name. They thought that an **established** ballerina should have a more Russian-sounding name. She didn't mind being called Maria, instead of her girlhood name of

> Because ballet was perfected in Russia and many famous dancers were Russian, non-Russian dancers often took Russian names.

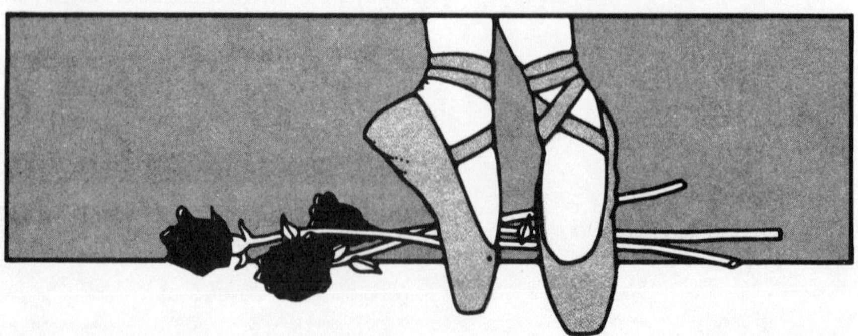

Betty Marie, but she insisted on maintaining the name of Tallchief. She was proud of it and wanted to **preserve** it.

Of the many triumphs of her career, one that meant the most to her was an invitation from the Osage Tribal Council in 1953 to return to Fairfax, Oklahoma, for a special ceremony naming her a Princess of the Osage.

Tip: Look for context clues in the passage to help you figure out the meaning of a word you do not know.

▶ **A.** On the line next to each word from the story in Column A, write the letter of its meaning listed in Column B.

	Column A	Column B
________	1. evident	a. completely devoted
________	2. anticipation	b. endurance; courage
________	3. engaged	c. to maintain; save
________	4. disciplinarians	d. obvious; easy to see
________	5. dedicated	e. occupied
________	6. fortitude	f. securely settled in a position
________	7. obscure	g. loud or prolonged applause
▶ ________	8. ovations	h. an action that is in preparation for a future action
________	9. established	i. not well-known or famous
________	10. preserve	j. those who demand obedience to strict rules and standards

When this word was used in the story, it described
- ☐ a kind of dance.
- ☐ audience reaction.

Knowing the meanings of the key words will help you to decide if each sentence is true or false.

▶ **B.** Read each sentence below. If it is true, write **T** on the line next to the sentence. Write **F** if it is false.

________ 1. Maria was willing to practice hard in anticipation of becoming a professional dancer.

________ 2. Maria's talent as a dancer was not evident.

________ 3. On school days she was not engaged in practicing.

________ 4. Because her teachers were disciplinarians, Maria did not have to meet their standards.

________ 5. The life of a professional dancer requires a great deal of fortitude.

________ 6. Maria's talent was recognized in both small parts and large.

________ 7. Other people suggested to Maria that she preserve her Indian name.

On a test, the context clues in a passage will often help you figure out the meaning of a new word.

lesson 7 Review

This lesson reviews the TIPS you have learned in this book. Use each TIP to answer the questions that follow it.

Tip **1. Look for prefixes, suffixes, and roots you know to help you figure out the meaning of an unfamiliar word.**
Write the meaning of each word. Circle all prefixes and suffixes.

a. collaborate ______________________________

b. familiarize ______________________________

c. realist ______________________________

d. disinterested ______________________________

e. monotonous ______________________________

Tip **2. Knowing a word's origin can often help you figure out its meaning.**
Choose the word from the box that matches each origin given below. Then write the meaning of the present-day word.

calico	camouflage	chronology	coleslaw	concern	concur

a. from French **camoufler**, "to disguise" ______________________________

Meaning: ______________________________

b. from Latin **con**, "together" + **currere**, "to run" ______________________________

Meaning: ______________________________

c. from Dutch **kool**, "cabbage" + **sla**, "salad" ______________________________

Meaning: ______________________________

d. from Greek **chron**, "time" + **ology**, "study of" ______________________________

Meaning: ______________________________

Tip **3. If a word has more than one meaning, be sure you understand which meaning it has in a given sentence.**
Write the number of the correct meaning on the line next to each sentence.
apply (ə plī') *v.* 1. to make practical or active use of. 2. to lay or spread on. 3. to be suitable or related. 4. to make a request or application.

___ a. Stacy will **apply** for a learner's permit tomorrow.

____ b. If you **apply** enough pressure, the window will open.

____ c. Those regulations **apply** only to campers, not counselors.

____ d. Aunt Alicia **applies** cream to her face every night before retiring.

Tip **4. Look for context clues to help you figure out the meaning of a word you do not know.**

Read each sentence. Underline the word that has the same meaning as the boldface word.

a. The witness's story was a little too **slick** to be believed.

slippery	logical	clever

b. The artist **regarded** the painting with a critical eye.

observed	respected	affected

c. Holding an unpopular opinion often takes a lot of **fortitude**.

sorrow	courage	attraction

Tip **5. Be careful to use homophones and other easily confused words correctly in your writing.**

Underline the word that correctly completes each sentence.

a. Jason was (continually, continuously) forgetting his homework assignments.

b. The (mishap, misshape) could have been avoided with a little foresight.

c. The play (affected, effected) the audience greatly.

Tip **6. Use precise words to make your writing clear and interesting.**

Choose the best word to complete each sentence.

a. Without thinking, Lindsay ______________ the secret. (proclaimed, blurted)

b. You forgot to walk the dog again; I can't understand your ______________ . (negligence, hostility)

c. The hot, humid weather made everyone feel ______________ . (sluggish, immobile)

Tip **7. Learn synonyms for words to build your vocabulary.**

Tip **8. Remember that antonyms are words that have opposite meanings.**

For each boldface word, circle its synonym and underline its antonym, if any is given.

a. **adroit**	nimble	clumsy	tense	transparent
b. **tedious**	peaceful	obscure	boring	modest
c. **ridicule**	greet	mock	complain	respect
d. **fragile**	tired	tough	plain	delicate
e. **preserve**	save	advise	rejoice	destroy

Post-Test

Choose the word or phrase that means the same, or about the same, as the underlined word in each sentence. Mark your choice in the answer rows.

1. The governor wore a cashmere coat.
   Ⓐ expensive Ⓒ bargain
   Ⓑ full-length Ⓓ wool

2. We had an insipid dinner at Val's house.
   Ⓔ uninteresting Ⓖ liquid
   Ⓕ overcooked Ⓗ burned

3. Everyone appreciates Inez's sociability.
   Ⓐ politics Ⓒ friendliness
   Ⓑ intelligence Ⓓ family

4. The victim gave a lucid account of the crime.
   Ⓔ crazy Ⓖ slow
   Ⓕ complicated Ⓗ clear

5. Plan for the future instead of lamenting the past.
   Ⓐ criticizing Ⓒ gossiping about
   Ⓑ mourning for Ⓓ relating

6. The meeting became quite clamorous.
   Ⓔ large Ⓖ solemn
   Ⓕnoisy Ⓗ star-studded

7. That drawing is the wrong dimension for this room.
   Ⓐ frame Ⓒ shape
   Ⓑ color Ⓓ size

8. The ballerina received an ovation.
   Ⓔ bouquet Ⓖ contract
   Ⓕ loud applause Ⓗ telegram

9. My brother Bill loves to dawdle.
   Ⓐ waste time Ⓒ work hard
   Ⓑ draw Ⓓ juggle

10. Their departure was quite abrupt.
    Ⓔ unhappy Ⓖ unexpected
    Ⓕ delightful Ⓗ smooth

ANSWER ROWS 1 ⒶⒷⒸⒹ 2 ⒺⒻⒼⒽ 3 ⒶⒷⒸⒹ 4 ⒺⒻⒼⒽ 5 ⒶⒷⒸⒹ
6 ⒺⒻⒼⒽ 7 ⒶⒷⒸⒹ 8 ⒺⒻⒼⒽ 9 ⒶⒷⒸⒹ 10 ⒺⒻⒼⒽ

Dictionary

abdicate (ab′ di kāt′), *v.* to resign from or give up (a throne or any high position of leadership).

abduct (ab dukt′), *v.* to carry off or kidnap by force or trickery.

abnormal (ab nôr′ məl), *adj.* not typical; different from what is normal.

abolish (ə bol′ ish), *v.* to do away with completely; put an end to.

abrasive (ə brā′ siv), *n.* a material or substance used for grinding, smoothing, or polishing.

abrupt (ə brupt′), *adj.* sudden or unexpected.

absence (ab′ səns), *n.* 1. the state of being away. 2. a lack; state of being without something.

abstain (ab stān′), *v.* to refrain from; deny oneself.

accelerate (ak sel′ ə rāt′), *v.* 1. to cause to move, develop, or happen more quickly. 2. to move faster.

adapt (ə dapt′), *v.* 1. to make suitable to special requirements or new conditions; adjust. 2. to adjust oneself to different conditions, new surroundings, etc.

adopt (ə dopt′), *v.* 1. to choose or take as one's own. 2. to become the legal parent of. 3. to accept or formally approve.

adorn (ə dôrn′), *v.* to decorate or add ornaments to.

adroit (ə droit′), *adj.* expert or nimble in use of one's hands.

advent (ad′ vent), *n.* the arrival or coming into being of something.

affect (ə fekt′), *v.* to act on; produce a change or effect in.

affirm (ə fûrm′), *v.* to state positively; maintain as true.

agitate (aj′ i tāt′), *v.* 1. to move, stir up, or shake. 2. to disturb or excite.

agonizing (ag′ ə nīz′ ing), *adj.* extremely painful; causing suffering.

animate (an′ ə māt′), *v.* 1. to give life to. 2. to make spirited and lively.

anticipation (an tis′ ə pā′ shen), *n.* 1. the act of looking forward to something; expectation. 2. an action that prepares for a future action.

apply (ə plī′), *v.* 1. to make practical or active use of. 2. to lay or spread on. 3. to be suitable or related. 4. to make a request or application.

aptness (apt′ nis), *n.* fitness or suitability.

aspire (ə spī ᵊr′), *v.* to aim for; to be ambitious to obtain something great.

beret (bə rā′), *n.* a soft, round cap that has no brim or visor, and fits snugly on the head.

blurt (blûrt), *v.* to say suddenly, often without thinking.

bouquet (bō kā′), *n.* a bunch of flowers.

boycott (boi′ kot), *v.* to refuse to buy, use, or deal with as a form of protest or pressure. [named after Charles C. Boycott, a land agent in County Mayo, Ireland, who refused to lower the rents]

calculation (kal′ kyə lā′ shən), *n.* 1. the act of figuring out mathematically. 2. an estimate; reasoning. 3. careful planning.

calico (kal′ ə kō′), *n.* cotton cloth, usually printed on one side with a colored pattern. [named after Calicut, the former name of a seaport of India]

camellia (kə mēl′ yə), *n.* an Asian shrub or tree with shiny evergreen leaves and large white, pink, or red flowers. [named after Georg Josef Kamel, a 17th-century Jesuit missionary who first described it]

camouflage (kam′ ə fläzh′), *n.* 1. a disguise that blends into the background or looks like something else. 2. the act or technique of disguising military equipment or uniforms so they cannot be easily seen by the enemy. —*v.* 3. to conceal or disguise by changing the appearance or covering up.

capitalism (kap′ i tᵊliz′ əm), *n.* an economic system in which most land and businesses are owned by individuals or companies rather than by the government.

cashmere (kazh′ mēr), *n.* fine, downy wool from the Kashmir goats of India, or fabric or yarn made from this wool. [named for Kashmir, a region of northern India and West Pakistan]

casual (kazh′ o͞o əl), *adj.* 1. happening by chance. 2. without serious intention; offhand.

causal (kô′ zəl), *adj.* involving or expressing a cause.

characterize (kar′ ik tə rīz′), *v.* to be typical of or peculiar to.

chronicle (kron′ i kəl), *n.* 1. a record of events; history. —*v.* 2. to record the events of a certain time.

chronology (krə nol′ ə jē), *n.* an order of events in time, from earliest to latest.

---

act, **ā**ble, d**â**re, **ä**rt; **e**bb, **ē**qual; **i**f, **ī**ce; h**o**t, **ō**ver, **ô**rder; **oi**l; b**o͝o**k; **o͞o**ze; **ou**t; **u**p, **û**rge;
ə = *a* as in *alone*; ᵊ as in *button* (but′ᵊn); **ch**ief; **sh**oe; **th**in; **t͟h**at; **zh** as in *measure* (me**zh**′ər)

clamorous (klam′ ər əs), *adj.* noisy or loudly demanding. **—clamorously**, *adv.*

clause (klôz), *n.* 1. a group of words containing a subject and a verb. 2. a part of a law, contract, treaty, or the like.

claws (klôz), *n.* sharp, usually curved nails on an animal's foot.

clique (klēk), *n.* a small group of people who are friendly with each other or work closely together and usually do not let outsiders join their activities.

coexist (kō′ ig zist′), *v.* to live together or at the same time.

cohesion (kō hē′ zhən), *n.* a sticking together.

coleslaw (kōl′ slô′), *n.* a salad of finely sliced or chopped raw cabbage. [from the Dutch word *koolsla*, which comes from *kool*, "cabbage" + *sla*, short for *salade*, "salad"]

collaborate (kə lab′ ə rāt′), *v.* to work together with others.

collage (kə läzh′), *n.* a work of art composed by pasting materials and objects on a surface.

compound (kom′ pound), *adj.* made of two or more parts put together.

comprehensible (kom′ pri hen′ sə bəl), *adj.* understandable; capable of being comprehended.

concern (kən sûrn′), *v.* 1. to be of interest or importance to; relate to; affect. 2. to worry or trouble. —*n.* 3. something that relates to or affects a person. 4. anxiety or worry.

concur (kən kûr′), *v.* to agree with.

conservatism (kən sûr′ və tiz′ əm), *n.* the quality of being opposed to social or political change.

continual (kən tin′ yo͞o əl), *adj.* happening at regular intervals; frequent or repeated.

continuous (kən tin′ yo͞o əs), *adj.* without stop or interruption.

controversy (kon′ trə vûr′ sē), *n.* a dispute or debate.

converge (kən vûrj′), *v.* to come together at a point.

converse[1] (kən vûrs′), *v.* to talk together; have a conversation.

converse[2] (kən vûrs′), *adj.* 1. opposite or contrary; turned around. —*n.* (kon′ vûrs). 2. something that is the opposite or reverse of another.

convert (kən vûrt′), *v.* to change into a different form or alter for a different use.

convey (kən vā′), *v.* 1. to carry, bring, or take from one place to another; conduct. 2. to communicate or transmit; to make known.

council (koun′ səl), *n.* 1. a group of persons called together to decide on or discuss something of importance. 2. a group of persons having the power to make laws or govern.

counsel (koun′ səl), *n.* 1. advice or opinion. —*v.* 2. to give advice to; advise.

coupe (ko͞op), *n.* a closed, two-door automobile.

crochet (krō shā′), *v.* to make needlework by looping thread or yarn with a needle having a hook on the end.

cruelty (kro͞o′ əl tē), *n.* behavior that causes pain or distress to others.

curry (kûr′ ē), *n.* 1. a yellowish powder made with several spices, used especially in the cookery of India. 2. food cooked and flavored with this powder. [from the Tamil word *kari*, "sauce"]

customary (kus′ tə mer′ ē), *adj.* usual; according to custom or habit.

cycle (sī′ kəl), *n.* 1. a period of time in which certain things repeat themselves in a certain way. 2. any complete series of occurrences that repeats itself. 3. a bicycle, tricycle, or similar wheeled vehicle.

dawdle (dôd′ ᵊl), *v.* to waste time; idle.

dedicated (ded′ ə kā′ təd), *adj.* completely devoted.

define (di fīn′), *v.* 1. to state or set forth the meaning of (a word or phrase). 2. to explain clearly. 3. to make clear the outline or form of: *a tower defined against the sky.*

deposit (di poz′ it), *n.* a natural accumulation or occurrence.

desert[1] (dez′ ərt), *n.* a very dry region with little or no vegetation.

desert[2] (di zûrt′), *v.* to leave or abandon.

dessert (di zûrt′), *n.* sweet food served as a last course.

deteriorate (di tēr′ ē ə rāt′), *v.* to become worse.

determine (di tûr′ min), *v.* 1. to settle or decide (as in a dispute). 2. to come to a conclusion; resolve. 3. to find out by observation or investigation. 4. to cause, affect, or control.

diatom (dī′ə tom′), *n.* any of numerous tiny one-celled water plants having a hard, two-piece outer covering.

dignity (dig′ ni tē), *n.* proud, noble, or honorable character.

dimension (di men′ shən), *n.* size or magnitude.

disciplinarian (dis′ ə ple nâr′ ē ən), *n.* a person who enforces discipline; one who demands obedience to strict rules and standards.

disclose (di sklōz′), *v.* to make known or reveal.

disinterested (dis in′ tə res′ tid), *adj.* impartial or without prejudice.

distinct (di stingkt′), *adj.* clear to the mind or senses; plain; unmistakable.

drone[1] (drōn), *n.* 1. a male bee. 2. a person who lives on the labor of others; loafer; idler.

---

act, **ā**ble, **dâ**re, **ä**rt; **e**bb, **ē**qual; **i**f, **ī**ce; h**o**t, **ō**ver, **ô**rder; **oi**l; b**o͝o**k; **o͞o**ze; **ou**t; **u**p, **û**rge; ə = *a* as in *alone*; ᵊ as in *button* (but′ᵊn); **ch**ief; **sh**oe; **th**in; **th**at; **zh** as in *measure* (me**zh**′ər)

drone[2] (drōn), *n.* 1. a low humming sound. —*v.* 2. to make a humming sound. 3. to speak in a monotonous tone.

effect (i fekt′), *n.* 1. something that is produced by a cause; result; consequence. —*v.* 2. to bring about or accomplish.

endeavor (en dev′ ər), *v.* 1. to make an effort; try; attempt. —*n.* 2. an attempt or effort.

engage (en gāj′), *v.* to occupy the attention or efforts of (a person or persons).

essential (ə sen′ shəl), *adj.* 1. absolutely necessary. 2. basic or fundamental.

establish (e stab′ lish), *v.* 1. to bring into being on a firm or permanent basis. 2. to settle securely in a position.

evident (ev′ i dənt), *adj.* obvious; easy to see; plain or clear.

evoke (i vōk′), *v.* to bring forth or call forth; suggest; produce.

facial (fa′ shəl), *adj.* of or located on the face.

faddist (fad′ ist), *n.* one who enthusiastically follows a fashion or a kind of behavior for a brief time.

familiarize (fə mil′ yə rīz′), *v.* to make well-acquainted with something.

fatigue (fə tēg′), *n.* 1. tiredness or weariness. —*v.* 2. to tire out.

feminism (fem′ ə niz′ əm), *n.* a belief in granting women the same rights as men, as in political or economic status.

feudalism (fyōōd′ ᵊliz′ əm), *n.* the social and economic system in medieval Europe in which a vassal held land from a lord in return for military service and other obligations.

flexible (flek′ sə bəl), *adj.* 1. capable of being bent. 2. capable of being changed or rearranged.

formerly (fôr′ mər lē), *adv.* in time past; earlier; once.

fortitude (fôr′ ti tōōd′), *n.* endurance; courage; strength of mind to bear pain or misfortune.

fractional (frak′ shə nᵊl), *adj.* small or insignificant.

fragile (fraj′ əl), *adj.* delicate or easily broken; frail.

functional (fungk′ shə nəl), *adj.* in working order; capable of performing.

global (glō′ bəl), *adj.* referring to the whole world; world-wide.

goulash (gōō′ läsh), *n.* a stew of beef or veal and vegetables, with paprika or other seasonings. [from the Hungarian phrase *gulyas hus*, "herdsman's meat"]

hail[1] (hāl), *v.* 1. to greet or welcome, especially by calling out. 2. to call out to in order to attract attention.

hail[2] (hāl), *n.* 1. rounded pieces of ice that fall from the sky like rain. —*v.* 2. to pour down hail.

harmonious (här mō′ nē əs), *adj.* 1. forming an agreeable combination or blend. 2. pleasant in sound. 3. sharing the same feelings or goals; friendly. **—harmoniously**, *adv.*

helipad (hel′ ə pad′), *n.* a small area for helicopters to land on or take off from.

hoard (hôrd), *n.* 1. a supply of money, food, etc., that is hidden or carefully guarded for future use. —*v.* 2. to gather and save, often secretly and greedily.

horde (hôrd), *n.* a large group; multitude; crowd.

hostility (ho stil′ i tē), *n.* unfriendliness; a hostile attitude.

hot line (hot′ līn′), *n.* 1. a direct Teletype or telephone line between two heads of state for instant communication in case of crisis. 2. any direct phone line for instant counseling or conferring.

humanity (hyōō man′ i tē), *n.* kindness or sympathy.

humility (hyōō mil′ i tē), *n.* modesty; lack of self-importance.

illusion (i lōō′ zhən), *n.* a false or erroneous idea or perception.

immobile (i mō′ bil), *adj.* 1. not moving; motionless. 2. not movable.

impact (im′ pakt), *n.* 1. effect or influence. 2. the striking of one object against another.

imply (im plī′), *v.* to hint or suggest.

impression (im presh′ ən), *n.* 1. a strong effect produced on the mind or feelings. 2. a vague or indistinct notion or belief. 3. a mark produced by pressure.

impulsive (im pul′ siv), *adj.* acting on impulse; moved by sudden inclination or emotion. **—impulsively**, *adv.*

indolent (in′ də lənt), *adj.* having a disposition to avoid work or exertion; lazy.

infer (in fûr′), *v.* to understand or conclude.

infinite (in′ fə nit), *adj.* 1. limitless or boundless. 2. exceedingly great.

inhabit (in hab′ it), *v.* to live or dwell in (a place).

inhibit (in hib′ it), *v.* to hold back, check, or restrain.

initial (i nish′ əl), *adj.* 1. of the beginning; first. —*n.* 2. the first letter of a word or name.

insipid (in sip′ id), *adj.* 1. without interesting or attractive qualities. 2. having little flavor. **—insipidly**, *adv.*

instantaneous (in′ stən tā′ nēəs), *adj.* occurring or completed in an instant. **—instantaneously**, *adv.*

integrity (in teg′ ri tē), *n.* honesty; holding to ethical or moral principles.

intricate (in′ trə kit), *adj.* complex; having many inter-related parts.

intrigue (in trēg′), *v.* to arouse the curiosity of; fascinate; attract.

invigorate (in vig′ə rāt), *v.* to give strength and vigor to; fill with energy.

jest (jest), *v.* to speak in a playful way; joke; tease.

ketchup (kech′ əp), *n.* a highly seasoned tomato sauce used on meat, fish, and such. [from the Chinese dialect word *ke-tsiap,* "pickled fish brine"]

lament (lə ment′), *v.* 1. to feel sorrow over; mourn for. 2. to wail; complain.

later (lā′ tər), *adv.* at a more advanced time.

latter (lat′ ər), *adj.* 1. the second mentioned of two (opposite of **former**). 2. more advanced in time: *the latter part of the month.*

leisurely (lē′ zhər lē), *adj.* without haste; slow; unhurried.

levee (lev′ ē), *n.* an embankment designed to prevent a river from overflowing.

liberalism (lib′ ər ə liz′ əm), *n.* the quality of favoring social or political change.

limerick (lim′ ər ik), *n.* a light, humorous verse of five lines. [named for Limerick, a county of Ireland]

logical (loj′ i kəl), *adj.* reasonable; that can be expected.

lucid (lo͞o′ sid), *adj.* 1. clear; transparent. 2. easily understood. 3. thinking clearly; rational. **—lucidly**, *adv.*

lynch (linch), *v.* to hang or otherwise kill a person by mob action and without legal authority. [perhaps named after Charles Lynch, an 18th-century Virginia planter and justice of the peace]

major (mā′ jər), *adj.* 1. great in importance, rank, or stature. 2. serious or dangerous; requiring attention. —*n.* 3. an officer's rank in the U.S. Army, Air Force, or Marines. 4. the subject field in which a college student specializes.

manner (man′ ər), *n.* 1. a way in which something happens or is done. 2. a way of acting or behaving.

manor (man′ ər), *n.* 1. an estate belonging to a lord in the Middle Ages. 2. any large, imposing house; mansion.

manuscript (man′ yə skript′), *n.* the written text of an author's work, prepared for publication.

marathon (mar′ ə thon′), *n.* 1. a long-distance foot race, especially one of 26 miles 385 yards. 2. any long contest of endurance. [so called after the 26-mile run of a Greek messenger from Marathon to Athens to bring news of the Greek victory over the Persians]

margin (mär′ jin), *n.* 1. a border or edge. 2. the space around the printed matter on a page. 3. an extra amount, as of time or money, beyond what is actually needed.

marmalade (mär′ mə lād′), *n.* a jellylike preserve of fruit, especially of oranges, that contains bits of rind. [French]

matchless (mach′ lis), *adj.* having no equal; incomparable.

medicinal (mə dis′ ə nᵊl), *adj.* referring to or containing a drug.

meltdown (melt′ doun), *n.* the melting of the core of a nuclear reactor.

microscopic (mī′ krə skop′ ik), *adj.* extremely small or fine; tiny.

militarism (mil′ i tə riz′ əm), *n.* 1. the policy of maintaining a powerful military force. 2. a tendency to regard military ideas as most important.

miner (mī′ nər), *n.* a person who works in a mine.

minor (mī′ nər), *adj.* 1. smaller or less important. —*n.* 2. a person under legal age.

mishap (mis′ hap), *n.* an unfortunate accident.

misshape (mis shāp′), *v.* to shape badly; deform.

mobilize (mo′ be līz′), *v.* to assemble and organize in readiness for action.

modest (mod′ ist), *adj.* 1. not vain or boastful. 2. simple in form or appearance. 3. not excessive. **—modestly**, *adv.*

monotonous (mə not′ ə nᵊs), *adj.* 1. lacking in variety; dull or boring. 2. continuing on the same tone. **—monotonously**, *adv.*

moonscape (mo͞on′ skāp), *n.* the surface of the moon or a picture of it.

moped (mō′ ped), *n.* a heavily built motorized bicycle. [from *mo(tor) ped(al)*]

negligence (neg′ li jəns), *n.* carelessness; irresponsibility.

obscure (əb skyo͝or′), *adj.* 1. not clear or straightforward. 2. not easily noticed or found. 3. not well-known or famous.

ombudsman (ôm′ bo͝odz man′), *n.* a public official who investigates citizens' complaints against government officials or agencies.

optimism (op′ tə miz′ əm), *n.* a tendency to look on the hopeful side of things.

ovation (ō vā′ shən), *n.* loud or prolonged applause; enthusiastic public welcome.

pacifist (pas′ ə fist), *n.* one who opposes war and violence.

paramedic (par′ ə med′ ik), *n.* a person trained to assist a physician and able to perform some kinds of medical tasks.

paramount (par′ ə mount′), *adj.* chief in importance; supreme.

passive (pas′ iv), *adj.* not reacting; acted upon rather than acting or causing action.

patience (pā′ shəns), *n.* the ability to put up with pain, delay, annoyance, or misfortune, without complaint or loss of temper.

peaked[1] (pēkt), *adj.* having a peak or point.

---

act, **ā**ble, d**â**re, **ä**rt; **e**bb, **ē**qual; **i**f, **ī**ce; h**o**t, **ō**ver, **ô**rder; **oi**l; b**o͝o**k; **o͞o**ze; **ou**t; **u**p, **û**rge; ə = *a* as in *alone*; ᵊ as in *button* (but′ᵊn); **ch**ief; **sh**oe; **th**in; **th**at; **zh** as in *measure* (me**zh**′ər)

peaked[2] (pē′ kid), *adj.* pale, sickly, or thin.

personal (pûr′ sə n'l), *adj.* belonging to or concerning a particular person.

personnel (pûr′ sə nel′), *n.* all the employees of a company or organization.

pessimism (pes′ ə miz′ əm), *n.* a tendency to see the gloomy side of things.

pigment (pig′ mənt), *n.* any of the substances that give color to living things.

plant (plant), *n.* 1. any member of the vegetable group of living things. 2. the buildings and equipment of a factory or other business. 3. a person placed in an audience to encourage applause or contribute to the action of the play. —*v.* 4. to put in the ground to grow. 5. to set firmly; put; place. 6. to place for the purpose of observing, spying, or informing.

porous (pôr′ əs), *adj.* full of pores; capable of allowing the passage of liquids or gases.

precede (pri sēd′), *v.* to go or come before.

preserve (pri zûrv′), *v.* to maintain or save.

printout (print′ out), *n.* the printed output of a computer.

probability (prob′ ə bil′ i tē), *n.* likelihood, chance.

proceed (prə sēd), *v.* to go forward or onward, especially after stopping; continue.

proclaim (prō klām′), *v.* to announce formally or publicly; declare.

propel (prə pel′), *v.* to cause to move forward or onward.

racism (rā′ siz əm), *n.* the belief that one's own race or ethnic group is superior.

ramble (ram′ bəl), *v.* to talk in an aimless way.

range (rānj), *n.* 1. the limits within which something varies, operates, or can be done. 2. a chain of mountains. 3. a large, open region for grazing livestock. 4. a large stove with burners and an oven.

rank[1] (rangk), *n.* social standing, class, or position.

rank[2] (rangk), *adj.* 1. growing quickly and coarsely: *rank weeds.* 2. having an unpleasantly strong smell or taste.

rationalize (rash′ ə n' liz′), *v.* to explain (an act) in a seemingly reasonable way.

realist (rē′ ə list), *n.* a person who faces facts as they are and avoids the imagined or impractical.

regard (ri gärd′), *v.* 1. to think of in a certain way. 2. to show respect or consideration for. 3. to look at; observe. —*n.* 4. thought, attention, or consideration.

relish (rel′ ish), *v.* 1. to enjoy. —*n.* 2. a liking or enjoyment of something.

renowned (ri nound′), *adj.* of a celebrated reputation; well-known; famous.

reproduce (rē′ prə dōōs′), *v.* to produce offspring or young.

resilient (ri zil′ yənt), *adj.* 1. having the power to return to the original shape or position after being bent or squeezed. 2. recovering readily (from illness, sorrow, etc.). —**resiliently**, *adv.*

ridicule (rid′ ə kyōōl′), *n.* 1. speech or action that mocks or makes fun of. —*v.* 2. to mock.

sabotage (sab′ ə täzh′), *n.* 1. intentional interference with production or work in a factory, such as by enemy agents during a war. 2. any deliberate effort to defeat or do harm to an undertaking. —*v.* 3. to injure or attack by sabotage.

scribe (skrīb), *n.* an author or writer, especially a news reporter.

sequoia (si kwoi′ ə), *n.* a large evergreen tree of California. [named after Sequoya, an American Indian leader and scholar]

sheer[1] (shēr), *adj.* 1. extremely thin and fine; transparent or almost transparent. 2. utter or absolute: *sheer nonsense.*

sheer[2] (shēr), *v.* to turn from a course; swerve.

situated (sich′ ōō ā′ tid), *adj.* placed or located.

skyjacker (skī′ jak ər), *n.* one who forcibly takes over an airplane in flight.

slick (slik), *adj.* 1. smooth and glossy; sleek. 2. slippery, especially from being covered with oil, ice, or water. 3. clever or tricky. —*n.* 4. a smooth or slippery place or spot.

sluggish (slug′ ish), *adj.* 1. lacking in energy. 2. moving slowly; having little motion.

sneer (snēr), *v.* to speak with scorn or contempt.

sociability (sō′ shə bil′ i tē), *n.* friendliness or agreeableness in company.

socialist (so′ shə list), *n.* one who favors an economic system in which the community as a whole rather than private interests controls land, production, etc.

soy (soi), *n.* a salty brown liquid sauce made by fermenting soybeans in brine. [from Japanese, *shō-yu*]

stability (stə bil′ i tē), *n.* steadiness; permanence; reliability.

stammer (stam′ ər), *v.* to speak with breaks or pauses, or with repetition of syllables; falter.

steep[1] (stēp), *adj.* having a sharp slant up and down.

steep[2] (stēp), *v.* to soak or be soaked in water or another liquid below the boiling point.

storm (stôrm), *v.* to show great anger; rant and rage.

succotash (suk′ ə tash′), *n.* a dish of corn kernels and lima beans cooked together. [from American Indian, the Narragansett word *msickquatash*, "boiled whole-grain corn (off the cob)"]

suite (swēt), *n.* 1. a number of related things forming a series or set: *a suite of rooms.* 2. a musical composition consisting of several short movements.

superpower (sōō′ pər pou′ ər), *n.* an extremely powerful nation; a nation capable of influencing the acts and policies of other nations.

surmount (sər mount′), *v.* to overcome or conquer.

sway (swā), *v.* 1. to influence. —*n.* 2. dominating power or influence.

taught (tôt), *v.* the past tense of **teach**.

taut (tôt), *adj.* tightly drawn; tense.

tedious (tē′ dē əs), *adj.* long and tiresome; boring.

theorize (thē′ ə rīz′), *v.* to form a theory or explanation.

tortilla (tôr tē′ yə), *n.* a round, flat bread made from coarse cornmeal, characteristic of Mexican cookery. [American Spanish, diminutive of Spanish *torta*, "a round cake"]

uninterested (un in′ tə res′ tid), *adj.* indifferent or without interest.

vocation (vō kā′ shən), *n.* one's profession, business, or occupation; calling.

wetland (wet′ land′), *n.* Usually **wetlands**. areas such as swamps or tidal flats containing much soil moisture.

yogurt (yo′ gərt), *n.* a custard-like food, prepared from milk curdled by bacteria. [from Turkish, *yōghurt*]

zucchini (zo͞o kē′ nē), *n.* a summer squash shaped like a cucumber and having a smooth, dark-green skin. [from the Italian *zucca*, "gourd"]

---

act, **ā**ble, d**â**re, **ä**rt; **e**bb, **ē**qual; **i**f, **ī**ce; h**o**t, **ō**ver, **ô**rder; **oi**l; b**o͝o**k; **o͞o**ze; **ou**t; **u**p, **û**rge; ə = *a* as in *alone*; ᵊ as in *button* (but′ᵊn); **ch**ief; **sh**oe; **th**in; **th**at; **zh** as in *measure* (me**zh**′ər)

Answer Key

Unit 1

Lesson 1

A. 1. co- 2. ab-

B.
1. abstain
2. converge
3. abduct
4. absence
5. abolishes
6. coexist
7. abnormal

C.
1. b
2. a
3. b
4. a
5. b
6. b
7. a

D.
1. coexist
2. abdicate
3. cohesion
4. collaborate
5. absence
6. converge

Lesson 2

A.
1. theorize
2. familiarize
3. rationalize
4. characterize

B.
1. facial
2. medicinal
3. functional
4. fractional

C.
1. characterize
2. facial
3. fractional
4. rationalize
5. theorize
6. familiarize
7. medicinal
8. functional

Lesson 3

A.
1. capital
2. conserve
3. fad
4. feminine
5. feudal
6. liberal
7. military
8. pacify or pacific
9. race
10. real
11. social

B.
1. liberalism
2. feminism
3. militarism
4. pacifist
5. capitalism
6. socialist
7. faddist
8. conservatism
9. Racism
10. realist

C.
1. capitalist
2. feminist
3. socialism
4. militarist

Lesson 4

A.
1. evoke
2. scribe
3. chronology
4. vocation
5. manuscript
6. chronicle

B.
1. evokes
2. manuscript
3. chronology
4. scribes
5. chronicle
6. vocation

C. Answers will vary.

Lesson 5

A.
1. ketchup
2. coleslaw
3. marmalade
4. goulash
5. soy
6. zucchini
7. curry
8. tortilla
9. yogurt
10. succotash

B.
1. zucchini
2. soy
3. coleslaw
4. ketchup
5. goulash
6. yogurt
7. tortillas
8. succotash
9. marmalade
10. curry

C.
1. banana
2. taco
3. chow mein
4. omelet
5. bagel
6. pizza

Lesson 6

A.
1. coupe
2. clique
3. crochet
4. collage
5. suite
6. levee
7. beret
8. camouflage
9. bouquet
10. sabotage

B.
1. collage
2. clique
3. sabotage
4. bouquet
5. suite
6. beret
7. camouflage
8. coupe
9. levee
10. crochet

Lesson 7

A.
1. limerick
2. cashmere
3. lynch
4. calico
5. sequoia
6. boycott
7. marathon
8. camellia

B.
1. N, camellia
2. P, cashmere
3. N, lynch
4. P, marathon
5. N, sequoia
6. N, boycott
7. P, calico
8. P, limerick

C.
1. sandwich
2. magnolia
3. Gypsy
4. graham

Lesson 8

A.
1. paramedic
2. meltdown
3. wetlands
4. printout
5. ombudsman
6. helipad
7. skyjacker
8. moonscape
9. hot line
10. superpowers
11. moped

B.
1. superpowers
2. skyjacker
3. meltdown
4. hot line
5. moonscape
6. moped
7. ombudsman
8. paramedics
9. helipad
10. wetlands

Lesson 9

A.
1. 1, verb
2. 2, adjective
3. 2, verb
4. 1, verb
5. 3, noun
6. 2, noun
7. 1, verb
8. 1, noun
9. 3, verb
10. 4, noun
11. 3, verb
12. 1, noun

B.
1. 3
2. 4
3. 3
4. 4
5. 2
6. 1

Lesson 10

A.
1. 1
2. 2
3. 1
4. 2
5. 2
6. 1
7. 1
8. 2
9. 1
10. 2
11. 2
12. 1
13. 1
14. 2

B. Answers will vary.

Lesson 11

A.
1. intricate
2. pigment
3. microscopic
4. adorn
5. reproduce
6. diatom
7. deposit
8. abrasive
9. porous
10. propel

B.
1. reproduce
2. pigment
3. abrasive
4. porous
5. intricate
6. microscopic
7. adorned
8. diatoms
9. propels
10. deposits

Lesson 12

A.
renowned - famous
customary - usual
distinct - clear
paramount - supreme
controversy - debate
logical - reasonable
dimension - size
matchless - incomparable
situated - placed
relished - enjoyed
swayed - influenced

B.
1. size
2. reasonable
3. enjoy
4. clear
5. debate
6. incomparable
7. placed
8. famous
9. usual
10. supreme
11. influence

C.
1. distinct
2. dimension
3. situated
4. renowned
5. customary
6. paramount
7. relished
8. matchless
9. controversy, logical
10. swayed

Lesson 13

A.
1. F R A C T I O N A L
2. R E A L I S T
3. P A C I F I S T
4. A B N O R M A L
5. F U N C T I O N A L
6. F A D D I S T
7. F E U D A L I S M
8. F A C I A L
9. C O E X I S T

possible answer: to produce offspring or young.

B.

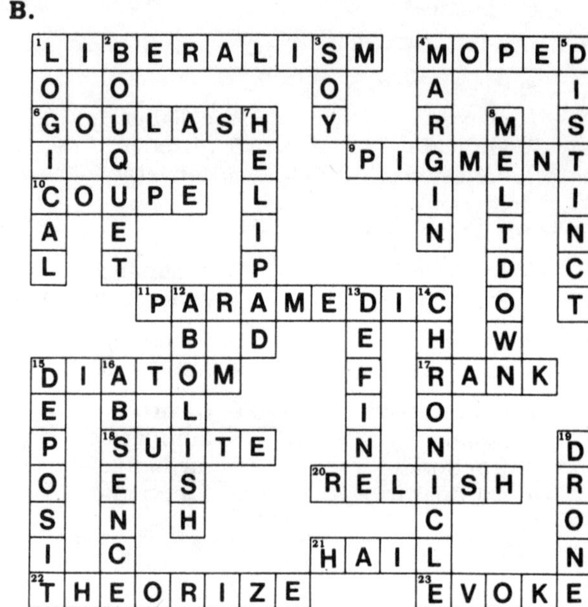

Unit 2

Lesson 1

A.
1. council
2. hoard
3. taut
4. clause
5. miner
6. Manor
7. claws

B.
1. hordes
2. minors
3. counsel
4. clause
5. taught
6. manner

Lesson 2

A.
1. a. disinterested
   b. uninterested
2. a. inferred
   b. implied
3. a. affect
   b. effect
4. a. continuous
   b. continual
5. a. proceeded
   b. preceded
6. a. personnel
   b. personal

B.
1. personnel
2. infer
3. uninterested
4. proceed
5. affect
6. continuous
7. preceding

Lesson 3

A.
1. a. later
   b. latter
2. a. adopt
   b. adapt
3. a. causal
   b. casual
4. a. misshape
   b. mishap
5. a. desert[2]
   b. dessert
   c. desert[1]
6. a. inhabit
   b. inhibit

B.
1. desert
2. inhabit
3. casual
4. adapted
5. latter
6. inhibits
7. mishap

Lesson 4

A.
1. stormed
2. proclaimed
3. disclose
4. rambled, affirmed
5. laments
6. blurted
7. sneered
8. jested
9. stammered

B. Answers will vary.

Lesson 5

A.
1. sociability
2. negligence
3. pessimism
4. cruelty
5. patience
6. hostility
7. humanity
8. optimism
9. dignity
10. integrity

B.
1. optimism
2. humanity
3. hostility
4. cruelty
5. patience
6. pessimism
7. sociability
8. Possible answers: humanity, dignity, integrity
9. Possible answers: dignity, humanity, integrity

Lesson 6

A.
1. monotonous
2. harmonious
3. instantaneous
4. insipid
5. clamorous
6. lucid
7. modestly
8. impulsively
9. resilient

B. Answers will vary.

Lesson 7

A.
1. leisurely
2. indolent
3. passive
4. sluggish
5. immobile

B.
1. animated
2. accelerate
3. agitate
4. invigorate
5. mobilized

C.
1. immobile
2. sluggish
3. invigorates
4. mobilize
5. leisurely
6. agitated
7. accelerate
8. indolent
9. animated
10. passive

Lesson 8

A. Answers will vary.

B. Answers will vary.

C. Answers will vary.

Lesson 9

A.
1. b
2. a
3. a
4. a
5. b
6. b

B.
1. red
2. round
3. go
4. stone
5. bushes
6. quickly
7. hidden
8. to the right
9. marker
10. large

C. Answers will vary.

D. Answers will vary.

Unit 3

Introduction

A.
1. peaceful
2. quarrel
3. began
4. stingy
5. available
6. expert
7. inadequate
8. simple
9. calm
10. accurate

B.

1.	2.	3.	4.	5.	6.	7.	8.
	A	I					G
	L	R	B				E
	I	R	E	R			N
A	K	I	G	A	C	N	E
M	E	T	A	P	H	O	R
P		A	N	I	A	I	O
L		T		D	R	S	U
E		E			M	Y	S

Lesson 1

A.
1. fascinated
2. first
3. overcome
4. aimed
5. earlier
6. necessary
7. weariness
8. attempt
9. fitness
10. figuring
11. painful

B.
1. intrigued
2. formerly
3. fatigue
4. agonizing
5. calculations
6. essential
7. initial
8. endeavor
9. aptness
10. surmounting
11. aspire

Lesson 2

A.
1. tedious
2. abrupt
3. advent
4. global
5. convert
6. comprehensible
7. impact
8. probability
9. infinite
10. conveyed

B.
1. sudden
2. change
3. understandable
4. world-wide
5. limitless
6. coming
7. communicated
8. likelihood
9. tiresome
10. effect

C. Answers will vary.

Lesson 3

A. 1. a 2. b 3. a 4. a 5. b 6. a 7. a 8. b 9. b

B.
1. humility
2. dawdle
3. adroit
4. deteriorate
5. flexible
6. illusion
7. fragile
8. ridicule

C.
1. humility
2. adroit
3. fragile
4. illusion
5. ridicule
6. dawdle
7. stability

Lesson 4

A. 1. 3 2. 1 3. 1 4. 6 5. 3 6. 3 7. 5 8. 4 9. 4 10. 2

B.
1. concern
2. plants
3. major
4. applied
5. cycle
6. range

Vocabulary Puzzle–Enrichment

1. wetland
2. bound base
3. borrowed
4. superpower
5. context
6. passive
7. optimism
8. major
9. uninterested
10. homograph
11. theorize

When I use a word, it means just what I choose it to mean-neither more nor less.

Lesson 5

A. 1. a 2. a 3. b 4. b 5. b 6. b 7. a 8. a 9. b 10. b 11. a 12. b

B. Possible answers:
1. by an extremely narrow margin; just barely
2. to become ruined (physically or morally)
3. with suspicion, or allowing for possible exaggeration

Lesson 6

A. 1. d 2. h 3. e 4. j 5. a 6. b 7. i 8. g 9. f 10. c

B. 1. T 2. F 3. F 4. F 5. T 6. T 7. F

Lesson 7

1. a. circle *col* and *ate;* to work together with others
   b. circle *ize;* to make well-acquainted with something
   c. circle *ist;* a person who faces facts
   d. circle *dis* and *ed;* impartial or without prejudice
   e. circle *mono* and *ous;* lacking in variety or with one tone only
2. a. camouflage: a disguise
   b. concur: to agree with
   c. coleslaw: a salad of raw cabbage
   d. chronology: an order of events in time
3. 4 a. 1 b. 3 c. 2 d.
4. a. clever
   b. observed
   c. courage
5. a. continually
   b. mishap
   c. affected
6. a. blurted
   b. negligence
   c. sluggish

7-8. a. circle nimble; underline clumsy
   b. circle boring
   c. circle mock; underline respect
   d. circle delicate; underline tough
   e. circle save; underline destroy

Illustrations on pages 35, 51, 64, 68, by JOHN HEINLY.

Vocabulary Puzzle–Enrichment

In Lewis Carroll's *Through the Looking Glass*, Humpty Dumpty had his own attitude toward vocabulary. Do this acrostic puzzle to find out what it is. Fill in the blanks below. Then transfer the letters into the correctly numbered box below. The words will spell out the quotation.

1. Modern word meaning an area like a swamp. ___ ___ ___ ___ ___ ___ ___ (1 2 3 4 5 6 7)
2. Root that must have a prefix or suffix. ___ ___ ___ ___ ___ ___ ___ ___ ___ (8 9 10 11 12 13 14 15 16)
3. Word that comes from another language. ___ ___ ___ ___ ___ ___ ___ ___ (17 18 19 20 21 22 23 24)
4. Modern word meaning an extremely powerful nation. ___ ___ ___ ___ ___ ___ ___ ___ ___ ___ (25 26 27 28 29 30 31 32 33 34)
5. Kind of clue that helps you figure out a word. ___ ___ ___ ___ ___ ___ ___ (35 36 37 38 39 40 41)
6. Antonym of *active*. ___ ___ ___ ___ ___ ___ ___ (42 43 44 45 46 47 48)
7. A tendency to look on the hopeful side of things. ___ ___ ___ ___ ___ ___ ___ ___ (49 50 51 52 53 54 55 56)
8. Word that can mean a rank in the army or important. ___ ___ ___ ___ ___ (57 58 59 60 61)
9. Word often confused with *disinterested*. ___ ___ ___ ___ ___ ___ ___ ___ ___ ___ ___ ___ (62 63 64 65 66 67 68 69 70 71 72 73)
10. Word that is spelled like another word but has a different meaning. ___ ___ ___ ___ ___ ___ ___ ___ ___ (74 75 76 77 78 79 80 81 82)
11. Word formed from *theory* + *ize*. ___ ___ ___ ___ ___ ___ ___ ___ (83 84 85 86 87 88 89 90)

1	74	85	37		46		62	15	23		43		22	31	61	73	,	64	51		57	67	80	6	70
59	26	25	41		32	82	5	38		52		35	84	9	18	55	28		88	71		83	49		
76	16	58	11		63	2	54	66	82	90	87		53	21	19	69		65	36	68		4	48	44	45

Answers on page 720

PRACTICING GRAMMAR

by Margarete Wright Pruce

Steps for Practicing Grammar

Note: Before you work on lessons 1 to 23, read the **Preview** on page 134.
Before you work on lessons 24 to 34, read the **Preview** on page 158.

1. Turn to the lesson you are going to do.
2. Read the definition and the example at the top of the page.
3. Do the **Identify** section of the lesson. Find the word or sentence described.
4. Do the **Apply** section of the lesson. Write the word or sentence described.
5. Now use the **Answer Key** to check your answers.
6. Count the number of correct answers. Fill in the number at the top of the lesson. Then turn to the **Progress Plotter** and shade it in to show how many items you answered correctly.
7. If you made any mistakes, go back and do the items again. Make sure you know how to do them.
8. After you have done *all* of the lessons in the book, read the **tips** contained on the **Preview** pages again. Now you are ready to take the **Final Test.**

Project Manager: *Marge M. Kennedy*

Text: Design and Production *Photo Plus Art, Inc.*

GRAMMAR

Table of Contents

PARTS OF SPEECH

Preview

When you study **grammar**, you learn how words work in sentences. The way a word is used in a sentence is called its **part of speech**.

Here are some tips to help you remember parts of speech:

1: Some words are used as names or in place of names.

When a word is used to name a person, place, thing, or idea, it is called a **noun**.

Susan B. Anthony fought for civil **rights**.

When a word is used to replace a noun, it is called a **pronoun**.

She fought for **them**.

2: Some words are used to tell about action.

When a word is used to tell what someone or something does, did, or will do, it is called an **action verb**.

She **fought** for civil rights.

3: Some words are used to describe.

When a word is used to point to or describe a noun, it is called an **adjective**.

She was **a strong** woman.

When a word is used to describe a verb, adjective, or other adverb, it is called an **adverb**.

She worked **very hard**.

4: Some words are used to connect.

Linking verbs connect the subject of a sentence to words after the verb.

She **was** a good speaker.

Conjunctions connect words, phrases, and sentences.

She traveled **and** spoke **because** she wanted to change the law.

Prepositions connect nouns and pronouns to other words in a sentence.

American women have voted **in** elections **since** 1920.

5: The same word may function as different parts of speech.

She had a **hard** (**adjective**) job. She worked **hard** (**adverb**).

LESSON 1

PARTS OF SPEECH

Common Nouns and Proper Nouns

Number Right: ____

A **noun** names a person, place, thing, or idea.

A noun that names a particular person, place, thing, or idea is a **proper noun** Proper nouns may include initials, abbreviations, and prepositions. The main words of a proper noun are always capitalized.

All other nouns are **common nouns.**

Common Nouns	Proper Nouns
minister	Reverend Martin Luther King, Jr.
bay	San Francisco Bay
country	United States of America
university	Yale University
capital	Washington, D.C.
hurricane	Hurricane David

Underline the common nouns. Circle the proper nouns.

1. The first settlement of Europeans in North America was in Jamestown, Virginia.
2. The territory called Virginia once included nine states.
3. The states are West Virginia, Kentucky, Illinois, Indiana, Michigan, Minnesota, Ohio, Wisconsin, and Virginia.
4. Because of this, Virginia is nicknamed "The Mother of States."
5. A Virginian, Thomas Jefferson, wrote the Declaration of Independence.

Write the common noun that best describes each proper noun.

6. Gettysburg Address **speech** — newspaper
7. Interstate 80 ______ — war
8. Memorial Day ______ — park
9. *New York Times* ______ — writer
10. Yellowstone National Park ______ — building
11. U.S.S. *Kitty Hawk* ______ — dam
12. Katherine Mansfield ______ — holiday
13. Civil War ______ — **speech**
14. Hoover Dam ______ — ship
15. White House ______ — highway

LESSON 2

PARTS OF SPEECH

Singular Nouns and Plural Nouns
Collective Nouns

Number Right: ____

A **singular noun** names one person, place, thing, or idea. A **plural noun** names more than one. A **collective noun**, such as *troop* or *audience*, is usually considered singular even though it names a group of more than one. Compare the singular and plural forms of these nouns:

Singular	Plural
audience	audiences
lunch	lunch**es**
day	day**s**
hobby	hobb**ies**
roof	roof**s**
wife	wi**ves**
solo	solo**s**
tomato	tomato**es**
volcano	volcano**s** *or* volcano**es**

Singular	Plural
foot	f**ee**t
woman	wom**e**n
cactus	cact**i** *or* cactus**es**
moose	moose
series	series
brother-in-law	brother**s**-in-law
runner-up	runner**s**-up
passerby	passer**s**by

Underline the singular nouns. Circle the plural nouns. Draw two lines beneath any collective nouns.

1. The troop pitched tents alongside the river.
2. A swarm of mosquitoes flew near each lantern.
3. A pack of coyotes howled at the moon.
4. The campers told stories around the campfire.
5. They used their knives to carve branches into whistles.

apply

Write the plural form of each singular noun.

6. half **halves**
7. family ____________
8. tax ____________
9. sister-in-law ____________
10. bench ____________
11. potato ____________
12. mouse ____________
13. child ____________
14. cactus ____________
15. tooth ____________
16. reindeer ____________
17. piano ____________
18. goose ____________
19. belief ____________
20. passerby ____________

LESSON

3

PARTS OF SPEECH

Subject Pronouns and Object Pronouns

Number Right: ____

A **pronoun** is a word that takes the place of a noun.

Pronouns that tell *whom* or *what* a sentence is about are **subject pronouns.** These subject pronouns are singular: **I, you, she, he,** and **it.** These are plural: **we, you,** and **they.**

Pablo waved. **He** waved. **Carol and I** called. **We** called.

Object pronouns tell *who* or *what* receives an action. Object pronouns are also used after prepositions. These object pronouns are singular: **me, you, her, him,** and **it.** These are plural: **us, you,** and **them.**

Justin threw **the ball** to **Pam.** Justin threw **it** to **her.**

Underline the subject pronouns. Circle the object pronouns. Then tell if the pronoun is *singular* or *plural.*

1. Most lakes do not have salt in them. ____________
2. The Great Salt Lake is unusual because it does contain salt. ____________
3. The first white man to see it was Jim Bridger. ____________
4. He reached the lake in 1824. ____________
5. Bridger tasted the water and thought an ocean lay before him. ____________

apply

Write the subject or object pronouns that replace the underlined words.

6. Ants live in tunneled cities. **They**
7. Some ants build the tunnels. ____________
8. Other ants bring food to the city. ____________
9. The queen ant lays the eggs. ____________
10. The queen is much larger than the other ants. ____________
11. The male usually has wings. ____________
12. The queen and the male don't do any work. ____________
13. All the work in the city is done by special workers. ____________
14. You and I seldom see the queen. ____________
15. The queen never leaves the city. ____________

LESSON 4

PARTS OF SPEECH

- Possessive Nouns
- Possessive Pronouns

Number Right: ____

A **possessive noun** shows ownership. A **possessive pronoun** takes the place of a possessive noun.

The Garcias' house is closer than **Meg's.** **Their** house is closer than **hers.**

Compare the singular and plural forms of these possessive words:

Possessive Nouns		Possessive Pronouns	
Singular	**Plural**	**Singular**	**Plural**
Tim Garcia**'s** tree**'s** woman**'s**	the Garcias**'** trees**'** women**'s**	my/mine his/her/hers/its your/yours	our/ours their/theirs your/yours

Underline the possessive nouns. Circle the possessive pronouns. Then tell if the possessive word is *singular* or *plural.*

1. Many presidents' wives have done important work. ____________
2. Eleanor Roosevelt worked for people's civil rights. ____________
3. Her work took her around the world. ____________
4. "Lady Bird" Johnson worked to beautify our cities. ____________
5. Betty Ford's concern was for the handicapped. ____________

apply

Write the possessive pronouns that replace the underlined words.

6. According to the ancient Romans' beliefs, Vulcan was the god of fire. ____their____
7. Vulcan's father was Jupiter, and his mother was Juno. ____________
8. These gods' names have become part of the English language. ____________
9. Your and my word for the sixth month is *June.* ____________
10. The word *June* was formed from Juno's name. ____________
11. The word *volcano* comes from a form of Vulcan's name. ____________
12. One planet's name is Jupiter. ____________
13. The Greeks' mythology is similar to the Romans'. ____________
14. However, the Greeks' names for the gods are different. ____________
15. In Greek mythology, Vulcan's name is Hephaestus. ____________

LESSON

5

PARTS OF SPEECH

- Reflexive Pronouns
- Intensive Pronouns

Number Right: ____

A **reflexive pronoun** refers to the subject. Singular reflexive pronouns end in **self.** These reflexive pronouns are singular: **myself, yourself, himself, herself,** and **itself.** Plural reflexive pronouns end in **selves.** These are plural: **ourselves, yourselves,** and **themselves.**

These same words are **intensive pronouns** when they are used to emphasize a noun or pronoun.

Reflexive: Tom saved **himself.** **They** praised **themselves.**

Intensive: Tom himself was unharmed. **They themselves** led the praise.

Underline the reflexive pronouns. Circle the intensive pronouns. Then write *singular* or *plural.*

1. Abraham Lincoln himself tried to prevent the Civil War. ____
2. He said, "A house divided against itself cannot stand." ____
3. He warned, "Familiarize yourselves with the chains of bondage." ____
4. Lincoln added, "Those who deny freedom to others deserve it not for themselves." ____
5. The war itself lasted four years. ____

Write the reflexive or intensive pronoun that refers to or emphasizes each underlined word.

6. Animals protect **themselves** in various ways.
7. A grasshopper hides ____ among twigs and leaves.
8. You ____ know that a bee protects ____ by stinging.
9. How do you think a stinkbug defends ____?
10. The female mallard duck camouflages ____ in her nest.
11. Sometimes, even the male mallard ____ can't find her!
12. Many animals defend ____ by fighting.
13. Others save ____ by running from danger.
14. An armadillo rolls ____ into a ball of armor.
15. We ____ use many defense techniques.

LESSON 6

PARTS OF SPEECH

- Principal Parts of Verbs
- Helping Verbs

Number Right: ____

A **verb** names an action or a state of being. All verbs have four forms, called the **principal parts.** Compare the four forms of these verbs:

Infinitive	Present Participle	Past	Past Participle
to laugh	laugh**ing**	laugh**ed**	laugh**ed**
to ride	rid**ing**	rode	rid**den**
to put	putt**ing**	put	put
to become	becom**ing**	became	become

The present participles and past participles are used with **helping verbs.** The helping verbs are **am, is, are, was, were, be, been, have, has,** and **had.**

Underline the helping verbs. Circle the main verbs.

1. Many animals are vanishing because people are hunting them.
2. Dodo birds, great auks, and quaggas have disappeared already.
3. The walrus and eagle populations have grown small.
4. Some animals have died because of water pollution and air pollution.
5. Many states are passing laws that are helping the animals.

Write the principal parts of each verb.

Infinitive	Present Participle	Past	Past Participle
6. to do	doing	did	done
7. to dance	______	______	______
8. to beg	______	______	______
9. to fry	______	______	______
10. to set	______	______	______
11. to begin	______	______	______
12. to come	______	______	______
13. to sit	______	______	______
14. to eat	______	______	______
15. to buy	______	______	______

LESSON

7

PARTS OF SPEECH

Action Verbs: Present, Past, and Future Tenses

Number Right: ____

An **action verb** tells what the subject *does, did,* or *will do.* The **tense** of a verb names the time of the action. All tenses are formed from the principal parts of verbs.

The **present tense** tells about an action that happens now.
The **past tense** tells about an action that already happened.
The **future tense** tells about an action that will happen.

Compare the present, past, and future tenses of these verbs:

Present	Past	Future	Present	Past	Future
laugh	laugh**ed**	**will** laugh	ride	r**o**de	**will** ride
fry	fr**ied**	**will** fry	put	put	**will** put
chop	chop**ped**	**will** chop	come	c**a**me	**will** come

Underline the action verbs. Then write *present, past,* or *future.*

1. Nearly five billion people live on our planet. ________________
2. That number will double by the year 2200. ________________
3. In Columbus's time, only 400 million people inhabited the earth. ________________
4. Today, large cities hold millions of people. ________________
5. Where will people live in the year 2200? ________________

apply Write the past- and future-tense forms of each action verb.

Present	Past	Future
6. find	**found**	**will find**
7. begin	________________	________________
8. see	________________	________________
9. set	________________	________________
10. beg	________________	________________
11. live	________________	________________
12. enjoy	________________	________________
13. cry	________________	________________
14. go	________________	________________
15. ride	________________	________________

LESSON

8

PARTS OF SPEECH

Action Verbs: Present-Perfect and Past-Perfect Tenses

Number Right: ____

The **present-perfect tense** tells about an action that *began in the past and is still going on,* or about an action that *happened at some indefinite time in the past.* This tense is formed by using the helping verb **have** or **has** with the past-participle form of the main verb.

People **have used** a written language for thousands of years.

The **past-perfect tense** tells about an action that *happened before another action.* This tense is formed by using the helping verb **had** with the past-participle form of the main verb.

Before they learned to write, cave dwellers **had drawn** pictures on walls to tell a story.

Underline the verbs in the present-perfect tense. Circle the verbs in the past-perfect tense.

1. The French Revolution began six years after the American Revolution had ended.
2. Had the Americans influenced the French?
3. Have you read about the French Revolution?
4. Many people have compared it to the American Revolution.
5. Did the French follow the example that the Americans had set?

apply

Fill in the present-perfect tense of each present-tense verb shown. Fill in the past-perfect tense of each past-tense verb shown.

6. People ___have lived___ in Hawaii for centuries. (live)
7. The first people who settled there ____________ from the Marquesas Islands. (came)
8. No European ____________ of Hawaii before 1778. (heard)
9. Few explorers ____________ the Pacific. (crossed)
10. In 1778, Captain Cook reached the islands. He ____________ from England. (sailed)
11. Before he left, he ____________ the islands. (renamed)
12. The natives ____________ the main island "Hawaii," but Cook decided to name the islands "The Sandwich Islands." (called)
13. By the 1880s, many Europeans ____________ to the islands. (flocked)
14. They called the islands by the name the natives ____________ them. (gave)
15. The name of the island group ____________ "Hawaii" to this day. (remains)

LESSON 9

PARTS OF SPEECH

Action Verbs: Present-Progressive and Past-Progressive Forms

Number Right: ____

There is a form of the present tense that tells about an action that *is continuing to happen* or *is about to happen.* It is called the **present progressive.** It is formed by using the helping verb **am, is,** or **are** with the present-participle form of the main verb.

I **am studying** French. She **is helping** me.

The past tense has a progressive form, too. The **past progressive** tells about an action that *was continuing to happen in the past.* It is formed by using the helping verb **was** or **were** with the present-participle form of the main verb.

The fire **was crackling.** The campers **were sitting** in a circle.

Underline the verbs in the present-progressive form. Circle the verbs in the past-progressive form.

1. In the early 1900s, transportation was changing.
2. People were trading horses for cars.
3. Blacksmiths were going out of business, and tire shops were opening.
4. Today, new businesses are growing because of new inventions, too.
5. Businesses are hiring people for jobs that didn't exist years ago.

apply

Fill in the present-progressive form of each present-tense verb shown. Fill in the past-progressive form of each past-tense verb shown.

6. Your body __is working__ even though you're not aware of it. (works)
7. Blood ________________ through your body at this moment. (moves)
8. Your lungs ________________ air. (inhale)
9. Stomach muscles ________________ your food. (digest)
10. Glands ________________ your body's temperature. (control)
11. Your senses ________________ to things around you. (react)
12. While you ________________ last night, your body continued its work. (slept)
13. You ________________ for part of the night. (dreamed)
14. The dreams ________________ you to relax. (helped)
15. Sleep ________________ you for a new day. (prepared)

LESSON 10 — PARTS OF SPEECH

Linking Verbs: Present and Past Tenses

Number Right: ____

Not all verbs tell about an action. Some verbs link, or connect, the subject of a sentence to other words in the sentence. These verbs are called **linking verbs.** Present-tense linking verbs tell what the subject *is* or *is like.* Past-tense linking verbs tell what the subject *was* or *was like.* All forms of the verb **be** are linking verbs when they are not part of an action verb. The verbs **seem** and **become** are also linking verbs.

Linking: He **is** funny. He **seems** funny. He **became** a clown.
Helping: He **is** juggling. He **was** taught at the circus.

The following verbs are linking verbs when they tell what the subject is like: **appear, feel, grow, look, remain, smell, sound, stay,** and **taste.** These verbs are action verbs when they tell what the subject does, did, or will do.

Linking: The bread **smells** good. It **remained** fresh.
Action: I **smell** the bread. I'll **remain** at home to eat it.

---

identify Underline the linking verbs. Circle the action verbs. Then write *present* or *past.*

1. Liberia is the oldest republic in Africa. ________________
2. Freed American slaves were the founders of this nation. ________________
3. Liberia became a republic in 1847. ________________
4. Many Liberians grow rubber trees. ________________
5. Others grow rich from mining iron ore. ________________

apply Fill in the word or words that make each verb a linking verb.

6. Tofu is ____a food____ from Japan. (a food, made from soybeans)
7. It is ________________. (easy to make, made easily)
8. Tofu tastes ________________. (carefully, good)
9. It feels ________________. (soft, immediately)
10. It looks ________________. (at you, creamy)
11. It appears ________________ to some people. (slippery, in supermarkets)
12. Tofu is often ________________ in soups. (stirred, an ingredient)
13. This food recently became ________________ in the United States. (over, popular)
14. It remains ________________ in Japan. (popular, in stores)
15. How long does tofu remain ________________? (here, fresh)

LESSON 11

PARTS OF SPEECH

Articles, Number Words, and Demonstrative Adjectives

Number Right: ____

Articles, number words, and **demonstrative adjectives** are words that point to nouns. The words **a, an,** and **the** are articles. *A* and *an* point to singular nouns. *The* points to singular or plural nouns.

Articles: The beetle is **a** pesty bug.

The number words **one, each,** and **every** point to singular nouns. The number words **two, many, few, both,** and **several** point to plural nouns. The number words **some, all, any, more,** and **most** point to singular or plural nouns.

Number Words: Every beetle has **four** wings.

The demonstrative adjectives **this** and **that** point to singular nouns. The demonstrative adjectives **these** and **those** point to plural nouns.

Demonstrative Adjectives: This insect ate **those** leaves.

---

identify Underline the articles, number words, and demonstrative adjectives. Draw an arrow to the nouns they point to.

1. A violin is an instrument with four strings.
2. This instrument is played with a bow.
3. As the bow touches each string, a sound is made.
4. All violins are made of some kind of wood.
5. These instruments are a part of every orchestra.

apply Fill in the words that point to singular or plural nouns.

6. The decimal system includes **ten** digits. (every, ten)
7. ________ digits are used to write all numbers. (This, These)
8. How do you write ________ number twenty-five? (the, those)
9. Do you write ________ ones? (each, twenty-five)
10. ________ number is written with two digits. (These, This)
11. The first digit, *2*, stands for ________ tens. (one, two)
12. ________ second digit, *5*, represents five ones. (The, Two)
13. ________ number from ten through 99 is written with two digits. (Every, Many)
14. Every number from 100 through 999 is written with ________ digits. (one, three)
15. Can ________ number be written as a fraction? (any, many)

LESSON 12

PARTS OF SPEECH

Indefinite Pronouns
Demonstrative Pronouns

Number Right: ____

An **indefinite pronoun** is a pronoun that does not name a specific person or thing. Indefinite pronouns often take the place of number words and nouns.

Number Word and Noun: Many flowers are in bloom.
Indefinite Pronouns: Many are in bloom. **Some** of them are red.

These indefinite pronouns are always singular: **one, each, everyone, everybody, everything, anyone, anybody, anything, someone, somebody, something, no one,** and **nobody.** These are always plural: **two, many, few, both,** and **several.** These may be singular or plural, depending on how they are used: **some, all, any, more, most,** and **none.**

A **demonstrative pronoun** is a pronoun that points out someone or something without naming it. Demonstrative pronouns often take the place of demonstrative adjectives and nouns. **This** and **that** are singular. **These** and **those** are plural.

Demonstrative Adjective and Noun: This rose is red.
Demonstrative Pronouns: This is red. **Those** are white.

Underline the indefinite and demonstrative pronouns. Circle the number words and demonstrative adjectives.

1. All chickens developed from the red jungle fowl.
2. Nobody knows when they developed into chickens.
3. Today, most jungle fowl are found in Asia.
4. Long ago, some were brought to Europe.
5. Others were brought to Africa.

Rewrite each sentence. Replace the underlined words with indefinite or demonstrative pronouns.

6. Many people are fashion-conscious.

   Many are fashion-conscious.

7. Some people spend hours each week choosing their wardrobes.

   ____

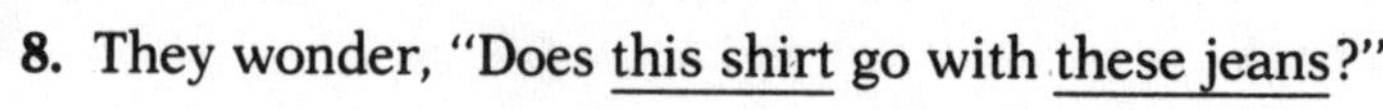

8. They wonder, "Does this shirt go with these jeans?"

   ____

9. Dressing is easier if several outfits can be mixed and matched.

   ____

10. Some colors go well with other colors.

   ____

LESSON 13 — PARTS OF SPEECH

Descriptive Adjectives

Number Right: ____

An **adjective** is a word that tells about a noun or pronoun.

Articles, number words, and demonstrative adjectives are kinds of adjectives. An adjective that describes a noun or a pronoun is a **descriptive adjective.** A descriptive adjective that is formed from a proper noun is a **proper adjective.** Descriptive adjectives go before nouns or after linking verbs.

Japanese gardens are **lovely.**

Underline the descriptive adjectives. Draw an arrow from each adjective to the noun or pronoun it describes.

1. The English language has an international background.
2. Foreign words including Latin prefixes are part of our language.
3. The word *ski* is a Norwegian word, and *yacht* is from the Dutch language.
4. Other common words, such as *yoga* and *rodeo*, come from different languages.
5. *Yoga* is a Hindi word, and *rodeo* is a Spanish word for a big round-up.

Circle the kind of adjective named in parentheses.

6. **National** / **Some** / **These** symbols are well-known. (descriptive)
7. **This** / **One** / **A** symbol of America is Uncle Sam. (number word)
8. His suit looks like an **American** / **original** / **early** flag. (proper)
9. Another American symbol is the **each** / **only** / **bald** eagle. (descriptive)
10. A **great** / **Russian** / **brown** bear symbolizes Russia. (proper)
11. **The** / **This** / **One** symbol of China is a dragon. (article)
12. **Some** / **Those** / **Olive** branches are a symbol for peace. (descriptive)
13. **The** / **A** / **One** well-known symbol means "we surrender." (number word)
14. The sign for surrendering is **this** / **a white** / **the** flag. (descriptive)
15. **The** / **This** / **A white** symbol is international. (demonstrative)

LESSON

14

PARTS OF SPEECH

Adjectives That Compare

Number Right: ____

Some descriptive adjectives can be used to compare nouns. An adjective that ends in **er** is **comparative.** It compares *two* people, places, or things. An adjective that ends in **est** is **superlative.** It compares *three or more* people, places, or things. Look at the base, comparative, and superlative forms of these adjectives:

Base	Comparative	Superlative
high	high**er**	high**est**
blue	blu**er**	blu**est**
thin	thin**ner**	thin**nest**

Base	Comparative	Superlative
pretty	prett**ier**	prett**iest**
good	**better**	**best**
bad	**worse**	**worst**

Underline the comparative adjectives. Circle the superlative adjectives.

1. The TV program with the highest ratings was "Roots."
2. It had a larger audience than any other TV program.
3. The longest telecast covered the Apollo XI moon mission of 1969.
4. That telecast was longer than any other on record.
5. Which do you think are the best and worst shows on TV?

Write the comparative and superlative forms of each adjective.

6. funny **funnier** **funniest**
7. few ____________ ____________
8. small ____________ ____________
9. good ____________ ____________
10. wise ____________ ____________
11. big ____________ ____________
12. stormy ____________ ____________
13. bad ____________ ____________
14. weak ____________ ____________
15. friendly ____________ ____________

LESSON 15

PARTS OF SPEECH

Adjectives with **More, Most, Less,** and **Least**

Number Right: ____

Longer adjectives use the word **more** or **less** instead of the **er** ending to form the comparative. They use the word **most** or **least** instead of the **est** ending for the superlative. The base form of the adjective does not change.

Base	Comparative	Superlative
energetic	**more/less** energetic	**most/least** energetic
attractive	**more/less** attractive	**most/least** attractive
interesting	**more/less** interesting	**most/least** interesting
helpful	**more/less** helpful	**most/least** helpful

Underline the comparative adjectives. Circle the superlative adjectives.

1. The least expensive car of all time was the 1922 Red Bug Buckboard.

2. It was less expensive than the Model T Ford.

3. The most costly car was the president's 1969 Lincoln Continental.

4. It was more expensive than other cars because it had armor plate.

5. The most durable car on record is the 1957 Mercedes 180D.

apply

Write a comparative and superlative form of each adjective.

6. difficult **more** *or* **less difficult** **most** *or* **least difficult**

7. practical ____________ ____________

8. lively ____________ ____________

9. common ____________ ____________

10. generous ____________ ____________

11. eager ____________ ____________

12. urgent ____________ ____________

13. famous ____________ ____________

14. secretive ____________ ____________

15. favorable ____________ ____________

LESSON 16 — PARTS OF SPEECH

Number Right: ____

Verbals: Participles as Adjectives

A **verbal** is a form of a verb that is used as another part of speech.

The past-participle form of a verb may be used as an adjective. Look at these sentences:

Past Participles as Main Verbs	Past Participles as Adjectives
They have **mashed** the turnips. The lake had **frozen.**	**Mashed** turnips are delicious. We skated on the **frozen** lake.

The present-participle form of a verb may be used as an adjective, too. Look at these sentences:

Present Participles as Main Verbs	Present Participles as Adjectives
The snow is **falling.** The dog was **howling** at the moon.	**Falling** snow is so quiet. The **howling** dog kept us awake.

Underline the past participles. Circle the present participles. Then write *verb* or *adjective.*

1. Potatoes are baked with their skins on. ____________
2. Baked potatoes are a healthful food. ____________
3. If you are boiling potatoes, you can remove the skins. ____________
4. You can prepare interesting dishes with potatoes. ____________
5. Fried potatoes are high in calories. ____________

In each sentence, a participle is used as a main verb. Rewrite each participle as an adjective with the noun it describes.

6. The drain had been clogged. **clogged drain**
7. Water had been running for over an hour. ____________
8. The bathtub had overflowed. ____________
9. The room became flooded. ____________
10. The floor is soaked. ____________
11. Things are floating in the room. ____________
12. The ceiling below is leaking. ____________
13. The problem is being corrected. ____________
14. The drain is now fixed. ____________
15. The water is draining. ____________

LESSON

17

PARTS OF SPEECH

Verbals: Gerunds Infinitives as Nouns

Number Right: ____

A **gerund** is a verb form ending in **ing** that is used as a noun. Each of these sentences contains a gerund:

> Many people enjoy **traveling.** Some travel by **sailing.**
> **Flying** is, of course, the fastest means of **traveling.**

An **infinitive** is another verb form that can be used as a noun. An infinitive is usually preceded by **to.** Infinitives are used as nouns in these sentences:

> Our club likes **to hike.** Our aim is **to succeed.**
> **To climb** that mountain is our goal.

Underline each gerund. Circle each infinitive used as a noun. Be careful not to underline participles or progressive verbs.

1. Waiting can be an exhausting experience.
2. To wait in line is boring.
3. Standing is often more tiring than walking.
4. Sometimes there is no choice but to stand.
5. At such times, moving your feet or wiggling your toes may help.

apply

Complete each sentence by filling in the gerund or infinitive form of the verb shown.

6. **Farming** is an important industry in Spain. (gerund of *farm*)
7. Spain is not able ______________ all of its food. (infinitive of *grow*)
8. Much of its land is used for ______________. (gerund of *graze*)
9. Therefore, Spain needs ______________ food. (infinitive of *import*)
10. The land is good for ______________ olives and grapes. (gerund of *grow*)
11. Spain is trying ______________ its crop production. (infinitive of *increase*)
12. ______________, however, is a prospering industry. (gerund of *fish*)
13. ______________ is another leading industry. (gerund of *mine*)
14. Also, countries like ______________ Spain's cork. (infinitive of *import*)
15. Much of the cork is used ______________ bottles. (infinitive of *seal*)

LESSON

18

PARTS OF SPEECH

Adverbs

Number Right: ____

An **adverb** is a word that describes a verb, an adjective, or another adverb. Adverbs can tell *how, when, how often, where,* and *how much.* The word *not* is an adverb of negation.

How: You can grow parsley **easily.** Soak the seeds **well.**

When: Leave them **overnight.** **Tomorrow,** plant them **immediately.**

How Often: Water them **weekly.** Pinch off the big leaves **often.**

Where: Plant them **outside.** Leave them **there.**

How Much: It is **very** easy to do.

Negation: It does **not** take much work.

---

identify Underline the adverbs. Draw an arrow from each adverb to the word it describes.

1. The town's mayor spoke quite confidently.
2. She said she was very pleased that so many people were there.
3. Then she abruptly introduced our extremely nervous class.
4. She said we were unusually civic-minded and especially clever.
5. We gratefully accepted the award, and everyone applauded loudly.

apply Circle the kind of adverb named in parentheses.

6. Echoes travel **quickly** / **loudly** / **forward.** (where)
7. Sounds do **not** / **usually** / **rarely** stand still. (negation)
8. In a canyon, sounds bounce **back** / **sharply** / **again.** (where)
9. This bouncing happens **early** / **there** / **continuously.** (how often)
10. Sounds bounce **again** / **down** / **well** in rocky canyons. (how)
11. The canyon walls must be **nicely** / **very** / **well** hard and bare. (how much)
12. A forested canyon **partly** / **completely** / **always** absorbs an echo. (how often)
13. In winter, echoes are heard **frequently** / **easily** / **well.** (how often)
14. **Then** / **Outside** / **These,** the trees are bare. (when)
15. Echoes can also be made **indoors** / **quickly** / **often** in an empty room. (where)

LESSON 19

PARTS OF SPEECH

Adverbs That Compare

Number Right: ____

Adverbs can be used to compare actions. A **comparative adverb** ends in **er** or begins with **more** or **less.** A **superlative** adverb ends in **est** or begins with **most** or **least.** Look at the base, comparative, and superlative forms of these adverbs:

Base	Comparative	Superlative
early	earl**ier**	earl**iest**
often	**more/less** often	**most/least** often
urgently	**more/less** urgently	**most/least** urgently
well	**better** *or* **less** well	**best** *or* **least** well
badly	**worse** *or* **least** badly	**worst** *or* **least** badly

Underline the comparative adverbs. Circle the superlative adverbs.

1. "Happy Birthday to You" is sung more frequently than any other song.
2. It is sung more often than "Auld Lang Syne."
3. "Auld Lang Syne" is most commonly sung on New Year's Eve.
4. National anthems are heard more regularly than most other songs.
5. "The Star-Spangled Banner" is most frequently played at American sporting events.

Write the comparative and superlative forms of each adverb.

6. far **farther** *or* **less far** **farthest** *or* **least far**
7. eagerly ____________ ____________
8. politely ____________ ____________
9. well ____________ ____________
10. often ____________ ____________
11. badly ____________ ____________
12. fast ____________ ____________
13. calmly ____________ ____________
14. intelligently ____________ ____________
15. late ____________ ____________

LESSON

20 PARTS OF SPEECH

Coordinating Conjunctions
Subordinating Conjunctions

Number Right: ____

A **conjunction** is a word that connects words, phrases, or sentences. The words **and, but, or, nor,** and **yet** are **coordinating conjunctions.**

Paint it blue **or** green, **but** paint it soon.

A **subordinating conjunction** connects a subordinate clause to an independent clause. (A subordinate clause that begins with a subordinating conjunction is an adverb clause. The whole clause functions as an adverb by telling *how, when,* etc.) The words **after, although, as, because, before, if, since, though, unless, until, when,** and **while** may be used as subordinating conjunctions to begin adverb clauses.

Paint the chair **because** it is peeling.
Paint it **when** you have time.

Underline each coordinating conjunction. Circle each subordinating conjunction.

1. The *achaeopteryx* had existed before humans and other mammals lived.
2. It wasn't a bird nor a reptile, although it looked like both.
3. The *archaeopteryx* couldn't fly well, yet it did have feathers.
4. Its head and tail were lizardlike, but it had wings.
5. This creature is interesting because it shows the development of birds from reptiles.

Connect each word group with the conjunction shown in parentheses.

6. fish / meat (and) **fish and meat**
7. my sister / your brother (or) ____________
8. The picnic was postponed / rain was forecasted. (because)

____

9. We knocked on the door / nobody answered. (but)

____

10. He worked / he listened to the radio. (while)

____

11. The crowd left / the game ended. (when) ____________
12. with a fork / with a spoon (or) ____________

LESSON

21

PARTS OF SPEECH

Interrogative Words
Relative Words

Number Right: ____

The words **who, whom, whose, what, which, when, where, how,** and **why** are **interrogative words** when they are used to begin questions. Interrogative words may function as pronouns, adjectives, or adverbs.

Pronouns: Who knows? **Whom** shall I ask? **Which** is mine?

Adjectives: Which hat is mine?

Adverbs: When did we meet? **How** did you like it?

These words and the word **that** are **relative words** when they are used to begin subordinate clauses. (A subordinate clause that begins with a relative word can be an adjective clause. The whole clause can function as an adjective by modifying a noun or pronoun.)

Paint the chair **that** is on the porch.

There was a time **when** the chair had been red.

Underline the interrogative words. Circle the relative words. Be careful not to circle any conjunctions.

1. Who is Pelé? He is an athlete who has played soccer.
2. Where was he born? He is from Brazil, which is in South America.
3. Where did he learn to play? He learned in the town where he grew up.
4. With whom did he play? He played with a team that was called the Santos.
5. When did Pelé join the Santos? He joined when he was 16 years old.

Rewrite each word group as a question. Be sure to put the words in the right order. Then complete each statement with a clause that begins with a relative word.

6. when New York was founded **When was New York founded?**

   At the time **when New York was founded**, it was called New Amsterdam.
7. who settled New York ____________________

   The people ____________________ were Dutch.
8. why it was given a Dutch name ____________________

   That is the reason ____________________.
9. by whom they were governed ____________________

   The leader ____________________ was Peter Minuit.
10. whose administration began in 1626 ____________________

    Minuit, ____________________, ruled until 1631.

LESSON 22 — PARTS OF SPEECH

Prepositions

Number Right: ____

A **preposition** is a word that connects a noun or pronoun to another word in the sentence. Prepositions usually tell about time or place.

After the next light, bear **to** the right and go **up** the hill.

Some common prepositions are **about, above, after, against, along, around, at, before, behind, below, beneath, beside, by, down, for, from, in, near, of, off, on, out, over, to, through, under, up, upon,** and **with.** Some of these words may be other parts of speech, depending on how they are used.

Prepositions: He went **up** the hill. He drove **under** the bridge.
Two-Word Verb: He **backed up** the car.
Infinitive: It was easy **to park.**
Adverb: He got **out** of the car.
Conjunction: After he had parked, he rang the bell.

Underline the prepositions.

1. They hunted down the lost dog from morning to night.
2. To help find him, they handed out his picture around the neighborhood.
3. People looked over the picture of the dog.
4. At nine o'clock, someone called out, "He's here!"
5. The dog was with a cat near a tree by the school.

Change the meaning of each sentence by replacing the preposition with the one in parentheses.

6. The car is parked ~~down~~ up that street. (up)
7. The mouse ran under the table. (over)
8. I can see better with these glasses. (without)
9. The keys are in the desk. (on)
10. King Kong climbed up the building. (down)
11. The squirrel scurried along the roof. (off)
12. Turn on the lights behind the stage. (above)
13. Your sneakers are beside the bed. (beneath)
14. She lives near that city. (in)
15. Take that to him. (from)

LESSON 23 — PARTS OF SPEECH

Review

Review Score: ____

A. Write the plural possessive form of each singular noun.

1. deer ____
2. scarf ____
3. brother-in-law ____

B. Write the pronouns that replace the underlined words.

4. Queen Victoria ruled England from 1837 to 1901. ____
5. Victoria's reign became known as the Victorian Age. ____
6. Many people in England admired Victoria. ____
7. Many places were named after Victoria. ____
8. Which places have you heard of? ____

C. Write the tense forms of each verb.

	Past	Present Perfect	Past Perfect
9. go	____	____	____
10. sit	____	____	____

D. Write the progressive forms of each verb.

	Present	Past
11. fly	*It* ____	*We* ____
12. win	*They* ____	*I* ____

E. Underline the adjectives. Circle the adverbs.

13. The cold wind howled loudly and fiercely on that wintry day.
14. Later, white snow quietly fell on the frozen earth.

F. Underline the participles used as adjectives. Circle the gerunds. Draw a box around the infinitives used as nouns.

15. A growing plant needs the shining sun.
16. If you are growing plants, place the seeds in dampened soil.
17. It's fun to garden.
18. Gardening is a relaxing pastime.

G. Use the abbreviations in parentheses to identify the parts of speech of the numbered words in the paragraph. (noun-*n;* pronoun-*pro;* action verb-*av;* linking verb-*lv;* adjective-*adj;* adverb-*adv;* conjunction-*conj;* preposition-*prep)* Write the abbreviations above the words.

The American (19) sculptor Patience Lovell Wright had gone (20) to (21) England before (22) the Revolutionary War began. Benjamin Franklin asked her (23) to do (24) some (25) spying (26) for the Americans (27) while (28) she lived there (29). Wright became (30) a spy.

SENTENCE STRUCTURE

Preview

When you study **grammar**, you learn how sentences are made. The way a sentence is made is called its **structure**.

Here are some tips to help you remember how sentences are made:

1: Every sentence has **two parts**.

The people in the United States | choose their leaders.

America | is a democracy.

2: The **subject** tells whom or what the sentence is about. The main word in the subject is the **simple subject**.

The people in the United States choose their leaders.

America is a democracy.

3: The **predicate** tells about the subject. (The predicate may contain an action verb or a linking verb.) The verb in the predicate is the **simple predicate**.

The people in the United States **choose their leaders**.

America **is a democracy.**

4: A linking verb may be followed by a noun that tells what the subject *is.* A linking verb may be followed by an adjective that tells what the subject *is like.*

America is a **democracy.**

Americans are **free**.

5: An action verb may be followed by a noun or pronoun. A noun or pronoun that tells who or what received the action is called a **direct object.**

The people in the United States choose their **leaders**.

A noun or pronoun that tells *to whom* or *for whom* an action is done is called an **indirect object**.

We give **them** our votes.

LESSON 24 — SENTENCE STRUCTURE

Kinds of Sentences

Number Right: ____

There are four kinds of sentences. A **declarative sentence** makes a statement. It ends with a period.

Fencing is an Olympic sport. The sword is called an *epée.*

An **interrogative sentence** is a sentence that asks for an answer. It ends with a question mark.

Have you watched a fencing event? It's graceful, isn't it?

An **imperative sentence** is a sentence that tells someone to do something. An imperative sentence may end with a period or an exclamation point.

Watch those fencers. Keep score. Look out! Begin!

An **exclamatory sentence** shows strong feeling. It ends with an exclamation point. An **interjection** is an exclamatory word or phrase that is used as a sentence, but it does not contain a verb.

What a great sport this is! On guard! Touché! Terrific!

Circle the punctuation mark at the end of each word group. Then write *declarative, interrogative, imperative, exclamatory,* or *interjection.*

1. Dinosaur eggs were discovered in France in 1961. ____________
2. What a discovery! ____________
3. They were a foot long and ten inches wide! ____________
4. Where can I find out more about them? ____________
5. Go to the public library. ____________

Make each word group a sentence or interjection by adding capital letters and punctuation marks.

6. Take a look at this. (imperative)
7. what a weird-looking dog (interjection)
8. let me see the picture (imperative)
9. it's a Shar-Pei, one of the rarest dogs in the world (declarative)
10. why is it so wrinkled (interrogative)
11. its thick skin protects it (declarative)
12. that's so strange (exclamatory)

LESSON 25 SENTENCE STRUCTURE

Simple Subjects and Complete Subjects

Number Right: ____

Every sentence has a naming part and a part that tells about the naming part. The naming part tells *what* or *whom* the sentence is about. It is called the **subject**. The whole subject of a sentence is the **complete subject**.

The people of ancient Egypt built the great pyramids.
Weren't **those huge stone pyramids** used as tombs?

The main word in the complete subject is the **simple subject.**

The **people** of ancient Egypt built the great pyramids.
Weren't those huge stone **pyramids** used as tombs?

In most imperative sentences, the simple subject is not said or written. In these sentences, the subject is **you.**

Tell me about the pyramids. **(You)** tell me about the pyramids.

Underline the complete subjects. Circle the simple subject in each complete subject. Fill in the simple subject *you* if the sentence is imperative.

1. ________ No two people have the same fingerprints.

2. ________ Look at your fingerprints.

3. ________ Those swirling marks will never change.

4. ________ Do newborn babies have fingerprints, too?

5. ________ Yes, every person is born with a unique set of fingerprints.

Rewrite each sentence using the simple subject only.

6. People in northern Europe believed in gods long ago.

People believed in gods long ago.

7. One of these gods was named Woden.

____

8. The wise Woden supposedly traveled everywhere.

____

9. The people of Scandinavia named a day after Woden.

____

10. "Wodnesdaeg," which we call "Wednesday," was named in Woden's honor.

____

LESSON 26 — SENTENCE STRUCTURE

Simple Predicates and Complete Predicates

Number Right: ____

The part of a sentence that tells about the subject is called the **predicate**. The whole predicate of a sentence is the **complete predicate**.

> **Have** you **visited the Smithsonian Institution**?
> The Smithsonian **is a museum**.

The action verb or linking verb in the complete predicate is the **simple predicate**.

> **Have** you **visited** the Smithsonian Institution?
> The Smithsonian **is** a museum.

Underline the complete predicates. Circle the simple predicate in each complete predicate.

1. America is a land of immigrants.
2. Immigrants invented new and useful things.
3. These people used America's many natural resources.
4. Other countries bought the immigrants' products.
5. America owes much to its immigrants.

Rewrite each sentence using the simple predicate only.

6. Astronomers study the stars. **Astronomers study.**
7. Some stars collapse into nothingness. ____
8. Astronomers define these as "black holes." ____
9. These holes swallow nearby stars. ____
10. Other stars explode into millions of pieces. ____
11. Exploding stars spray space with meteors. ____
12. Meteors seldom hit the earth. ____
13. They often nick the moon, though. ____
14. Have you noticed the craters on the moon in pictures? ____
15. Meteors dug the holes on the moon's surface. ____

LESSON 27

SENTENCE STRUCTURE

Compound Subjects and Compound Predicates

Number Right: ____

Sometimes there is more than one main word in the subject. A complete subject that has two or more simple subjects is called a **compound subject.** The simple subjects are joined by a coordinating conjunction. They share the same predicate.

Ducks and geese swim well. Can **chickens and turkeys** swim?

Sometimes there is more than one verb in the predicate. A complete predicate that has two or more simple predicates is called a **compound predicate**. The simple predicates are joined by a coordinating conjunction. They share the same subject.

Holland's windmills **pump** water **and grind** wheat.
Can windmills **make** electricity **or do** other things?

Underline the compound subjects. Circle the compound predicates.

1. The Space Shuttle orbits like a spaceship and lands like a plane.
2. American satellites and Russian satellites orbit the earth.
3. Did Skylab 1 or Skylab 2 fall from the sky in 1979?
4. Saturn V stands over 363 feet tall and weighs more than 82 tons.
5. The Boeing 747 and the Concord seat hundreds and travel quickly.

Rewrite each sentence pair as one sentence with a compound subject or compound predicate. Use the conjunction shown in parentheses.

6. Calculators add figures. Calculators subtract figures. (and)
   Calculators add and subtract figures.
7. Microcomputers can store data. Microcomputers give back data. (or)
   ____
8. Telephones send messages. Telegraphs send messages. (and)
   ____
9. Photocopiers photograph pictures. Photocopiers develop pictures. (and)
   ____
10. Typewriters print words. Word processors print words. (or)
   ____

LESSON 28

SENTENCE STRUCTURE

Predicate Nouns and Predicate Adjectives

Number Right: ____

A noun that follows a linking verb tells what the subject *is, was,* or *will be.* It is called a **predicate noun.** Adjectives may modify predicate nouns.

S	LV		N	LV	S		N
That tourist	is	a	**Canadian.**	Isn't	Montreal	a Canadian	**city?**

An adjective that follows a linking verb tells what the subject *is like, was like,* or *will be like.* It is called a **predicate adjective.**

S	LV	A	S	LV	A	LV	S	A
That goose	is	**Canadian.**	It	grew	**large.**	Isn't	it	**pretty?**

Underline the predicate nouns. Circle the predicate adjectives.

1. Gooseberries are fruit. Their name sounds silly.
2. Fully ripe gooseberries taste sweet. They always look green.
3. Unripe gooseberries are very tart. An unripe berry is hard.
4. A ripe gooseberry feels soft. Ripe gooseberries are delicious.
5. Gooseberries are a favorite fruit in England.

Circle the predicate named in parentheses.

6. Some people in New Orleans are **Creoles** / **interesting.** (noun)
7. The Creole people are **international** / **an international group.** (adjective)
8. Creoles were **European, African, and American Indian** / **Europeans, Africans, and American Indians.** (nouns)
9. The Creole language is **a mixture of languages** / **special.** **(noun)**
10. Creole food is **famous** / **a mixture of French, Spanish, African, and American Indian cooking.** (adjective)
11. Many Creole dishes have become **popular** / **popular foods.** (noun)
12. Creole gumbo is **hearty** / **a thick soup.** (adjective)
13. Jambalaya is **spicy** / **an original Creole dish.** (noun)
14. Fried crayfish is **tasty** / **another specialty.** (noun)
15. Rice has always been **popular** / **a dish** in New Orleans. (adjective)

LESSON

29 SENTENCE STRUCTURE

- Direct Objects and Indirect Objects
- Transitive Verbs and Intransitive Verbs

Number Right: ____

A noun or pronoun that receives the action of a verb is called a **direct object.** The direct object usually follows the action verb. In an interrogative sentence, the object may come before the verb.

S AV DO	DO S AV
Doug read a **story.**	**What** did he read?

An **indirect object** tells *to whom* or *for whom* an action was done. The indirect object goes between the verb and the direct object.

S AV IO DO	S AV IO DO
Doug read **us** a story.	He sent **himself** a letter.

An action verb that has a direct object is called a **transitive verb.** In the sentences above, *read* and *sent* are transitive. An action verb that has no object is an **intransitive verb.** (Linking verbs are always intransitive.) In the sentences below, *read* is intransitive.

S AV	S AV	S AV
Doug read quickly.	He read to us.	Who read?

Underline the direct objects. Circle the indirect objects. Then tell if the verb is *transitive* or *intransitive.*

1. Advertisers sell us products every day. ________________
2. Commercials promise you and me better lives. ________________
3. Do the right jeans really win us friends? ________________
4. We should ask ourselves such questions. ________________
5. Otherwise, we might spend foolishly. ________________

Rewrite each sentence by changing the underlined phrase to an indirect object. Then label each direct and indirect object.

6. Juan wrote a letter to his senator.

   IO DO
   Juan wrote his senator a letter.

7. The senator sent a long reply to Juan.

   ____

8. Juan read its contents to us. ____

9. The senator had sent an invitation to Juan to visit the capital.

   ____

10. He showed the invitation to the entire school.

    ____

LESSON 30 SENTENCE STRUCTURE

Number Right: ____

Prepositional Phrases

A **prepositional phrase** contains a preposition, an object of the preposition, and any words that modify the object. In the sentences that follow, *at* is the preposition, and *desk* is the object of the preposition. A prepositional phrase can be used as an adjective if it modifies a noun or as an adverb if it modifies a verb.

Adjective Phrase (modifies man): Ask the man **at the red desk.**
Adverb Phrase (tells where): We asked **at the red desk.**

Do not confuse a prepositional phrase with a subordinate clause or an infinitive. An infinitive such as *to go* acts as a noun. A subordinate clause has its own subject and verb. A prepositional phrase has neither a subject nor a verb.

Prepositional Phrase: After lunch, we plan to go home.
Subordinate Clause: After we eat, we plan to go home.

Underline each prepositional phrase. Circle the object of the preposition. Then write *adjective* or *adverb.*

1. George Washington Carver was born a slave in Missouri. ____________
2. He attended Iowa State College and was graduated in 1894. ____________
3. After he was graduated, he worked at the greenhouse there. ____________
4. Booker T. Washington invited him to teach at Tuskegee Institute. ____________
5. Today, Tuskegee houses a museum of Carver's many discoveries. ____________

Circle a prepositional phrase to complete each sentence.

6. An emperor **of India** / **long ago** built a magnificent tomb.
7. The tomb was built **to last** / **for his wife.**
8. It was made **before he died** / **of white marble.**
9. It was completed **after twenty years** / **after his wife died.**
10. The emperor didn't name the tomb **until it was finished** / **until its completion.**
11. It has been called the Taj Mahal **since 1653** / **since he built it.**
12. The word "Taj" came **to mean "crown"** / **from the Indian word for "crown."**
13. "Mahal" was the name **of his wife** / **the emperor chose.**
14. The Taj Mahal is **in Agra, India** / **the most expensive gift ever given.**
15. Tourists **often** / **from many countries** visit the Taj Mahal.

LESSON 31

SENTENCE STRUCTURE

Simple Sentences and Compound Sentences

Number Right: ____

A **simple sentence** has only one complete subject and one complete predicate.

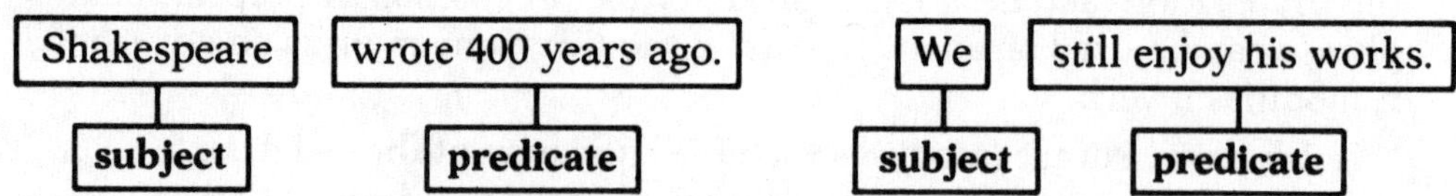

A **compound sentence** is made up of two simple sentences that are joined by a coordinating conjunction. A comma is usually placed in front of the conjunction.

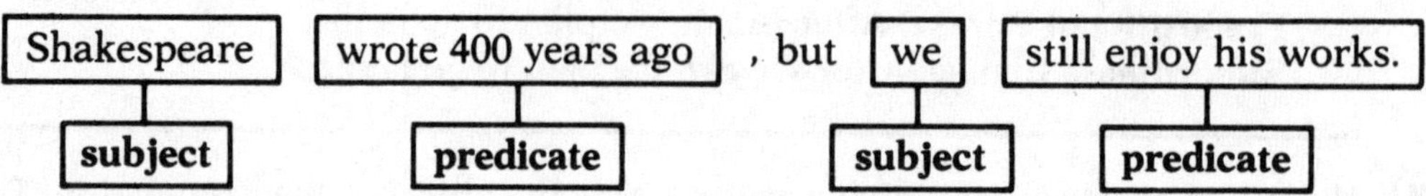

A simple sentence can have a compound subject or a compound predicate. Do not confuse such a sentence with a compound sentence.

---

identify Tell if each sentence is *simple* or *compound.*

1. There are about 30,000 kinds of fish, but only 4,000 species live in North American waters. ________________
2. Some fish live only in warm water, but others survive in cold water. ________________
3. All fish can swim, but some can also crawl. ________________
4. Most fish cannot see well, and some are almost blind. ________________
5. However, fish have excellent senses of taste and touch. ________________
6. Fish can also hear, and they are sensitive to vibration. ________________
7. The spines in the fins may be bony or soft. ________________
8. Fish have no scales when hatched, but most develop scales quickly. ________________
9. Some fish have rough scales, and others have smooth scales. ________________
10. You can tell the age of a fish by counting the number of rings left from the growth of scales. ________________

Go on to the next page.

Write each sentence pair as a compound sentence. Use the conjunction shown in parentheses.

11. The Renaissance began in the 1300s. It lasted through the 1600s. (, and)

    The Renaissance began in the 1300s, and it lasted through the 1600s.

12. The movement began in Italy. It spread throughout Europe. (, but)

13. Great art was being produced. Science was moving forward. (, and)

14. Leonardo da Vinci is known as a great Renaissance painter. He was also an inventor. (, but)

15. Much of da Vinci's art has been lost. Two great works still exist. (, but)

16. One is the *Mona Lisa.* The other is *The Last Supper.* (, and)

17. He also drew sketches of an airplane. The model was never built. (, but)

18. Leonardo wrote his ideas in notebooks. They were difficult to read. (, but)

19. He wrote everything backwards. A mirror was needed to read them. (, and)

20. You can see da Vinci's work in museums. You can see copies in an encyclopedia. (, or)

LESSON 32

SENTENCE STRUCTURE

Independent Clauses and Subordinate Clauses
Simple Sentences and Complex Sentences

Number Right: ____

A **clause** is a group of words that has a subject and a predicate. An **independent clause** expresses a complete thought and can stand alone. When it stands alone, it is a simple sentence.

We played word games after dinner.

A **subordinate clause** does not express a complete thought and cannot stand alone. A subordinate clause begins with a subordinating conjunction or a relative word. It is always joined to an independent clause. A sentence that contains an independent clause and one or more subordinate clauses is called a **complex sentence.**

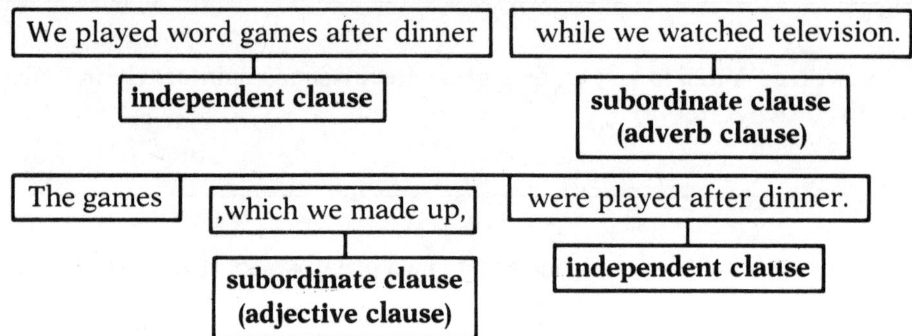

Do not confuse a subordinate clause with a prepositional phrase. A phrase such as *after dinner* does not contain a subject or a verb.

Underline the subordinate clause if the sentence has one. Then tell if the sentence is *simple* or *complex.*

1. When you look into a kaleidoscope, you see colored designs. ________________
2. As you turn the kaleidoscope, the design changes. ________________
3. A kaleidoscope consists of a tube that holds mirrors and ground glass. ________________
4. The pieces of glass reflect against the mirrors when light hits them. ________________
5. The light enters the tube through a piece of clear glass. ________________
6. At the other end of the tube is a peek hole. ________________
7. As you peer through the peek hole with one eye, you must close the other eye. ________________
8. Many designers use kaleidoscopes while they work. ________________
9. They copy the patterns for wallpaper, carpets, and fabric. ________________
10. The first kaleidoscope that was patented was designed by Sir David Brewster in 1817. ________________

Go on to the next page.

Rewrite each simple sentence as a complex sentence. Use the subordinate clause in parentheses.

11. There has been garbage. (since humans began living)

    Since humans began living, there has been garbage.
    or: **There has been garbage since humans began living.**

12. People made garbage dumps. (after cities had been formed)

13. People had thrown garbage into the street. (before there were dumps)

14. Many people became ill. (because the garbage carried disease)

15. Modern cities are reusing garbage. (whenever they can)

16. Garbage is being used as fuel. (because oil is expensive)

17. Garbage can create a lot of heat. (that is needed)

18. Aluminum cans can be reused. (after they are melted down)

19. Recycling garbage makes sense. (although it, too, is expensive)

20. There would be more fuel and fewer dumps. (if more cities would recycle their garbage)

LESSON 33

SENTENCE STRUCTURE

- Complete Sentences
- Sentence Fragments
- Run-On Sentences

Number Right: ____

A **complete sentence** must have a subject and a predicate. It must also make sense by itself. A group of words that is punctuated as though it were a sentence but is not complete is called a **sentence fragment.**

Complete Sentence: She mounted the horse and rode away.
Fragment (Missing a Subject): She mounted the horse. **And rode away.**

Complete Sentences: Ella enjoys riding. Pedro rides, too.
Fragment (Missing a Predicate): Ella enjoys riding. **Pedro, too.**

Complete Sentence: They ride after they groom their horses.
Fragment (Subordinate Clause): They ride. **After they groom their horses.**
Fragment (Prepositional Phrase): They ride. **After dinner.**

A **run-on** is the opposite of a sentence fragment. In a run-on sentence, two sentences are written as though they were one sentence, and a comma is put where a period should be. You can correct a run-on sentence in three ways. You can write two simple sentences, or you can write one compound sentence or one complex sentence.

Run-on: Tomatoes grow on vines, parsnips grow underground.
Two Sentences: Tomatoes grow on vines. Parsnips grow underground.
Compound Sentence: Tomatoes grow on vines, and parsnips grow underground.
Complex Sentence: Tomatoes grow on vines while parsnips grow underground.

Write *sentence, fragment,* or *run-on.*

1. Lesotho is a mountainous country. ____________

2. Near the southern tip of Africa. ____________

3. Lesotho was a British colony, it became independent in 1966. ____________

4. It is completely surrounded. ____________

5. By the Republic of South Africa. ____________

6. Lesotho is called the Switzerland of Africa. ____________

7. Because it has steep mountains. ____________

8. Lesotho exports wool, this nation exports beef, too. ____________

9. Lesotho has a pleasant climate, many people are farmers. ____________

10. Industry is not well-developed in Lesotho. ____________

Go on to the next page.

Correct each sentence fragment by using it in a complete sentence. Correct each run-on by writing two simple sentences, one compound sentence, or one complex sentence.

11. Insects have six legs, spiders have eight legs.

Insects have six legs, but spiders have eight legs.
or: **Insects have six legs. Spiders have eight legs.**
or: **Insects have six legs while spiders have eight legs.**

12. Wolf spiders catch insects. By chasing them.

13. Some spiders can dive into water, they can grab fish.

14. Some spiders trap insects. In webs made of silk.

15. The silk comes from the back. Of the spider's body.

16. The silk liquid becomes thread. When air touches it.

17. Garden spiders' webs are sticky, black widows' webs are knotty.

18. Raft spiders make boats of silk. And go fishing for insects.

19. Most spiders have eight eyes, they can see in many directions.

20. Spiders are *arachnids.* Scorpions, too.

LESSON 34 — SENTENCE STRUCTURE

Review

Review Score: ___

A. Underline the simple subjects. Circle the simple predicates. If the sentence is imperative, fill in the simple subject.

1. ____ In Europe, many old churches have gargoyles.
2. ____ These grotesque stone statues sit on the church roofs.
3. ____ Have you ever seen one?
4. ____ Look for pictures of them in an encyclopedia.

B. Underline the predicate nouns. Circle the predicate adjectives. Draw a box around the direct objects. Put an X over the indirect objects.

5. Chard is a vegetable.
6. It tastes delicious.
7. It is leafy, like lettuce.
8. Some restaurants serve us chard in our salads.
9. Chard gives salads a unique flavor.

C. Underline the prepositional phrases. Circle the object of each preposition. Then tell if the phrase is used as an adjective or as an adverb.

10. The top of that hedge needs clipping.

____

11. Do not clip below the upper branches.

____

D. Write *S* if the words make a sentence. Write *F* if the words are a sentence fragment. Write *R* if the words are a run-on.

12. In less than a month after eggs are laid. ____
13. The chicks must be kept warm, they should be kept at 90° F. ____
14. The hen may keep the chicks warm. ____

E. Underline the independent clauses.

15. The Chinese had printed books before the Europeans learned printing.
16. After Gutenberg invented the printing press, books became common.
17. When books became available, more people learned how to read.
18. Would the world be different if people could not read and write?

F. Underline the transitive verb. Circle the intransitive verb.

19. Giant squid and sperm whales fight sometimes.
20. The squid squeezes the whale with its arms.

Name ______________________________ Progress Plotter 

Number Right	Lesson 1	Lesson 2	Lesson 3	Lesson 4	Lesson 5	Lesson 6	Lesson 7	Lesson 8	Lesson 9	Lesson 10	Lesson 11	Lesson 12	Lesson 13	Lesson 14	Lesson 15	Lesson 16	Lesson 17	Number Right
20																		20
19																		19
18																		18
17																		17
16																		16
15																		15
14																		14
13																		13
12																		12
11																		11
10																		10
9																		9
8																		8
7																		7
6																		6
5																		5
4																		4
3																		3
2																		2
1																		1

PARTS OF SPEECH

Number Right	Lesson 18	Lesson 19	Lesson 20	Lesson 21	Lesson 22	Lesson 23	Lesson 24	Lesson 25	Lesson 26	Lesson 27	Lesson 28	Lesson 29	Lesson 30	Lesson 31	Lesson 32	Lesson 33	Lesson 34	Number Right
20						Review Score: ___											Review Score: ___	20
19																		19
18																		18
17																		17
16																		16
15																		15
14																		14
13																		13
12																		12
11																		11
10																		10
9																		9
8																		8
7																		7
6						PARTS OF SPEECH											SENTENCE STRUCTURE	6
5																		5
4																		4
3																		3
2																		2
1																		1
							SENTENCE STRUCTURE											

GRAMMAR

Final Test Name________________

Directions: Read each sentence below. Choose the word or phrase that best describes the underlined word. Fill in the letter of your answer in the answer row.

1 One of Peru's bridges was made from egg whites in 1610.
Ⓐ common noun
Ⓑ possessive noun
Ⓒ proper adjective
Ⓓ possessive pronoun

2 Builders used 10,000 of them to make the bridge.
Ⓔ subject pronoun
Ⓕ possessive pronoun
Ⓖ object pronoun
Ⓗ reflexive pronoun

3 Mice belong to the same family as squirrels.
Ⓐ proper noun
Ⓑ plural noun
Ⓒ possessive noun
Ⓓ collective noun

4 The Chinese were printing books 500 years before Europeans.
Ⓔ past-progressive form of verb
Ⓕ present-progressive form of verb
Ⓖ present-perfect tense verb
Ⓗ past-perfect tense verb

5 The British word for a car trunk is "boot."
Ⓐ present-tense action verb
Ⓑ infinitive
Ⓒ present-progressive form of verb
Ⓓ linking verb

6 In Iceland, the sun shines 24 hours a day during the summer.
Ⓔ subordinating conjunction
Ⓕ coordinating conjunction
Ⓖ preposition
Ⓗ adverb

7 Tidal waves move faster than cars.
Ⓐ comparative form of adjective
Ⓑ superlative form of adjective
Ⓒ comparative form of adverb
Ⓓ superlative form of adverb

8 Indians in South America ate baked potatoes 400 years ago.
Ⓔ past-perfect tense of verb
Ⓕ participle used as adjective
Ⓖ infinitive
Ⓗ gerund

9 The had baked the potatoes in ashes.
Ⓐ past-perfect tense of verb
Ⓑ past-progressive form of verb
Ⓒ participle used as adjective
Ⓓ infinitive

10 After he had invented the light bulb, Edison invented a switch to turn on the light.
Ⓔ preposition
Ⓕ coordinating conjunction
Ⓖ subordinating conjunction
Ⓗ adverb

(Go on to the next page.)

ANSWER ROWS:
1 Ⓐ Ⓑ Ⓒ Ⓓ **2** Ⓔ Ⓕ Ⓖ Ⓗ **3** Ⓐ Ⓑ Ⓒ Ⓓ **4** Ⓔ Ⓕ Ⓖ Ⓗ **5** Ⓐ Ⓑ Ⓒ Ⓓ
6 Ⓔ Ⓕ Ⓖ Ⓗ **7** Ⓐ Ⓑ Ⓒ Ⓓ **8** Ⓔ Ⓕ Ⓖ Ⓗ **9** Ⓐ Ⓑ Ⓒ Ⓓ **10** Ⓔ Ⓕ Ⓖ Ⓗ

Directions: Read each word group below. Choose the phrase that best describes the underlined words. Fill in the letter of your answer in the answer row.

11 The earthworm has no lungs, it breathes through its skin.
- Ⓐ compound sentence
- Ⓑ complex sentence
- Ⓒ simple sentence
- Ⓓ run-on

12 Most people do not remember their dreams.
- Ⓔ direct object
- Ⓕ predicate noun
- Ⓖ prepositional phrase
- Ⓗ indirect object

13 Rice the main food of people in China.
- Ⓐ simple sentence
- Ⓑ compound sentence
- Ⓒ fragment
- Ⓓ run-on

14 The chocolate in a candy bar comes from cocoa beans.
- Ⓔ simple subject
- Ⓕ compound subject
- Ⓖ complete subject
- Ⓗ simple predicate

15 Before clocks were invented, people had used sundials to tell time.
- Ⓐ simple sentence
- Ⓑ independent clause
- Ⓒ subordinate clause
- Ⓓ prepositional phrase

16 If you file alphabetically, you place the letter *E* before the letter *G*.
- Ⓔ independent clause
- Ⓕ subordinate clause
- Ⓖ prepositional phrase
- Ⓗ direct object

17 The inventor of the movie camera was Thomas Edison.
- Ⓐ predicate noun
- Ⓑ predicate adjective
- Ⓒ direct object
- Ⓓ indirect object

18 A spider has eight legs, but an insect has six.
- Ⓔ simple sentence
- Ⓕ compound sentence
- Ⓖ complex sentence
- Ⓗ run-on

19 The sun gives the earth warmth and light.
- Ⓐ predicate noun
- Ⓑ direct object
- Ⓒ indirect object
- Ⓓ object of preposition

20 Dogs smell very well but see poorly.
- Ⓔ simple predicate
- Ⓕ compound predicate
- Ⓖ complete subject
- Ⓗ predicate adjective

Final Test Score: ______

ANSWER ROWS:
11 Ⓐ Ⓑ Ⓒ Ⓓ **12** Ⓔ Ⓕ Ⓖ Ⓗ **13** Ⓐ Ⓑ Ⓒ Ⓓ **14** Ⓔ Ⓕ Ⓖ Ⓗ **15** Ⓐ Ⓑ Ⓒ Ⓓ
16 Ⓔ Ⓕ Ⓖ Ⓗ **17** Ⓐ Ⓑ Ⓒ Ⓓ **18** Ⓔ Ⓕ Ⓖ Ⓗ **19** Ⓐ Ⓑ Ⓒ Ⓓ **20** Ⓔ Ⓕ Ⓖ Ⓗ

ANSWER KEY

Lesson 1

1. settlement Europeans North America Jamestown, Virginia
2. territory Virginia states
3. states West Virginia Kentucky Illinois Indiana Michigan Minnesota Ohio Wisconsin Virginia
4. Virginia "The Mother of States"
5. Virginian Thomas Jefferson Declaration of Independence

6. speech 7. highway 8. holiday
9. newspaper 10. park 11. ship
12. writer 13. war 14. dam 15. building

Lesson 2

1. troop tents river
2. swarm mosquitoes lantern
3. pack coyotes moon
4. campers stories campfire
5. knives branches whistles

6. halves 7. families 8. taxes
9. sisters-in-law 10. benches 11. potatoes
12. mice 13. children 14. cacti *or* cactuses
15. teeth 16. reindeer 17. pianos
18. geese 19. beliefs 20. passersby

Lesson 3

1. them (plural) 2. it (singular)
3. it (singular) 4. He (singular)
5. him (singular)

6. They 7. them 8. it 9. them 10. She
11. He 12. They 13. them 14. We 15. it

Lesson 4

1. presidents' (plural) 2. people's (plural)
3. Her work (singular) 4. our (plural)
5. Ford's (singular)

6. their 7. His 8. Their 9. Our 10. her
11. his 12. Its 13. theirs 14. their 15. his

Lesson 5

1. himself (singular) 2. itself (singular)
3. yourselves (plural) 4. themselves (plural)
5. itself (singular)

6. themselves 7. itself 8. yourself itself
9. itself 10. herself *or* itself
11. himself *or* itself 12. themselves
13. themselves 14. itself 15. ourselves

Lesson 6

1. are vanishing are hunting
2. have disappeared 3. have grown
4. have died 5. are passing are helping

6. doing	did	done
7. dancing	danced	danced
8. begging	begged	begged
9. frying	fried	fried
10. setting	set	set
11. beginning	began	begun
12. coming	came	come
13. sitting	sat	sat
14. eating	ate	eaten
15. buying	bought	bought

Lesson 7

1. live (present) 2. will double (future)
3. inhabited (past) 4. hold (present)
5. will live (future)

6. found will find 7. began will begin
8. saw will see 9. set will set
10. begged will beg 11. lived will live
12. enjoyed will enjoy 13. cried will cry
14. went will go 15. rode will ride

Lesson 8

1. had ended 2. Had influenced
3. have read 4. have compared
5. had set

6. have lived 7. had come 8. had heard
9. had crossed 10. had sailed
11. had renamed 12. had called
13. had flocked 14. had given
15. has remained

Lesson 9

1. was changing 2. were trading
3. were going were opening
4. are growing 5. are hiring

6. is working 7. is moving
8. are inhaling 9. are digesting
10. are controlling 11. are reacting
12. were sleeping 13. were dreaming
14. were helping 15. was preparing

Lesson 10

1. is (present) 2. were (past)
3. became (past) 4. grow (present)
5. grow (present)

6. a food 7. easy to make 8. good 9. soft
10. creamy 11. slippery 12. an ingredient
13. popular 14. popular 15. fresh

Lesson 11

1. A violin an instrument four strings
2. This instrument a bow
3. the bow each string a sound
4. All violins some kind
5. These instruments a part every orchestra

6. ten 7. These 8. the 9. twenty-five
10. This 11. two 12. The 13. Every
14. three 15. any

Lesson 12

1. All 2. Nobody 3. most 4. some 5. Others
6. Many are fashion-conscious.
7. Some spend hours each week choosing their wardrobes.
8. They wonder, "Does this go with these?"
9. Dressing is easier if several can be mixed and matched.
10. Some go well with others.

Lesson 13

1. English language international background
2. Foreign words Latin prefixes
3. Norwegian word Dutch language
4. common words different languages
5. Hindi word Spanish word big round-up

6. National 7. One 8. American
9. bald 10. Russian 11. The
12. Olive 13. One 14. a white 15. This

Lesson 14

1. highest 2. larger 3. longest
4. longer 5. best worst

6. funnier funniest 7. fewer fewest
8. smaller smallest 9. better best
10. wiser wisest 11. bigger biggest
12. stormier stormiest 13. worse worst
14. weaker weakest 15. friendlier friendliest

Lesson 15

1. least expensive 2. less expensive
3. most costly 4. more expensive
5. most durable

6. more/less difficult most/least difficult
7. more/less practical most/least practical
8. more/less lively most/least lively
9. more/less common most/least common
10. more/less generous most/least generous
11. more/less eager most/least eager
12. more/less urgent most/least urgent
13. more/less famous most/least famous
14. more/less secretive most/least secretive
15. more/less favorable most/least favorable

Lesson 16

1. baked (verb) 2. Baked (adjective)
3. boiling (verb) 4. interesting (adjective)
5. Fried (adjective)

6. clogged drain 7. running water
8. overflowed bathtub 9. flooded room
10. soaked floor 11. floating things
12. leaking ceiling 13. corrected problem
14. fixed drain 15. draining water

Lesson 17

1. Waiting 2. To wait 3. Standing walking
4. to stand 5. moving wiggling

6. Farming 7. to grow 8. grazing 9. to import
10. growing 11. to increase 12. Fishing
13. Mining 14. to import 15. to seal

Lesson 18

1. spoke quite confidently
2. very pleased so many were there
3. Then abruptly introduced extremely nervous
4. unusually civic-minded especially clever
5. gratefully accepted applauded loudly

6. forward 7. not 8. back 9. continuously
10. well 11. very 12. always
13. frequently 14. Then 15. indoors

Lesson 19

1. more frequently 2. more often
3. most commonly 4. more regularly
5. most frequently

6. farther/less far farthest/least far
7. more/less eagerly most/least eagerly
8. more/less politely most/least politely
9. better *or* less well best *or* least well
10. more/less often most/least often
11. worse *or* less badly worst *or* least badly
12. faster/less fast fastest/least fast
13. more/less calmly most/least calmly
14. more/less intelligently most/least intelligently
15. later/less late latest/least late

Lesson 20

1. before and 2. nor although
3. yet 4. and but 5. because

6. fish and meat
7. my sister or your brother
8. The picnic was postponed because rain was forecasted.
9. We knocked on the door, but nobody answered.
10. He worked while he listened to the radio.
11. The crowd left when the game ended.
12. with a fork or with a spoon

Lesson 21

1. Who is who has 2. Where was which is
3. Where did where he
4. whom that 5. When did
6. When was New York founded?
At the time *when New York was founded,* it was called New Amsterdam.
7. Who settled New York?
The people *who settled New York* were Dutch.
8. Why was it given a Dutch name?
That is the reason *why it was given a Dutch name.*
9. By whom were they governed?
The leader *by whom they were governed* was Peter Minuit.
10. Whose administration began in 1626?
Minuit, *whose administration began in 1626,* ruled until 1631.

Lesson 22

1. from to 2. around 3. of 4. At
5. with near by
6. up that street 7. over the table
8. without these glasses 9. on the desk
10. down the building 11. off the roof
12. above the stage 13. beneath the bed
14. in that city 15. from him

Lesson 23 Review

See page 721

Lesson 24

1. declarative 2. interjection 3. exclamatory
4. interrogative 5. imperative
6. Take a look at this.
7. What a weird-looking dog!
8. Let me see the picture. *or*
Let me see the picture!
9. It's a Shar-Pei, one of the rarest dogs in the world.
10. Why is it so wrinkled?
11. Its thick skin protects it.
12. That's so strange!

Lesson 25

1. No two people 2. You
3. Those swirling marks
4. newborn babies 5. every person
6. People believed in gods long ago.
7. One was named Woden.
8. Woden supposedly traveled everywhere.
9. People named a day after Woden.
10. "Wodnesdaeg" was named in Woden's honor.

Lesson 26

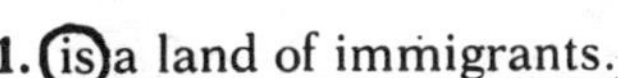
1. is a land of immigrants.
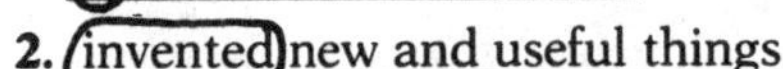
2. invented new and useful things
3. used America's many natural resources
4. bought the immigrants' products
5. owes much to its immigrants
6. Astronomers study. 7. Some stars collapse.
8. Astronomers define. 9. These holes swallow.
10. Other stars explode. 11. Exploding stars spray.
12. Meteors seldom hit. 13. They often nick.
14. Have you noticed? 15. Meteors dug.

Lesson 27

1. orbits and lands
2. American satellites and Russian satellites
3. Skylab 1 or Skylab 2 4. stands and weighs
5. The Boeing 747 and the Concord
6. Calculators add and subtract figures.
7. Microcomputers can store or give back data.
8. Telephones and telegraphs send messages.
9. Photocopiers photograph and develop pictures.
10. Typewriters or word processors print words.

Lesson 28

1. fruit silly 2. sweet green 3. tart hard
4. soft delicious 5. fruit
6. Creoles 7. international
8. Europeans, Africans, and American Indians
9. a mixture of languages 10. famous
11. popular foods 12. hearty
13. an original Creole dish
14. another specialty 15. popular

Lesson 29

1. us products (transitive)
2. you and me lives (transitive)
3. us friends (transitive)
4. ourselves questions (transitive)
5. (intransitive)
6. Juan wrote his senator a letter. (IO: senator; DO: letter)
7. The senator sent Juan a long reply. (IO: Juan; DO: reply)
8. Juan read us its contents. (IO: us; DO: contents)
9. The senator had sent Juan an invitation to visit the capital. (IO: Juan; DO: invitation)
10. He showed the entire school the invitation. (IO: school; DO: invitation)

Lesson 30

1. in Missouri (adverb) 2. in 1894 (adverb)
3. at the greenhouse (adverb)
4. at Tuskegee Institute (adverb)
5. of Carver's many discoveries (adjective)

6. of India 7. for his wife
8. of white marble 9. after twenty years
10. until its completion 11. since 1653
12. from the Indian word for "crown"
13. of his wife 14. in Agra, India
15. from many countries

Lesson 31

1. compound 2. compound
3. compound 4. compound
5. simple 6. compound
7. simple 8. compound
9. compound 10. simple

11. The Renaissance began in the 1300s, and it lasted through the 1600s.
12. The movement began in Italy, but it spread throughout Europe.
13. Great art was being produced, and science was moving forward.
14. Leonardo da Vinci is known as a great Renaissance painter, but he was also an inventor.
15. Much of da Vinci's art has been lost, but two great works still exist.
16. One is the *Mona Lisa*, and the other is *The Last Supper*.
17. He also drew sketches of an airplane, but the model was never built.
18. Leonardo wrote his ideas in notebooks, but they were difficult to read.
19. He wrote everything backwards, and a mirror was needed to read them.
20. You can see da Vinci's work in museums, or you can see copies in an encyclopedia.

Lesson 32

1. When you look into a kaleidoscope (complex)
2. As you turn the kaleidoscope (complex)
3. that holds mirrors and ground glass (complex)
4. when light hits them (complex)
5. (simple)
6. (simple)
7. As you peer through the peek hole with one eye (complex)
8. while they work (complex)
9. (simple)
10. that was patented (complex)

Note: *For sentences 11 through 16 and 18 through 20, the subordinate clause may also follow the independent clause.*

11. Since humans began living, there has been garbage.
12. After cities had been formed, people made garbage dumps.
13. Before there were dumps, people had thrown garbage into the street.
14. Because the garbage carried disease, many people became ill.
15. Whenever they can, modern cities are reusing garbage.
16. Because oil is expensive, garbage is being used as fuel.
17. Garbage can create a lot of heat that is needed.
18. After they are melted down, aluminum cans can be reused.
19. Although it, too, is expensive, recycling garbage makes sense.
20. If more cities would recycle their garbage, there would be more fuel and fewer dumps.

Lesson 33

1. sentence 2. fragment
3. run-on 4. sentence
5. fragment 6. sentence
7. fragment 8. run-on
9. run-on 10. sentence

Note: *Sentences 11, 13, 17, and 19 may be written as simple, compound, or complex sentences.*

11. Insects have six legs, but spiders have eight legs.
12. Wolf spiders catch insects by chasing them.
13. Some spiders can dive into water where they can grab fish.
14. Some spiders trap insects in webs made of silk.
15. The silk comes from the back of the spider's body.
16. The silk liquid becomes thread when air touches it.
17. Garden spiders' webs are sticky, but black widows' webs are knotty.
18. Raft spiders make boats of silk and go fishing for insects.
19. Because most spiders have eight eyes, they can see in many directions.
20. Spiders are *arachnids*. Scorpions are *arachnids*, too.

Lesson 34 Review

See page 721

GRAMMAR

Enrichment

Activities

Use the **tips** on pages 2 and 26 to help you do this page.

A. The poem "Jabberwocky" by Lewis Carroll is filled with nonsensical words. See if you can name the parts of speech of the underlined words.

'Twas brillig (1), and the slithy (2) toves
Did gyre and gimble (3) in the wabe (4);
All mimsy (5) were the borogoves (6),
And (7) the mome (8) raths outgrabe.

1. ______________________
2. ______________________
3. ______________________
4. ______________________
5. ______________________
6. ______________________
7. ______________________
8. ______________________

B. Make at least five sentences from this word wheel. Begin with the word in the middle. Use one word from each ring. Each word you use must touch the word before and after it. One sentence is done for you.

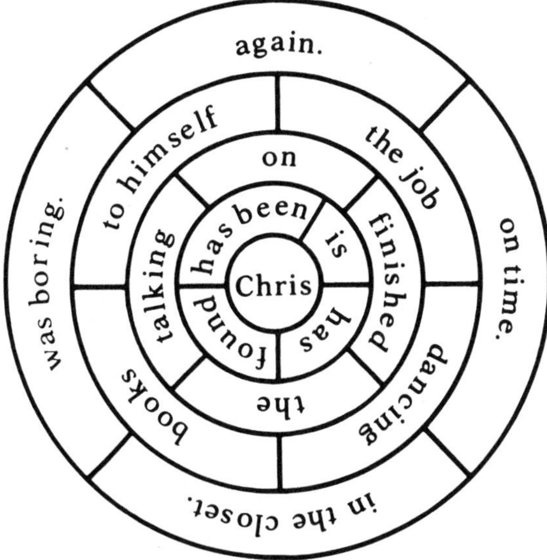

1. **Chris has finished the job on time.**
2. ______________________
3. ______________________
4. ______________________
5. ______________________

Answers on page 721

PRACTICING CAPITALIZATION and PUNCTUATION

by Burton Goodman

Steps for Practicing Capitalization and Punctuation

Note: Before you work on lessons 1 to 7, read the **Preview** on page 184. Before you work on lessons 8 to 20, read the **Preview** on page 198.

1. Turn to the lesson you are going to do.
2. Read the rule and the example at the top of the page.
3. Do the **Find** section of the lesson. Circle the letters of the sentences that are correct.
4. Do the **Fix** section of the lesson. Add capital letters or punctuation marks where they are needed.
5. Turn the page to the **Write** section. Write the words or sentences on the lines. Look back at the rules if you need to.
6. Now use the **Answer Key** to check your answers.
7. Count the number of correct answers. Fill in the number at the top of the lesson. Then turn to the **Progress Plotter** and shade it in to show how many items you answered correctly.
8. If you made any mistakes, go back and do the items again. Make sure you know how to do them.
9. After you have done *all* of the lessons in the book, read the **tips** contained on the **Preview** pages again. Now you are ready to take the **Final Test.**

Project Manager: *Marge M. Kennedy*

Text: Design and Production *Photo Plus Art, Inc.*

CAPITALIZATION AND PUNCTUATION

Table of Contents

CAPITALIZATION

Preview

Writers use capital letters to signal that they have begun a new sentence. They also use capital letters to signal that a word or phrase names a particular person, place, or thing. When you study **capitalization,** you learn to use the signals that good writers use.

Here are some tips to help you remember when to use capital letters:

1: Every sentence begins with a capital letter. Some sentences contain quotations. The sentence or sentence part within the quotation marks also begins with a capital letter.

The librarian said, "**H**ere is the card catalog."

2: Every word that names a particular person begins with a capital letter. The names of people include titles that are in front of a person's name and initials that stand for names. Do *not* capitalize titles that are not in front of names.

Reverend **J**. **H**arvard helped start the first library in America in 1648 when he gave 400 books to the president of a college.

3: Every word that names a particular place begins with a capital letter. The names of places include streets, cities, states, countries, continents, schools, parks, buildings, bodies of water, mountains, and monuments.

The school in **C**ambridge, **M**assachusetts, was renamed **H**arvard **U**niversity in his honor. The first national library, **T**he **L**ibrary of **C**ongress, was established in 1800.

4: Every word that names a particular thing begins with a capital letter. The names of things include days, months, holidays, events, eras, nationalities, languages, particular groups, and titles of written works. When you write titles, capitalize the *first, last,* and *all important* words. Do *not* capitalize other words in the titles.

It was burned down by the **B**ritish during the **W**ar of 1812 and was rebuilt in 1815. A copy of the **D**eclaration of **I**ndependence can be seen there.

LESSON 1

CAPITALIZATION

- The First Word in a Sentence
- The Word *I*

Number Right: ____

Begin the first word in a sentence with a capital letter.

Under a microscope, blood appears to be yellow.

Always capitalize the word *I*.

That is what **I** learned when **I** used a microscope.

In each group, circle the letter of the sentence that is capitalized correctly.

1. a. how does the skeleton protect the body?
   b. The brain is protected by the hard bones of the skull.
   c. the lungs and heart are shielded by the ribs.

2. a. I decided that i would enter the race.
   b. For months, i practiced every day.
   c. When I won, I was glad I'd worked so hard.

3. a. "How many elephants can you put in an empty cage?" I asked.
   b. My friend said, "i don't know."
   c. "Only one," i said, "because after that, the cage isn't empty."

4. a. In first-aid class, i learned how to help an accident victim.
   b. First, I was told, keep the person still.
   c. then, cover the victim with a blanket to keep him or her warm.

5. a. the white shark is a large, hungry animal.
   b. no matter how much it eats, it is never satisfied.
   c. It spends most of its time searching for food.

Fix the mistakes in these sentences. Cross out the small letters and write capital letters above them.

6. everything in nature is either in motion or at rest.

7. your feet contain one-fourth of the bones in your body.

8. i joined the chorus because i like to sing.

9. if i had three wishes, i'd wish for three more wishes.

10. what is the difference between a microscope and a telescope?

On the lines, write the sentences correctly. Be sure to begin each sentence with a capital letter and to capitalize the word *I*.

11. the center of an atom is called the nucleus.

____

12. since i started jogging, i feel great!

____

13. the color blue attracts mosquitoes.

____

14. in the last year, i've grown three inches.

____

15. water is an excellent conductor of electricity.

____

16. i'm so full that i think i'll skip dessert.

____

17. elephants sleep only two to three hours each night.

____

18. if i could meet any person in history, whom would i choose?

____

19. history repeats itself.

____

20. more than 15,000 people are bitten by deadly cobras each year.

____

LESSON

2

CAPITALIZATION

- Names, Initials, and Titles of People
- Days, Months, and Holidays

Number Right: ___

Capitalize the names, titles, and initials of people. Some last names need two capital letters. Do *not* capitalize titles that appear alone or after names.

In 1868, **G**eneral **U**lysses **S.** **G**rant became president.
In 1896, **P**resident **W**illiam **M**c**K**inley was elected.

Begin the names of days, months, and holidays with capital letters.

The first **T**uesday after the first **M**onday in **N**ovember is **E**lection **D**ay.

In each group, circle the letter of the sentence that is capitalized correctly.

1. a. When did general George Washington cross the Delaware?
   b. When did benedict arnold become a traitor?
   c. When did King George III, England's king, admit defeat?
2. a. Amelia Earhart made a solo flight across the Atlantic in 1932.
   b. In 1937, Ms. earhart attempted a round-the-world flight.
   c. She and fred Noonan, her navigator, disappeared over the Pacific.
3. a. The month of September is named for the Latin word for *seven.*
   b. The month of october is named for the Latin word that means *eight.*
   c. November and december are named for *nine* and *ten.*
4. a. Potato chips were invented by mr. George crum.
   b. A process for freezing food was invented by Mr. clarence birdseye.
   c. The shopping cart was invented by Mr. Sylvan N. Goldman.
5. a. The fourth thursday in November is Thanksgiving Day.
   b. The second Monday in October is Columbus Day.
   c. On July 4, Independence day is celebrated.

Fix the mistakes in these sentences. Cross out the small letters and write capital letters above them.

6. Name the discovery for which sir isaac newton is most famous.
7. One of the first movie stars was w. c. fields.
8. Federal holidays, such as new year's, are observed in every state.
9. From 1939 to 1975, justice william o. douglas served on the Supreme Court.
10. president wilson instituted mother's day as a national holiday.

On the lines below, write the words and initials that need capital letters. You do not have to write sentences. Be sure to add capital letters where they are needed.

11. The teddy bear was named after president theodore roosevelt.

____

12. England's queen victoria ruled from 1837 to 1901.

____

13. The first arbor day was celebrated on april 10, 1872.

____

14. mother's day and memorial day are both celebrated in may.

____

15. The leader of the Nez Percé Indians was chief joseph.

____

16. When will fire prevention week be observed this year?

____

17. president dwight d. eisenhower was known by the nickname ike.

____

18. ms. susan b. anthony was born on february 15, 1820.

____

19. Winter begins in december and ends in march.

____

20. mr. thomas a. edison, inventor of the phonograph, was partially deaf.

____

LESSON 3

CAPITALIZATION

- Particular Places
- Particular Events and Eras

Number Right: ____

Capitalize the names and abbreviations of particular places, such as streets, cities, states, countries, continents, planets, bodies of water, mountains, buildings, and monuments.

New Orleans	Switzerland	MacArthur Park
South Dakota	Saturn	Statue of Liberty

Capitalize the names of particular events and eras.

World War II	World Series	Iron Age
Battle of Bull Run	Olympic Games	Great Depression

In each group, circle the letter of the sentence that is capitalized correctly.

1. a. In Yosemite national park, there are giant redwood trees.
   b. Yellowstone National Park has geysers and hot springs.
   c. The colorado river flows through Grand canyon national Park.
2. a. The largest cities in Nebraska are omaha and Lincoln.
   b. The largest cities in new hampshire are Manchester and Nashua.
   c. Phoenix and Tucson are the largest cities in Arizona.
3. a. About 6,000 Americans died in battle during the revolutionary War.
   b. More than 50,000 Americans died in World War I.
   c. Nearly 300,000 Americans died in World war II.
4. a. The world series is played every year.
   b. The Kentucky derby is also an annual event.
   c. The Olympic Games are held every four years.
5. a. The capital of Belgium is Brussels.
   b. Copenhagen is the capital of denmark.
   c. The capital of India is new Delhi.

Fix the mistakes in these sentences. Cross out the small letters and write capital letters above them.

6. The pacific ocean is almost twice as large as the atlantic ocean.
7. Both the liberty bell and independence hall are in philadelphia.
8. During the ice age, the world was covered with ice.
9. The allegheny river flows into the ohio river.
10. stockholm, sweden, is nearly 10,000 miles from melbourne, australia.

On the lines, write the words that need capital letters. Be sure to capitalize the names of particular places and events.

11. Bricks were used in egypt 7,000 years ago.

____

12. The louisiana purchase was made in 1803.

____

13. The smallest continents are europe and australia.

____

14. The bronze age followed the stone age.

____

15. At the smithsonian institution in washington, d.c., you can see the Wright brothers' plane.

____

16. The united states bought alaska from russia for $7,200,000.

____

17. The largest lake in connecticut is candlewood lake.

____

18. The battle of gettysburg lasted three days.

____

19. How many presidents attended the united states military academy at west point?

____

20. During the great depression, thousands of people were out of work.

____

LESSON

4 CAPITALIZATION

- Nationalities and Languages
- Particular Groups

Number Right: ____

Capitalize the names of nationalities and languages.

Italian	**N**orse	**S**outh **A**merican

Capitalize the names of particular groups.

Boy **S**couts of **A**merica	**T**exans	**C**heyenne **I**ndian tribe
Whigs	**R**ed **S**ox	**C**onfederate soldiers
League of **N**ations	**Q**uakers	**B**olshoi **B**allet

In each group, circle the letter of the sentence that is capitalized correctly.

1. **a.** The spanish bayonet is a tree with sword-shaped leaves.
   b. The Chinese evergreen will grow in either water or soil.
   c. The japanese maple is a beautiful, fragile tree.
2. **a.** Leo Tolstoy, a russian author, wrote powerful novels.
   b. Georgia O'Keeffe, an American artist, is known for her paintings of flowers.
   c. Beethoven, a german composer, wrote symphonies.
3. **a.** Spanish explorers settled in south america.
   b. Therefore, in most latin american countries, people speak Spanish.
   c. In Brazil, however, the national language is Portuguese.
4. **a.** President Zachary Taylor was a member of the Whigs.
   b. President Ulysses S. Grant was a republican.
   c. President James Buchanan was a democrat.
5. **a.** The word *stadium* comes from the latin language.
   b. The word *umbrella* comes from the Italian language.
   c. The word *democracy* has its origin in the greek language.

Fix the mistakes in these sentences. Cross out the small letters and write capital letters above them.

6. In the Civil War, the confederate soldiers wore gray uniforms.
7. Fireworks are part of the chinese New Year celebration.
8. The store sells colombian, brazilian, and venezuelan coffees.
9. The two major american political parties are the democrats and the republicans.
10. The montreal canadiens are a canadian hockey team.

On the lines, write the names of nationalities, languages, and particular groups. Be sure to add capital letters where they are needed.

11. Yogurt was originally a turkish food.

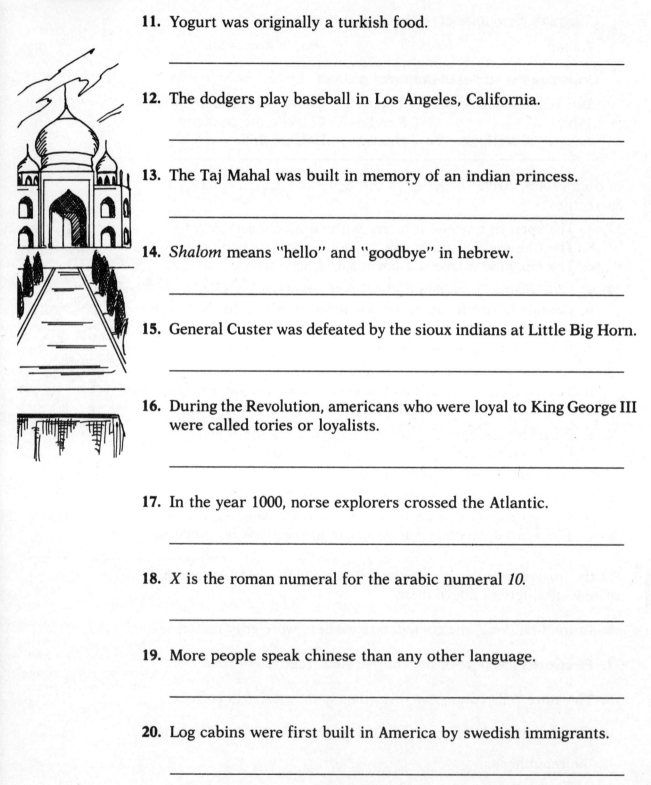

12. The dodgers play baseball in Los Angeles, California.

13. The Taj Mahal was built in memory of an indian princess.

14. *Shalom* means "hello" and "goodbye" in hebrew.

15. General Custer was defeated by the sioux indians at Little Big Horn.

16. During the Revolution, americans who were loyal to King George III were called tories or loyalists.

17. In the year 1000, norse explorers crossed the Atlantic.

18. *X* is the roman numeral for the arabic numeral *10*.

19. More people speak chinese than any other language.

20. Log cabins were first built in America by swedish immigrants.

LESSON

5

CAPITALIZATION

- Titles of Written Works
- Titles of Documents

Number Right: ___

Capitalize the *first, last,* and *all important words* in the titles of books, magazines, newspapers, movies, stories, poems, songs, television programs, reports, and documents.

A Tale** of **Two Cities
Declaration of **I**ndependence

Do *not* capitalize the word *magazine* unless it is part of the title.

***N**ewsweek* magazine

In each group, circle the letter of the title that is capitalized correctly.

1. a. *Giants in The Earth*
   b. *Giants In The Earth*
   c. *Giants in the Earth*

2. a. "The Ransom Of Red Chief"
   b. "The Ransom of Red Chief"
   c. "the Ransom of Red Chief"

3. a. *Sports Illustrated* magazine
   b. *Sports illustrated* magazine
   c. *sports illustrated* magazine

4. a. "The Ten O'Clock News"
   b. "The Ten o'clock News"
   c. "The ten o'clock news"

5. a. *The Miami herald*
   b. *The Miami Herald*
   c. *The miami Herald*

Fix the mistakes in these sentences. Cross out the small letters and write capital letters above them.

6. Did cowboys really sing "home on the range," or is that a modern song?

7. Amy wrote a report entitled "changing liquids to gas."

8. A lion named Elsa is the central character in the movie called *born free.*

9. Isn't "the night the bed fell" an amusing short story?

10. *the laziest man in the world* is a play about Benjamin Franklin.

On the lines, write the titles correctly. Be sure to begin the *first, last,* and *all important words* with capital letters.

11. Many people who jog read *runner's world* magazine.

____

12. Booker T. Washington's autobiography is called *up from slavery.*

____

13. "using the ocean for farming" was the title of Jill's report.

____

14. *star wars* has made more money than any other movie.

____

15. In *seventeen* magazine, you can read about fashions.

____

16. *the red badge of courage* is a novel about the Civil War.

____

17. *camelot* is a play that tells the story of King Arthur and Sir Lancelot.

____

18. *my side of the mountain* was a wonderful book.

____

19. The first crossword puzzle appeared in the *new york world* in 1913.

____

20. We call our class newspaper *the spectator.*

____

LESSON

6

CAPITALIZATION

First Word of a Direct Quotation

Number Right: ____

Begin the first word of a direct quotation with a capital letter.

William Shakespeare said, "**T**o thine own self be true."

In each pair, circle the letter of the sentence that is capitalized correctly.

1. **a.** Langston Hughes wrote, "hold fast to dreams."
   b. He concluded, "If dreams die, life is a broken-winged bird that cannot fly."

2. **a.** "Did you know that fish cough?" asked Harriet.
   b. Pat replied, "now I do!"

3. **a.** "Where are the canned beets?" asked the shopper.
   b. The clerk answered, "they're in the next aisle."

4. **a.** "What kind of animal can jump higher than a house?" asked Nelson.
   b. Meredith answered, "any animal can. Houses can't jump."

5. **a.** Benjamin Franklin said, "there are no gains without pains."
   b. He also said, "If a man could have half his wishes, he would double his troubles."

Fix the mistakes in these sentences. Cross out the small letters and write capital letters above them.

6. "what number do you want?" asked the telephone operator.

7. Henry David Thoreau said, "if a man does not keep pace with his companions, perhaps it is because he hears a different drummer."

8. Kathleen asked, "has anyone seen my new notebook?"

9. Franklin D. Roosevelt declared, "the only thing we have to fear is fear itself."

10. Speaking about women's rights, Abigail Adams warned, "we will not hold ourselves bound by any laws in which we have no voice."

On the lines, write the sentences correctly. Be sure to use capital letters to begin direct quotations.

11. Juliet told Romeo, "parting is such sweet sorrow."

____

12. "what is the Roman numeral for one hundred?" asked Carly.

____

13. The fans shouted, "we're number one!"

____

14. "how are you feeling today?" asked the nurse.

____

15. The coach stated, "the best defense is a good offense."

____

16. Thomas Edison said, "genius is one percent inspiration and ninety-nine percent perspiration."

____

17. The police officer asked, "did anyone witness the accident?"

____

18. "passengers, please move to the rear," requested the driver.

____

19. A wise person once said, "a stitch in time saves nine."

____

20. "a house divided against itself cannot stand," said Lincoln.

____

LESSON 7

CAPITALIZATION

Review

Review Score: ___

A. Fix the mistakes in these sentences. Cross out the small letters that should be capitals and write capital letters above them.

1. The aztec indian tribe once dominated mexico.
2. Their empire extended from the pacific ocean to the gulf of mexico.
3. The aztec capital was called tenochtitlan.
4. This city was on an island in lake texcoco.
5. In 1517, spaniards invaded mexico.
6. In february, 1519, an explorer named hernando cortes set out to invade the aztec city.
7. He reached tenochtitlan in november.
8. He took montezuma, the aztec emperor, as a hostage.
9. The aztecs revolted in june of 1520 and drove the spaniards out.
10. In may, 1921, cortes returned, and by august, he had destroyed the aztec city.

B. Find the mistakes in these sentences. Circle the words that should begin with capital letters.

11. Mountain climbing began as a sport in europe in the 1800s.
12. Since then, mountains in asia, africa, and the americas have been climbed.
13. One of the most famous climbers was sir edmund p. hillary of new zealand.
14. On may 29, 1953, he reached the peak of mount everest in the himalaya range.
15. The sierra club of north america leads many mountain-climbing expeditions today.

C. Write these sentences on a separate piece of paper. Use capital letters where they are needed.

16. edna st. vincent millay was an american poet.
17. She was born in rockland, maine, in 1892.
18. She was graduated from vassar college in 1917.
19. In 1920, she published a book entitled *a few figs from thistles.*
20. Another book, *conversations at midnight,* contains poems about world war II.

PUNCTUATION

Preview

Writers use punctuation marks to signal that they have ended a sentence. They also use punctuation marks to signal that a word, phrase, or sentence should be read in a certain way. When you study **punctuation**, you learn to use the signals that good writers use.

Here are some tips to remember about using punctuation marks:

1: Periods, question marks, and exclamation points are signals to *stop*. A semicolon may be used in place of a period when you write two closely related sentences. Periods are also used after abbreviations and initials.

Some people say that Mr. Abner Doubleday invented baseball; others say that the sport grew out of an old British game.

2: Commas are signals to *pause*. The following paragraph shows some of the uses of commas.

Historians agree, however, that Alexander Cartwright, a New York sportsman, wrote the first official rules and formed the first baseball club in 1845. On June 19, 1846, his team played in Hoboken, New Jersey, at Elysian Fields, but the other team won the game. Although today's rules resemble Cartwright's, baseball has changed.

3: Apostrophes are signals that letters have been left out of words or that words are being used to show ownership.

All of Cartwright's rules aren't followed today.

4: Quotation marks are signals that certain words are the exact words of a speaker. Quotation marks also signal that a title is the name of a short work. (To signal that a title names a long work, use an underline.)

Baseball umpires shout, "Strike three! You're out!"

One chapter in <u>The History of Baseball</u> is called "The Babe Ruth Era."

5: A colon signals that a list, an exact time, or a business letter is about to follow:

These positions are held by players: pitchers, catchers, basemen, and fielders.

3:15 A.M. Dear Mr. Seaver:

LESSON

8

PUNCTUATION

Number
Right: ____

End Marks

Put a period (.) at the end of a sentence that tells something or that gives a command.

Salmon can swim upstream.
Tell me why they make their long journey.

Put a question mark (?) at the end of a sentence that asks a question.

Why do salmon swim against the current?
They return to their birthplace, don't they?

Put an exclamation point (!) at the end of a word, phrase, or sentence that shows surprise or strong feeling. Use an exclamation point when you write a command that shows strong feeling.

Wow! That must be difficult!
Imagine swimming *up* a waterfall!

In each pair, circle the letter of the sentence that has the correct end mark.

1. **a.** Congress passes laws.
   b. Which branch of the government interprets the laws.
2. **a.** What is unusual about the way frogs breathe?
   b. Frogs can breathe through both their skin and their lungs?
3. **a.** Are there ways to purify sea water?
   b. Scientists have been working on this problem for years?
4. **a.** Can a snake look like a stick!
   b. Watch out for that snake!
5. **a.** Which sense develops first in human beings.
   b. The sense of smell is the first sense to develop.

Fix the mistakes in these sentences. Add the correct end marks.

6. Chicago is an important transportation center, isn't it
7. On your mark, get set, go
8. Owls can see as well in the daytime as they can at night
9. When did the Battle of Gettysburg take place
10. Plants that lived thousands of years ago have turned into fossil fuel

On the lines, write the sentences correctly. Be sure to include the right end marks.

11. Blood is six times heavier than water

____

12. The sunflower is the state flower of Kansas

____

13. That's truly amazing

____

14. Why is freedom of speech important to a democracy

____

15. It is impossible to rhyme the word *orange* with any other English word

____

16. Hurry, or we'll be late

____

17. Air pollution and water pollution are problems in our society

____

18. What are the main exports of Japan

____

19. Hooray Our track team finished first

____

20. Which part of a newspaper presents opinions

____

LESSON

9

PUNCTUATION

Periods in Abbreviations and Initials

Number Right: ___

Put a period after the abbreviation of a person's title and after an initial.

Mr. Rudolph C. K. Diesel invented the diesel engine.

Use periods when you write the time of day.

A.M. (*ante meridiem*) P.M. (*post meridiem*)

Put a period after the abbreviation of an address or a company name in the heading of a letter or on an envelope. Do *not* use periods after the two-letter abbreviations of states.

Atlas Painting Corp. 14-01 7th Ave. St. Louis, MO	Park Products, Inc. 13 W. Sommers St. Cheyenne, WY

In each pair, circle the letter of the sentence or address that is punctuated correctly.

1. a. Abraham Lincoln debated Stephen A Douglas in 1858.
   b. In 1860, Lincoln ran against Mr. Douglas and Mr. John C. Breckinridge.
2. a. Samson Auto Wreckers, Inc
   b. Dean's Glass and Mirror Co.
3. a. In 1909, Robert E Peary reached the North Pole.
   b. Two years later, Mr. Roald Amundsen explored the South Pole.
4. a. 22 Old Country Rd
   b. 85 Market Pl.
5. a. Elizabeth C. Stanton was a pioneer for women's rights.
   b. Another well-known suffragette was Ms. Lucretia C Mott.

Fix the mistakes in these sentences and addresses. Add periods where they are needed.

6. Dr Martin Luther King, Jr , was born in Atlanta, Georgia.
7. The first woman to serve in Congress was Ms Jeannette Rankin.
8. Lawrence Business Machines, Inc
73 Horatio St
St Louis, MO
9. If you work from 9:00 A M to 5:00 P M on weekdays, how many hours do you work each week?
10. Mr P T Barnum founded the three-ring circus in 1871.

On the lines, write the titles, initials, times, and address abbreviations correctly. Be sure to use periods after each abbreviation.

11. Mr Elisha G Otis invented the passenger elevator.

____

12. Morse code was named for its inventor, Samuel F B Morse.

____

13. Rapid Cleaners, Inc ______________________________

14-91 W Marcy Pl ______________________________

St Paul, MN ______________________________

14. Ms Victoria C Woodhull ran for president in 1872.

____

15. At 4:30 P M, the basketball game will begin.

____

16. Mr C W Post invented a breakfast cereal made of corn flakes.

____

17. Rafael Roofing Co ______________________________

99 Fourth Ave ______________________________

Mt Adams, NH ______________________________

18. "Generally, privates awaken at 6:00 A M," said the sergeant.

____

19. Mary E Walker was a surgeon during the Civil War.

____

20. Quick Copy Printing Corp ______________________________

135-01 N Central Blvd ______________________________

St Petersburg, FL ______________________________

LESSON

10 PUNCTUATION

- Commas in Dates
- Commas in Place Names

Number Right: ____

When you write dates and addresses, separate every item with a comma.

On December 17, 1903, the Wright brothers made history.

In Kitty Hawk, North Carolina, they flew their plane a distance of 120 feet.

In each group, circle the letter of the sentence that is punctuated correctly.

1. a. The Battle of Bunker Hill took place on June 17, 1775.
   b. The Battle of Lexington was fought on April 19 1775.
   c. April 19, 1775 is also the date of the Battle of Concord.

2. a. A 1,200-pound pizza was baked in Little Rock Arkansas.
   b. A 440-pound beefburger was made at Blackpond, England.
   c. An 8,100-pound ice-cream sundae was made in Northampton Massachusetts.

3. a. Maine entered the Union on March 15 1820.
   b. On March 3 1845, Florida entered the Union.
   c. On August 21, 1959, Hawaii became the fiftieth state.

4. a. Athens Greece is 671 miles from Cairo Egypt.
   b. It is nearly 1,000 miles from Lisbon, Portugal to London England.
   c. How far is it from Mobile, Alabama, to Denver, Colorado?

5. a. When it is noon in Jacksonville, Florida, it's 9:00 A.M. in San Diego, California.
   b. When it is noon in Pueblo, Colorado, it's 2:00 P.M. in Newark New Jersey.
   c. When it is noon in Baltimore, Maryland it's 11:00 A.M. in St. Louis, Missouri.

Fix the mistakes in these sentences. Add commas where they are needed.

6. On September 1 1923 an earthquake took 100,000 lives in Tokyo Japan.

7. Babe Ruth's last home run was on May 25 1935 in Pittsburgh Pennsylvania.

8. Louisa May Alcott was born on November 29 1832 in Germantown Pennsylvania.

9. On July 7 1905 the temperature in Parker Arizona was 127 degrees.

10. Napoleon was defeated at Waterloo on June 18 1815.

On the lines, write the sentences correctly. Be sure to use commas when you write dates and places.

11. Paris France is known as "The City of Light."

12. The "unsinkable" *Titanic* sank on April 15 1912.

13. On July 20 1969 an astronaut first set foot on the moon.

14. The longitude of Reno Nevada is 120 degrees.

15. General Lee surrendered to General Grant at Appomattox Virginia

16. Butte Montana is 5,765 feet above sea level.

17. President Kennedy was born on May 29 1917 in Brookline Massachusetts.

18. The Astrodome is in Houston Texas.

19. Death Valley California is the lowest point in the United States.

20. The Boston Tea Party took place on December 16 1773 in Boston Massachusetts.

LESSON 11

PUNCTUATION

Commas in a Series

Number Right: ____

Use commas to separate three or more items in a series.

Salt is found in mines, oceans, and in the Great Salt Lake.

In each group, circle the letter of the sentence that is punctuated correctly.

1. a. The planets closest to the sun are Mercury, Venus Earth and Mars.
   b. Mercury has a thick, white, cloudy atmosphere.
   c. Mars appears to be covered with rock sand, and soil.

2. a. Willie Mays played baseball with skill grace, and energy.
   b. He was an outstanding hitter fielder and base runner.
   c. He led his league in home runs in 1955, 1962, 1964, and 1965.

3. a. In science, we learned about elements compounds, and mixtures.
   b. Oxygen, hydrogen, iron, and sulfur are elements.
   c. Water salt, and carbon dioxide are compounds.

4. a. A newspaper contains news, advertisements, and editorials.
   b. There are also articles about sports, education theater, and movies.
   c. A good news story tells *who, what, when where* and *why.*

5. a. Three kinds of clouds are *stratus, cumulus,* and *cirrus.*
   b. Stratus clouds are long smooth and low.
   c. Cirrus clouds are thin wispy, and high.

Fix the mistakes in these sentences. Add commas where they are needed.

6. You need talent drive and luck to succeed in the theater.

7. The main ingredients in mayonnaise are oil vinegar and egg yolk.

8. The heart lungs stomach and skin are organs of the body.

9. The doctor said, "Drink liquids take aspirin and get plenty of rest."

10. Ounces pounds tons grams and milligrams are units of measure.

On the lines, write the sentences correctly. Be sure to use commas to separate items in a series.

11. Books may be classified by title subject or author.

12. Green plants produce sugar starch and oxygen.

13. Frogs toads and salamanders are all amphibians.

14. The compass points are North South East and West.

15. Corn wheat and soybeans are major products of Illinois.

16. Squirrels eat berries nuts insects and plants.

17. The Painted Desert the Petrified Forest and London Bridge are in Arizona.

18. Do you like chess checkers or bingo?

19. The colors in a rainbow are red orange yellow green blue indigo and violet.

20. The storm snarled traffic caused flooding and produced delays.

LESSON 12

PUNCTUATION

- Commas in Direct Address
- Commas in Apposition
- Commas after *Yes* and *No*

Number Right: ____

Use a comma to set off a name in direct address.

What is Mark Twain's real name, Jeremy?

Use commas to set off a word or a group of words that has the same meaning as other words in a sentence *only if* the words are not essential to the meaning of the sentence.

Mark Twain, an American author, was named Samuel Clemens.

The American author Mark Twain was named Samuel Clemens.

Use commas after the *yes* and *no* in a sentence.

Yes, Twain wrote *The Adventures of Tom Sawyer.*

In each group, circle the letter of the sentence that is punctuated correctly.

1. **a.** Florida, a sunny state, has a 1,350-mile coastline.
b. Alaska, the largest state gets the least sunshine.
c. Rhode Island the smallest state is not really an island.

2. **a.** Marco Polo, an Italian explorer traveled to China.
b. The Spanish explorer Ponce de Leon traveled to Puerto Rico.
c. Henry Hudson an English sailor, explored parts of North America.

3. **a.** Ellen who invented boxing gloves?
b. Boxing gloves were invented by Jack Broughton, Robert.
c. Ellen you're right.

4. **a.** Gerald Ford, a lawyer became the thirty-eighth president.
b. James Carter, a peanut farmer, became the thirty-ninth president.
c. Ronald Reagan, a Hollywood star became the fortieth president.

5. **a.** Yes I was happy with my report card.
b. No I didn't fail any subjects.
c. Yes, it was the best report card I'd ever received.

Fix the mistakes in these sentences. Add commas where they are needed.

6. Opossums furry mammals play dead when they're afraid.

7. Did you finish your science project Kevin?

8. Enamel the material on the surface of teeth is very hard.

9. Justine will you be at the library this afternoon?

10. Yes a senator serves a six-year term.

On the lines, write the sentences correctly. Be sure to add commas where they are needed.

11. The dodo an awkward bird is extinct.

____

12. Yes the square root of 64 is 8.

____

13. Bill have you seen my baseball glove?

____

14. Hydrogen a gas is colorless and odorless.

____

15. What score did you bowl yesterday Valerie?

____

16. The largest planet Jupiter has at least fourteen moons.

____

17. No I can't stay for the rehearsal today Luis.

____

18. Coal decayed plant material is used for fuel.

____

19. Theresa let's go to the museum tonight.

____

20. Buck Rogers a fictional character travels through time and space.

____

LESSON

13

PUNCTUATION

- Commas in Transitional Expressions
- Commas with the Word *Too*

Number Right: ____

Use commas to set off words and phrases such as *however, therefore, nevertheless, for example, of course, on the contrary, in general,* and *in fact.*

> Of course, every football team hopes to play in the Super Bowl.
> Only two teams, however, can compete.

Use commas to set off the word *too* when it means *also.*

> Fans, too, hope their team will participate.

In each group, circle the letter of the sentence that is punctuated correctly.

1. **a.** Generally speaking most people do not think highly of pigs.
b. Pigs however, are very intelligent animals.
c. Of course, not many people have a pig as a pet.

2. **a.** Reading, of course, can help you find information.
b. However, reading can be entertaining too.
c. Therefore it is important to be able to read well.

3. **a.** Christopher Columbus in fact was an Italian explorer.
b. He sailed under the Spanish flag, however.
c. Therefore he claimed the New World for Spain.

4. **a.** I too, like country music.
b. However, I enjoy listening to rock music, too.
c. In fact I enjoy all kinds of music.

5. **a.** Ants as you know are very powerful for their size.
b. In fact an ant can pull a load fifty times its weight.
c. Ants are very industrious, too.

Fix the mistakes in these sentences. Add commas where they are needed.

6. The airplane of course has made the world smaller too.

7. It is important therefore that you write to your senator.

8. We too agreed with the decision.

9. On the contrary cities have grown in population.

10. However much water is stored in cactus plants.

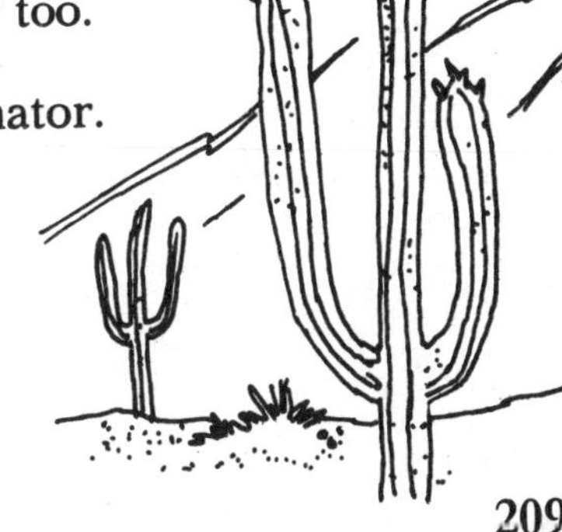

On the lines, write the sentences correctly. Be sure to add commas where they are needed.

11. In fact we were surprised when we won second place.

____

12. Benjamin Franklin for example was an inventor too.

____

13. Of course whales must breathe air above water.

____

14. It is necessary therefore to conserve our natural resources.

____

15. Are you going to the concert too?

____

16. In general I agree with your point of view.

____

17. Coffee however is America's most popular drink.

____

18. Nevertheless rain is necessary.

____

19. They too will support our candidate.

____

20. Therefore it is possible to send satellites into space.

____

LESSON 14

PUNCTUATION

- Commas in Compound Sentences
- Commas in Complex Sentences
- Commas after Introductory Phrases

Number Right: ____

Use a comma before the words *and, but,* and *or* to separate the main clauses in a compound sentence.

An insect has six legs, and a spider has eight legs.
Spiders weave webs, but insects do not.

Use a comma to separate phrases and clauses to make the meaning of a sentence clear.

After eating, insects rest.
After they eat insects, spiders rest.

In each pair, circle the letter of the sentence that is punctuated correctly.

1. **a.** Before striking a rattlesnake, twists itself into a coil.
   b. Before striking, a rattlesnake makes a warning sound.
2. **a.** Milk contains many vitamins, and minerals but it has no vitamin C.
   b. Milk is used to make butter and cheese, but corn oil is used to make margarine.
3. **a.** Congress passes laws, and the president has the power to veto them.
   b. The president can veto a bill and Congress can overrule his veto.
4. **a.** As the lights began to dim, the audience grew quiet.
   b. As the curtain rose the audience, applauded.
5. **a.** When volcanoes erupt lava, and ash spill from the earth's core.
   b. When earthquakes occur, the earth's crust cracks.

Fix the mistakes in these sentences. Add commas where they are needed.

6. When the moon hides the sun it is called a *solar eclipse.*
7. You can lead a horse to water but you cannot make it drink.
8. Before you strum your guitar must be properly tuned.
9. The coach sent in the players and the quarterback called the signals.
10. We will see the Grand Canyon or we may go to Yellowstone National Park.

On the lines, write the sentences correctly. Be sure to add commas where they are needed.

11. After swallowing the bird looked around for more crumbs.

___

12. The puppeteer pulled a string and the tiny clown jumped.

___

13. Although we decided to return the park was closed.

___

14. When the power failed the city grew dark.

___

15. If we pollute our rivers the fish will die.

___

16. The largest planet is Jupiter and Mercury is the smallest planet.

___

17. The locusts ate the entire crop and the farmer was unable to stop them.

___

18. Rats are related to mice but rats are larger and more dangerous.

___

19. Are there any tickets left or have they all been sold?

___

20. Green is a mixture of yellow and blue and orange is a mixture of yellow and red.

___

LESSON 15

PUNCTUATION

Apostrophes in Contractions
Apostrophes to Show Possession

Number Right: ____

Use an apostrophe (') when you write a contraction.

It isn't always easy to find a job after school.

Use an apostrophe and *s* to show possession.

A student**'s** time for work is limited.

When a word that means *more than one* ends in *s*, use only an apostrophe. When a proper noun ends in *s*, use an apostrophe and *s*.

Most boys' and girls' jobs are part-time.

Agnes**'s** job begins at 4:30 P.M.

In each group, circle the letter of the sentence that is punctuated correctly.

1. **a.** A giraffe's long neck contains only seven bones.
b. A giraffes' heart may weigh as much as twenty-five pounds.
c. A giraffes legs may be six feet long.

2. **a.** Its not the size of the dog in the fight that counts.
b. Its' the size of the fight in the dog.
c. In other words, it's more important to be brave than it is to be big.

3. **a.** James's brother borrowed Bess's hammer.
b. Besses sister borrowed James' saw.
c. Who has Bess's hammer and James saw?

4. **a.** If youre leaving, don't forget to lock the door.
b. If you're staying, don't lock the door.
c. If youre going to come home late, dont forget to call.

5. **a.** Frog's babies are called *tadpoles.*
b. A frogs' tongue is long and sticky.
c. Frogs' legs are muscular and powerful.

Fix the mistakes in these sentences. Add apostrophes where they are needed. Add *s* where needed, too.

6. Insects cant close their eyes because they dont have eyelids.

7. A babys skeleton has more bones than an adults.

8. Im surprised that you werent at Michaels party.

9. Columbus ships traveled at a rate of about three miles per hour.

10. If you didnt have muscles, you wouldnt be able to move.

On the lines, write the contractions or words that show possession. Be sure to use apostrophes and to add *s* where needed.

11. About 97 percent of the worlds water is saltwater.

____

12. Dont you think well finish on time?

____

13. Its true that an elephants body is covered with hair.

____

14. Dont count your chickens before theyre hatched.

____

15. The average adults brain weighs three pounds.

____

16. It hasnt rained since last months hurricane.

____

17. Hes a wolf dressed in sheeps clothing!

____

18. Arent those Thomas friends in the car?

____

19. Anne Franks diary wasnt discovered until after the war.

____

20. Our dogs bite is worse than its bark.

____

LESSON 16

PUNCTUATION

- Quotation Marks with Direct Quotations
- Commas and End Marks with Quotations

Number Right: ___

Put quotation marks (" ") around the exact words of a speaker. When a quote comes at the beginning of a sentence, put a comma or an end mark *before* the second quotation mark. When a quote comes at the end of a sentence, use a comma to introduce the quotation, and put the quotation mark *after* the end marks.

"When things go wrong, what can you always count on?" asked Gene.
Debbie answered, "Your fingers."

In each pair, circle the letter of the sentence that is punctuated correctly.

1. a. Patrick Henry stated, "I am not a Virginian, but an American.
   b. Thomas Paine said, "The harder the conflict, the more glorious the triumph."
2. a. What does the word *hula* mean in Hawaiian? asked Janet.
   b. "The word *hula* means *dancing*," answered Lisa.
3. a. "I object!" the lawyer shouted firmly.
   b. "Objection sustained! replied the judge.
4. a. "Is Miami the capital of Florida?" asked Joanie.
   b. No, the capital of Florida is Tallahassee, said Craig.
5. a. "Why does a dog wag its tail?" joked Sue Ann.
   b. Because no one else will do it! answered Dennis.

Fix the mistakes in these sentences. Add punctuation marks where they are needed.

6. Helen Keller said I learned from life itself.
7. A Chinese proverb states One picture is worth more than ten thousand words.
8. I hope I can make the team said the player.
9. Dr. Martin Luther King, Jr., exclaimed I have been to the mountaintop!
10. Mrs. Melendez said A thundercloud contains about 100,000 tons of water.

On the lines, write the sentences correctly. Be sure to put quotation marks around the exact words of the speaker. Use commas and end marks where they are needed.

11. As he rode through Boston, Paul Revere announced The British are coming!

____

12. Did you know that honeybees are deaf asked Roger.

____

13. If the shoe fits, wear it said the salesperson.

____

14. The druggist said Shake the medicine well before using it.

____

15. I'm late exclaimed the White Rabbit.

____

16. Sandy asked Why does it always rain on holidays?

____

17. We're counting on you the manager told the pitcher.

____

18. The waiter said Your food will be here shortly.

____

19. No country has more earthquakes than Japan stated Terry.

____

20. Stone walls do not a prison make, said the poet.

____

LESSON 17

PUNCTUATION

Titles of Written Works

Number Right: ____

Underline the titles of books, magazines, newspapers, plays, and movies. (An underline takes the place of *italics*.)

Johnny Tremain is a novel about the Revolutionary War.

Do *not* underline the word *magazine* unless it is a part of the title.

National Geographic magazine tells about many nations.

Put quotation marks around the titles of stories, poems, songs, reports, and television shows.

"Oh Captain! My Captain!" is a poem by Walt Whitman.

In each group, circle the letter of the title that is written correctly.

1. a. The Gift of the Magi is probably O. Henry's best-known short story.
   b. Another familiar O. Henry story is "After Twenty Years."
   c. More O. Henry stories are in the book entitled "The Four Million."
2. a. "Watchdog" is an amusing poem by Richard Armour.
   b. Ogden Nash's poem The Duck is also humorous.
   c. "The Spider," a poem by Robert Coffin, is serious, however.
3. a. "TV Guide" magazine offers television listings.
   b. "Popular Mechanics" magazine contains articles about machinery.
   c. Field & Stream magazine deals with outdoor life.
4. a. John Donne wrote a poem called "Death Be Not Proud."
   b. John Gunther wrote a novel named "Death Be Not Proud."
   c. The movie "Death Be Not Proud" was based on Gunther's book.
5. a. My uncle is a reporter for the Boston Globe.
   b. He used to work for the Chicago Tribune.
   c. He also has many friends on "The Detroit Free Press."

Fix the mistakes in these sentences. Add underlines and quotation marks where they are needed.

6. José's report was entitled Solutions to Traffic Problems.
7. The Open Window, a short story by Saki, has a surpise ending.
8. The movie King Kong was first made in 1933.
9. Every evening, my family watches The Seven O'Clock News.
10. The Drama Club's next play will be Peter Pan.

On the lines, write the titles correctly. Be sure to use underlines or quotation marks where they are needed.

Books, Movies, Plays, Magazines, and Newspapers

11. White Fang

____

12. 2001: A Space Odyssey

____

13. Fiddler on the Roof

____

14. Popular Science

____

15. Los Angeles Times

____

Poems, Stories, Television Shows, Reports, and Songs

16. Old Ironsides

____

17. The Necklace

____

18. Monday Night Football

____

19. Ways of Using Solar Energy

____

20. Oh, Susanna!

____

LESSON

18

PUNCTUATION

- Colon to Introduce a List
- Colon in Time of Day
- Semicolon between Sentences

Number Right: ____

Use a colon (:) to introduce a list.

Tornadoes occur in these states: Kansas, Iowa, Texas, and Oklahoma.

Use a colon between the hour and the minute when you write the time of day.

Most tornadoes occur between 7:00 A.M. and 12:00 P.M.

Use a semicolon (;) to connect sentences that are closely related.

Tornadoes are violent windstorms; they occur on land.

In each pair, circle the letter of the sentence that is punctuated correctly.

1. **a.** These countries are in Asia; China, Korea, Japan, and India.
b. The following are also in Asia: Burma, Cambodia, and Thailand.

2. **a.** A young person has twenty-eight teeth: an adult has thirty-two.
b. Help prevent tooth decay; brush frequently.

3. **a.** The factory doors open at 8 00 A.M.
b. At 4:30 P.M., the workday ends.

4. **a.** Mammals are warm-blooded: reptiles are cold-blooded.
b. These animals are reptiles: alligators, lizards, snakes, and turtles.

5. **a.** California is bordered on the north by Oregon; to the south is Mexico.
b. The Pacific is to the west of California: Nevada and Oregon are to the east.

Fix the mistakes in these sentences. Add punctuation marks where they are needed.

6. The human body performs these functions automatically swallowing, breathing, and digesting.

7. The most common American last name is *Smith* next comes *Johnson.*

8. It is possible to classify flavors as follows sweet, sour, bitter, and salty.

9. Suddenly, dark clouds appeared it began to rain.

10. Benjamin Franklin was the following statesman, scientist, writer, and inventor.

On the lines, write the sentences correctly. Be sure to use colons and semicolons where they are needed.

11. James Madison was the shortest president President Lincoln was the tallest.

____

12. The experiment required the following sand, gravel, chalk, and water.

____

13. Many people do not accept criticism some do.

____

14. It's exactly 7 00 P.M. it's time to go.

____

15. The hummingbird is an amazing bird it can fly backward.

____

16. The following are metric weights grams, milligrams, and kilograms.

____

17. Suddenly there was a loud crash everyone jumped.

____

18. These are some kinds of dogs poodles, collies, and terriers.

____

19. Dreaming is essential to good health everyone dreams.

____

20. Here are some favorite American writers Mark Twain, Edgar Allan Poe, and Emily Dickinson.

____

LESSON 19

PUNCTUATION

- Friendly Letters
- Business Letters

Number Right: ____

Use a comma after the greeting of a friendly letter.

Dear Dale, Dear Uncle Frank, Dear Dad,

Use a colon after the greeting of a business letter.

Dear Sirs: Dear Mrs. Oliver: To Whom It May Concern:

Use a comma after the closing of any letter.

Very truly yours, Love, Your student,

In each group, circle the letter of the greeting or closing that is punctuated correctly.

1. a. Dear Marty;
   b. Dear Mollie.
   c. Dear Yvonne,

2. a. Sincerely yours.
   b. Your friend,
   c. Respectfully yours:

3. a. Dear Mom,
   b. Dear Dad:
   c. Dear Uncle Josh.

4. a. Dear Dr. Rivera.
   b. Dear Mrs. Carr:
   c. Dear Mr. Lyle;

5. a. Your pal
   b. Affectionately:
   c. Your neighbor,

January 8, 199__
Dear Marco,
Thanks for

Fix the greetings and closings below. Add commas or colons where they are needed.

6. Dear Aunt Veronica

7. Your friend

8. Dear Senator Curtis

9. Very truly yours

10. To Whom It May Concern

On the right-hand side of the page, complete the letters. Be sure to use commas and colons where they are needed.

11. Dear Maria
I can hardly wait to see you in February. Don't forget to bring warm clothing.
12. Your pen pal
Nancy

____
I can hardly wait to see you in February. Don't forget to bring warm clothing.
____
Nancy

13. Dear Mrs. Rowens
Thank you for letting our class visit your office. We had a wonderful time.
14. Sincerely
Lee Thomas

____
Thank you for letting our class visit your office. We had a wonderful time.
____
Lee Thomas

15. To the Editor
I strongly agree with your editorial about the summer playground program. More attention must be paid to this city's parks.
16. Sincerely yours
Dave Reiss

____
I strongly agree with your editorial about the summer playground program. More attention must be paid to this city's parks.
____
Dave Reiss

17. Dear Customer Relations Manager
I am returning the enclosed book. Pages 29–36 are missing. Please send me another copy.
18. Yours truly
Theresa Gavros

____
I am returning the enclosed book. Pages 29–36 are missing. Please send me another copy.
____
Theresa Gavros

19. Dear Mom
I'm visiting Cindy after class. I will be home for dinner.
20. Love
Teddy

____
I'm visiting Cindy after class. I will be home for dinner.
____
Teddy

LESSON 20 — PUNCTUATION

Review

Review Score: ___

A. Put end marks where they are needed.

1. Ducks have webbed feet, don't they ___
2. Loons also have webbed feet ___
3. Look ___ What a beautiful loon ___

B. Put punctuation marks where they are needed in this name and address.

4. Mr P D Ferndale
5. 9 E Forest Ave
6. Chicago IL

C. Put punctuation marks where they are needed in this letter.

7. April 16 1985
8. Dear Mr Ferndale
9. Enclosed is my check for two tickets to the 8 30 P M Pink Mink concert.
10. Yours truly

Carol Anderson

D. Put punctuation marks where they are needed in these sentences.

11. The Liberty Bell Americas most famous bell is in Philadelphia Pennsylvania.
12. On July 8 1776 it rang for the first time and it was rung every July 8 until 1835.
13. As it rang the bell cracked.
14. The crack hasnt ever been repaired.
15. However the bell has been struck on a few special occasions since.
16. The inscription on it says Proclaim liberty throughout the land unto all the inhabitants thereof.
17. It has been known by these three names the Old State House Bell the Bell of the Revolution and Old Independence.
18. In fact it wasnt called the Liberty Bell until 1839.
19. The bell is made of iron copper and tin.
20. Kevin have you read The Liberty Bell a book about this bell?

Name ______________________________ Progress Plotter 

Number Right	Lesson 1	Lesson 2	Lesson 3	Lesson 4	Lesson 5	Lesson 6	Lesson 7	Lesson 8	Lesson 9	Lesson 10	Lesson 11	Lesson 12	Lesson 13	Lesson 14	Lesson 15	Lesson 16	Lesson 17	Lesson 18	Lesson 19	Lesson 20	Number Right
20							Review Score: ____ CAPITALIZATION													Review Score: ____ PUNCTUATION	20
19																					19
18																					18
17																					17
16																					16
15																					15
14																					14
13																					13
12																					12
11																					11
10																					10
9																					9
8																					8
7																					7
6																					6
5																					5
4																					4
3																					3
2																					2
1																					1
	CAPITALIZATION							PUNCTUATION													

CAPITALIZATION AND PUNCTUATION

Final Test Name ______________________

Directions: Read each sentence. Decide which word in the sentence should be capitalized. Fill in the letter for your answer in the answer row. If no word should be capitalized, fill in the letter for the choice marked *None.*

1 A doctor used the first artificial heart in 1969. *None*
Ⓐ Ⓑ Ⓒ Ⓓ

2 "I have a dream," said dr. Martin Luther King, Jr. *None*
Ⓔ Ⓕ Ⓖ Ⓗ

3 The british word for *apartment* is *flat*. *None*
Ⓐ Ⓑ Ⓒ Ⓓ

4 *The red Pony* is a novel by John Steinbeck. *None*
Ⓔ Ⓕ Ⓖ Ⓗ

5 Paul Revere said, "one if by land; two if by sea." *None*
Ⓐ Ⓑ Ⓒ Ⓓ

6 The tallest waterfall on earth is Angel falls in Venezuela. *None*
Ⓔ Ⓕ Ⓖ Ⓗ

7 Pioneer day is a legal holiday in Utah. *None*
Ⓐ Ⓑ Ⓒ Ⓓ

8 During New England autumns, maple leaves turn red. *None*
Ⓔ Ⓕ Ⓖ Ⓗ

9 Snoopy often does battle with the Red baron. *None*
Ⓐ Ⓑ Ⓒ Ⓓ

10 The Olympic games are played every four years. *None*
Ⓔ Ⓕ Ⓖ Ⓗ

(Go on to the next page.)

ANSWER ROWS:

1 Ⓐ Ⓑ Ⓒ Ⓓ 2 Ⓔ Ⓕ Ⓖ Ⓗ 3 Ⓐ Ⓑ Ⓒ Ⓓ 4 Ⓔ Ⓕ Ⓖ Ⓗ 5 Ⓐ Ⓑ Ⓒ Ⓓ

6 Ⓔ Ⓕ Ⓖ Ⓗ 7 Ⓐ Ⓑ Ⓒ Ⓓ 8 Ⓔ Ⓕ Ⓖ Ⓗ 9 Ⓐ Ⓑ Ⓒ Ⓓ 10 Ⓔ Ⓕ Ⓖ Ⓗ

Directions: Read each sentence. Look at the underlined part. If the part does not have the correct punctuation, choose the answer that shows the correct punctuation and fill in the letter of your choice in the answer row. If there are no errors, fill in the letter for the choice marked *Correct*.

11 On April 14 1894 the first motion picture was shown.

Ⓐ April 14, 1894
Ⓑ April 14 1894,
Ⓒ April 14, 1894,
Ⓓ *Correct*

12 A Northerner wrote the Southern Civil War song *Dixie.*

Ⓔ "Dixie." Ⓖ Dixie.
Ⓕ "*Dixie*." Ⓗ *Correct*

13 Jesse Owens an Olympic track star won a race against a horse.

Ⓐ Owens an Olympic track star, won
Ⓑ Owens, an Olympic track star, won
Ⓒ Owens, an Olympic track star won
Ⓓ *Correct*

14 After eating a baby usually naps.

Ⓔ eating, a baby
Ⓕ eating a, baby
Ⓖ eating a baby,
Ⓗ *Correct*

15 Detroit Michigan was occupied by the British during the War of 1812.

Ⓐ Detroit, Michigan,
Ⓑ Detroit, Michigan
Ⓒ Detroit Michigan,
Ⓓ *Correct*

16 These three birds cant fly penguins, ostriches, and emus.

Ⓔ can't fly, Ⓖ cant fly:
Ⓕ can't fly: Ⓗ *Correct*

17 A great Russian writer said The world will be saved by beauty.

Ⓐ said, "The world will be saved by beauty."
Ⓑ said, "The world will be saved by beauty".
Ⓒ said "The world will be saved by beauty."
Ⓓ *Correct*

18 Citizens have a right to vote they also have an obligation to vote.

Ⓔ vote, they Ⓖ vote: they
Ⓕ vote; they Ⓗ *Correct*

19 Generally speaking, most people prefer daylight to darkness.

Ⓐ speaking most
Ⓑ speaking most,
Ⓒ speaking; most
Ⓓ *Correct*

20 When it is 8 15 P M in New York, what time is it in California?

Ⓔ 8:15 P M Ⓖ 8:15 P.M.
Ⓕ 815 P.M. Ⓗ *Correct*

STOP

Final Test Score: ______

ANSWER ROWS: **11** Ⓐ Ⓑ Ⓒ Ⓓ **12** Ⓔ Ⓕ Ⓖ Ⓗ **13** Ⓐ Ⓑ Ⓒ Ⓓ **14** Ⓔ Ⓕ Ⓖ Ⓗ **15** Ⓐ Ⓑ Ⓒ Ⓓ
16 Ⓔ Ⓕ Ⓖ Ⓗ **17** Ⓐ Ⓑ Ⓒ Ⓓ **18** Ⓔ Ⓕ Ⓖ Ⓗ **19** Ⓐ Ⓑ Ⓒ Ⓓ **20** Ⓔ Ⓕ Ⓖ Ⓗ

ANSWER KEY

Lesson 1

1. b 2. c 3. a 4. b 5. c

6. Everything in nature is either in motion or at rest.

7. Your feet contain one-fourth of the bones in your body.

8. I joined the chorus because I like to sing.

9. If I had three wishes, I'd wish for three more wishes.

10. What is the difference between a microscope and a telescope?

11. The center of an atom is called the nucleus.
12. Since I started jogging, I feel great!
13. The color blue attracts mosquitoes.
14. In the last year, I've grown three inches.
15. Water is an excellent conductor of electricity.
16. I'm so full that I think I'll skip dessert.
17. Elephants sleep only two to three hours each night.
18. If I could meet any person in history, whom would I choose?
19. History repeats itself.
20. More than 15,000 people are bitten by deadly cobras each year.

Lesson 2

1. c 2. a 3. a 4. c 5. b

6. Name the discovery for which Sir Isaac Newton is most famous.

7. One of the first movie stars was W. C. Fields.

8. Federal holidays, such as New Year's are observed in every state.

9. From 1939 to 1975, Justice William O. Douglas served on the Supreme Court.

10. President Wilson instituted Mother's Day as a national holiday.

11. President Theodore Roosevelt 12. Queen Victoria 13. Arbor Day; April 14. Mother's Day; Memorial Day; May 15. Chief Joseph 16. Fire Prevention Week 17. President Dwight D. Eisenhower; Ike 18. Ms. Susan B. Anthony; February 19. December; March 20. Mr. Thomas A. Edison

Lesson 3

1. b 2. c 3. b 4. c 5. a

6. The Pacific Ocean is almost twice as large as the Atlantic Ocean.

7. Both the Liberty Bell and Independence Hall are in Philadelphia.

8. During the Ice Age, the world was covered with ice.

9. The Allegheny River flows into the Ohio River.

10. Stockholm, Sweden, is nearly 10,000 miles from Melbourne, Australia.

11. Egypt 12. Louisiana Purchase 13. Europe; Australia 14. Bronze Age; Stone Age 15. Smithsonian Institution; Washington, D.C. 16. United States; Alaska; Russia 17. Connecticut; Candlewood Lake 18. Battle of Gettysburg 19. United States Military Academy; West Point 20. Great Depression

Lesson 4

1. b 2. b 3. c 4. a 5. b

6. In the Civil War, the Confederate soldiers wore gray uniforms.

7. Fireworks are part of the Chinese New Year celebration.

8. The store sells Colombian, Brazilian, and Venezuelan coffees.

9. The two major American political parties are the Democrats and the Republicans.

10. The Montreal Canadiens are a Canadian hockey team.

11. Turkish 12. Dodgers 13. Indian 14. Hebrew 15. Sioux Indians 16. Americans; Tories; Loyalists 17. Norse 18. Roman; Arabic 19. Chinese 20. Swedish

Lesson 5

1. c 2. b 3. a 4. a 5. b

6. Did cowboys really sing "Home on the Range," or is that a modern song?

7. Amy wrote a report entitled "Changing Liquids to Gas."

8. A lion named Elsa is the central character in the movie called *Born Free.*

9. Isn't "The Night the Bed Fell" an amusing short story?

10. *The Laziest Man in the World* is a play about Benjamin Franklin.

11. *Runner's World* 12. *Up From Slavery* 13. "Using the Ocean for Farming" 14. *Star Wars* 15. *Seventeen* 16. *The Red Badge of Courage* 17. *Camelot* 18. *My Side of the Mountain* 19. *New York World* 20. *The Spectator*

Lesson 6

1. b 2. a 3. a 4. a 5. b

6. "What number do you want?" asked the telephone operator.

7. Henry David Thoreau said, "If a man does not keep pace with his companions, perhaps it is because he hears a different drummer."
8. Kathleen asked, "Has anyone seen my new notebook?"
9. Franklin D. Roosevelt declared, "The only thing we have to fear is fear itself."
10. Speaking about women's rights, Abigail Adams warned, "We will not hold ourselves bound by any laws in which we have no voice."
11. Juliet told Romeo, "**P**arting is such sweet sorrow."
12. "**W**hat is the Roman numeral for one hundred?" asked Carly.
13. The fans shouted, "**W**e're number one!"
14. "**H**ow are you feeling today?" asked the nurse.
15. The coach stated, "**T**he best defense is a good offense."
16. Thomas Edison said, "**G**enius is one percent inspiration and ninety-nine percent perspiration."
17. The police officer asked, "**D**id anyone witness the accident?"
18. "**P**assengers, please move to the rear," requested the driver.
19. A wise person once said, "**A** stitch in time saves nine."
20. "**A** house divided against itself cannot stand," said Lincoln.

Lesson 7 Review

See page 722

Lesson 8

1. a **2.** a **3.** a **4.** b **5.** b

6. Chicago is an important transportation center, isn't it?
7. On your mark, get set, go!
8. Owls can see as well in the daytime as they can at night.
9. When did the Battle of Gettysburg take place?
10. Plants that lived thousands of years ago have turned into fossil fuel.
11. Blood is six times heavier than water.
12. The sunflower is the state flower of Kansas.
13. That's truly amazing!
14. Why is freedom of speech important to a democracy?
15. It is impossible to rhyme the word *orange* with any other English word.
16. Hurry, or we'll be late!
17. Air pollution and water pollution are problems in our society.
18. What are the main exports of Japan?
19. Hooray! Our track team finished first!
20. Which part of a newspaper presents opinions?

Lesson 9

1. b **2.** b **3.** b **4.** b **5.** a

6. Dr. Martin Luther King, Jr., was born in Atlanta, Georgia.
7. The first woman to serve in Congress was Ms. Jeannette Rankin.
8. Lawrence Business Machines, Inc.
   73 Horatio St.
   St. Louis, MO
9. If you work from 9:00 A.M. to 5:00 P. M. on weekdays, how many hours do you work each week?
10. Mr. P. T. Barnum founded the three-ring circus in 1871.

11. Mr. G. **12.** F. B. **13.** Inc. W. Pl. St. **14.** Ms. C. **15.** P. M. **16.** C. W. **17.** Co. Ave. Mt. **18.** A.M. **19.** E. **20.** Corp. N. Blvd. St.

Lesson 10

1. a **2.** b **3.** c **4.** c **5.** a

6. On September 1, 1923, an earthquake took 100,000 lives in Tokyo, Japan.
7. Babe Ruth's last home run was on May 25, 1935, in Pittsburgh, Pennsylvania.
8. Louisa May Alcott was born on November 29, 1832, in Germantown, Pennsylvania.
9. On July 7, 1905, the temperature in Parker, Arizona, was 127 degrees.
10. Napoleon was defeated at Waterloo on June 18, 1815.
11. Paris, France, is known as "The City of Light."
12. The "unsinkable" *Titanic* sank on April 15, 1912.
13. On July 20, 1969, an astronaut first set foot on the moon.
14. The longitude of Reno, Nevada, is 120 degrees.
15. General Lee surrendered to General Grant at Appomattox, Virginia.
16. Butte, Montana, is 5,765 feet above sea level.
17. President Kennedy was born on May 29, 1917, in Brookline, Massachusetts.
18. The Astrodome is in Houston, Texas.
19. Death Valley, California, is the lowest point in the United States.
20. The Boston Tea Party took place on December 16, 1773, in Boston, Massachusetts.

Lesson 11

1. b **2.** c **3.** b **4.** a **5.** a

6. You need talent, drive, and luck to succeed in the theater.
7. The main ingredients in mayonnaise are oil, vinegar, and egg yolk.

8. The heart,lungs,stomach,and skin are organs of the body.
9. The doctor said, "Drink liquids,take aspirin, and get plenty of rest."
10. Ounces,pounds,tons,grams,and milligrams are units of measure.
11. Books may be classified by title, subject, or author.
12. Green plants produce sugar, starch, and oxygen.
13. Frogs, toads, and salamanders are all amphibians.
14. The compass points are North, South, East, and West.
15. Corn, wheat, and soybeans are major products of Illinois.
16. Squirrels eat berries, nuts, insects, and plants.
17. The Painted Desert, the Petrified Forest, and London Bridge are in Arizona.
18. Do you like chess, checkers, or bingo?
19. The colors in a rainbow are red, orange, yellow, green, blue, indigo, and violet.
20. The storm snarled traffic, caused flooding, and produced delays.

Lesson 12

1. a 2. b 3. b 4. b 5. c

6. Opossums,furry mammals,play dead when they're afraid.
7. Did you finish your science project,Kevin?
8. Enamel,the material on the surface of teeth, is very hard.
9. Justine,will you be at the library this afternoon?
10. Yes,a senator serves a six-year term.
11. The dodo, an awkward bird, is extinct.
12. Yes, the square root of 64 is 8.
13. Bill, have you seen my baseball glove?
14. Hydrogen, a gas, is colorless and odorless.
15. What score did you bowl yesterday, Valerie?
16. The largest planet, Jupiter, has at least fourteen moons.
17. No, I can't stay for the rehearsal today, Luis.
18. Coal, decayed plant material, is used for fuel.
19. Theresa, let's go to the museum tonight.
20. Buck Rogers, a fictional character, travels through time and space.

Lesson 13

1. c 2. a 3. b 4. b 5. c

6. The airplane,of course,has made the world smaller,too.
7. It is important,therefore,that you write to your senator.
8. We,too,agreed with the decision.
9. On the contrary,cities have grown in population.
10. However,much water is stored in cactus plants.
11. In fact, we were surprised when we won second place.
12. Benjamin Franklin, for example, was an inventor, too.
13. Of course, whales must breathe air above water.
14. It is necessary, therefore, to conserve our natural resources.
15. Are you going to the concert, too?
16. In general, I agree with your point of view.
17. Coffee, however, is America's most popular drink.
18. Nevertheless, rain is necessary.
19. They, too, will support our candidate.
20. Therefore, it is possible to send satellites into space.

Lesson 14

1. b 2. b 3. a 4. a 5. b

6. When the moon hides the sun,it is called a *solar eclipse.*
7. You can lead a horse to water,but you cannot make it drink.
8. Before you strum,your guitar must be properly tuned.
9. The coach sent in the players,and the quarterback called the signals.
10. We will see the Grand Canyon,or we may go to Yellowstone National Park.
11. After swallowing, the bird looked around for more crumbs.
12. The puppeteer pulled a string, and the tiny clown jumped.
13. Although we decided to return, the park was closed.
14. When the power failed, the city grew dark.
15. If we pollute our rivers, the fish will die.
16. The largest planet is Jupiter, and Mercury is the smallest planet.
17. The locusts ate the entire crop, and the farmer was unable to stop them.
18. Rats are related to mice, but rats are larger and more dangerous.
19. Are there any tickets left, or have they all been sold?
20. Green is a mixture of yellow and blue, and orange is a mixture of yellow and red.

Lesson 15

1. a 2. c 3. a 4. b 5. c

6. Insects can't close their eyes because they don't have eyelids.
7. A baby's skeleton has more bones than an adult's.
8. I'm surprised that you weren't at Michael's party.

9. Columbus's ships traveled at a rate of about three miles per hour.
10. If you didn't have muscles, you wouldn't be able to move.

11. world's **12.** Don't; we'll **13.** It's; elephant's **14.** Don't; they're **15.** adult's
16. hasn't; month's **17.** He's; sheep's
18. Aren't; Thomas's **19.** Frank's; wasn't
20. dog's

Lesson 16

1. b **2.** b **3.** a **4.** a **5.** a

6. Helen Keller said, "I learned from life itself."
7. A Chinese proverb states, "One picture is worth more than ten thousand words."
8. "I hope I can make the team," said the player.
9. Dr. Martin Luther King, Jr., exclaimed, "I have been to the mountaintop!"
10. Mrs. Melendez said, "A thundercloud contains about 100,000 tons of water."
11. As he rode through Boston, Paul Revere announced, "The British are coming!"
12. "Did you know that honeybees are deaf?" asked Roger.
13. "If the shoe fits, wear it," said the salesperson.
14. The druggist said, "Shake the medicine well before using it."
15. "I'm late!" exclaimed the White Rabbit.
16. Sandy asked, "Why does it always rain on holidays?"
17. "We're counting on you," the manager told the pitcher.
18. The waiter said, "Your food will be here shortly."
19. "No country has more earthquakes than Japan," stated Terry.
20. "Stone walls do not a prison make," said the poet.

Lesson 17

1. b **2.** a **3.** c **4.** a **5.** a

6. José's report was entitled "Solutions to Traffic Problems."
7. "The Open Window," a short story by Saki, has a surprise ending.
8. The movie <u>King Kong</u> was first made in 1933.
9. Every evening, my family watches "The Seven O'Clock News."
10. The Drama Club's next play will be <u>Peter Pan</u>.

11. <u>White Fang</u> **12.** <u>2001: A Space Odyssey</u>
13. <u>Fiddler on the Roof</u> **14.** <u>Popular Science</u>
15. <u>Los Angeles Times</u> **16.** "Old Ironsides"
17. "The Necklace" **18.** "Monday Night Football" **19.** "Ways of Using Solar Energy"
20. "Oh, Susanna!"

Lesson 18

1. b **2.** b **3.** b **4.** b **5.** a

6. The human body performs these functions automatically: swallowing, breathing, and digesting.
7. The most common American last name is *Smith*; next comes *Johnson*.
8. It is possible to classify flavors as follows: sweet, sour, bitter, and salty.
9. Suddenly, dark clouds appeared; it began to rain.
10. Benjamin Franklin was the following: statesman, scientist, writer, and inventor.
11. James Madison was the shortest president; President Lincoln was the tallest.
12. The experiment required the following: sand, gravel, chalk, and water.
13. Many people do not accept criticism; some do.
14. It's exactly 7:00 P.M.; it's time to go.
15. The hummingbird is an amazing bird; it can fly backward.
16. The following are metric weights: grams, milligrams, and kilograms.
17. Suddenly there was a loud crash; everyone jumped.
18. These are some kinds of dogs: poodles, collies, and terriers.
19. Dreaming is essential to good health; everyone dreams.
20. Here are some favorite American writers: Mark Twain, Edgar Allan Poe, and Emily Dickinson.

Lesson 19

1. c **2.** b **3.** a **4.** b **5.** c

6. Dear Aunt Veronica,
7. Your friend,
8. Dear Senator Curtis:
9. Very truly yours,
10. To Whom It May Concern:

11. Dear Maria, **12.** Your pen pal, **13.** Dear Mrs. Rowens: **14.** Sincerely, **15.** To the Editor: **16.** Sincerely yours, **17.** Dear Customer Relations Manager: **18.** Yours truly, **19.** Dear Mom, **20.** Love,

Lesson 20 Review

See page 722

Enrichment

Activities

Use the **tips** on pages 2 and 16 to help you do this page.

Create a page for your own yearbook. Fill in the information, using capital letters and punctuation marks correctly.

Yearbook - 198___

A record of ________________ class at ________________________
teacher's name — name of school

Paste your photo here

Background Information

Name: ________________________
first middle last

Birthdate: ________________________
day month date year

Time of Birth: ________________________
hour minute before or after noon

Place of Birth: ________________________
city state

Personal Interests

- The three television programs I enjoy most are ____________ ____________ and ____________
- My favorite book ________________ was written by ________________
- The place I would most like to visit is ________________________ and the person I would most like to meet is ________________________

Predictions

- If I become famous my picture will be on the cover of ________________ the accompanying story will tell how I ________________________
- If I meet a classmate twenty years from now he or she will probably say ____________ ____________________________________
- I will celebrate New Years Day in the year 2000 by ________________________

Answers on page 723

PRACTICING STANDARD USAGE

by Judith J. Thoms

Steps for Practicing Standard Usage

Note: Before you work on lessons 1 to 11, read the **Preview** on page 234. Before you work on lessons 12 to 20, read the **Preview** on page 256.

1. Turn to the lesson you are going to do.
2. Read the rule and the example at the top of the page.
3. **Complete** the sentences in the first part of the lesson. Write the correct words on the lines.
4. Turn the pages to the second part of the lesson. **Choose** the letter of the correct word, and circle the letter.
5. **Check** the paragraphs in the third part of the lesson. If a word is correct, write **C** on the line. If it is not correct, write the correct word.
6. Now use the **Answer Key** to check your answers.
7. Count the number of correct answers. Fill in the number at the top of the lesson. Then turn to the **Progress Plotter** and shade it in to show how many items you answered correctly.
8. If you made any mistakes, go back and do the items again. Make sure you know how to do them.
9. After you have done *all* of the lessons in the book, read the **tips** contained on the **Preview** pages again. Now you are ready to take the **Final Test.**

Project Manager: *Marge M. Kennedy*

Text: Design and Production *Photo Plus Art, Inc.*

STANDARD USAGE

Table of Contents

SUBJECT-VERB AGREEMENT / IRREGULAR VERBS

Preview

Every sentence contains a verb. When you study **standard usage**, you learn to use verbs correctly to make good sentences.

Here are some tips to remember about using verbs in sentences:

1: Use verbs that end in **s** to tell what *one* person or thing does now or is now.

A state **belongs** to the Union.
A state **has** a governor.
A city or a town **has** a mayor.
Each **is** elected.

2: Use verbs that do *not* end in **s** to tell what *two or more* people or things do now or are now. Also use verbs that do *not* end in **s** when the subject is *I* or *you*.

Fifty states **belong** to the Union.
States **have** governors. I **vote**.
A governor and a mayor **represent** us.
Some **are** Democrats, and some **are** Republicans.

3: In some sentences, the subject is separated from the verb. In some sentences, the subject is after the verb. Find the subject of the sentence before you decide which form of the verb to use.

The **governor** of each of the states **is** elected.
Two senators from every state **are** chosen.

Does the governor live in the state capital?
Do the senators live in Washington, D.C.?

There **is one governor**.
There **are two senators**.

4: Most verbs that tell about the past end in **ed** or **d**. Some verbs that tell about the past do *not* end in **ed** or **d**. Use the right form of the verb.

The governor **was** elected.
Senators **were** elected, too.
We **chose** them.
We **have given** them our votes.

LESSON 1

SUBJECT-VERB AGREEMENT

Simple Subjects and Verbs Together

Number Right: ____

Most verbs have two present-tense forms, such as **travel** and **travels**. When the subject of a sentence is *he, she, it,* or a singular noun, use the form that ends in **s.** When the subject is *I, you, they, we,* or a plural noun, use the form that does not end in **s.**

The moon travels around the earth.
The planets travel around the sun.

---

complete Complete each sentence. Write the correct form of the verb on the line.

1. Our hearts ________________ hard. (work, works)
2. The right side ________________ blood from the body. (get, gets)
3. It ________________ this blood to the lungs. (pump, pumps)
4. The lungs ________________ oxygen to the blood. (give, gives)
5. They ________________ carbon dioxide from the blood. (take, takes)
6. Then the blood ________________ to the left side of the heart. (return, returns)
7. The left side ________________ the blood to the rest of the body. (pump, pumps)
8. Veins ________________ the blood to the heart. (bring, brings)
9. Arteries ________________ the blood away from the heart. (carry, carries)
10. Your heart ________________ about 100,000 times a day. (beat, beats)

choose Circle the letter of the verb that agrees with each subject.

11. Most crabs ____ other small shellfish.
    a. lives on b. eat c. consumes d. dines on

12. The coconut crab ____ on some tropical islands.
    a. reside b. inhabit c. dwell d. lives

13. It ____ palm trees to get coconuts.
    a. crawl up b. climbs c. go up d. ascend

14. Coconut crabs ____ the coconuts with their strong claws.
    a. crack b. crushes c. pinches d. cuts

15. They ____ the sweet meat of the coconuts.
    a. devours b. consumes c. eat d. dines on

Read the paragraphs. If an underlined word is correct, write **C** on the line at the right. If it is not correct, write the correct form of the verb.

All animals needs (16) food to survive. In the winter, animals require (17) more energy to keep their bodies warm in cold weather. Food give (18) them energy.

However, in winter, it become (19) more difficult for many animals to find food. Many animals copes (20) with this problem by hibernating. They eat (21) a great deal of food in the fall. Then they sleeps (22) through the winter. Their body temperature fall (23), and their heartbeat slows (24) down. They burns (25) less energy and are able to survive in this way until the spring.

16. ____________
17. ____________
18. ____________
19. ____________
20. ____________
21. ____________
22. ____________
23. ____________
24. ____________
25. ____________

LESSON 2

SUBJECT-VERB AGREEMENT

Compound Subjects and Verbs Together

Number Right: ____

When two or more subjects are joined by *and*, use the same verb form as you would use with a plural subject.

A doctor and a nurse help patients.
Doctors and nurses help patients.

When two or more subjects are joined by *or* or *nor*, use the same verb form as you would use with the subject that is right before the verb.

Either a doctor or a nurse gives advice.
The nurses or a doctor gives advice.
The doctor or the nurses give advice.

---

complete Complete each sentence. Write the correct form of the verb on the line.

1. An adult and a child ______________ different amounts of food. (require, requires)

2. A child or a teenager ______________ more food than an adult. (need, needs)

3. Starches, sugars, and fats ______________ energy. (provide, provides)

4. Bread or cereal ______________ you starch. (give, gives)

5. Rice and potatoes ______________ starch, too. (contain, contains)

6. Milk and meat ______________ some fat. (contain, contains)

7. Butter or oil ______________ fat also. (provide, provides)

8. Either animal protein or vegetable protein ______________ things the body needs to grow and maintain itself. (give, gives)

9. Cheese, eggs, fish, milk, and meat ______________ as sources of animal protein. (serve, serves)

10. Beans, nuts, grain, and vegetables ______________ vegetable protein. (provide, provides)

Circle the letter of the verb that agrees with each subject.

11. A cabinetmaker and a carpenter ____ woodworking tools.
 a. needs b. makes use of c. use d. works with

12. Either a handsaw or an electric saw ____ the wood.
 a. divide b. part c. cuts d. slice

13. Nails, screws, and glue ____ pieces of wood together.
 a. keeps b. hold c. binds d. puts

14. A vise or clamp ____ pieces of wood in place.
 a. keeps b. squeeze c. maintain d. hold

15. Metal files or sandpaper ____ surfaces smooth.
 a. get b. makes c. keep d. rub

Read the paragraphs. If an underlined word is correct, write **C** on the line at the right. If it is not correct, write the correct form of the verb.

If you or I want (16) to save trees, we can recycle paper. Used paper and paper products become (17) new paper in a paper-processing plant. First, newspapers and other used paper goes (18) into a pulper. There, chemicals and water removes (19) the ink. The paper and chemicals turns (20) into pulp. Staples and paper clips come (21) out of the pulp in a large whirling machine.

Next, the ink and dirty water needs (22) to be squeezed out. Then a screen or other sifter distribute (23) the pulp in a large sheet. The pulp and more water then go (24) into a pressing machine. Recycled paper or cardboard emerge (25) from this machine.

16. ____________
17. ____________
18. ____________
19. ____________
20. ____________
21. ____________
22. ____________
23. ____________
24. ____________
25. ____________

LESSON 3

SUBJECT-VERB AGREEMENT

Subjects Separated from Verbs

Number Right: ____

The subject and verb in a sentence must agree. Even when the subject and verb are separated, the verb must agree with the subject, not with the words in between.

Canals take the place of streets in Venice.
Canals in Venice **take** the place of streets.

A visitor rides in a *gondola,* or taxi-boat.
A visitor who is sightseeing **rides** in a *gondola.*

The boats glide through the canals.
The boats simply **glide** through the canals.

---

complete Complete each sentence. Write the correct word on the line.

1. We usually ____________ of the sun as a ball of light. (think, thinks)
2. However, dark patches of gas also ____________ on the sun's surface. (form, forms)
3. The patches of gas ____________ dark because they are cooler than the rest of the sun. (appear, appears)
4. Scientists who study the sun ____________ these dark places *sunspots.* (call, calls)
5. The position of the sunspots ____________. (vary, varies)
6. The size and number of sunspots also ____________ over the years. (change, changes)
7. Over an eleven-year period, the number of sunspots ____________ to about one hundred. (increase, increases)
8. The number of patches ____________ to about five over the next eleven years. (decrease, decreases)
9. Each period of eleven years ____________ a sunspot cycle. (form, forms)
10. Scientists who have studied the sun ____________ when these cycles take place, but they don't know why. (know, knows)

choose Circle the letter of the verb that agrees with each subject.

11. The action of weather on rocks ____ them into soil.
    a. turn b. change c. make d. converts

12. The surface of the rocks slowly ____ away.
    a. get blown b. wash c. wears d. blow

13. Water and glaciers also ____ soil by eroding rocks.
    a. form b. creates c. becomes d. makes

14. Soil that is good for growing ____ oxygen and minerals.
    a. require b. needs c. use d. get

15. Plants and animals, as they decay in the soil, ____ it to become fertile.
    a. help b. causes c. gets d. requires

Read the paragraphs. If an underlined word is correct, write **C** on the line at the right. If it is not correct, write the correct word.

The forces of supply and demand governs (16) the price and supply of most goods. The supply of apples, for example, refer (17) to the number of apples for sale. The demand for apples mean (18) the number of people who want to buy them.

If the supply of apples increase (19), people who sell them starts (20) to lower their price. As the price of apples go (21) down, the demand for them goes (22) up. A low price for apples usually encourage (23) people to buy.

The forces of the marketplace works (24) well when the supply of a product equal (25) the demand for it.

16. ____________
17. ____________
18. ____________
19. ____________
20. ____________
21. ____________
22. ____________
23. ____________
24. ____________
25. ____________

LESSON 4

SUBJECT-VERB AGREEMENT

Indefinite Pronoun Subjects

Number Right: ____

Indefinite pronouns do not refer to particular people, places, or things. These indefinite pronouns are always singular: *each, either, neither, one, everyone, everybody, anyone, anybody, someone, somebody, no one,* and *nobody. None* is usually singular, but in some cases, *none* is plural. When the subject is singular, use the verb form that ends in **s**.

Everyone tries. No one gives up.
None gives up. None of the team gives up.
None of the runners give up.

These indefinite pronouns are always plural: *both, few, others, many,* and *several.* These indefinite pronouns are usually plural, but in some cases, they may be singular: *some, all, any,* and *most.* When the subject is plural, use the verb form that does not end in **s**.

Many try. A few give up.
Most try. Some of them give up.
Some of the team gives up.

---

complete Complete each sentence. Write the correct verb on the line.

1. Everyone ________________ to have good luck. (want, wants)
2. Some ____________ that they can influence their luck. (believe, believes)
3. Many ____________ it's good luck to find a four-leaf clover. (think, thinks)
4. Others ________________ a rabbit's foot for good luck. (carry, carries)
5. Someone ______________ on wood to prevent bad luck. (knock, knocks)
6. Another ________________ it's good luck to put a shiny penny in a new wallet. (think, thinks)
7. A few ________________ making important decisions on Friday the thirteenth. (avoid, avoids)
8. Some ________________ rice at a bride and groom to bring them good luck. (throw, throws)
9. Many ________________ that if you forget to take an umbrella, it will rain. (say, says)
10. Almost all of us ________________ some superstitions. (follow, follows)

Circle the letter of the verb that agrees with each subject.

11. Everyone ____ from inventions made in earlier times.
a. profit **b.** benefits **c.** smart **d.** rich

12. Nobody ____ to reinvent the wheel.
a. needs **b.** going **c.** want **d.** plan

13. Everybody ____ a language that was made up by others.
a. know **b.** use
c. learns **d.** develop

14. Many ____ telephones, television, and computers.
a. enjoys **b.** owns **c.** use **d.** wants

15. Few ____ life without these conveniences.
a. knows **b.** recall
c. remembers **d.** thinks about

Read the paragraphs. If an underlined word is correct, write **C** on the line at the right. If it is not correct, write the correct form of the verb.

Everyone need (16) exercise to be healthy. Some simply walk (17) to and from school. Others jogs (18) every day. Most gets (19) some exercise in gym classes.

A few takes (20) special classes in gymnastics, dance, or self-defense. One swim (21). Another skates (22). Some plays (23) team sports. Others rides (24) bikes. Everyone benefit (25) from regular exercise.

16. ____________

17. ____________

18. ____________

19. ____________

20. ____________

21. ____________

22. ____________

23. ____________

24. ____________

25. ____________

LESSON 5

SUBJECT-VERB AGREEMENT

- The Verbs **Have** and **Do**
- The Verb **Be**

Number Right: ____

The verbs **have** and **do** have two present-tense forms. The verb **be** has three present-tense forms and two past-tense forms. The chart below shows the verb forms that agree with each subject.

SUBJECTS	PRESENT OF HAVE	PRESENT OF DO	PRESENT OF BE	PAST OF BE
I *he, she, it* singular nouns	have has has	do does does	am is is	was was was
you, they, we plural nouns compound subject joined by *and*	have have have	do do do	are are are	were were were

complete Complete each sentence. Write the correct form of the verb on the line.

1. The first computer ________________ built in 1944. (was, were)
2. Early computers ________________ very large. (was, were)
3. New computers ________________ much smaller. (is, are)
4. A computer ________________ "think" on its own. (don't, doesn't)
5. It ________________ to be given instructions by people. (have, has)
6. A computer ____________ useful for many kinds of work. (is, are)
7. Computers ________________ things thousands of times faster than people. (does, do)
8. Computers ________________ replaced people in some jobs. (have, has)
9. The increased use of computers ________________ created many jobs, too. (have, has)
10. Learning to work with computers ________________ difficult. (isn't, aren't)

choose Circle the letter of the verb that agrees with each subject.

11. Most astronomers ____ sleep on clear nights.
a. doesn't **b.** hasn't **c.** don't **d.** haven't

12. They ____ to be awake while the stars can be seen.
a. has **b.** have **c.** got **d.** must

13. Powerful telescopes ____ used to look into space.
a. is **b.** be **c.** was **d.** are

14. Astronomers ____ many things to study the stars.
a. do **b.** does **c.** got **d.** has

15. They can tell how far away, how big, and how old a star ____.
a. are **b.** is **c.** be **d.** were

Read the paragraphs. If an underlined word is correct, write **C** on the line at the right. If it is not correct, write the correct form of the verb.

Australia have (16) many interesting animals. Some of these animals isn't (17) found in any other part of the world. You was (18) probably quite young when you learned that kangaroos has (19) pouches. Many other Australian mammals, including the koala bear, also has (20) pouches.

Most mammals in the world don't (21) lay eggs. However, the platypus and echidna does (22). A platypus have (23) fur, a duck's bill, and webbed feet. An echidna, or spiny anteater, be (24) hatched inside its mother's pouch. It ain't (25) ready to leave the pouch until it is several weeks old.

16. ____________________

17. ____________________

18. ____________________

19. ____________________

20. ____________________

21. ____________________

22. ____________________

23. ____________________

24. ____________________

25. ____________________

LESSON 6

SUBJECT-VERB AGREEMENT

- Sentences with **Here** and **There**
- Question Sentences

Number Right: ____

When a sentence begins with **here** or **there**, neither of these words is the subject. The subject comes after the verb. Even when the subject follows the verb, the verb must agree with the subject.

Here **is the book.**
There **are eight chapters** in it.
Here **comes the teacher.**

In a question sentence, the subject usually comes after the verb. Even when the subject follows the verb, the verb must agree with the subject.

Who **is the author**?
Where **does the story** take place?
Who **are the main characters**?

---

complete Complete each sentence. Write the correct form of the verb on the line.

1. There ____________ basic facts to be learned about every country. (are, is)
2. Here ____________ some questions about Canada. (is, are)
3. What ____________ the capital of Canada? (is, are)
4. What languages ____________ Canadians speak? (do, does)
5. What form of government ____________ Canadians have? (do, does)
6. Who ____________ Canada's prime minister? (is, are)
7. What ____________ the difference between Canada's provinces and territories? (is, are)
8. What ____________ Canada's chief crops and industries? (is, are)
9. What ____________ the Canadian flag look like? (do, does)
10. What ____________ Canada's national holidays? (is, are)

Circle the letter of the verb that agrees with each subject.

11. Here ____ some old riddles.
    a. is b. was c. are d. be

12. When ____ a door not a door? (When it is ajar.)
    a. are b. is c. be d. were

13. What ____ a giraffe have that no other animal has? (Baby giraffes.)
    a. do b. don't c. are d. does

14. Where ____ a 1,000-pound gorilla eat? (Anywhere it wants to.)
    a. do b. don't c. does d. have

15. Where ____ a fish get money? (At the riverbank.)
    a. does b. don't c. do d. be

Read the list below. If an underlined word is correct, write **C** on the line at the right. If it is not correct, write the correct word.

Vacation Check List

Here <u>are</u> (16) a list to check before you go on vacation:

- ☐ <u>Has</u> (17) you told your neighbors that you will be gone?
- ☐ <u>Does</u> (18) they know where to reach you in an emergency?
- ☐ <u>Do</u> (19) you have to stop any deliveries?
- ☐ <u>Is</u> (20) all the lights out?
- ☐ <u>Are</u> (21) any faucets leaking?
- ☐ <u>Are</u> (22) the gas shut off?
- ☐ <u>Have</u> (23) the plants been watered?
- ☐ <u>Is</u> (24) all the doors and windows locked?
- ☐ <u>Is</u> (25) your mailbox empty?

16. ________________
17. ________________
18. ________________
19. ________________
20. ________________
21. ________________
22. ________________
23. ________________
24. ________________
25. ________________

LESSON 7

IRREGULAR VERBS

Drive, Fall, Come, and Other Verbs

Number Right: ____

To form the past and past participle of most verbs, you add **-ed** to the present-tense form, as in **need, needed,** and **have needed.** This chart shows the forms of some irregular verbs. The past forms are used alone. The past-participle forms are used with helping verbs, such as *has, have, had, am, is, are, was, were, be,* and *been.*

PRESENT	PAST	PAST PARTICIPLE
drive	drove	driven
write	wrote	written
ride	rode	ridden
eat	ate	eaten
give	gave	given
forgive	forgave	forgiven
fall	fell	fallen
take	took	taken
shake	shook	shaken
see	saw	seen
come	came	come
become	became	become
run	ran	run

complete Complete each sentence. Write the correct form of the verb on the line.

1. The Romans ______________ control of Britain in A.D. 43. (took, taken)
2. After 400 years, the Roman Empire ______________. (fell, fallen)
3. Angles, Saxons, and other German tribes then ______________ to Britain. (came, come)
4. The Angles ______________ the most land. (took, taken)
5. Angle-land ______________ known as England. (became, become)
6. The Scandinavians ______________ in the ninth century. (came, come)
7. The Normans, a French tribe, ______________ over in 1066. (took, taken)
8. During their rule, most things were ______________ in French. (wrote, written)
9. The Normans were not ______________ out. (drove, driven)
10. Gradually, the Normans and the Anglo-Saxons ______________ one people. (became, become)

Circle the letter of the verb that goes in each sentence.

11. Indian names have been ____ to countries, states, and cities.
a. gived **b.** gave **c.** given **d.** gaved

12. The word *Canada* was ____ from the Iroquois word *Kanada,* meaning "a group of huts."
a. took **b.** taked **c.** taken **d.** tooked

13. The Delaware, Illinois, and Massachusetts tribes ____ their names to states.
a. gave **b.** given **c.** gived **d.** gaved

14. The cities Miami, Wichita, and Omaha also ____ Indian names.
a. taked **b.** took **c.** taken **d.** tooked

15. *Man-a-hat-ta,* or *The Island of the Hills,* ____ Manhattan in New York.
a. becomed **b.** become **c.** became **d.** becamed

Read the paragraphs. If an underlined word is correct, write **C** on the line at the right. If it is not correct, write the correct form of the verb.

The ancient Greeks seen (16) the sun as a god, Helios, who drived (17) a chariot. During the day, four wild horses runned (18) ahead of the chariot, pulling it across the sky. Night fell (19) when Helios reached his evening palace. Then his tired horses falled (20) into the sea for a bath.

After the horses had shook (21) themselves off, they eated (22) and rested. Meanwhile, Helios told his daughters all he had saw (23) that day.

When the time comed (24) for Helios and his steeds to return to the east, they sailed to their morning palace in a golden boat. As the day dawned, they rode (25) across the sky once more.

16. ____________
17. ____________
18. ____________
19. ____________
20. ____________
21. ____________
22. ____________
23. ____________
24. ____________
25. ____________

LESSON 8

IRREGULAR VERBS

Throw, Begin, Sink, and Other Verbs

Number Right: ____

This chart shows the past and past-participle forms of some irregular verbs.

PRESENT	PAST	PAST PARTICIPLE
throw	threw	thrown
know	knew	known
blow	blew	blown
draw	drew	drawn
show	showed	shown
fly	flew	flown
begin	began	begun
swim	swam	swum
sink	sank *or* sunk	sunk
drink	drank	drunk
ring	rang	rung
sing	sang *or* sung	sung
shrink	shrank *or* shrunk	shrunk *or* shrunken
swing	swung	swung

complete Complete each sentence. Write the correct form of the verb on the line.

1. Pollution ________________ to be a major problem in the nineteenth century. (began, begun)
2. As factories ________________ more numerous, pollution became common. (grew, grown)
3. Dirty smoke was ________________ into the air. (blew, blown)
4. Waste products from industry were ________________ into streams and lakes. (threw, thrown)
5. People in crowded cities ______________ untreated water. (drank, drunk)
6. In the twentieth century, cars and airplanes ________________ gas and smoke into the air. (threw, thrown)
7. People ________________ dirty air into their lungs. (drew, drawn)
8. The problems of pollution have not ________________. (shrank, shrunk)
9. However, people have ________________ to try to do something about pollution. (began, begun)
10. Organizations that fight pollution have ______________. (grew, grown)

Circle the letter of the verb that goes in each sentence.

11. The story of Atlantis was ____ to the ancient Greeks.
 a. knowed b. knew c. knows d. known
12. They said the island-nation had ____ into a powerful empire.
 a. growed b. grown c. grewed d. grew
13. According to legend, it ____ into the Atlantic Ocean.
 a. sank b. sinked c. sunked d. sanked
14. It has never been ____ that Atlantis actually existed.
 a. shown b. shew c. showed d. showned
15. Some think it was really a Greek island that ____ up in a volcano.
 a. blown b. blowed c. blewn d. blew

Read the paragraphs. If an underlined word is correct, write **C** on the line at the right. If it is not correct, write the correct form of the verb.

It is hard to put down the *Guinness Book of World Records* once you have began (16) reading. Are these facts knowed (17) to you?

- The heaviest bell in the world is showed (18) in Moscow. This 216-ton bell rung (19) first in 1735. It isn't ringed (20) any more.
- In 1979, Mollie Jackson swinged (21) on a swing for 185 hours straight. In the same year, S.A.E.W. Perera sung (22) a song for 134 hours!
- In 1978, Penny Dean swum (23) across the English Channel in seven hours, forty minutes. In 1981, an unusual plane flew (24) across the Channel. It was flied (25) by solar energy.

16. ____________
17. ____________
18. ____________
19. ____________
20. ____________
21. ____________
22. ____________
23. ____________
24. ____________
25. ____________

LESSON 9

IRREGULAR VERBS

Go, Break, Lose, and Other Verbs

Number Right: ____

This chart shows the past and past-participle forms of some irregular verbs.

PRESENT	PAST	PAST PARTICIPLE
go	went	gone
do	did	done
get	got	got *or* gotten
forget	forgot	forgotten
freeze	froze	frozen
break	broke	broken
speak	spoke	spoken
choose	chose	chosen
steal	stole	stolen
tear	tore	torn
wear	wore	worn
lose	lost	lost
feed	fed	fed
lead	led	led
hear	heard	heard
send	sent	sent
lend	lent	lent
dig	dug	dug
leave	left	left

complete Complete each sentence. Write the correct form of the verb on the line.

1. Archeologists have ________________ to faraway places. (went, gone)
2. Some have ________________ expeditions. (led, leaded)
3. Others have ________________ up ancient ruins. (digged, dug)
4. They study civilizations that were ________________. (lost, losted)
5. They find tools that were ________________ behind. (left, leaved)
6. Carefully, they restore items that were ______________. (broke, broken)
7. They can learn what people ________________ for a living. (did, done)
8. They can even tell what clothing was ________________. (wore, worn)
9. They also determine what language had been ____________. (spoke, spoken)
10. Some of these languages are not ______________ today. (heared, heard)

Circle the letter of the verb that goes in each sentence.

11. Many people have ____ about hypnosis.
a. heared **b.** heard **c.** hear **d.** hears

12. Some people have ____ to be hypnotized.
a. chose **b.** choosed **c.** chosen **d.** choosen

13. Once they have ____ into a trance, they are very relaxed.
a. went **b.** goed **c.** go **d.** gone

14. Hypnosis can also help people remember things they have ____.
a. forget **b.** forgotten **c.** forgets **d.** forgetted

15. People in a trance can speak and be ____ to.
a. speaked **b.** spoke **c.** spoken **d.** speaken

Read the paragraphs. If an underlined word is correct, write **C** on the line at the right. If it is not correct, write the correct form of the verb.

You may have heared [16] of the Bermuda Triangle. You would outline it if you goed [17] from Bermuda to Florida to Puerto Rico. Since 1854, more than fifty ships and planes have went [18] there, never to return. Most of them have leaved [19] no trace. Few pilots or captains ever sended [20] out distress signals. They were never heard [21] from again.

Some people have choosed [22] to believe that the ships and planes were stealed [23] by creatures from outer space. Probably, they were lost [24] in sudden storms. The waves then sended [25] the wreckage to the bottom of the sea.

16. ____________

17. ____________

18. ____________

19. ____________

20. ____________

21. ____________

22. ____________

23. ____________

24. ____________

25. ____________

LESSON 10

IRREGULAR VERBS

Say, Bring, Hurt, and Other Verbs

Number Right: ____

This chart shows the past and past-participle forms of some irregular verbs.

PRESENT	PAST	PAST PARTICIPLE
say	said	said
pay	paid	paid
find	found	found
stand	stood	stood
tell	told	told
sell	sold	sold
make	made	made
bring	brought	brought
think	thought	thought
buy	bought	bought
teach	taught	taught
catch	caught	caught
fight	fought	fought
beat	beat	beat *or* beaten
The present, past, and past-participle forms of these verbs are the same: *hurt, cost, hit, let, cut, put, set, bet,* and *burst.*		

complete Complete each sentence. Write the correct form of the verb on the line.

1. Ben Franklin was ____________ the craft of printing. (teached, taught)
2. At seventeen, he ______________ out for Philadelphia. (set, setted)
3. By the time he was twenty-four, he had ______________ his own print shop. (buyed, bought)
4. He printed and ______________ an almanac. (selled, sold)
5. *Poor Richard's Almanack* ______________ people about the weather. (telled, told)
6. Franklin also _________ many wise sayings in his almanac. (put, putted)
7. One of them ______________, "Early to bed and early to rise, makes a man healthy, wealthy, and wise." (sayed, said)
8. Franklin ______________ for thrift and hard work. (standed, stood)
9. Many people ______________ attention to Franklin. (payed, paid)
10. He ______________ about many changes in the new nation. (bringed, brought)

Circle the letter of the verb that goes in each sentence.

11. Some astronomers say they have ____ black holes in space.
a. found **b.** finded **c.** finds **d.** finded

12. A black hole is ____ when a star collapses.
a. maked **b.** maded **c.** made **d.** beginned

13. When this happens, a huge mass is ____ into a very small space.
a. broughten **b.** bringed **c.** brung **d.** brought

14. Even light is ____ by the strength of its gravity.
a. catch **b.** catched **c.** caught **d.** caughten

15. Black holes can't be ____ easily because no light can escape from them.
a. finded **b.** found **c.** finden **d.** finds

Read the paragraphs. If an underlined word is correct, write **C** on the line at the right. If it is not correct, write the correct form of the verb.

The Revolutionary War was fighted (16) from 1775 to 1781. The British had said (17) that higher taxes should be payed (18) by the American colonies.

The colonists letted (19) the British know that these taxes were unacceptable. The ties between Britain and the colonies were officially cutted (20) on July 4, 1776, when the Declaration of Independence was signed. All thirteen colonies standed (21) together in opposing British rule.

George Washington was putted (22) in charge of the American troops. Many of his troops were hit (23) by gunfire. Washington himself was never hurted. (24) The British were finally beated, (25) and Washington accepted their surrender.

16. ____________

17. ____________

18. ____________

19. ____________

20. ____________

21. ____________

22. ____________

23. ____________

24. ____________

25. ____________

LESSON 11 — SUBJECT-VERB AGREEMENT/IRREGULAR VERBS

Review

Review Score: ____

A. Write the correct present form of each verb.

1. Two bureaus of the Treasury Department ________ money in the United States. (make, makes)
2. One ________________ coins. (make, makes)
3. Another ________________ paper money. (print, prints)
4. The date on which a coin was made ________ on the front of a coin. (is, are)
5. A picture and the value of the coin ________________ shown on the reverse side. (is, are)
6. The phrase *e pluribus unum* ________ been engraved on coins, too. (has, have)
7. The meaning of these Latin words ________ "out of many, one." (is, are)
8. A five-dollar bill or a penny ________________ Lincoln's likeness. (have, has)
9. There ________ pictures of other famous Americans on different bills. (is, are)
10. ________________ you know whose picture is on a one-hundred dollar bill? (Do, Does)

B. Write the correct past or past-participle form of each verb.

11. Early American colonists ________________ for things in several ways. (paid, payed)
12. Some ________________ things with Indian *wampum.* (buyed, bought)
13. Others used money that ________ from Spain or England. (come, came)
14. Spanish money was ________ to America by traders. (brung, brought)
15. They ________________ business in the Caribbean. (done, did)
16. The Spanish *peso,* or silver dollar, ________________ a commonly used coin. (became, become)
17. It was sometimes ________ into eight pie-shaped wedges. (cutted, cut)
18. These wedges were ________ as *pieces of eight.* (knew, known)
19. During the Revolution, Congress ________________ paper money. (made, maked)
20. Each bill had the value of Spanish dollars ________________ on it. (wrote, written)

PRONOUNS / WORD CHOICE

Preview

Every sentence is made of words. When you study **standard usage**, you learn to choose the right words to make good sentences.

Here are some tips to remember about using words in sentences:

1: Use the right pronoun to take the place of a noun. Different pronouns can take the place of the same noun, depending on how each pronoun is used in a sentence. See how the pronouns *he, him, his,* and *himself* all take the place of the noun *Peter*.

Peter listens to music when **he** studies.
Peter's friends study with **him**.
Peter's radio is on **his** shelf.
Peter built the radio **himself**.

2: Use the right word to describe. Some describing words have two forms, such as *soft* and *softly*. Use the form that does *not* end in **ly** to tell *what kind*. Use the form that ends in **ly** to tell *how*.

Peter likes **soft** music.
He plays the radio **softly**.

3: Use only one word that means "no" to make a sentence mean "no."

He **doesn't** ever play tapes.
He **never** plays tapes.

4: Use the right word when you write a word that sounds like another word.

Whose record is playing now?
Who's singing?

Use the right word when you use a word that is easily confused with another word.

Peter likes all music, **except** opera.
He **accepts** invitations to many concerts.

LESSON 12

PRONOUNS

Subject and Object Pronouns

Number Right: ____

Pronouns take the place of nouns. Use these pronouns in place of nouns that are used as subjects:

I **he** **she** **you** **it** **we** **they**

Use these pronouns in place of nouns that are used as objects:

me **him** **her** **you** **it** **us** **them**

When you use *we* or *us* with the nouns they stand for, use the same pronouns you would use alone. When you use *I* or *me* with nouns or other pronouns, name yourself last.

We baseball players started a team.
The game was won by **us players.**
He and I are outfielders.
The game depends on **him and me**.

---

complete Complete each sentence. Write the correct pronoun on the line.

1. ____________ students took part in an experiment. (We, Us)

2. One of ____________ was told to describe an object without naming it. (we, us)

3. ____________ described its color, shape, and size. (She, Her)

4. The rest of ____________ students weren't allowed to ask any questions about the object. (we, us)

5. ____________ were told to guess what the object was. (We, Us)

6. Few of ____________ guessed correctly. (we, us)

7. Then ____________ repeated the experiment. (we, us)

8. This time, we were allowed to ask ____________ questions. (she, her)

9. My classmates and ____________ were then able to guess correctly. (I, me)

10. The experiment taught my friends and ____________ the importance of asking questions. (I, me)

Circle the letter of the pronoun that goes in each sentence.

11. ____ Americans sometimes eat food on the run.
a. Us **b.** Them **c.** We **d.** That

12. There are many fast-food restaurants for ____ people on the go.
a. we **b.** them **c.** that **d.** us

13. These restaurants make it easy for you and ____ to eat and run.
a. I **b.** they **c.** me **d.** we

14. If you or ____ want a quick snack, we can even eat standing up.
a. me **b.** I **c.** us **d.** them

15. ____ hamburger-lovers rarely have to wait long for lunch.
a. We **b.** Them **c.** Us **d.** This

Read the paragraphs. If an underlined word or words are correct, write **C** on the line at the right. If they are not correct, or if they are in the wrong order, write them correctly.

Us [16] newspaper readers like comic strips. Pollsters have surveyed us [17] readers. The surveys show that the comics are the part of the paper that we [18] like the best.

Comic strips became popular soon after them [19] began to appear in 1895. The first comic strip showed a boy dressed in yellow. Him [20] was called the Yellow Kid. Him [21] and his creator became famous almost overnight.

Me and you [22] can read many comic strips today. Some of they [23] are adventure stories. Others are meant to make we [24] readers laugh. A few of them even poke fun at you and I. [25]

16. ____________________
17. ____________________
18. ____________________
19. ____________________
20. ____________________
21. ____________________
22. ____________________
23. ____________________
24. ____________________
25. ____________________

LESSON 13

PRONOUNS

Reflexive and Intensive Pronouns

Number Right: ____

These pronouns are used to refer to singular pronouns or nouns:

myself **herself** **himself** **yourself** **itself**

These pronouns are used to refer to plural pronouns or nouns:

ourselves **themselves** **yourselves**

Do *not* use these pronouns in place of subject or object pronouns Never say, "Maria and *myself* went to the museum." Never say, "The guide showed Maria and *myself* the painting." Say:

Maria and **I** went to the museum.
The guide showed Maria and **me** the painting.

---

complete Complete each sentence. Write the correct pronoun on the line.

1. Margaret Bourke-White made ______________ famous as a photographer. (herself, herselves)
2. She first attracted attention to ______________ by photographing coal miners. (herself, herselves)
3. The subject ______________ was interesting. (itself, itselves)
4. Her dramatic use of lighting made the portraits ______________ works of art. (themselves, theirselves)
5. As a reporter covering World War II, she found ______________ in many dangerous situations. (herself, herselves)
6. She photographed the battles ______________. (theirself, themselves)
7. Her camera captured soldiers as they saw ______________. (theirselves, themselves)
8. When she met Gandhi, an Indian leader, she photographed ______________. (him, himself)
9. She wrote and photographed pictures for many books ______________. (herself, herselves)
10. One of her books is called *Portrait of* ______________. *(Meself, Myself)*

choose Circle the letter of the pronoun that goes in each sentence.

11. Pets can't take care of ____.
a. theirself **b.** theirselves **c.** themself **d.** themselves

12. If you have a pet, you know ____ the care it requires.
a. youself **b.** youselves **c.** yourself **d.** itself

13. An animal can't hunt food for ____ in your home.
a. hisself **b.** itself **c.** theirself **d.** themself

14. In many cities, dogs can't go for walks by ____.
a. themselves **b.** theirselves **c.** themself **d.** theirself

15. My dog and ____ like to take long walks together.
a. myself **b.** himself **c.** me **d.** I

Read the paragraphs. If an underlined word is correct, write **C** on the line at the right. If it is not correct, write the correct word.

King Midas had a chance to make hisself [16] rich. In return for a favor, the god Dionysus asked him, "What do you want for youself [17]?"

"I want more gold for meself [18]," Midas replied. "Everything I touch should turn itself [19] to gold." Dionysus granted Midas's wish.

At first, Midas was pleased with hisself [20]. He found himself [21] surrounded with gold. The flowers theirselves [22] turned to gold at his touch. However, when his daughter turned to gold herself [23], Midas realized what a fool he had made of hisself [24]. He begged for help. Dionysus said, "Wash yourself [25] in the River Pactolus, and all will be as before."

16. ______________

17. ______________

18. ______________

19. ______________

20. ______________

21. ______________

22. ______________

23. ______________

24. ______________

25. ______________

LESSON

14 PRONOUNS

Pronoun Agreement

Number Right: ____

Masculine pronouns refer to masculine nouns, and feminine pronouns refer to feminine nouns. Singular pronouns refer to singular nouns and pronouns and to singular nouns joined by *or.*

Andrew rides **his bicycle. He** rides **it.**

Lisa rides **her** bike or her motorcycle. **She** rides **it.**

Plural pronouns refer to plural nouns and pronouns and to nouns and pronouns joined by *and.*

Some students have **cars. They** have **them.**

Lisa and I have **our** licenses.

---

complete Complete each sentence. Write the correct pronoun on the line.

1. People build canals to help ________ go from one body of water to another. (it, them)
2. A ship may go through canals as ________ travels. (they, it)
3. Many canals have *locks* in ________. (it, them)
4. A lock connects two bodies of water when ________ are at different heights. (it, they)
5. A lock has watertight gates at both ends of ________. (it, them)
6. When a ship sails into a lock, the gates shut after ________. (it, them)
7. Water then flows *into* the lock or *out* of ________. (them, it)
8. The ship moves up or down according to ________ route. (their, its)
9. The Panama Canal has twelve locks in ________. (him, it)
10. Canals aid ships by making ________ journeys shorter. (its, their)

choose Circle the letter of the pronoun that goes in each sentence.

11. A cassowary is a large bird that makes ____ home in Australia.
    a. their b. its c. our d. your

12. Cassowaries don't fly, but ____ can run extremely fast.
    a. it b. they c. you d. we

13. Cassowaries have bony helmets on ____ heads.
    a. its b. their c. our d. your

14. If a cassowary is attacked, ____ can become very dangerous.
    a. they b. we c. it d. them

15. A cassowary kicks with ____ strong legs and sharp claws.
    a. their b. its c. your d. our

Read the list. If an underlined word is correct, write **C** on the line at the right. If it is not correct, write the correct word.

What to Do on a Rainy Day

- Find a book or magazine and read them (16).
- Take your (17) umbrella and walk outside.
- Find your loose photos and put it (18) into albums.
- Think of a food you like and make them (19).
- Call some friends and invite him (20) over.
- Check your plants and repot it (21) if necessary.
- Turn on the radio or record player and listen to it (22).
- Write a letter or a postcard and mail them (23).
- Look in your closet and clean them (24).
- Write a list of your friends' birthdays so you'll remember it (25).

16. ____________
17. ____________
18. ____________
19. ____________
20. ____________
21. ____________
22. ____________
23. ____________
24. ____________
25. ____________

LESSON

15 WORD CHOICE

Adjectives and Adverbs

Number Right: ____

Adjectives tell about nouns. Here are some adjectives that can be used to describe nouns:

good **fast** **warm** **careful** **slow**

Adverbs tell about verbs, adjectives, or other adverbs. Some adverbs are formed by adding **-ly** to adjectives. Here are some adverbs that can be used to describe verbs and adjectives:

well **fast** **warmly** **carefully** **slowly** *or* **slow**

Complete each sentence. Write the correct word on the line.

1. The first Frisbees were ______________ aluminum pie plates. (plain, plainly)
2. Some students at Yale University discovered that the pie plates flew ______________. (good, well)
3. They sailed ______________ through the air. (graceful, gracefully)
4. Some ______________ manufacturers began to produce plastic Frisbees. (clever, cleverly)
5. The new sport caught on ______________. (quick, quickly)
6. ______________, there were Frisbee players all over the country. (Sudden, Suddenly)
7. To throw a Frisbee ______________, you have to spin it away from you. (good, well)
8. Most players ______________ play "catch." (simple, simply)
9. You may have to run ______________ to catch a Frisbee. (fast, fastly)
10. A good Frisbee player reacts ______________. (quick, quickly)

choose Circle the letter of the word that goes in each sentence.

11. The rules of chess can be learned ____.
a. quick **b.** rapid **c.** easily **d.** thorough

12. Each type of chessman moves ____.
a. certain **b.** careful **c.** different **d.** differently

13. The *rook,* for example, can only move in ____ lines.
a. narrowly **b.** straight **c.** diagonally **d.** straightly

14. The ____ *knight* can make L-shaped moves.
a. useful **b.** usefully **c.** dependably **d.** strongly

15. A *bishop* can move ____, going either forward or backward.
a. diagonally **b.** horizontal **c.** diagonal **d.** good

Read the paragraphs. If an underlined word is correct, write **C** on the line at the right. If it is not correct, write the correct word.

If you want to write good (16), you should first think clear (17) about your purpose for writing. Do you want to educate, persuade, or entertain your readers? Consider careful (18) who your readers will be.

Don't expect to write quick (19). Plan your work thoughtful (20), write a rough (21) draft, and then revise it. The important (22) thing is to express yourself as good (23) as possible. When you are satisfied, make a final copy that is neatly (24) and correct (25).

16. ____________________

17. ____________________

18. ____________________

19. ____________________

20. ____________________

21. ____________________

22. ____________________

23. ____________________

24. ____________________

25. ____________________

LESSON 16

WORD CHOICE

Comparative and Superlative Forms

Number Right: ____

Adjectives and adverbs can be used to compare. Adjectives that compare two things end in **-er** or begin with **more** or **less.**

better **faster** **warmer** **more careful** **slower**

Adjectives that compare three or more things end in **-est** or begin with **most** or **least.**

best **fastest** **warmest** **most careful** **slowest**

Adverbs that compare two actions end in **-er** or begin with **more** or **less.**

better **faster** **more warmly** **less carefully** **slower** *or* **more slowly**

Adverbs that compare three or more actions end in **-er** or begin with **most** or **least.**

best **fastest** **most warmly** **least carefully** **slowest** *or* **most slowly**

---

complete Complete each sentence. Write the correct words on the lines.

1. Ostriches are now the ____________ birds in the world. (larger, largest)
2. The extinct moa bird was ____________ than the ostrich. (taller, tallest)
3. The extinct elephant bird was ____________ than the ostrich. (heavier, heaviest)
4. Dinosaur eggs were ____________ than ostrich eggs. (bigger, biggest)
5. Today, however, ostriches lay the ____________ eggs of any bird or reptile. (larger, largest)
6. Ostriches have the ____________ eyelashes of any bird. (thicker, thickest)
7. Their eyesight is ____________ than that of many other animals. (better, best)
8. The female ostrich has a ____________ coat than the male. (duller, dullest)
9. Ostriches can run ____________ than any other bird. (faster, fastest)
10. They live ____________ than most other birds, too. (longer, longest)

Circle the letter of the word that goes in each sentence.

11. Thomas Edison may have been the world's ____ inventor.
a. greater **b.** most greatest **c.** greatest **d.** more greater

12. His ____ invention was the electric light.
a. more important **b.** importantest
c. most important **d.** most best

13. He himself thought the record player was his ____ invention.
a. bestest **b.** best **c.** most best **d.** most bestest

14. He made other people's inventions work ____, too.
a. more better **b.** most best **c.** better **d.** gooder

15. He made telephones and movie cameras work ____ than they had before.
a. more efficiently **b.** efficienter
c. more efficienter **d.** most efficient

Read the paragraphs. If an underlined word is correct, write **C** on the line at the right. If it is not correct, write the correct word.

Advertisements promise us a gooder [16] life. They show people using products that make their clothes cleaner [17] and their teeth more brighter [18] than ever before.

People who appear in ads tell us why their products are the most best [19]. They always look more happier [20] and appear more attractive [21] after using the product.

Some commercials stress that their products are of the most highest [22] quality. Others emphasize that they sell for the most lowest [23] prices. One of the most quickest [24] ways to interest someone in a product is to offer it at a lower [25] price than usual.

16. ______________
17. ______________
18. ______________
19. ______________
20. ______________
21. ______________
22. ______________
23. ______________
24. ______________
25. ______________

LESSON 17

WORD CHOICE

Double Negatives

Number Right: ____

To make a sentence mean "no," use only one negative word.

We have **no** homework.	We **haven't** any homework.
That bothered **no one.**	That **didn't** bother anyone.
There is **nothing** to do.	There **isn't** anything to do.
We have **none.**	We **don't** have any.
I can **hardly** wait.	I **can't** wait.
I'm **never** bored.	I'm **not** ever bored.

complete Complete each sentence. Write the correct word on the line.

1. The moon doesn't have ____________ atmosphere. (any, no)

2. This means that there isn't ____________ air to breathe. (any, no)

3. Because there isn't ____________ air, sounds can't travel either. (any, no)

4. Nobody ____________ breathe on the moon without an oxygen tank. (can, can't)

5. ____________ can't talk on the moon without a radio. (Nobody, A person)

6. From the moon, the sky doesn't ____________ appear any color other than black. (ever, never)

7. There isn't ____________ living on the moon. (nothing, anything)

8. A person walking on the moon hardly weighs ____________. (anything, nothing)

9. If you looked for water on the moon, you wouldn't find ____________. (any, none)

10. There isn't ____________ on the earth that gets as hot or as cold as the moon. (no place, anyplace)

Circle the letter of the word or words that go in each sentence.

11. Most people don't know ____ about mushrooms.
a. nothing **b.** no information **c.** anything **d.** no facts

12. Some mushrooms shouldn't ____ be eaten.
a. ever **b.** not **c.** never **d.** hardly

13. There isn't ____ remedy for their poison.
a. scarcely no **b.** no **c.** any **d.** hardly no

14. There are many tasty mushrooms that don't contain ____ poison.
a. any **b.** none of the **c.** no **d.** hardly any

15. If you're not familiar with a mushroom, don't eat ____ of it.
a. none **b.** any **c.** no part **d.** no piece

Read the paragraphs. If an underlined word is correct, write **C** on the line at the right. If it is not correct, write the correct word.

Without muscles, you couldn't never (16) move. Some muscles don't hardly (17) move unless you want them to. Without these muscles, you couldn't throw nothing (18). Other muscles don't need no (19) conscious control. You don't never (20) need to remember to tell your heart to beat, for example.

Most people aren't never (21) aware of their muscles until they become sore. You shouldn't never (22) start any vigorous exercises without warming up first. Warm-up exercises shouldn't (23) barely strain your muscles. If you don't never (24) stretch your muscles too fast, you probably won't get no (25) cramps.

16. ____________

17. ____________

18. ____________

19. ____________

20. ____________

21. ____________

22. ____________

23. ____________

24. ____________

25. ____________

LESSON 18

WORD CHOICE

Homophones

Number Right: ____

Some words sound alike but are spelled differently and have different meanings. This chart shows when to use each word.

WORDS	MEANINGS	EXAMPLES
to too two	part of an infinitive; toward also; more than enough the number 2	Some plan **to** go **to** college. Trade schools are good, **too**. It takes **two** years to complete junior college.
its it's	belonging to it it is	A whale holds **its** breath underwater. **It's** able to swim great distances.
their there they're	belonging to them a place; a word that begins a sentence they are	Some scientists work in **their** labs. They go **there** to study. **There** are others who work outdoors. **They're** interested in nature.
whose who's	belonging to whom who is	**Whose** sneakers are these? **Who's** planning to jog today?
your you're	belonging to you you are	I like **your** new car. **You're** a good driver.

Complete each sentence. Write the correct word on the line.

1. How fast does ______________ hair grow? (you're, your)
2. Most people's hair grows about ___________ inches in four months. (to, too, two)
3. Some people think that's ___________ fast. (to, too, two)
4. _____________ the ones who don't like haircuts. (Their, There, They're)
5. Some people let _____________ hair grow long. (their, there, they're)
6. Others think that __________ better to cut hair often. (its, it's)
7. ______________ are some who like cutting hair. (Their, There, They're)
8. ______________ barbers and hair stylists. (Their, There, They're)
9. ______________ business is haircutting. (Their, There, They're)
10. ______________ your hair stylist? (Whose, Who's)

Circle the letter of the word that goes in each sentence.

11. ____ are many varieties of fish.
a. They're **b.** There **c.** Their **d.** There're

12. A sea horse is a fish ____ head looks like the head of a horse.
a. whose **b.** who is **c.** who's **d.** who'se

13. ____ tail is like a snake's.
a. It's **b.** It is **c.** Its **d.** Its'

14. Sea horses curl ____ tails around seaweed to anchor themselves.
a. they're **b.** their **c.** there'er **d.** there

15. ____ found in nearly all warm seas.
a. Their **b.** They're **c.** There are **d.** There

Read the paragraphs. If an underlined word is correct, write **C** on the line at the right. If it is not correct, write the correct word.

Vitamins in food are to (16) small too (17) see, but they're (18) they're (19). If you receive too (20) little of a certain vitamin in your food, you may need to take vitamin tablets.

If your (21) eating a balanced diet, they're (22) are enough vitamins in you're (23) food. Then its (24) probably not necessary to take vitamin pills. Anybody whose (25) not sure what a balanced diet consists of should consult an encyclopedia or another reference book.

16. ________________

17. ________________

18. ________________

19. ________________

20. ________________

21. ________________

22. ________________

23. ________________

24. ________________

25. ________________

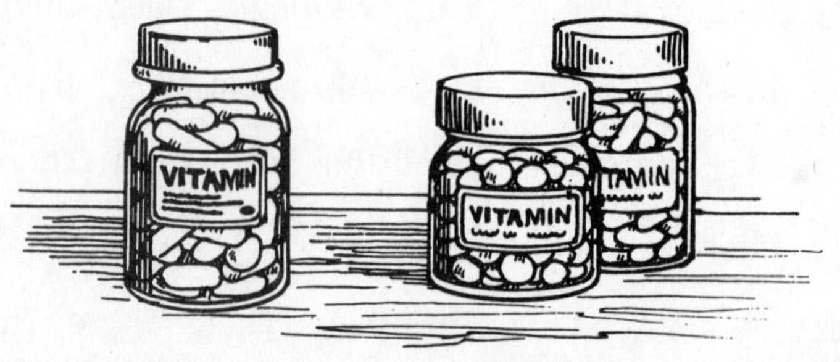

LESSON 19

WORD CHOICE

Confusing Pairs

Number Right: ____

The chart below shows the meanings of easily confused words. Read the examples to see when to use each word.

WORDS	MEANINGS	EXAMPLES
lay, laid, laid lie, lay, lain	to put or place to be at rest	They **laid** their pencils down. They **lay** down and rested.
sit, sat, sat, set, set, set	to rest to put or arrange	We **sat** by the fire. We **set** our sleeping bags down.
accept except	to agree to all but this one	I don't **accept** your opinion. I agree with everyone **except** you.
then than	at that time; next used after a comparative word	First dive, and **then** swim. Wading is easier **than** swimming.
between among	connecting two people or things connecting more than two people or things	Let's divide the work **between** you and me. Let's divide the work **among** the three of us.

complete Complete each sentence. Write the correct word on the line.

1. More ____________ one person plans a new building. (then, than)
2. Many developers discuss the plans __________ themselves. (between, among)
3. Then they ____________ down with an architect. (sit, set)
4. The architect surveys the place where the building will be _________. (sit, set)
5. The architect ______________ draws plans for the building. (then, than)
6. He or she may make more ____________ one design. (then, than)
7. One design is then _______________. (excepted, accepted)
8. ______________ the developers and the architect show the plans to several contractors. (Than, Then)
9. Each of the contractors ____________ a price for the work. (sits, sets)
10. All the bids ______________ one are rejected, and the construction begins. (accept, except)

Circle the letter of the word that goes in each sentence.

11. How do you tell the distance ____ two places on a globe?
   a. among b. between c. than d. amongst

12. It's easier to do ____ you might think.
   a. then b. next c. than d. from what

13. Simply ____ a piece of string on the globe so that it touches each place.
   a. lie b. lain c. lay d. laid

14. Mark the string and ____ it next to the distance scale on the globe.
   a. set b. sat c. sit d. setted

15. ____ you can measure the string along the scale.
   a. Than b. That c. This d. Then

Read the paragraphs. If an underlined word is correct, write **C** on the line at the right. If it is not correct, write the correct word.

Have you ever lain (16) your keys on a table and then (17) searched for them everywhere accept (18) where you left them? Of course, they were lying (19) in one place all the time. Did you ever search between (20) all your papers for a homework assignment only to find that it disappeared somewhere between (21) home and school? Have you ever set (22) down to watch your favorite show just as the phone rang?

There are some days when life seems harder then (23) ever. On days like these, if something can go wrong, then (24) it will. The only thing to do is to except (25) it. Tomorrow is another day.

16. ____________
17. ____________
18. ____________
19. ____________
20. ____________
21. ____________
22. ____________
23. ____________
24. ____________
25. ____________

LESSON

20 PRONOUNS / WORD CHOICE

Review

Review Score: ____

A. Write the pronoun that completes each sentence.

1. The starling is a black bird. ________ is known for its song. (It, They)
2. Starlings make ________ nests in hollow trees. (its, their)
3. Sometimes, they don't build their nests ________ . (theirselves, themselves)
4. A starling may make ________ home by stealing another bird's nest. (its, their)
5. A female starling lays four to six eggs in ________ lifetime. (her, their)
6. Starlings are helpful birds because ________ eat insects. (they, them)
7. ________ can see starlings almost everywhere in the United States. (Me and you, You and I)
8. Millions of ________ live here. (themselves, them)

B. Write the adjective or adverb that completes each sentence.

9. Caves are ________ places. (beautiful, beautifully)
10. Stones that look like icicles hang ________ from the roofs of caves. (beautiful, beautifully)
11. You can see these stones ________ in Carlsbad Caverns in New Mexico. (well, good)
12. Another ________ place to see them is in Mammoth Cave in Kentucky. (well, good)

C. Write the word that compares in each sentence.

13. Stainless steel is ________ than most other kinds of steel. (more stronger, stronger)
14. It resists rust ________ than other kinds of steel. (better, best)
15. It can be cleaned the ________ , too. (easiest, most easily)

D. Write the word that makes each sentence mean "no."

16. Surfing isn't ________ easy sport. (an, no)
17. A person who can't swim, shouldn't ________ surf. (ever, never)
18. There isn't ________ more exciting than riding a big wave. (nothing, anything)

E. Write the right word in each sentence.

19. ________ party are you attending? (Whose, Who's)
20. I ________ John's invitation. (accepted, excepted)

Name ______________________________ Progress Plotter

Number Right ↑

25
24
23
22
21
20
19
18
17
16
15
14
13
12
11
10
9
8
7
6
5
4
3
2
1

Lesson 1	Lesson 2	Lesson 3	Lesson 4	Lesson 5	Lesson 6	Lesson 7	Lesson 8	Lesson 9	Lesson 10	Lesson 11	Lesson 12	Lesson 13	Lesson 14	Lesson 15	Lesson 16	Lesson 17	Lesson 18	Lesson 19	Lesson 20
SUBJECT-VERB AGREEMENT						IRREGULAR VERBS				SUBJECT-VERB AGREEMENT/IRREGULAR VERBS Review Score: ____	PRONOUNS			WORD CHOICE					PRONOUNS/WORD CHOICE Review Score: ____

STANDARD USAGE

Final Test Name ______________________

Directions: Read each sentence. Choose the word or words that go in each sentence. Fill in the letter of your answer in the answer row.

1 One of my friends ________ performing in the play.
Ⓐ is
Ⓑ are
Ⓒ be
Ⓓ were

2 In the 1500s, traders first ________ coffee to Europe.
Ⓔ brang
Ⓕ bringed
Ⓖ brung
Ⓗ brought

3 Some birds ________ fly.
Ⓐ does not
Ⓑ doesn't
Ⓒ done
Ⓓ don't

4 There ________ no penguins at the North Pole.
Ⓔ are
Ⓕ is
Ⓖ be
Ⓗ was

5 Marco Polo ________ to China in the thirteenth century.
Ⓐ gone
Ⓑ goed
Ⓒ has went
Ⓓ went

6 Where ________ meteors come from?
Ⓔ does
Ⓕ done
Ⓖ do
Ⓗ doed

7 The sun or the moon ________ light.
Ⓐ are
Ⓑ give
Ⓒ shine
Ⓓ provides

8 Some lobsters in the ocean ________ three feet long.
Ⓔ is
Ⓕ be
Ⓖ are
Ⓗ was

9 Who ________ the first airplane?
Ⓐ flown
Ⓑ flew
Ⓒ flied
Ⓓ flyed

10 The dog and the cat ________ become friendly.
Ⓔ have
Ⓕ has
Ⓖ hasn't
Ⓗ does

(Go on to the next page.)

ANSWER ROWS:
1 Ⓐ Ⓑ Ⓒ Ⓓ   2 Ⓔ Ⓕ Ⓖ Ⓗ   3 Ⓐ Ⓑ Ⓒ Ⓓ   4 Ⓔ Ⓕ Ⓖ Ⓗ   5 Ⓐ Ⓑ Ⓒ Ⓓ
6 Ⓔ Ⓕ Ⓖ Ⓗ   7 Ⓐ Ⓑ Ⓒ Ⓓ   8 Ⓔ Ⓕ Ⓖ Ⓗ   9 Ⓐ Ⓑ Ⓒ Ⓓ   10 Ⓔ Ⓕ Ⓖ Ⓗ

Directions: Read each sentence. Choose the word or words that go in each sentence. Fill in the letter of your answer in the answer row.

11 Onions get ________ strong smell from the sulphur in them.
Ⓐ its
Ⓑ there
Ⓒ their
Ⓓ they're

12 A newborn panda bear is smaller ________ a stick of butter.
Ⓔ then
Ⓕ accept for
Ⓖ thin
Ⓗ than

13 George W. Carver made the peanut a cash crop almost by ________ .
Ⓐ hisself
Ⓑ himself
Ⓒ himselves
Ⓓ themselves

14 Rice is the ________ food in the world.
Ⓔ popularest
Ⓕ more popular
Ⓖ most popular
Ⓗ most popularly

15 ________ saw an ostrich.
Ⓐ She and I
Ⓑ She and myself
Ⓒ Me and her
Ⓓ Her and me

16 A male peacock has colorful feathers on ________ tail.
Ⓔ her
Ⓕ their
Ⓖ his
Ⓗ himself

17 You shouldn't ________ ride a bike on a highway.
Ⓐ never
Ⓑ not
Ⓒ not ever
Ⓓ ever

18 Skating is good exercise for ________ .
Ⓔ you and myself
Ⓕ you and me
Ⓖ you and I
Ⓗ me and you

19 Cork floats ________ .
Ⓐ fine
Ⓑ well
Ⓒ good
Ⓓ goodly

20 Ben Franklin liked turkeys. He wanted ________ to be the national bird.
Ⓔ themselves
Ⓕ it
Ⓖ them
Ⓗ they

STOP

Final Test Score: ________

ANSWER ROWS:
11 Ⓐ Ⓑ Ⓒ Ⓓ 12 Ⓔ Ⓕ Ⓖ Ⓗ 13 Ⓐ Ⓑ Ⓒ Ⓓ 14 Ⓔ Ⓕ Ⓖ Ⓗ 15 Ⓐ Ⓑ Ⓒ Ⓓ
16 Ⓔ Ⓕ Ⓖ Ⓗ 17 Ⓐ Ⓑ Ⓒ Ⓓ 18 Ⓔ Ⓕ Ⓖ Ⓗ 19 Ⓐ Ⓑ Ⓒ Ⓓ 20 Ⓔ Ⓕ Ⓖ Ⓗ

Lesson 1

1. Our hearts **work** hard.
2. The right side **gets** blood from the body.
3. It **pumps** this blood to the lungs.
4. The lungs **give** oxygen to the blood.
5. They **take** carbon dioxide from the blood.
6. Then the blood **returns** to the left side of the heart.
7. The left side **pumps** the blood to the rest of the body.
8. Veins **bring** the blood to the heart.
9. Arteries **carry** the blood away from the heart.
10. Your heart **beats** about 100,000 times a day.

11. b **12.** d **13.** b **14.** a **15.** c

16. need **17.** C **18.** gives
19. becomes **20.** cope **21.** C
22. sleep **23.** falls **24.** C **25.** burn

Lesson 2

1. An adult and a child **require** different amounts of food.
2. A child or a teenager **needs** more food than an adult.
3. Starches, sugars, and fats **provide** energy.
4. Bread or cereal **gives** you starch.
5. Rice and potatoes **contain** starch, too.
6. Milk and meat **contain** some fat.
7. Butter or oil **provides** fat also.
8. Either animal protein or vegetable protein **gives** things the body needs to grow and maintain itself.
9. Cheese, eggs, fish, milk, and meat **serve** as sources of animal protein.
10. Beans, nuts, grain, and vegetables **provide** vegetable protein.

11. c **12.** c **13.** b **14.** a **15.** b

16. C **17.** C **18.** go **19.** remove
20. turn **21.** C **22.** need
23. distributes **24.** C **25.** emerges

Lesson 3

1. We usually **think** of the sun as a ball of light.
2. However, dark patches of gas also **form** on the sun's surface.
3. The patches of gas **appear** dark because they are cooler than the rest of the sun.
4. Scientists who study the sun **call** these dark places *sunspots.*
5. The position of the sunspots **varies.**
6. The size and number of sunspots also **change** over the years.
7. Over an eleven-year period, the number of sunspots **increases** to about one hundred.
8. The number of patches **decreases** to about five over the next eleven years.
9. Each period of eleven years **forms** a sunspot cycle.
10. Scientists who have studied the sun **know** when these cycles take place, but they don't know why.

11. d **12.** c **13.** a **14.** b **15.** a

16. govern **17.** refers **18.** means
19. increases **20.** start **21.** goes
22. C **23.** encourages **24.** work
25. equals

Lesson 4

1. Everyone **wants** to have good luck.
2. Some **believe** that they can influence their luck.
3. Many **think** it's good luck to find a four-leaf clover.
4. Others **carry** a rabbit's foot for good luck.
5. Someone **knocks** on wood to prevent bad luck.
6. Another **thinks** it's good luck to put a shiny penny in a new wallet.
7. A few **avoid** making important decisions on Friday the thirteenth.
8. Some **throw** rice at a bride and groom to bring them good luck.
9. Many **say** that if you forget to take an umbrella, it will rain.
10. Almost all of us **follow** some superstitions.

11. b **12.** a **13.** c **14.** c **15.** b

16. needs **17.** C **18.** jog **19.** get
20. take **21.** swims **22.** C **23.** play
24. ride **25.** benefits

Lesson 5

1. The first computer **was** built in 1944.
2. Early computers **were** very large.
3. New computers **are** much smaller.
4. A computer **doesn't** "think" on its own.
5. It **has** to be given instructions by people.
6. A computer **is** useful for many kinds of work.
7. Computers **do** things thousands of times faster than people.

8. Computers **have** replaced people in some jobs.
9. The increased use of computers **has** created many jobs, too.
10. Learning to work with computers **isn't** difficult.

11. c **12.** b **13.** d **14.** a **15.** b

16. has **17.** aren't **18.** were
19. have **20.** have **21.** C **22.** do
23. has **24.** is **25.** isn't

Lesson 6

1. There **are** basic facts to be learned about every country.
2. Here **are** some questions about Canada.
3. What **is** the capital of Canada?
4. What languages **do** Canadians speak?
5. What form of government **do** Canadians have?
6. Who **is** Canada's prime minister?
7. What **is** the difference between Canada's provinces and territories?
8. What **are** Canada's chief crops and industries?
9. What **does** the Canadian flag look like?
10. What **are** Canada's national holidays?

11. c **12.** b **13.** d **14.** c **15.** a

16. is **17.** Have **18.** Do **19.** C
20. Are **21.** C **22.** Is **23.** C
24. Are **25.** C

Lesson 7

1. The Romans **took** control of Britain in A.D. 43.
2. After 400 years, the Roman Empire **fell.**
3. Angles, Saxons, and other German tribes then **came** to Britain.
4. The Angles **took** the most land.
5. Angle-land **became** known as England.
6. The Scandinavians **came** in the ninth century.
7. The Normans, a French tribe, **took** over in 1066.
8. During their rule, most things were **written** in French.
9. The Normans were not **driven** out.
10. Gradually, the Normans and the Anglo-Saxons **became** one people.

11. c **12.** c **13.** a **14.** b **15.** c

16. saw **17.** drove **18.** ran **19.** C
20. fell **21.** shaken **22.** ate
23. seen **24.** came **25.** C

Lesson 8

1. Pollution **began** to be a major problem in the nineteenth century.
2. As factories **grew** more numerous, pollution became common.
3. Dirty smoke was **blown** into the air.
4. Waste products from industry were **thrown** into streams and lakes.
5. People in crowded cities **drank** untreated water.
6. In the twentieth century, cars and airplanes **threw** gas and smoke into the air.
7. People **drew** dirty air into their lungs.
8. The problems of pollution have not **shrunk.**
9. However, people have **begun** to try to do something about pollution.
10. Organizations that fight pollution have **grown.**

11. d **12.** b **13.** a **14.** a **15.** d

16. begun **17.** known **18.** shown
19. rang **20.** rung **21.** swung
22. sang **23.** swam **24.** C **25.** flown

Lesson 9

1. Archeologists have **gone** to faraway places.
2. Some have **led** expeditions.
3. Others have **dug** up ancient ruins.
4. They study civilizations that were **lost**.
5. They find tools that were **left** behind.
6. Carefully, they restore items that were **broken**.
7. They can learn what people **did** for a living.
8. They can even tell what clothing was **worn.**
9. They also determine what language had been **spoken.**
10. Some of these languages are not **heard** today.

11. b **12.** c **13.** d **14.** b **15.** c

16. heard **17.** went **18.** gone
19. left **20.** sent **21.** C **22.** chosen
23. stolen **24.** C **25.** sent

Lesson 10

1. Ben Franklin was **taught** the craft of printing.
2. At seventeen, he **set** out for Philadelphia.
3. By the time he was twenty-four, he had **bought** his own print shop.

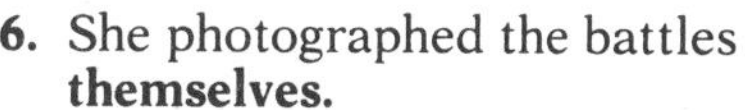

4. He printed and **sold** an almanac.
5. *Poor Richard's Almanack* **told** people about the weather.
6. Franklin also **put** many wise sayings in his almanac.
7. One of them **said,** "Early to bed and early to rise, makes a man healthy, wealthy, and wise."
8. Franklin **stood** for thrift and hard work.
9. Many people **paid** attention to Franklin.
10. He **brought** about many changes in the new nation.

11. a **12.** c **13.** d **14.** c **15.** b

16. fought **17.** C **18.** paid **19.** let
20. cut **21.** stood **22.** put **23.** C
24. hurt **25.** beaten

Lesson 11 Review

See page 724

Lesson 12

1. **We** students took part in an experiment.
2. One of **us** was told to describe an object without naming it.
3. **She** described its color, shape, and size.
4. The rest of **us** students weren't allowed to ask any questions about the object.
5. **We** were told to guess what the object was.
6. Few of **us** guessed correctly.
7. Then **we** repeated the experiment.
8. This time, we were allowed to ask **her** questions.
9. My classmates and **I** were then able to guess correctly.
10. The experiment taught my friends and **me** the importance of asking questions.

11. c **12.** d **13.** c **14.** b **15.** a

16. We **17.** C **18.** C **19.** they
20. He **21.** He **22.** You and I
23. them **24.** us **25.** you and me

Lesson 13

1. Margaret Bourke-White made **herself** famous as a photographer.
2. She first attracted attention to **herself** by photographing coal miners.
3. The subject **itself** was interesting.
4. Her dramatic use of lighting made the portraits **themselves** works of art.
5. As a reporter covering World War II, she found **herself** in many dangerous situations.
6. She photographed the battles **themselves.**
7. Her camera captured soldiers as they saw **themselves.**
8. When she met Gandhi, an Indian leader, she photographed **him.**
9. She wrote and photographed pictures for many books **herself.**
10. One of her books is called *Portrait of* **Myself**.

11. d **12.** c **13.** b **14.** a **15.** d

16. himself **17.** yourself **18.** myself
19. C **20.** himself **21.** C
22. themselves **23.** C **24.** himself
25. C

Lesson 14

1. People build canals to help **them** go from one body of water to another.
2. A ship may go through canals as **it** travels.
3. Many canals have *locks* in **them.**
4. A lock connects two bodies of water when **they** are at different heights.
5. A lock has watertight gates at both ends of **it.**
6. When a ship sails into a lock, the gates shut after **it.**
7. Water then flows *into* the lock or *out* of **it.**
8. The ship moves up or down according to **its** route.
9. The Panama Canal has twelve locks in **it.**
10. Canals aid ships by making **their** journeys shorter.

11. b **12.** b **13.** b **14.** c **15.** b

16. it **17.** C **18.** them **19.** it
20. them **21.** them **22.** C **23.** it
24. it **25.** them

Lesson 15

1. The first Frisbees were **plain** aluminum pie plates.
2. Some students at Yale University discovered that the pie plates flew **well.**
3. They sailed **gracefully** through the air.
4. Some **clever** manufacturers began to produce plastic Frisbees.
5. The new sport caught on **quickly**.
6. **Suddenly,** there were Frisbee players all over the country.
7. To throw a Frisbee **well,** you have to spin it away from you.
8. Most players **simply** play "catch."

9. You may have to run **fast** to catch a Frisbee.
10. A good Frisbee player reacts **quickly.**

11. c **12.** d **13.** b **14.** a **15.** a

16. well **17.** clearly **18.** carefully
19. quickly **20.** thoughtfully **21.** C
22. C **23.** well **24.** neat **25.** C

Lesson 16

1. Ostriches are now the **largest** birds in the world.
2. The extinct moa bird was **taller** than the ostrich.
3. The extinct elephant bird was **heavier** than the ostrich.
4. Dinosaur eggs were **bigger** than ostrich eggs.
5. Today, however, ostriches lay the **largest** eggs of any bird or reptile.
6. Ostriches have the **thickest** eyelashes of any bird.
7. Their eyesight is **better** than that of many other animals.
8. The female ostrich has a **duller** coat than the male.
9. Ostriches can run **faster** than any other bird.
10. They live **longer** than most other birds, too.

11. c **12.** c **13.** b **14.** c **15.** a

16. better **17.** C **18.** brighter
19. best **20.** happier **21.** C
22. highest **23.** lowest **24.** quickest
25. C

Lesson 17

1. The moon doesn't have **any** atmosphere.
2. This means that there isn't **any** air to breathe.
3. Because there isn't **any** air, sounds can't travel either.
4. Nobody **can** breathe on the moon without an oxygen tank.
5. **A person** can't talk on the moon without a radio.
6. From the moon, the sky doesn't **ever** appear any color other than black.
7. There isn't **anything** living on the moon.
8. A person walking on the moon hardly weighs **anything.**
9. If you looked for water on the moon, you wouldn't find **any.**
10. There isn't **anyplace** on the earth that gets as hot or as cold as the moon.

11. c **12.** a **13.** c **14.** a **15.** b

16. ever **17.** don't **18.** anything
19. any **20.** ever **21.** ever **22.** ever
23. should **24.** ever **25.** any

Lesson 18

1. How fast does **your** hair grow?
2. Most people's hair grows about **two** inches in four months.
3. Some people think that's **too** fast.
4. **They're** the ones who don't like haircuts.
5. Some people let **their** hair grow long.
6. Others think that **it's** better to cut hair often.
7. **There** are some who like cutting hair.
8. **They're** barbers and hair stylists.
9. **Their** business is haircutting.
10. **Who's** your hair stylist?

11. b **12.** a **13.** c **14.** b **15.** b

16. too **17.** to **18.** C **19.** there
20. C **21.** you're **22.** there **23.** your
24. it's **25.** who's

Lesson 19

1. More **than** one person plans a new building.
2. Many developers may discuss plans **among** themselves.
3. Then they **sit** down with an architect.
4. The architect surveys the place where the building will be **set.**
5. The architect **then** draws plans for the building.
6. He or she may make more **than** one design.
7. One design is then **accepted.**
8. **Then** the developers and the architect show the plans to several contractors.
9. Each of the contractors **sets** a price for the work.
10. All the bids **except** one are rejected, and the construction begins.

11. b **12.** c **13.** c **14.** a **15.** d

16. laid **17.** C **18.** except
19. laying **20.** among **21.** C **22.** sat
23. than **24.** C **25.** accept

Lesson 20 Review

See page 724

Enrichment

Use the tips on pages 234 and 256 to help you do this page.

Riddle: Look at this group of words. As you study it, can you find why it's unusual? In fact, it is so uncommon that your probability of finding a group similar to it is about a million to two. Why is it so unusual?

_____ 1 _____ 2 _____ 3 _____ 4 _____ 5

_____ 6 _____ 7 _____ 8, _____ 9 _____ 10.

By choosing the right words to complete these sentences, you can answer the riddle. Write each answer choice on the line above the number of the sentence.

1. The alphabet has twenty-six letters in _____. (them, it)
2. It _____ contain an equal number of vowels and consonants. (don't, doesn't)
3. All English words _____ at least one vowel. (have, has)
4. The words *I* and *a* are examples of words that don't have _____ consonants. (any, no)
5. The word *alphabet* comes from the first two letters _____ Greek alphabet, *alpha* and *beta.* (off the, of the)
6. The English word that is spoken _____ is the word *I.* (most commonly, commonest)
7. The word that is _____ most often is *the.* (wrote, written)
8. One _____ appears in almost every English sentence. (letters, letter)
9. Can you guess _____ letter is used most frequently? (witch, which)
10. The letter that appears in most sentences _____. (are *e,* is *e*)

Answers on page 724

SPECTRUM WRITING

CONTENTS: Each Lesson is four pages.

Project Editor: Sandra Kelley
Text: Written by Ambrose J. Burfoot, Ted Bartoletta, and Victor Perpetua
Design and Production by A Good Thing, Inc.
Illustrated by Sally Springer, Doug Cushman, Karen Pietrobono,
Kris Boyd, Anne Stockwell

unit 1
Writing in Sequence

Things to Remember About Writing in Sequence

Sequence tells the order of events.

Writing

- Use chronological, or time, order to sequence events.
- Use logical order to sequence a description.
- Vary a chronological sequence of events in a story by using flashbacks to tell about something that happened earlier, by telling about simultaneous actions in different places, or by foreshadowing future action.
- Use chronological or logical order in an outline to help you organize ideas for a report. Follow your outline when you write your report.

Revising

- Add adverbs to your writing to give specific information about *how, when,* or *where.*
- Use specific verbs to do the job of a verb-adverb combination, when possible.

lesson

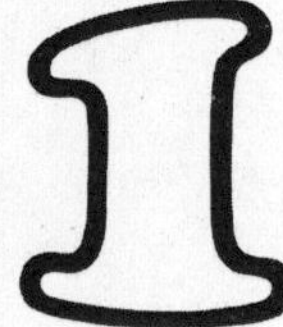

Writing in chronological or logical order

Wanda Wechsler, controversial underwater painter, had a long and interesting life. If you were going to write a short biography of her, it would make sense to describe the events of her life in the sequence in which they happened. This time sequence is called **chronological order.**

A. On the lines below, number the events of Wanda Wechsler's life in chronological order.

______ Started painting under water while in high school

______ Moved to French Riviera to escape criticism

______ Born in Boise, Idaho, on February 1, 1890, during unusually heavy rainstorm

______ Became very excited when she spilled paints in the sink in nursery school

______ Died at eight-five, rich and happy, in French villa

______ Experimented in France with sprays, oils, acrylics

______ Later work hailed by critics as "masterpieces of form and content"

______ Won watercolor contest in elementary school

______ As a baby, never wanted to get out of her bath

______ First paintings jeered at by critics as "washed out"

Short biographies, such as those found in who's who books, the *Dictionary of American Biographies*, or obituary columns of newspapers, usually start with a sentence that includes information about why the person was important. Then they go on to tell about events in the person's life in chronological order. Wanda Wechsler's biography might begin like this.

> Wanda Wechsler, the controversial underwater painter, was born in Boise, Idaho, on February 1, 1890, during an unusually heavy rainstorm. This may, in some way, have influenced her lifelong involvement with water. Her mother said that as far back as she could remember, Wanda had always loved water. "As a baby, she never wanted to get out of her bath," Mrs. Wechsler recalled.

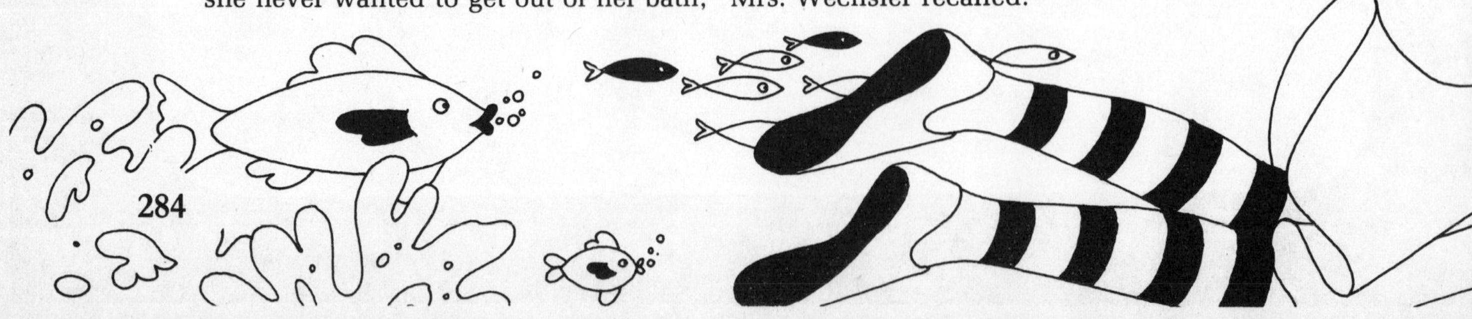

B. Refer to the paragraph at the bottom of page 2 to answer these questions.

1. Which phrase tells what Wanda Wechsler was famous as?

____

2. Underline the sentences in the paragraph that were *not* in the list of events in part **A.** How do the sentences you underlined help show a connection between the events?

____

C. Write up the rest of Wanda Wechsler's life, based on the events listed in part **A.** You may add more details if you wish. Try to use words and phrases that show how one event is related to another in time, such as *after that, during this time,* or *finally.* You may also wish to add phrases that show how one event influenced another, such as *because of this, since then,* or *as a result.*

____

____

____

____

____

____

____

____

____

____

For some kinds of writing, such as biographies and directions, it makes sense to use chronological order to organize your material. Other kinds of writing can be organized in **logical order.** Suppose you wanted to describe Wanda Wechsler's painting pictured below. You might start by stating your general impression of it and then go on to tell in more detail what you see. You could describe it from top to bottom, from left to right, from large forms to small forms, or in some other such logical order.

D. Refer to the picture above to do the activities below.

1. Write a title for the painting in the space at the bottom of the frame.
2. Write a description of the painting for a catalog of Wanda Wechsler's major works. Start with an overall impression, then go on to describe the main features of the painting in an order that seems logical to you.

E. Read the list of topics below. Put an *L* in front of the topics that might best be described in logical order and a *C* in front of the topics that could be described in chronological order.

_______ a stage set you painted

_______ a day's trip

_______ the plot of a story

_______ a new outfit you bought

_______ how the tiger got stripes

_______ your favorite recipe

_______ wallpaper you designed

_______ your house or apartment

_______ how spiders weave webs

_______ the gym decorated for a dance

F. Choose one of the topics in part **E.** List below the main things you will want to say about it. Then number them in logical or chronological order.

____

____

____

____

____

____

____

____

____

Write On

Choose one of the following.

1. Write up the topic you chose for part **F**, using the sequence you planned. Add details and transition words (like *first, next, on the top,* or *to the left.*)
2. What are your ambitions in life? Pretend that you have achieved one of your goals, and write a fictional autobiography in chronological order for the *Dictionary of American Biographies.* Think of everything you needed to do or sacrifice to reach your goal. Be imaginative. Give yourself an interesting life.

You can sequence events by using chronological, or time, order. You can sequence a description by using some kind of logical order.

lesson

Varying the sequence of events

Most stories are told from the beginning to the end in a fairly straightforward chronological progression. However, to achieve certain effects, there are several ways a storyteller can vary the sequence of events.

One way is to start the story somewhere near the middle or the end and then show earlier events in what is called a **flashback.** Read this selection.

> Hurtling through space, Captain Corcoran shifted moodily in his seat, then released the restraining buckle at his waist and floated slowly out of his chair toward the control panel. He selected his favorite tape, "The Midnight Rose," and propelled himself to the center of the cabin, trying to put all thoughts of earth and home out of his mind. As the music began, he started to dance—very slowly, since sudden movements could send him crashing into the walls. He was like a diver in slow motion or a dolphin in a small tank, gracefully stretching his body, expertly gliding along the wall without ever touching it.
>
> As he turned a slow somersault, he found himself thinking of his pole vaulting. He had always felt that gravity was some sort of enemy restraining him, holding him back, keeping him from flying. It had been exhilarating to propel himself over that bar the first time, to be free of gravity, if only for a split second. After his first jump, he had sat on the grass and thought for a long time. What if he could really get away from gravity and could float? Corcoran bumped softly against the wall. The music had stopped, but he wasn't aware just when.

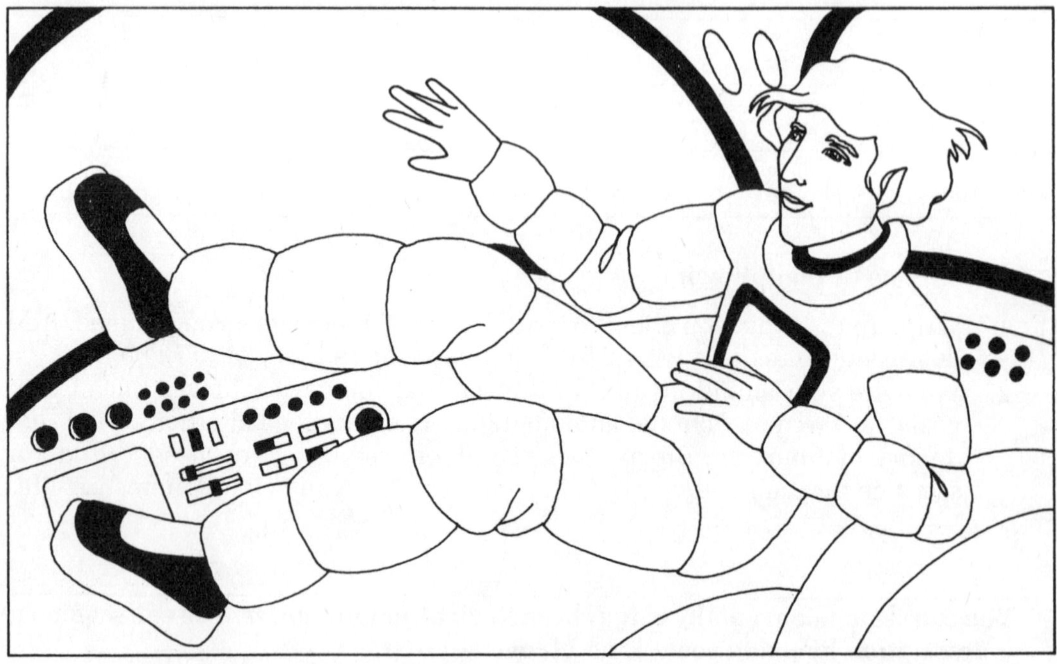

A. Think about how you might convert the scene you just read into a movie.

1. Where would the movie scene start?

___

2. What scene would you cut to for the flashback?

___

3. What does the flashback reveal about Captain Corcoran?

___

B. Suppose you were going to start a story using a flashback. Circle one of the characters below and think of a present-time situation you could put him or her in that might require an explanation. Then think of a time your character could "flash back" to, or remember, that would explain something about the present.

a gossip columnist	a private detective	a comic-book illustrator
a stunt flyer	a blind musician	a fortuneteller

Present time situation: ___

___

Flashback to: ___

___

Another way an author can depart from a strictly chronological order is to report on **simultaneous actions,** two events happening at the same time in two different places. Read this selection.

> Streaking through space in a silvery ship, concealed by the tail of a comet, the Earth Raiders have been able to approach our fragile planet undetected and are preparing to deal it a vital blow.
>
> At this moment, on a high mountain peak, Colleen MacGregor turns her telescope to focus on Saturn.

C. Suppose that the passage above began a comic strip called "The Earth Raiders." Answer the questions below.

1. What do you think Colleen would discover in the comic strip panels that follow this introduction?

___

___

2. What effect is an author able to create by reporting on simultaneous action?

___

___

D. Below is a phrase to begin the second paragraph of a story. Think about what could be happening in the first paragraph that might create some anxiety in our minds about what was going on at the ranch. Then fill in your descriptions of two simultaneous actions on the lines provided.

____

____

____

____

Meanwhile, back at the ranch, ______________________

____

____

____

____

Sometimes authors give hints about something that is going to happen. Usually, the author shares these hints with the reader while the characters in the story are unaware of them or don't realize their importance. The use of clues about future events is called **foreshadowing.** Read this selection.

> A faint but distinct whirring sound woke Harriet. "I must have been dreaming," she mused. Glancing at her watch, she realized with alarm that she had dozed off on the beach and that she would be late for supper. She got up, stretched, shook out her towel, and pulled her sweatshirt over her head. She had just started up the slope leading to the beach house when she stepped on something sticky. She leaned over and pulled a light green substance off her bare foot. "Gum!" she thought in disgust. "Who on earth would have left a wad of gum out here?"

E. Think about how the story above might continue.

1. What two things in the story would you expect to have explained as you read further?

   ____

2. If this story were a movie, think of something the camera could show next that Harriet would be unaware of. What would it be?

   ____

   ____

   ____

F. Suppose you were making a movie in which one of the following dangers was in store for the main character. How would you foreshadow the danger?

a robbery a visit of a creature from outer space a shark

____

____

____

____

____

Choose one of the following.

1. Write a short story using the flashback situation you thought of in part **B.**
2. Continue the "Meanwhile, back at the ranch" story you started in part **D** using more scenes of simultaneous action.
3. Continue the story you started in part **F.** How does the main character escape from danger? Or is it too late?

A chronological sequence of events in a story can be varied by using flashbacks to tell about something that happened earlier, by telling about simultaneous actions in different places, or by foreshadowing future action.

lesson 3

Writing and following an outline

An **outline** is a valuable writing tool, especially when you are organizing material for a report. If you are attempting to cover too much in your report, your outline will help you see this. Your outline can also help you identify areas that you must research more thoroughly; it will point out gaps or weak links in your report.

First you must determine the sequence of your outline. Certain topics lend themselves to certain kinds of sequence—for example, a history or biography can be neatly arranged in chronological order.

A. The topics below belong to an outline for "The History of Comics." Use chronological order to rearrange the main heads and subheads into a clear order. Write the topics next to the correct numbers and letters below.

"Mutt and Jeff" first daily in 1907
New comics combine humor with satire
The earliest comics
"Superman" and "Prince Valiant" follow in thirties
Adventure strips of the thirties
Some old comics continue in the seventies
"Hogan's Alley" first comic in 1895
"Dick Tracy" started in 1931
Modern comics

The History of Comics

I. ____________________

A. ____________________

B. ____________________

II. ____________________

A. ____________________

B. ____________________

III. ____________________

A. ____________________

B. ____________________

Other kinds of outlines can be organized in some kind of logical order. In any outline, you must be certain that the main heads are all parallel and that each subhead is placed under the appropriate main head.

B. Suppose you are writing a report about modern American music. Which of the following would be appropriate, parallel main heads? Write the Roman numerals I, II, III, and IV in front of your choices.

______ The Beatles	______ French ballads	______ Early Egyptian music
______ Folk music	______ Rock music	______ Scott Joplin
______ Show music	______ Piano music	______ Country/Western music

C. Once the main heads are arranged, you can fill in the subheads and the sub-subheads, or details, below them. Fill in the subheads and details below in the logical spaces in the outline. (Hint: Look for three parallel subheads first, and then fill in the details that go with each subhead.)

Woody Guthrie	Western prairie songs	Imported folk songs
Mexican songs	Famous folk singers	Songs native to America
Joan Baez	New England sea chanteys	Pete Seeger
English ballads	Black American spirituals	West Indian calypso

I. Folk Music

A. ______________________________

1. ______________________________

2. ______________________________

3. ______________________________

B. ______________________________

1. ______________________________

2. ______________________________

3. ______________________________

C. ______________________________

1. ______________________________

2. ______________________________

3. ______________________________

Be sure your report follows the order of your outline, unless you make a decision to reorganize it. Use each main head as the main idea of a paragraph, and use the subheads as details. Don't leave out any subheads, and don't write facts in one paragraph that belong in a different section.

D. Below are part of the outline on American folk music and a paragraph based on it. Read them, and answer the questions that follow.

C. Songs native to America
   1. Western prairie songs
   2. New England sea chanteys
   3. Black American spirituals

People sang as they worked, and many American folk songs developed out of work situations. Cowhands sang songs like "The Chisholm Trail" and "Streets of Laredo" to quiet the cattle or to help fill the lonely hours on the trail. Spirituals, like "Go Down, Moses" and "Swing Low, Sweet Chariot," although religious in content, were often sung to accompany the ship loading and plantation work done by slaves and later free workers in the South. During the Depression years of the thirties, Woody Guthrie traveled among migrant workers. His songs, like "This Land Is Your Land," told of the beauty of the American country.

1. Which is the main idea of the paragraph?

___

2. Which subhead was left out?

___

3. Underline the sentences that fit under a different section, according to the outline in part **C.**

___

4. Under which part of the outline do these sentences belong?

___

The writer may decide to move these sentences or to reorganize the outline.

E. Choose your favorite kind of modern American music from the main heads in part **B.** Write part of an outline about your topic on the lines below. You may wish to choose musical styles, songs, or performers to outline.

My favorite music: ______________________

A. ______________________

1. ______________________

2. ______________________

3. ______________________

F. Now write a paragraph that follows your outline for part **E.**

____

____

____

____

____

____

____

Write On

Choose one of the topics below or a topic that you are especially interested in. If you need to, research facts to make an outline for your topic. Sequence your outline in chronological or logical order. Then write a short report based on your outline.

My Favorite Sport (its history or famous players)
UFOs (or other strange phenomena)
A biography of a famous person
An Event That Changed History

In an outline, you use chronological or logical order to help you organize ideas for a report. Follow your outline when you write your report.

lesson

Revising

Adding adverbs

Adverbs tell how, when, where. Some adverbs are single words and some are phrases.

	How	When	Where
Adverbs	gingerly	yesterday	outside
Adverbial phrases	without a trace	on July 4th	above the clouds

A. Fill in the blanks in the sentences below with one-word adverbs or with phrases. In the parentheses after each sentence, write whether your adverb tells when, where, or how.

1. The game began ______________________________. (____________)
2. She screamed ______________________________. (____________)
3. Igor arrived ______________________________. (____________)
4. The snow stopped ______________________________. (____________)
5. The workers sang ______________________________. (____________)

Well-used adverbs can make your writing more descriptive and clear. But it is easy to overuse adverbs. Inexperienced writers tend to use too many adverbs to make up for poor verb selection. Notice how one specific verb can take the place of each verb–adverb combination below.

walked slowly—strolled	spoke loudly—yelled
did very well—excelled	taught again—reviewed

B. The paragraph below contains too many adverbs. Read completely through the paragraph once and then revise it by crossing out unnecessary adverbs. You can also cross out verb–adverb (or verbal–adverb) combinations and substitute more specific verbs (or verbals).

Paco first heard the strange noise as he was sitting easily on the sofa, lightly holding the evening newspaper in his hand. He wanted to read it carefully because he was wishing strongly to find a sale on stereo equipment. Then he heard the noise once more. He finally decided that he had better look closely, so he walked softly through the hallway until he gradually reached the bathroom. Then he stopped to listen attentively once again. No doubt about it: A scratching sound was coming regularly from the bathroom. Paco quickly decided that a bold approach would work best, so he bravely opened the door and moved directly into the bathroom.

C. On the lines below, write two more sentences about Paco. First, tell what he found in the bathroom. Then tell what he did about it. Use at least one how, one when, and one where adverb.

___

___

___

___

Look over the papers you have written for this unit. See which ones have too many adverbs that can be replaced with specific verbs. See which ones may need more adverbs to pinpoint how, when, or where something happened. Choose one paper to revise.

Add adverbs to your writing to give specific information about how, when, or where. But don't overuse adverbs. A specific verb may often do the job of a verb-adverb combination.

Post-Test

1. Decide whether the topics below are best written in chronological or logical order. Write C for chronological or L for logical on each blank.

   _____ a. a biography   _____ c. a description of a ball game

   _____ b. a description of a city   _____ d. a description of the planet Jupiter

2. Choose one of the topics below. Organize your ideas about the topic in outline form on the blanks below.

   a. clothing styles b. computers c. team sports

   ____________________ ____________________

   ____________________ ____________________

   ____________________ ____________________

   ____________________ ____________________

3. Write a short anecdote about one of the following: your first day at a new school, a blind date, or going to a party where you don't know anyone. Start from a present-time situation, and use the flashback technique.

4. Rewrite each sentence. Replace the underlined verb-adverb combinations with specific verbs.

   a. The assembly <u>greeted</u> the president <u>enthusiastically.</u>

   ____

   b. Jean <u>wrote</u> a note <u>carelessly</u> to her homeroom teacher.

   ____

   c. Tony <u>differed strongly</u> with Denis over which football team was the best.

   ____

unit 2
Writing About Cause and Effect

Things to Remember When Writing About Cause and Effect

A **cause** tells why something happens. An **effect** is what happens.

Writing 

- Use the topic sentence in a cause-and-effect paragraph to describe a cause with the other sentences giving effects, or to describe an effect with the other sentences giving causes.
- Place the topic sentence either first or last in the paragraph.
- Let the reader discover the cause or causes when you write a mystery. Make the crime or fearful situation your effect.
- Go from the effects you observe to their probable causes when writing about a scientific experiment.
- When you write syllogisms, begin with a generalization and then reason your way to a specific conclusion.

Revising 

- Use connecting words, such as prepositions, conjunctions, and relative pronouns, to link sentences and to make cause-and-effect relationships clear.

lesson

Writing topic sentences in cause and effect paragraphs

We see **causes** and **effects** every day. Alarm clocks wake us up; rain causes us to open umbrellas; hunger causes us to eat. Much of our writing involves describing causes and effects.

One very common method of organizing paragraphs is from cause to effect. In some paragraphs the first several sentences state obvious, observable causes. The final sentence **(the topic sentence)** then describes the effect of these causes.

A. Read the following sentences, which make up the beginning of a paragraph. Think about what effect these causes will most likely have. Then underline the best topic sentence of the three choices listed below the paragraph.

Several consecutive years of drought have made life miserable for lettuce farmers in Southern California. At the same time fertilizer prices have doubled as the cost of oil skyrocketed. Labor expenses have risen, too, as the result of union-organizing drives.

1. As a result, many farmers have decided to grow oranges instead of lettuce.
2. These rising costs are forcing farmers to think about buying more land so they can harvest larger crops.
3. It's no wonder, then, that consumers are paying more for a head of lettuce now than they did three years ago.

In other cause-and-effect paragraphs, the topic sentence gives the cause. Then several effects are listed to complete the paragraph.

B. The topic sentence is missing from the paragraph below. Read the effects and figure out the most likely cause. Then fill in the best topic sentence from those below the paragraph.

____

How do we know? One sure indicator is the sale of sporting goods equipment, which has been rising at the rate of 15 percent over the past five years. Sales of running shoes particularly have been so strong that factories can't keep up with the demand. Tennis, bicycling, backpacking, and soccer equipment are also selling at higher-than-ever-before levels. Members of the medical profession supply more confirmation that millions of Americans have a regular exercise program. Cardiologists, for example, are reporting for the first time since World War II a decrease in heart attack rates.

1. Americans have always been great sports enthusiasts.
2. At last Americans have begun to exercise regularly.
3. Heart disease is less of a problem now than it once was.

C. The following sentences from a cause-and-effect paragraph are scrambled. Number the sentences in the correct order. Start by identifying the topic sentence and deciding where it should go in the paragraph.

______ By morning, Johnny felt as if he were sleeping in a cold puddle.

______ It began when he tried to set up his tent and discovered that he didn't have a centerpole.

______ The raw oatmeal he ended up eating for breakfast made him feel slightly sick.

______ One night of camping was enough to turn Johnny into a nervous wreck.

______ Although the sky was clear and starry for a while, a drenching rain soon started, pouring through the sides of his tent and soaking his sleeping bag.

______ He thought that a hearty breakfast would make him feel better—until he tried to light his camp stove and found that it was out of gas.

______ He solved that crisis by tying the tent to a couple of trees, but then he learned that you can never rely on the weather forecast.

D. Look back at part **C** to answer these questions.

1. Was the topic sentence in part **C** a cause or an effect?

____

2. Did you place it first or last in the paragraph?

____

You have seen that cause-and-effect paragraphs can be organized in several ways. The topic sentence can come first. If it states a cause, it is followed by several sentences that give effects. If it states an effect, it is followed by several sentences that give causes. When the topic sentence comes last, it usually states the effect of the causes listed in the preceding sentences.

E. The two paragraphs below are each missing a topic sentence. Read the paragraph, adding up the causes or effects. Then fill in an appropriate topic sentence on the blank lines. In the parentheses, write whether your topic sentence is a cause or an effect.

____

______________________________________ (__________)

When the magician tried to make a coin disappear, several coins fell out of his sleeve. Then he tapped his top hat to make a rabbit appear. When he lifted the hat, however, there was nothing under it. As he started to leave the stage, the magician collided with the rabbit, hopping out from behind the magician's cabinet.

The day after the early peas were planted, twelve inches of snow fell on the field. Then followed two months of sunny, dry days that first melted the snow and turned the field into a mudpack, and then baked the soil and roasted the shallow roots of the pea plants. The sun kept away the fungus diseases, but it also wilted the uppermost leaves of the plant. ______________________________

____

______________________________________ (__________)

F. Choose one of the topic sentences below and put an X next to it. Decide whether it describes a cause or an effect. If it describes a cause, list several possible effects on the blank lines. If it describes an effect, list several possible causes.

______ It was the worst storm in several years.

______ I never laughed so hard.

______ Having only one bathroom can be a problem.

______ So now we have a pet raccoon (or other pet).

______ Of all days to oversleep, why did I pick Friday?

______ I haven't spoken to Dana since that day.

____

____

____

____

____

____

Write On Choose one of the other topic sentences from part **F** to develop into a paragraph. Or, if you like, think of your own topic sentence. Decide whether to put the topic sentence first or last. Then, to complete the paragraph, add several sentences that give causes or effects.

In a cause-and-effect paragraph, the topic sentence may describe a cause with the other sentences giving effects, or it may describe an effect with the other sentences giving causes. The topic sentence may come first or last in the paragraph.

---

lesson

2 Writing a mystery

Mystery stories often begin with effects—a murder, a robbery, a kidnapping. Then the rest of the story tells how the cause or causes were discovered. Mysteries like these are often called **whodunits.** In a whodunit, the detective plays an important role. He or she must put the clues together to form a chain of effects and causes that lead back to the person who committed the crime.

A. Number this chain of causes and effects in the correct order to solve "The Case of the Missing Necklace."

______ The butler was the only one with the key to Lord Lumley's room.

______ Footprints in the dirt near the bushes were made by size 13 boots.

______ Both a necklace and its case were taken from Lady Lumley's room.

______ The detective then determined that the size 13 boots belonged to the chauffeur.

______ Muddy size 13 boots were found in Lord Lumley's room.

______ The case was found discarded in the bushes under her window.

______ The butler claimed he lent the key to the chauffeur.

______ However, Lord Lumley was away, and his room was locked.

The thief was ______________________________

The most important character in a whodunit is usually the detective. The detective may be a police officer, a private detective, or someone who specializes in solving crimes. Or the detective may be an amateur—perhaps someone who poses no threat and whom people would talk to freely, or perhaps someone with special powers. Read this description of one detective.

> Ponsonby looked rather fat and stupid as he slumped in his chair. But beneath the small, close-set eyes and bald head, his steel trap of a mind was racing to put the clues together. Suddenly he sat up straight and smiled, fingering his red beard. "I've got the answer, inspector," he drawled.

B. Choose a character to be your detective. Put an X next to one of the people below or write in your own idea. Then describe your detective's appearance and skills on the lines below.

______ a former pickpocket	______ a little old lady
______ a girl with a photographic memory	______ a fortuneteller
______ A Navajo police officer	______ a French detective

Own idea: ______________________________

____

____

____

____

C. Choose a situation below or think up your own. Then briefly outline the plot, giving the chain of causes and effects that lead to a solution of the crime.

______ A priceless stamp has been stolen from the post office.

______ The governor's daughter has been kidnapped.

______ All the cows on a ranch have been poisoned.

______ All the residents of one apartment building have been robbed on consecutive Tuesday nights.

____

____

____

____

Another kind of mystery is a **horror story.** Read the following.

Out of the fog, the footsteps came closer. Jenny wanted to scream, but no sound came through her clenched teeth. Then, from the mists, she saw a huge, caped figure and heard its cackling laugh. As it lunged toward her, everything went black.

Horror stories create fearful situations by using things that people are afraid of—places like dark alleys, creatures like bats and vampires, events like thunderstorms.

D. Make a list of at least five things people are afraid of. Think about frightening places, creatures, and events.

____

____

____

____

____

In a horror story, the hero/heroine is often just an ordinary person who is affected by the fearful situation. This person must find the cause and stop it.

E. Choose a hero/heroine for your horror story—perhaps it is you yourself or someone you know well. Write a short description of your hero/heroine below.

____

____

____

____

____

F. Now choose the fearful situation—perhaps from those you listed for part **D.** Explain in a few sentences how your hero/heroine will overcome the horror.

G. Write the opening for your horror story, in which your hero/heroine realizes that something is wrong.

Write On

Choose one of the following.

1. Develop your whodunit story from parts **B** and **C.** Include at least three clues that lead the detective to find the solution.
2. Write the horror story you started in part **G.** Show how the hero/heroine overcomes the fearful situation.

Mystery stories include whodunits and horror stories. In a mystery, the effect is the crime or fearful situation. The cause or causes must be discovered.

---

lesson

3 Writing about cause and effect in science

Scientists often use cause and effect in their work. In order to find causes, they sometimes set up experiments in which they use two groups (of animals, plants, and so on) and treat each group differently. Then the scientists observe the effects. If there are not too many variables—that is, if the two groups and their treatment are similar enough—the scientists can determine what caused the different effects they observed.

A. Read the following description of an experiment. On the lines below, tell whether you think Carlotta Braun's conclusion is warranted and why. Is it based on absolute proof of a cause-and-effect relationship? Or are there too many variables?

Carlotta Braun conducted an experiment with white mice to determine if there was any relationship between their weight, reward foods, and speed of learning a maze. She constructed a simple maze and tested two groups of mice—a "fat" group and a "thin" group. The "fat" mice were given a piece of cake if they correctly ran through the maze. The "thin" mice received some carrot. When her results showed that the "thin" mice learned the maze much faster than the "fat" mice, Carlotta concluded that carrots are "brain food."

____

____

____

____

B. Read the two selections that follow. Then, on the lines, write a final sentence for each. Be sure your sentence reflects the correct cause of the effects that are described in the paragraphs.

1. How does sunlight affect plant growth? A group of students at Franklin Junior High decided to find out. One Monday morning they planted three dozen sunflower seeds in identical clay pots. They gave them exactly the same amounts of water and fertilizer. The students put twelve of the pots in a dark closet and left them there. They put twelve pots outside for just two hours a day. They put the final twelve outside for six hours a day.

After three weeks the plants in the closet were dead. The plants receiving two hours of sunlight daily averaged 4.3 inches in height, while the ones receiving six hours of sunlight were 7.1 inches tall on the average.

____

____

____

2. Dr. Ralph Lowell received a grant from the National Foot Care Association to test his theory of foot blisters. They were caused, he believed, not by friction, but by the color of the socks or shoes worn.

To examine this theory Dr. Lowell devised a questionnaire that he distributed to a thousand students at the state university. He asked each of these students to mail the questionnaire back to him anytime in the next year that they got blisters.

At the end of the twelve-month period he had received seventy-four reports of blisters. In every single case the student got blisters from playing a sport, going on a long hike, dancing, or taking part in some similar activity. The students got blisters while wearing white socks, brown socks, green socks, argyle socks, no socks, black shoes, red shoes, sneakers, and just about every other possible color of socks and shoes.

___

___

___

The **syllogism** is a favorite device of scientists who are testing their theories. A syllogism is an argument consisting of three parts—the major premise, the minor premise, and the conclusion. The major premise states a given generalization. The minor premise states a specific situation. The conclusion follows logically from the first two parts. Here are examples of correct and faulty syllogisms.

Correct

All *A* is *B*.	All dogs are animals.
This is *A*.	This is a dog.
Therefore it is *B*.	It is an animal.

Faulty

All *A* is *B*.	All dogs are animals.
This is *B*.	This is an animal.
Therefore it is *A*.	It is a dog.

Obviously, there are other animals besides dogs.

C. Use the examples above to help you decide whether each syllogism below is correct or faulty. If it is correct, write C on the line. If it is faulty, write F.

_____ 1. All scientists use computers.
Justina Morales uses computers.
Therefore, Justina Morales is a scientist.

_____ 2. All green plants contain chlorophyll.
This plant is green.
Therefore, it contains chlorophyll.

_____ 3. Homes heated by 100 percent solar energy don't burn oil.
This is a 100 percent solar-heated home.
Therefore, it doesn't burn oil.

_____ 4. All machines produce heat.
This object is producing heat.
Therefore, it is a machine.

_______ 5. The planets in our solar system revolve around the sun.
Uranus is a planet in our solar system.
Therefore, it revolves around the sun.

_______ 6. Citrus fruits contain vitamin C.
Grapefruit is a citrus fruit.
Therefore, it contains vitamin C.

_______ 7. All squares are rectangles.
This is a rectangle.
Therefore, it is a square.

_______ 8. All water contains oxygen.
This contains oxygen.
Therefore, it is water.

D. On the lines below, construct two syllogisms of your own. Use two of the generalizations below or think of your own generalizations. Be sure your minor premise and conclusions follow logically from the generalizations.

All plants produce carbon dioxide.
All birds hatch from eggs.
All matter is composed of atoms.
All satellites revolve around planets.

Syllogism 1: ____

____

____

Syllogism 2: ____

____

____

Write On Write a fictional account of a real scientific discovery. Choose one of the situations below or think of your own. Before you begin, decide whether your paragraph will move from cause to effect or effect to cause. Consider also whether the topic sentence should come at the beginning or end of the paragraph. Finally, be certain your sentences follow each other in a logical progression.

Two wheels are first attached to a wagon.
Someone first goes up into the air in a balloon.
Someone first makes fire.
Someone discovers that frozen water makes ice.

Most scientific writing involves cause and effect. In experiments, scientists go from the effects they observe to their probable causes. In syllogisms, scientists begin with a generalization and then reason their way to a specific conclusion.

Revising

Using connecting words to show cause and effect

Simple cause-and-effect relationships are clearest when ideas are tied together by connecting words. Read the following two groups of short sentences. Is the cause-and-effect relationship expressed clearly in each group?

1. Fran hit a long homerun. The ball crashed through the Krupsaks' picture window. Mr. Krupsak ran out of the house yelling.
2. The storm developed slowly. The Canadian cold front stalled over Lake Michigan. A temperature inversion stopped weather movements into New England.

Now read the following revisions of these sentences. Note the subordinate conjunctions, prepositions, and relative pronouns that are underlined. These are **connecting words.**

1. <u>Because</u> Fran hit a long homerun <u>that</u> crashed through the Krupsaks' picture window, Mr. Krupsak ran out of the house yelling.
2. The slowness of the storm's development was <u>due to</u> a Canadian cold front <u>that</u> stalled over Lake Michigan <u>while</u> a temperature inversion stopped weather movements into New England.

A. Rewrite the following groups of sentences as single sentences with connecting words. Try to make your sentences as varied as possible.

1. The roads were icy. Louanne lost control of the car. It skidded into a guardrail.

____

____

2. The oven thermometer was broken. Claude had no way to gauge the oven temperature. The cake came out as hard as a rock.

____

____

3. Several icebergs drifted into heavily traveled shipping zones. The Coast Guard had to tow them away.

____

____

4. The air pollution index was at the "dangerous" level. Several people collapsed. They had to be rushed to the hospital.

____

____

5. The noise level was intolerable. Arnold couldn't concentrate. He failed the test.

____

____

6. The winning time for the race was slow. The horses found the track thick and muddy. Rain had been falling since midnight.

____

____

7. The crowd pushed forward eagerly. Everyone stood on tiptoes. They were all trying to catch sight of the movie stars.

____

____

8. Sandy had used bits of wood, leaves, and flowers in her picture. It was the most unusual work of art in the contest. The judges awarded her first prize.

____

____

Write On Look back at the "Write On" activities you have done for this unit. Have you clearly shown cause-and-effect relationships? Choose one that isn't as clear as it could be. When you find short, choppy, or unclear sentences, revise them by using connecting words.

Use connecting words, such as prepositions, conjunctions, and relative pronouns, to link sentences and to make cause-and-effect relationships clear.

Post-Test

1. Read these facts about muscles and exercise:

During exercise, muscles produce lactic acid for extra energy.
The body needs more oxygen to get rid of the lactic acid.

a. Now think of a reason why you start breathing hard when you exercise. Write your reason as a topic sentence.

____

b. Write a sentence about the effect of hard breathing.

____

2. Read the following paragraph. Then write a reasonable conclusion.

During the robbery, the dog never barked. Neither the door nor the window had been forced open. The thief evidently found the jewels immediately: there were no signs of a search.

Therefore, ____.

3. Supply the missing line in each syllogism below.

a. All mammals nourish their young with milk.

____

Therefore, the whale is a mammal.

b. Pure water boils at 100° C.
This water sample boils at 100° C.

Therefore, ____

4. Write a paragraph explaining why the discovery of fire was vitally important to humanity.

unit 3

Writing Details

Things to Remember About Writing with Details

Details are small bits of information.

Writing

- List all the details you can think of about your topic. Decide on your point of view and write a topic sentence. Then choose the details that support your topic sentence. Rank them in order of importance. Cross out those that give little support to the topic sentence.
- Keep in mind the mood you want to create when you choose details to describe the setting, character, or situation.

Revising

- Use modifiers to make your writing clear and specific.
- Remove unnecessary modifiers and misplaced or dangling modifiers.

lesson

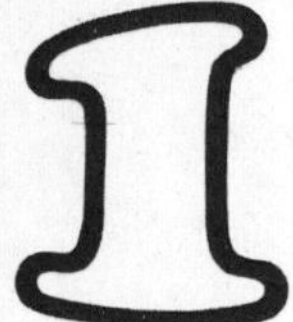

Choosing the important details

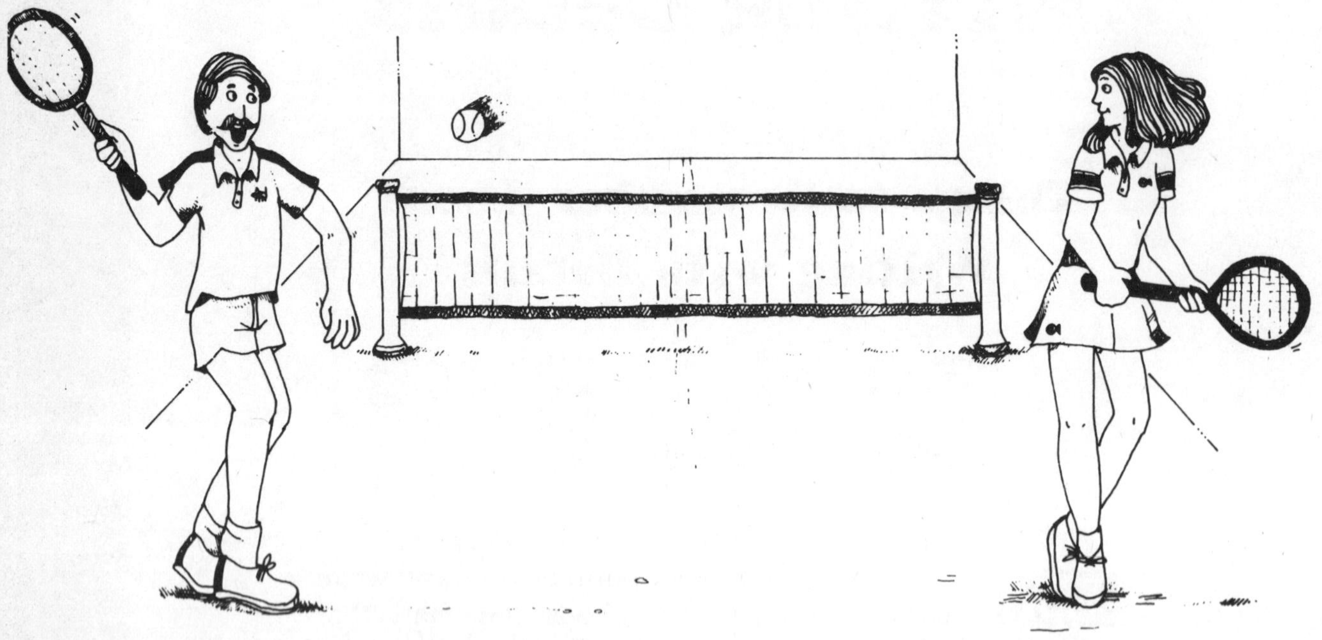

Do you see anything wrong with this picture of a tennis game? The players are using their rackets to hit the ball back and forth. But they don't seem to know that in tennis the object of the game is to hit the ball over the net.

A. Choose two of the games below. For each, state the object of the game—what you must do to score points or to win.

bowling basketball dominoes football

1. ______________________________

____

2. ______________________________

____

When you are giving the rules for a game, remember that the object of the game is most important and is usually stated first. Then the necessary **details** are selected.

B. Four details about playing tennis are listed below. Choose the two that you would need to know in order to play the game. Put an X next to the necessary rules.

______ 1. The ball must land within the boundaries of your opponent's half of the court.

______ 2. A serve that the opponent can't touch is called an *ace*.

______ 3. In keeping score, the term *love* means "zero."

______ 4. After the serve, the receiver must hit the ball on the first bounce.

C. Suppose you have been hired to write nationally distributed directions for a game. Choose one of the games below, or think of a fairly simple game you know.

relay race   checkers   tic-tac-toe   volleyball

All your rules must fit on one card. Therefore you must select only the necessary details and write them in logical order. You may wish to list all the details on scrap paper first and then select and number the most important ones to write on the card below. If you feel that illustrations will help you eliminate wordy descriptions, include notes for the illustrations.

Rules for the Game of ______________________

Object of the game: ______________________

____

Rules: ______________________

____

____

____

____

____

____

____

____

Notes for illustrations: ______________________

____

Choosing details is also important in paragraph or theme writing. Follow the suggestions below to select details for a paragraph.

1. List all the details you can think of about your topic.
2. Decide on your point of view and write a topic sentence.
3. Then choose the details that support your topic sentence, and rank them in order of importance.

D. On the lines below, list the details of something you have strong feelings about, such as a trip you've taken, a dream you've had, or a person you just met. List as many details as you can—at least twelve. Don't worry about their order or importance.

____

____

____

____

____

____

____

____

____

____

____

____

____

____

E. Now decide on your point of view about the subject you chose for part **D.** Write a topic sentence that supports your viewpoint. For example, "It was the worst nightmare I've ever had" or "Although we've just met, I'm sure ______ will become one of my best friends." Write your topic sentence on the lines below.

____

____

____

F. Now look back at the details you listed in part **D.** Cross out those that don't support your topic sentence, or that give it little support. Do you have five or six details left? If not, add some below.

____

____

____

G. Number all your details in order of importance. Then, on the lines below, write a paragraph using your topic sentence and supporting details from parts **D, E,** and **F.**

____

____

____

____

____

____

____

____

____

____

Write On

Choose one of the subjects below, and follow the procedures you used in parts **D** through **G** to write a paragraph. Use a separate sheet of paper.

A person who makes me angry (happy, sad)
A place I (love, hate) to be
My (most, least) favorite possession

When you write the rules of a game, give the object of the game and then give the necessary, important details in logical order. When you write about a topic, choose details that support your topic sentence.

lesson

Using details to create a mood

The **mood** you wish to create influences the details you choose in a description.

A. Read the two paragraphs below and answer the questions that follow them.

The sun beat down on the city. Clothes stuck to people's backs. Tempers flared, and arguments could be heard on one steaming block after another.

The warming rays of the sun caressed the city streets. In the parks, people splashed in water or basked in the glowing sun. Cheery words were exchanged as people picnicked and relaxed on this beautiful summer day.

1. What are both paragraphs about?

____

2. What mood does the first paragraph describe?

____

3. List two details the writer chose to create the mood.

____

4. What mood does the second paragraph describe?

____

5. List two details the writer chose to create the mood.

____

B. Choose two of the following situations. Write two short paragraphs for each. In the first paragraph, choose details to create a favorable mood. In the second paragraph, choose details to create an unfavorable mood.

a rainy day	eating breakfast
staying up late	dressing up in your best clothes

Topic 1: ______________________________

Favorable: ______________________________

____

____

____

____

Unfavorable: ______________________________

____

____

____

____

Topic 2: ______________________________

Favorable: ______________________________

____

____

____

____

Unfavorable: ______________________________

____

____

____

____

You know that the details you choose can help you create a mood. Look at the picture above. It shows someone approaching a house. When you describe the setting and the character, you can use different details, depending on the kind of story you want to write.

C. Suppose you want to write a mystery story. How would you describe the man to make him seem mysterious? Is he wearing a disguise? What might be in the bag he is carrying? What crime or horror might be awaiting him in the house? Write a short description of the character and setting on the lines below.

____

____

____

____

____

____

____

____

D. Suppose you want to write a romance. How would you describe the man to make him seem romantic? How would you describe the setting? Is someone waiting inside the house for him? How does he feel? What's in the bag he's carrying? Write your description on the lines that follow.

____

____

E. Suppose you want to write an adventure story. How would you describe the man to make him seem adventurous? Is he a sea captain, a spy, a deposed king? What is in his bag? What adventure awaits him in the house? Write your description on the lines below.

Write On

Choose one of the following to write on a separate sheet of paper. Be sure to use details to create a mood.

1. Write a story based on the character and setting you described for part **C,** part **D,** or part **E.**
2. Write about yourself. Describe a situation in which some circumstance causes your mood to change—perhaps from anger to sorrow or from fear to happiness.

You should keep in mind the mood you want to create when you choose details to describe a setting, character, or situation. For example, you will want a different mood for a mystery than you would for a romance or an adventure story.

lesson

3 Writing details for a science-fiction story

Fact: People have flown to and landed on the moon.

Fantasy: Each person who lands on the moon is captured by moon creatures and replaced with a creature that has the same form as the human.

A **science-fiction story** is a balance between fact and fantasy. The facts come from your knowledge of people, events, and environments. The fantasy begins when you change those facts in an unusual and unexpected way.

A. Write some science-fiction ideas of your own. Use the three facts listed below, but change each one in an imaginative way to turn it from fact to fantasy.

1. Fact: If you could travel backward in time, you might meet one of your own ancestors.

Your fantasy: ____

____

____

2. Fact: In the future, more information may be stored in computers than in books.

Your fantasy: ______________________________

____

____

3. Fact: The population of the world is growing faster than the production of food.

Your fantasy: ______________________________

____

____

B. Now try using a fact of your own to create a fantasy.

Fact: ______________________________

____

Fantasy: ______________________________

____

____

Choosing the right details for a science-fiction story can make both the fact and the fantasy seem convincing. Science-fiction writers use and adapt details from their own experience. That's why they sometimes create new worlds by making changes in familiar environments. Frank Herbert's *Dune* is a good example. Herbert takes a desert environment and creates an entire planet that lacks water. He can use desert nomads—the way they hunt, grow crops, dress, and travel—as models for dwellers on his planet.

C. You will now begin to create your own science-fiction world—your own planet. First, think of one outstanding feature about your planet. Perhaps its size or shape is special. Suppose the planet were a cube with two-inch sides? Suppose only six creatures lived on the cube, one on each surface? Or perhaps it is the air, the water, the plants, or the creatures of your planet that are special in some way. On the lines below, tell what is most unusual about your planet.

____

____

____

____

____

D. Now add details about your planet. Start by brainstorming the categories below and writing two or three details for each. Think about the relationships among the categories. For example, climate will influence clothing, clothing may affect social customs, customs could change the ways families live together, and so on. Try to relate your details in a consistent way. On the last six lines, add other categories as you think of them.

Shape and size of planet: ______________________________

____

Terrain: ______________________________

____

Climate: ______________________________

____

Foliage: ______________________________

____

Appearance of creatures who live there: ______________________________

____

Dwellings: ______________________________

____

Clothes: ______________________________

____

Transportation: ______________________________

____

____

____

____

____

____

____

E. When you write a science-fiction story, the world, creatures, and events you describe must be vivid enough for your readers to picture. Think of yourself on a rocket about to make a visit to your imaginary planet. Write a vivid description of what you see as you approach the planet and land there.

Write On Choose one of the following.

1. Think of a problem or plot that is suggested by the planet you have created. Write a short story telling how the problem is solved.
2. Choose one of the fantasies you wrote for part **A** or part **B**, and write a story based on it.

A science-fiction story is a balance between fact and fantasy. Choosing the right details for the story can make both the fact and the fantasy seem convincing.

Revising

Using modifiers

We use **modifiers** in our writing for the same reason that we use details. Both modifiers and details make our writing specific. Modifiers—which may be adjectives, adverbs, phrases, or clauses—develop, restrict, or otherwise modify the meanings of words in sentences.

One danger in using modifiers is the tendency to use too many in trying to make our writing colorful. Consider the sentence below and its revision.

> The long-distance marathon runner, exhausted from fatigue, finally collapsed past the finish line marking the end of the race, narrowly beating his equally tired opponent by slim seconds.
>
> The marathon runner collapsed past the finish line, beating his opponent by seconds.

The underlined words in the first sentence are **redundant.** Other specific words in the sentence make them unnecessary—for example, *marathon* indicates "long distance."

A. Revise each sentence below to remove unnecessary modifiers. Keep enough modifiers to make the sentence clear and specific; strengthen nouns and verbs if necessary.

1. A dog-eared old book with the pages folded back and an old stained cover on top lay sitting on the dusty desk that hadn't been dusted in weeks.

____

____

2. A large, colorful crowd of gaily dressed dancers crowded onto the dance floor and danced as the loud music blared and the bright lights flashed.

____

____

3. The cold, freezing children huddled under the warm, cosy quilt that kept them warm in the icy, frigid room that had no heat.

____

____

A modifier should be placed as close as possible to the word it modifies; a **misplaced modifier** makes a sentence ambiguous. If there is no word in the sentence that a modifier can sensibly modify, we say the modifier is **dangling.** In that case, you must rewrite the sentence. Look at the examples at the top of the next page.

Misplaced: The astronomer sighted a comet through her telescope that she could not identify.
Revised: Through her telescope the astronomer sighted a comet that she could not identify.
Dangling: Unable to identify it, the comet must be unknown.
Revised: Since she was unable to identify it, the comet must be unknown.

B. Revise each sentence below to correct the misplaced or dangling modifier.

1. Coming in view of the landing sight, my fears were confirmed.

___

2. Armed aliens crouched behind the hills, who were ready to attack at any moment.

___

___

3. My partner Lom decided to stay in the spaceship, who was not feeling well.

___

___

4. Being in Lom's pocket, I could not use the radio to get help.

___

___

5. I knew that someday I would tell of my adventures in space in the comfort of my own home.

___

___

Write On

Look over the papers you have written for this unit. Check to see that you have modifiers to make your sentences clear and specific but have not used any unnecessary modifiers. Also look for misplaced or dangling modifiers to correct. Choose one paper and revise it.

Use modifiers to make your writing clear and specific, but don't use unnecessary modifiers. Check your writing to be sure to have no misplaced or dangling modifiers.

Post-Test

1. Check the details below that would be most suitable for a report on wildlife management in a national park.

   ______ a. Sixty miles of hiking trails are open to the public.

   ______ b. The bear population has increased 25% since 1980.

   ______ c. Camping is permitted from May to October.

   ______ d. Coyotes have moved into the area.

2. Imagine a wild, windswept landscape on a dark, stormy night. Write a descriptive paragraph about it. Choose details that will create one of the following moods. Write the letter of the mood you chose next to your paragraph.

   a. a feeling of horror

   b. a feeling of romance

   c. a feeling of adventure

3. Some scientists believe that space cities, built in large cylinders or spheres, will be the homes of the future. Complete the sentences below by writing two details about life in a space city.

   a. The best thing about living in a space city is ______________________

   ____.

   b. The worst thing about a space city is ______________________

   ____.

4. Rewrite each sentence to correct unnecessary or misplaced modifiers.

   a. Senator Seal is the strongest champion of wildlife in Congress.

   ____

   b. The exhausted and weary sailor told an incredible, hard-to-believe tale of survival on a liferaft in his hospital room.

   ____

   ____

unit 4
Writing Comparisons

Things to Remember About Writing Comparisons

Comparisons shows likenesses. **Contrasts** show differences.

Writing

- Look for similarities when you compare. Look for differences when you contrast.
- Explain the unfamiliar by comparing it to the familiar.
- Use point-by-point order or parallel order when writing a comparison-and-contrast paragraph.
- Use figurative language such as similes, metaphors, and personification to make your comparisons more imaginative and interesting.
- Avoid mixing metaphors.
- Use analogies to clarify and add emotional appeal to an argument. Base your analogies on a comparison of a partial similarity between otherwise unlike things.

Revising

- Replace dull, unnecessary adjectives with fresh adjectives and similes to make your descriptions clear and vivid.
- Form concrete modifiers by adding endings to strong nouns and verbs.

lesson

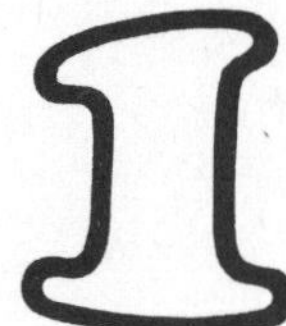

Comparing and contrasting in writing

When you **compare**, you look for similarities. Comparison of the little known to the well known can be very helpful. For example, an okapi can be compared to a giraffe, and an emu to an ostrich. If the boy in the picture had heard these comparisons, he would have been able to identify each animal.

A. Choose two of the unfamiliar things below. Write a one-sentence description in which you compare each to a better-known thing. You may use your dictionary.

dhow blintze serape samisen

1. ______________________________

____

2. ______________________________

____

Comparison can also help define two similar objects more exactly. A paper clip and a staple might not seem to have that much in common until they are compared completely in form and function.

B. Choose two of the following pairs to compare. List at least three similarities between the objects in each pair.

an apple and a pear
kickball and soccer
running and walking
a potato and a rutabaga
TV and movies
tea and coffee

1. ______________________________

____

____

____

2. ______________________________

____

____

____

Contrast tells how one thing is different from another. Sometimes it is helpful to explain something by contrasting it with something it is *not*.

C. Choose two of the following pairs to contrast. Tell three ways in which they are different. For example, to contrast the sun and the moon, you could say that the earth orbits the sun while the moon orbits the earth. You could also contrast the sizes of the sun and the moon and their distances from the earth. You could note that the sun is a star and the moon is not.

tennis and badminton
Chinese and Italian food
spring and autumn
the East Coast and West Coast
tragedy and comedy
birth and death

1. ______________________________

____

____

____

2. ______________________________

____

____

____

Once you have decided on the similarities and differences of the two objects you are comparing, you are ready to develop your comparisons and contrasts into a paragraph. There are two ways of doing this: by using point-by-point order or by using parallel order. In the first, you skip back and forth between object *A* and object *B*, comparing and contrasting them one point at a time. In the second, you describe all the points of object *A*, then you move on to object *B*, describing its points in the same order.

D. Choose one pair that you compared in part **B** or contrasted in part **C.** On the lines below, write a paragraph that compares them in point-by-point order.

____

____

____

____

____

____

____

____

E. Choose another pair from part **B** or part **C.** On the lines below, write a paragraph that compares them in parallel order.

____

____

____

____

____

____

____

____

You can help explain something unfamiliar by comparing and contrasting it to something familiar. Sometimes, you might want to recall the familiar past and then describe how it has changed.

F. Read the following paragraph and answer the questions below.

A modern newspaper office is different from the office that many of us picture in our minds. But the difference may not be quickly grasped by a quick visit. Rows of desks and wire-service terminals still fill the office. Telephones still constantly ring. Reporters with half-empty coffee cups still scurry in a thousand different directions. But the typewriters—some of them do not even use paper! Frequently, all the typewriters in an office are electric, and their hum has become another voice in the office din. Some have special keys with special symbols. A story is typed on a piece of paper and then "read" by a computer. Other typewriters are tied into computer screens: as a story is typed, it appears on the screen and is "remembered" by the computer. The newspaper itself may be printed from "pictures" sent by the computer. A computer may play a large role in bringing your daily paper to you.

1. List two ways in which a modern newspaper office is similar to an older office.

____

____

2. List two ways in which a modern newspaper office is different from an older office.

____

____

Write a paragraph in which you compare or contrast how you look now with how you looked five years ago. Or compare and contrast your appearance now with the way you hope to look five years from now.

When you compare, you look for similarities. When you contrast, you look for differences. Comparisons and contrasts often help to explain the unfamiliar by comparing it to the familiar. A comparison-and-contrast paragraph can be in point-by-point order or parallel order.

lesson

Writing with figurative language

The Eagle

He clasps the crag with crooked hands;
Close to the sun in lonely lands,
Ringed with the azure world he stands.

The wrinkled sea beneath him crawls;
He watches from his mountain walls,
And like a thunderbolt he falls.

—Alfred, Lord Tennyson

This poem, like many others, makes its point by using **figurative language** instead of straight description. Figurative language includes **similes, metaphors,** and **personification.**

A. Look for comparisons in the poem and answer the questions below.

1. In a simile, two unlike things are compared by using *like* or *as*. Write a simile from the poem.

____

2. Tell how you think the two parts of the simile are alike.

____

____

3. In personification, an animal or nonliving thing is compared to a human by giving it some human characteristic. Write an example of personification from the poem.

____

A metaphor is different from a simile in that it does not state a comparison with the words *as* or *like*. Thus the comparison is less direct; it is harder to see that a comparison is being made. A metaphor says that one thing is the same as another. The word *metaphor* comes from the Greek word meaning "to transfer." When you use a metaphor, therefore, you transfer the meaning from one thing and apply it to the other.

B. Read these metaphors. Then answer the questions below.

The world is nothing but an endless seesaw.

—Michel de Montaigne

Friends are thermometers by which we may judge the temperature of our fortunes.

—Countess of Blessington

1. Do you think the world is like a seesaw? If so, in what way? If not, what would you compare the world to?

____

____

2. Do you agree with the second metaphor? If so, why? If not, what do you think friends are like?

____

____

C. Read each comparison below. Put an S in front of each simile, an *M* in front of each metaphor, and a *P* in front of each example of personification. Then, on the blank line, explain the comparison.

_____ 1. Knowledge is the food of the soul. (Plato)

____

____

_____ 2. Youth like summer morn, age like Winter weather (William Shakespeare)

____

_____ 3. Money is a good servant, but a bad master. (H. G. Bohn)

____

_____ 4. Let the rain sing you a lullaby. (Langston Hughes)

____

____

Figurative language is often found in poetry, but similes, metaphors, and even personification can give any descriptive writing more impact.

D. Select three of the pairs below (or choose your own pairs) and write a sentence about each pair. One of the sentences should use a simile; one, a metaphor; and one, personification.

a kite and a hawk	a friend and a bridge	a dancer and a meadow
night and a person	a skyscraper and a mountain	electricity and a stream

1. ____

____

2. ____

____

3. ____

____

There is one error to guard against when using figurative language. It is **mixing metaphors.** A mixed metaphor can best be described by looking at the example below.

In every shy person, there is a hidden tiger just waiting to take flight.

Do tigers fly? This mixed metaphor can be corrected by changing the sentence in one of two ways.

In every shy person, there is a hidden tiger just waiting to spring out.
In every shy person, there is a hidden eagle just waiting to take flight.

E. Rewrite each sentence below to correct the mixed metaphor.

1. Like a ship in full sail, he confidently went about feathering his nest.

____

2. She was an eager beaver, always ready to grab the ball and run with it.

____

3. The clock's ticking reminded him of the beating of a drum that pounded against the shore of his brain.

____

____

4. Her smile was the sunshine that brightened our days and lit up the darkest nights.

____

____

F. Each statement below can be made more imaginative and interesting. Rewrite each, using the information in it as the basis for a figurative statement.

1. The melting snow added to the water in the river.

2. He hammered nails into the wood.

3. We were without electricity for several hours.

4. I stubbed my toe on a brick.

5. The sunset was quite colorful.

Choose one of the subjects below to write about in an imaginative way—or use the picture on this page. To give your description impact, think of at least one metaphor, one simile, and one statement using personification. Then include your figurative language in a poem or prose description of your subject.

a city at twilight	a wild animal
a storm	a jet plane

Figurative language includes similes, metaphors, and personification. Figurative comparisons can make descriptions more imaginative and interesting.

lesson

3 Writing analogies

captain : ship = mayor : city

The words above are called an **analogy.** The analogy can be read as a sentence: "Captain is to ship as mayor is to city." The symbol : stands for the words "is to," which express a relationship. The relationships on both sides of the equal sign must be similar. What is the relationship between a captain and a ship? The captain is the chief executive who runs the ship. What about a mayor and a city? The mayor is the chief executive who runs the city. Are the relationships on either side of the equal sign similar? Yes—so the analogy works.

bud : flower = child : ______________________

To complete an analogy, you must understand the relationship between the first two words. What is the relationship between a bud and a flower? A bud is small; it will develop into a flower. What will a child develop into? Fill in the word on the blank line above.

A. Now use the method above to complete the analogies below.

1. bull : cow = rooster : ______________________
2. elephant : mammal = ostrich : ______________________
3. cold : hot = young : ______________________
4. small : little = easy : ______________________
5. night : moon = day : ______________________
6. dish : cupboard = ______________________ : wallet
7. artist : painting = ______________________ : snapshot
8. doctor : hospital = waiter : ______________________
9. pond : lake = hill : ______________________
10. mail carrier : deliver = ballerina : ______________________

B. The analogies below have been started, but you must complete each to show a similar relationship.

1. man : woman = ____________________ : ____________________

2. calf : cow = ____________________ : ____________________

3. smooth : rough = ____________________ : ____________________

4. violin : orchestra = ____________________ : ____________________

5. farmer : crop = ____________________ : ____________________

6. cherry : pie = ____________________ : ____________________

7. cook : ____________________ = ____________________ : ____________________

In an analogy, unlike things are compared by looking for ways in which they are alike. Analogies can be used in writing to clarify a point or to make an emotional appeal. When analogies are used in writing, all four parts are not always expressed. Compare the two sentences below. The second is an analogy.

> It is important to use seat belts because it has been proven that they reduce serious injuries in auto accidents.
>
> Not wearing seat belts is like jumping off a cliff and expecting to land in a net.

C. Choose two of the items below. Write a one-sentence analogy for each.

littering	wearing new shoes	being late
not doing homework	listening to rock music	going to the dentist

1. ____

____

2. ____

____

A **fable** and a **parable** are both special types of analogies in story form. Both fables and parables illustrate lessons or moral truths that we can apply to our lives. In a fable, the characters are usually animals.

D. Read the short fable below and answer the questions that follow it.

A donkey was relaxing between two bales of hay. He became hungry and eyed first one bale and then the other. Both looked delicious, and the donkey could not decide which one he should eat. It was such a difficult decision for the donkey to make that he gave up and starved to death.

1. What do you think is the moral of this fable?

____

2. How could you relate this fable to your own life?

____

____

____

Now read this parable.

A man had three daughters. The two eldest never stopped telling him how much they loved him, but the youngest was silent. The father bragged about his two wonderful older daughters, but he had nothing good to say about the youngest. Then the man became ill. The two older daughters never came to see their father. They were too busy with their friends and entertainments. But the youngest daughter nursed her father and took care of him until he was better.

E. Write a moral for the parable at the bottom of page 60.

____

____

____

F. Choose one of the morals below. Write a short fable or parable to illustrate it.

Look before you leap.
Kindness can often accomplish more than strength.
Beware of flatterers.
All that glitters is not gold.

____

____

____

____

____

____

____

____

____

____

____

____

Write On

Choose a moral that has special meaning for you. Write it on another sheet of paper. Then write a fable or parable to illustrate the moral.

Analogies are comparisons based on a partial similarity between otherwise unlike things. An analogy can clarify and add emotional appeal to an argument. Parables and fables are stories which make analogies to illustrate lessons or moral truths.

Revising

Choosing adjectives

Adjectives are an important part of any writing that compares or contrasts objects. Well selected and wisely used, they add color, detail, and exactness to your writing. However, poorly chosen, overused adjectives make writing vague and cloudy instead of sharp and focused.

Read the following two sentences. In which are the adjectives better chosen?

> The big, slow boat churned lazily up the long, winding river as the still, hot sun shone down on the many resting vacationers.
>
> The huge boat churned lazily up the river as the sun shone down like a brilliant lamp on the vacationers.

The second sentence says almost everything that the first says and does it more clearly. *Huge* creates a sharper contrast with the slow, lazy images of the rest of the sentence. The simile "like a brilliant lamp" says that the sun is still, close, and intense; and it says it with an exact, concrete image.

A. Rewrite the following sentences. Eliminate unnecessary adjectives and substitute stronger ones or figurative language to make each image more concrete.

1. The long, interconnected freight train pulled gradually out of the dark, smelly, windswept freightyard and began its long, jerky journey to the faraway East Coast.

 ____

 ____

2. The manicured, lush green golf course was overrun by pushing, eager fans who wanted to see every measured inch of the swings of their favorite professional golfers.

 ____

 ____

3. The shy, quiet girl looked down at her new pink ballroom dancing shoes as the muscled, ramrod-straight young man in a perfectly tailored black tuxedo walked toward her across the polished wooden dance floor.

 ____

 ____

 ____

One way to make your descriptions fresh is to replace stale adjectives like *big, loud, old* with carefully chosen, concrete modifiers. You can form interesting modifiers by adding endings such as those below to strong nouns and verbs.

soup—soupy fog   thunder—thundering train   fade—faded pattern

B. Add an ending to change each word below to a modifier. Also write a noun it might modify. Think of two fresh modifiers of your own for numbers 7 and 8.

1. brood____ ____________	5. scratch____ ____________
2. grouch____ ____________	6. crack____ ____________
3. carpet____ ____________	7. ________ing ____________
4. howl____ ____________	8. ________ed ____________

C. The paragraph below is an example of writing that is colorless and dull for lack of adjectives. Rewrite it, adding fresh adjectives to create a concrete picture.

Adela reached the station early. It was big inside. Little light came into the open space. It smelled bad, and noises echoed off the ceiling. There was some linoleum on the floor. Adela sat on a bench and read a magazine as she waited for the train.

Write On Look over the papers you have written for this unit. Check for descriptions that need more concrete images. Choose one paper, and revise it.

By replacing dull, unnecessary adjectives with fresh adjectives and similes, you can make your descriptions clear and vivid. Many concrete modifiers can be formed by adding endings to strong nouns and verbs.

Post-Test

1. Rewrite each comparison below. Make sure you unmix the metaphors.
   a. Jamie's speech was a beacon that stirred us to action.

   ____

   b. Lana's voice was a silver bell with a surprisingly sharp edge.

   ____

   c. Detective Bunsen's hawklike profile reminded me of a cheetah stalking its prey.

   ____

2. Complete these one-sentence analogies.
   a. For shy Lucy, going to a party was like ______________________________.

   b. Max took games seriously: playing chess with him was like ______________________________.

   c. Justin's idea of a "little" snack was like ______________________________.

3. Write comparisons for the following:
   a. tennis ball and boomerang (simile)

   ____

   b. subway train and snake (metaphor)

   ____

   c. tree swaying in the wind and a dancer (personification)

   ____

4. Write a short fable or parable illustrating the following moral:
   As you make your bed, so shall you lie in it.

unit 5

Writing Facts and Opinions

Things to Remember About Writing Facts and Opinions

A **fact** is an objective statement that can be tested or checked. An **opinion** is a subjective statement that expresses someone's feelings or ideas.

Writing

- Use facts that answer the questions *who, what, when, where,* and *why* in news stories. Do not include opinions unless they are in quotations. Use a lead paragraph to capture the reader's attention.
- State your opinions on controversial community issues in letters to the editor of a newspaper. Base your opinions on facts.
- Combine facts about your candidate and the issues, as well as opinions about the candidate, when you write school campaign speeches.

Revising

- Use specific nouns and verbs to make your sentences clear and accurate.

lesson

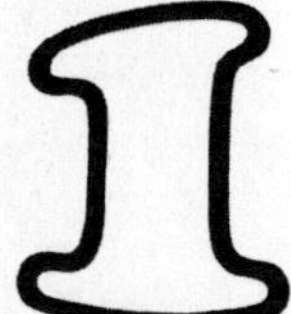

Writing a news article

News articles consist of facts that answer the *wh* questions **who, what, when, where,** and **why.**

A. Read the following news story openings. Decide which question words each opening answers and write them on the line below.

1. At noon on April 4th, Martian Scouts, velvet Venusians, and purple Plutonian plants took part in the annual Alien Day Parade.

___

2. Mayor Rita Greensleeves announced that she will not buy another trained cougar.

___

3. The town raccoon-watching committee watched into the wee hours of Sunday morning, but officials report no raccoons were sighted.

___

4. "I used trained monkeys to rob the night deposit box so I wouldn't get caught," the criminal sobbed as he was led away this morning.

___

B. Choose two of the above statements. Add made-up facts that answer the *wh* questions that the original statement leaves unanswered. For example, sentence 1 does not tell where or why the parade was held. Rewrite each statement as you add the necessary facts, but remember to include the original information. You may want to use two sentences to include all the facts.

1. ___

___

___

2. ___

___

___

A news reporter must distinguish between facts and opinions. A **statement** of fact is a statement that can be verified (checked) by observation, testing, or reference to records. Whenever possible, the reporter should tell the reader the source of his or her information. A reporter also keeps notes that list the sources of information.

A reporter should not express her or his own opinions in a news article, although the reporter might quote an opinion of a person being written about. Read these two opinions from news articles.

"The Millburn railroad station is being ruined by this ugly, disgusting graffiti and the hoodlums who put it there," Mayor LaCosta complained yesterday. "It is a blight, and it must be stopped."

Things go from bad to worse in Millburn these days. Take the railroad station, for example. It's a jungle of ugly colors and mindless scrawls. Any delinquents old enough to hold a can of spray paint must think they have the right to make their stupidity public.

The first statement could be checked by talking with Mayor LaCosta. The mayor's statement is an opinion, but it is a fact that the mayor said it. The second statement is the reporter's opinion and should not appear in a straight news story.

C. Decide whether the following statements are facts or opinions. In front of each fact, write *F*. On the line below the statement, tell how it could be checked. In front of each opinion, write *O*. On the line below, explain why it is an opinion.

______ 1. The people of San Francisco pay more sales tax in one month than the entire population of Bolivia pays in one year.

____

______ 2. We pay a small fortune for professional dog-catching services, yet the city is completely overrun by increasing bands of dirty, nasty mongrels.

____

______ 3. Watching TV is, of course, a waste of time. But if you must waste your time this way, you might as well watch color TV—it's much better than black and white.

____

______ 4. Mrs. Quinn told the city council that graffiti was all right in its place. She said it would be good if the teenagers had a special place set aside for graffiti.

The opening of a news article is called a **lead.** Just as most writers work to develop interesting openings, most reporters try hard to come up with good leads for their stories. In a newspaper filled with many articles, the lead often determines whether or not a particular story will be read. Some leads are explosive, like the first example below. Others are more intriguing or thoughtful, like the second version.

> Shouting "Not in our town you don't!" an angry mob stormed city hall this morning protesting a proposal to build a jail on the outskirts of town. "I got kids to think of," speaker after speaker told the applauding crowd. Amid the din of honking horns, police in riot gear held back the crowd to keep the road open.

> A crowd of an estimated three hundred men, women, and children gathered outside city hall this morning to protest a proposal to build a correctional facility on the edge of the city. Speaker after speaker voiced concern for the safety of their homes and children. Helmeted police were on the scene and worked authoritatively to keep the road open and traffic moving.

The type of story often determines the type of lead. It is important that a lead give some facts and point to, or "lead" to, the rest of the story.

D. Write leads for two of the following stories. One lead should be explosive. The other lead should be more thoughtful. Include additional information to answer some *wh* questions in each lead.

1. An earthquake occurs near the site of a nuclear power plant. Officials are afraid that radioactive waste is leaking into a nearby river.
2. Four young boys are found adrift at sea after being missing for a week. They claim they were carried off to sea while playing in an old boat on the beach.
3. Two fifteen-year-old girls find one million dollars in cash in an old suitcase in a deserted garage. The police have no information about the money, and the girls will get it if it is not claimed within two months.
4. An unidentified flying object was seen in downtown Chicago by about four thousand people. Strange musical sounds and flashing patterns of lights were reported. The Air Force is investigating.

1. ______________________________

____

____

____

____

2. ______________________________

____

____

____

____

Read the following ridiculous headlines and try to imagine the content of the news article that would follow them.

ROB JOHNSON TELLS BROTHER TO KEEP HAMSTERS OUT OF BEDROOM
CHERYL MIRANDA BUYS NEW SNEAKERS—SIZE 8C
HOWIE BERGER ASKS RACHEL BREEN TO MOVIES
MRS. BETTY RILEY CLAIMS SHE WILL BAKE CAKE FRIDAY

Write the article which goes with one of these silly headlines. Or think of an everyday occurrence that happens in your home or school and write about it in a news article. Include facts; quote an opinion; and pay special attention to the lead.

A news article contains facts that answer the questions who, what, when, where, and why. It should not include opinions—except in quotations. It is important that the lead paragraph of a news story interest the readers.

---

lesson 2

Writing an editorial

Most sections of a newspaper—world news, local news, business, weather—are made up of objective or factual articles. The reporter presents information that is known to be true.

Most newspapers also have an **editorial** page. On this page the editors and other writers give their opinions on events in the news. In the lead of an editorial, a writer usually reports some basic facts about the subject. The writer also provides a clue about his or her opinions on the subject.

A. Read the following editorial lead. List the fact or facts the writer reports. What is the writer's opinion?

> The general national unemployment rate has gradually yet steadily fallen for the last eighteen months. It now rests at 5.2 percent. However, the persistence of a jobless rate approaching 30 percent for inner-city youths remains one of the nation's most troubling social problems.

Fact: ______________________________

____

Opinion: ______________________________

____

B. Here is the first sentence of an editorial lead. It contains a fact.

> Today's students enjoy almost four months of vacations and holidays each year.

Write a second sentence for this lead. The second sentence should let your readers know your opinion about this subject.

____

____

C. Practice writing the beginning of an editorial. Choose one of the facts below to write about in the lead. Use the possible opinions to help form your own opinion or opinions. Write at least three sentences on the lines below.

Fact	Possible Opinions
In recent years there has been a 25 percent increase in school violence.	Violent students should be punished more severely. School principals should eliminate conditions that lead to violence. Violence is increasing everywhere; the government should do something.
Junior high school students are joining more competitive sports teams.	Competition is good; it helps develop people's characters. Competition is bad; it makes you dislike other people. Competition is bad because someone always has to lose.
Many eighth graders have no money to buy things that they want and need.	Eighth graders who want money should earn it. Eighth graders are not responsible enough to handle money wisely. All eighth graders should have a minimum allowance provided by their parents or guardians.

____

____

____

____

____

How do editors choose the subjects of their editorials? They usually choose subjects that are important both to them and to the people in the community. If an issue is important, there is usually something **"at stake."** That means that depending on how the issue turns out, people in the community tend to gain or lose something—usually money, power, freedom, or security.

D. What is important to you? List at least five things about which you have a firm opinion or would write an editorial. You may want to think of issues in your community or school.

___

___

___

___

___

Editorials are often written when there is a strong difference of opinion that is dividing a community. Important issues over which many people differ are said to be **controversial.** The writer of the editorial often hopes to persuade a majority of people to agree with either one or the other side of an issue.

E. Read these two editorial leads, each from a different newspaper. Then answer the questions below.

Teachers and other school employees should be allowed to strike for better salaries and working conditions. The right to strike is a right all Americans must have.

Teachers and other school officials have a special responsibility to their students. Teachers have no right to let their salary demands interfere with the educational development of the nation's youth.

1. What facts are these editorials discussing?

___

2. What is the opinion of the first editorial?

___

3. What is the opinion of the second editorial?

___

F. Choose one of the following controversies. Write an editorial lead that expresses your opinion.

Pro	Con
Girls should compete against boys in organized athletics.	Girls should not compete against boys in organized athletics.
The city should cut taxes so citizens will have more money to spend on what they want.	In order to have enough money to provide services to the people, the city should not cut taxes.
The government should spend more on missiles to protect our nation.	The government should spend more on schools to provide better education.

When issues are controversial, emotions run at a high level. That means that unrealistic demands, threats, or predictions of disaster will sometimes appear in editorials. Most readers, however, will not be convinced or persuaded by an editorial unless it is based on facts and logical thought. An editorial must list in order the reasons that lead to an opinion.

Choose one of the controversial issues you have written or thought about in this lesson. Write an editorial that logically states the issue and your opinion.

Editorials state the opinions of editors and other writers on important, controversial community issues. An editorial should be based on facts and written logically.

lesson

3 Writing a campaign speech

It is election day in Ocean City. The town is about to elect a mayor. The polls show that two candidates are running neck and neck—each has 35 percent of the vote with 30 percent undecided. Since you are a professional speechwriter, each candidate has asked for your help. You must choose to support one, and then write the speeches that will help him or her get elected. Here's a rundown on the candidates and their qualifications.

Floyd P. Jolly	Ina O. Hartfelter
Qualifications	**Qualifications**
Has served as mayor for two terms (eight years)	Has a law degree and a degree in city planning
As a native and lifelong resident, he knows the town of Ocean City	Has been a councilwoman for four years in the city government
Has learned a great deal about management, building one clam stand into a statewide chain of seafood restaurants	Has taken an active role in improving the Ocean City school system ever since she moved to town five years ago

As a speechwriter you will also be interested in the personal qualities of the candidate you will support. Read the following lists. Think about which qualities you would emphasize if you had to introduce the candidate to a large crowd of people.

Jolly	**Hartfelter**
Very friendly; people like him Practical; a self-made millionaire Independent; thinks people should take care of themselves rather than let the government do it Hardworking; but always has time for fishing or a game of golf Married; enjoys holidays with his four grown children	Intelligent; has an excellent academic background and holds three advanced degrees Hardworking; usually works eighty hours a week, not including weekends Compassionate; wants the city to do more for the old and poor Single; has a few good friends; lives alone; rarely takes a vacation

A. Your first job as a speechwriter is to introduce your candidate to a large gathering of voters at a local beach. Choose a candidate. Then decide what qualities and qualifications you wish to emphasize in your introduction. Write the introduction here.

Ocean City has its share of important issues and controversies. These issues have become important in the campaign because the candidates disagree over them. Read about the issues and the opinions of the candidates.

Issue	Jolly's Opinions	Hartfelter's Opinions
Offshore oil drilling near Ocean City's beaches	Yes. The oil rigs are necessary. They will provide jobs, and the country needs oil.	No. There is no evidence that there is oil there. The rigs are loud and ugly. If oil is found, spills could ruin the beaches.
Proposed 50 percent cut of local property taxes	Yes. People deserve to keep more of their hard-earned money. Government tends to waste money anyway.	No. Ocean City needs that tax money to pay for police and fire protection, as well as to improve libraries, schools, and senior citizen centers.
Ban smoking in all city buildings	No. Smokers have rights too, and it would be too difficult to enforce.	Yes. It is unfair to make others breathe stale, smoky air.
Benson-Green Housing Renewal Site	No. The buildings are too old to save. Tear them down and put up the high rises as originally planned.	Yes. There are enough high rises already. Let residents who reconstruct old houses keep them.

B. Your candidate wants you to write some campaign "literature." It is a leaflet that will tell about the opinions of your candidate on the major issues. The leaflet will be handed to people on the street. Write the opening paragraph for this leaflet.

Your candidate has been asked to speak to the Chamber of Commerce. The governor will be there, and the event will be televised. Your candidate has asked you to write a great speech for the occasion.

Most good political speeches contain the right combination of factual details and well-expressed opinions. Those in office usually stress their fine records of accomplishment. Those out of office usually stress the poor record of the officeholder, the problems to be dealt with, and the solutions they propose to initiate. Political speeches often include both issues and personal details about the candidates. They appeal to the emotions as well as to the intellect. The use of repetition in a speech helps a candidate make her or his point.

C. Examine your candidate's opinions on page 76. Then plan or outline the speech your candidate will give on the lines below.

____

____

____

____

____

____

____

Now write the actual speech. Stick to the outline that you wrote in part **C.** Remember to give facts as well as opinions. Repeat the important points that your candidate wants to make.

A political speech combines facts about the candidate and the issues, as well as opinions and personal qualities. Such speeches often appeal to both the intellect and the emotions.

Revising

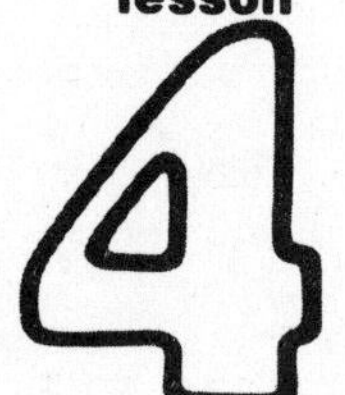

lesson 4

Using specific nouns and verbs

A reporter must provide facts that are clear and accurate. One good way to do this is to use **specific nouns** in news articles, editorials, and other writing. Compare these sentences.

The guy running for city office promised a lot of things.
Mayoral candidate Floyd P. Jolly promised to cut taxes, build high-rise housing, and develop offshore oil wells.

A. Next to each general noun below write three specific nouns.

1. flower __________ __________ __________
2. drink __________ __________ __________
3. trash __________ __________ __________
4. transportation __________ __________ __________
5. disease __________ __________ __________

B. Each sentence below can be made more specific. Replace each underlined vague word with a more specific word.

1. The big red <u>building</u> on Benson Street is 150 years old. __________
2. Those oil rigs make a loud <u>noise</u> when they drill. __________
3. <u>They</u> work hard. __________
4. Ms. Hartfelter is giving a speech <u>someplace</u> tonight. __________
5. It will be about the <u>place</u> where senior citizens live. __________

Your writing will also be more exact if you choose **specific verbs.** One specific verb can often do the job of a vague verb and an adverb. Compare these sentences.

Vague: Mayor Jolly <u>went quickly</u> to Washington.

Better: Mayor Jolly <u>flew</u> to Washington.

C. Next to each general verb that follows, write three specific verbs.

1. walk __________ __________ __________
2. talk __________ __________ __________

3. eat ______ ______ ______

D. Revise each sentence below by replacing the underlined word or words with a more specific verb.

1. Ms. Hartfelter said, "We must improve our schools!" ______

2. Mayor Jolly, who weighs over two hundred pounds, walked slowly toward the banquet table. ______

3. He ate quickly and talked loudly throughout the meal.

   ______ ______

4. The mayor's aides talked softly about a new poll which said Ms. Hartfelter was running slightly ahead of the mayor. ______

E. The sentence below is vague.

He didn't like it when he heard it.

Revise the sentence to make it tell more. The sentence should be clear and accurate. Then use the sentence as the topic sentence of a paragraph. Add several sentences of your own, remembering to use specific nouns and verbs.

______

______

______

______

______

______

Write On

Look at the "Write On" exercises you have completed for this unit. Choose one to revise. Make it more accurate by using specific nouns and verbs.

Use specific nouns and verbs to make your sentences clear and accurate.

Post-Test

1. Read each sentence below. Write N if the sentence belongs to a news story. Write E if it belongs to an editorial.

   _____ a. "I think our city should give small businesses a tax break," said Mayor Roche.

   _____ b. More should be done to stop small businesses from leaving our city.

   _____ c. Scientists believe there is a small but real chance that a large asteroid may someday collide with Earth.

   _____ d. As if unemployment, pollution, and the threat of war weren't enough to worry about, now, it seems, we should be developing "anti-asteroid" missiles.

2. For each fact below, write an opinion.

   a. Teenagers spend large sums of money playing video games.

   ____

   b. Many types of math problems can be done easily on inexpensive pocket calculators.

   ____

   c. Fewer students are applying to the more expensive private colleges.

   ____

3. Write a campaign speech promoting yourself as principal-for-a-day. Mention your qualifications, personal qualities, and ideas.

4. Rewrite these sentences, using specific nouns or verbs for the underlined words.

   a. We <u>saw</u> an <u>animal</u> hiding in a tree.

   ____

   b. The writer <u>gave a prepared talk</u> about her childhood in <u>the South.</u>

   ____

unit 6

Making Your Point in Writing

Things to Remember About Making Your Point in Writing

The **purpose** of a piece of writing may be to inform, to entertain, to express feelings or opinions, or to persuade.

Writing

- Create a positive or negative feeling when you write descriptions of people, places, or things by using words that have positive or negative connotations, such as *healthy* or *lazy*.
- Write better reviews by including a short summary of the work, your opinions, and your reasons for them. Then suggest whether others would enjoy it.
- Make your letters of application brief and to the point. State what the job is, how you found it, and what your qualifications are.

Revising

- Combine short sentences and omit words that are repeated often to give your paragraphs better rhythm.

lesson

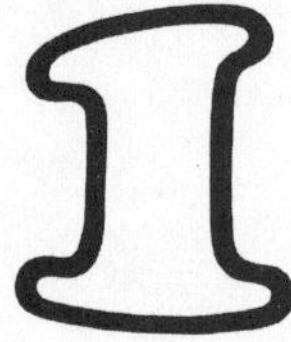

Using the denotation and connotation of words

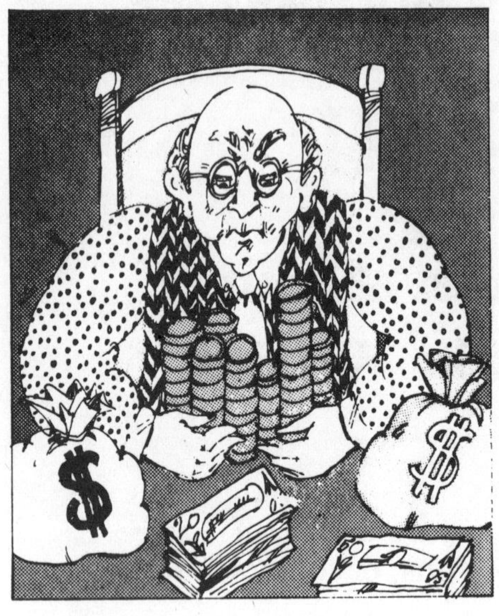

This is the story of Ephraim Ruddy, a stingy, miserly old man.

This is the story of Ephraim Ruddy, a man who is thrifty and careful with his money.

How do you feel about Ephraim Ruddy after looking at the picture and reading the sentence on the left? Do you get the same feeling from the picture and sentence on the right? *Stingy, miserly, thrifty,* and *careful with money* all have the same basic meaning or **denotation.** But they differ in their **connotation,** the positive or negative feelings they give. Here are some other words with similar meanings but different connotations.

Positive	**Negative**
easygoing	lazy
ambitious	aggressive

Carefully selecting the exact words you want when writing helps you to make your point. You can create positive or negative feelings about characters in your writing, depending on the words you use to describe them.

A. Below and on the next page, you will find sentences that describe people using words with positive connotations. These words are underlined. Rewrite each sentence to give it a negative connotation.

1. Oliver <u>takes pride in his work.</u>

____

2. Todd takes pride in his appearance.

____

3. Penelope is persistent.

____

4. Helga has a healthy appetite.

____

A place, like a person, can be described by using positive or negative words. Read this paragraph.

I visited my cousin Alana in her cramped apartment for the first time tonight. As I entered the messy one-room apartment, I was surprised. Alana had been living there for only three weeks. Magazines and newspapers were strewn on the coffee table. Dishes were dumped in the sink. The furniture was ancient. The view from the front window was bleak. I couldn't stay very long, but I did wish Alana the best of luck.

B. Answer these questions about the paragraph above.

1. What did the writer think about the appearance of Alana's apartment?

____

2. Underline the words in the paragraph that helped you know how the writer felt.
3. Do the words the writer used convey a positive or a negative connotation?

____

C. Below are several sentences from the paragraph. Rewrite each sentence so that it conveys a positive connotation. An example has been done for you.

I visited my cousin Alana in her cramped apartment for the first time tonight.
I visited my cousin Alana in her cozy apartment for the first time tonight.

1. As I entered the messy one-room apartment, I was surprised.

____

2. Magazines and newspapers were strewn on the coffee table.

____

3. Dishes were dumped in the sink.

____

4. The furniture was ancient.

____

5. The view from the front window was bleak.

____

Ad writers use words with positive connotations ("plus-loaded" words) and negative connotations ("minus-loaded" words) to try to make you buy a product. Plus-loaded words are used to describe either the product itself or how you will feel or look using the product. Minus-loaded words often describe the way you must feel or look if you aren't using the product.

D. Read the ads below. Underline the plus-loaded words and phrases. Circle the minus-loaded ones. Keep in mind that names of products can also be loaded.

a.

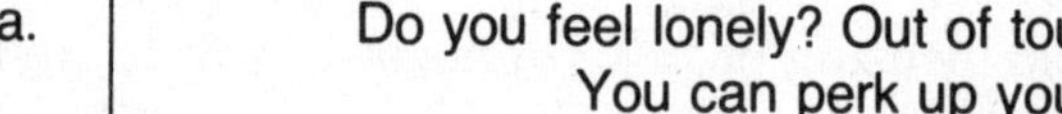

Do you feel lonely? Out of touch? Do people find you boring?
You can perk up your life! Win new friends!
Be the talk of the town!

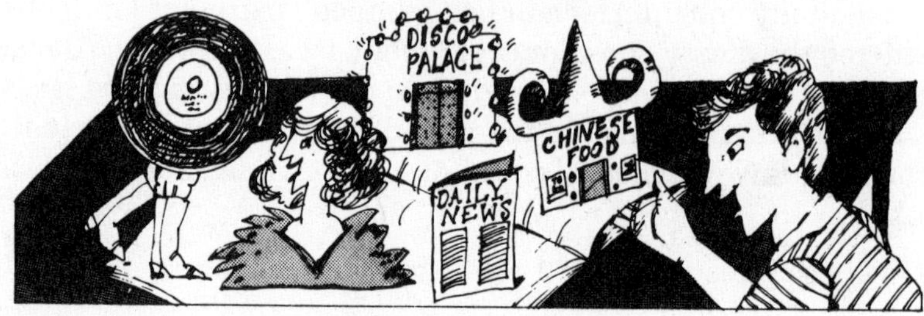

Subscribe to **GOOD IMPRESSIONS**—
the magazine that keeps you up-to-date on
news, hit records, discos, and places to eat.

b.

Are there days when everything rubs you the wrong way?
No need to despair any longer.
Rid yourself of minor aches and pains with

SUNSHINE Liniment Ointment.

No need to rub it in. Just pour it on.
Watch your troubles float away and your shining smile return!

c.

The **SLIM-TRIM** Store offers you a golden opportunity.
The latest in slick T-shirts, stylish jeans, chic jackets,
at low, low prices to fit your budget.
Everything we sell makes you look and feel **SLIM** AND **TRIM**!!!

Come see us soon at our new store in the Cross-Country Shopping Center.

E. Below are products that need advertising. Give each one a name. Write two or three plus-loaded words you would use to describe it. Then write two or three minus-loaded words to tell how the consumer would look or feel without the product.

1. a school ring

   Name: ______________________________

   Plus-loaded words: ______________________________

   Minus-loaded words: ______________________________

2. a typewriter with a circular keyboard

   Name: ______________________________

   Plus-loaded words: ______________________________

   Minus-loaded words: ______________________________

3. a hand computer that gives answers in three languages

   Name: ______________________________

   Plus-loaded words: ______________________________

   Minus-loaded words: ______________________________

4. a snowmaking machine

   Name: ______________________________

   Plus-loaded words: ______________________________

   Minus-loaded words: ______________________________

5. a how-to book on winning contest prizes

   Name: ______________________________

   Plus-loaded words: ______________________________

   Minus-loaded words: ______________________________

Write On

Choose one of the following.

1. Pick a person or place to describe. On a separate sheet of paper, write two descriptions. In one description, use words with positive connotations. Then write about the same subject using words with negative connotations.
2. Pick a product to describe. Write your description in the form of an ad. Use plus- and minus-loaded words.

When you write descriptions of people, places, or things, you can create a positive or negative feeling by using words that have positive or negative connotations.

lesson

2 Writing a review

Have you ever read a movie review that made the movie sound so exciting that you just had to see it? Have you ever read a review of a TV show that kept you from watching it?

People write reviews of movies, TV shows, books, and plays. A **review** summarizes facts about a work—characters, plot, setting, style, sets, performers, and so on. It states opinions and gives reasons for them. And it suggests whether or not other people should read or see the work.

Here is part of a review of a new book.

Donna Blakely's first book, *Echoes of the Past,* is a spine-tingling thriller. I was spellbound as I followed twenty-year-old Tess D'Aubermont on her ominous journey. Her family and friends were sure that she was crazy, but she knew she wasn't. She knew her visions were real—and she would convince everyone, if it was the last thing she ever did.

The seemingly serene setting of the small New England town contrasts with Tess's turmoil. Will she find the reasons for her visions? Is someone playing a trick on her? Or is the quiet seaside house really haunted? Does Tess really belong to the past, a past of 150 years ago?

Looking for answers to these questions—and carried along by the well-written narrative—I read *Echoes of the Past* in one sitting. I found Tess D'Aubermont a convincing character, strong willed and courageous. She stood out more than any other character in the book. In fact, I would have liked to have learned more about the other characters. Still, I applaud Donna Blakely's first book and hope that another is on its way.

A. Look back at the review to answer the following questions.

1. List three facts the reviewer gives you about the book.

___

___

___

2. What does the reviewer say the book is about?

____

____

3. What is the reviewer's general opinion of the book? How is this opinion supported?

____

____

____

4. List one thing that the reviewer does not like about the book.

____

5. Does the reviewer seem to recommend the book to other people? Explain your answer.

____

____

B. Now imagine that you are a critic. You are in the audience watching the one-act play pictured below. Use the illustration to answer the questions on the next page.

1. Briefly describe the characters and setting of the play.

2. What do you think the play is about?

3. What seems to be the audience's reaction to the play?

4. What else would you need to include about the play if you were actually writing a review of it?

C. Think of four books you've read, four movies you've seen, and four TV shows you've watched. List them on the lines below. Then rate them 1 to 4, starting with 1 for your favorite.

Books

Movies

TV Shows

D. Use the lists you made in part **C** as you follow the directions below.

1. Choose one of the movies or TV shows. Tell where and when you saw it. Or choose one of the books and tell when you read it.

2. Write a short paragraph that tells what the film, TV show, or book was about. Be sure not to give away the ending.

3. List several things that you liked about the movie, TV show, or book.

4. List several things that you didn't like about the film, TV show, or book.

Write On

On a separate sheet of paper, write a review of the movie, TV show, or book you chose in part **D.** Include your short summary of the plot. You may wish to describe in more detail one scene that stands out in your mind. Then write your opinions of the show. If you chose a film or TV show, give your opinions about performers, plot, sets, costumes and dialogue. If you chose a book, discuss the characters, plot, setting and writing style. End by telling whether or not you think others would enjoy the work.

A review usually includes a short summary of the work, the reviewer's opinions and the reasons for them, and a suggestion as to whether others would enjoy it.

lesson

Writing a letter of application

Are you interested in getting a part-time job? A summer job? A weekend job? When you apply for a job, one of the first steps is to write a **letter of application.**

It is important to keep several points in mind when you write a letter of application. You should have the correct spelling of the name of the person you are writing to, as well as the correct address. You should state the job you are applying for. You should include how you found out about the job and why you think you're qualified for it. You should also decide what the point of your letter is. Are you asking for an application form, or do you wish to set up an appointment? Once you decide what the point is, get to it quickly. Your letter should not be more than a page long.

Read the sample letter below.

48 South Bend Drive
Bay Ridge, KY 40012
June 11, 19____

Ms. Louise Seiden
Manager
Paradise Bake Shop
3 Twin Oaks Shopping Center
Bay Ridge, KY 40012

Dear Ms. Seiden:

Yesterday I was in the Twin Oaks Shopping Center and saw the sign in your bake shop window for a summer assistant. I am interested in applying for the job. Although I've never worked in a bake shop, I have always helped out at home and am a fast learner. I live across the street from the shopping center and can always be at work on time. I also do not have a sweet tooth, so I wouldn't be eating as I work!

I would like to set up an appointment to introduce myself to you. I can meet with you after school hours or on weekends. My home phone number is 089-3636. Thank you for taking the time to read this letter.

Very truly yours,
Alexander Gold
Alexander Gold

A. Use the sample letter on page 90 to answer these questions.

1. Is this letter written in the form of a friendly letter or a business letter?

___

2. How did Alexander find out about the job?

___

3. What does Alexander feel his qualifications are for this job?

___

___

___

4. What is the point of Alexander's letter?

___

5. What other kind of information did Alexander give in his letter?

___

Now ask yourself the question, "Why should anyone hire me?" The best way to demonstrate your qualifications is to show that you have performed similar duties in the past. This doesn't mean that you had to have a job exactly like the one you're applying for. But everyone has skills learned from past experience that can be applied to new situations.

If you have helped in your parent's home workshop, then you probably know about tools. This knowledge would be something to mention if you were applying for work in a gas station. If you have supervised a table at a bake sale, then you've shown you can handle and account for money. That would be a plus for a job as a cashier or a salesclerk. If you frequently take care of younger brothers or sisters, then you've shown responsibility in supervising youngsters, a necessary skill for a playground supervisor or a camp counselor.

Also consider your personal characteristics. Are you a hard worker? Creative or artistic? Willing to take on responsibility? Able to work with people? You should be able to prove to someone who doesn't know you that you have these characteristics.

B. On the lines below, write down qualifications and personal characteristics you have that you think would make someone want to hire you.

___

___

___

___

___

Below is an imaginary section of classified ads from a newspaper, the *Clarion*. Read the ads. Do any of them appeal to you?

HELP WANTED
at the
METRO BIKE SHOP
21 Park Drive East
Choose your own hours.
Write to: Bob Hanle

Ms. Angela Pagano
needs an
Assistant Salesperson
at the
Golden Arches Shoe Shop
41 Triangle Lane
Part-time hours

Do you like cars?
Do you like to see them look brand new?
The **CLEAN 'N' SHINY** Car Wash
wants you!
Weekends only.
Send for application.
2 West End Road
L. Beech, Manager

THE PIZZA PALACE
needs someone to make
local deliveries.
H. Hertlischek
721 White Street
Evening hours only.

Ye Olde Ice Cream Shoppe
needs reliable person to work counter.
Weekends only.
33 Belt Blvd.
S. Georgiades, Owner.

The Seascape Library
has a position available.
We need someone to conduct a
Saturday morning
story hour.
1330 Willow Lane
Mr. Roy Petro, Librarian

PART-TIME JOB AVAILABLE
at
House of Records
Hours: 3–6 p.m., Mon. thru Sat.
We're located at 666 Main St.
Make an app't with R. Gomez.

YOUTH needed to help with
Summer Lunch Program
for kids 5–9 years old.
Start at 10 a.m.
Finish at 2 p.m.
People's Firehouse, Inc.
212 Northside Ave.
Director: Fred Dunlop

CASHIER/PACKER needed at
H & M Supermarket
15 Knob Hill Square
Saturdays and Sundays
Martha Kawada, Manager

VERY BUSY
Veterinarian's Office needs summer receptionist to answer phones and make appointments
Dr. Sarah Steiner
89 Middletown Rd.
(four-day work week)

We need someone who can run a
copying machine!
Full-time summer position
Speedy Copy Center
13 Highwater St.
Request for application from
Mr. S. Flint.

Goody's Card Shop
55 Park Drive West
needs someone to handle
new deliveries.
Send inquires to Ms. C. Wendell.

C. Choose one of the ads listed above. Imagine that you are writing a letter of application for the job. Then answer the questions below.

1. Who will you write your letter to? (If this person has a title, be sure to include it.)

____

2. What is the address you are writing to? (Use your own town, city, or neighborhood. Don't forget the state and zip code.)

____

____

3. How did you find out about this job?

____

____

4. List the qualifications you feel you have for this job.

____

____

____

5. List personal characteristics that you feel would be good for this job.

____

____

____

6. What is the point of your letter?

____

Write On

On a separate sheet of paper, write a letter of application for the job you chose above. Incorporate your answers to the questions in part **C.** Make sure you write a business letter. (On page 123 of the Handbook, you will find more information on writing business letters.)

Writing a letter of application is one of the first steps you usually take when applying for a job. A letter of application should be brief and to the point. It should state what the job is, how you found out about it, and what your qualifications are for the job.

lesson 4

Revising

Sentence and paragraph rhythm

The sentences below are from the beginning of a paragraph.

Winters in Connecticut become unbearable. I think of summers spent in leisurely sailing. I think of summers spent in leisurely sunbathing.

When winters in Connecticut become unbearable, I think of summers spent in leisurely sailing and sunbathing.

The three short sentences above have been combined into one longer, smoother sentence. In the longer sentence, some of the repeated words were eliminated and the connection between the sentences was made clearer. Too many short, choppy sentences spoil a paragraph's rhythm.

A. The sentences below continue the paragraph. Combine each group into one sentence that sounds both smooth and clear.

1. I have memories of sun-filled days. The memories get me through the slush. They also get me through the cold.

2. Winter may have pleasures for some. I find myself concentrating on ways to keep warm. I also try to keep dry.

3. I like to curl up. I read a good book. I sit in front of a fire. The fire is roaring.

4. My book is forgotten. I dream of summer. I finally feel warmth. I feel contentment. They steal over me.

Notice that you've created two very different characters, both using the word *I*. Each *I* has a different **point of view.** They are **narrators** of scenes you've imagined. Many people think that the narrator is really the writer. But usually a narrator is as much a creation of the author's imagination as the story itself.

Also notice that you've written about the same day from two different points of view. Any event can be seen from several points of view.

C. Think once again about your celebrity. Can you imagine at least two other people who would have different points of view about the world tour? Jot them down below and add a few notes about each point of view.

Good diaries always remain fresh. Each entry is usually written shortly after the events described took place. This is a portion of Samuel Pepys's diary written more than three hundred years ago. It remains as alive now as when it was first written.

> Anon the house grew full, and the candles light, and the King, Queen and all the ladies set. And it was indeed a glorious sight to see Mrs. Stewart in black and white lace and her head and shoulders dressed with diamonds. . . . Mrs. Stewart danced mighty finely, and many French dances, especially one the King called the New Dance, which was very pretty.

Diaries written ten, fifty, or a hundred years ago show history as it was lived. If you read a diary written during the Civil War, you realize that the war was not just an old story—for five years it was part of everyday life in America. Here's a quote from the diary of Sarah Morgan, who lived in Louisiana during the Civil War.

> Cousin Will saw one lying dead without a creature by to notice when he died. Another was dying, and muttering to himself as he lay too far gone to brush the flies out of his eyes and mouth, while no one was able to do it for him. Cousin Will helped him, though. . . . Oh, I wish these poor men were safe in their own land! It is heartbreaking to see them die here like dogs, with no one to say Godspeed.

Historical characters can become living people when you know what they felt and suffered.

D. Imagine someone living during the Civil War: for example, a general leading his men on an exhausting march, a Southern belle, an ex-slave fighting in the Union army, a plantation owner, or a foreign visitor. Write a diary entry that tells some of your character's experiences. What is your character's opinion of the war? Is your character involved or merely an observer? How does your character get along with the people around him or her?

____

____

____

____

____

____

____

____

____

____

E. You yourself are a historical figure. You are living history right now. Much of what you do and think could happen only today. You belong to the time you live in. Jot down events in a typical day. Then underline the events or phrases that show that you are living in the 1980s.

____

____

____

____

____

____

____

____

____

____

Write On

Choose one of the activities below.

1. Think of a favorite historical character, someone you admire very much. Imagine that you were able to meet this person. Describe your historic meeting in a diary entry. What was this person like? What did you talk about? What were your feelings when you met this person? Was this person like what you expected?
2. A diary can show that a person's private life may be very different from her or his public life. A diary of a great singer, for example, could be filled with fears of not being good enough. Write a brief story in which you discover another person's diary. What do you learn about this person? How does it change your feelings about him or her?

Diaries are brief records of everyday life. A fictional diary can give a detailed account of a character's point of view.

---

lesson

2 Writing first-person and third-person narratives

Imagine that you are hearing a story read aloud. The voice you hear is the narrator's, telling the story in his or her own words. In a **first-person narrative,** the narrator uses the words *I, me, my,* and *mine.* In a third-person narrative, characters are referred to as *he* or *she.* In the **third-person narrative,** *I* is used only in dialogue or letters.

A. Read the following excerpts. Write *FP* if the passage comes from a first-person narrative and *TP* if it comes from a third-person narrative.

_____ 1. The schoolmaster was leaving the village, and everybody seemed sorry. (Thomas Hardy, *Jude the Obscure*)

_____ 2. I got another barber that comes over from Carterville and helps me out Saturdays, but the rest of the time I can get along all right alone. (Ring Lardner, "The Haircut")

_____ 3. When I was a child, I used to go to the seaside for the holidays. (Beatrix Potter, "Tale of Little Pig Robinson")

_____ 4. It is a truth universally acknowledged, that a single man in possession of a good fortune must be in want of a wife. (Jane Austen, *Pride and Prejudice*)

If you listen to the voices speaking in the lines above, you can tell that each narrator is very different. First-person narratives usually sound very much like a normal speaking voice. Third-person narratives are usually—though not always—more formal.

A writer is careful about choosing the right narrator for a story. The narrator gives the story a specific quality. Depending on the choice of words the narrator uses, the story can be serious or funny, simple or complicated. Sometimes it is a good idea to try several narrators for a story to find out which one suits it best.

Use the picture below to give you ideas for parts **B, C,** and **D.**

B. A remark about football turns a big Thanksgiving dinner into a family brawl. Write a paragraph, giving a humorous first-person account of the beginning of the dinner. The narrator is an involved participant in the football discussion in which some of the guests are supporting opposite teams, while some hate football.

C. Now write another account of the dinner from the point of view of someone not involved in the fight: a small child or an out-of-town visitor. The fight is at its fiercest now: people are arguing about football, TV, and who took the last turkey wing.

D. By dessert, no one is talking to anyone else. Describe the scene in a third-person account.

A third-person narrative can be **subjective** or **omniscient.** In a subjective third-person narrative, the story is seen from the point of view of one person. In an omniscient third-person account, the narrator seems to know how all the characters feel.

E. Read the two quotes below. Write O if the passage seems to be written from an omniscient viewpoint and S if it seems to be a subjective narrative.

______ 1. Alice was beginning to get very tired of sitting by her sister on the bank, and of having nothing to do: once or twice she had peeped into the book her sister was reading, but it had no pictures or conversations in it, "and what is the use of a book," thought Alice, "without pictures or conversations?" (Lewis Carroll, *Alice's Adventures in Wonderland*)

______ 2. Once upon a time a father had two sons. The oldest was clever and wise and could do anything, but the younger son was stupid and couldn't understand anything—people used to look at him and say, "Oh, there's a son who is going to give his father trouble." (The Brothers Grimm, "The Boy Who Set Out to Learn Fear")

Have you ever been in an embarrassing situation—for example, walking down the street with a gaping hole in your jeans, or forgetting lines in a school play? Your "point of view" in those situations becomes wildly off-target because you're nervous. You may think that everybody is staring at you or talking about you.

A character's point of view can provide a story in itself. A story which concentrates on a character's feelings and thoughts is often called a **character study.**

F. Write a third-person subjective account of a character who has to deliver ten thousand dollars to a large train station. The money is stored in a large supermarket bag so it won't look suspicious. Still, the character thinks that every passerby knows there's money in that bag. Describe your character's fears and suspicions.

____

____

____

____

____

____

____

____

____

____

G. Any group of strangers gathered together—in a waiting room, for example, or on a bus or ship—can be the subject of a story. Although they are physically close, their thoughts and lives are separate. Write a paragraph or two from an omniscient viewpoint: describe two strangers, and give some details about their thoughts. Do they notice one another? Are they preoccupied with worries? Daydreaming?

Choose one of the story ideas you used in this lesson: the Thanksgiving fight, the money in the bag, or the two strangers in one place. Work out a plot with a climax and a conclusion. Then decide from which point of view you will narrate the story. On another sheet of paper, write your story. Keep your point of view consistent.

A narrative may be written from the first-person, third-person subjective, or third-person omniscient point of view, depending on the writer's goals.

lesson

3 Writing about your life

The story of your life is the story you know best of all. Unlike most writing assignments, this one requires no investigation of secondary sources. As the writer of your **autobiography,** you may find that you have far too much information to handle well. Where should you begin? What are the important events? Who were the important influences? How can you begin to put it all on paper?

You could of course, simply begin with your earliest memories and write everything that you can recall in the sequence that the events actually happened. But an autobiography is more than simply the retelling of events in your life.

Your task in this lesson will be to select an important phase from your past, describe it in detail, and answer the question: What did it mean?

What is a phase? In this case, a **phase** is simply a portion of your life with a beginning and an end. A summer might be a phase in your life. Your adaptation to a school or the birth of one of your brothers or sisters could also be a phase.

A. Jot down a few events or feelings in your life that you particularly remember.

____

____

____

____

____

B. Choose one of the events from part **A** to become the phase you will write about. In the space below, briefly describe the phase. Note the events and the approximate dates on which the phase started and ended.

____

____

____

____

____

____

C. What was the nature of this phase? Did you learn something about yourself? Did you grow up, or learn a new skill?

____

____

____

____

____

D. Now that you have begun to define the change you experienced during this phase of your life, you should write a statement of the theme of this autobiographical phase. The theme could be friendship, learning, or loss. It should capture the meaning of the phase for you.

____

____

____

In order for your readers to know how you changed during this phase, they should have some idea of what you were like before the phase.

E. Describe briefly your feelings before this phase. In your description make it clear why this phase was important to you.

____

____

____

____

F. The changes you underwent during this phase were largely produced by important people and events at that time in your life. List the persons that influenced you during this period. Describe each person and the particular events that person is linked to. Then describe the influence that person had on you.

Person: ______________________________

____

____

Person: ______________________________

____

____

Person: ______________________________

____

____

G. List in chronological order the important events that took place during this phase of your life. After each event, describe your reaction to it.

Event: ______________________________

____

Event: ______________________________

____

Event: ______________________________

____

Event: ______________________________

Event:

H. You learned how it is possible to describe the same event from different points of view. Other people may have different viewpoints about your phase than you do. In fact, your own point of view may have changed. You may have been unhappy about this period of your life while you were living it and discovered later how valuable it was to you. Your autobiography should be written from your present point of view. What is your viewpoint about this phase of your life now?

I. What makes you remember this phase today? Do people remind you? Are you reminded by sights and sounds that recall that period of your life? Do you compare present experiences to that time in your life?

Write On

Using the ideas and information you have written above, you should be able to write several paragraphs about your autobiographical phase. As you write, try to combine the telling of the events with your interpretation of their significance.

An autobiography is the story of one's life: it tells both the events and the significance of those events in a person's life.

Revising

lesson

Polishing your writing

When you have finished your first draft of a story or an essay, it is a good idea to reread what you have written and revise it until it's as good as you can make it.

A. The rules below review some of the guidelines for revising that you have studied in this book. Use them to help you revise the sentences beneath each rule.

1. Add adverbs and adverbial phrases to sentences to give specific information about how, when, and where.

   The batter hit the ball.

   ____

   ____

2. Use connecting words, such as prepositions, conjunctions, and relative pronouns, to link sentences and make relationships clear.

   Shop for winter clothes now. Spring clothes are already out.
   Winter clothes are on clearance sale. You can get some real bargains.

   ____

   ____

   ____

3. Don't overload your sentences with too many modifiers.

   On top of the old, antique, battered desk lay an old worn diary which was an old brown book with two faded photographs about fifty years old inside of the diary.

   ____

   ____

4. Rewrite sentences to correct misplaced or dangling modifiers.

   Desperately clinging to life rafts, the Coast Guard cutter approached the survivors.
   Wrapped in blankets to keep warm, the cutter headed into port.

   ____

   ____

   ____

5. Replace dull adjectives with fresh adjectives and similes.

   Staying in the big old house made Kerry feel strange.

   ____

   ____

6. Use specific nouns and verbs to make your sentences clear and accurate.

   Everyone will go there tonight.

   ____

   ____

7. Combine sentences and omit or change repeated words to improve paragraph rhythm.

   I eat breakfast. I get on my bicycle. I ride north. I ride on country roads. The roads are long and winding. I see woods. I see farms. The farms have red barns. The barns are off in the distance.

   ____

   ____

   ____

   ____

B. Revise the paragraph below, combining sentences and changing words until it sounds just right to you.

The night was dark. The night was chilly. She heard something at her window. Suddenly, a figure leapt there. Screaming loudly, the bedroom door flew open. It was the police. They were there. She was safe.

____

____

____

____

____

Write On

Go over all the papers you wrote this year and pick one you would like to improve. Revise it, keeping in mind the guidelines you have studied in this book. When your paper says just what you want it to say, make a neat copy.

Revise your writing until it says exactly what you want it to say.

Post-Test

1. Read the paragraph below. Then write a first-person narrative about the incident from the point of view of one of the people involved.

   A commercial jet carrying 348 people made an emergency landing yesterday when the landing gear did not work properly. Airport officials say the pilot made a skillful "bellylanding." Some minor injuries were reported, but no one was seriously hurt. Passengers were quickly evacuated from the plane.

2. Read this diary excerpt. Tell whose point of view the excerpt could describe.

   Today, the egg shows signs of hatching. If the egg doesn't hatch within 72 hours, I'll have to help it, but I don't want to rush things. I'm not going to leave the lab until it's over. If the chick hatches, it will be the first crested sandhopper ever born in captivity.

   ____

3. Read each quote below. Write S if it is a subjective narrative, or O if it is omniscient.

   _____ a. When Leslie entered the office, she saw a brusque, stocky man who barely gave her a glance. She gulped and wondered what chance she had to win the music scholarship.

   _____ b. Derek and Fran soon launched into their favorite topic: Dr. Dower. Unfortunately, both of them were too busy to notice Mrs. Dower, who had sat down in the row ahead of them.

4. Revise this paragraph.

   My parents were both in the Army. They traveled a lot. I was born in France. My brother was born in Germany. Living in different places, other cultures became familiar to us. Making new friends was sometimes hard and difficult. It was an absorbing, interesting life.

   ____

   ____

   ____

   ____

   ____

Writing Handbook

When your writing says exactly what you want it to say, it is a good idea to proofread to look for errors you might have made in capitalization, punctuation, or word usage. The following pages include rules for using capital letters, punctuation marks, and word forms correctly. Use this handbook as a reference whenever you have any questions. When you feel you know the rules, turn to page 124 and take the proofreading test there.

PART 1 **CAPITALIZATION**

1. The first word of every sentence begins with a capital letter.

   The players were in a huddle. What would they do?

   The first word of a direct quotation begins with a capital letter.

   The quarterback said, "Let's fake a pass."

2. In the titles or subtitles of works, the first, the last, and any important words begin with capital letters. "Important words" means all words except *a, an, the;* coordinate conjunctions; prepositions of four letters or less; and *to* in an infinitive.

   I Know Why the Caged Bird Sings (book)
   The Merchant of Venice (play)
   "I Like to See It Lap the Miles" (poem)
   the *Daily Clarion* (newspaper; *the* not part of title)

3. Every word or abbreviation in a proper noun begins with a capital letter (except *of, the, and*). A proper noun names a particular person, animal, place, or thing.

   James E. Carter, Jr.
   Bogotá, Colombia (city/country)
   Pacific Ocean (body of water)
   Merritt Parkway (road)
   the *Monitor* (boat)
   the Magna Charta (document)
   Sunkist oranges (brand name)
   Friday, May 11 (day/month)
   Passover (holiday)
   the American Revolution (historic event)
   Christianity (religion)
   the Red Cross (organization)
   Jefferson High School (institution)
   the Democratic Party (political party)
   the Photography Club (club)
   Sears, Roebuck and Co. (company)

   Do not begin a common noun with a capital letter, even when it refers to a proper noun just mentioned. A common noun is a general noun (see page 120).

   We swam in the Pacific Ocean. The ocean was rough.

4. Titles and ranks (and their abbreviations) begin with capital letters when they occur with names.

   General Douglas MacArthur
   Professor Emilia Ruiz
   Dr. Horace Chang, Jr.
   Mary, Queen of Scots

Ranks or titles that appear alone do not begin with capital letters.

The queen gave a speech. Where's the doctor?

You may capitalize family relationship words that appear alone if they are used as names.

I asked Dad for a loan.

5. Do not capitalize the words for directions unless they are being used as parts of names or to name specific geographic places.

They went west. They live on West Street. They visited the West.

PART 2 PUNCTUATION

Apostrophes (')

1. An apostrophe is used to show the possessive form of a noun.

Reiko's ring the horses' saddles the men's lockers

2. An apostrophe is used in a contraction to show that a letter or letters have been left out.

don't (do not) let's (let us) they're (they are)

Colons (:)

1. A colon is used to introduce a list.

The campers took the following items: one tent, three sleeping bags, a stove, and some pots.

2. A colon is sometimes used to introduce a direct quotation. (A comma would also be correct; a colon simply makes a stronger pause.)

Abraham Lincoln said: "The ballot is stronger than the bullet."

Commas (,)

1. A comma is used to separate two independent clauses linked by a coordinate conjunction.

The car stopped, and a woman jumped out.

2. Commas are used to separate items in a series.

She carried flowers, chocolates, and fruit.

It is not necessary to use commas in a series if coordinate conjunctions are used between all items.

Bring flowers or chocolates or fruit.

3. A comma is used to separate coordinate adjectives (adjectives of equal force that separately modify the same noun).

An old, tattered book lay on the desk.

Do not use a comma to separate adjectives that are not coordinate.

Its cover was dull olive green.

4. Commas are used to set off modifying phrases and clauses when they come before the main clause.

   To solve the case, Miss Marple needed more clues.
   Standing outside the door, she heard every word.
   Behind the bookcase next to the far wall, there was a safe.
   When she entered the room, the safe was open.

   A comma is not required after a short introductory adverbial phrase.

   Behind the bookcase there was a safe.

5. Commas are used to set off nonrestrictive modifying appositives, phrases, and clauses. A nonrestrictive element is one that merely adds information to the word it follows.

   My favorite singer, Diana Ross, made that record.
   One skater, wearing a red scarf, is waving to you.
   That car, which has a dented fender, should be repaired.

   Do not set off restrictive modifying appositives, phrases, and clauses with commas. A restrictive element restricts, or limits, the meaning of the word it follows.

   We saw the singer Diana Ross in person.
   The skater wearing a red scarf is my cousin.
   The car that has a dented fender belongs to Tim.

6. Commas are used to set off parenthetic words and expressions—words and expressions that interrupt the sentence.

   No, I am not going. I will, of course, if you insist.

7. Commas are used to set off a direct quotation that is not a grammatical part of the entire sentence.

   The coach said, "Winning isn't everything."

   When the quotation is a grammatical part of the sentence, do not use commas unless the sentence structure makes them necessary.

   The coach told the team that "winning isn't everything."

8. Commas are used in dates to separate the day's name from the month, the day's number from the year, and the end of the date from the rest of the sentence.

   On June 19, 1846, the first organized baseball game was played.

9. Commas are used in street addresses to separate the street from the town or city, the town or city from the state or country, the state from the country, and the end of the address from the rest of the sentence.

   We moved to 129 Union Street, Columbus, Ohio, two years ago.
   My sister went to Cambridge, England, for her junior year in college.

10. Commas are used to set off a person's title or rank when it follows the name.

    Martin Luther King, Jr., was a great man.

11. Commas are used to set off the name of a person directly addressed (spoken to).

Fetch the ball, Rags. Brigitta, please answer the phone.

Exclamation Points (!)

An exclamation point always follows an exclamation and sometimes follows an imperative sentence.

How lovely you look! Nuts! Stop that!

Italics/Underlining

1. The titles of longer works—books, longer poems, plays, films, works of art, symphonies, magazines, and newspapers—are italicized (or underlined in handwriting or typewriting). The names of ships, planes, and spacecraft are also italicized (or underlined).

   Frankenstein was written by Mary Shelley in 1818.
   The space module *Eagle* was the first craft to land on the moon.

2. Words as words and letters as letters are italicized (or underlined).

   What word besides *abstemious* has *a*, *e*, *i*, *o*, and *u* in order?

Periods (.)

1. A period always follows a declarative sentence and usually follows an imperative sentence.

   Five English words begin with *gh*. Name them.

2. Periods are used in most abbreviations. (Note: *Miss* is not an abbreviation.)

   Mrs. Mr. Rev. Sgt. Ph.D. N.J. Mich.
   Rd. Tpke. Can. Eur. A.D. P.M. R.S.V.P.

   Some abbreviations and acronyms (words formed from the first letters of each important word in a term) do not use periods. Official post office abbreviations accompanied by zip codes do not use periods. If in doubt, check your dictionary.

   rpm (revolutions per minute) Norfolk, VA 23518
   NBC (National Broadcasting Company) Springfield, MO 65803

Question Marks (?)

A question mark follows an interrogative sentence.

What is the tallest mountain in the world?

Quotation Marks (" ") (' ')

1. Quotation marks are used to set off a direct quotation.

   Luis asked, "Did you see my keys?"

2. Quotation marks are used to set off the titles of stories, short poems, articles, chapters, essays, songs, TV shows, and other short works.

   "The Lottery" is a story by Shirley Jackson.

3. Quotation marks are used to set off coined words or words intended to mean something different from what they normally mean.

   The "orchestra" consisted of two guitars and a kazoo.

4. Single quotation marks are used inside double quotation marks.

   "I hope to appear on 'The Gong Show' soon," said Uncle Egbert.

NOTE: A comma or a period *always* goes inside of a closing quotation mark. A semicolon or a colon *always* goes outside a closing quotation mark. A question mark or an exclamation point goes either inside or outside a closing quotation mark, depending on whether or not it is part of the quotation.

He sang "Three Blind Mice." We begged, "Will you please stop?"
Kristin said, "I can't stand it"; I said, "I agree."
Does he know "Row, Row Your Boat"?

Semicolons (;)

1. A semicolon is used to separate two independent, related clauses when a coordinate conjunction is not used.

   The car stopped; immediately a woman jumped out.

2. Semicolons are used to separate items in a series when at least one element already has a comma.

   We have cheese, tuna, or egg sandwiches; tossed salad; and sherbet.

PART 3 USAGE

Adjectives and Adverbs

1. An adjective modifies a noun, a pronoun, or a gerund.

   His loud snoring woke the whole family.

   An adverb or adverbial phrase tells how, how often, when, or where. Most adverbs and adverbials modify verbs.

   Trucks rumble noisily past my house every morning.

   A common error that many people make is to use adjectives when they should use adverbs. Remember, adjectives do not modify verbs.

   Trucks rumble noisily (not *noisy*). She dances well (not *good*).

2. Both adjectives and adverbs can be used to show comparisons. There are two degrees of comparison: comparative and superlative. Comparative degree is used to compare two items. Superlative degree is used to compare three or more items. Rules for showing comparison are as follows.

   a. For all one-syllable and some two-syllable adjectives and adverbs, add *-er* for the comparative and *-est* for the superlative.

Peter came early.
Vera came earlier than Pete.
Ichi came earliest of all.

The lamp is bright.
The streetlight is brighter than the lamp.
The moon is brightest of all.

b. For all other adjectives and adverbs, use the word *more* for the comparative and the word *most* for the superlative.

Pete walks quickly.	The flowered dress is vivid.
Vera walks more quickly than Pete.	The yellow dress is more vivid.
Ichi walks most quickly of all.	The red dress is most vivid of all.

c. A few adjectives and adverbs show comparative and superlative degrees by changing form completely.

	Comparative	Superlative
good / well	better	best
bad	worse	worst
little (meaning *few*)	less	least

A common error that many people make is to use a double comparative or superlative form.

Vera walks more faster than Pete. The sun is the most brightest star.

Agreement

1. A present-tense verb must agree with its subject. The simple form of the verb is used with *I*, *you*, and all plural subjects. The *s* form is used with all singular subjects except *I* and *you*.

I like peanuts.	He likes peanuts.
You like peanuts.	Elinor likes peanuts
Squirrels like peanuts.	That bluejay likes peanuts.

Sometimes the word *Here* or *There* is used as a sentence starter. In this case, the verb agrees with the subject that follows.

Here is the bacon, and there are the eggs.

For more information on present-tense verb forms, see page 122.

2. A pronoun must agree with the noun or other pronoun to which it refers.

When Aunt Lula came, she brought gifts. (*She* refers to *Aunt Lula*).
I opened my gift. It was a tape recorder. (*It* refers to *gift*).
The twins loved their new sweaters. (*Their* refers to *twins*).

For more information on pronouns, see page 121.

3. Many people make agreement errors with singular indefinite pronouns (see the list on page 121). Remember: A singular indefinite pronoun is not affected by any adjective phrase that comes after it.

Neither of the boys likes his old sweaters anymore. (Do not be confused by the adjective phrase *of the boys;* the subject *neither* is singular.)
Everybody was surprised to hear his or her voice on tape.

A few indefinite pronouns may be either singular or plural (see the list on page 121). With these pronouns, the adjective phrases are helpful.

All of the food is gone. All of the peanuts are gone.

4. Nouns or pronouns joined by *and* form a compound expression that is plural.

   Aunt Lula and Uncle Ben like to cook.
   They and I make a good chili.

   If the expression joined by *and* names a single thing, it is singular.

   Peanut butter and jelly is my favorite sandwich.

5. Singular nouns or pronouns joined by *or* or *nor* form a compound expression that is singular.

   Neither Ray nor Roy likes his peanut butter sandwich.

   Plural nouns or pronouns joined by *or* or *nor* form a compound expression that is plural.

   Neither the twins nor their friends like their peanut butter sandwiches.

   You should avoid constructions in which a singular is joined to a plural by *or* or *nor*. However, the rule for such a case is that the verb or any pronoun agrees with the closer word.

   Acceptable: Neither the twins nor Aunt Lula likes her peanut butter sandwich.
   Better: The twins don't like their peanut butter sandwich, and neither does Aunt Lula.
   Acceptable: Neither Aunt Lula nor the twins like their peanut butter sandwiches.
   Better: Aunt Lula doesn't like her peanut butter sandwich, and neither do the twins.

Comparison (See Adjectives and Adverbs on page 117.)

Dangling Modifiers (See Unit 3, page 47.)

Double Negatives

1. Using more than one negative word in a clause is considered a mistake.

   They don't want nothing. should be changed to:
   They don't want anything. OR They want nothing.

2. The words *barely, hardly,* and *scarcely* are half negatives and also should not appear together with another negative word.

   They hardly ate nothing. should be changed to:
   They hardly ate anything.

Fragments

A sentence fragment is a group of words that, though punctuated like a sentence, does not express a complete thought.

A large bouquet of roses. As soon as I got home.

In general, you should avoid sentence fragments in your writing. However, fragments are sometimes acceptable—in realistic dialogue, for example.

"What did you buy your mother?" "A large bouquet of roses."
"When did you give them to her?" "As soon as I got home."

Misplaced Modifiers (See Unit 3, page 47.)

Negatives (See Double Negatives, page 119.)

Nouns

1. A noun names a person, an animal, a place, a thing, or an idea.

   The boy and his dog enjoyed their new freedom in the country.

2. A noun can be either common or proper. A proper noun is the name of a particular person, animal, place, or thing. The first letter is always capitalized (see page 113).

   Brigitta Rags Bogotá Chevrolet

   A common noun is any other noun.

   girl dog city car

3. A noun can be singular (one) or plural (more than one). The rules for spelling the plural forms of nouns follow.

   a. In most cases, the plural form is made by adding *-s* to the singular.

   girl, girls dog, dogs car, cars

   b. When a singular noun ends in a consonant plus *y*, the plural is formed by changing the *y* to *i* and adding *-es*.

   city, cities factory, factories country, countries

   c. When a singular noun ends in a consonant plus *o*, the plural is sometimes formed by adding *-es*. Check your dictionary.

   torpedo, torpedoes echo, echoes motto, mottoes

   d. When a singular noun ends in *f* or *fe*, the plural is sometimes formed by changing the *f* or *fe* to *v* and adding *-es*. Check your dictionary.

   life, lives shelf, shelves wife, wives

   e. Irregular plurals are formed in various ways. Whenever you are not sure, check your dictionary.

   tooth, teeth phenomenon, phenomena sheep, sheep

4. A noun can be made into a possessive to show ownership. A singular noun is made into a possessive by adding an apostrophe (') and an *s*.

   the thief's mask the boss's office Bess's scarf

   To form the possessive of a plural noun that ends in *s*, just add an apostrophe.

   the thieves' masks the bosses' offices the girls' scarves

If the plural form does not end in s, add an apostrophe and an s to form the possessive.

the sheep'<u>s</u> wool　　the people'<u>s</u> choice　　the children'<u>s</u> games

Plurals (See Agreement, page 118, and Nouns, page 120.)

Possession (See Nouns, page 120, and Pronouns below.)

Pronouns

1. Pronouns have subject, object, and possessive forms. Many people have difficulty using the forms of pronouns correctly, especially when they occur in compound subjects or objects.

   a. Use subjective forms of pronouns that are subjects of sentences or predicate nominatives (following linking verbs).

   Dad and <u>I</u> mowed the lawn.　　The car washers were Milt and <u>she</u>.

   b. Use objective forms of pronouns that are objects of verbs, prepositions, or verbals.

   Let's take Lorraine and <u>them</u> to the game.　(direct object)
   Send Brenda or <u>him</u> the package.　(indirect object)
   Throw the pass to Lacey or <u>me</u>.　(object of a preposition)
   After seeing Jamie and <u>her</u>, Ralph left.　(object of a verbal)

2. Possessive pronouns, like possessive nouns, show ownership. But unlike possessive nouns, possessive pronouns do not have any apostrophes.

   <u>His</u> tickets are now <u>theirs</u>.　　<u>My</u> watch lost <u>its</u> crystal.

   A common error people make is to confuse certain possessive pronouns with contractions that they sound like.

   <u>Their</u> house is oddly furnished.　(*Their* is a possessive pronoun.)
   <u>They're</u> buying a new three-legged chair.　(*They're* is a contraction for *they are.*)
   <u>Your</u> watch is slow.　(*Your* is a possessive pronoun.)
   <u>You're</u> always late.　(*You're* is a contraction for *you are.*)

3. An indefinite pronoun refers to an unspecified person, place, or thing. Most indefinite pronouns are always singular, some can be singular or plural, and a few are always plural. For a discussion of agreement with indefinite pronouns, see page 118.

INDEFINITE PRONOUNS					
Always Singular			**Singular or Plural**		**Always Plural**
another	everybody	no one	all	most	both
anybody	everyone	nothing	any	none	few
anyone	everything	one	enough	some	many
anything	much	other	more	such	several
each	neither	somebody			
either	nobody	someone			
		something			

Run Ons

A run-on sentence is a sentence in which two or more independent clauses are joined together without correct punctuation.

> Pablo's pencil broke he used his pen.
> Pablo's pencil broke, he used his pen.

The above run-on sentence could be corrected as follows:

a. Add a semicolon to show that the two independent clauses are related. (You may also add a conjunctive adverb.)

   Pablo's pencil broke; he used his pen.
   Pablo's pencil broke; therefore, he used his pen.

b. Add a coordinate conjunction between the two independent clauses.

   Pablo's pencil broke, and he used his pen.

c. Add a subordinate conjunction to one of the clauses.

   When Pablo's pencil broke, he used his pen.

d. If the two independent clauses are unrelated, make them into separate sentences.

   Run on: Pablo's pencil broke I used green ink.
   Corrected: Pablo's pencil broke. I used green ink.

Verbs

Verbs have five forms.

a. The simple form is used for present tense with plural subjects, *I*, and *you*. (It is sometimes called the plural form.) It is also used after all helping verbs except forms of *have* and *be*.

   I sneeze. They sneeze. Will you sneeze?

b. The *-s* form is the simple form plus *-s*. It is used for present tense with singular subjects (except *I* and *you*). (It is sometimes called the singular form.)

   Molly sneezes. She sneezes.

c. The *-ing* form, or the present participle, is the simple form plus *-ing*. It is used after the helping verb *be* to form the progressive tenses. For spelling changes in the *ing* form, consult your dictionary.

d. The *-ed* ending is used for both the past tense and the past participle, but these are actually different forms. The past tense *-ed* form stands alone.

   He sneezed. They sneezed. We sneezed. I sneezed.

   Notice that the same past-tense form is used for all subjects. The only exception is *be*.

   I was You (or plural subjects) were He (or singular subjects) was

   For spelling changes in the past tense, consult your dictionary.

e. The past participle (also *-ed* ending) is used after the helping verb *have.*

I have sneezed. She has sneezed. I had sneezed.

f. Irregular verbs are verbs that do not form their past tense and past participle (*-ed*) forms in the regular way. The term does not apply to mere spelling changes (*carry* to *carried*, for example) but to complete irregularity. Often, irregular verbs have two different forms for past tense and past participle.

I went there; I have gone there.

For irregular verb forms,consult your dictionary.

NOTE: Make sure you do not confuse the simple past tense with the past participle when they are different.

Wrong: I have wrote the letter.
Correct: I have written the letter.

PART IV **Letter Forms**

1. Most business letters have six parts arranged in the following way.

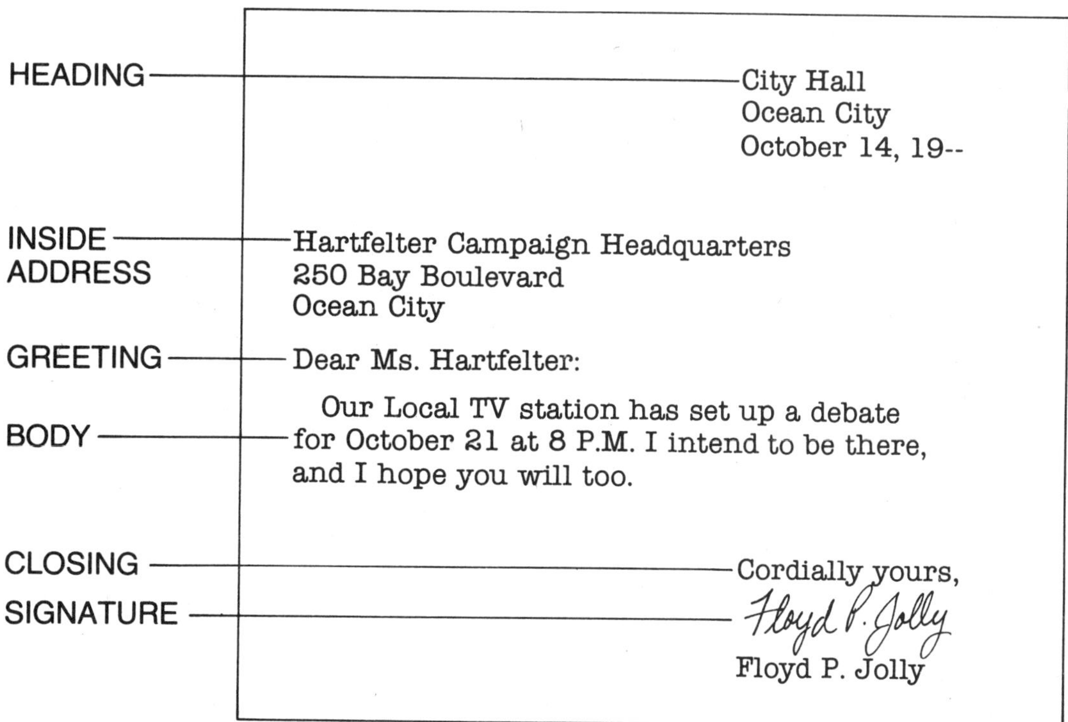

HEADING — City Hall
Ocean City
October 14, 19--

INSIDE ADDRESS — Hartfelter Campaign Headquarters
250 Bay Boulevard
Ocean City

GREETING — Dear Ms. Hartfelter:

BODY — Our Local TV station has set up a debate for October 21 at 8 P.M. I intend to be there, and I hope you will too.

CLOSING — Cordially yours,

SIGNATURE — Floyd P. Jolly
Floyd P. Jolly

2. A colon is used following the greeting of a formal business letter.

3. Most friendly letters have five parts arranged in the following way.

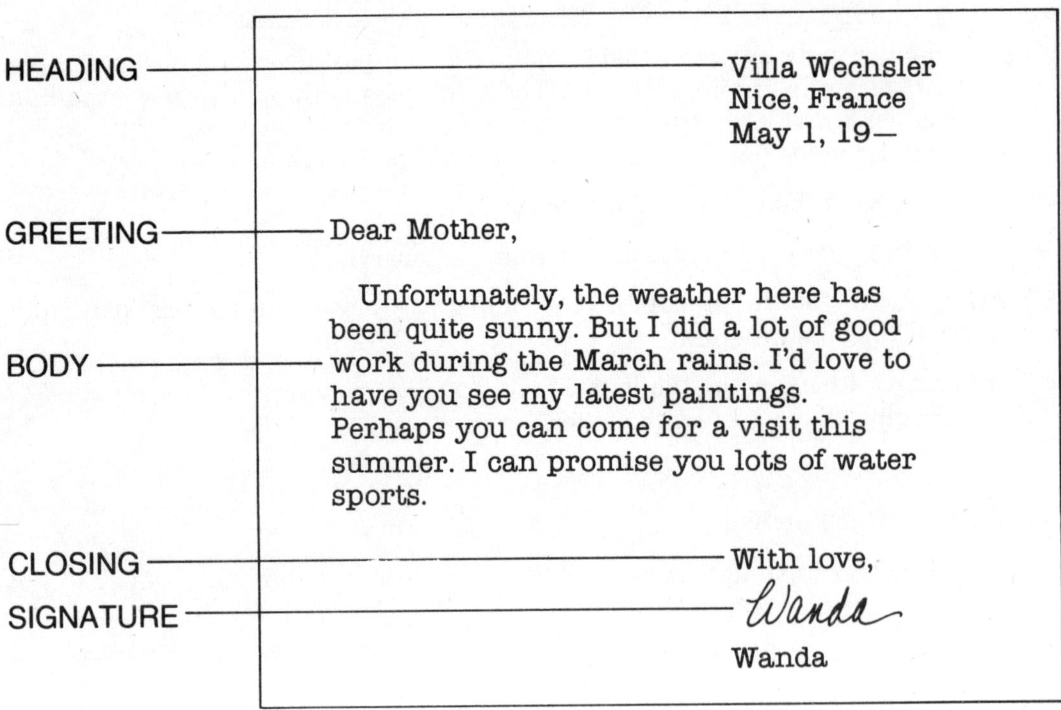

HEADING
Villa Wechsler
Nice, France
May 1, 19—
GREETING
Dear Mother,
BODY
Unfortunately, the weather here has been quite sunny. But I did a lot of good work during the March rains. I'd love to have you see my latest paintings. Perhaps you can come for a visit this summer. I can promise you lots of water sports.
CLOSING
With love,
SIGNATURE
Wanda
Wanda

4. Commas are used following the greeting of a friendly letter, and following the closing of any letter.

A. How good a proofreader are you? Can you find and correct the twenty-five errors in the passage below?

The most popularest rodent in the world mickey mouse, was born in 1928. He maked his screen debut in Steamboat Willie, the first cartoon to use sound Walt Disney, the man who drawed Mickey also provided the mouses voice. Since his first film was released. Mickey has made countless, other films and has became world famous. Now Mickey's big ears bow tie and white gloves is recognized everywhere. Can their be anyone who don't know and love this mouse among mouses. the ageless star now have two homes. Disneyland in Anaheim, California, was opened on July 17 1955, and Disney World in Orlando florida, was opened in 1971.

Unit 1

Lesson 1

A. 5, 7, 1, 3, 10, 8, 9, 4, 2, 6

B. 1. the controversial underwater painter
2. In the paragraph you should have underlined sentences 2 and 3. The underlined sentences help to show a connection between the events by telling us what effect water had in shaping her career.

C. ⇨⇦ Whenever you see this symbol, check with your teacher.

D. ⇨⇦

E.

L or C	C
C	L
C	L
L	C
C	L

F. ⇨⇦

Lesson 2

A. 1. The movie scene might begin with Captain Corcoran floating around in his space capsule.
2. his first pole vault.
3. The flashback reveals his longstanding desire to escape from gravity.

B. ⇨⇦

C. 1. She might discover the approach of the Earth Raiders.
2. The author can create a fast pace and a tension between the two events.

D. ⇨⇦

E. 1. what caused the whirring sound and what the "gum" really is
2. ⇨⇦

F. ⇨⇦

Lesson 3

A. I. The earliest comics
- A. "Hogan's Alley" first comic in 1895
- B. "Mutt and Jeff" first daily in 1907

II. Adventure strips of the thirties
- A. "Dick Tracy" started in 1931
- B. "Superman" and "Prince Valiant" follow in thirties

III. Modern comics
- A. Some old comics continue in the 70's
- B. New comics combine humor with satire

B. I. Folk music　III. Rock music
II. Show music　IV. Country/Western music

C. I. Folk music
- A. Famous folk singers
  1. Woody Guthrie
  2. Joan Baez
  3. Pete Seeger
- B. Imported folk songs
  1. Mexican songs
  2. English ballads
  3. West Indian calypso
- C. Songs native to America
  1. Western prairie songs
  2. New England sea chanteys
  3. Black American spirituals

D. 1. The main idea of the paragraph is that American folk songs developed out of work situations.
2. The subhead that was left out was: New England sea chanteys
3. You should have underlined the last two sentences.
4. These sentences belong under I. A. 1.

E. ⇨⇦　**F.** ⇨⇦

Lesson 4

A. ⇨⇦

B. You might have crossed out the following adverbs: *easily, lightly, strongly, closely, softly, gradually, attentively, regularly, bravely, directly*. Substitutions will vary.

C. ⇨⇦

Unit 2

Lesson 1

A. 3　**B.** 2　**C.** 5, 2, 7, 1, 4, 6, 3

D. 1. effect　2. first

E. Your answer for the first paragraph should be similar to one of these: *The magician's first night on stage was a disaster. (effect)* OR *That magician needed more practice. (cause)* Your answer to the second paragraph should be similar to this: *The farmer lost the entire crop of peas that year. (effect)*

F. ⇨⇦

Lesson 2

A. 6, 3, 1, 8, 4, 2, 7, 5
The thief was the chauffeur.

B. ⇨⇦　**C.** ⇨⇦

D. You might have listed haunted houses, mountaintops, wolves, sharks, hurricanes, fires, and so on.

E. ⇨⇦　**F.** ⇨⇦　**G.** ⇨⇦

Lesson 3

A. Your answer should have been that Carlotta Braun's conclusion is not warranted because there are too many variables: the mice were not the same size and they were each given different food.

B. 1. Your answer might be that sunflower seeds grow best when they are exposed to lots of sunlight.
2. Your answer should be that foot blisters are caused by friction, not by the color of the socks or shoes worn.

C. 1. F
2. C
3. C
4. F
5. C
6. C
7. F
8. F

D.

Lesson 4

A.

Unit 3

Lesson 1

A. 1. Bowling: The person who knocks down the most pins with a ball in ten frames, or rounds, is the winner.
2. Basketball: The team that throws the most balls into the basket wins.
3. Dominoes: Players must try to get rid of their dominos by playing those with sections identical to the end dominoes on the board.
4. Football: Teams score points by getting the ball over the opposing team's goal line and by kicking the ball over the opposing team's goal post.

B. You should have put an X next to 1 and 4.

C. D. E. F. G.

Lesson 2

A. 1. Both paragraphs are about the effect the hot sun has on the people who live in the city.
2. The mood of the first paragraph is anger and hostility.
3. tempers, arguments, sticky clothes
4. The mood of the second paragraph is one of serenity or joy.
5. people in parks, cheery words, picnicking

B. C. D. E.

Lesson 3

A. B. C. D. E.

Lesson 4

A. Your answers should be similar to these:
1. A dog-eared old book with a stained cover lay on the dusty desk.
2. A crowd of gaily dressed couples danced as the music blared and lights flashed.
3. The half-frozen children huddled under the warm quilt because the room was unheated.

B. 1. As I came in view of the landing sight, my fears were confirmed.
2. Armed aliens, who were ready to attack at any moment, crouched behind the hills.
3. My partner Lom, who was not feeling well, decided to stay in the spaceship.
4. Since the radio was in Lom's pocket, I could not use it to get help.
5. I knew that someday in the comfort of my own home I would tell of my adventures in space.

Unit 4

Lesson 1

A. 1. A dhow is a type of sailing vessel used by Arabs.
2. A blintze is like a thin pancake folded around a filling such as cheese or fruit.
3. A serape is a blanketlike shawl.
4. A samisen is a guitarlike Japanese musical instrument.

B. C. D. E.

F. 1. They both have rows of desks, ringing phones, scurrying reporters.
2. A modern office has humming electric typewriters, and typewriters which are tied into computer screens.

Lesson 2

A. 1. like a thunderbolt he falls
2. The eagle's sudden flight is compared to a sudden bolt of lightning.
3. "He clasps the crag with crooked hands" or "The wrinkled sea beneath him crawls."

B.

C. 1. M - Just as food nourishes the body, knowledge nourishes the mind, or soul.
2. S - Youth is like a summer morn because summer is the time when nature blooms. Age is like winter because nature begins to wither and die just like an old person.
3. P - Money is given human qualities of serving man, but when it is allowed to control man it is a bad master.
4. P - The rain is being compared to someone singing a lullaby because when rain falls steadily against a windowpane it can have a soothing rhythm.

D.

E. Your answers may be similar to these:
1. Like a fearless eagle, he confidently went about feathering his nest.
2. She was an eager beaver, always ready to build a new dam.
3. The clock's ticking reminded him of the beating of a drum.
4. Her smile was the sunshine that brightened our days.

F.

Lesson 3

A. 1. hen
2. bird
3. old
4. simple
5. sun
6. money
7. photographer
8. restaurant
9. mountain
10. dance

B. Here are some possible examples. Your answers may be different.
1. boy : girl
2. baby : mother
3. crooked : straight
4. singer : chorus
5. carpenter : furniture
6. tomato : salad
7. cook : kitchen = judge : courtroom

C.

D. 1. Your answer may be similar to this: Lack of decision may cost you your life.
2.

E. Your answer may be similar to this: Action speaks louder than words.

F.

Lesson 4

A. Here are some possible answers:
   1. The winding freight train chugged slowly out of the dismal freightyard and began a lengthy journey to the East Coast.
   2. The luxurious golf course was overrun by enthusiastic fans who wanted to observe every move made by their favorite professional golfers.
   3. The timid girl stared at her new pink dancing shoes as a brawny young man in a black tuxedo strode toward her.

B. 1. brooding 2. grouchy 3. carpeted 4. howling 5. scratchy 6. cracking or cracked 7. 8.

C.

Unit 5

Lesson 1

A. 1. when, who, what
   2. who, what
   3. who, what, when
   4. what, who, when

B.

C. 1. *F* - This statement could be checked by checking data on San Francisco's and Bolivia's sales tax.
   2. *O* - This statement is an opinion because it uses such words as *small fortune, dirty*, and *nasty*.
   3. *O* - This statement is an opinion because it uses such phrases as "a waste of time."
   4. *F* - This statement is a fact because you can always check the information with Mrs. Quinn.

D.

Lesson 2

A. Fact: The national unemployment rate has fallen steadily for the last eighteen months, it rests at 5.2%, and the jobless rate is 30% for city youths.
   Opinion: The writer feels that the jobless rate for city youth is one of our nation's most troubling social problems.

B. C. D.

E. 1. The right of teachers and school employees to strike
   2. Everyone has the right to strike.
   3. Teachers and other school officials do not have the right to strike if it interferes with the educational development of the nation's youth.

F.

Lesson 3

A. B. C.

Lesson 4

A. Answers will vary. Here are some samples:
   1. tulip, rose, daffodil
   2. milk, coffee, tea
   3. broken bottles, old newspapers, potato peels
   4. car, bus, subway
   5. cancer, measles, chickenpox

B. Answers will vary. Here are some possibilities:
   1. courthouse, store, apartment house
   2. boom, bang
   3. plumbers, dentists, police officers
   4. at the Town Hall, at the Civic Center
   5. institutions, homes, hospitals

C. Answers will vary. Here are some possibilities:
   1. stroll, tread, saunter
   2. chatter, prate, gab
   3. gobble, chew, devour

D. Your answers may be similar to these:
   1. stated, demanded
   2. sauntered, strolled, shuffled
   3. bolted or gulped his food, shouted or yelled
   4. whispered

E.

Unit 6

Lesson 1

A. Answers should be similar to these:
   1. Oliver is a braggart.
   2. Todd is conceited.
   3. Penelope is a nag.
   4. Helga is a pig.

B. 1. The writer thought the room was a mess and very depressing to be in.
   2. cramped, messy, strewn, dumped, ancient, and bleak
   3. negative

C. 1. For *messy* you might substitute *lived-in*.
   2. For *strewn* you might substitute *displayed*.
   3. For *dumped* you might substitute *piled neatly*.
   4. For *ancient* you might substitute *antique*.
   5. For *bleak* you might substitute *serene*.

D. a. You should have underlined: *perk up, new friends, talk of the town, Good Impressions, up-to-date*.
   You should have circled: *lonely, out of touch, boring*.
   b. You should have underlined: *Sunshine, float away, shining smile*. You should have circled: *rubs you the wrong way, despair, aches and pains*.
   c. You should have underlined: *Slim-Trim, golden opportunity, latest, slick, stylish, chic, low prices, Slim and Trim, new*. There are no minus-words in the ad.

E.

Lesson 2

A. 1. Possible answers are: the name of the book, the author, the main character, and the setting.
   2. The reviewer says the book is a thriller about a young woman who is trying to find out where her visions come from.
   3. The reviewer liked the book because it was well written and the main character was convincing.

4. The reviewer feels that the other characters did not stand out enough.
5. The reviewer recommends the book to other people by applauding the book and hoping another is on its way.

B. 1. The setting is a futuristic home. The characters are two people and two robots.
2. You may say it's about the future struggle between people and machines.
3. The audience is laughing and seems to be enjoying the play.
4. You would need to include your own opinion and the reasons for your views.

Lesson 3

A. 1. business letter
2. Alexander saw a sign in the bake shop window.
3. He has helped out at home, he is a fast learner, he lives across the street from the shopping center and can always be at work on time, and he does not have a sweet tooth.
4. Alexander is asking to set up an appointment.
5. He told Ms. Seiden when he could meet with her and gave her his telephone number.

Lesson 4

A. Here are some possible answers:
1. The memories of sun-filled days get me through the slush and the cold.
2. Although winter may have pleasures for some, I find myself concentrating on ways to keep warm and dry.
3. I like to curl up with a good book in front of a roaring fire.
4. My book forgotten, I dream of summer and finally feel warmth and contentment stealing over me.

B. Answers should be similar to this:
As Simone stepped off the plane, she was greeted by tall tropical plants and sweet-smelling air. From the airport, she could see the green mountains rising in the background. She couldn't wait to get to her room, unpack her bags, and take a long swim in the ocean. Simone felt so lucky to be home again, where she was the most comfortable. She had enjoyed her visit with her grandmother, but she wouldn't trade living on this island for anything!

Unit 7

Lesson 1

A. B. C. D. E.

Lesson 2

A. TP 1. FP 2. FP 3. TP 4.
B. C. D. E. S 1. O 2.
F. G.

Lesson 3

A. D. G.
B. E. H.
C. F. I.

Lesson 4

A. Your answers may be similar to these:
1. In the ninth inning the batter hit the ball hard into the bleachers.
2. Shop for winter clothes now when spring clothes are already out. Since winter clothes are on clearance sale, you can get some real bargains.
3. On top of the old battered desk lay a worn-out brown diary which had two faded 50-year-old photographs inside.
4. The Coast Guard cutter approached the survivors who were desperately clinging to life rafts.
With the survivors wrapped in blankets to keep warm, the cutter headed into port.
5. Staying in the haunted house made Kerry feel as if he was going to jump out of his skin.
6. Everyone in the class will go to Jim's Halloween party tonight.
7. After breakfast, I get on my bicycle and ride north on long, winding country roads. I see woods and farms with red barns off in the distance.

B. Here is one possible revision:
The night was dark and chilly when Sarah heard a noise outside her window. Suddenly, a mysterious figure leapt into the bedroom. When Sarah screamed loudly, the bedroom door flew open. The police rushed in, and she was safe.

Writing Handbook

A. The most popular~~est~~ rodent in the world, Mickey Mouse, was born in 1928. He made ~~maked~~ his screen debut in Steamboat Willie, the first cartoon to use sound. Walt Disney, the man who drew ~~drawed~~ Mickey, also provided the mouse's voice. Since his first film was released, Mickey has made countless other films and has become world famous. Now Mickey's big ears, bow tie, and white gloves are ~~is~~ recognized everywhere. Can there ~~their~~ be anyone who doesn't ~~don't~~ know and love this mouse among mice? ~~mouses.~~ The ageless star now has ~~have~~ two homes. Disneyland in Anaheim, California, was opened on July 17, 1955, and Disney World in Orlando, Florida, was opened in 1971.

Post-Test Answers; pg 298

1. a. C
   b. L
   c. C
   d. L
2. Outlines will vary. Students should include at least two main heads (Roman numerals) followed by subheads (capital letters). Sub-subheads should have arabic numbers.
3. Anecdotes will vary. The first sentences should refer to the present-time situation which leads into the "flashback" with transition words or sentences.
4. Answers may vary.
   a. The assembly cheered the president.
   b. Jean scribbled a note to her homeroom teacher.
   c. Tony argued with Denis over the best football team.

Post-Test Answers; pg 314

1. Wording mary vary slightly.
   a. People start panting during hard exercise because their bodies need more oxygen.
   b. The increased oxygen helps remove the lactic acid that is produced by the muscles.
2. Answers may vary slightly.
   Therefore, the thief must have been someone familiar with the house.
3. a. The whale nourishes its young with milk.
   b. Therefore this water sample is pure.
4. Paragraphs will vary. Students may begin with a cause topic sentence, such as *The discovery of fire changed history.* The rest of the paragraph may list effects of the discovery of fire.

Post-Test Answers; pg 330

1. b and d.
2. Paragraphs will vary. Make sure that the details chosen are appropriate to the mood the student wants to create.
3. Answers will vary. Possible answers:
   a. ...you can see the stars so clearly.
   b. ...the landscape is artificial.
4. Answers may vary slightly.
   a. In Congress, Senator Seal is the strongest champion of wildlife.
   b. From the hospital room, the exhausted sailor told an incredible tale of survival on a liferaft.

Post-Test Answers; pg 346

1. Answers may vary.
   a. Jamie's speech was a beacon that lit our course of action.
   b. Lana's voice was usually gentle, but sometimes it could cut like a knife.
   c. Detective Bunsen reminded me of a cheetah stalking its prey.
2. Possible answers:
   a. ...plunging from the high diving board.
   b. ...declaring war.
   c. like a week's groceries for most people.
3. Possible answers:
   a. The tennis ball kept returning like a boomerang.
   b. The subway train is a long, steel snake winding under the city.
   c. The tree was a dancer in a long rustling skirt.
4. Paragraphs will vary. The fable or parable can be a humorous, imaginative, or literal illustration of the moral.

Post-Test Answers; pg 362

1. a. N
   b. E
   c. N
   d. E
2. Answers will vary. Be sure that each opinion relates to the fact.
3. Speeches will vary. The best speeches will include specific qualifications and ideas, as well as facts to support them.
4. Possible answers:
   a. We spied a monkey hiding in a tree.
   c. The writer lectured on her childhood in Mississippi.

Post-Test Answers; pg 378

1. Answers will vary. Possible answers:
   a. Jeffery is so concerned about other people's affairs.
   b. Shawna always dresses casually.
2. Ads will vary. The best ads will use loaded words in imaginative, catchy ways.
3. Answers will vary. Some possible answers:
   a. babysitting experience
   b. good with figures
   c. take care of neighbors' yards
4. Students should mention two of the following: The author's name, reasons for the reviewer's opinion, and suggestions as to whether others will like the book are all missing.
5. Answers will vary slightly. Possible answer:
   After the concert started, Linda's violin string snapped. She had to go backstage to get a new string. The audience grew restless until Linda returned. Then the orchestra started from the beginning.

Post-Test Answers; pg 394

1. Paragraphs will vary. Students may write f from the point of view of a crew member, passenger, or airport employee.
2. The point of view is probably that of a biologist working in a zoo.
3. a. S
   b. O
4. Answers will vary. A possible answer:
   Since my parents were both in the army, they traveled a lot. I was born in France and my brother was born in Germany. Living different countries, we became familiar with other cultures. Although making new friends was sometimes difficult, it was an interesting life.

Writing Puzzle Answers

1. **Write in clear but interesting order.**
2. **Create a mood with details.**
3. **Use specific words.**
4. **Write vivid descriptions.**
5. **Base your opinions on facts.**
6. **The words you choose should make your point.**
7. **Create a consistent point of view.**

Writing Puzzle

Can you unravel the secrets of good writing? Use the clues to help you.

1. Order interesting but clear in Write. (maybe the other way around)

2. ETAERC A DOOM HTIW SLIATED (reverse gears)

3. Seu cciifeps drsow (scrambled eggs)

4. Wrt vvd dscrptns. (vowel drop-outs)

5. Basyouopiiononfctsernsa. (bad sequence)

6. 20 8 5 23 15 18 4 19 25 15 21 3 8 15 15 19 5 (number-letter code)
19 8 15 21 12 4 13 1 11 5 25 15 21 18 16 15 9 14 20

7. XIVZGV Z XLMHRHGVMG KLRMG LU ERVD (letter-letter code)

Answers on page 412

Steps for Practicing Math

Do each step with a number. If you are working on speed, do the steps marked with * too.

1. Find the right page.

   * Get a watch or timer.

2. Study the sample at the top of the page carefully.

   * Start timing.

3. Do all the exercises on the page. Work carefully.

   * Stop timing. Find the Scoreboard at the bottom of the page. Shade in the number of minutes you took to do the page. Did you beat the starred time?

4. Get your Answer Key. Find the right place and check your answers.

5. Write the number of answers you got right in the Scoreboard.

6. Find the Progress Plotter at the back of this book. Find the right place and shade in the number of answers you got right.

7. Correct any items you got wrong.

Author: Margie Hayes Richmond

Knowing Place Value

Lesson 1

The standard number for
three hundred twenty-four billion, seven hundred thirty-one million, eighty-four thousand, one hundred fifty-one is 324,731,084,151.

The chart shows the place value of each digit.

Billions			Millions			Thousands			Ones		
Hundreds	Tens	Ones	Hundreds	Tens	Ones	Hundreds	Tens	Ones	Hundreds	Tens	Ones
3	2	4	7	3	1	0	8	4	1	5	1

Match. Write the letter of the correct standard number in the blank.

1. nine hundred thirty thousand, five hundred ten ______
2. 4 ten millions 5 millions 3 ten thousands 6 thousands 8 hundreds 2 tens ______
3. 70,000,000 + 2,000,000 + 800,000 + 7,000 + 300 + 5 ______
4. one hundred million, thirty-seven thousand, ninety-one ______
5. 4 thousands 5 hundreds 8 tens 3 ones ______

a. 72,807,305
b. 4583
c. 930,510
d. 100,037,091
e. 45,036,820

In what place is the 6 in each numeral below? Write the correct letter in the blank.

6. 406,481 ______
7. 98,620,523 ______
8. 62,024,531,789 ______
9. 62,859 ______
10. 7604 ______

a. hundred thousands
b. ten billions
c. hundreds
d. thousands
e. ten thousands

Write > or < in each ☐

11. 39,673 ☐ 93,769
12. 941,003 ☐ 479,892
13. 30,000 ☐ 3547
14. 86,419 ☐ 86,320

Which number is the greatest? Circle the letter.

15. a. 4173 b. 9101 c. 5672
16. a. 617,201 b. 6,719 c. 67,196

Which number is the least? Circle the letter.

17. a. 71,369,420 b. 501,278,512
18. a. 37,426 b. 34,733 c. 134,733

Scoreboard												
Minutes	7	8	9	☆10	11	12	13	14	15	16	17	Number Right ______

Lesson 2	Rounding Numbers	

819,146 rounded to the nearest thousand is 819,000.

693,729,243 rounded to the nearest thousand is 693,729,000.

18,876,919 rounded to the nearest million is 19,000,000.

3,964,519,637 rounded to the nearest million is 3,965,000,000.

Round each to the nearest thousand.

1. 3249 ______ **2.** 2901 ______ **3.** 21,940 ______ **4.** 1856 ______

5. 39,461 ______ **6.** 113,598 ______ **7.** 9703 ______ **8.** 61,165,789 ______

Match each sentence to a number rounded to the nearest million.
Write the letter in the blank.

9. 1,260,000 new radios are sold each week. ______

10. 13,195,000 people stay in motels each week. ______

11. Children ride 63,600,000 miles on school buses each week. ______

12. Everyday 10,930,000 cows are milked. ______

13. 19,178,000 photographs are taken daily. ______

14. An average of 176,810,950 eggs are laid every day. ______

15. 2,176,130 couples get married each year. ______

16. 3,724,825 people give blood each year. ______

17. 79,934,246 people ride a bus to work each week. ______

18. Each week 8,189,041 people ride in a taxi. ______

19. People pay $121,080,000 in tolls each day. ______

20. 20,440,000 animals are left in animal shelters each year. ______

a. 64,000,000
b. 19,000,000
c. 121,000,000
d. 177,000,000
e. 1,000,000
f. 11,000,000
g. 80,000,000
h. 20,000,000
i. 13,000,000
j. 2,000,000
k. 8,000,000
l. 4,000,000

Scoreboard												
Minutes	7	8	9	☆ 10	11	12	13	14	15	16	17	Number Right ______

Knowing Exponents

Lesson 3

$3 \times 3 =$ 9 $\qquad 3^2 =$ 9

$3 \times 3 \times 3 =$ 27 $\qquad 3^3 =$ 27

Rewrite. Use exponents.

1. 5×5 ______

2. 2×2 ______

3. $2 \times 2 \times 2$ ______

4. $5 \times 5 \times 5 \times 5 \times 5 \times 5 \times 5 \times 5 \times 5 \times 5$ ______

5. $4 \times 4 \times 4$ ______

6. $3 \times 3 \times 3 \times 3$ ______

7. 10×10 ______

8. $2 \times 2 \times 2 \times 2 \times 2$ ______

Write the standard number.

9. 4^2 ______

10. 10^2 ______

11. 1^3 ______

12. 4^3 ______

13. 2^2 ______

14. 5^2 ______

15. 2^3 ______

16. 10^3 ______

17. 2^4 ______

18. 6^2 ______

19. 4^5 ______

20. 5^1 ______

Scoreboard												
Minutes	7	8	9	☆10	11	12	13	14	15	16	17	Number Right ______

Lesson 4	Adding and Subtracting Whole Numbers	

```
   36,491        36,491        93,703        93,703
 + 89,879      + 89,879      − 16,931      − 16,931
               126,370                      76,772
```

Add.

```
1.    46,935    2.   440,917    3.   74,687    4.    82,606
    + 17,362      + 336,491        + 27,898        + 10,603

5.  4,963,501   6.    36,954    7.     4173    8.      2073
  + 6,207,399       + 10,903           6190            5986
                                     + 4638          + 5097
```

Subtract.

```
9.      6903   10.    71,903   11.    2000   12.    55,491
      − 5118         − 6,909        − 1730        − 45,362

13.  865,000   14.    62,691   15.  49,621   16.  1,719,632
   − 309,713        −  9,904      − 21,798      − 1,706,384
```

Add or subtract.

17. 3651 + 7986 = ______ **18.** 25,163 − 7981 = ______

19. 41,963 + 2001 + 719 = ______ **20.** 41,792 − 1863 = ______

Scoreboard												
Minutes	11	12	13	☆ 14	15	16	17	18	19	20	21	Number Right ______

Multiplying and Dividing Whole Numbers

Lesson 5

```
              1 2
              3 6
   937        937          74 ) 2090        28 R18
 ×  39      ×  39                       74 ) 2090
             8433                            148
            2811                             610
           36,543                            592
                                              18
```

Multiply.

1. 170 × 6
2. 549 × 7
3. 526 × 3
4. 79 × 72
5. 507 × 79
6. 4693 × 51
7. 936 × 14
8. 786 × 78
9. 632 × 871
10. 7849 × 623

Divide.

11. 9) 10,108
12. 7) 398
13. 92) 598
14. 65) 32,695
15. 83) 8184
16. 79) 54,115
17. 61) 15,433
18. 87) 6008
19. 189) 118,125
20. 796) 189,060

Scoreboard												
Minutes	19	☆ 20	21	22	23	24	25	26	27	28	29	Number Right ______

Lesson 6	Adding Integers	

$^{+}1 + {}^{+}4 =$ +5

$^{-}3 + {}^{-}2 =$ −5

$^{+}5 + {}^{-}4 =$ +1

$^{-}6 + {}^{+}2 =$ −4

Add.

1. $^{+}6 + {}^{+}6 =$ ______
2. $^{-}8 + {}^{-}8 =$ ______
3. $^{+}4 + {}^{+}5 =$ ______
4. $^{+}6 + {}^{+}10 =$ ______
5. $^{-}8 + {}^{-}2 =$ ______
6. $^{+}1 + {}^{-}3 =$ ______
7. $^{-}9 + {}^{+}7 =$ ______
8. $^{-}1 + {}^{+}9 =$ ______
9. $^{+}8 + {}^{-}2 =$ ______
10. $^{+}5 + {}^{-}5 =$ ______
11. $^{-}11 + {}^{-}1 =$ ______
12. $^{-}4 + {}^{+}7 =$ ______
13. $^{+}3 + {}^{+}23 =$ ______
14. $^{-}2 + {}^{-}13 =$ ______
15. $^{-}5 + {}^{-}6 =$ ______
16. $^{+}6 + {}^{-}7 =$ ______
17. $^{+}10 + {}^{+}10 =$ ______
18. $^{-}100 + {}^{+}100 =$ ______
19. $^{-}35 + {}^{-}2 =$ ______
20. $^{+}16 + {}^{-}17 =$ ______

Scoreboard												
Minutes	15	☆ 16	17	18	19	20	21	22	23	24	25	Number Right ______

Subtracting Integers

Lesson 7

$^{+}1 - {}^{+}3 =$ $^{+}1 + {}^{-}3 = {}^{-}2$

$^{-}2 - {}^{-}6 =$ $^{-}2 + {}^{+}6 = {}^{+}4$

$0 - {}^{+}5 =$ $0 + {}^{-}5 = {}^{-}5$

Subtract.

1. $^{+}5 - {}^{+}2 =$ ______
2. $^{-}1 - {}^{+}7 =$ ______
3. $^{-}3 - {}^{-}2 =$ ______
4. $^{-}9 - {}^{+}3 =$ ______
5. $^{-}6 - {}^{-}6 =$ ______
6. $^{+}6 - {}^{+}4 =$ ______
7. $^{+}10 - {}^{-}10 =$ ______
8. $^{+}8 - {}^{-}9 =$ ______
9. $^{+}5 - {}^{+}5 =$ ______
10. $^{-}4 - {}^{+}7 =$ ______
11. $^{+}4 - {}^{-}8 =$ ______
12. $^{-}7 - {}^{-}7 =$ ______
13. $0 - {}^{-}4 =$ ______
14. $^{-}9 - {}^{-}3 =$ ______
15. $^{+}1 - {}^{+}11 =$ ______
16. $^{+}5 - {}^{-}10 =$ ______
17. $^{-}8 - {}^{+}9 =$ ______
18. $^{+}12 - 0 =$ ______
19. $^{+}7 - {}^{-}1 =$ ______
20. $^{-}15 - {}^{-}13 =$ ______

Scoreboard												
Minutes	15	16	17	☆18	19	20	21	22	23	24	25	Number Right ______

Lesson 8	Multiplying Integers	

$^{+}4 \times {}^{+}5 =$ $^{+}20$

$^{-}6 \times {}^{-}7 =$ $^{+}42$

$^{-}3 \times {}^{+}2 =$ $^{-}6$

$^{+}5 \times {}^{-}5 =$ $^{-}25$

Multiply.

1. $^{+}2 \times {}^{+}2 =$ ______
2. $^{-}4 \times {}^{-}5 =$ ______
3. $^{-}6 \times {}^{-}3 =$ ______
4. $^{+}7 \times {}^{+}2 =$ ______
5. $^{-}1 \times {}^{-}10 =$ ______
6. $^{-}3 \times {}^{+}4 =$ ______
7. $^{-}2 \times {}^{-}4 =$ ______
8. $^{+}7 \times {}^{-}1 =$ ______
9. $^{-}3 \times {}^{+}10 =$ ______
10. $^{+}6 \times {}^{-}1 =$ ______
11. $^{+}3 \times {}^{+}3 =$ ______
12. $^{-}5 \times {}^{+}2 =$ ______
13. $^{+}10 \times {}^{-}1 =$ ______
14. $^{-}8 \times {}^{-}2 =$ ______
15. $^{-}9 \times 0 =$ ______
16. $^{-}4 \times {}^{+}5 =$ ______
17. $^{+}7 \times {}^{+}6 =$ ______
18. $^{+}9 \times {}^{-}8 =$ ______
19. $^{+}12 \times {}^{+}2 =$ ______
20. $^{-}10 \times {}^{+}10 =$ ______

Scoreboard												
Minutes	15	☆16	17	18	19	20	21	22	23	24	25	Number Right ______

Dividing Integers

Lesson 9

$^{+}12 \div {}^{+}6 = {}^{+}2$

$^{+}16 \div {}^{-}2 = {}^{-}8$

$^{-}18 \div {}^{+}3 = {}^{-}6$

$^{-}10 \div {}^{-}5 = {}^{+}2$

Divide.

1. $^{+}12 \div {}^{+}4 =$ ______ **2.** $^{-}20 \div {}^{+}5 =$ ______ **3.** $^{+}10 \div {}^{-}2 =$ ______

4. $^{+}25 \div {}^{+}5 =$ ______ **5.** $^{-}28 \div {}^{-}7 =$ ______ **6.** $^{-}18 \div {}^{-}3 =$ ______

7. $^{+}21 \div {}^{-}7 =$ ______ **8.** $^{-}9 \div {}^{-}3 =$ ______ **9.** $^{-}100 \div {}^{+}10 =$ ______

10. $^{-}12 \div {}^{+}1 =$ ______ **11.** $^{+}15 \div {}^{+}3 =$ ______ **12.** $^{+}10 \div {}^{-}5 =$ ______

13. $^{-}12 \div {}^{-}2 =$ ______ **14.** $^{-}18 \div {}^{+}6 =$ ______ **15.** $^{-}48 \div {}^{+}6 =$ ______

16. $^{-}63 \div {}^{-}7 =$ ______ **17.** $^{+}72 \div {}^{-}8 =$ ______ **18.** $^{+}22 \div {}^{+}2 =$ ______

19. $^{-}10 \div {}^{-}1 =$ ______ **20.** $^{+}48 \div {}^{-}4 =$ ______

Scoreboard												
Minutes	15	☆16	17	18	19	20	21	22	23	24	25	Number Right ______

Lesson 10	Adding and Subtracting Fractions and Mixed Numbers

$$\begin{array}{r} \frac{5}{6} = \frac{5}{6} \\ +\frac{2}{3} = \frac{4}{6} \\ \hline \frac{9}{6} = 1\frac{3}{6} = 1\frac{1}{2} \end{array}$$

$$\begin{array}{r} 5\frac{1}{4} = 5\frac{5}{20} = 4\frac{25}{20} \\ -1\frac{4}{5} = 1\frac{16}{20} = 1\frac{16}{20} \\ \hline 3\frac{9}{20} \end{array}$$

Add. Write each answer in lowest terms.

1. $\frac{2}{3} + \frac{3}{4}$
2. $\frac{6}{7} + \frac{1}{14}$
3. $3\frac{1}{2} + \frac{5}{6}$
4. $\frac{3}{7} + 3\frac{1}{3}$
5. $9\frac{1}{8} + \frac{5}{12}$
6. $\frac{4}{5} + \frac{3}{8}$
7. $2\frac{1}{2} + 3\frac{1}{9}$
8. $8\frac{1}{3} + 4\frac{7}{12}$
9. $5\frac{4}{15} + 6\frac{1}{5}$
10. $3\frac{7}{10} + 9\frac{3}{5}$

Subtract. Write each answer in lowest terms.

11. $\frac{7}{8} - \frac{2}{3}$
12. $\frac{3}{7} - \frac{1}{14}$
13. $2\frac{3}{4} - \frac{3}{7}$
14. $8\frac{1}{3} - 4\frac{1}{2}$
15. $6\frac{3}{8} - 5\frac{1}{3}$
16. $9 - 5\frac{7}{8}$
17. $6\frac{3}{8} - 2$
18. $4\frac{3}{5} - 3\frac{2}{3}$
19. $2\frac{1}{8} - 1\frac{1}{3}$
20. $3\frac{7}{8} - 1\frac{3}{5}$

Scoreboard												
Minutes	15	16	☆ 17	18	19	20	21	22	23	24	25	Number Right ______

Multiplying Fractions and Mixed Numbers

Lesson **11**

$\frac{3}{7} \times \frac{5}{6} = \frac{\overset{1}{\cancel{3}}}{7} \times \frac{5}{\underset{2}{\cancel{6}}} = \frac{5}{14}$

$1\frac{1}{3} \times 4\frac{1}{5} = \frac{4}{\underset{1}{\cancel{3}}} \times \frac{\overset{7}{\cancel{21}}}{5} = \frac{28}{5} = 5\frac{3}{5}$

Multiply. Write each answer in lowest terms.

1. $\frac{1}{3} \times \frac{1}{5} =$ ______

2. $\frac{4}{7} \times 2\frac{1}{2} =$ ______

3. $\frac{2}{3} \times \frac{5}{12} =$ ______

4. $3\frac{1}{4} \times 5\frac{1}{3} =$ ______

5. $\frac{3}{5} \times 5 =$ ______

6. $\frac{1}{2} \times \frac{5}{7} =$ ______

7. $1\frac{3}{8} \times 4\frac{1}{2} =$ ______

8. $\frac{1}{8} \times 7\frac{1}{4} =$ ______

9. $1\frac{1}{2} \times 7 =$ ______

10. $3\frac{1}{3} \times \frac{5}{6} =$ ______

11. $\frac{6}{7} \times \frac{3}{8} =$ ______

12. $\frac{1}{8} \times 4 =$ ______

13. $\frac{7}{10} \times 2\frac{1}{2} =$ ______

14. $7\frac{1}{5} \times \frac{5}{10} =$ ______

15. $\frac{1}{4} \times \frac{3}{8} =$ ______

16. $10 \times 4\frac{3}{5} =$ ______

17. $1\frac{1}{3} \times 1\frac{1}{2} =$ ______

18. $\frac{4}{5} \times 1 =$ ______

19. $4\frac{2}{3} \times 2\frac{5}{8} =$ ______

20. $3\frac{1}{3} \times 2\frac{1}{8} =$ ______

Scoreboard												
Minutes	19	☆20	21	22	23	24	25	26	27	28	29	Number Right ______

Lesson 12	Dividing Fractions and Mixed Numbers

$$4\frac{2}{3} \div \frac{1}{3} = \frac{14}{3} \div \frac{1}{3} = \frac{14}{\cancel{3}_1} \times \frac{\cancel{3}^1}{1} = \frac{14}{1} = 14$$

Divide. Write each answer in lowest terms.

1. $\frac{1}{3} \div \frac{1}{2} =$ ______
2. $\frac{2}{7} \div \frac{3}{5} =$ ______
3. $\frac{1}{2} \div 4 =$ ______
4. $6\frac{2}{3} \div 4 =$ ______
5. $\frac{2}{7} \div 2\frac{1}{2} =$ ______
6. $\frac{3}{8} \div \frac{5}{8} =$ ______
7. $7\frac{2}{3} \div 4\frac{1}{4} =$ ______
8. $\frac{2}{5} \div \frac{2}{7} =$ ______
9. $\frac{4}{9} \div \frac{4}{10} =$ ______
10. $\frac{6}{7} \div 12 =$ ______
11. $\frac{7}{8} \div \frac{3}{10} =$ ______
12. $\frac{1}{8} \div \frac{3}{4} =$ ______
13. $2\frac{3}{10} \div \frac{1}{5} =$ ______
14. $\frac{4}{7} \div 2 =$ ______
15. $6\frac{1}{4} \div 4\frac{1}{2} =$ ______
16. $9 \div \frac{3}{14} =$ ______
17. $1\frac{5}{6} \div 3\frac{1}{2} =$ ______
18. $6 \div \frac{1}{4} =$ ______
19. $2\frac{1}{7} \div \frac{3}{4} =$ ______
20. $5\frac{5}{8} \div 2\frac{1}{4} =$ ______

Scoreboard												
Minutes	19	20	21	☆22	23	24	25	26	27	28	29	Number Right ______

Writing and Rounding Decimals

Lesson 13

The standard number for
nine thousand four hundred sixty-three millionths is 0.009463.

ones	tenths	hundredths	thousandths	ten thousandths	hundred thousandths	millionths
0	0	0	9	4	6	3

Write the standard number for each.

1. Fifty-three thousandths ______
2. Nine hundred four ten thousandths ______
3. Six and five thousand eighty-two millionths ______
4. 0.001 + 0.00002 ______
5. 100 + 6 + 0.4 + 0.07 + 0.009 ______
6. six thousand and eighty-three thousandths ______

a. 0.00102
b. 106.479
c. 0.053
d. 6.005082
e. 6000.083
f. 0.0904

Match each underlined digit to its place value. Write the correct letter in the blank.

7. 3.7600<u>9</u> ______
8. 6<u>0</u>02.31 ______
9. 0.00400<u>1</u> ______
10. 8.49<u>6</u>7 ______
11. 2<u>0</u>.05 ______
12. 0.<u>1</u>09 ______
13. 1.745<u>2</u>3 ______
14. 9.3<u>6</u> ______

a. millionths
b. hundreds
c. thousandths
d. hundred thousandths
e. ones
f. hundredths
g. tenths
h. ten thousandths

Round each number to the nearest whole number.

15. 6.009 ______

16. 1.5 ______

Round each number to the nearest tenth.

17. 0.666 ______

18. 7.14 ______

Round each number to the nearest hundredth.

19. 0.005 ______

20. 1.096 ______

Scoreboard												
Minutes	11	12	☆13	14	15	16	17	18	19	20	21	Number Right ______

Lesson 14	Adding and Subtracting Decimals	

```
    5.04        1 1                 4.7        6 9 10
  + 4.996       5.040             - 0.066      4.700
                + 4.996                       - 0.006
                10.036                          4.694
```

Add.

```
1.    4.67     2.   0.451    3.   7.63     4.   80.060
    + 0.38        + 0.096       + 0.745       +  7.304

5.   9.8376    6.   8.047    7.  0.5071    8.    6.062
   + 0.6012       + 0.9         + 0.2429        + 7.07
```

9. 4.329 + 0.188 = ______

10. 6.743 + 0.01 = ______

Subtract.

```
11.   6.701    12.  9.007    13.  4.75     14.   7.837
    - 5.833       - 0.6         - 1.6329       - 1.641

15.   10.17    16.  7.032    17.  0.4032   18.   0.6
    -  4.16       - 0.41        - 0.398        - 0.059
```

19. 2.4007 − 1.325 = ______

20. 7.83 − 4.003 = ______

Scoreboard											
Minutes	15	☆16	17	18	19	20	21	22	23	24	25	Number Right ______

Multiplying Decimals

Lesson 15

```
  3.042        3.042       0.002       0.002
×     8      ×     8     ×   0.3     ×   0.3
            24.326                   0.0006
```

Multiply.

```
1.   5.13    2.  6.33    3.  4.98    4.  37.002    5.  3.712
   ×    6      × 0.7       × 0.9       ×      4      × 0.68

6.   7.39    7.  0.004   8.  2.46    9.  0.02     10.  1.115
   × 0.09      × 0.08      × 100       × 0.9           × 400

11.  3.925   12. 4.318   13. 0.604   14. 0.0309   15.  0.66
   ×   7.7     ×   5.6     ×   1.2      ×   0.7        × 4.2
```

16. 5.91 × 0.06 = ______

17. 2.41 × 6 = ______

18. 0.756 × 0.9 = ______

19. 0.0304 × 1000 = ______

20. 0.042 × 0.4 = ______

Scoreboard												
Minutes	19	20	21	☆22	23	24	25	26	27	28	29	Number Right ______

Lesson 16	Dividing Decimals	

Divide.

$4\overline{)4.2}$

$$\begin{array}{r} 1.05 \\ 4\overline{)4.20} \\ \underline{4} \\ 2 \\ \underline{0} \\ 20 \\ \underline{20} \end{array}$$

Round the quotient to the nearest tenth.

$3\overline{)2}$

$$\begin{array}{r} 0.66 \approx 0.7 \\ 3\overline{)2.00} \\ \underline{0} \\ 20 \\ \underline{18} \\ 20 \\ \underline{18} \\ 2 \end{array}$$

1. $3\overline{)4.2}$ **2.** $7\overline{)0.0343}$ **3.** $8\overline{)1.2}$ **4.** $13\overline{)3.913}$

5. $2\overline{)0.007}$ **6.** $16\overline{)3.2}$ **7.** $9\overline{)6.381}$ **8.** $10\overline{)2.5}$

9. $17\overline{)5.1}$ **10.** $40\overline{)28}$ **11.** $14\overline{)5.39}$ **12.** $15\overline{)17.25}$

Divide. Round each quotient to the nearest tenth.

13. $9\overline{)2}$ **14.** $32\overline{)44.6}$ **15.** $2\overline{)0.1}$ **16.** $7\overline{)3}$

Divide. Round each quotient to the nearest hundredth.

17. $4\overline{)3.7}$ **18.** $3\overline{)1}$ **19.** $22\overline{)3.5}$ **20.** $6\overline{)19.3}$

Scoreboard											
Minutes	19	20	21	☆22	23	24	25	26	27	28	29	Number Right ______

Dividing Decimals by Decimals

Lesson 17

Round the quotient to the nearest hundredth.

$0.08\overline{)0.4}$ $\quad$ $0.08\overset{5}{\overline{)0.40}}$ (40)

$1.2\overline{)0.389}$ $\quad$ $1.2\overset{0.324 \approx 0.32}{\overline{)0.3890}}$ (36, 29, 24, 50, 48, 2)

Divide.

1. $0.4\overline{)3.2}$
2. $0.02\overline{)0.7}$
3. $0.5\overline{)1.2}$
4. $0.06\overline{)0.3}$
5. $1.2\overline{)0.36}$
6. $0.01\overline{)7.089}$
7. $4.5\overline{)9}$
8. $0.7\overline{)50.4}$
9. $0.1\overline{)0.072}$
10. $1.4\overline{)0.574}$
11. $1.5\overline{)18}$
12. $0.004\overline{)0.1}$

Divide. Round each quotient to the nearest tenth.

13. $0.6\overline{)100}$
14. $0.07\overline{)2}$
15. $0.2\overline{)1.93}$
16. $1.4\overline{)3.18}$

Divide. Round each quotient to the nearest hundredth.

17. $0.9\overline{)20}$
18. $4.3\overline{)16.48}$
19. $0.03\overline{)0.5}$
20. $2.3\overline{)4.2}$

Scoreboard												
Minutes	23	24	☆25	26	27	28	29	30	31	32	33	Number Right ______

Lesson 18	Writing Fractions and Decimals

Write 0.625 as a fraction in lowest terms.

$$0.625 = \frac{625}{1000} = \frac{5}{8}$$

Write $\frac{1}{3}$ as a decimal.

$$\frac{1}{3} \rightarrow 3\overline{)1.000} = 0.333 \rightarrow 0.\overline{3}$$

$$\begin{array}{r} 9 \\ \hline 10 \\ 9 \\ \hline 10 \\ 9 \\ \hline 1 \end{array}$$

Write each decimal as a fraction in lowest terms.

1. 0.25 = ______ **2.** 0.05 = ______ **3.** 7.75 = ______ **4.** 6.25 = ______

5. 4.125 = ______ **6.** 0.9 = ______ **7.** 0.363 = ______ **8.** 1.7 = ______

Write each fraction as a decimal.

9. $\frac{1}{4}$ = ______ **10.** $\frac{3}{8}$ = ______ **11.** $\frac{2}{3}$ = ______ **12.** $\frac{1}{20}$ = ______

13. $\frac{71}{100}$ = ______ **14.** $\frac{1}{10}$ = ______ **15.** $\frac{4}{9}$ = ______ **16.** $\frac{4}{3}$ = ______

17. $\frac{1}{11}$ = ______ **18.** $\frac{5}{6}$ = ______ **19.** $\frac{7}{25}$ = ______ **20.** $\frac{1}{9}$ = ______

Scoreboard												
Minutes	15	☆ 16	17	18	19	20	21	22	23	24	25	Number Right ______

Writing Decimals and Fractions as Percents

Lesson 19

0.53 = 53%

0.275 = 27.5%

$\frac{2}{5} \rightarrow 5\overline{)2.00}$ = 0.40 = 40%

20
0
0

$\frac{1}{3} \rightarrow 3\overline{)1.00}$ = $0.33\frac{1}{3} = 33\frac{1}{3}\%$

9
10
9
1

Write each decimal as a percent.

1. 0.23 = ______
2. 4.35 = ______
3. 0.666 = ______
4. 0.01 = ______
5. 0.17 = ______
6. 0.005 = ______
7. 3 = ______
8. 1.25 = ______
9. 0.625 = ______
10. 0.07 = ______

Write each fraction as a percent.

11. $\frac{7}{100}$ = ______
12. $\frac{1}{4}$ = ______
13. $\frac{2}{3}$ = ______
14. $\frac{3}{25}$ = ______
15. $\frac{4}{5}$ = ______
16. $\frac{3}{2}$ = ______
17. $\frac{3}{8}$ = ______
18. $\frac{5}{6}$ = ______
19. $\frac{5}{5}$ = ______
20. $\frac{1}{6}$ = ______

Scoreboard												
Minutes	11	12	13	☆14	15	16	17	18	19	20	21	Number Right ______

Lesson 20	Writing Percents as Decimals and Fractions	

Write as a decimal.

$85\% = \underline{0.85}$

$137\% = \underline{1.37}$

$2\frac{1}{2}\% = \underline{2.5\% = 0.025}$

Write as a fraction in lowest terms.

$75\% = \frac{75}{100} = \frac{3}{4}$

$33\frac{1}{3}\% = \frac{33\frac{1}{3}}{100} = 33\frac{1}{3} \div 100 = \frac{100}{3} \times \frac{1}{100} = \frac{1}{3}$

Write as a decimal.

1. $69\% =$ ______
2. $7.8\% =$ ______
3. $100\% =$ ______
4. $30\% =$ ______
5. $0.75\% =$ ______
6. $33.3\% =$ ______
7. $10\% =$ ______
8. $3\frac{1}{2}\% =$ ______
9. $67.55\% =$ ______
10. $\frac{1}{2}\% =$ ______

Write as a fraction in lowest terms.

11. $7\% =$ ______
12. $10\% =$ ______
13. $125\% =$ ______
14. $16\% =$ ______
15. $50\% =$ ______
16. $40\% =$ ______
17. $333\% =$ ______
18. $66\frac{2}{3}\% =$ ______
19. $8\frac{1}{3}\% =$ ______
20. $95\% =$ ______

Scoreboard												
Minutes	11	12	13	☆14	15	16	17	18	19	20	21	Number Right ______

Using Percents

Lesson 21

30% of 50 is what number?

$0.30 \times 50 = 15.00$

What percent of 25 is 5?

$\frac{5}{25} = \frac{20}{100} = 20\%$

40% of what number is 32?

$0.40\overline{)32.00} = 80.$

320
0
0

Solve.

1. 20% of 60 is what number? ______
2. What percent of 15 is 12? ______
3. 50% of 10 is what number? ______
4. 30% of what number is 24? ______
5. What percent of 70 is 35? ______
6. 75% of 100 is what number? ______
7. 10% of what number is 9? ______
8. 25% of 40 is what number? ______
9. What percent of 100 is 20? ______
10. What percent of 5 is 2? ______
11. 49 is 35% of what number? ______
12. 6 is 30% of what number? ______
13. 15% of 30 is what number? ______
14. What number is 20% of 5? ______
15. 25% of what number is 75? ______
16. 50% of what number is 25? ______
17. 18 is 10% of what number? ______
18. 1% of what number is 80? ______
19. What percent of 20 is 4? ______
20. 2% of 32 is what number? ______

Scoreboard												
Minutes	23	24	☆ 25	26	27	28	29	30	31	32	33	Number Right ______

Lesson 22

Ratio and Proportion

□□□ △△△△ △△△△

The ratio of □ to △ is 3 to 8.

The ratio can be written as $\frac{3}{8}$.

Two ratios that are equal form a proportion.

Cross multiply to tell whether these ratios form a proportion.

$\frac{3}{8}$? $\frac{9}{24}$

$3 \times 24 = 8 \times 9$

$72 = 72$

$\frac{3}{8} = \frac{9}{24}$

Write the ratio of □ to △ for each.

1. □ △△△ ______

2. □□□□□ △△△△△△ ______

3. □□□□□□□□ △△△△△△△△△ ______

4. □□□ △△△△△△△△△ ______

Tell whether each pair of ratios forms a proportion. Write = or ≠ in each □.

5. $\frac{2}{3}$ □ $\frac{4}{9}$	6. $\frac{3}{7}$ □ $\frac{21}{28}$	7. $\frac{7}{8}$ □ $\frac{14}{16}$	8. $\frac{1}{2}$ □ $\frac{49}{100}$
9. $\frac{2}{25}$ □ $\frac{4}{100}$	10. $\frac{3}{9}$ □ $\frac{1}{3}$	11. $\frac{3}{4}$ □ $\frac{30}{40}$	12. $\frac{1}{5}$ □ $\frac{4}{100}$
13. $\frac{2}{12}$ □ $\frac{3}{18}$	14. $\frac{25}{30}$ □ $\frac{2}{5}$	15. $\frac{5}{6}$ □ $\frac{2}{3}$	16. $\frac{4}{5}$ □ $\frac{16}{20}$
17. $\frac{6}{11}$ □ $\frac{18}{33}$	18. $\frac{4}{9}$ □ $\frac{20}{36}$	19. $\frac{33}{100}$ □ $\frac{330}{1000}$	20. $\frac{6}{25}$ □ $\frac{30}{100}$

Scoreboard

Minutes	11	☆12	13	14	15	16	17	18	19	20	21	Number Right ____

Solving Proportions

Lesson 23

$$\frac{3}{6} = \frac{10}{n}$$
$$3 \times n = 6 \times 10$$
$$3 \times n = 60$$
$$n = 20$$

Solve the proportions.

1. $\frac{6}{9} = \frac{n}{6}$
2. $\frac{5}{6} = \frac{n}{12}$
3. $\frac{2}{n} = \frac{3}{12}$
4. $\frac{4}{8} = \frac{5}{n}$
5. $\frac{n}{6} = \frac{3}{4}$
6. $\frac{1}{4} = \frac{7}{n}$
7. $\frac{n}{10} = \frac{30}{100}$
8. $\frac{3}{n} = \frac{1}{20}$
9. $\frac{2}{3} = \frac{5}{n}$
10. $\frac{1}{25} = \frac{3}{n}$
11. $\frac{2}{n} = \frac{3}{15}$
12. $\frac{3}{n} = \frac{1}{5}$
13. $\frac{7}{14} = \frac{n}{4}$
14. $\frac{n}{8} = \frac{9}{24}$
15. $\frac{6}{n} = \frac{2}{6}$
16. $\frac{12}{25} = \frac{4}{n}$
17. $\frac{4}{12} = \frac{3}{n}$
18. $\frac{90}{n} = \frac{9}{10}$
19. $\frac{n}{2} = \frac{5}{16}$
20. $\frac{3}{2} = \frac{n}{6}$

Scoreboard												
Minutes	15	☆ 16	17	18	19	20	21	22	23	24	25	Number Right ______

Lesson 24	Solving Addition Equations	

$$n + 4 = 7$$
$$n + 4 - 4 = 7 - 4$$
$$n = 3$$

Solve for n.

1. $n + 1 = 4$	**2.** $3 + n = 7$	**3.** $n + 3 = 4$
4. $2 + n = 8$	**5.** $n + 5 = 15$	**6.** $n + 8 = 24$
7. $4 + n = 9$	**8.** $3 + n = 10$	**9.** $n + 1 = 6$
10. $9 + n = 17$	**11.** $1 + n = 99$	**12.** $n + 12 = 24$
13. $100 + n = 200$	**14.** $20 + n = 25$	**15.** $n + 15 = 21$
16. $7 + n = 27$	**17.** $25 + n = 31$	**18.** $n + 92 = 96$
19. $n + 12 = 18$	**20.** $0 + n = 3$	

Scoreboard

Minutes	11	☆ 12	13	14	15	16	17	18	19	20	21	Number Right ______

Solving Subtraction Equations

Lesson 25

$$n - 4 = 7$$
$$n - 4 + 4 = 7 + 4$$
$$n = 11$$

Solve for *n*.

1. $n - 1 = 2$
2. $n - 2 = 5$
3. $n - 8 = 17$
4. $n - 8 = 3$
5. $n - 4 = 8$
6. $n - 6 = 1$
7. $n - 3 = 7$
8. $n - 13 = 2$
9. $n - 12 = 8$
10. $n - 2 = 98$
11. $n - 25 = 50$
12. $n - 70 = 77$
13. $n - 14 = 30$
14. $n - 19 = 10$
15. $n - 3 = 1$
16. $n - 25 = 100$
17. $n - 8 = 18$
18. $n - 5 = 0$
19. $n - 4 = 4$
20. $n - 7 = 1$

Scoreboard												
Minutes	11	12	13	☆14	15	16	17	18	19	20	21	Number Right ______

Lesson 26	Solving Multiplication Equations	

$$4n = 32$$

$$\frac{4n}{4} = \frac{32}{4}$$

$$n = 8$$

Solve for *n*.

1. $6n = 24$

2. $7n = 77$

3. $8n = 32$

4. $5n = 20$

5. $2n = 2$

6. $3n = 60$

7. $9n = 81$

8. $3n = 42$

9. $5n = 100$

10. $6n = 72$

11. $4n = 100$

12. $10n = 100$

13. $12n = 60$

14. $7n = 49$

15. $100n = 500$

16. $24n = 48$

17. $25n = 75$

18. $20n = 80$

19. $5n = 40$

20. $4n = 36$

Scoreboard												
Minutes	11	12	☆13	14	15	16	17	18	19	20	21	Number Right ______

Solving Division Equations

Lesson **27**

$$\frac{n}{12} = 3$$

$$12 \cdot \frac{n}{12} = 12 \cdot 3$$

$$n = 36$$

Solve for *n*.

1. $\frac{n}{3} = 6$

2. $\frac{n}{8} = 2$

3. $\frac{n}{5} = 4$

4. $\frac{n}{6} = 2$

5. $\frac{n}{30} = 10$

6. $\frac{n}{10} = 4$

7. $\frac{n}{10} = 10$

8. $\frac{n}{1} = 1$

9. $\frac{n}{9} = 3$

10. $\frac{n}{4} = 2$

11. $\frac{n}{9} = 7$

12. $\frac{n}{8} = 6$

13. $\frac{n}{5} = 5$

14. $\frac{n}{15} = 5$

15. $\frac{n}{7} = 6$

16. $\frac{n}{1} = 9$

17. $\frac{n}{10} = 1$

18. $\frac{n}{3} = 8$

19. $\frac{n}{4} = 4$

20. $\frac{n}{5} = 9$

Scoreboard												
Minutes	11	12	13	☆ 14	15	16	17	18	19	20	21	Number Right ______

Lesson 28	Solving Equations

$n + 4 = 9$	$n - 8 = 9$	$5n = 30$	$\frac{n}{7} = 3$
$n + 4 - 4 = 9 - 4$	$n - 8 + 8 = 9 + 8$	$\frac{5n}{5} = \frac{30}{5}$	$7 \cdot \frac{n}{7} = 7 \cdot 3$
$n = 5$	$n = 17$	$n = 6$	$n = 21$

Solve for *n*.

1. $n + 6 = 16$
2. $n - 5 = 20$
3. $4n = 16$
4. $\frac{n}{4} = 8$
5. $n - 3 = 7$
6. $n + 92 = 98$
7. $n - 25 = 75$
8. $6n = 60$
9. $\frac{n}{50} = 2$
10. $\frac{n}{3} = 11$
11. $8n = 56$
12. $n + 0 = 7$
13. $n - 1 = 0$
14. $\frac{n}{7} = 1$
15. $3n = 12$
16. $37 + n = 41$
17. $\frac{n}{2} = 5$
18. $\frac{n}{7} = 3$
19. $n - 1 = 99$
20. $16n = 48$

Scoreboard

Minutes	11	12	13	14	☆ 15	16	17	18	19	20	21	Number Right ______

Measuring Length, Mass, and Capacity

Lesson 29

1000 mm = 1 m	There are 1000 millimeters in 1 meter.
100 cm = 1 m	There are 100 centimeters in 1 meter.
1000 m = 1 km	There are 1000 meters in 1 kilometer.
1000 g = 1 kg	There are 1000 grams in 1 kilogram.
1000 mg = 1 g	There are 1000 milligrams in 1 gram.
1000 mL = 1 L	There are 1000 milliliters in 1 liter.

Fill in the blanks.

1. 2.7 kg = ______ g
2. 5200 mm = ______ cm
3. 426 m = ______ km
4. 623.1 mm = ______ m
5. 27 L = ______ mL
6. 2 km = ______ m
7. 129 mm = ______ cm
8. 113 cm = ______ m
9. 9200 m = ______ km
10. 100 mg = ______ g
11. 0.752 L = ______ mL
12. 2.71 kg ______ g

Which measurement is greater? Circle it.

13. 200 g or 1 kg
14. 10 mm or 10 km
15. 5 L or 3 mL
16. 8721 mg or 9 g
17. 1000 mm or 95 cm
18. 105 cm or 1000 mm
19. 6.53 cm or 7 m
20. 4 km or 400 m

Scoreboard												
Minutes	11	☆12	13	14	15	16	17	18	19	20	21	Number Right ______

Lesson 30

Finding Area

Rectangle

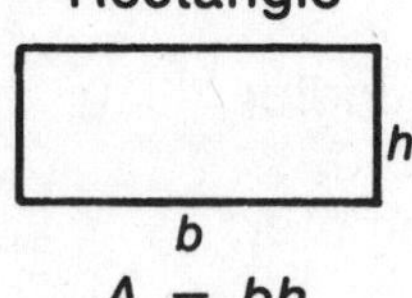

$A = bh$

Parallelogram

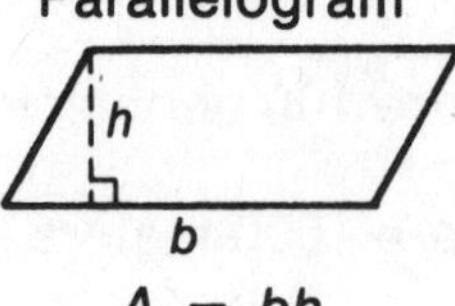

$A = bh$

Triangle

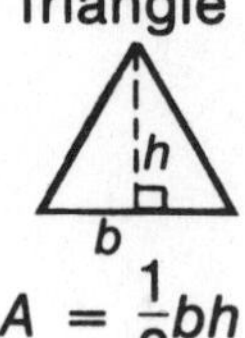

$A = \frac{1}{2}bh$

Trapezoid

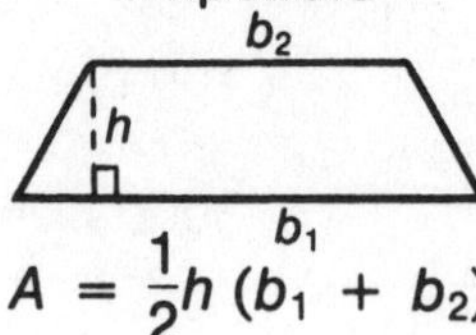

$A = \frac{1}{2}h\,(b_1 + b_2)$

Find the area.

1.

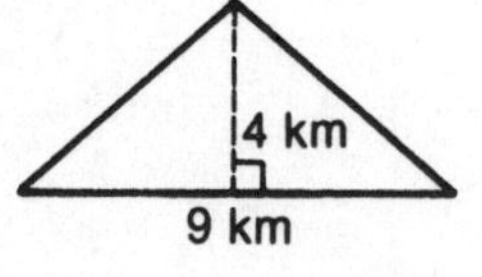

$A =$ ______

2.

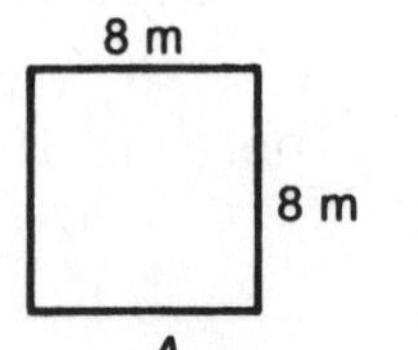

$A =$ ______

3.

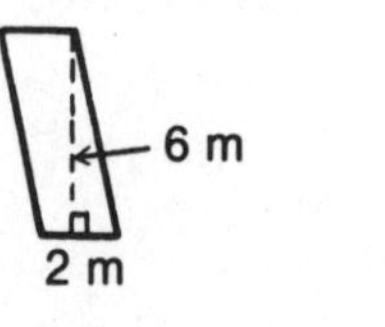

$A =$ ______

4.

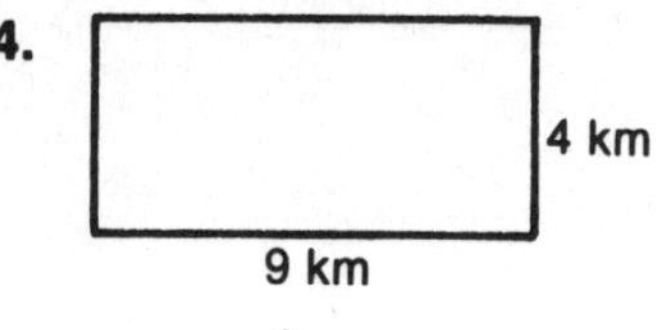

$A =$ ______

5.

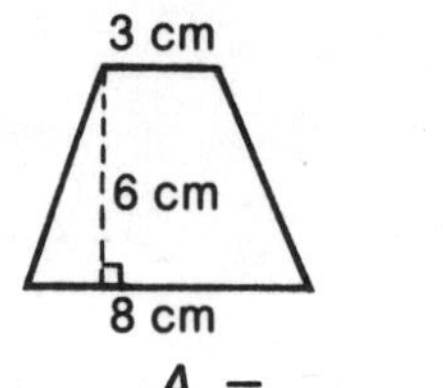

$A =$ ______

6.

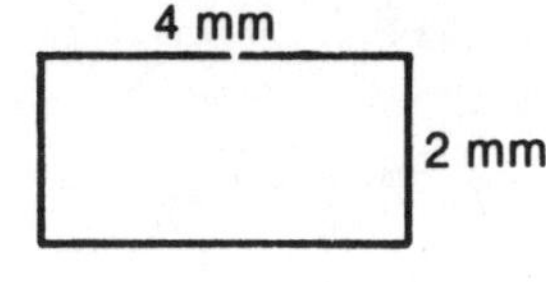

$A =$ ______

7.

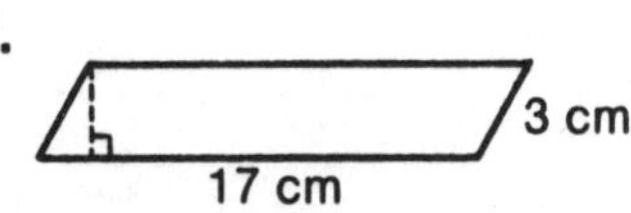

$A =$ ______

8.

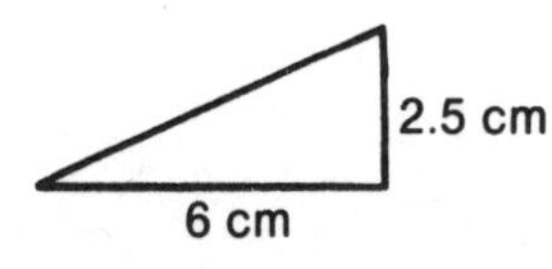

$A =$ ______

9.

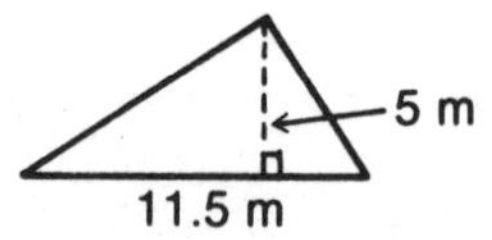

$A =$ ______

10.

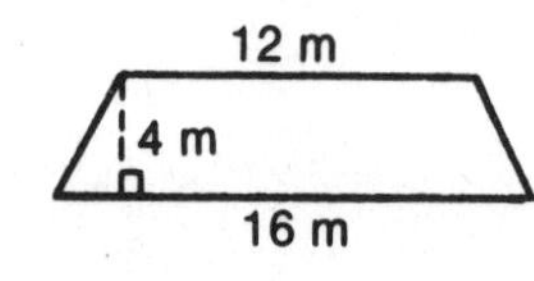

$A =$ ______

11.

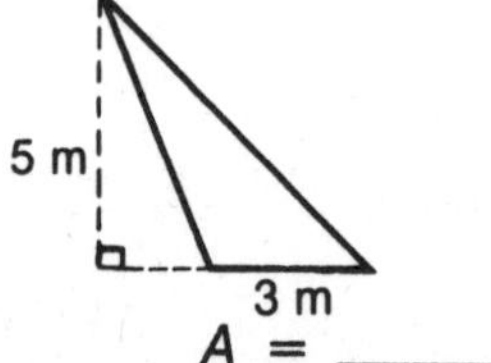

$A =$ ______

12.

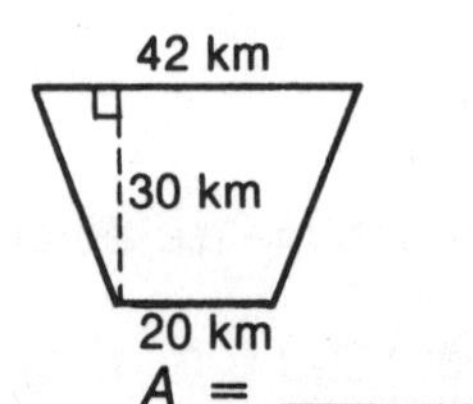

$A =$ ______

13. A square is 6.3 km on a side. $A =$ ______

14. The height of a triangle is 48 mm and its base is 75 mm. $A =$ ______

15. The base of a parallelogram is 50 km and its height is 50 km. $A =$ ______

16. The height of a trapezoid is 4 cm, one base is 8 cm, and the other base is 4 cm. $A =$ ______

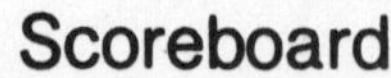

Scoreboard												
Minutes	15	16	17	☆18	19	20	21	22	23	24	25	Number Right ______

Finding Circumference and Area of a Circle

Lesson **31**

$C = \pi d$

$C = 3.14 \cdot 10$

$C = 31.4$ m

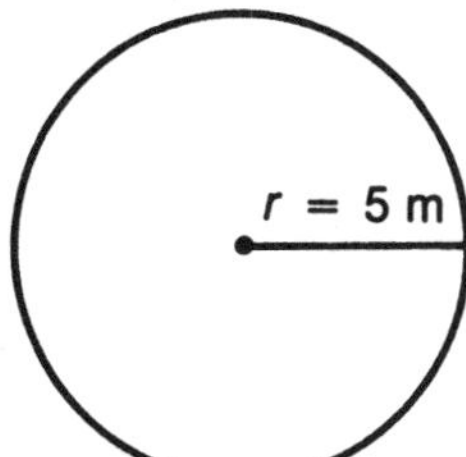

$A = \pi r^2$

$A = 3.14 \cdot 5 \cdot 5$

$A = 3.14 \cdot 25$

$A = 78.5$ m^2

Find the circumference. Use 3.14 for π.

1. 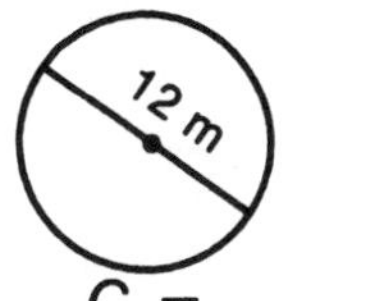

$C =$ ______

2. 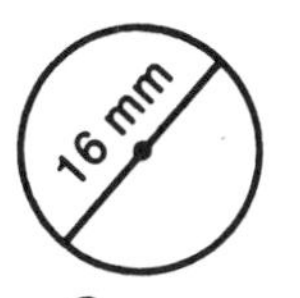

$C =$ ______

3. 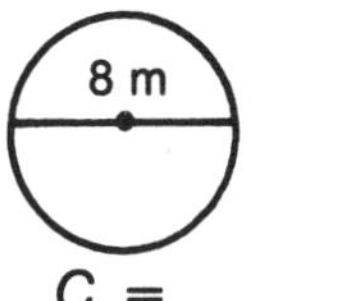

$C =$ ______

4. 

$C =$ ______

5. 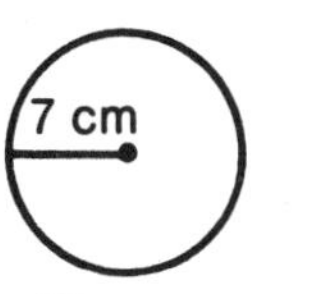

$C =$ ______

6. 

$C =$ ______

7. $r = 10$ m

$C =$ ______

8. $r = 35$ mm

$C =$ ______

9. $d = 3.5$ km

$C =$ ______

Find the area. Use 3.14 for π.

10. 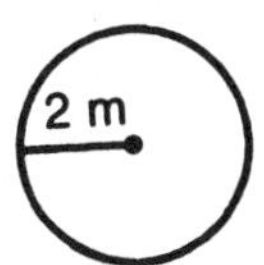

$A =$ ______

11. 

$A =$ ______

12. 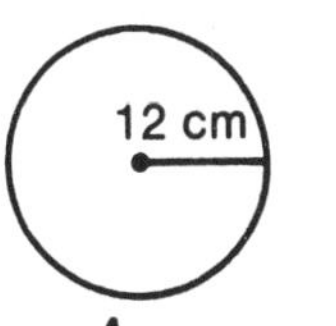

$A =$ ______

13. 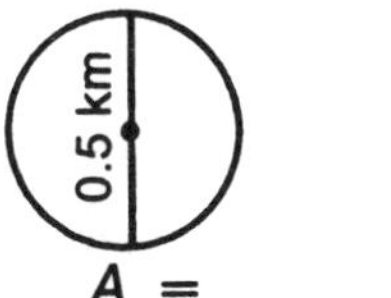

$A =$ ______

14. 

$A =$ ______

15. 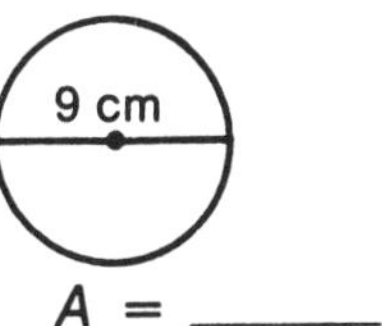

$A =$ ______

16. $r = 1$ mm

$A =$ ______

17. $r = 0.3$ mm

$A =$ ______

18. $d = 100$ km

$A =$ ______

Scoreboard												
Minutes	15	16	17	☆ 18	19	20	21	22	23	24	25	Number Right ______

Lesson 32

Finding Volume

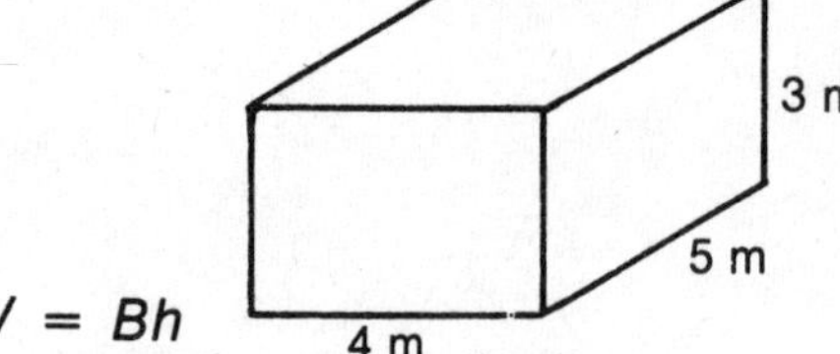

$V = Bh$
$V =$ Area of base • height
$V = (5m \cdot 4m) \cdot 3m$
$V =$ 60m³

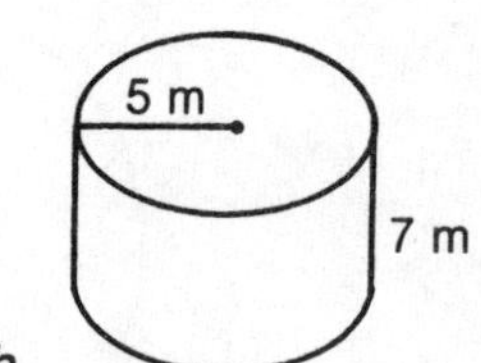

$V = Bh$
$V =$ Area of base • height
$V = 3.14 \cdot (5m \cdot 5m) \cdot 7m$
$V =$ 549.5m³

Find the volume of the prisms.

1.

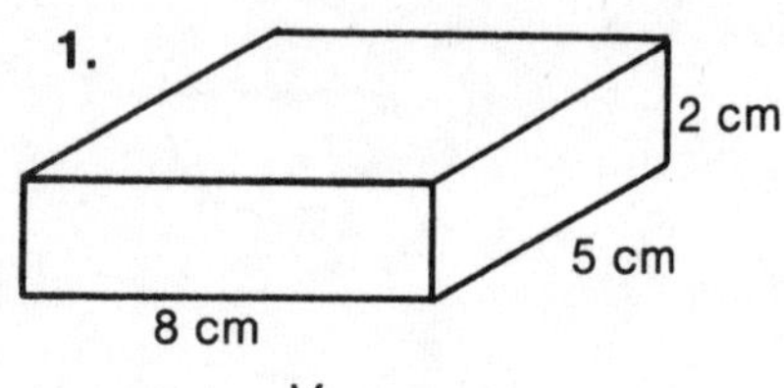

$V =$ ______

2.

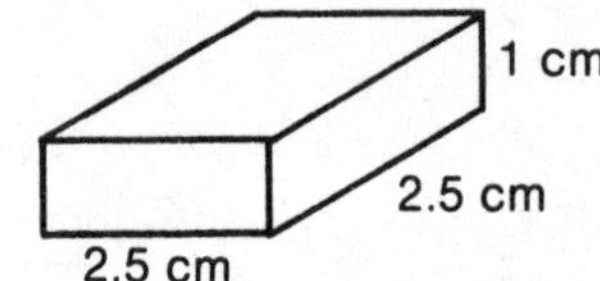

$V =$ ______

3.

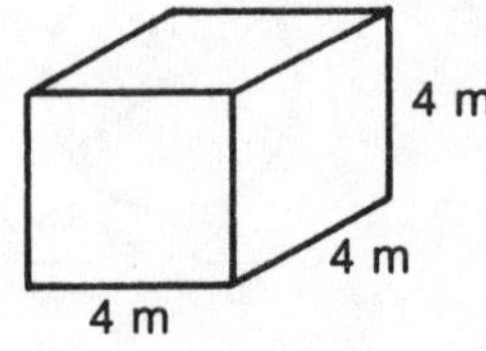

$V =$ ______

4. length: 10 m
width: 5 m
height: 3 m

Volume: ______

5. length: 6 km
width: 7 km
height: 2 km

Volume: ______

6. length: 20 mm
width: 8 mm
height: 4 mm

Volume: ______

7. length: 3 cm
width: 9 cm
height: 11 cm

Volume: ______

8. length: 8 cm
width: 8 cm
height: 8 cm

Volume: ______

9. length: 15 m
width: 10 m
height: 7.5 m

Volume: ______

Find the volume of the cylinders to the nearest hundredth. Use 3.14 for π.

10.

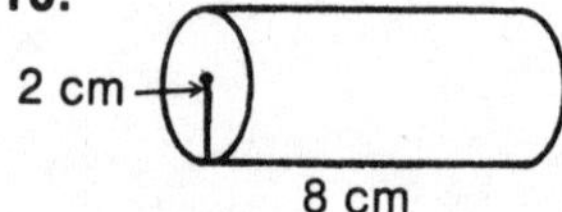

$V =$ ______

11.

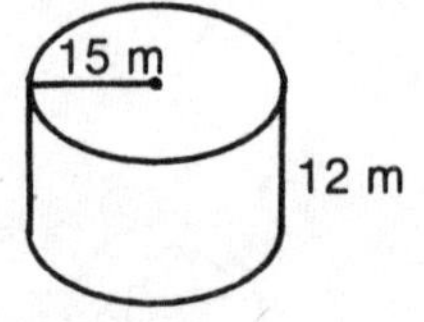

$V =$ ______

12.

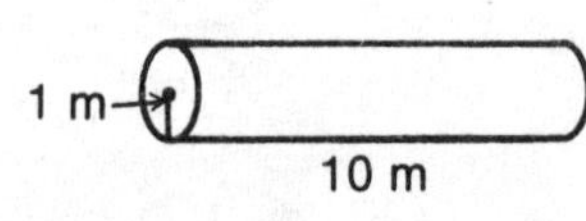

$V =$ ______

13. radius: 7 cm
height: 4 cm

Volume: ______

14. radius: 10 mm
height: 12 mm

Volume: ______

15. diameter: 10 m
height: 1 m

Volume: ______

Scoreboard												
Minutes	19	☆ 20	21	22	23	24	25	26	27	28	29	Number Right ______

Identifying Angles

Lesson
33

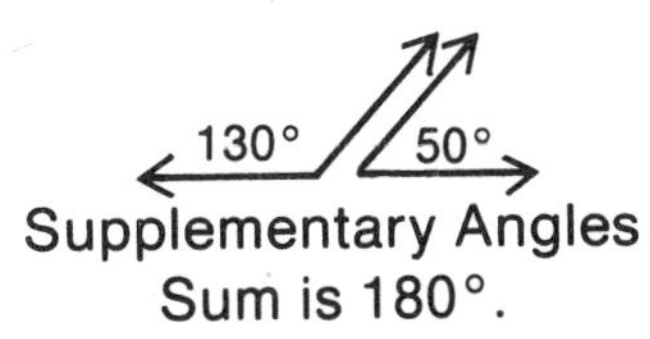

Supplementary Angles
Sum is 180°.

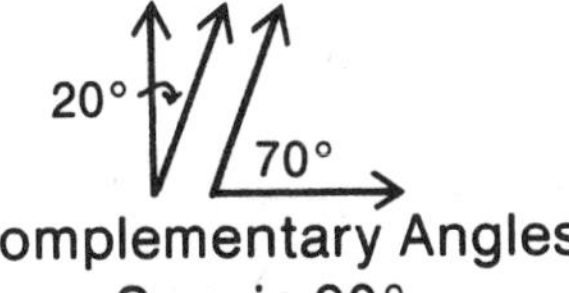

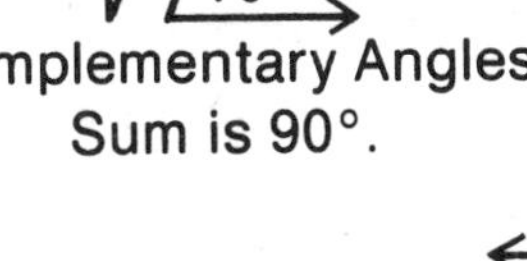
Complementary Angles
Sum is 90°.

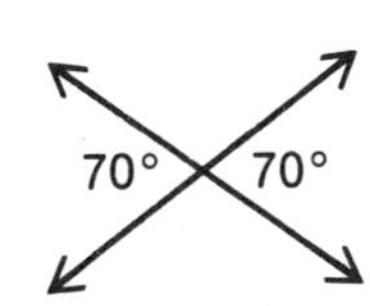

Vertical Angles

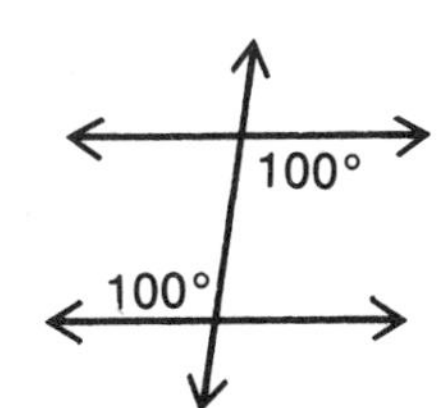

Alternate Interior Angles

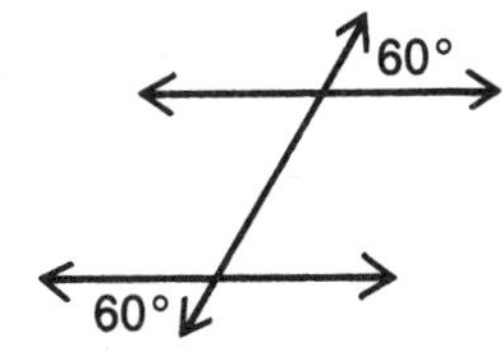

Alternate Exterior Angles

Identify each pair of angles. Write the correct letter in the blank.

a. Supplementary
b. Complementary
c. Vertical
d. Alternate Interior
e. Alternate Exterior

1. 

____

2. 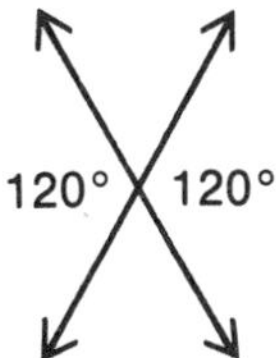

____

3. 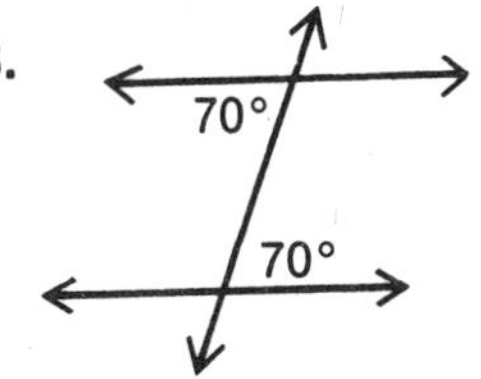

____

4. 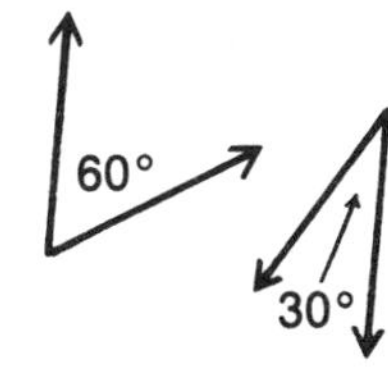

____

Find the measure of each angle marked *x*.

5. 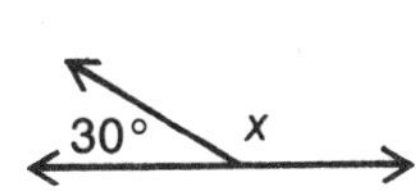

____

6. 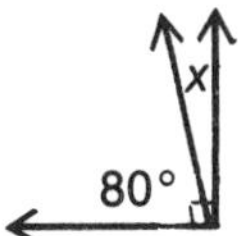

____

7. 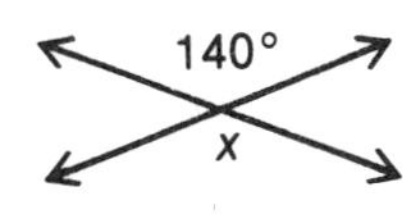

____

8. 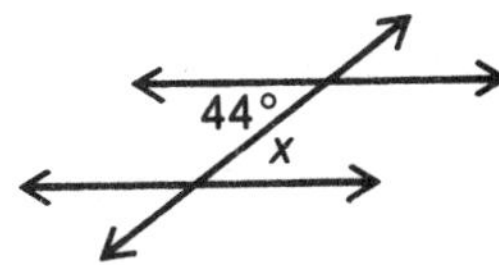

____

9. 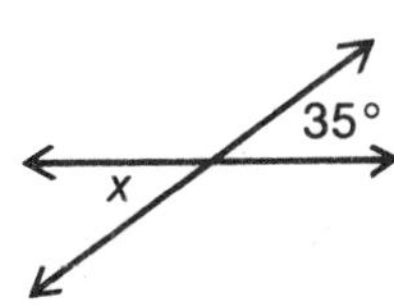

____

10. 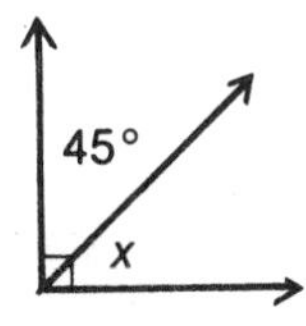

____

11. 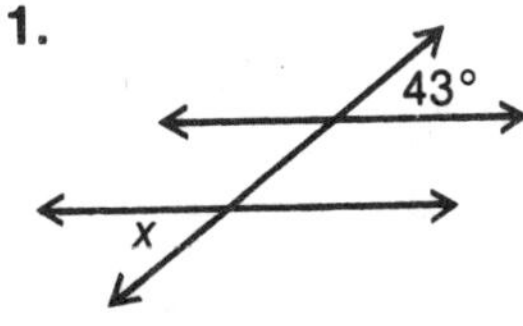

____

12. 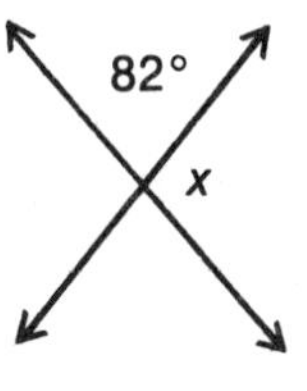

____

Scoreboard											
Minutes	11	☆ 12	13	14	15	16	17	18	19	20	21	Number Right ______

Lesson 34

Solving Word Problems

A full cord of wood is 4 feet high, 8 feet long, and 4 feet deep. What is the volume of a full cord of wood?

$V = lwh$
$V = 4 \cdot 8 \cdot 4$
$V = 128$ cu ft

Solve.

1. Scott burns 1 cord of wood every 30 days. If he plans to burn wood for 120 days, how many cords will he need? ______

2. A face cord of wood is 4 feet high, 8 feet long, and 1 foot deep. What is the volume of a face cord of wood? ______

3. Clare has stored 4 full cords of wood for winter. A full cord is worth $85 where she lives. What is the value of the wood she has stored? ______

4. Mike has cut 8 face cords of wood. He sells them in the city for $65 a face cord. His transportation costs are $114.30. How much will he earn after paying transportation costs? ______

5. The Wangs had 205 gallons of oil in their fuel tank. Pappas Oil Company delivered 175 more gallons. If oil costs $1.05 a gallon, what is the value of the oil in their tank? ______

6. This year the Wangs spent $1200 for heating. This was 75% of what they spent last year. How much were their heating costs last year? ______

7. Joellen bought an electric heater. The heater cost $44 and the sales tax was 7%, what was the total cost of the heater? ______

8. A unit of wood is 2 feet high, 2 feet wide, and 1 foot deep. What is the volume of a unit of wood? ______

Scoreboard												
Minutes	15	16	17	☆18	19	20	21	22	23	24	25	Number Right ______

Solving Word Problems

Lesson 35

John is a waiter in a restaurant. He works 4.5 hours on Monday, 4 hours on Tuesday, 5.5 hours on Wednesday, 8 hours on Friday, and 4 hours on Saturday. How many hours each week does John work?

4.5 + 4 + 3.5 + 8 + 4 = *24 hours*

Solve.

1. John earns \$4.20 an hour. How much is John's salary for a 24-hour work week? ______

2. Marie earns \$72 a week. She saves $\frac{1}{6}$ of her weekly salary. How many weeks will it take her to save \$60? ______

3. Every week Fred works $4\frac{1}{4}$ hours on Wednesday, $3\frac{3}{4}$ hours on Thursday, and 8 hrs. on Friday. What fraction of his weekly pay is earned on Friday? ______

4. Fred earns \$56 a week. 0.0613 of his pay is taken out for Social Security. To the nearest cent, how much is taken out each week? ______

5. Glenn earns \$95 a week. 0.08 of his salary is withheld for taxes. How much is withheld each week? ______

6. Kim earns \$100 each week. \$6.13 is taken out for Social Security and \$8 is taken out for taxes. How much money does Kim bring home? ______

7. Celeste works 20 hours a week. She earns about \$50 in tips a week. About how much does she earn in tips per hour? ______

8. Marie works 48 weeks each year and earns about \$60 in tips each week. She saves $\frac{1}{10}$ of her tip money to pay taxes. How much does she save for taxes each year? ______

Scoreboard												
Minutes	19	☆ 20	21	22	23	24	25	26	27	28	29	Number Right ______

Lesson 36

Solving Percent Problems

Saul put 20 kilograms of bird seed in the feeder. He estimated that blue jays ate 40% of it. About how many kilograms of bird seed did the blue jays eat?

40% of 20

$0.40 \times 20 = 8$ kg

Solve.

1. Eve counted 20 birds at her feeder one day. Four of the birds were chickadees. What percent of the birds were chickadees? _______

2. Oscar thinks squirrels ate 90% of the feed from his bird feeder one week. He had put out 8 kilograms of feed. How much did the squirrels eat? _______

3. Carlos thought that 50% of the birds which came to his feeder were starlings. If 100 birds visited the feeder, how many were starlings? _______

4. Naomi made jars of bird food for gifts. She added 1 cup of sunflower seeds to 4 cups of the ready-made mix. What percent of her mix was sunflower seeds? _______

5. Rusty bought a 10-kilogram bag of bird seed. 30% of it was used in 2 days. How many kilograms of bird seed did he have left? _______

6. Donna estimated that 400 birds came to her feeder in one week. She only saw 4 cardinals. What percent of the birds were cardinals? _______

7. Ivan mixes his feed so that it is 25% sunflower seeds. He used 6 kg of sunflower seeds in his mixture. What was the total weight of his mixture? _______

8. Mr. Vine spent $3.75 for bird seed at the grocery store. How much was his total grocery bill if 5% of the total was spent on bird seed? _______

Scoreboard												
Minutes	19	20	21	☆ 22	23	24	25	26	27	28	29	Number Right _______

Using Maps

Lesson 37

Since 1 cm = 150 km on this map, what distance would 2.5 cm represent?

$$\begin{array}{r} 150 \\ \times\ 2.5 \\ \hline 750 \\ 300\ \\ \hline 375.0 \text{ km} \end{array}$$

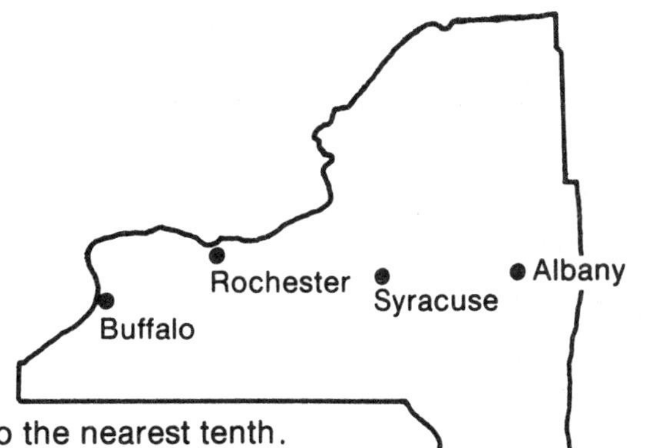

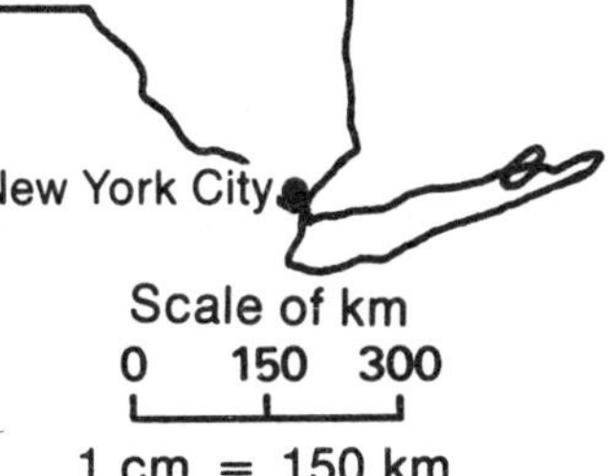

Use the map to fill in the chart. Round each answer to the nearest tenth.

	From	To	Length on Map	Actual Distance
1.	Buffalo	Rochester	1.5 cm	______
2.	Rochester	Syracuse	2 cm	______
3.	Syracuse	Albany	1.7 cm	______
4.	Albany	New York City	3 cm	______
5.	New York City	Buffalo	______	913 km
6.	New York City	Rochester	______	747 km
7.	New York City	Syracuse	______	548 km

Use the chart and map to solve.

8. Is Rochester closer to Buffalo or to Syracuse? ______

9. About how many kilometers is it from Buffalo to Albany? ______

10. Mr. Alonzo drove from Buffalo to Rochester in 3 hours. What was his rate of speed? ______

11. Ms. Fair drove at a rate of 75 kilometers per hour. About how long did it take her to drive from Albany to New York City? ______

12. The Whitenecks can drive an average 75 kilometers per hour. If they leave New York City and drive 10 hours, can they be in Buffalo? ______

Scoreboard												
Minutes	15	☆ 16	17	18	19	20	21	22	23	24	25	Number Right ______

Lesson 38	Solving Problems about Measurement

Wade is working on a circular fish bowl for his Hobby Club project. He wants to put red tape around its top which has a diameter of 20 cm. How much tape does he need?

$$C = \pi d$$
$$C = 3.14 \cdot 20$$
$$C = 62.8 \text{ cm}$$

Solve.

1. Rosa is working on a rectangular fish tank that is 15 cm wide and 20 cm long. How much tape will she need to put all around the top of the tank? ______

2. Pepe is building a planter with a circular bottom. The diameter of the bottom is 40 cm. What is the area of the bottom of the planter? ______

3. Otto is making a circular tray for a planter. If the tray has a radius of 30 cm, will it be large enough for a planter that has a 58-cm diameter? ______

4. The bottom of Kate's rectangular planter is 1.2 m by 0.25 m. What is its area? ______

5. Lena's cube-shaped planter is 22 cm on each side. What is its volume? ______

6. Lena plans to fill her 22-cm cube to within 2 cm of the top. How many cubic centimeters of dirt will Lena need? ______

7. One package of water plants is recommended for 3000 cubic centimeters of water in a fish tank. How many packages of plants will be needed for a 45 cm by 70 cm tank that is filled to a depth of 10 cm? ______

8. Craig made a cylinder-shaped sand candle. The radius of its base is 4 cm; its height is 18 cm. How many cubic centimeters of sand did he use? ______

Scoreboard												
Minutes	19	20	21	☆22	23	24	25	26	27	28	29	Number Right ______

Using Circle and Bar Graphs

Lesson 39

Last year Podun's Trash Company collected 1500 tons of trash. The circle graph shows the kinds of trash collected.

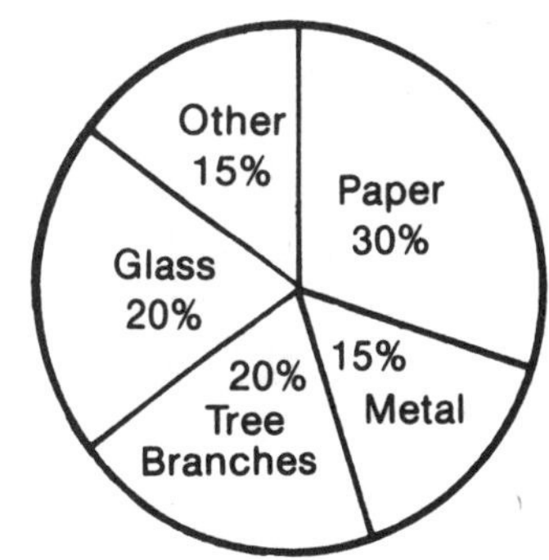

Use the information above to solve.

1. Podun's sold the glass and metal to Bailey Recycling, Inc. What percentage of trash was sold to Bailey's? ______
2. What percent of the trash collected was not metal? ______
3. How many tons of paper did Podun's collect last year? ______
4. One half of the paper was sold. What percent of the total trash collected was that? ______
5. How many tons of glass did they collect? ______

Solve by using the information shown in the bar graph.

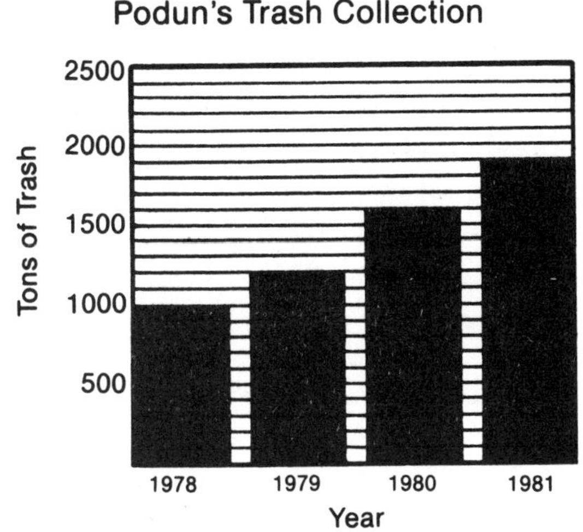

6. How many tons of trash were collected in 1979? ______
7. How many more tons of trash were collected in 1980 than in 1978? ______
8. In 1978, 45% of the trash collected was paper. How many tons of paper were collected? ______
9. In what year was the increase over the previous year the greatest? ______
10. Suppose Podun's collects 25% more trash in 1982 than in 1981. How many tons will they collect in 1982? ______

Scoreboard												
Minutes	15	☆ 16	17	18	19	20	21	22	23	24	25	Number Right ______

Progress Plotter

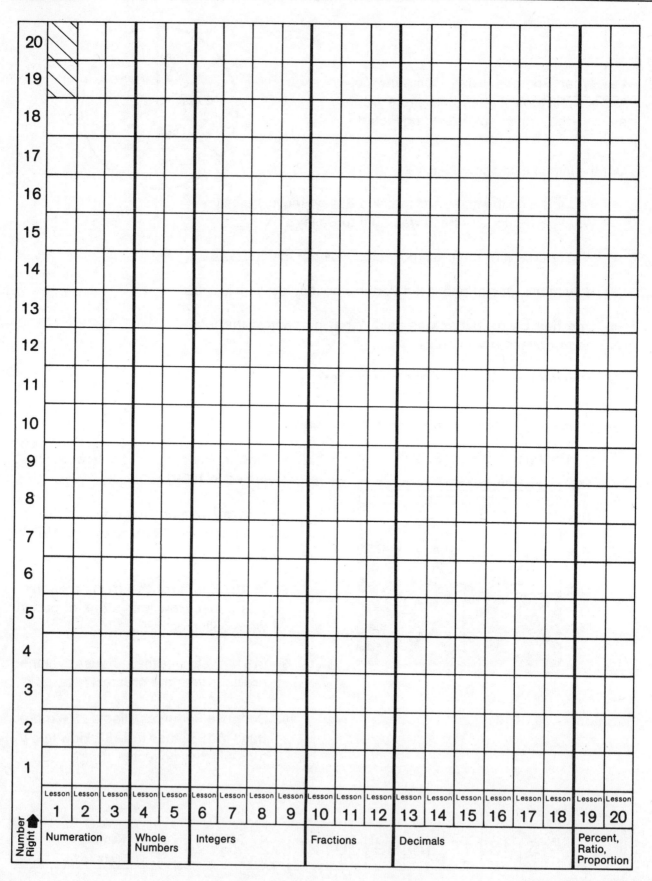

Number Right	Lesson 1	Lesson 2	Lesson 3	Lesson 4	Lesson 5	Lesson 6	Lesson 7	Lesson 8	Lesson 9	Lesson 10	Lesson 11	Lesson 12	Lesson 13	Lesson 14	Lesson 15	Lesson 16	Lesson 17	Lesson 18	Lesson 19	Lesson 20
20																				
19																				
18																				
17																				
16																				
15																				
14																				
13																				
12																				
11																				
10																				
9																				
8																				
7																				
6																				
5																				
4																				
3																				
2																				
1																				
	Numeration			Whole Numbers		Integers				Fractions			Decimals						Percent, Ratio, Proportion	

Name ____________________________________

Lesson 21	Lesson 22	Lesson 23	Lesson 24	Lesson 25	Lesson 26	Lesson 27	Lesson 28	Lesson 29	Lesson 30	Lesson 31	Lesson 32	Lesson 33	Lesson 34	Lesson 35	Lesson 36	Lesson 37	Lesson 38	Lesson 39	Number Right
																			20
																			19
																			18
																			17
																			16
																			15
																			14
																			13
																			12
																			11
																			10
																			9
																			8
																			7
																			6
																			5
																			4
																			3
																			2
																			1
Percent, Ratio, Proportion continued			Equations					Geometry and Measurement					Problem Solving						

Answer Key

	Lesson 1	Lesson 2	Lesson 3	Lesson 4	Lesson 5	Lesson 6	Lesson 7	Lesson 8	Lesson 9	Lesson 10
1.	c	3000	5^2	64,297	1020	$^+12$	$^+3$	$^+4$	$^+3$	$1\frac{5}{12}$
2.	e	3000	2^2	777,408	3843	$^-16$	$^-8$	$^+20$	$^-4$	$\frac{13}{14}$
3.	a	22,000	2^3	102,585	1578	$^+9$	$^-1$	$^+18$	$^-5$	$4\frac{1}{3}$
4.	d	2000	5^{10}	93,209	5688	$^+16$	$^-12$	$^+14$	$^+5$	$3\frac{16}{21}$
5.	b	39,000	4^3	11,170,900	40,053	$^-10$	0	$^+10$	$^+4$	$9\frac{13}{24}$
6.	d	114,000	3^4	47,857	239,343	$^-2$	$^+2$	$^-12$	$^+6$	$1\frac{7}{40}$
7.	a	10,000	10^2	15,001	13,104	$^-2$	$^+20$	$^+8$	$^-3$	$5\frac{11}{18}$
8.	b	61,166,000	2^5	13,156	61,308	$^+8$	$^+17$	$^-7$	$^+3$	$12\frac{11}{12}$
9.	e	e	16	1785	550,472	$^+6$	0	$^-30$	$^-10$	$11\frac{7}{15}$
10.	c	i	100	64,994	4,889,927	0	$^-11$	$^-6$	$^-12$	$13\frac{3}{10}$
11.	$<$	a	1	270	1123R1	$^-12$	$^+12$	$^+9$	$^+5$	$\frac{5}{24}$
12.	$>$	f	64	10,129	56R6	$^+3$	0	$^-10$	$^-2$	$\frac{5}{14}$
13.	$>$	b	4	555,287	6R46	$^+26$	$^+4$	$^-10$	$^+6$	$2\frac{9}{28}$
14.	$>$	d	25	52,787	503	$^-15$	$^-6$	$^+16$	$^-3$	$3\frac{5}{6}$
15.	b	j	8	27,823	98R50	$^-11$	$^-10$	0	$^-8$	$1\frac{1}{24}$
16.	a	l	1000	13,248	685	$^-1$	$^+15$	$^-20$	$^+9$	$3\frac{1}{8}$
17.	a	g	16	11,637	253	$^+20$	$^-17$	$^+42$	$^-9$	$4\frac{3}{8}$
18.	b	k	36	17,182	69R5	0	$^+12$	$^-72$	$^+11$	$\frac{14}{15}$
19.		c	1024	44,683	625	$^-37$	$^+8$	$^+24$	$^+10$	$\frac{19}{24}$
20.		h	5	39,929	237R408	$^-1$	$^-2$	$^-100$	$^-12$	$2\frac{11}{40}$

Answer Key

	Lesson ⬇11	Lesson 12	Lesson 13	Lesson 14	Lesson 15	Lesson 16	Lesson 17	Lesson 18	Lesson 19	Lesson 20
1.	$\frac{1}{15}$	$\frac{2}{3}$	c	5.05	30.78	1.4	8	$\frac{1}{4}$	23%	0.69
2.	$1\frac{3}{7}$	$\frac{10}{21}$	f	0.547	4.431	0.0049	35	$\frac{1}{20}$	435%	0.078
3.	$\frac{5}{18}$	$\frac{1}{8}$	d	8.375	4.482	0.15	2.4	$7\frac{3}{4}$	66.6%	1
4.	$17\frac{1}{3}$	$1\frac{2}{3}$	a	87.364	148.008	0.301	5	$6\frac{1}{4}$	1%	0.3
5.	3	$\frac{4}{35}$	b	10.4388	2.52416	0.0035	0.3	$4\frac{1}{8}$	17%	0.0075
6.	$\frac{5}{14}$	$\frac{3}{5}$	e	8.947	0.6651	0.2	708.9	$\frac{9}{10}$	0.5%	0.333
7.	$6\frac{3}{16}$	$1\frac{41}{51}$	d	0.7500	0.00032	0.709	2	$\frac{363}{1000}$	300%	0.1
8.	$\frac{29}{32}$	$1\frac{2}{5}$	b	13.132	246	0.25	72	$1\frac{7}{10}$	125%	0.035
9.	$10\frac{1}{2}$	$1\frac{1}{9}$	a	4.517	0.018	0.3	0.72	0.25	62.5%	0.6755
10.	$2\frac{7}{9}$	$\frac{1}{14}$	c	6.753	446	0.7	0.41	0.375	7%	0.005
11.	$\frac{9}{28}$	$2\frac{11}{12}$	e	0.868	30.2225	0.385	12	$0.\overline{6}$	7%	$\frac{7}{100}$
12.	$\frac{1}{2}$	$\frac{1}{6}$	g	8.407	24.1808	1.15	25	0.05	25%	$\frac{1}{10}$
13.	$1\frac{3}{4}$	$11\frac{1}{2}$	h	3.1171	0.7248	0.2	166.7	0.71	$66\frac{2}{3}\%$	$1\frac{1}{4}$
14.	$3\frac{3}{5}$	$\frac{2}{7}$	f	6.196	0.02163	1.4	28.6	0.1	12%	$\frac{4}{25}$
15.	$\frac{3}{32}$	$1\frac{7}{18}$	6	6.01	2.772	0.1	9.7	$0.\overline{4}$	80%	$\frac{1}{2}$
16.	46	42	2	6.622	0.3546	0.4	2.3	$1.\overline{3}$	150%	$\frac{2}{5}$
17.	2	$\frac{11}{21}$	0.7	0.0052	14.46	0.93	22.22	$0.\overline{09}$	$37\frac{1}{2}\%$	$3\frac{33}{100}$
18.	$\frac{4}{5}$	24	7.1	0.541	0.6804	0.33	3.83	$0.8\overline{3}$	$83\frac{1}{3}\%$	$\frac{2}{3}$
19.	$12\frac{1}{4}$	$2\frac{6}{7}$	0.01	1.0757	30.4	0.16	16.67	0.28	100%	$\frac{1}{12}$
20.	$7\frac{1}{12}$	$2\frac{1}{2}$	1.10	3.827	0.0168	3.22	1.83	$0.\overline{1}$	$16\frac{2}{3}\%$	$\frac{19}{20}$

Answer Key

	Lesson 21	Lesson 22	Lesson 23	Lesson 24	Lesson 25	Lesson 26	Lesson 27	Lesson 28	Lesson 29	Lesson 30
1.	12	$\frac{1}{3}$	$n = 4$	$n = 3$	$n = 3$	$n = 4$	$n = 18$	$n = 10$	2700	18 km^2
2.	80%	$\frac{5}{6}$	$n = 10$	$n = 4$	$n = 7$	$n = 11$	$n = 16$	$n = 25$	520	64 m^2
3.	5	$\frac{8}{9}$	$n = 8$	$n = 1$	$n = 25$	$n = 4$	$n = 20$	$n = 4$	0.426	12 m^2
4.	80	$\frac{3}{9}$	$n = 10$	$n = 6$	$n = 11$	$n = 4$	$n = 12$	$n = 32$	0.6231	36 km^2
5.	50%	$\neq$	$n = 4.5$	$n = 10$	$n = 12$	$n = 1$	$n = 300$	$n = 10$	27,000	33 cm^2
6.	75	$\neq$	$n = 28$	$n = 16$	$n = 7$	$n = 20$	$n = 40$	$n = 6$	2000	8 mm^2
7.	90	$=$	$n = 3$	$n = 5$	$n = 10$	$n = 9$	$n = 100$	$n = 100$	12.9	51 cm^2
8.	10	$\neq$	$n = 60$	$n = 7$	$n = 15$	$n = 14$	$n = 1$	$n = 10$	1.13	7.5 cm^2
9.	20%	$\neq$	$n = 7.5$	$n = 5$	$n = 20$	$n = 20$	$n = 27$	$n = 100$	9.2	28.75 m^2
10.	40%	$=$	$n = 75$	$n = 8$	$n = 100$	$n = 12$	$n = 8$	$n = 33$	0.1	56 m^2
11.	140	$=$	$n = 10$	$n = 98$	$n = 75$	$n = 25$	$n = 63$	$n = 7$	752	7.5 m^2
12.	20	$\neq$	$n = 15$	$n = 12$	$n = 147$	$n = 10$	$n = 48$	$n = 7$	2710	930 km^2
13.	4.5	$=$	$n = 2$	$n = 100$	$n = 44$	$n = 5$	$n = 25$	$n = 1$	1 kg	39.69 km^2
14.	1	$\neq$	$n = 3$	$n = 5$	$n = 29$	$n = 7$	$n = 75$	$n = 7$	10 km	1800 mm^2
15.	300	$\neq$	$n = 18$	$n = 6$	$n = 4$	$n = 5$	$n = 42$	$n = 4$	5 L	2500 km^2
16.	50	$=$	$n = 8\frac{1}{3}$	$n = 20$	$n = 125$	$n = 2$	$n = 9$	$n = 4$	9 g	24 cm^2
17.	180	$=$	$n = 9$	$n = 6$	$n = 26$	$n = 3$	$n = 10$	$n = 10$	1000 mm	
18.	8000	$\neq$	$n = 100$	$n = 4$	$n = 5$	$n = 4$	$n = 24$	$n = 21$	105 cm	
19.	20%	$=$	$n = 0.625$	$n = 6$	$n = 8$	$n = 8$	$n = 16$	$n = 100$	7 m	
20.	0.64	$\neq$	$n = 9$	$n = 3$	$n = 8$	$n = 9$	$n = 45$	$n = 3$	4 km	

Answer Key

	Lesson 31	Lesson 32	Lesson 33	Lesson 34	Lesson 35	Lesson 36	Lesson 37	Lesson 38	Lesson 39
1.	37.68 m	80 cm^3	a	4 cords	$100.80	20%	225 km	70 cm	35%
2.	50.24 mm	6.25 cm^3	c	32 cu ft	5 weeks	7.2 kg	300 km	1256 cm^2	85%
3.	25.12 m	64 m^3	d	$340	$\frac{1}{2}$	50 starlings	255 km	yes	450 tons
4.	31.4 km	150 m^3	b	$405.70	$3.43	20%	450 km	0.3 m^2	15%
5.	43.96 cm	84 km^3	150°	$399	$7.60	7 kg	6.1 cm	10,648 cm^3	300 tons
6.	25.12 m	640 mm^3	10°	$1600	$85.87	1%	5.0 cm	9680 cm^3	1200 tons
7.	62.8 m	297 cm^3	140°	$47.08	$2.50	24 kg	3.7 cm	10.5 packages	600 tons
8.	219.8 mm	512 cm^3	44°	4 cu ft	$288	$75	Buffalo	904.32 cm^3	450 tons
9.	10.99 km	1125 m^3	35°				780 km		1980
10.	12.56 m^2	100.48 cm^3	45°				75 kph		2375 tons
11.	200.96 mm^2	8478 m^3	43°				6 hours		
12.	452.16 cm^2	31.4 m^3	98°				no		
13.	0.19625 km^2	615.44 cm^3							
14.	28.26 mm^2	3768 mm^3							
15.	63.585 cm^2	78.5 m^3							
16.	3.14 mm^2								
17.	0.2826 m^2								
18.	7850 km^2								
19.									
20.									

PRACTICING PROBLEM SOLVING

Contents

Project Editors: Lynne Lewin, Dorothy McDermott

Text: Developed by The Garber Group
Written By Merrily P. Hansen and Maryann Marrapodi
Design and Production by Thomas Vroman Associates, Inc.

How to Use This Book

This book will help you learn how to solve word problems. It also will let you practice what you learn.

Follow these steps for Practicing Problem Solving:

1. Find the lesson you are going to do.
2. Read problem 1 carefully.
3. Then read the THINK section under the problem. Read all the choices and pick the best one. Write the letter for your answer in box 1 for THINK.
4. Now read the ANSWER section. Figure out the answer to the problem. You can do any scratch work right on the page. Write your answer in box 1 for ANSWER.
5. Do the rest of the problems the same way you did the first one. Work carefully. Remember to complete both the THINK and ANSWER sections of each problem.
6. Turn to the Answer Key. Find the right place and check your answers.
7. Count the number of correct answers. Fill in the number you got right in the box labeled Number Right. The highest score is 12.
8. Turn to the Progress Plotter on page 3. Shade it in to show how many answers you got right.
9. If you got any problems wrong, go back and try them again. Make sure you know how to do them.

The title of each lesson tells you something that will help you solve the problems in that lesson.

Under the titles of some lessons are special notes you will want to remember whenever you solve word problems. These special notes are called **TIPS**. Pay attention to the **TIPS**. They will be reviewed in the last lesson of the book and on the back cover.

A TIP looks like this: Tip

Before you start, think of what you know that will help you solve word problems:

- You know how to write ratios.
- You know how to solve problems with more than one step.
- You know how to use a graph to find facts.

Progress Plotter

12										
11										
10										
9										
8										
7										
6										
5										
4										
3										
2										
1										
	LESSON 1	LESSON 2	LESSON 3	LESSON 4	LESSON 5	LESSON 6	LESSON 7	LESSON 8	LESSON 9	LESSON 10

12										
11										
10										
9										
8										
7										
6										
5										
4										
3										
2										
1										
	LESSON 11	LESSON 12	LESSON 13	LESSON 14	LESSON 15	LESSON 16	LESSON 17	LESSON 18	LESSON 19	LESSON 20

LESSON 1

Choose the Correct Operation

1. The diameter of the moon is 2160 mi. The diameter of the earth is 7927 mi. How many miles longer is the diameter of the earth than the diameter of the moon?

THINK: To solve this problem you should
a. divide.
b. subtract.
c. add.

ANSWER: The diameter of the earth is ____ mi longer.

---

2. The moon revolves around the earth at a speed of 2299 miles per hour. How many miles does the moon travel in 24 hours?

THINK: To solve this problem you should
a. multiply.
b. subtract.
c. add.

ANSWER: It travels ____ mi in 24 hours.

---

3. The crew of Apollo 11 brought 47 lb of rocks back from the moon. The Apollo 16 crew brought back 213 lb of moon rocks, and the Apollo 17 crew brought back 250 lb of moon rocks. What was the total weight of the lunar rocks brought back to earth by these Apollo crews?

THINK: To solve this problem you should
a. multiply.
b. add.
c. divide.

ANSWER: They brought back ____ lb of lunar rocks in all.

	1	2	3	4	5	6	Number Right
THINK:							
ANSWER:							

4. Objects on the earth weigh 6 times more than they do on the moon. If some rocks weigh 177 lb on the moon, how many pounds do they weigh on earth?

THINK: To solve this problem you should
a. multiply.
b. divide.
c. subtract.

ANSWER: They weigh _____ lb on earth.

---

5. Apollo 14's voyage to the moon and back took 216 hours. How many days did the voyage take?

THINK: To solve this problem you should
a. add.
b. divide.
c. multiply.

ANSWER: It took _____ days.

---

6. An Apollo spacecraft must reach a speed of 5281 miles per hour in order to escape the moon's gravity and return to the earth. At this rate how far could it travel in 24 hours?

THINK: To solve this problem you should
a. subtract.
b. multiply.
c. divide.

ANSWER: It could travel _____ mi in 24 hours.

LESSON 2

Choose the Correct Equation

 An equation will help you to find the answer to a word problem.

1. The zookeepers prepared a 6.4-m by 8.35-m cage for the giant pandas the zoo was receiving from China. What was the area of the floor of the cage?

THINK: Which equation fits the problem?

a. $8.35 - 6.4 = \square$
b. $6.4 + \square = 8.35$
c. $6.4 \times 8.35 = \square$

ANSWER: The area of the floor of the cage was ______ m^2.

---

2. On their trip from China, each panda ate a total of 21.375 kg of bamboo shoots in 2.5 days. What was the average amount each panda ate each day?

THINK: Which equation fits the problem?

a. $21.375 \div 2.5 = \square$
b. $21.375 + \square = 2.5$
c. $2.5 \times 21.375 = \square$

ANSWER: The average amount each panda ate each day was ______ kg.

---

3. One of the pandas arrived at the zoo in a cage that weighed 28.2 kg. The total weight of the cage and the panda was 139.03 kg. How many kilograms did the panda weigh?

THINK: Which equation fits the problem?

a. $139.03 - 28.2 = \square$
b. $139.03 + 28.2 = \square$
c. $139.03 \div \square = 28.2$

ANSWER: The panda weighed ______ kg.

	1	2	3	4	5	6	Number Right
THINK:							
ANSWER:							

4. The female panda weighed 106.9 kg, and the male panda weighed 3.93 kg more than that. How many kilograms did the male panda weigh?

THINK: Which equation fits the problem?

a. $106.9 \div 3.93 = \square$

b. $106.9 + 3.93 = \square$

c. $106.9 - 3.93 = \square$

ANSWER: The male panda weighed ______ kg.

---

5. A baby panda is 0.95 m tall. It is expected to reach a height of 1.4 m when full-grown. How many more meters is the baby panda expected to grow?

THINK: Which equation fits the problem?

a. $1.4 \times 0.95 = \square$

b. $1.4 + \square = 0.95$

c. $1.4 - 0.95 = \square$

ANSWER: It is expected to grow ______ more meters.

---

6. The zookeepers were told that each panda would eat a total of 61.25 kg of bamboo shoots a week. How many kilograms of bamboo shoots should they order to feed each panda for 12.5 weeks?

THINK: Which equation fits the problem?

a. $61.25 - 12.5 = \square$

b. $61.25 \div 12.5 = \square$

c. $61.25 \times 12.5 = \square$

ANSWER: They should order ______ kg of bamboo shoots.

LESSON 3

Estimate

1. An early computer could solve 300 multiplication problems in a second. About how many multiplication problems could it solve in 28.75 seconds?

THINK: Which numbers should you use to estimate the answer?
a. 20 and 400
b. 30 and 300
c. 2900 and 300

ANSWER: It could solve about _____ problems.

---

2. One programmer used 235.5 ft of magnetic tape to enter information into a computer. Another programmer used 376.75 ft of magnetic tape. About how many feet of tape did they use all together?

THINK: Which numbers should you use to estimate the answer?
a. 300 and 400
b. 300 and 200
c. 200 and 400

ANSWER: They used about _____ ft of tape all together.

---

3. Ms. Chung spent 8.25 hours writing a computer program and 17.5 hours debugging it. About how many more hours did she spend debugging the program than writing it?

THINK: Which numbers should you use to estimate the answer?
a. 80 and 10
b. 800 and 200
c. 10 and 20

ANSWER: She spent about _____ more hours debugging the program.

	1	2	3	4	5	6	Number Right
THINK:							
ANSWER:							

4. The printer attached to one computer typed 927 characters in 31.35 seconds. About how many characters did it type each second?

THINK: Which numbers should you use to estimate the answer?

a. 900 and 30
b. 1000 and 40
c. 900 and 3000

ANSWER: It typed about ______ characters each second.

---

5. Some computers can read information stored on a disk at a rate of 345,000 characters per second. About how many characters can these computers read in 11.02 seconds?

THINK: Which numbers should you use to estimate the answer?

a. 400,000 and 100
b. 300,000 and 10
c. 400,000 and 1100

ANSWER: They can read about ______ characters in 11.02 seconds.

---

6. Lab workers can make 490 memory chips from a piece of polished silicon 14.4 inches long. About how long is each of the memory chips?

THINK: Which numbers should you use to estimate the answer?

a. 20 and 400
b. 10 and 500
c. 140 and 500

ANSWER: Each chip is about ______ in. long.

LESSON 4

Solve Two-Step Problems

 To solve a problem with more than one step, you must solve one problem and use the answer to solve another problem.

1. Mr. Sancho teaches 5 Spanish classes a day. Each class has 27 students. Ms. Bailey teaches Spanish to 150 students a day. How many more students does Ms. Bailey teach each day than Mr. Sancho?

THINK: To solve this problem you should
a. multiply then subtract.
b. subtract then add.
c. divide then subtract.

ANSWER: She teaches _____ more students each day.

---

2. One Spanish class learned 130 new Spanish words in September, 175 in October, 246 in November, and 165 in December. What was the average number of new Spanish words the students learned each month?

THINK: To solve this problem you should
a. add then subtract.
b. add then multiply.
c. add then divide.

ANSWER: They learned an average of _____ new Spanish words each month.

---

3. The students in Mr. Sancho's advanced Spanish class read 8 pages of *Don Quixote* in class for each of 16 days. They also read 47 pages as a homework assignment. How many pages did they read in all?

THINK: To solve this problem you should
a. multiply then add.
b. add then subtract.
c. subtract then multiply.

ANSWER: They read _____ pages in all.

	1	2	3	4	5	6	Number Right
THINK:							
ANSWER:							

4. Ms. Bailey distributed 150 copies of a Spanish textbook to her students. She gave out the same number of books to each of her 5 classes. She also distributed 30 Spanish-English dictionaries to each class. How many books in all were distributed to each class?

THINK: To solve this problem you should
a. multiply then subtract.
b. divide then add.
c. add then multiply.

ANSWER: ______ books in all were distributed to each class.

---

5. A committee of students made 36 yarn pictures as decorations for the fiesta. They used 86 ft of red yarn, 76 ft of green yarn, 82 ft of blue yarn, 84 ft of yellow yarn, and 104 ft of orange yarn for the pictures. What was the average number of feet of yarn used for each picture?

THINK: To solve this problem you should
a. multiply then add.
b. add then divide.
c. subtract then add.

ANSWER: An average of ______ ft of yarn was used for each picture.

---

6. Another committee of students made 15 piñatas for a fiesta. Each piñata weighed 5 lb when empty and 11 lb when filled with prizes. What was the total weight of the prizes used to fill all the piñatas?

THINK: To solve this problem you should
a. add then multiply.
b. multiply then add.
c. subtract then multiply.

ANSWER: The total weight of the prizes was

______ lb.

LESSON 5

Choose the Correct Equation

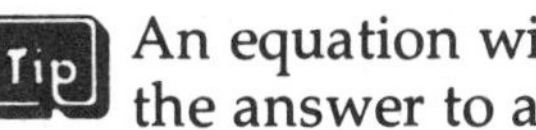

Tip An equation will help you to find the answer to a word problem.

1. Bob and Pia worked on a model airplane for $3\frac{1}{4}$ hours on Saturday and $2\frac{1}{3}$ hours on Sunday. For how many hours did they work on the model in all?

THINK: Which equation fits the problem?

a. $2\frac{1}{3} + \square = 3\frac{1}{4}$

b. $3\frac{1}{4} - \square = 2\frac{1}{3}$

c. $3\frac{1}{4} + 2\frac{1}{3} = \square$

ANSWER: They worked on the plane for ______ hours in all.

---

2. The wingspan of the model plane was $32\frac{2}{3}$ in. long. The total length of the plane was $41\frac{1}{6}$ in. long. How many inches longer was the plane than its wingspan?

THINK: Which equation fits the problem?

a. $32\frac{2}{3} \times \square = 41\frac{1}{6}$

b. $41\frac{1}{6} \div \square = 32\frac{2}{3}$

c. $41\frac{1}{6} - 32\frac{2}{3} = \square$

ANSWER: The plane was ______ in. longer than its wingspan.

---

3. The two friends used a strip of plastic $5\frac{1}{4}$ in. long to cut windows for their model. Each window was $\frac{3}{4}$ in. long. How many windows could they cut out of the plastic?

THINK: Which equation fits the problem?

a. $5\frac{1}{4} \div \frac{3}{4} = \square$

b. $5\frac{1}{4} \times \frac{3}{4} = \square$

c. $\frac{3}{4} \div 5\frac{1}{4} = \square$

ANSWER: They could cut ______ windows out of the plastic.

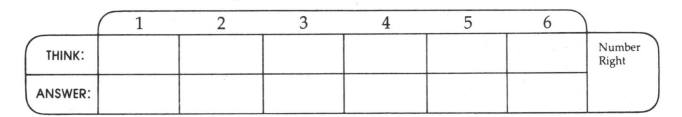

	1	2	3	4	5	6	Number Right
THINK:							
ANSWER:							

4. Pia spent $\frac{1}{2}$ hour gluing the windows on the plane and $\frac{1}{3}$ hour painting their frames light blue. How much more time did she spend gluing the windows on the plane than painting the frames?

THINK: Which equation fits the problem?

a. $\frac{1}{2} - \frac{1}{3} = \square$

b. $\frac{1}{2} \times \frac{1}{3} = \square$

c. $\frac{1}{3} - \frac{1}{2} = \square$

ANSWER: She spent ______ of an hour more gluing the windows on the plane.

---

5. Bob mixed $3\frac{1}{2}$ oz of gray paint with $1\frac{2}{3}$ oz of silver paint to get the correct color for the body of the plane. How many ounces of paint did he mix all together?

THINK: Which equation fits the problem?

a. $3\frac{1}{2} + 1\frac{2}{3} = \square$

b. $3\frac{1}{2} \times 1\frac{2}{3} = \square$

c. $3\frac{1}{2} - \square = 1\frac{2}{3}$

ANSWER: He mixed ______ oz of paint all together.

---

6. Pia used a total of $7\frac{1}{2}$ oz of white paint to make some new colors. She used $\frac{3}{4}$ of an ounce to make each new color. How many new colors did she make?

THINK: Which equation fits the problem?

a. $7\frac{1}{2} \times \frac{3}{4} = \square$

b. $7\frac{1}{2} \div \frac{3}{4} = \square$

c. $7\frac{1}{2} - \frac{3}{4} = \square$

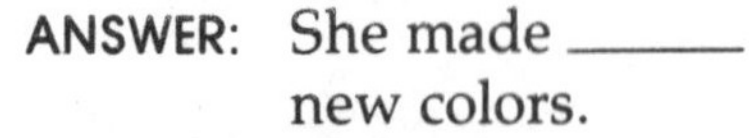

ANSWER: She made ______ new colors.

Find the Missing Information

1. Jeremy made 8 banners for the medieval fair. How many yards of felt did he use all together?

Use the information you chose to compute the answer.

THINK: Choose the information that is needed to solve the problem.

a. Each banner was made with 3 colors of felt.
b. Each of the 8 banners represented a different guild.
c. Each banner took $1\frac{3}{4}$ yd of felt.

ANSWER: He used ______ yd of felt all together.

---

2. A group of students used $2\frac{1}{4}$ lb of tabs from juice cans to make each suit of armor. How many pounds of tabs did they use for all of the suits?

THINK: Choose the information that is needed to solve the problem.

a. They made 26 suits of armor.
b. Each suit was $4\frac{1}{2}$ ft long.
c. They used 1500 tabs for each suit.

ANSWER: They used ______ lb of tabs all together.

---

3. Wendy cut 3 shields of equal length from a piece of cardboard. How long was each shield?

THINK: Choose the information that is needed to solve the problem.

a. The cardboard weighed $1\frac{1}{2}$ lb.
b. The cardboard was $10\frac{1}{2}$ ft long.
c. The cardboard was $\frac{1}{4}$ in. thick.

ANSWER: Each shield was ______ ft long.

	1	2	3	4	5	6	Number Right
THINK:							
ANSWER:							

4. The members of the Candlemaker's Club used $31\frac{1}{4}$ lb of wax to make candles. How much did each candle weigh?

THINK: Choose the information that is needed to solve the problem.

a. They made 4 different styles of candles.
b. Some candles were $3\frac{1}{2}$ in. in diameter.
c. They made 50 candles of equal weight.

ANSWER: Each candle weighed ______ lb.

---

5. In the archery contest, Lou shot an arrow $14\frac{1}{3}$ feet farther than Kyle. How far did Lou shoot the arrow?

THINK: Choose the information that is needed to solve the problem.

a. Kyle's arrow weighed $5\frac{1}{2}$ oz.
b. Kyle shot his arrow $46\frac{1}{4}$ ft.
c. Kyle's arrow was $14\frac{1}{2}$ in. in length.

ANSWER: Lou shot the arrow ______ ft.

---

6. Sam pinned his opponent to the ground in the wrestling contest in exactly $4\frac{1}{2}$ minutes. How much longer did Mack take to pin his opponent than Sam?

THINK: Choose the information that is needed to solve the problem.

a. Mack's opponent weighed $112\frac{1}{4}$ lb.
b. Mack was $60\frac{3}{4}$ in. tall.
c. Mack pinned his opponent in $7\frac{3}{4}$ minutes.

ANSWER: It took Mack ______ more minutes than Sam.

LESSON 7

Read and Use a Diagram

Jessica's Wallhanging

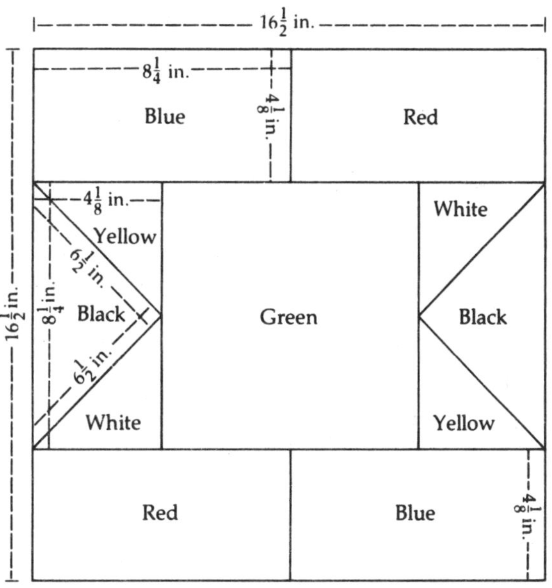

1. Jessica plans to cover her patchwork wallhanging with a sheet of glass. How many square inches of glass does she need?

THINK: You should look for

a. the length and width of each side of the green square.
b. the length and width of each side of the blue rectangles.
c. the length and width of the wallhanging.

ANSWER: She needs _____ sq. in. of glass.

---

2. A friend offered Jessica a strip of velvet to frame the edges of the wallhanging. How many inches long should the strip be?

THINK: You should look for

a. the length of each side of the wallhanging.
b. the length of each rectangle in the wallhanging.
c. the total number of rectangles in the wallhanging.

ANSWER: It should be _____ in. long.

	1	2	3	4	5	6	Number Right
THINK:							
ANSWER:							

3. Jessica outlined the green square with black silk cord. How many inches of cord did she use?

THINK: You should look for
a. the length of the sides of the wallhanging.
b. the length of the sides of the green square.
c. the length of the sides of the black triangles.

ANSWER: She used ______ in. of cord.

---

4. How many inches of white ribbon did Jessica need to separate both sets of blue and red rectangles from each other?

THINK: You should look for
a. the length of the side shared by each blue and red rectangle.
b. the difference between the length and the width of the blue rectangle.
c. the length of each side of the blue and red rectangles.

ANSWER: She needed ______ in. of ribbon.

---

5. What length of ribbon did Jessica need to trim the borders of each black triangle?

THINK: You should look for
a. the length of all the triangles.
b. the number of triangles in the wallhanging.
c. the length of each side of a black triangle.

ANSWER: She needed ______ in. of ribbon.

---

6. Jessica used a total of $4\frac{1}{2}$ ft of thread to embroider a design in each triangular section of the wallhanging. She used the same amount of thread for each design. How much thread did she use to embroider one design?

THINK: You should look for
a. the lengths of the sides of each triangle in the wallhanging.
b. the number of yellow triangles in the wallhanging.
c. the number of triangular sections in the wallhanging.

ANSWER: She used ______ ft of thread.

LESSON 8

Identify Extra Information

1. Ships crossing the Panama Canal have to travel 80 km from the Atlantic side to the Pacific side. The tides have an average height of 0.61 m a day on the Atlantic side of the canal and 3.8 m a day on the Pacific side. How many more meters do the tides average on the Pacific side?

THINK: Which information is not needed for solving the problem?
a. the height of the tides on the Atlantic side of the canal
b. the height of the tides on the Pacific side of the canal
c. the distance between the Atlantic and Pacific sides of the canal

ANSWER: Tides average ______ more meters on the Pacific side.

---

2. The Panama Canal is 81.6 km long. It is 13 m deep at its shallowest point. The Suez Canal is 80.3 km longer than the Panama Canal. How many kilometers long is the Suez Canal?

THINK: Which information is not needed for solving the problem?
a. the length of the Panama Canal
b. the depth of the Panama Canal at its shallowest point
c. the length of the Suez Canal

ANSWER: The Suez Canal is ______ km long.

---

3. The longest ship canal in the world is the St. Lawrence Seaway, which is 724 km in length. The Chesapeake and Delaware Canal is 137.1 m wide and 23 km long. How many kilometers longer is the St. Lawrence Seaway than the Chesapeake and Delaware Canal?

THINK: Which information is not needed for solving the problem?
a. the width of the Chesapeake and Delaware
b. the length of the St. Lawrence Seaway Canal
c. the length of the Chesapeake and Delaware Canal

ANSWER: The St. Lawrence Seaway is ______ km longer.

	1	2	3	4	5	6	Number Right
THINK:							
ANSWER:							

4. The Suez Canal opened in 1869. At 161.9 km in length, it is 4 times as long as Canada's Welland Canal. How many kilometers long is the Welland Canal?

THINK: Which information is not needed for solving the problem?

a. the year the Suez Canal opened
b. the length of the Suez Canal
c. how many times longer the Suez Canal is than the Welland Canal

ANSWER: The Welland Canal is ______ km long.

---

5. A ship took 10.5 hours to travel through the Albert Canal in Belgium. The Albert Canal is 128.1 km long and 5.03 m deep. At the rate of how many kilometers per hour did the ship travel through the canal?

THINK: Which information is not needed for solving the problem?

a. the length of the canal
b. the amount of time it took for the ship to travel through the canal
c. the depth of the canal

ANSWER: It traveled through the canal at a rate of ______ km/h.

---

6. Locomotives called "mules" help pull ships through the Panama Canal at a speed of 24.1 km/h. Ships are pulled through a series of 4 locks. How many kilometers can a ship travel in 1.5 hours?

THINK: Which information is not needed for solving the problem?

a. the number of locks in the canal
b. the speed of the ships when pulled by mules
c. the amount of time the ship is traveling

ANSWER: A ship can travel ______ km in 1.5 hours.

Read and Use a Table

Speed Records of Certain Aviators

Aviator	Year	Speed (Miles Per Hour)	Country in Which Flight Originated
J. Doolittle	1932	294.38	United States
F. Everest	1953	755.14	United States
E. Joersz	1976	2196.17	United States
G. Mosolov	1959	1483.85	Russia
A. Santos-Dumont	1906	25.66	France
R. Stephens	1965	2070.1	United States
J. Vedrines	1912	108.18	France
F. Wendel	1939	469.22	Germany
H. Wilson	1945	606.25	England

1. In which year was the fastest speed listed in the table recorded?

THINK: You should look first for
a. the column labeled *Speed*.
b. the column labeled *Year*.
c. the column labeled *Aviator*.

ANSWER: The fastest speed listed on the chart was recorded in ______.

---

2. Doolittle set his speed record in 1932. What was his speed?

THINK: You should look for
a. the column labeled *Speed*.
b. the column labeled *Year*.
c. the highest speed listed on the table.

ANSWER: His speed was ______ mph.

	1	2	3	4	5	6	Number Right
THINK:							
ANSWER:							

3. Which aviator set a speed record that was 728.71 mph less than the speed record set by Mosolov?

THINK: You should look for
a. a speed of 728.71 mph.
b. a speed greater than 728.71 mph.
c. Mosolov's speed record.

ANSWER: _____ set a speed record 728.71 mph less than Mosolov's.

---

4. If Santos-Dumont traveled 64.15 mi at his record speed, for how many hours did he fly?

THINK: You should look for
a. Santos-Dumont's record speed.
b. the year in which Santos-Dumont set his record.
c. the country in which the flight originated.

ANSWER: He flew for _____ hours.

---

5. Whose speed record did Wilson break by exactly 137.03 mph?

THINK: You should look for
a. Wilson's speed record.
b. a speed greater than 137.03 mph.
c. a speed less than 137.03 mph.

ANSWER: He broke _____ speed record.

---

6. If Stephens traveled at his record speed for 3.25 hours, how far would he travel?

THINK: You should look for
a. the speed of any aviator on the table.
b. the speed listed for Stephens.
c. the highest speed on the table.

ANSWER: He would travel _____ mi.

Read and Use a Double Line Graph

Tip Sometimes you must read two sets of information on a graph to answer a word problem.

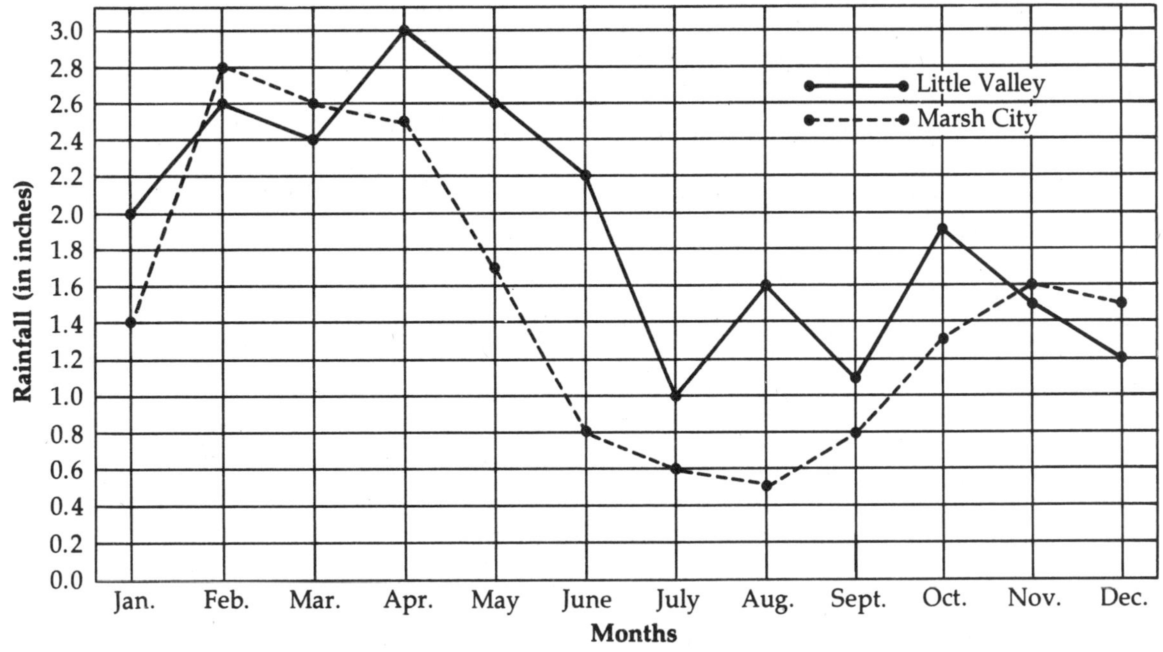

1. Which city had the greatest average rainfall in November?

THINK: You should look for
- a. the highest point on the graph.
- b. the higher point for November.
- c. the lower point for November.

ANSWER: ______ had the greatest average rainfall in November.

---

2. How many inches fewer did it rain in Marsh City in August than in February?

THINK: You should look for
- a. the points that show Marsh City's rainfall for August and February.
- b. the points that show Little Valley's rainfall for August and February.
- c. the highest and lowest points on the graph.

ANSWER: It rained ______ in. fewer in August.

	1	2	3	4	5	6	Number Right
THINK:							
ANSWER:							

3. How many more inches did it rain in Little Valley in May than in October?

THINK: You should look for

a. the points that show the rainfall in Marsh City for May and October.
b. the highest and lowest points on the line that represents Little Valley's rainfall.
c. the points that show the rainfall in Little Valley for May and October.

ANSWER: It rained ______ more inches in May.

---

4. What was the total number of inches of rain in Marsh City during June, July, and August?

THINK: You should look for

a. the points for June, July, and August on both lines.
b. the points that show the rainfall in Marsh City for June, July, and August.
c. the points that show the rainfall in Little Valley for June, July, and August.

ANSWER: It rained ______ in. during June, July, and August.

---

5. How many more inches did it rain during the month of greatest rainfall in Little Valley than the month of least rainfall in Marsh City?

THINK: You should look for

a. the highest point on the line representing Little Valley and the lowest point on the line representing Marsh City.
b. the highest point on the line representing Little Valley and the highest point on the line representing Marsh City.
c. the highest and lowest points on the line representing Little Valley.

ANSWER: It rained ______ more inches.

---

6. What was the total amount of rainfall for the year in Marsh City?

THINK: You should look for

a. the number of inches of rain in each month shown by the broken line on the graph.
b. the number of inches of rain in each month shown by the solid line on the graph.
c. the number of inches of rain in each month shown by both the broken line and the solid line on the graph.

ANSWER: The total rainfall was ______ in.

Solve Multi-Step Problems

To solve a problem with more than one step, you must solve one problem and use the answer to solve another problem.

1. Mr. Astin wanted a camera and lens that sold for $525. He could either pay the total amount at the time of purchase, or he could agree to pay the store $135 down and $40 a month for 12 months. How much money could he save by paying the total amount at the time of purchase?

THINK: The first thing you should do is
a. find the difference in cost between the two payment plans.
b. find the cost of the items under the installment plan.
c. find the average cost per month.

ANSWER: He could save ______ by paying the total amount.

---

2. A videotape recorder was on sale for $1250. Dr. Marshall paid $75 down and $58.50 for 22 months. Mrs. Kent bought the same videotape recorder, but she paid in full at the time of purchase. How much more money did Dr. Marshall pay for the videotape recorder than Mrs. Kent?

THINK: The first thing you should do is
a. find the difference in cost between the two plans.
b. find the total cost for Dr. Marshall.
c. find the total cost of both plans together.

ANSWER: Dr. Marshall paid ______ more than Mrs. Kent.

---

3. Mr. Sachs bought a microcomputer for $1100 and a small printer for $450. He paid $300 down and agreed to pay the balance of the bill in 8 equal monthly payments. Assuming that the owner of the store did not charge him interest, how much money did Mr. Sachs pay each month?

THINK: After you find the total cost of the items you should
a. find the average cost of the items.
b. find the difference between the total bill and the down payment.
c. find the difference between the cost of the items.

ANSWER: He paid ______ each month.

	1	2	3	4	5	6	Number Right
THINK:							
ANSWER:							

4. Norm agreed to pay a total of $224 in 8 equal monthly payments for his new television set, plus an additional $1.35 a month for a service contract. He put aside $51 a month to cover this and other installment payments. How much money did he have left over for his other payments?

THINK: The first thing you should do is
a. find the monthly payment for the television set.
b. find his total installment payments per month.
c. find the amount of money left over each month.

ANSWER: He had ______ left over for his other payments.

---

5. Ms. Watts bought a movie camera and a projector. She could pay for these articles by putting $100 down and paying $84 a month for 10 months, or she could borrow $800 from the bank and repay the loan at a rate of $92 a month for 10 months. How much money will she save by borrowing from the bank?

THINK: The first thing you should do is
a. find the cost of the items under each of the two plans.
b. find the interest rate charged by the bank.
c. find the actual cost of theitems if paid in full at time of purchase.

ANSWER: She will save ______.

---

6. Mr. Wong bought a stereo receiver for $579 and a pair of speakers for $379. He paid $55.78 in sales tax on this purchase. He gave the clerk $150 in cash and a check for $800. How much more money did he need to pay the bill in full?

THINK: After you find the total amount of the purchase you should
a. find the cost of each item.
b. find the total amount Mr. Wong paid the clerk.
c. find the cost of the bill on the installment plan.

ANSWER: He needed ______ more.

LESSON 12

Use a Proportion to Solve Problems

Tip: Sometimes you can write a **proportion** to solve a word problem.

1. Helene placed a 6-g weight 33 cm from the fulcrum of a balance. How far from the fulcrum should she place a 4-g weight in order for the two weights to balance each other?

THINK: Which proportion fits the problem?

a. $\frac{6}{33} = \frac{x}{4}$

b. $\frac{33}{6} = \frac{4}{x}$

c. $\frac{6}{33} = \frac{4}{x}$

ANSWER: She should place the weight ______ cm from the fulcrum.

---

2. Carrie balanced a 15-g weight and a 25-g weight. She placed the 25-g weight 80 cm from the fulcrum. How far from the fulcrum did she place the 15-g weight?

THINK: Which proportion fits the problem?

a. $\frac{25}{80} = \frac{15}{x}$

b. $\frac{25}{15} = \frac{x}{80}$

c. $\frac{25}{80} = \frac{x}{15}$

ANSWER: She placed the 15-g weight ______ cm from the fulcrum.

---

3. One student experimented with balancing a 30-g weight and a 60-g weight. He placed the 30-g weight 24 cm from the fulcrum. How far from the fulcrum did he place the 60-g weight?

THINK: Which proportion fits the problem?

a. $\frac{30}{24} = \frac{60}{x}$

b. $\frac{24}{30} = \frac{60}{x}$

c. $\frac{30}{60} = \frac{x}{24}$

ANSWER: He placed the 60-g weight ______ cm from the fulcrum.

	1	2	3	4	5	6	Number Right
THINK:							
ANSWER:							

4. Mr. Schorr assigned a group of students the task of balancing a 64-g weight and a 56-g weight. He placed the 64-g weight 32 cm from the fulcrum. How far from the fulcrum did the students have to place the 56-g weight?

THINK: Which proportion fits the problem?

a. $\frac{64}{32} = \frac{x}{56}$

b. $\frac{64}{32} = \frac{56}{x}$

c. $\frac{64}{56} = \frac{x}{32}$

ANSWER: They had to place the 56-g weight ______ cm from the fulcrum.

---

5. A student placed an 18-g weight 60 cm from the fulcrum. She balanced it by placing a second weight 10 cm from the fulcrum. How many grams did the second weight weigh?

THINK: Which proportion fits the problem?

a. $\frac{18}{60} = \frac{x}{10}$

b. $\frac{60}{18} = \frac{x}{10}$

c. $\frac{60}{18} = \frac{10}{10}$

ANSWER: It weighed ______ g.

---

6. Roberto placed a 48-g weight 90 cm from the fulcrum. Sarah balanced the lever by placing a weight 15 cm from the fulcrum. How much did Sarah's weight weigh?

THINK: Which proportion fits the problem?

a. $\frac{48}{90} = \frac{15}{x}$

b. $\frac{90}{48} = \frac{x}{15}$

c. $\frac{48}{90} = \frac{x}{15}$

ANSWER: It weighed ______ g.

LESSON 13

Estimate

1. Ms. Golden earns $1000 each month after taxes. From this amount she must pay $275.12 for rent and $87.50 for transportation and utilities. How much does she have left each month to spend for other things?

THINK: The best estimate of the answer is
a. $700.
b. $600.
c. $500.

ANSWER: She has ______ left to spend each month.

---

2. One month Ms. Golden had $640 left after paying her bills. From that amount, she set aside $124 for food, $68 for recreation, and $183 for clothing. She deposited the balance of the money in her savings account. How much money did she deposit in the savings account?

THINK: The best estimate of the answer is
a. $270.
b. $130.
c. $180.

ANSWER: She deposited ______ in her account.

---

3. Ms. Golden wanted to save $800 for a vacation. She deposited $16 a week for each of 19 weeks into a special vacation club account. How much more money did she need for her vacation?

THINK: The best estimate of the answer is
a. $300
b. $500.
c. $250.

ANSWER: She needed ______ more.

	1	2	3	4	5	6	Number Right
THINK:							
ANSWER:							

4. When Ms. Golden decided to move, she knew she could pay no more than one week's salary for rent. After she received a raise, Ms. Golden took home $1173.56 a month. How much could she afford to pay for rent then?

THINK: The best estimate of the answer is
a. $250.
b. $200.
c. $300.

ANSWER: She could afford to pay ______.

---

5. Ms. Golden bought a car and paid back a $1350-loan in 12 equal monthly payments. She also spent $47 each month for gas and services for the car. What was the total amount of money that she spent on car expenses each month?

THINK: The best estimate of the answer is
a. $160.
b. $100.
c. $250.

ANSWER: She spent a total of ______ each month on car expenses.

---

6. At the end of the year, Ms. Golden had $1674 in her savings account. Her goal is to have $3500 saved by the end of next year. She put a $500 gift into her account. The rest she will add in equal parts each month. How much money will she have to save each month in order to reach her goal?

THINK: The best estimate of the answer is
a. $200.
b. $150.
c. $100.

ANSWER: She will have to save ______ each month.

LESSON 14

Choose the Correct Equation

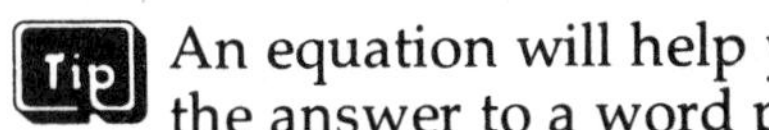
An equation will help you to find the answer to a word problem.

1. In October, 975 students entered a Walk-a-Thon. Only 24% of them did not complete the event. How many students did not finish the Walk-a-Thon?

THINK: Which equation fits the problem?

a. $975 \times 0.24 = \square$

b. $975 - 0.24 = \square$

c. $975 \div 0.24 = \square$

ANSWER: ______ students did not finish.

---

2. Of the 975 students in the Walk-a-Thon, 68% were more than ten years old. How many students were over ten years of age?

THINK: Which equation fits the problem?

a. $975 \div 0.68 = \square$

b. $975 \times 0.68 = \square$

c. $975 + 0.68 = \square$

ANSWER: ______ students were more than ten years old.

---

3. A local restaurant pledged a gift equal to 15% of the total amount of money raised by all the students in the Walk-a-Thon. The students raised a total of $4516. How much did the restaurant contribute?

THINK: Which equation fits the problem?

a. $\$4516 - \square = 0.15$

b. $\square \times 0.15 = 4516$

c. $4516 \times 0.15 = \square$

ANSWER: It contributed ______.

	1	2	3	4	5	6	Number Right
THINK:							
ANSWER:							

STUDENT WALK FOR HEALTH
JOIN THE WALK-A-THON *SIGN UP NOW!*
SUNDAY 8:00 A.M. OCTOBER 14
STARTING AT JUNIPER PARK LAKESIDE

4. Of the students in this year's Walk-a-Thon, 750 had been in previous Walk-a-Thons. Out of this number 32% had been in more than two previous Walk-a-Thons. How many students had participated in more than two previous Walk-a-Thons?

THINK: Which equation fits the problem?

a. $0.32 \div 750 = \square$

b. $750 \times \square = 0.32$

c. $750 \times 0.32 = \square$

ANSWER: ______ students had participated in more than two previous Walk-a-Thons.

---

5. Freemont Junior High School has an enrollment of 768 students. Of this number 25% entered the Walk-a-Thon. How many students entered the Walk-a-Thon?

THINK: Which equation fits the problem?

a. $768 \times 0.25 = \square$

b. $768 \times \square = 0.25$

c. $\square \times 0.25 = 768$

ANSWER: ______ students from Freemont entered the Walk-a-Thon.

---

6. There were 450 adult volunteers at the Walk-a-Thon. Of this number 60% of the adults were women. How many women served as volunteers for the Walk-a-Thon?

THINK: Which equation fits the problem?

a. $450 \div 0.6 = \square$

b. $450 \times 0.6 = \square$

c. $450 \times 6.0 = \square$

ANSWER: ______ women served as volunteers for the Walk-a-Thon.

LESSON 15

Read and Use a Circle Graph

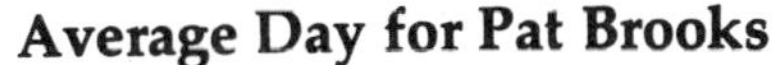

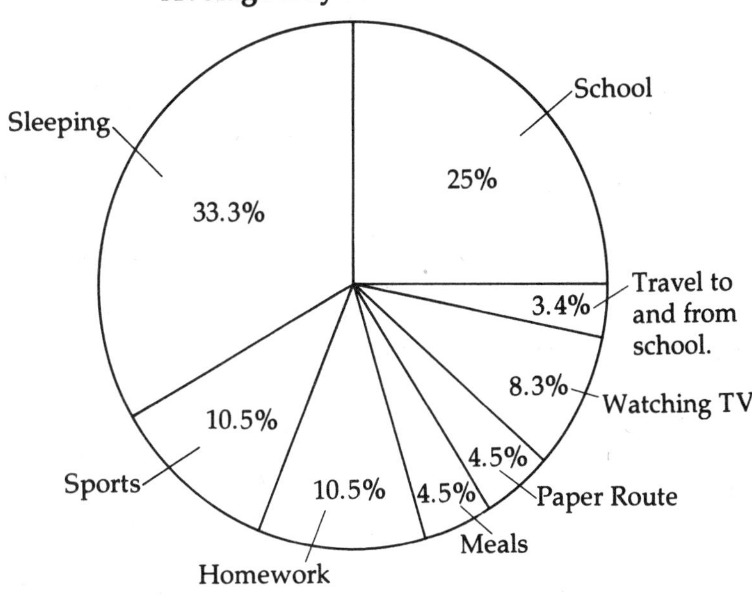

1. On which activity does Pat spend more than 25% of an average day?

THINK: You should look for
- a. the segment that represents 25%.
- b. the segment that represents more than 25%.
- c. the segment that represents less than 25%.

ANSWER: The activity in which he spends more than 25% of an average day is ______.

---

2. On how many different activities does Pat spend less than 5% of an average day?

THINK: You should look for
- a. the number of segments that represent less than 5%.
- b. the number of segments that represent 5%.
- c. the number of segments that represent more than 5%.

ANSWER: He spends less than 5% of an average day on each of ______ different activities.

	1	2	3	4	5	6	Number Right
THINK:							
ANSWER:							

3. What percentage of a day does Pat spend on school and homework combined?

THINK: You should look for
a. the segment labeled *School.*
b. the segments labeled *Homework* and *Sports.*
c. the segments labeled *School* and *Homework.*

ANSWER: He spends _____ of a day on school and homework combined.

---

4. What greater percentage of his day does Pat spend on sports than watching TV?

THINK: You should look for
a. the segments labeled *School* and *Watching TV.*
b. the segments labeled *Sports* and *Watching TV.*
c. the segments labeled *Sleeping* and *Watching TV.*

ANSWER: He spends _____ more of his day on sports than watching TV.

---

5. On weekends Pat watches twice the amount of TV than is shown on the graph. What percentage of a day does Pat spend watching TV on a weekend?

THINK: You should look for
a. the segment labeled *Watching TV.*
b. the segment that represents 10.5% of his day.
c. the segment labeled *Sleeping.*

ANSWER: He spends _____ of a day watching TV on a weekend.

---

6. After sleeping what percentage of Pat's time in an average day is left for other activities?

THINK: You should look for
a. the segment labeled *Sports.*
b. the segment labeled *Sleeping.*
c. the segment labeled *School.*

ANSWER: _____ of an average day is left for other activities.

LESSON 16

Solve Two-Step Problems

 To solve a problem with more than one step, you must solve one problem and use the answer to solve another problem.

1. The results of a survey taken of the 900 students at Baxter Junior High showed that 432 students were studying a foreign language. What percentage of students were not studying a foreign language?

THINK: To find the answer you should
a. add then subtract.
b. subtract then divide.
c. subtract then multiply.

ANSWER: ______ of the students were not studying a foreign language.

---

2. The survey also showed that 70% of the 900 students either took a bus or rode a bike to school. The rest of the students walked. How many of the students walked to school?

THINK: To find the answer you should
a. subtract then divide.
b. subtract then multiply.
c. add then multiply.

ANSWER: ______ students walked to school.

---

3. The survey indicated that 8% of the 900 students were in the band and another 18% were in the Pep Club. How many students were in either the band or the Pep Club?

THINK: To find the answer you should
a. subtract then add.
b. multiply then subtract.
c. add then multiply.

ANSWER: ______ students were in either the band or the Pep Club.

	1	2	3	4	5	6	Number Right
THINK:							
ANSWER:							

4. Another fact shown by the survey was that 35% of the 900 students planned on working next summer. Of this number 20% planned to work outdoors. How many students planned to work outdoors?

THINK: To find the answer you should
a. multiply then divide.
b. multiply then multiply.
c. divide then multiply.

ANSWER: ______ students planned to work outdoors.

---

5. It was also learned that woodworking classes were taken by 432 of the 900 students, while another 18% of the students took electrical shop classes. What percentage of the students took woodworking or electrical shop classes?

THINK: To find the answer you should
a. divide then add.
b. multiply then add.
c. subtract then add.

ANSWER: ______ of the students took woodworking or electrical shop classes.

---

6. The survey revealed that 20% of the 900 students lived more than a mile from school. Of those students 85% took a bus to school. How many students living more than a mile away took a bus to school?

THINK: To find the answer you should
a. divide then add.
b. subtract then divide.
c. multiply then multiply.

ANSWER: ______ students living more than a mile away took a bus to school.

LESSON 17

Read and Use a Map

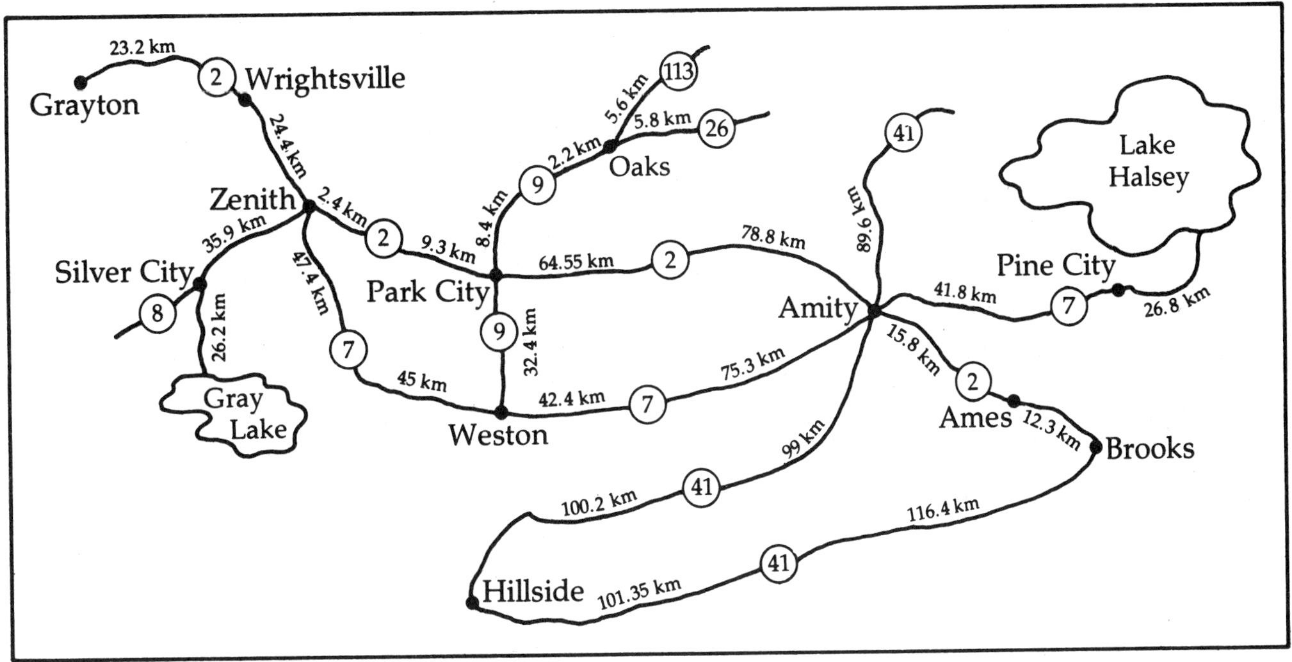

1. How many routes pass through Amity?

THINK: You should look for
a. any dot on the map.
b. the dot in the northwest corner of the map.
c. the dot that represents Amity.

ANSWER: ______ routes pass through Amity.

---

2. Which route connects Route 7 and Route 2?

THINK: You should look for
a. Route 7 and Route 8.
b. Route 2 and Route 41.
c. Route 7 and Route 2.

ANSWER: Route ______ connects Routes 7 and 2.

	1	2	3	4	5	6	Number Right
THINK:							
ANSWER:							

3. How many kilometers do you have to drive to get from Zenith to Brooks if you take Route 2?

THINK: You should look for

a. the distances between Brooks and all other cities.
b. the distance between Brooks and Zenith.
c. the distances between Zenith and all other cities.

ANSWER: You have to drive ______ km.

---

4. Once a month Mr. Ortiz drives from Amity to visit his children in Weston, and then goes on to Park City. He returns to Amity directly from Park City. How many kilometers does he drive when making a round trip?

THINK: You should look for

a. the distances along Route 2 and Route 7 only.
b. the distances between Amity and Weston, and Amity and Park City.
c. the distances between Amity and Weston, Weston and Park City, and Park City and Amity.

ANSWER: He drives ______ km when making a round trip.

---

5. Donny rode his bike from Wrightsville to Zenith at an average speed of 8 km/h. How long did it take him to make this trip?

THINK: You should look for

a. the distance between Wrightsville and Grayton.
b. the distance between Wrightsville and Zenith.
c. the name of the road between Wrightsville and Zenith.

ANSWER: It took him ______ hours.

---

6. Mr. Tobin drove the entire length of Route 7. How many kilometers did he drive all together?

THINK: You should look for

a. the names of the cities along Route 7.
b. all of the distances marked between points along Route 7.
c. the number of roads that branch off from Route 7.

ANSWER: He drove ______ km all together.

LESSON 18 Use a Proportion to Solve Problems

Tip Sometimes you can write a **proportion** to solve a word problem.

1. Mr. Kee designed a plan of a town park in a scale of 1 in. = 1.5 yd. He drew a line 75.5 in. long to represent the northern boundary of the playground area. How many yards did this boundary line actually represent?

THINK: Which proportion fits the problem?

a. $\frac{1}{1.5} = \frac{x}{75.5}$

b. $\frac{1}{1.5} = \frac{75.5}{x}$

c. $\frac{1.5}{1} = \frac{x}{7.5}$

ANSWER: The boundary line represented

_____ yd.

---

2. One architect suggested that a spray pool 6 yd wide should be included in the town park. How many inches wide was the pool in the plan?

THINK: Which proportion fits the problem?

a. $\frac{1}{1.5} = \frac{x}{6}$

b. $\frac{1.5}{1} = \frac{x}{6}$

c. $\frac{1}{1.5} = \frac{6}{x}$

ANSWER: The pool was

_____ in. wide in the plan.

---

3. Mr. Kee designed a fountain 10.5 yd in diameter. What was the diameter of the drawing of this fountain?

THINK: Which proportion fits the problem?

a. $\frac{1}{1.5} = \frac{10.5}{x}$

b. $\frac{1}{1.5} = \frac{x}{10.5}$

c. $\frac{1.5}{1} = \frac{x}{10.5}$

ANSWER: The drawing was

_____ in. in diameter.

	1	2	3	4	5	6	Number Right
THINK:							
ANSWER:							

4. A flowerbed was drawn on the plan using lines 9 in. on each side. How many yards on each side will the actual flowerbed be?

THINK: Which proportion fits the problem?

a. $\frac{1}{1.5} = \frac{x}{9}$

b. $\frac{1.5}{1} = \frac{9}{x}$

c. $\frac{1}{1.5} = \frac{9}{x}$

ANSWER: The actual flowerbed will be ______ yd on each side.

---

5. A brick path 33 yd long was planned for the area near the flowerbed. How many inches long did Mr. Kee draw the path?

THINK: Which proportion fits the problem?

a. $\frac{1}{1.5} = \frac{33}{x}$

b. $\frac{1.5}{1} = \frac{x}{33}$

c. $\frac{1}{1.5} = \frac{x}{33}$

ANSWER: He drew the path ______ in. long.

---

6. Mr. Kee drew a line 22.8 in. long to represent a bandshell for the park. How many yards long will the bandshell actually be built?

THINK: Which proportion fits the problem?

a. $\frac{1}{1.5} = \frac{22.8}{x}$

b. $\frac{1}{1.5} = \frac{x}{22.8}$

c. $\frac{1.5}{1} = \frac{22.8}{x}$

ANSWER: The bandshell will actually be built ______ yd long.

Estimate

1. A car traveling at a rate of 64 km/h needs a braking distance of 38.4 m on a wet road surface and 28.8 m on a dry road surface. How many more meters are needed to stop on a wet road surface than on a dry road surface?

THINK: The best estimate of the answer is
a. 30 m.
b. 20 m.
c. 10 m.

ANSWER: ______ more meters are needed to stop on a wet road surface.

---

2. Miss Woods traveled a distance of 116 km. The first time she braked, her car required 17.85 m to come to a full stop. It needed only 11.7 m the second time. How many meters of braking distance did the car require in all?

THINK: The best estimate of the answer is
a. 1 m.
b. 30 m.
c. 10 m.

ANSWER: The car required ______ m of braking distance in all.

---

3. Mr. Sullivan's heavy car requires 88.2 m of braking distance when he drives at 112 km/h. Mr. Watson's compact car requires 7.95 fewer meters of braking distance for the same speed. How many meters of braking distance does Mr Watson's car require?

THINK: The best estimate of the answer is
a. 100 m.
b. 90 m.
c. 80 m.

ANSWER: Mr. Watson's car requires ______ m of braking distance.

	1	2	3	4	5	6	Number Right
THINK:							
ANSWER:							

4. One car took 67.2 m to stop after the brakes were applied. The driver applied the brakes 7 times in all. How many meters of braking distance did the driver require all together?

THINK: The best estimate of the answer is
a. 470 m.
b. 100 m.
c. 80 m.

ANSWER: The driver required ______ m of braking distance all together.

---

5. Mrs. Bennet's car required 73.8 m of braking distance when traveling at a speed of 97.3 km/h. Mr. Bennet's van required 16.43 more meters of braking distance at the same speed. How many meters of braking distance did Mr. Bennet's van require?

THINK: The best estimate of the answer is
a. 50 m.
b. 90 m.
c. 120 m.

ANSWER: It required ______ m of braking distance.

---

6. A car needs a braking distance of 117.6 m for a speed of 112 km/h. The same car requires 79.2 fewer meters of braking distance for a speed of 64 km/h. How many meters of braking distance are required at this speed?

THINK: The best estimate of the answer is
a. 180 m.
b. 40 m.
c. 20 m.

ANSWER: ______ m of braking distance are required at this speed.

Solve Multi-Step Problems

 To solve a problem with more than one step, you must solve one problem and use the answer to solve another problem.

1. Last week Mr. Jenks earned a regular salary of $125.40 for working 5 days a week as a garage attendant. He also divided $18.75 a day in tips with 3 other attendants. What was his total daily take-home pay?

THINK: The first thing you should do is
a. find his regular daily salary.
b. find his weekly income in tips.
c. find the average amount of each tip.

ANSWER: His total daily take-home pay was ______.

---

2. Keller's Garage charges $1.25 for the first hour of parking and $0.75 for each additional hour. Mr. Isley parks his car in the garage for 8 hours a day, 5 days a week. How much money does he save by paying a weekly parking rate of $30.00?

THINK: The first thing you should do is
a. find the monthly parking rate for Keller's Garage.
b. find the amount Mr. Isley would pay under the daily plan.
c. find the amount Mr. Isley pays each year.

ANSWER: He saves ______.

---

3. Ms. Long parked her car in a garage that charged $1.20 for the first hour and $0.90 for each additional hour. When she returned from shopping, she gave the attendant $10.00. He gave her $3.40 change. For how many hours did she park her car?

THINK: After you find the total amount she paid for parking you should
a. subtract the amount she paid for the first hour.
b. find the cost for each hour.
c. find the daily parking rate.

ANSWER: She parked her car for ______ hours.

	1	2	3	4	5	6	
THINK:							Number Right
ANSWER:							

4. Mr. Young parked his car in a lot that charged $1.75 for the first hour and $0.85 for each additional hour. He left his car in the lot for 8 hours. How much change did he receive from a ten-dollar bill?

THINK: The first thing you should do is
a. find the amount of change he received.
b. find the cost of parking for 8 hours.
c. find the rate for each hour.

ANSWER: He received ______ change.

---

5. Smith's Parking Lot charges $0.75 for the first 0.5 of an hour, $0.60 for the second 0.5 of an hour, and $0.40 for each additional hour or part of an hour. Ernie paid $2.95 to park his car. For how long was his car parked in the lot?

THINK: The first thing you should do is
a. find the total cost for parking.
b. find the amount of change he received from a five-dollar bill.
c. find the cost for the first hour.

ANSWER: His car was parked in the lot for ______ hours.

---

6. The rates at a parking lot in Center City are $0.85 for the first 0.5 of an hour, $0.60 for the second 0.5 of an hour, and $0.35 for each additional hour or part of an hour. Ms. Adams parked her car for 5 hours. How much did she pay to park her car?

THINK: After you find the cost for the first hour you should
a. find the additional cost for 4 hours.
b. find the average hourly rate.
c. find the cost for 3 hours.

ANSWER: She paid ______ to park her car.

LESSON

21 Review

This lesson reviews the **TIPS** you have learned in this book. Use each **TIP** to help you solve these problems. Circle the letter for your answer in the THINK section. Write your answer in the ANSWER section.

A. An equation will help you to find the answer to a word problem.

1. The largest cave system in the U.S.A is 181.4 miles long. It is 2.5 times longer than the longest cave in Switzerland. How long is the cave in Switzerland?

THINK: Which equation fits the problem?
a. $181.4 \times 2.5 = \square$
b. $181.4 \div 2.5 = \square$
c. $2.5 \div 181.4 = \square$

ANSWER: The cave in Switzerland is ______ miles long.

B. To solve a problem with more than one step, you must solve one problem and use the answer to solve another problem.

2. Scott made $201 every 2 weeks in the summer. His hourly rate was $3.35. On the average, how many hours did he work each week?

THINK: To find the answer you should
a. divide then divide again.
b. divide then multiply.
c. multiply then divide.

ANSWER: Scott works ______ hours each week.

Tip

C. Sometimes you must read two sets of information on a graph to answer a word problem.

3. What was the difference between the highest score in the second semester and the lowest score in the first semester?

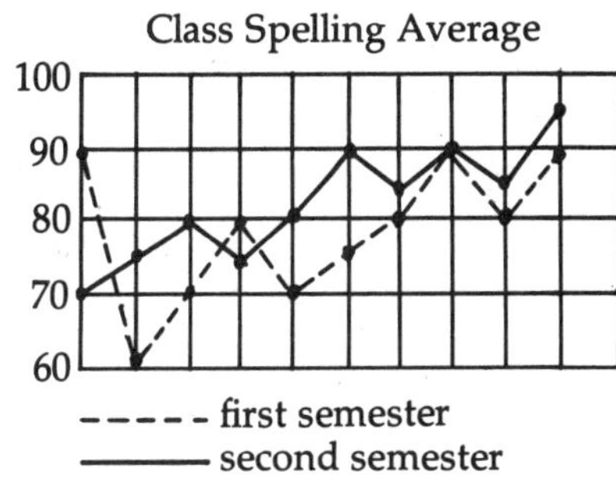

THINK: You should look for
a. the highest and lowest points on the line representing the first semester.
b. the highest and lowest points on the line representing the second semester.
c. the highest point on the line representing the second semester and the lowest point on the line representing the first semester.

ANSWER: The difference was ______ points.

D. Sometimes you can write a <u>proportion</u> to solve a word problem.

4. On a map 1 inch = 400 miles. The Nile River is 16.7 inches long on the map. What is the actual length of the Nile?

THINK: Which proportion fits the problem?

a. $\frac{1}{400} = \frac{16.7}{x}$ b. $\frac{1}{400} = \frac{x}{16.7}$ c. $\frac{16.7}{400} = \frac{x}{1}$

ANSWER: The actual length of the Nile is ______ miles.

Post-Test

Score ____

Choose the correct answers. Mark your answers in the answer rows below.

1. A cement block weighs 40 lb. How many 40-lb cement blocks are there in 2000 lb? Choose the correct equation.

   A $2000 \times \square = 40$
   B $40 \times \square = 2000$
   C $40 \div \square = 2000$
   D $\square = 40 \times 2000$
   E none of these

2. Mr. Finn bought 850 cement blocks for his summer cabin. They cost $612.50. What was the cost of each block?

   A $0.75
   B $1.33
   C $237.50
   D $0.85
   E none of these

3. Mr. Alonzo bought 17 dozen eggs at $1.15 a dozen. How much change did he get back from his $20 bill? To solve this problem you should

   A add then subtract.
   B subtract then multiply.
   C divide then multiply.
   D multiply then subtract.
   E none of these

4. Mr. Finn paid $25 an hour for a bulldozer to clear a lot. It took 7 hours. He paid $28 an hour for a backhoe to dig the foundation. It took 6 hours. How much did it cost in all?

   A $293
   B $343
   C $168
   D $175
   E none of these

5. The mason laid 285 blocks on Monday and 211 blocks on Tuesday. Out of 850 blocks, about how many are left?

   A 350 blocks
   B 300 blocks
   C 200 blocks
   D 450 blocks
   E none of these

6. Tickets for the ballgame are $6.40 for children and $9.70 for adults. Ms. Foy paid $45.00 for tickets for her husband, her children, and herself. How many children's tickets did she buy?

   A 3 tickets
   B 4 tickets
   C 5 tickets
   D 6 tickets
   E none of these

ANSWER ROWS:
1. Ⓐ Ⓑ Ⓒ Ⓓ Ⓔ 2. Ⓐ Ⓑ Ⓒ Ⓓ Ⓔ 3. Ⓐ Ⓑ Ⓒ Ⓓ Ⓔ
4. Ⓐ Ⓑ Ⓒ Ⓓ Ⓔ 5. Ⓐ Ⓑ Ⓒ Ⓓ Ⓔ 6. Ⓐ Ⓑ Ⓒ Ⓓ Ⓔ

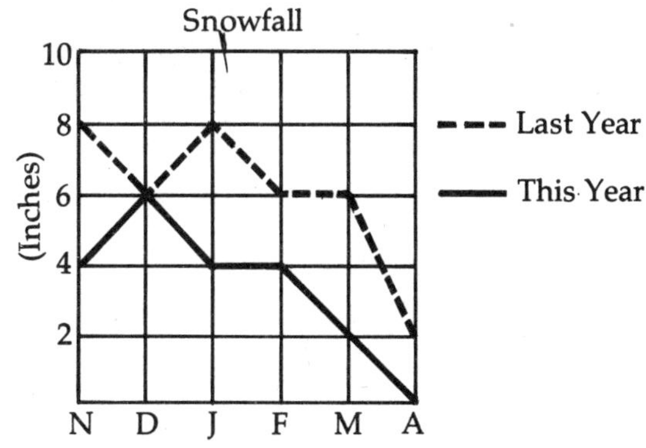

7. How much more snow fell last year in April than this year in April?

A 0 inches
B 2 inches
C 4 inches
D 6 inches
E none of these

8. A mason lays 250 blocks in 7 hours. How long will it take him to lay 850 blocks? Choose the correct proportion.

A $\frac{250}{7} = \frac{m}{850}$
B $\frac{250}{850} = \frac{m}{7}$
C $\frac{250}{7} = \frac{850}{m}$
D $\frac{250}{1} = \frac{850}{m}$
E none of these

9. On a map Lesford is 2.5 cm from Lakeland. The scale of the map is 1 cm = 10.5 km. How far is Lesford from Lakeland?

A 8 km
B 4.2 km
C 13 km
D 26.25 km
E none of these

10. Mrs. Sacks bought 12.6 lb of meat for \$23.70. What was the cost per lb? The best estimate of the answer is

A \$1.50
B \$2.00
C \$3.50
D \$5.00
E none of these

11. Ms. Diaz rented a car for 7¢ a mile. She drove 78.5 mi, 82.3 mi, and 91.9 mi. How much did she pay for the car? The best estimate of the answer is

A \$10
B \$15
C \$25
D \$50
E none of these

12. How much change should Al get from \$10.00 if he buys 4.36 lb of chicken at \$1.36 per lb?

A \$5.93
B \$4.07
C \$5.92
D \$4.08
E none of these

ANSWER ROWS: 7. Ⓐ Ⓑ Ⓒ Ⓓ Ⓔ 8. Ⓐ Ⓑ Ⓒ Ⓓ Ⓔ 9. Ⓐ Ⓑ Ⓒ Ⓓ Ⓔ
10. Ⓐ Ⓑ Ⓒ Ⓓ Ⓔ 11. Ⓐ Ⓑ Ⓒ Ⓓ Ⓔ 12. Ⓐ Ⓑ Ⓒ Ⓓ Ⓔ

Answer Key

		1	2	3	4	5	6
1	THINK	b	a	b	a	b	b
	ANSWER	5767	55,176	510	1062	9	126,744
2	THINK	c	a	a	b	c	c
	ANSWER	53.44	8.55	110.83	110.83	0.45	765.625
3	THINK	b	c	c	a	b	b
	ANSWER	9000	600	10	30	3,000,000	.02
4	THINK	a	c	a	b	b	c
	ANSWER	15	179	175	60	12	90
5	THINK	c	c	a	a	a	b
	ANSWER	$5\frac{7}{12}$	$8\frac{1}{2}$	7	$\frac{1}{6}$	$5\frac{1}{6}$	10
6	THINK	c	a	b	c	b	c
	ANSWER	14	$58\frac{1}{2}$	$3\frac{1}{2}$	$\frac{5}{8}$	$60\frac{7}{12}$	$3\frac{1}{4}$
7	THINK	c	a	b	a	c	c
	ANSWER	$272\frac{1}{4}$	66	33	$8\frac{1}{4}$	$21\frac{1}{4}$	$\frac{3}{4}$
8	THINK	c	b	a	a	c	a
	ANSWER	3.19	161.9	701	40.475	12.2	36.15
9	THINK	a	b	c	a	a	b
	ANSWER	1976	294.38	Everest	2.5	Wendel's	6727.825
10	THINK	b	a	c	b	a	a
	ANSWER	Marsh City	2.3	0.7	1.9	2.5	18.1

		1	2	3	4	5	6
11	THINK	b	b	b	a	a	b
	ANSWER	$90	$112	$156.25	$21.65	$20	$63.78
12	THINK	c	a	a	b	a	c
	ANSWER	22	48	48	28	3	8
13	THINK	b	a	b	c	a	c
	ANSWER	$637.38	$265	$496	$293.39	$159.50	$110.50
14	THINK	a	b	c	c	a	b
	ANSWER	234	663	$677.40	240	192	270
15	THINK	b	a	c	b	a	b
	ANSWER	sleeping	3	35.5%	2.2%	16.6%	66.7%
16	THINK	b	b	c	b	a	c
	ANSWER	52%	270	234	63	66%	153
17	THINK	c	c	b	c	b	b
	ANSWER	3	9	183.15	293.45	3.05	278.7
18	THINK	b	a	b	c	c	a
	ANSWER	113.25	4	7	13.5	22	34.2
19	THINK	c	b	c	a	b	b
	ANSWER	9.6	29.55	80.25	470.4	90.23	38.4
20	THINK	a	b	a	b	c	a
	ANSWER	$29.76	$2.50	7	$2.30	5	$2.85
21	THINK	b	a	c	a		
	ANSWER	72.56	30	35	6680		

Skills Sharpener
INDIA ASOKA

Post Test
1. B 2. E 3. D 4. B 5. A 6. B 7. B 8. C 9. D 10. B 11. C 12. B

Skills Sharpener Enrichment

Solve each problem. Write the letter for each problem on the line over its answer to complete:

The earliest preserved samples of present number symbols are found on stone columns erected in 250 B.C. by King ______ .

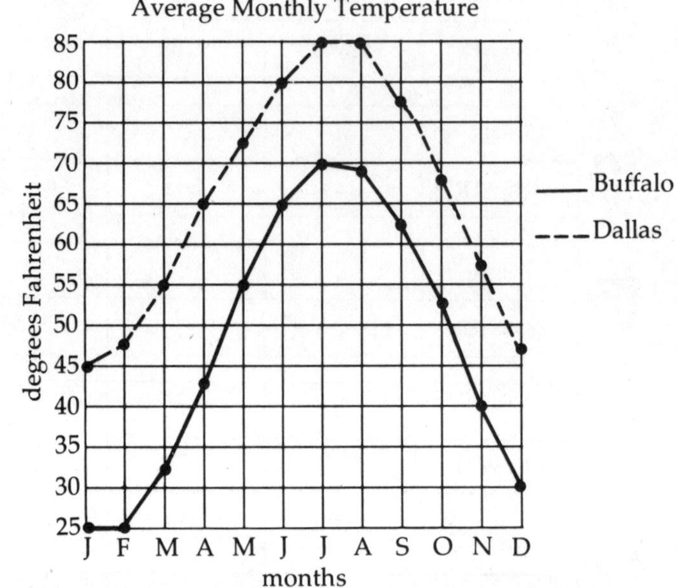

K How much higher was the average monthly temperature in Dallas than in Buffalo in January? What equation would you use to solve this problem?

S In January the average temperature in the Millers' house in Buffalo was 45° warmer than the average outdoor temperature. What equation would you use to find the average temperature in the Millers' house in January?

O When the Fahrenheit temperature drops 9°, the Celsius temperature drops 5°. The average Fahrenheit temperature in Dallas dropped 18° from October to December. How many degrees Celsius did the temperature drop?

D How much higher is the average temperature for June in Dallas than in Buffalo?

I The Millers estimated that the furnace ran 60% of the days last year in their Buffalo home. How many days did the furnace run?

A The Browns estimated that the furnace in their Dallas home ran 35% of the days last year and that their air conditioner ran 20% of the days. How many days did either the furnace or the air conditioner run?

N What is the difference between the highest monthly temperature in Dallas and the lowest monthly temperature in Buffalo?

ANSWER:

___	___	___	___	___		___	___	___	___	___
219	60° F	15° F	219	201		201	45+25 = □	10° C	45−25 = □	201

PRACTICING MATH APPLICATIONS

by Carolyn Aho and Alexis Aquino-Mackles

Contents

How to Use This Book

This book will help you learn how to solve some problems. Follow these steps for Practicing Math Applications:

1. Turn to the lesson you are going to do.
2. Find the PRACTICE part of the lesson. Study the first exercise; it has been worked out for you.
3. Do the rest of the exercises on the page. Work carefully.
4. Turn the page to the APPLY part of the lesson. Do all the exercises on the page.
5. Follow your teacher's directions for checking your answers.
6. Count the number of correct answers for each part of the lesson.
7. Turn to the Progress Plotter on page 2. Shade it in to show how many items you got right in each part of the lesson.
8. If you got any items wrong, go back and try them again. Make sure you know how to do them.

A **TIP** looks like this: Tip

In some lessons, you will find special notes that you will want to remember whenever you solve problems. These special notes are called **TIPS.** Pay attention to the **TIPS.** They will be reviewed in the last lesson of the book and on the back cover.

Before you start, think of what you know that will help you solve problems:

- You know how to add, to subtract, to multiply, and to divide whole numbers, mixed numbers, fractions, and decimals.
- You know how to write ratios.
- You probably know how to solve problems with proportions.

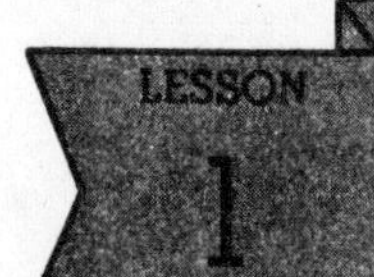

LESSON 1 Knowing Place Value

PRACTICE

Billions			Millions			Thousands			Ones		
2	8	3	9	3	1	2	4	6	1	7	5

What is the digit in the

1. thousands place? ________
2. millions place? ________
3. ten millions place? ________
4. ten billions place? ________
5. hundred millions place? ________
6. hundred billions place? ________

In the number in the chart, what is the value of the

7. 9? ________
8. 6? ________
9. 8? ________
10. 4? ________
11. 5? ________
12. 7? ________

Write the number that is 100,000 more.

13. 476,083 ________
14. 70,654 ________
15. 982,436 ________

Write the number that is 10,000,000 more.

16. 13,278,406 ________
17. 456,681 ________
18. 99,001,659 ________

Fill in the missing numbers in each pattern.

19. 7,319,084
    7,329,084
    ____
    7,349,084
    ____

20. 936,470
    936,370
    ____
    ____
    936,070

21. 29,017,852
    ____
    ____
    29,020,852
    ____

Round each number.

		nearest thousand	nearest million	nearest billion
22.	8,635,482,731			
23.	42,919,756,380			

APPLY

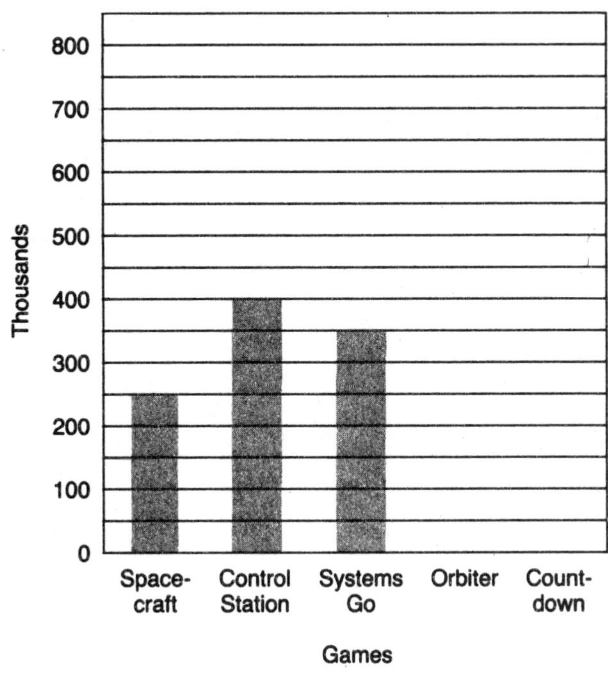

Use the bar graph to find the number of games produced.

How many

1. Space Craft games? ____________
2. Control Station games? ____________
3. Systems Go games? ____________

Draw bars to show the number produced.

4. Orbiter: three times as many as Space Craft. How many? ____________
5. Count Down: one hundred fifty thousand less than Orbiter. How many? ____________

Use the line graph to find the sales for each month.

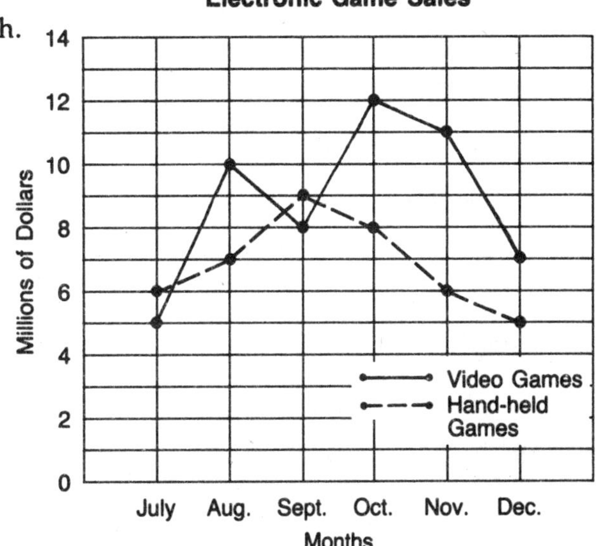

How much for hand-held games

6. in July? ____________
7. in September? ____________
8. in November? ____________

How much for video games

9. in August? ____________
10. in October? ____________
11. in December? ____________
12. Compare the highest monthly sales for each type of game. What is the difference in the amount of sales for each?

____

LESSON 2 Adding and Subtracting

PRACTICE

Find the sums and differences.

1.	2.	3.	4.	5.
5498	7002	65,371	$5123	$98.61
+7316	+ 498	−26,084	− 679	− 4.50
12,814				

6.	7.	8.	9.	10.
$72	$309	674,324	$55.79	$394.98
34	52	5,632	1.42	475.31
80	840	27,081	8.07	9.83
+ 6	+ 117	+460,050	+ 25.90	+ 621.06

11. 16,302 + 2107 + 48,199 = ______ **12.** $375.21 + $514 + $1077.16 = ______

13. 5891 + 30,056 + 43,279 = ______ **14.** 88,560 + 358 + 9203 = ______

15.	16.	17.	18.	19.
9020	3668	80,025	$1134	$9206
−7504	− 79	− 347	− 95	− 1348

20.	21.	22.	23.	24.
71,407	$510.36	$490.82	$500.02	$9607.04
− 1,368	− 214.57	− 53.07	− 289.13	− 717.05

25. 26,302 − 17,984 = ______ **26.** 43,008 − 8,212 = ______

27. $18,343.27 − $2754.88 = ______ **28.** $60,845.97 − $14,377.18 = ______

Round the answers to these problems to the nearest thousand.

29. Problem 15 ______ **30.** Problem 16 ______ **31.** Problem 17 ______ **32.** Problem 18 ______

APPLY

1. The R and J Boat Dealers deposited $48,936 in checks and $4371 in cash. What was their total deposit?

   ____

2. The bank lent the *Yachting News* $65,450 for remodeling and a word processor. The word processor cost $13,460. How much did the *Yachting News* spend for remodeling?

   ____

3. One day a total of $274,918 was deposited by three companies. Boat Builders, Inc. deposited $74,386 and Linda's Colorful Sail Company deposited $13,495. How much was the third deposit from Ms. Maria Boat Decorating Company?

   ____

4. Susan and Mike are planning to buy a water sports store for $87,300. They have $19,560 and need a loan for the rest. How much must they borrow from the bank?

   ____

Fill in each missing balance on the check record.

	Check Number	Date	Description of Transaction	Payment Debit	Deposit Credit	Balance
						1501.00
5.	131	1/5	Joseph and Company	126.25		1374.75
6.	132	1/5	Water Department	18.50		
7.					50.00	
8.	133	1/5	Post Office	10.25		
9.					100.00	
10.	134	1/6	Rosie's Galley	145.75		
11.	135	1/10	J & C Rigging	210.25		
12.					50.00	
13.	136	1/12	Steven's Marine Dealers	350.50		

LESSON 3

Multiplying and Dividing

PRACTICE

Find the products and quotients.

1. 936 × 28
7488
1872
26,208

2. 39 × 42

3. 501 × 74

4. 68 × 59

5. 7011 × 80

6. 105 × 86

7. 4372 × 7

8. 627 × 103

9. 5422 × 31

10. 10,243 × 215

11. 19)1439

12. 40)2491

13. 22)4158

14. [illegible])3730

15. 60)73,990

16. 64)19,328

17. 300)11,100

18. 325)22,432

Circle the approximate answer that is closest to the correct answer.
Do not work the problem . . . estimate!

19. 412 × 48 a. 20,000 b. 2000 c. 16,000 d. 1800

20. 42,297 ÷ 613 a. 7000 b. 600 c. 70 d. 700

APPLY

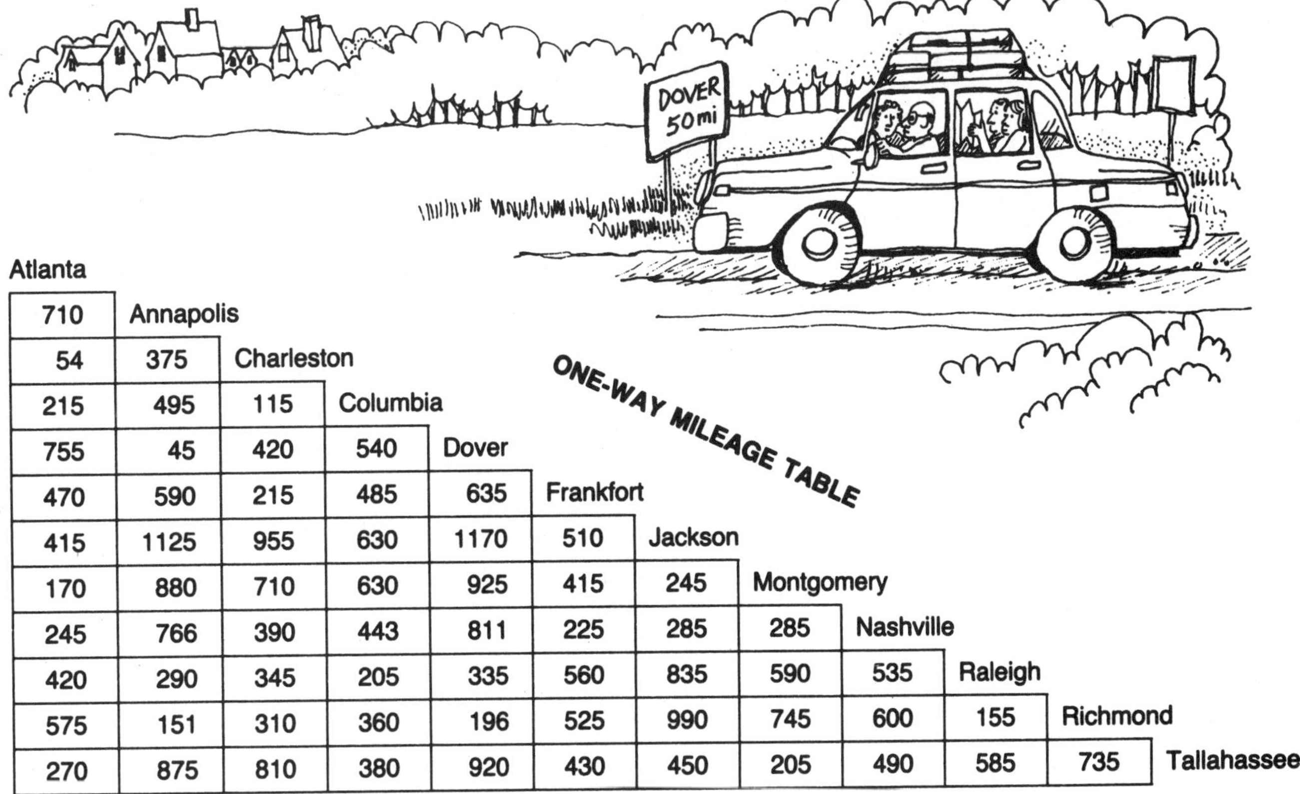

ONE-WAY MILEAGE TABLE

	Atlanta	Annapolis	Charleston	Columbia	Dover	Frankfort	Jackson	Montgomery	Nashville	Raleigh	Richmond
Annapolis	710										
Charleston	54	375									
Columbia	215	495	115								
Dover	755	45	420	540							
Frankfort	470	590	215	485	635						
Jackson	415	1125	955	630	1170	510					
Montgomery	170	880	710	630	925	415	245				
Nashville	245	766	390	443	811	225	285	285			
Raleigh	420	290	345	205	335	560	835	590	535		
Richmond	575	151	310	360	196	525	990	745	600	155	
Tallahassee	270	875	810	380	920	430	450	205	490	585	735

The Diner family toured the capitals of the southeast states. They drove 8 hours each day at an average speed of 50 mph.

Use the mileage table above to complete this chart. Round all minutes to the nearest hour.

		One-Way Distance	Round-Trip Distance	Total Time (days and hours)
1.	Raleigh to Jackson			
2.	Montgomery to Annapolis			
3.	Frankfort to Atlanta			
4.	Tallahassee to Dover			
5.	Dover to Atlanta			
6.	Nashville to Charleston			
7.	Richmond to Nashville			
8.	Columbia to Annapolis			

LESSON 4

Adding/Subtracting Mixed Numbers

PRACTICE

Find each sum or difference. Write it in lowest terms.

1. $\begin{array}{r} 5\frac{3}{6} \\ +6\frac{7}{8} \\ \hline \end{array}$ $= 5\frac{12}{24}$, $= 6\frac{21}{24}$, $11\frac{33}{24} = 12\frac{3}{8}$

2. $\begin{array}{r} 9\frac{1}{12} \\ -3\frac{5}{12} \\ \hline \end{array}$

3. $\begin{array}{r} \frac{1}{9} \\ +\frac{5}{6} \\ \hline \end{array}$

4. $\begin{array}{r} 10\frac{5}{16} \\ -\ 2\frac{11}{16} \\ \hline \end{array}$

5. $\begin{array}{r} \frac{7}{8} \\ -\frac{1}{2} \\ \hline \end{array}$

6. $\begin{array}{r} 35\frac{1}{6} \\ -\ 2\frac{5}{9} \\ \hline \end{array}$

7. $\begin{array}{r} 42\frac{7}{12} \\ +13\frac{11}{12} \\ \hline \end{array}$

8. $\begin{array}{r} 608\frac{1}{2} \\ +\ 74\frac{3}{10} \\ \hline \end{array}$

9. $\frac{3}{5} - \frac{4}{15} =$ ________

10. $5\frac{1}{4} + 6\frac{3}{4} =$ ________

11. $\frac{3}{4} + \frac{1}{3} + \frac{1}{12} =$ ________

12. $4\frac{3}{8} - \frac{5}{6} =$ ________

13. $49\frac{5}{16} - 11\frac{9}{16} =$ ________

14. $\frac{2}{3} + \frac{7}{9} + \frac{5}{6} =$ ________

15. $\begin{array}{r} 9\frac{1}{8} \\ 7\frac{5}{8} \\ +80\frac{7}{8} \\ \hline \end{array}$

16. $\begin{array}{r} 6\frac{11}{12} \\ 7\frac{7}{12} \\ +9 \\ \hline \end{array}$

17. $\begin{array}{r} 35\frac{5}{6} \\ 8\frac{1}{2} \\ +74\frac{3}{4} \\ \hline \end{array}$

18. $\begin{array}{r} 4\frac{3}{5} \\ 56 \\ +\ 3\frac{1}{3} \\ \hline \end{array}$

19. $\begin{array}{r} 84\frac{9}{10} \\ +19\frac{1}{5} \\ \hline \end{array}$

20. $\begin{array}{r} 27\frac{7}{16} \\ -12\frac{5}{8} \\ \hline \end{array}$

21. $\begin{array}{r} 35\frac{1}{2} \\ +28\frac{2}{5} \\ \hline \end{array}$

22. $\begin{array}{r} 90\frac{1}{18} \\ -84\frac{11}{12} \\ \hline \end{array}$

Who am I?

23. I am $17\frac{3}{8}$ less than $50\frac{1}{16}$.

I am ______.

24. I am $24\frac{3}{15}$ greater than $9\frac{4}{5}$.

I am ______.

APPLY

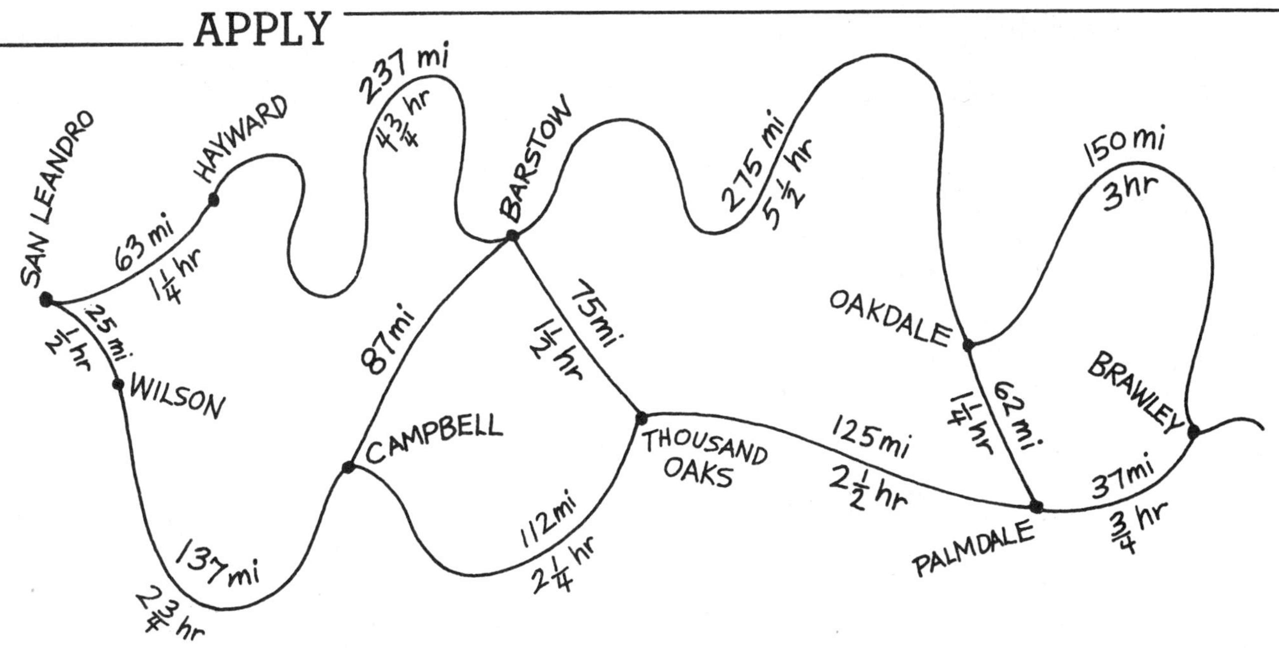

Use the map to answer these questions.

1. Frank and Millie drove from Barstow to Brawley by way of Thousand Oaks. How much time did their trip take? __________

2. Which of these two routes takes less time? __________

Melodie's route	San Leandro — Hayward — Barstow
Bea's route	San Leandro — Wilson — Campbell — Barstow

How much less time? __________

3. Helen and Sid drove from Brawley to Campbell by way of Palmdale and Thousand Oaks. How many miles did they drive in all? __________

   How much time did the trip take? __________

4. Warren left Oakdale at 7 A.M., worked one hour in Barstow and then drove to Hayward. At what time did Cheryl have to leave San Leandro in order to arrive in Haywood at the same time as Warren did? __________

5. Which of these two routes takes more time? __________
   How much more time? __________

Josh and Marian's Route	Brawley — Oakdale — Barstow
Scott and Zachary's Route	Brawley — Palmdale — Thousand Oaks — Barstow

LESSON 5

Multiplying/Dividing Mixed Numbers

PRACTICE

Find each product. Write it in lowest terms.

1. $\frac{7}{8} \times \frac{1}{2} =$ $\frac{7}{16}$ 2. $\frac{13}{20} \times 40 =$ ______ 3. $2\frac{3}{4} \times 6 =$ ______

4. $15 \times \frac{9}{20} =$ ______ 5. $\frac{8}{9} \times \frac{1}{6} =$ ______ 6. $2\frac{1}{2} \times 5\frac{3}{5} =$ ______

7. $6\frac{1}{4} \times 7\frac{1}{5} =$ ______ 8. $10\frac{5}{6} \times 3\frac{1}{3} =$ ______ 9. $1\frac{2}{3} \times 3\frac{3}{8} =$ ______

Find each quotient. Write it in lowest terms.

10. $5 \div \frac{1}{5} =$ ______ 11. $\frac{3}{5} \div \frac{2}{3} =$ ______ 12. $16 \div 2\frac{1}{2} =$ ______

13. $8\frac{5}{8} \div 3 =$ ______ 14. $\frac{7}{8} \div \frac{3}{4} =$ ______ 15. $3\frac{4}{15} \div 1\frac{5}{9} =$ ______

16. $4\frac{1}{2} \div 1\frac{1}{2} =$ ______ 17. $4\frac{4}{9} \div 4\frac{4}{5} =$ ______ 18. $9\frac{3}{4} \div 2\frac{7}{16} =$ ______

19. $9\frac{7}{14} \div \frac{4}{5} =$ ______ 20. $8\frac{3}{4} \div 2\frac{1}{3} =$ ______ 21. $7\frac{1}{5} \div 4 =$ ______

Find the prime factorization of each number.

22.

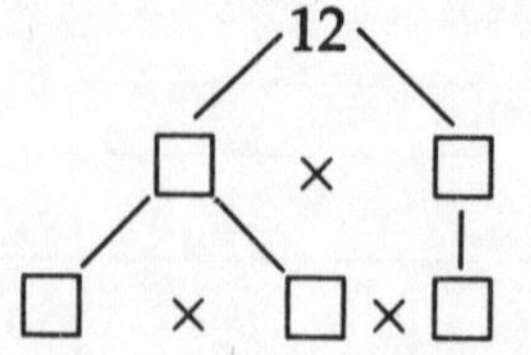

12 = ______

23.

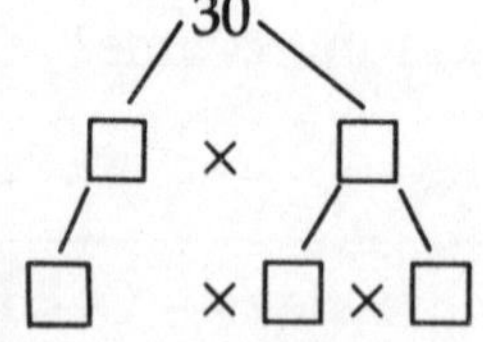

30 = ______

24.

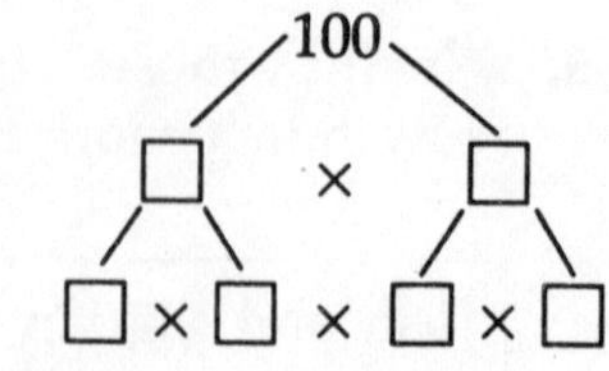

100 = ______

APPLY

A total of 50 people were at the class party.

Solve these problems.

1. Arlene's cake recipe calls for $15\frac{3}{4}$ cups of flour and $10\frac{1}{2}$ cups of sugar. It makes enough to serve 100 people. How much flour and sugar will she need for a cake that serves 50?

 ____

2. June and Pat made enough punch so that each person could have $2\frac{1}{2}$ cups. How much punch did they make in all?

 ____

3. Mr. Gregorio donated the sandwich meat for the party. He sent one quarter pound per person. How much meat did he donate in all?

 ____

4. The Mateo Product Company donated $6\frac{1}{2}$ lb of oranges, $7\frac{1}{2}$ lb of bananas, and $4\frac{3}{4}$ lb of apples for fruit salad. About how much would each person at the party receive, if each one received the same amount?

 ____

5. Frances, Gilbert, and Frank each worked $2\frac{3}{4}$ hours at the party. How much time did they work all together?

 ____

6. Beverly and Bill cut two-thirds of a 10-lb piece of cheese. How many pounds of cheese did they cut?

 ____

7. Joe painted for $2\frac{1}{2}$ hours each day for five days. Roberto painted for $3\frac{1}{4}$ hours less than Joe. How many hours did they both paint altogether?

 ____

8. Valerie and Steven waxed the floors. They bought a gallon of wax on sale for $\frac{1}{3}$ off the regular price of $12.75. How much change did they get back from $20?

 ____

LESSON 6

Writing Decimals

PRACTICE

Write the decimal for each.

1. six and two tenths 6.2
2. six and two hundredths ______
3. six and two thousandths ______
4. six and two ten thousandths ______
5. five hundred seventy-two thousandths ______
6. nine hundred six and nine hundred six thousandths ______
7. thirty and seven hundred ninety-one ten thousandths ______
8. one million and one hundredth ______

Change these decimals to fractions.
Use denominators of 10, 100 or 1000.

9. 0.4 = ______ 10. 0.04 = ______ 11. 0.004 = ______ 12. 0.35 = ______

13. 0.135 = ______ 14. 1.8 = ______ 15. 1.89 = ______ 16. 1.876 = ______

17. 5.29 = ______ 18. 9.076 = ______ 19. 0.03 = ______ 20. 6.38 = ______

Round each decimal.

		Nearest Whole Number	Nearest Tenth	Nearest Hundredth	Nearest Thousandth
21.	6.1439				
22.	8.7362				
23.	0.5179				

Build a number. Write the decimal point in the correct place.

24. Put 9 in the ones place
 0 in the tenths place
 5 in the tens place
 7 in the hundredths place
 1 in the hundreds place

______

25. Put 4 in the tenths place
 3 in the ones place
 2 in the thousandths place
 3 in the ten thousandths place
 2 in the hundredths place
 8 in the hundreds place
 6 in the tens place

______

APPLY

Write the place for each contestant.

1.

LONG JUMP		
Place	Name	Longest Jump
_____	Matt	2.69 m
_____	Carol	2.79 m
_____	Jack	2.51 m
_____	Susan	2.6 m

Look at the chart in exercise 1.

2. Round these jumps to the nearest tenth.

1st place _____________

2nd place _____________

3.

HIGH JUMP		
Place	Name	Highest Jump
_____	Paul	1.31 m
_____	Pat	1.28 m
_____	Gigi	1.29 m
_____	Annette	1.35 m

Look at the chart in exercise 3.

4. Round these jumps to the nearest tenth.

1st place _____________

2nd place _____________

Write the place for each contestant.

5.

60-METER DASH		
Place	Name	Fastest Time (sec)
_____	Hiro	4:51
_____	Gary	4:39
_____	Simone	4:33
_____	Nancy	4:4

Look at the chart for exercise 5.

6. What is the difference in seconds between the times of the 1st- and 3rd-place contestants?

____

7.

400-METER RELAY		
Place	School Name	Fastest Time (min)
_____	Princeton Ave.	1:14
_____	Summerville	1:19
_____	Stage	1:37
_____	Lawrence	1:25

Look at the chart for exercise 7.

8. How many more seconds did the 4th-place contestant take than the 1st-place contestant?

____

LESSON 7

Adding and Subtracting Decimals

PRACTICE

Find the sums.

1. 5.763 + 1.249 = 7.012

2. 8.05 + 7.9641

3. \$423.07 + 94.96

4. 781.783 + 450.2

5. \$36.50 + 7.53 + 0.93 + 1.26

6. \$0.32 + 0.88 + 0.25 + 0.17

7. 4.65 + 8.096 + 60.001 + 16.8

8. \$9.25 + 0.12 + 0.35 + 4.98

9. 0.7 + 0.43 + 5.62 = ________

10. 1.9 + 0.2 + 0.401 + 8.6 = ________

11. 8.73 + 9.5 + 2.7 = ________

12. 0.14 + 0.23 + 0.65 = ________

Find the differences.

13. 7.8898 − 6.0769

14. 3.25 − 1.621

15. 24.003 − 1.65

16. 0.47 − 0.079

17. \$199.46 − 2.79

18. \$2507.21 − 1376.78

19. 0.6 − 0.455

20. 5.3 − 4.8983

Round the answers to the following problems to the nearest whole number.

21. Problem 5 ________

22. Problem 6 ________

23. Problem 7 ________

24. Problem 8 ________

APPLY

FROM	TO	5% TAX
$.01	$.10	$.00
.11	.27	.01
.28	.47	.02
.48	.67	.03
.68	.87	.04
.88	.99	.05

AM'T. SALE	5% TAX
$ 1.00	$ .05
2.00	.10
3.00	.15
4.00	.20
5.00	.25
6.00	.30
7.00	.35
8.00	.40
9.00	.45
10.00	.50
11.00	.55
12.00	.60
13.00	.65
14.00	.70
15.00	.75
16.00	.80
17.00	.85
18.00	.90
19.00	.95
20.00	1.00
21.00	1.05
22.00	1.10
23.00	1.15
24.00	1.20
25.00	1.25
26.00	1.30
27.00	1.35
28.00	1.40
29.00	1.45
30.00	1.50
31.00	1.55
32.00	1.60
33.00	1.65
34.00	1.70
35.00	1.75
36.00	1.80
37.00	1.85
38.00	1.90
39.00	1.95

Fill in the blanks in these bills. Use the tax chart.

1.
```
   WONG'S
    Paper
  Supplies
    $5.01
     2.49
     7.76
     0.80

Sub-
Total_______
Tax  _______
Total_______
```

2.
```
    ENDO'S
 Electronics
   $10.89
    21.25
     4.66
     3.05
     8.30

Sub-
Total_______
Tax  _______
Total_______
```

3.
```
  RUSSELL'S
    Toys
    $2.55
     4.98
     0.29
     1.79
     4.88

Sub-
Total_______
Tax  _______
Total_______
```

Solve these problems. Use the tax chart, if needed.

4. David and Douglas paid $18.47 plus tax for electronic supplies. What was their total bill?

____

5. Mary Jo paid $21.75 for math games. Tax was $1.09. How much change did she get from twenty-five dollars?

____

6. Dorothy bought paper supplies for $24.88 before sales tax. How much change did she get from three ten-dollar bills?

____

7. Jeff and Ricardo bought notebooks for $2.50 and $2.95 at Wong's and a $17.50 drilling game at Russell's. How much did they spend with tax at each store?

____

What did they buy?

8. Tom spent $9.29 including tax. _______________

9. Victor spent $15.96 including tax. _______________

10. Anita spent $16.11 including tax. _______________

LESSON 8

Multiplying Decimals

PRACTICE

Finish each pair of problems.

1. $9 \times 0.6 =$ 5.4

   $9 \times \frac{6}{10} =$ $\frac{54}{10} = 5\frac{4}{10}$

2. $0.8 \times 0.7 =$ ______

   $0.8 \times \frac{7}{10} =$ ______

3. $4.3 \times 9.5 =$ ______

   $4\frac{3}{10} \times 9\frac{5}{10} =$ ______

4. $0.07 \times 0.04 =$ ______

   $\frac{7}{100} \times \frac{4}{100} =$ ______

5. $62 \times 0.09 =$ ______

   $62 \times \frac{9}{100} =$ ______

6. $85.03 \times 0.4 =$ ______

   $85\frac{3}{100} \times \frac{4}{10} =$ ______

Find the products.

7. 5.78×59

8. 46.58×82

9. 46.8×6.4

10. 72.9×1.7

11. 12.94×3.9

12. 85.43×50.1

13. 0.356×76

14. 31.298×8

15. 0.297×7.8

16. 7.12×6.31

17. 3.0712×2.45

18. 4.003×1.08

Multiply by powers of 10.

19. $4.73 \times 10^0 =$ ______

    $4.73 \times 10^1 =$ ______

    $4.73 \times 10^2 =$ ______

20. $9.019 \times 10^1 =$ ______

    $9.019 \times 10^2 =$ ______

    $9.019 \times 10^3 =$ ______

21. $0.25806 \times 10^4 =$ ______

    $0.25806 \times 10^5 =$ ______

    $0.25806 \times 10^6 =$ ______

22. $3.125479 \times 10^3 =$ ______

    $3.125479 \times 10^5 =$ ______

    $3.125479 \times 10^7 =$ ______

APPLY

Use the page of the school paper to solve these problems.

What is the area of the

1. film store ad? ________

2. computer store ad? ________

3. want ad? ________

4. larger picture? ________

   smaller picture? ________

5. news story? ________

What is the

6. length of the page? ________

7. width of the page? ________

8. area of all the ads? ________

HARRISON FILMS
1440 Harrison Street
Your Film Supplies at Discount Prices
Super II Color

11 cm

WILSON'S TEAM WINS

Robert's Computers
135 VAN NESS AVE.
GAMES
MICROS DISCS
Ask for Diane or Mark

15.5 cm

WALTER'S FUNNIES
11th and Harrison Sts.
☆☆☆
Stop after school for some laughs!
World's best collection of funnies

The First Floor Magic Store
The Best in Magic Tricks

8 cm

WANT AD
Student to work after school. South of Market Music
call: 863-4223

5.5 cm

5.5 cm | 5.5cm | 5.5cm | 5.5cm | 5.5cm

If ads cost \$0.095 per square centimeter, how much do these ads cost? (Round answers to the nearest cent.)

9. Robert's Computers ____________

10. Walter's Funnies ____________

11. Want Ad ____________

12. The 1st Floor Magic Store ____________

LESSON 9

Dividing Decimals

PRACTICE

Find the quotients.

1. $6\overline{)4.50}$ (worked example: 0.75; 42; 30; 30)

2. $6\overline{)45}$

3. $2\overline{)1.36}$

4. $2\overline{)13.6}$

5. $4\overline{)0.5}$

6. $4\overline{)5}$

7. $8\overline{)2.3}$

8. $8\overline{)23}$

9. $17\overline{)\$66.13}$

10. $24\overline{)55.2}$

11. $36\overline{)2.7}$

12. $25\overline{)81.4}$

Divide by powers of ten.

13. 48.99 ÷ 10 = ______________

48.99 ÷ 10^1 = ______________

14. 70,883 ÷ 100 = ______________

70,883 ÷ 10^2 = ______________

15. 9700 ÷ 1000 = ______________

9700 ÷ 10^3 = ______________

16. 10,498 ÷ 10,000 = ______________

10,498 ÷ 10^4 = ______________

Divide and round each quotient.

		Quotient	Nearest Whole Number	Nearest Tenth	Nearest Hundredth
17.	6.84 ÷ 10				
18.	930.7 ÷ 100				

APPLY

1. What was the total amount that Betty paid for four Top 10 albums and two tapes?

   ____

2. What is the total cost of three country music albums and three posters?

   ____

3. Which costs more, two Top 10 albums, or one tape and one poster? How much more?

   ____

4. How much change did Don get from $30.00 if he bought three tapes?

   ____

5. What two items did Ester buy if she spent $6.88?

   ____

6. What is the difference in cost between 1 dozen 2-for-$4.75 pieces of sheet music and 1 dozen 3-for-$7.00 pieces of sheet music?

   ____

Round each answer up to the next cent.

7. Which is the better buy, the 2-for-$4.75 or the 3-for-$7.00 sheet music?

   ____

8. David and Diane bought two Top 10 albums, one country music album and 2 pieces of sheet music. What was the average cost of each item?

   ____

LESSON 10

Dividing Decimals

PRACTICE

Divide. Check your answers.

1. $0.9\overline{)2.718}$
2. $2.4\overline{)37.44}$
3. $0.04\overline{)1.808}$
4. $0.68\overline{)5.916}$
5. $9.6\overline{)3648}$
6. $0.52\overline{)468}$
7. $30\overline{)222}$
8. $0.73\overline{)5037}$
9. $1.19\overline{)725.9}$

Write each fraction as a terminating decimal.

10. $\frac{3}{8}$ = ________
11. $\frac{7}{8}$ = ________
12. $\frac{3}{5}$ = ________
13. $\frac{1}{10}$ = ________
14. $\frac{9}{10}$ = ________
15. $\frac{3}{4}$ = ________

Write each fraction as a repeating decimal.

16. $\frac{1}{3}$ = ________
17. $\frac{2}{3}$ = ________
18. $\frac{1}{6}$ = ________
19. $\frac{1}{9}$ = ________
20. $\frac{4}{9}$ = ________
21. $\frac{1}{12}$ = ________

Give the starting number.

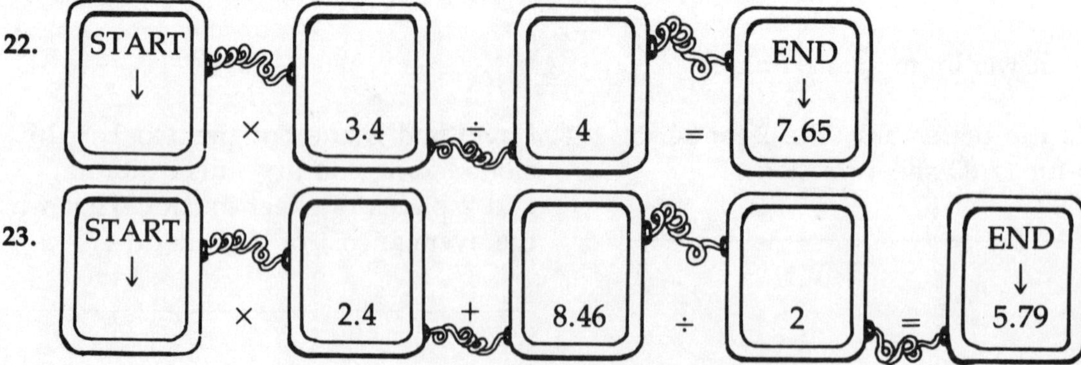

APPLY

Tip Sometimes when you solve a problem, you find a **terminating decimal**; sometimes you find a **repeating decimal**. Round a repeating decimal.

Complete the chart. Find the miles per gallon for each car. Round your answers to the nearest tenth.

	Car	Miles Driven	Gallons of Gas Used	Miles per Gallon
1.	Craig's *Minnow*	143.7	11.9	
2.	Pam's *Red Snapper*	231	13.2	
3.	Kelly's *Wheels*	284.2	16.9	
4.	Scott's *Silver Streak*	335.5	12.2	
5.	Brian's *Pony*	291.2	10.4	
6.	Mamie's *Cream Puff*	225.5	20.5	
7.	Emil's *Cyclone*	166.6	17	

Solve these problems.

8. Alan is paid $3.75 per hour. If he earned a total of $63.75, how many hours did he work? ____________

9. Gabriella worked 14 hours. She earned a total of $53.20. How many more hours must she work in order to earn $76.00 in all? ____________

10. Mrs. Cole gets an average of 19.2 mpg. She drove 24,000 miles for her job last year. How many gallons of gas did she use? ____________

11. Janet's car expenses for the year were $3990. She drove 5000 miles less than Mrs. Cole did. What were her expenses per mile? ____________

12. During one quarter-hour period, sales at Sandy's gas station were: $17.85, $5.00, $20.00, $15.45, $10.75, and $19.00. What was the average amount of each sale? ____________

LESSON 11

Adding/Subtracting Integers

PRACTICE

Find the sums and differences.

1. $^{-}12 + {}^{+}4 =$ ______ **2.** $^{+}8 + {}^{-}5 =$ ______ **3.** $^{-}7 + {}^{-}9 =$ ______

4. $^{+}13 + {}^{-}13 =$ ______ **5.** $^{-}25 + {}^{+}5 =$ ______ **6.** $^{+}8 + {}^{-}7 =$ ______

7. $^{-}9 + {}^{+}16 =$ ______ **8.** $^{-}64 + {}^{+}40 =$ ______ **9.** $^{-}12 + {}^{-}18 =$ ______

10. $^{-}5 - {}^{+}14 =$ ______ **11.** $^{+}1 - {}^{+}15 =$ ______ **12.** $^{-}8 - {}^{+}9 =$ ______

13. $^{+}1 - {}^{+}5 =$ ______ **14.** $^{-}9 - {}^{+}3 =$ ______ **15.** $^{-}15 - {}^{-}8 =$ ______

16. $^{+}40 - {}^{+}51 =$ ______ **17.** $^{-}3 - {}^{-}8 =$ ______ **18.** $^{-}13 - {}^{-}19 =$ ______

19. $^{+}10 - {}^{-}8 =$ ______ **20.** $^{+}64 - {}^{+}84 =$ ______ **21.** $^{-}27 - {}^{-}78 =$ ______

22. $\begin{array}{r} ^{-}5 \\ ^{+}8 \\ + \ ^{+}7 \\ \hline \end{array}$ **23.** $\begin{array}{r} ^{-}9 \\ ^{+}16 \\ ^{-}4 \\ + \ ^{-}7 \\ \hline \end{array}$ **24.** $\begin{array}{r} ^{+}33 \\ ^{-}16 \\ ^{+}9 \\ + \ ^{-}10 \\ \hline \end{array}$ **25.** $\begin{array}{r} ^{+}14 \\ ^{-}9 \\ + \ ^{-}11 \\ \hline \end{array}$ **26.** $\begin{array}{r} ^{-}3 \\ ^{+}5 \\ + \ ^{-}6 \\ \hline \end{array}$

Compare. Write >, <, or =.

27. $^{-}4$ ◯ $^{-}5$ **28.** $^{-}19$ ◯ $^{-}19$ **29.** $^{+}1.52$ ◯ 0

$^{+}4$ ◯ $^{+}5$ $^{-}19$ ◯ $^{-}18$ $^{-}2.5$ ◯ $^{-}2.25$

$^{-}4$ ◯ $^{+}5$ $^{-}54$ ◯ $^{+}55$ $^{+}3.78$ ◯ $^{-}3.9$

$^{+}4$ ◯ $^{-}5$ $^{-}1$ ◯ $^{+}3$ $^{-}5.5$ ◯ $^{-}5\frac{1}{2}$

APPLY

Tip When you **add or subtract integers**, remember that positive integers are greater than zero and that negative integers are less than zero.

Solve these problems.

On Monday the temperature was ⁻2°C. The temperature went down 3°C each day for the next three days. Then it went up 5°C on each of the next two days. Fill in the chart. Record the temperature changes.

	Day of the Week	Temperature
1.		
2.		
3.		
4.		
5.		
6.		

7. Mark drove 18 km to the east, 11 km to the west, 10 km more to the west, and 8 km to the east. How far was he from his starting point after driving all these distances? ______

8. Mt. McKinley is 4418 m above sea level. Death Valley is 86 m below sea level. How much higher is Mt. McKinley than Death Valley? ______

9. At the end of June, Norma's savings account had a balance of $50. During July, she deposited $35, withdrew $25, withdrew $15, deposited $45, and withdrew $15. What was her balance at the end of July? ______

Karen's bank statement looked like this. Fill in the missing amounts.

	Month	Balance	Monthly Change
		$242	
10.	August	$169	⁻$73
11.	September	$369	
12.	October	$219	
13.	November	$138	
14.	December	$182	

LESSON 12

Multiplying/Dividing Integers

PRACTICE

Find the products.

1. $^{-}5 \times {}^{-}7 =$ $^{+}35$
2. $^{+}4 \times {}^{-}12 =$ ______
3. $^{-}10 \times {}^{-}20 =$ ______
4. $0 \times {}^{-}9 =$ ______
5. $^{-}8 \times ({}^{+}4 \times {}^{+}3) =$ ______
6. $({}^{-}9 \times {}^{-}2) \times {}^{+}6 =$ ______
7. $^{+}3 \times {}^{+}9 =$ ______
   $^{-}3 \times {}^{-}9 =$ ______
   $^{+}3 \times {}^{-}9 =$ ______
   $^{-}3 \times {}^{+}9 =$ ______
8. $^{+}15 \times {}^{+}7 =$ ______
   $^{-}15 \times {}^{-}7 =$ ______
   $^{+}15 \times {}^{-}7 =$ ______
   $^{-}15 \times {}^{+}7 =$ ______
9. $^{-}11 \times {}^{+}6 =$ ______
   $^{-}6 \times {}^{+}11 =$ ______
   $^{-}11 \times {}^{-}6 =$ ______
   $^{+}6 \times {}^{+}11 =$ ______

Find the quotients.

10. $^{+}36 \div {}^{-}9 =$ ______
11. $^{-}50 \div {}^{+}5 =$ ______
12. $^{-}81 \div {}^{-}9 =$ ______
13. $\frac{^{-}30}{^{+}6} =$ ______
14. $\frac{^{+}63}{^{-}7} =$ ______
15. $\frac{^{-}48}{^{-}8} =$ ______

Write *positive* or *negative* in each blank.

16. The product of two positive numbers is a ______ number.
17. The product of two negative numbers is a ______ number.
18. The product of a positive number and a negative number is a ______ number.
19. The quotient of two positive numbers is a ______ number.
20. The quotient of two negative numbers is a ______ number.
21. The quotient of a positive number and a negative number is a ______ number.

What is the end number?

22.

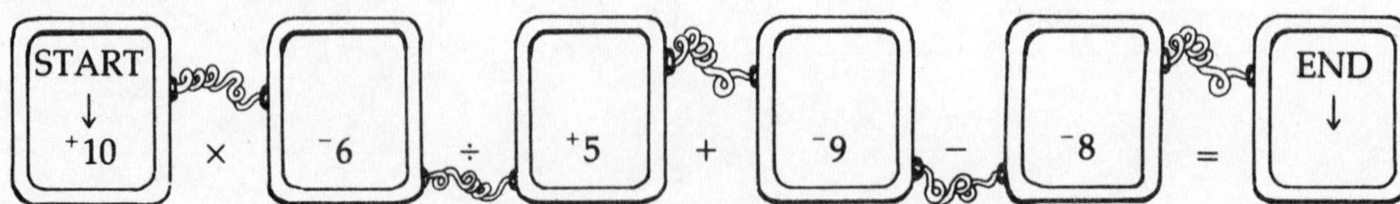

APPLY

When you **multiply or divide integers** and the signs are the same, the answer is positive. When the signs are different, the answer is negative.

Solve these problems.

1. Tomas bought Memory Bank stock for $26 a share. It dropped $2 a day for seven days. Then it went up $4 a day for the next 5 days. What is the current selling price per share? __________

2. Ginna bought Data Action stock for $15 a share. It went up $1.25 a day for the next 5 days. Then it went up another $2.10. What is the current selling price per share? __________

3. Scott and Samantha drove 275 km south each day for 3 days. Then they drove 125 km west. How far did they travel in all? __________

4. Cherlyn and Jack ran 12 blocks east, 10 blocks south, 14 blocks west, and 10 blocks north. How many blocks were they from their starting point? __________

5. Clifford's first dive this week was 25 m below sea level. His second and third dives were 18 m and 32 m below sea level. What was his average dive? __________

6. The bottom floor of the Caldwell Building is 15 m below ground level. The top of the building is 60 m above ground level. If each floor is 7.5 m high, how many floors are in the building? __________

7. The temperature is now 0°C. It has risen 3°C each hour. What was the temperature four hours ago? __________

LESSON 13

Solving Equations

PRACTICE

Solve these equations.

1. $n + 5 = 22$

   $n + 5 - 5 = 22 - 5$

   $n = 17$

2. $6 + n = 58$

3. $(9 + 5) + y = 37$

4. $18 + b = 37$

5. $b + 18 = 67$

6. $35 + (6 + r) = 85$

7. $a - 7 = 16$

8. $49 - a = 42$

9. $(183 - 50) + c = 155$

10. $38 - (7 - 2) = n$ $n =$ ______

    $(38 - 7) - 2 = n$ $n =$ ______

11. $(29 + 18) + 26 = m$ $m =$ ______

    $29 + (18 + 26) = m$ $m =$ ______

12. $70 - (34 + 8) = x$ $x =$ ______

    $(70 - 34) + 8 = x$ $x =$ ______

13. $56 + (19 - 7) = y$ $y =$ ______

    $(56 + 19) - 7 = y$ $y =$ ______

14. $97 - (0 + 6) = a$ $a =$ ______

    $(97 - 0) + 6 = a$ $a =$ ______

15. $80 + (34 - 25) = h$ $h =$ ______

    $(80 + 34) - 25 = h$ $h =$ ______

Write and solve an equation for each sentence.
Use n for the variable.

16. 8 more than a number is 42.

    ____

17. 9 less than a number is 11.

    ____

18. 78 more than a number is 205.

    ____

19. 69 less than a number is 314.

    ____

20. 24 increased by a number is 50.

    ____

21. 89 minus a number is 76.

    ____

APPLY

Tip When you use an **equation** to solve a problem, you should add or subtract the same number on both sides of the equation.

Write and solve an equation for each problem. Use *n* for the variable.

1. The outside temperature has dropped 12°F since noon. If the temperature now reads 38°F, what was it at noon?

   ____

2. The temperature at 7 A.M. was ⁻10°F. By 11 A.M. it had gone up 4°F. What is the temperature at 11 A.M.?

   ____

3. Jean's age plus 8 years is the same as George's age. Jean's age is 15. What is George's age?

   ____

4. Laura is 5 years younger than Rosie. If Laura is 24 years old, how old is Rosie?

   ____

5. Kenny gained 8.25 pounds. Before the gain he weighed 110.5 pounds. How much does he weigh now?

   ____

6. Marty spent $10.35. He now has $17.65. How much did he have before?

   ____

7. John and Sylvia have 76 tapes in their library. They lent some tapes to friends and have 49 left. How many did they lend?

   ____

8. Kevin and Mike must drive 268 miles today. They drove 133 miles before lunch. How many more miles do they have left?

   ____

LESSON 14

Solving Equations

PRACTICE

Solve these equations.

1. $7x = 70$

$\frac{7x}{7} = \frac{70}{7}$

$x = 10$

2. $15x = 75$

3. $^{-}12x = 72$

4. $25y = 175$

5. $90y = 540$

6. $38y = 342$

7. $40z = 960$

8. $25z = 625$

9. $60z = 3000$

10. $7b = 28$

11. $27 = 3b$

12. $72 = 9b$

13. $0.4r = 3.6$

14. $8.2r = 1.23$

15. $3.6r = 10.8$

16. $4t - 7 = 13$

17. $24 + 8t = 40$

18. $76 - 6t = 34$

Evaluate each expression if $a = 4$ and $b = 6$.

19. a^2

20. b^2

21. $a \times b$

22. $3a + b$

23. $5a - 3b$

24. $(6a - 10) - b$

APPLY

Tip When you use an **equation** to solve a problem, you should add, subtract, or multiply the same number on both sides of the equation.

Write and solve an equation for each problem. Use *n* for the variable.

1. Maritza packed 4 times as many boxes on Wednesday as she did on Tuesday. On Tuesday she packed 7 boxes. How many did she pack on Wednesday?

   ____

2. Julia worked three times as long as Louie. Louie worked 10.5 hours. How long did Julia work?

   ____

3. The class cleaned 10 desks on Monday. By Friday they had cleaned 38. How many were cleaned after Monday?

   ____

4. Cindy packed 15 books less than Jennifer. If Jennifer packed 52 books, how many did Cindy pack?

   ____

5. Virginia painted for twice as many hours as Phillip did. Phillip painted for three and a quarter hours. For how long did Virginia paint?

   ____

6. 250 of the 925 chairs in the auditorium were cleaned by Thursday. How many were left to clean?

   ____

7. Mia worked a total of 41 hours during cleanup week. She worked 5 daily shifts plus 6 hours of overtime. How long was each daily shift?

   ____

8. Jessie worked a total of 25 hours cleaning the outside of the school. He worked 3 regular shifts plus 7 hours of overtime. How long were his regular shifts?

   ____

LESSON 15

Solving Equations

PRACTICE

Solve these equations.

1. $\frac{a}{4} = 9$

2. $\frac{b}{7} = 9$

3. $\frac{c}{3} = 15$

4. $\frac{d}{6} = 8$

5. $\frac{x}{10} = 12$

6. $\frac{y}{4} = 2$

7. $5 = \frac{r}{10}$

8. $6 = \frac{s}{7}$

9. $1 = \frac{t}{4}$

10. $18 = \frac{n}{4}$

11. $\frac{m}{8} = 7$

12. $9 = \frac{p}{25}$

13. $\frac{s}{4} - 9 = 1$

14. $35 = 20 + \frac{t}{5}$

15. $110 - \frac{v}{7} = 105$

Evaluate each expression if $a = 4$ and $b = 6$.

16. $\frac{6a}{b}$

17. $\frac{200}{2a}$

18. $\frac{60}{2b}$

19. $\frac{12b}{2a}$

20. $\frac{20a}{8}$

21. $\frac{40a}{10}$

APPLY

Tip When you use an **equation** to solve a problem, you should divide by the same number on both sides of the equation.

Write each of the following as a mathematical expression. Use n for the variable.

1. 4 students shared some money evenly. __________

2. $0.25 was left over when some money was divided between two people. __________

3. A number of doughnuts were divided into dozens. __________

4. 38 more than a number of books __________

5. $0.68 less than an amount of money __________

6. 5 times a number of hours __________

7. 48 drinks shared equally among a number of people __________

8. A number of packages was divided evenly among 3 boxes. __________

9. 7 more than twice a number of books __________

Write and solve an equation for each problem. Use n for the variable.

10. One class has 96 books. There are three times as many books as students. How many students are in the class? __________

11. The length of a room is 6 meters less than twice the width. If the length is 26 meters, find the width. __________

LESSON 16

Writing Ratios and Proportions

PRACTICE

Write a rate for each.

1. 55 miles per hour $\frac{55}{1}$

2. 24 miles per gallon ________

3. 8 cans for $1.79 ________

4. 6 for a half-dollar ________

5. 30 students for each teacher ________

6. 45 feet every fifteen seconds ________

Complete the equal ratios.

7. $\frac{5}{9} = \frac{10}{18} = \frac{\square}{\square} = \frac{\square}{36} = \frac{25}{\square}$

8. $\frac{3}{5} = \frac{6}{\square} = \frac{9}{\square} = \frac{\square}{20} = \frac{\square}{\square}$

9. $\frac{15}{10} = \frac{\square}{8} = \frac{\square}{6} = \frac{\square}{4} = \frac{3}{\square}$

10. $\frac{12}{16} = \frac{\square}{12} = \frac{\square}{8} = \frac{3}{\square} = \frac{\square}{\square}$

11. $\frac{16}{4} = \frac{8}{2} = \frac{\square}{1} = \frac{\square}{0.5} = \frac{\square}{\square}$

12. $\frac{0.2}{0.4} = \frac{0.4}{0.8} = \frac{\square}{1.2} = \frac{0.8}{\square} = \frac{\square}{\square}$

Use cross products to find if the ratios are equal. Write = or ≠.

13. $\frac{8}{12} \bigcirc \frac{3}{4}$

14. $\frac{7}{9} \bigcirc \frac{27}{36}$

15. $\frac{1}{4} \bigcirc \frac{3}{12}$

16. $\frac{8}{3} \bigcirc \frac{54}{21}$

17. $\frac{28}{15} \bigcirc \frac{9}{5}$

18. $\frac{16}{2} \bigcirc \frac{8}{1}$

19. $\frac{20}{32} \bigcirc \frac{5}{8}$

20. $\frac{1}{3} \bigcirc \frac{8}{24}$

Solve each proportion for n.

21. $\frac{3}{25} = \frac{9}{n}$

22. $\frac{1}{4} = \frac{n}{120}$

23. $\frac{5}{6} = \frac{90}{n}$

24. $\frac{9}{8} = \frac{n}{144}$

25. $\frac{1.5}{3} = \frac{6}{n}$

26. $\frac{n}{15} = \frac{24}{9}$

27. $\frac{1}{n} = \frac{3}{3.6}$

28. $\frac{45}{6} = \frac{n}{4}$

APPLY

Tip Sometimes to solve a **rate, distance,** or **time** problem, you can write and solve a **proportion.** To solve a proportion, find cross products, then divide.

Write and solve a proportion for each problem.

1. The Connolly family drove 362.4 km in 6 hours. What was their average speed per hour? __________

2. The Pardee family drove for 7.5 hours at an average speed of 66 km/h. At that rate, how far did they drive in all? __________

3. Libby's goal is to ski the 10-km cross-country race in 50 minutes. In order to do this, how many kilometers must she average per minute? __________

4. Sarah skied the 50-km cross-country course at an average speed of 0.25 km per minute. At that rate, how much time did it take her to finish the course? __________

5. Gayle ran for 1 minute and 20 seconds at an average speed of 5 m per second. At that rate, how far did he run in all? __________

6. Keith's goal is to run 1500 m in 6 minutes. In order to do this, how many meters per minute must he average? __________

7. Suzette drew a map that had a scale of 5 mm = 80 km. What is the actual distance of a length that is 75 mm on the map? __________

8. Lorraine built a model of a house. The scale was 10 mm = 8.5 m. The actual house is 42.5 m long. What is the length of the model? __________

LESSON 17

Percents, Ratios, and Decimals

PRACTICE

Complete the chart.

		Ratio	Lowest-Terms Fraction	Percent	Decimal
1.	Compare 15 to 100	$\frac{15}{100}$	$\frac{3}{20}$	15%	0.15
2.	Compare 17 to 100				
3.	Compare 2 to 100				
4.	Compare 3 to 100				
5.	Compare 95 to 100				
6.	Compare 87 to 100				
7.	Compare 125 to 100				
8.	Compare 180 to 100				

Write as a percent.

9. $\frac{1}{5}$ ______ **10.** $\frac{2}{5}$ ______ **11.** $\frac{3}{5}$ ______ **12.** $\frac{8}{5}$ ______

13. $\frac{3}{4}$ ______ **14.** $\frac{4}{4}$ ______ **15.** $\frac{7}{4}$ ______ **16.** $\frac{8}{4}$ ______

Write as a fraction in lowest terms.

17. $33\frac{1}{3}\%$ ______ **18.** $66.\overline{6}\%$ ______ **19.** $16\frac{2}{3}\%$ ______ **20.** $83.\overline{3}\%$ ______

21. $41\frac{2}{3}\%$ ______ **22.** $58.\overline{3}\%$ ______ **23.** $12\frac{1}{2}\%$ ______ **24.** 37.5% ______

Write as a percent. Round to the nearest tenth of a percent.

25. 0.7156 ______ **26.** 1.2536 ______ **27.** 0.3895 ______ **28.** 4.0083 ______

APPLY

Use the picture graphs to answer these questions. Round all decimals to the nearest whole number. Express all fractions in lowest terms.

Survey of Number of Cars Owned by Families

No cars	
One car	
Two cars	
Three or more cars	
Each represents 100 families	

1. How many families were in the survey?

   ____

2. What does represent? ________

What fraction of the families

3. have no cars? ________
4. have one car? ________
5. have three or more cars? ________
6. How many families have two cars?

   ____

Survey of Number of Home Video Games Owned by Families

no games	
one game	
two games	
three or more games	
Each represents 20 families	

7. What does represent? ________
8. What does represent? ________
9. What is the total number of families represented by this survey?

   ____

What percent of the families

10. have no home video games? ________
11. have one home video game? ________
12. have two or more home video games?

    ____

LESSON 18

Finding the Percent of a Number

PRACTICE

Write an equivalent fraction problem, then solve.

1. 20% of 85

$\frac{1}{5} \times 85 = 17$

2. 50% of 46

3. 25% of 540

4. $33\frac{1}{3}$% of 246

5. $66\frac{2}{3}$% of 24

6. $12\frac{1}{2}$% of 120

Write an equivalent decimal problem, then solve.

7. 10% of 9.7

$0.10 \times 9.7 = 0.97$

8. 76% of 300

9. 150% of 800

10. 39% of 73

11. 5.2% of 95

12. 4.7% of 980

Write and solve a proportion for each.
Use *n* as the variable.

13. 4% of 1500

$\frac{4}{100} = \frac{n}{1500}$; $n = 60$

14. 10% of 789

15. 5.2% of 9000

16. 8% of 178

17. 72% of 260

18. 4.8% of 670

Solve the following problem in three different ways.

20% of 49 = ___?___

19. Change the percent to a fraction and solve. ____________________

20. Change the percent to a decimal and solve. ____________________

21. Write a proportion and solve. ____________________

APPLY

Tip To find a **percent of a number**, change the percent to a fraction or a decimal and multiply.

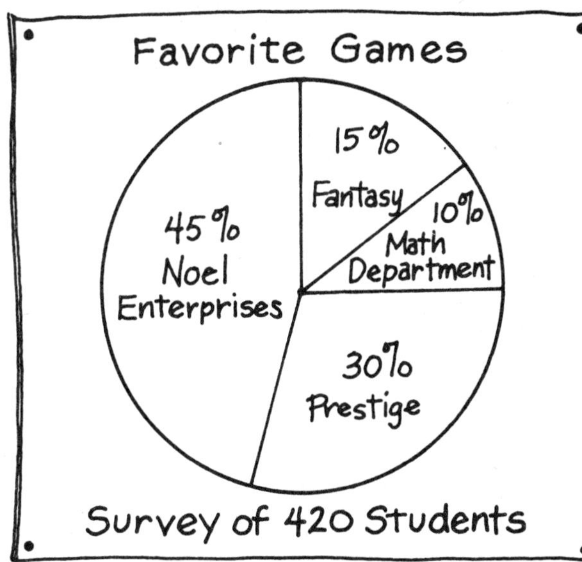

Use the circle graphs to answer these questions.

How many students prefer the game named

1. Fantasy? ________
2. Noel Enterprises? ________
3. Prestige? ________
4. Math Department? ________

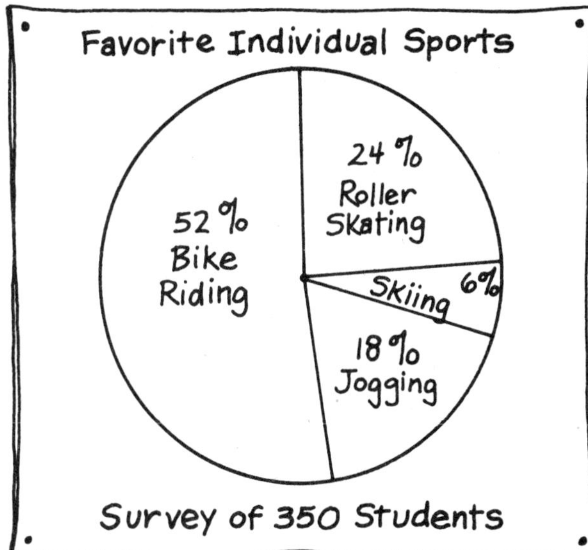

How many students prefer the sport of

5. bike riding? ________
6. roller skating? ________
7. skiing? ________
8. jogging? ________

Favorite Musical Groups

24% 22nd Street

48% Lopez and Adams

8% Ron, Tom and Rich

20% Windows

Survey of 575 Students

How many students prefer the musical group named

9. Lopez and Adams? ________
10. Windows? ________
11. Ron, Tom and Rich? ________
12. 22nd Street? ________

LESSON 19

Finding the Percent

PRACTICE

Fill in the blanks on the chart.
Round answers to the nearest tenth of a percent.

		Equation	Ratio	Solution
1.	What percent of 100 is 7?	$n\% \cdot 100 = 7$	$n\% = \frac{7}{100}$	7%
2.	What percent of 30 is 1?			
3.	What percent of 66 is 264?			
4.	88 is what percent of 176?			
5.	30 is what percent of 250?			
6.	What percent of 75 is 66?			
7.	43.2 is what percent of 96?			

Solve.

8. $n\% \cdot 94 = 37.6$

9. $n\% \cdot 50 = 55$

10. $n\% \cdot 90 = 135$

11. $n\% \cdot 45.5 = 91$

12. $n\% \cdot 75 = 90$

13. $n\% \cdot 125 = 213.5$

14. $n\% \cdot 63 = 52.5$

15. $n\% \cdot 18 = 99$

16. $n\% \cdot 75 = 150$

Choose the best answer to fill the blank.

17. \$0.35 is ______ of \$2.20
a. a little more than 15%
b. a little less than 15%

18. \$0.25 is ______ of \$1.60
a. a little more than 15%
b. a little less than 15%

19. \$0.70 is ______ of \$4.80.
a. a little more than 15%
b. a little less than 15%

20. \$2.15 is ______ of \$14.40
a. a little more than 15%
b. a little less than 15%

APPLY

Numbers of People Crossing the Bridge to the City Each Morning

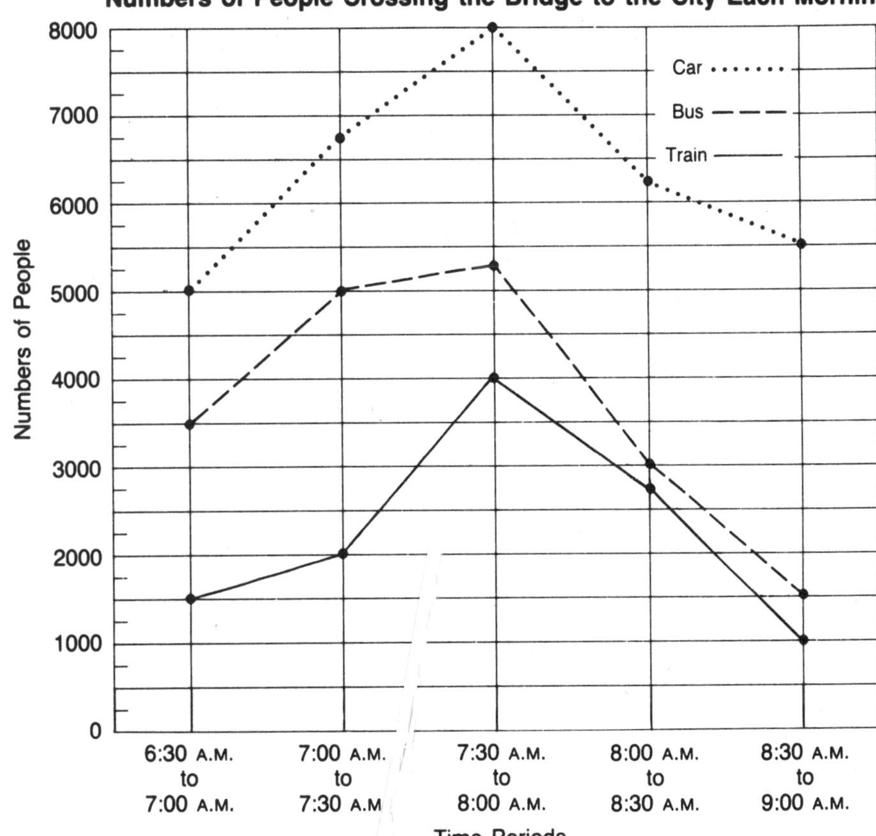

Use the line graph to answer these questions.

1. In which time period do the most people cross the bridge in the morning? ____________

What percent of the total number of people represented on the graph who cross the bridge by car travel between

2. 6:30-7:00 A.M.? ______ 3. 7:30-8:00 A.M.? ______ 4. 8:30-9:00 A.M.? ______

What percent of the total number of people represented on the graph who cross the bridge by bus travel between

5. 7:00-7:30 A.M.? ______ 6. 8:00-8:30 A.M.? ______ 7. 8:30-9:00 A.M.? ______

8. What percent of the people who travel across the bridge by train travel at the heaviest traffic period? ____________

LESSON 20

Finding a Number

PRACTICE

Write an equivalent fraction problem, then solve.

1. 80% of n = 144

$\frac{4}{5}n = 144$

$n = 144 \times \frac{5}{4}$

$n = 180$

2. 48% of n = 24

3. 32% of n = 288

4. 75% of n = 48

5. $33\frac{1}{3}$% of n = 290

6. $62\frac{1}{2}$% of n = 110

Write an equivalent decimal problem, then solve.

7. 40% of n = 250

$n = \frac{250}{0.4}$

$n = 625$

8. 76% of n = 608

9. 84% of n = 109.2

10. 77% of n = 69.3

11. 19% of n = 11.4

12. 15% of n = 146.4

Write a proportion problem, then solve.

13. 90% of n = 45

$\frac{45}{n} = \frac{90}{100}$

$90n = 4500$

$n = 50$

14. 25% of n = 375

15. 5% of n = 10

16. 250% of n = 120

17. 95% of n = 285

18. 12.5% of n = 64

Write a number sentence and solve.

19. If 30% of a number is $7.50, what is the number? ____________

20. If 75% of a number is $600.00, what is the number? ____________

APPLY

Write and solve an equation for each of these problems.

1. Kirsti and John left a 15% tip of $5.15 for their dinner. What was the amount of their bill? __________

2. Hunter received a 15% tip of $28.35 for waiting on a table of ten people. What was the cost of the dinner excluding tip? __________

3. The O'Brien family's dinner check came to $125. They left an additional $22.50 tip. What percent of the total dinner check did they leave as a tip? __________

4. Kathy, Skip, and Billy received a total of $104 in tips for working at a large party. The check for the party totaled $650. What percent of the check did they receive? __________

5. Susan deposited part of her salary in a savings account that paid a yearly interest rate of 7.75%. If she received $186 interest in one year, what was her total savings? __________

6. Howard manages the kitchen. He saved $14, or 5%, off the regular price of some food items. What was the regular price of these items? __________

7. Beth earned $259.20. She put 50% of that money away to buy a 10-speed bike. The bike she hopes to buy sells for $160 plus 6% tax. How much more money does she need to save? __________

8. Nick and Tim own the Elm Restaurant. Each year, they pay 4.38% of the total value of the property in taxes. Last year they paid $7665 in taxes. What is the value of their property? __________

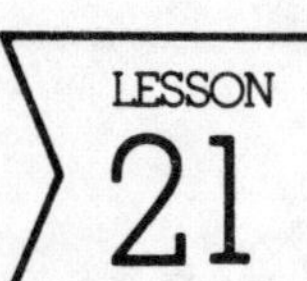

Review

This lesson reviews the **TIPS** you have learned in this book. Use each **TIP** to help you solve these problems.

Tip A. Sometimes when you solve a problem, you find a terminating decimal; sometimes you find a repeating decimal. Round a repeating decimal.

1. Mrs. Hill bought 3 lb of ground beef for her family of 8. How much ground beef was that per person? ________

Tip B. When you add or subtract integers, remember that positive integers are greater than zero and that negative integers are less than zero.

2. The daily temperatures for one week were: $^-3$°C, $^+7$°C, $^+10$°C, $^-4$°C, and $^-5$°C. What was the average daily temperature? ________

Tip C. When you multiply or divide integers and the signs are the same, the answer is positive. When the signs are different, the answer is negative.

3. The price of a share of Fergitron stock has dropped $4 a share for 5 days. What is the change in the price of a share of stock? ________

Tip D. When you use an equation to solve a problem, you should add, subtract, multiply, or divide the same number from both sides of the equation.

4. Peter and Andrea washed 15 windows. Peter washed 6 windows. How many did Andrea wash? ________

Tip E. Sometimes to solve a rate, distance, or time problem, you can write and solve a proportion. To solve proportion, find cross products, then divide.

5. Bill drove 137 miles in 4 hours. How long should it take him to drive 87 more miles? ________

Tip F. To find a percent of a number, change the percent to a fraction or a decimal and multiply.

6. A waitress received a tip of 15% at one table. The bill was $60. What was the tip? ________

Post-Test

Score ________

Solve each problem. Mark your answers in the answer rows below.

1. Mrs. Jones bought 3 bushels of apples for $20.00. How much is that per bushel?

   A $6.67
   B $7.66
   C $6.66
   D $20.00
   E none of these

2. The temperature was $^{-}14$°C. It rose 3°C per hour for 4 hours. What was the temperature at the end of 4 hours?

   A $^{-}11$°C
   B $^{-}26$°C
   C $^{-}2$°C
   D $^{+}2$°C
   E none of these

3. Connemara stock cost $63 a share. The price fell $4 a day for 11 days. What was the price then?

   A $11
   B $44
   C $19
   D $107
   E none of these

4. Paul weighs 108 lb. Four years earlier he weighed 60 lb. How much did he gain per year? Which is the correct equation?

   A $108 - 60 - x$
   B $60 + 4x = 108$
   C $60 - 4x = 108$
   D $4x = 108 + 60$
   E none of these

5. How much weight did Paul gain each year? Use the equation you chose in problems 4.

   A 12 lb
   B 48 lb
   C 42 lb
   D 4 lb
   E none of these

6. Les drove 14 miles in 20 min. How long would it take him to drive 77 miles?

   A 5 hr 50 min
   B 54 min
   C 2 hr
   D 1 hr 50 min
   E none of these

7. A class of 350 students elected a president. 44% voted for Paula. How many students voted for Paula?

   A 140 students
   B 148 students
   C 394 students
   D 154 students
   E none of these

8. Elise took a trip of 178 miles. When she had driven 103 miles, what percentage of the trip was completed?

   A 73%
   B 75%
   C 103%
   D 28%
   E none of these

ANSWER ROWS:
1. Ⓐ Ⓑ Ⓒ Ⓓ Ⓔ 2. Ⓐ Ⓑ Ⓒ Ⓓ Ⓔ 3. Ⓐ Ⓑ Ⓒ Ⓓ Ⓔ 4. Ⓐ Ⓑ Ⓒ Ⓓ Ⓔ
5. Ⓐ Ⓑ Ⓒ Ⓓ Ⓔ 6. Ⓐ Ⓑ Ⓒ Ⓓ Ⓔ 7. Ⓐ Ⓑ Ⓒ Ⓓ Ⓔ 8. Ⓐ Ⓑ Ⓒ Ⓓ Ⓔ

ANSWER KEY

LESSON 1

Practice

1. 6 **2.** 1 **3.** 3 **4.** 8 **5.** 9 **6.** 2 **7.** 900,000,000 **8.** 6000 **9.** 80,000,000,000 **10.** 40,000 **11.** 5 **12.** 70 **13.** 576,083 **14.** 170,654 **15.** 1,082,436 **16.** 23,278,406 **17.** 10,456,681 **18.** 109,001,659 **19.** 7,339,084; 7,359,084 **20.** 936,270; 936,170 **21.** 29,018,852; 29,019,852; 29,021,852 **22.** 8,635,483,000; 8,635,000,000; 9,000,000,000 **23.** 42,919,756,000; 42,920,000,000; 43,000,000,000

Apply

1. 250,000 **2.** 400,000 **3.** 350,000 **4.** 750,000 **5.** 600,000 **6.** six million **7.** nine million **8.** six million **9.** ten million **10.** twelve million **11.** seven million **12.** three million

LESSON 2

Practice

1. 12,814 **2.** 7500 **3.** 39,287 **4.** \$4444 **5.** \$94.11 **6.** \$192 **7.** \$1318 **8.** 1,167,087 **9.** \$91.18 **10.** \$1501.18 **11.** 66,608 **12.** \$1966.37 **13.** 79,226 **14.** 98,121 **15.** 1516 **16.** 3589 **17.** 79,678 **18.** \$1039 **19.** \$7858 **20.** 70,039 **21.** \$295.79 **22.** \$437.75 **23.** \$210.89 **24.** \$8889.99 **25.** 8318 **26.** 34,796 **27.** \$15,588.39 **28.** \$46,468.79 **29.** 2000 **30.** 4000 **31.** 80,000 **32.** 1000

Apply

1. \$53,307 **2.** \$51,990 **3.** \$187,037 **4.** \$67,740 **5.** \$1374.75 **6.** \$1356.25 **7.** \$1406.25 **8.** \$1396.00 **9.** \$1496.00 **10.** \$1350.25 **11.** \$1140.00 **12.** \$1190.00 **13.** \$839.50

LESSON 3

Practice

1. 26,208 **2.** 1638 **3.** 37,074 **4.** 4012 **5.** 560,880 **6.** 9030 **7.** 30,604 **8.** 64,581 **9.** 168,082 **10.** 2,202,245 **11.** 75 R14 **12.** 62 R11 **13.** 189 **14.** 532 R6 **15.** 1233 R10 **16.** 302 **17.** 37 **18.** 69 R7 **19.** a **20.** c

Apply

1. 835 mi; 1670 mi; 4 days, 1 hr **2.** 880 mi; 1760 mi; 4 days, 3 hrs **3.** 470 mi; 940 mi; 2 days, 3 hrs **4.** 920 mi; 1840 mi; 4 days, 5 hrs **5.** 755 mi; 1510 mi; 3 days, 6 hrs **6.** 390 mi; 780 mi; 2 days **7.** 600 mi; 1200 mi; 3 days **8.** 495 mi; 990 mi; 2 days, 4 hrs

LESSON 4

Practice

1. $12\frac{3}{8}$ **2.** $5\frac{2}{3}$ **3.** $\frac{17}{18}$ **4.** $7\frac{5}{8}$ **5.** $\frac{3}{8}$ **6.** $32\frac{11}{18}$ **7.** $56\frac{1}{2}$ **8.** $682\frac{4}{5}$ **9.** $\frac{1}{3}$ **10.** 12 **11.** $1\frac{1}{6}$ **12.** $3\frac{13}{24}$ **13.** $37\frac{3}{4}$ **14.** $2\frac{5}{18}$ **15.** $97\frac{5}{8}$ **16.** $23\frac{1}{2}$ **17.** $119\frac{1}{12}$ **18.** $63\frac{14}{15}$ **19.** $104\frac{1}{10}$ **20.** $14\frac{13}{16}$ **21.** $63\frac{14}{15}$ **22.** $5\frac{5}{36}$ **23.** $32\frac{11}{16}$ **24.** 34

Apply

1. $4\frac{1}{2}$ hours **2.** Bea's route; one hour less **3.** 262 miles; $5\frac{1}{4}$ hours **4.** 6:10 P.M. **5.** Josh and Marian's route; $3\frac{3}{4}$ hours

LESSON 5

Practice

1. $\frac{7}{16}$ **2.** 26 **3.** $16\frac{1}{2}$ **4.** $6\frac{3}{4}$ **5.** $\frac{4}{27}$ **6.** 14 **7.** 45 **8.** $36\frac{1}{9}$ **9.** $5\frac{5}{8}$ **10.** 25 **11.** $\frac{9}{10}$ **12.** $6\frac{2}{5}$ **13.** $2\frac{7}{8}$ **14.** $1\frac{1}{6}$ **15.** $2\frac{1}{10}$ **16.** 3 **17.** $\frac{25}{27}$ **18.** 4 **19.** $11\frac{7}{8}$ **20.** $3\frac{3}{4}$ **21.** $1\frac{4}{5}$ **22.** $12 = 2 \times 2 \times 3$ **23.** $30 = 5 \times 3 \times 2$ **24.** $100 = 5 \times 5 \times 2 \times 2$

Apply

1. $7\frac{3}{8}$ c flour; $5\frac{1}{4}$ c sugar **2.** 125 c punch **3.** $12\frac{1}{2}$ lb meat **4.** $\frac{3}{4}$ lb per person **5.** $8\frac{1}{4}$ hours **6.** $6\frac{2}{3}$ **7.** $21\frac{3}{4}$ hours **8.** \$14.75

ANSWER KEY

LESSON 6

Practice

1. 6.2 **2.** 6.02 **3.** 6.002 **4.** 6.0002 **5.** 0.572 **6.** 906.906 **7.** 30.0791 **8.** 1,000,000.01 **9.** $\frac{4}{10}$ **10.** $\frac{4}{100}$ **11.** $\frac{4}{1000}$ **12.** $\frac{35}{100}$ **13.** $\frac{135}{1000}$ **14.** $1\frac{8}{10}$ **15.** $1\frac{89}{100}$ **16.** $1\frac{876}{1000}$ **17.** $5\frac{29}{100}$ **18.** $9\frac{76}{1000}$ **19.** $\frac{3}{100}$ **20.** $6\frac{38}{100}$ **21.** 6; 6.1; 6.14; 6.144 **22.** 9; 8.7; 8.74; 8.736 **23.** 1; 0.5; 0.52; 0.518 **24.** 159.07 **25.** 863.4223

Apply

1. 2nd; 1st; 4th; 3rd **2.** 2.8 m; 2.7 m **3.** 2nd; 3rd; 4th; 1st **4.** 1.4 m; 1.3 m **5.** 4th; 2nd; 1st; 3rd **6.** 0.06 seconds **7.** 1st; 2nd; 4th; 3rd **8.** 23 seconds

LESSON 7

Practice

1. 7.012 **2.** 16.0141 **3.** $518.03 **4.** 1231.983 **5.** $46.22 **6.** $1.62 **7.** 89.547 **8.** $14.70 **9.** 6.75 **10.** 11.101 **11.** 20.93 **12.** 1.02 **13.** 1.8129 **14.** 1.629 **15.** 22.353 **16.** 0.391 **17.** $196.67 **18.** $1130.43 **19.** 0.145 **20.** 0.4017 **21.** 46 **22.** 2 **23.** 90 **24.** 15

Apply

1. $16.06; $0.80; $16.86 **2.** $48.15; $2.41; $50.56 **3.** $14.49; $0.73; $15.22 **4.** $19.39 **5.** $2.16 **6.** $3.88 **7.** $5.72; $18.38 **8.** AAA batteries and AA batteries **9.** AA batteries and recharger **10.** Calculator and AAA batteries

LESSON 8

Practice

1. 5.4; $5\frac{4}{10}$ **2.** 0.56; $\frac{56}{100}$ **3.** 40.85; $40\frac{85}{100}$ **4.** 0.0028; $\frac{28}{1000}$ **5.** 5.58; $5\frac{58}{100}$ **6.** 34.012; $34\frac{12}{100}$ **7.** 341.02 **8.** 3819.56 **9.** 299.52 **10.** 123.93 **11.** 50.466 **12.** 4280.043 **13.** 27.056 **14.** 250.384 **15.** 2.3166 **16.** 44.9272 **17.** 7.524440 **18.** 4.32324 **19.** 4.73; 47.3; 473 **20.** 90.19; 901.9; 9019 **21.** 2580.6; 25,806; 2,580,060 **22.** 3,125.479; 312,547.9; 31,254,790

Apply

1. 121 cm^2 **2.** 170.5 cm^2 **3.** 30.25 cm^2 **4.** 181.5 cm^2; 170.5 cm^2 **5.** 308 cm^2 **6.** 40 cm **7.** 27.5 cm **8.** 440 cm^2 **9.** $16.20 **10.** $7.05 **11.** $2.87 **12.** $4.18

LESSON 9

Practice

1. 0.75 **2.** 7.5 **3.** 0.68 **4.** 6.8 **5.** 0.125 **6.** 1.25 **7.** 0.2875 **8.** 2.875 **9.** $3.89 **10.** 2.3 **11.** 0.075 **12.** 3.256 **13.** 4.899; 4.899 **14.** 708.83; 708.83 **15.** 9.7; 9.7 **16.** 1.0498; 1.0498 **17.** 0.684; 1; 0.7; 0.68 **18.** 9.307; 9; 9.3; 9.31

Apply

1. $43.42 **2.** $31.35 **3.** 2 Top 10 records; $1.31 **4.** $6.15 **5.** 1 poster and one piece of sheet music (at 2 for $4.75) **6.** 50¢ **7.** 3 for $7 **8.** $4.89

LESSON 10

Practice

1. 3.02 **2.** 15.6 **3.** 45.2 **4.** 8.7 **5.** 380 **6.** 900 **7.** 7.4 **8.** 6900 **9.** 610 **10.** 0.375 **11.** 0.875 **12.** 0.6 **13.** 0.1 **14.** 0.9 **15.** 0.75 **16.** $0.\overline{3}$ **17.** $0.\overline{6}$ **18.** $0.1\overline{6}$ **19.** $0.\overline{1}$ **20.** $0.\overline{4}$ **21.** $0.08\overline{3}$ **22.** 9 **23.** 1.3

Apply

1. 12.1 **2.** 17.5 **3.** 16.8 **4.** 27.5 **5.** 28 **6.** 11 **7.** 9.8 **8.** 17 hours **9.** 6 more hours **10.** 1250 gallons **11.** 21¢ **12.** $14.68

LESSON 11

Practice

1. $^{-}8$ **2.** $^{+}3$ **3.** $^{-}16$ **4.** 0 **5.** $^{-}20$ **6.** $^{+}1$ **7.** $^{+}7$ **8.** $^{-}24$ **9.** $^{-}30$ **10.** $^{-}19$ **11.** $^{-}14$ **12.** $^{-}17$ **13.** $^{-}4$ **14.** $^{-}12$ **15.** $^{-}7$ **16.** $^{-}11$ **17.** $^{+}5$ **18.** $^{+}6$ **19.** $^{+}18$ **20.** $^{-}20$ **21.** $^{+}51$ **22.** $^{+}10$ **23.** $^{-}4$ **24.** $^{+}16$ **25.** $^{-}6$ **26.** $^{-}4$ **27.** $>; <; <; >$ **28.** $=; <; <; <$ **29.** $>; <; >; =$

Apply

1. Monday; $^{-}2$°C **2.** Tuesday; $^{-}5$°C **3.** Wednesday; $^{-}8$°C **4.** Thursday; $^{-}11$°C **5.** Friday; $^{-}6$°C **6.** Saturday; $^{-}1$°C **7.** 5 km **8.** 4504 m **9.** \$75 **10.** $^{-}$\$73 **11.** $^{+}$\$200 **12.** $^{-}$\$150 **13.** $^{-}$\$81 **14.** $^{+}$\$44

LESSON 12

Practice

1. 35 **2.** $^{-}48$ **3.** 200 **4.** 0 **5.** $^{-}96$ **6.** 108 **7.** $^{+}27$; $^{+}27$; $^{-}27$; $^{-}27$ **8.** $^{+}105$; $^{+}105$; $^{-}105$; $^{-}105$ **9.** $^{-}66$; $^{-}66$; $^{+}66$; $^{+}66$ **10.** $^{-}4$ **11.** $^{-}10$ **12.** 9 **13.** $^{-}5$ **14.** $^{-}9$ **15.** 6 **16.** positive **17.** positive **18.** negative **19.** positive **20.** positive **21.** negative **22.** $^{-}13$

Apply

1. \$32 **2.** \$23.35 **3.** 950 km **4.** 2 blocks **5.** 25 m below sea level **6.** 10 floors **7.** $^{-}12$°C

LESSON 13

Practice

1. 17 **2.** 52 **3.** 23 **4.** 19 **5.** 49 **6.** 44 **7.** 23 **8.** 7 **9.** 22 **10.** 33; 29 **11.** 73; 73 **12.** 28; 44 **13.** 68; 68 **14.** 91; 103 **15.** 89; 89 **16.** $8 + n = 42; n = 34$ **17.** $n - 9 = 11;$ $n = 20$ **18.** $n + 78 = 205; n = 127$ **19.** $n - 69 = 314; n = 383$ **20.** $24 + n = 50; n = 26$ **21.** $89 - n = 76; n = 13$

Apply

1. $n - 12 = 38; n = 50$°F **2.** $^{-}10 + {}^{+}4 = n;$ $n = 6$ **3.** $15 + 8 = n; n = 23$ **4.** $n - 5 = 24; n = 29$ **5.** $110.5 + 8.25 = n$ **6.** n − \$10.35 = \$17.65; n = \$28.00 **7.** $76 - n = 49; n = 27$ **8.** $n + 133 = 268;$ $n = 135$

LESSON 14

Practice

1. 10 **2.** 5 **3.** 6 **4.** 7 **5.** 6 **6.** 9 **7.** 24 **8.** 25 **9.** 50 **10.** 4 **11.** 9 **12.** 8 **13.** 9 **14.** 0.15 **15.** 3 **16.** 5 **17.** 2 **18.** 7 **19.** 16 **20.** 36 **21.** 24 **22.** 18 **23.** 2 **24.** 8

Apply

1. $4 \times 7 = n; n = 28$ **2.** $3 \times 10.5 = n;$ $n = 31.5$ **3.** $n + 10 = 38; n = 28$ **4.** $52 - 15 = n; n = 37$ **5.** $2 \times 3\frac{1}{4} = n;$ $n = 6\frac{1}{2}$ **6.** $925 - 250 = n; n = 675$ **7.** $5n + 6 = 41; n = 7$ **8.** $3n + 7 = 25;$ $n = 6$

LESSON 15

Practice

1. 36 **2.** 63 **3.** 45 **4.** 48 **5.** 120 **6.** 8 **7.** 50 **8.** 42 **9.** 4 **10.** 72 **11.** 56 **12.** 225 **13.** 40 **14.** 75 **15.** 35 **16.** 4 **17.** 25 **18.** 5 **19.** 9 **20.** 10 **21.** 16

Apply

1. $\frac{n}{4}$ **2.** $\frac{n}{2} + 0.25$ **3.** $\frac{n}{12}$ **4.** $n + 38$ **5.** $n - 0.68$ **6.** $5n$ **7.** $\frac{48}{n}$ **8.** $\frac{n}{3}$ **9.** $2n + 7$ **10.** $3n = 96; n = 32$ **11.** $2n - 6 = 26;$ $n = 16$

LESSON 16

Practice

1. $\frac{55}{1}$ **2.** $\frac{24}{1}$ **3.** $\frac{8}{1.79}$ **4.** $\frac{6}{0.450}$ **5.** $\frac{30}{1}$ **6.** $\frac{45}{15}$ **7.** $\frac{15}{27}; \frac{20}{36}; \frac{25}{45}$ **8.** $\frac{6}{10}; \frac{9}{15}; \frac{12}{20}; \frac{15}{25}$ **9.** $\frac{12}{8}; \frac{9}{6}; \frac{6}{4}; \frac{3}{2}$ **10.** $\frac{9}{12}; \frac{6}{8}; \frac{3}{4}; \frac{1.5}{2}$ **11.** $\frac{4}{1}; \frac{2}{0.5}; \frac{1}{0.25}$ **12.** $\frac{0.6}{1.2}; \frac{0.8}{1.6};$ $\frac{1}{2}$ **13.** ≠ **14.** ≠ **15.** = **16.** ≠ **17.** ≠ **18.** = **19.** = **20.** = **21.** 75 **22.** 30 **23.** 108 **24.** 162 **25.** 12 **26.** 40 **27.** 1.2 **28.** 30

Apply

1. 60.4 km/h **2.** 495 km **3.** 0.2 km **4.** 200 minutes **5.** 400 m **6.** 250 m **7.** 1200 km **8.** 50 mm

LESSON 17

Practice

1. $\frac{15}{100}; \frac{3}{20};$ 15%; 0.15 **2.** $\frac{17}{100}; \frac{17}{100};$ 17%; 0.17 **3.** $\frac{2}{100}; \frac{1}{50};$ 2%; 0.2 **4.** $\frac{3}{100}; \frac{3}{100};$ 3%; 0.3

5. $\frac{95}{100}$; $\frac{19}{20}$; 95%; 0.95 **6.** $\frac{87}{100}$; $\frac{87}{100}$; 87%; 0.87

7. $\frac{125}{100}$; $\frac{5}{4}$; 125%; 1.25 **8.** $\frac{180}{100}$; $\frac{9}{5}$; 180%; 1.8

9. 20% **10.** 40% **11.** 60% **12.** 160%

13. 75% **14.** 100% **15.** 175% **16.** 200%

17. $\frac{1}{3}$ **18.** $\frac{2}{3}$ **19.** $\frac{1}{6}$ **20.** $\frac{5}{6}$ **21.** $\frac{5}{12}$ **22.** $\frac{7}{12}$

23. $\frac{1}{8}$ **24.** $\frac{3}{8}$ **25.** 71.6% **26.** 125.4% **27.** 39%

28. 400.8%

Apply

1. 1000 **2.** 50 families **3.** $\frac{3}{20}$ **4.** $\frac{7}{20}$ **5.** $\frac{1}{10}$

6. 400 **7.** 10 families **8.** 5 families **9.** 400

10. 32.5% **11.** 11.25% **12.** 20%

LESSON 18

Practice

1. $\frac{1}{5} \times 85 = 17$ **2.** $\frac{1}{2} \times 46 = 23$

3. $\frac{1}{4} \times 540 = 135$ **4.** $\frac{1}{3} \times 246 = 82$

5. $\frac{2}{3} \times 24 = 16$ **6.** $\frac{1}{8} \times 120 = 15$

7. $0.10 \times 9.7 = 0.97$ **8.** $0.76 \times 300 = 228$

9. $1.5 \times 800 = 1200$ **10.** $0.39 \times 73 = 28.47$

11. $0.052 \times 95 = 4.94$ **12.** $0.047 \times 980 = 46.06$

13. $\frac{4}{100} = \frac{n}{1500}; n = 60$ **14.** $\frac{10}{100} = \frac{n}{789}; n = 78.9$

15. $\frac{5.2}{100} = \frac{n}{9000}; n = 468$ **16.** $\frac{8}{100} = \frac{n}{178}; n = 14.24$

17. $\frac{72}{100} = \frac{n}{260}; n = 187.2$ **18.** $\frac{4.8}{100} = \frac{n}{670}; n = 32.16$

19. $\frac{1}{5} \times 49 = 9\frac{4}{5}$ **20.** $0.2 \times 49 = 9.8$

21. $\frac{20}{100} = \frac{n}{49}; n = 9.8$

Apply

1. 63 **2.** 189 **3.** 126 **4.** 42 **5.** 182 **6.** 84
7. 21 **8.** 63 **9.** 276 **10.** 115 **11.** 46 **12.** 138

LESSON 19

Practice

1. $n\% \cdot 100 = 7; n\% = \frac{7}{100}$; 7%

2. $n\% \cdot 30 = 1; n\% = \frac{1}{30}$; 3%

3. $n\% \cdot 264 = 66; n\% = \frac{66}{264}$; 25%

4. $88 = n\% \cdot 176; n\% = \frac{88}{176}$; 5%

5. $30 = n\% \cdot 250; n\% = \frac{30}{250}$; 12%

6. $n\% \cdot 75 = 66; n\% = \frac{66}{75}$; 88%

7. $43.2 = n\% \cdot 96; n\% = \frac{43.2}{96}$; 45% **8.** 40%

9. 110% **10.** 150% **11.** 20% **12.** 120%

13. 170% **14.** $n = 83\%$ **15.** $n = 55\%$

16. $n = 200\%$ **17.** a **18.** a **19.** b **20.** b

Apply

1. 7:30–8:00 A.M. **2.** 16% **3.** 26% **4.** 15%
5. 27% **6.** 16% **7.** 8% **8.** 36%

LESSON 20

Practice

1. $\frac{4}{5}n = 144; n = 180$ **2.** $\frac{24}{50}n - 24; n = 50$

3. $\frac{8}{25}n = 288; n = 900$ **4.** $\frac{3}{4}n = 48; n = 64$

5. $\frac{1}{3}n = 290; n = 870$ **6.** $\frac{5}{8}n = 110; n = 176$

7. $0.4n = 250; n = 625$ **8.** $0.76 \times n = 608;$

$n = 800$ **9.** $0.84n = 109.2; n = 130$

10. $0.77n = 69.3; n = 90$ **11.** $0.19n = 11.4;$

$n = 60$ **12.** $0.15n = 146.4; n = 976$

13. $\frac{45}{n} = \frac{90}{100}; n = 50$ **14.** $\frac{375}{n} = \frac{25}{100};$

$n = 1500$ **15.** $\frac{10}{n} = \frac{5}{100}; n = 200$

16. $\frac{120}{n} = \frac{250}{100}; n = 48$ **17.** $\frac{285}{n} = \frac{95}{100}; n = 300$

18. $\frac{64}{n} = \frac{12.5}{100}; n = 512$ **19.** $25.00 **20.** $800.00

Apply

1. $34.33 **2.** $189 **3.** 18% **4.** 16% **5.** $2400
6. $280 **7.** $40 **8.** $175,000.00

LESSON 21

1. 0.375 lb **2.** $^{+}5$°C **3.** $^{-}\$20$ **4.** 9 windows
5. $2\frac{1}{2}$ hours **6.** $9

Skills Sharpener

Solve each problem. Write the letter for each problem on the line over its answer to complete:

The set of all natural numbers, zero, and the negative numbers is called ________.

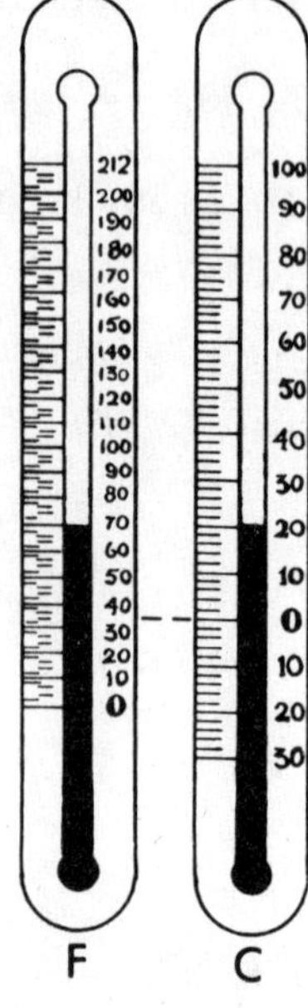

R 1 Fahrenheit degree is equivalent to $\frac{5}{9}$ Celsius degrees. Write $\frac{5}{9}$ as a decimal.

N 1 Celsius degree is equivalent to $\frac{9}{5}$ Fahrenheit degrees. Write $\frac{9}{5}$ as a decimal.

E On three consecutive nights the low temperature was $^{+}7$°F, $^{-}11$°F, and $^{-}2$°F. What was the average low temperature?

T To get the temperature in degrees Fahrenheit, multiply the temperature in degrees Celsius by $\frac{9}{5}$ and add 32. The temperature is 10°C. What is the temperature in degrees Fahrenheit?

G The temperature dropped 6°C in 3 hours. It continues to drop at the same rate. How much more will it drop in 2 more hours?

I A thermometer cost $15.75. The sales tax was 7%. What was the total cost?

S The regular price of a thermometer was $9.60. The sale price is 15% off. What is the sale price?

ANSWER:

___	___	___	___	___	___	___	___
$16.86	1.8	50°F	$^{-}2$°F	4°C	$^{-}2$°F	0.6	$8.15

Answers on page 557

Table of Contents

Spectrum Test Prep

The Program That Teaches Test-Taking Achievement

For over two decades, McGraw-Hill has helped students perform their best when taking standardized achievement tests. Over the years, we have identified the skills and strategies that students need to master the challenges of taking a standardized test. Becoming familiar with the test-taking experience can help ensure your child's success.

Spectrum Test Prep covers all test skill areas

Spectrum Test Prep contains the subject areas that are represented in the five major standardized tests. *Spectrum Test Prep* will help your child prepare for the following tests:

- California Achievement Tests® (CAT/5)
- Comprehensive Tests of Basic Skills (CTBS/4)
- Iowa Tests of Basic Skills® (ITBS, Form K)
- Metropolitan Achievement Test (MAT/7)
- Stanford Achievement Test(SAT/9)

Spectrum Test Prep provides strategies for success

Many students need special support when preparing to take a standardized test. *Spectrum Test Prep* gives your child the opportunity to practice and become familiar with:

- General test content
- The test format
- Listening and following standard directions
- Working in structured settings
- Maintaining a silent, sustained effort
- Using test-taking strategies

Spectrum Test Prep is comprehensive

Spectrum Test Prep provides a complete presentation of the types of skills covered in standardized tests in a variety of formats. These formats are similar to those your child will encounter when testing. The subject areas covered in this book include:

- Reading
- Language Arts
- Math

Spectrum Test Prep gives students the practice they need

Each student lesson provides several components that help develop test-taking skills:

- An **Example,** with directions and sample test items
- A **Tips** feature, that give test-taking strategies
- A **Practice** section, to help students practice answering questions in each test format

Each book gives focused test practice that builds confidence:

- A **Test Yourself** lesson for each unit gives students the opportunity to apply what they have learned in the unit
- A **Test Practice** section gives students the experience of a longer test-like situation.
- A **Progress Chart** for students to note and record their own progress.

Spectrum Test Prep is the first and most successful program ever developed to help students become familiar with the test-taking experience. *Spectrum Test Prep* can help to build self-confidence, reduce test anxiety, and provide the opportunity for students to successfully show what they have learned.

A Message to Parents and Teachers:

- **Standardized tests: the yardstick for your child's future**

  Standardized testing is one of the cornerstones of American education. From its beginning in the early part of this century, standardized testing has gradually become the yardstick by which student performance is judged. For better or worse, your child's future will be determined in great part by how well she or he performs on the standardized test used by your school district.

- **Even good students can have trouble with testing**

  In general, standardized tests are well designed and carefully developed to assess students' abilities in a consistent and balanced manner. However, there are many factors that can hinder the performance of an individual student when testing. These might include test anxiety, unfamiliarity with the test's format, or failing to understand the directions.

  In addition, it is rare that students are taught all of the material that appears on a standardized test. This is because the curriculum of most schools does not directly match the the content of the standardized test. There will certainly be overlap between what your child learns in school and how he or she is tested, but some materials will probably be unfamiliar.

- ***Ready to Test* will lend a helping hand**

  It is because of the shortcomings of the standardized testing process that *Spectrum Test Prep* was developed. The lessons in the book were created after a careful analysis of the most popular achievement tests. The items, while different from those on the tests, reflects the types of material that your child will encounter when testing. Students who use *Spectrum Test Prep* will also become familiar with the format of the most popular achievement tests. This learning experience will reduce anxiety and give your child the opportunity to do their best on their next standardized test.

We urge you to review with your child the Message to Students and the feature "How to Use This Book" on pages 7-9. The information on these pages will help your child to use this book and develop important test-taking skills. We are confident that following the recommendations in this book will help your child to earn a test score that accurately reflects his or her true ability.

A Message to Students:

Frequently in school you will be asked to take a standardized achievement test. This test will show how much you know compared to other students in your grade. Your score on a standardized achievement test will help you teachers plan your education. It will also give you and your parents an idea of what your learning strengths and weaknesses are.

This book will help you do your best on a standardized achievement test. It will show you what to expect on the test and will give you a chance to practice important reading and test-taking skills. Here are some suggestions you can follow to make the best use of *Spectrum Test Prep.*

Plan for success

- You'll do your best if you begin studying and do one or two lessons in this book each week. If you only have a little bit of time before a test is given, you can do one or two lessons each day.
- Study a little bit at a time, no more than 30 minutes a day. If you can, choose the same time each day to study in a quiet place.
- Keep a record of your score on each lesson. The charts on pp. 154–156 of this book will help you do this.

On the day of the test . . .

- Get a good night's sleep the night before the test. Have a light breakfast and lunch to keep from feeling drowsy during the test.
- Use the tips you learned in *Spectrum Test Prep.* The most important tips are to skip difficult items, take the best guess when you're unsure of the answer, and try all the items.
- Don't worry if you are a little nervous when you take an achievement test. This is a natural feeling and may even help you stay alert.

How to Use This Book

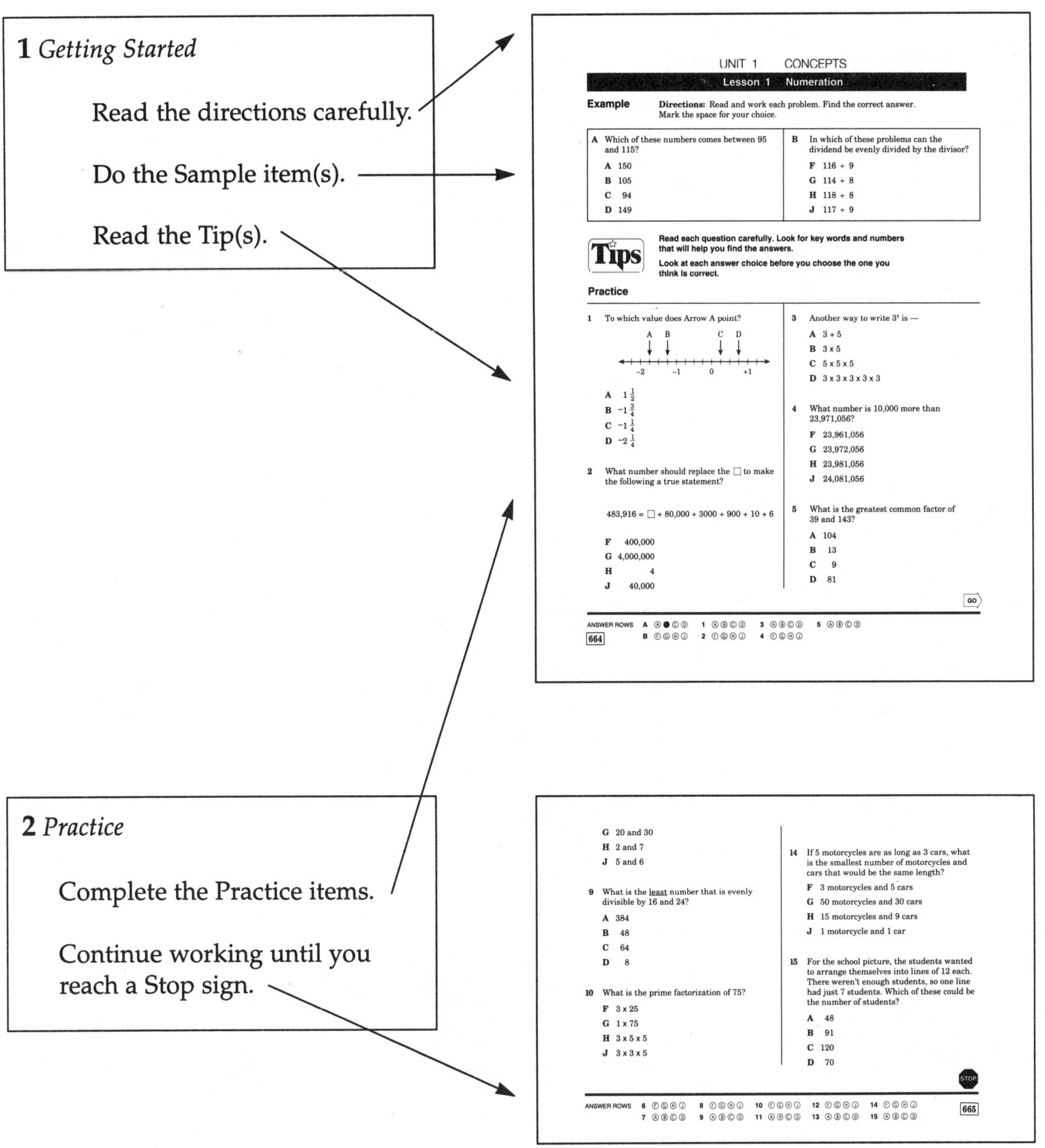

1 *Getting Started*
Read the directions carefully.
Do the Sample item(s).
Read the Tip(s).
2 *Practice*
Complete the Practice items.
Continue working until you reach a Stop sign.

UNIT 1 CONCEPTS

Lesson 1 Numeration

Example **Directions:** Read and work each problem. Find the correct answer. Mark the space for your choice.

A Which of these numbers comes between 95 and 115?

A 150
B 105
C 94
D 149

B In which of these problems can the dividend be evenly divided by the divisor?

F 116 ÷ 9
G 114 ÷ 8
H 118 ÷ 8
J 117 ÷ 9

Tips

Read each question carefully. Look for key words and numbers that will help you find the answers.

Look at each answer choice before you choose the one you think is correct.

Practice

1 To which value does Arrow A point?

A $1\frac{1}{2}$
B $-1\frac{3}{4}$
C $-1\frac{1}{4}$
D $-2\frac{1}{4}$

2 What number should replace the □ to make the following a true statement?

483,916 = □ + 80,000 + 3000 + 900 + 10 + 6

F 400,000
G 4,000,000
H 4
J 40,000

3 Another way to write 3^5 is —

A 3 + 5
B 3 x 5
C 5 x 5 x 5
D 3 x 3 x 3 x 3 x 3

4 What number is 10,000 more than 23,971,056?

F 23,961,056
G 23,972,056
H 23,981,056
J 24,081,056

5 What is the greatest common factor of 39 and 143?

A 104
B 13
C 9
D 81

GO

ANSWER ROWS A Ⓐ●ⒸⒹ 1 ⒶⒷⒸⒹ 3 ⒶⒷⒸⒹ 5 ⒶⒷⒸⒹ
B ⒻⒼⒽⒿ 2 ⒻⒼⒽⒿ 4 ⒻⒼⒽⒿ

664

G 20 and 30
H 2 and 7
J 5 and 6

9 What is the least number that is evenly divisible by 16 and 24?

A 384
B 48
C 64
D 8

10 What is the prime factorization of 75?

F 3 x 25
G 1 x 75
H 3 x 5 x 5
J 3 x 3 x 5

14 If 5 motorcycles are as long as 3 cars, what is the smallest number of motorcycles and cars that would be the same length?

F 3 motorcycles and 5 cars
G 50 motorcycles and 30 cars
H 15 motorcycles and 9 cars
J 1 motorcycle and 1 car

15 For the school picture, the students wanted to arrange themselves into lines of 12 each. There weren't enough students, so one line had just 7 students. Which of these could be the number of students?

A 48
B 91
C 120
D 70

STOP

ANSWER ROWS 6 ⒻⒼⒽⒿ 8 ⒻⒼⒽⒿ 10 ⒻⒼⒽⒿ 12 ⒻⒼⒽⒿ 14 ⒻⒼⒽⒿ
7 ⒶⒷⒸⒹ 9 ⒶⒷⒸⒹ 11 ⒶⒷⒸⒹ 13 ⒶⒷⒸⒹ 15 ⒶⒷⒸⒹ

665

3 *Check It Out*

Check your answers by turning to the Answer Key at the back of the book.

Keep track of how you're doing by marking the number right on the Progress Charts on pages 154-156.

Mark the lesson you completed on the table of contents for each section.

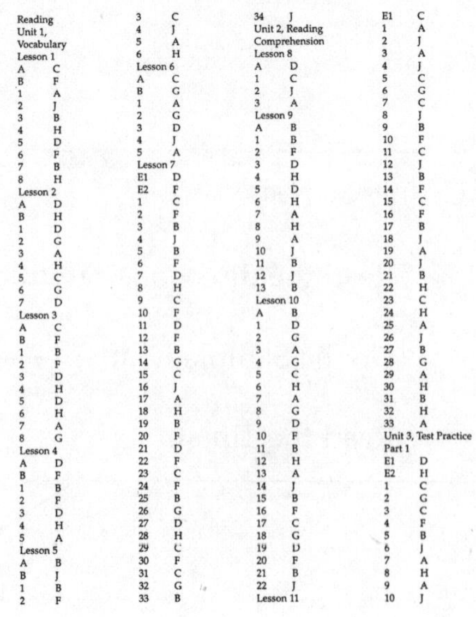

Answer Keys

Reading Unit 1, Vocabulary	
Lesson 1	
A	C
B	F
1	A
2	J
3	B
4	H
5	D
6	F
7	B
8	H
Lesson 2	
A	D
B	H
1	D
2	G
3	A
4	H
5	C
6	G
7	D
Lesson 3	
A	C
B	F
1	B
2	F
3	D
4	H
5	D
6	H
7	A
8	G
Lesson 4	
A	D
B	F
1	B
2	F
3	D
4	H
5	A
Lesson 5	
A	B
B	J
1	B
2	F
3	C
4	J
5	A
6	H
Lesson 6	
A	C
B	G
1	A
2	G
3	D
4	J
5	A
Lesson 7	
E1	D
E2	F
1	C
2	F
3	B
4	J
5	B
6	F
7	D
8	H
9	C
10	F
11	D
12	F
13	B
14	G
15	C
16	J
17	A
18	H
19	B
20	F
21	D
22	F
23	C
24	F
25	B
26	G
27	D
28	H
29	C
30	F
31	C
32	G
33	B
34	J
Unit 2, Reading Comprehension	
Lesson 8	
A	D
1	C
2	J
3	A
Lesson 9	
A	B
1	B
2	F
3	D
4	H
5	D
6	H
7	A
8	H
9	A
10	J
11	B
12	J
13	B
Lesson 10	
A	B
1	D
2	G
3	A
4	G
5	C
6	H
7	A
8	G
9	D
10	F
11	B
12	H
13	A
14	J
15	B
16	F
17	C
18	G
19	D
20	F
21	B
22	J
Lesson 11	
E1	C
1	A
2	J
3	A
4	J
5	C
6	G
7	C
8	J
9	B
10	F
11	C
12	J
13	B
14	F
15	C
16	F
17	B
18	J
19	A
20	J
21	B
22	H
23	C
24	H
25	A
26	J
27	B
28	G
29	A
30	H
31	B
32	H
33	A
Unit 3, Test Practice	
Part 1	
E1	D
E2	H
1	C
2	G
3	C
4	F
5	B
6	J
7	A
8	H
9	A
10	J

709

Reading Progress Chart

Circle your score for each lesson. Connect your scores to see how well you are doing.

Unit 1 Lesson 1	Lesson 2	Lesson 3	Lesson 4	Lesson 5	Lesson 6	Lesson 7	Unit 2 Lesson 8	Lesson 9	Lesson 10	Lesson 11
8 7 6 5 4 3 2 1	7 6 5 4 3 2 1	8 7 6 5 4 3 2 1	5 4 3 2 1	6 5 4 3 2 1	5 4 3 2 1	34 33 32 31 30 29 28 27 26 25 24 23 22 21 20 19 18 17 16 15 14 13 12 11 10 9 8 7 6 5 4 3 2 1	3 2 1	13 12 11 10 9 8 7 6 5 4 3 2 1	22 21 20 19 18 17 16 15 14 13 12 11 10 9 8 7 6 5 4 3 2 1	33 32 31 30 29 28 27 26 25 24 23 22 21 20 19 18 17 16 15 14 13 12 11 10 9 8 7 6 5 4 3 2 1

714

Table of Contents
Reading

571

Skills

Reading

VOCABULARY

Identifying synonyms
Identifying words with similar meanings
Identifying antonyms
Identifying multi-meaning words
Identifying words in paragraph context
Identifying word meaning from a clue
Identifying words from a defining statement

READING COMPREHENSION

Recognizing story structures
Differentiating between fact and opinion
Understanding literary devices
Identifying story genres
Recognizing details
Understanding events
Drawing conclusions
Applying story information
Deriving word or phrase meaning
Understanding characters
Sequencing ideas
Making inferences
Making comparisons
Generalizing from story information
Identifying strategic reading techniques
Choosing the best title for a story
Using a story web
Understanding the author's purpose
Understanding feelings
Understanding the main idea

Language Arts

LANGUAGE MECHANICS

Identifying the need for punctuation marks (period, question marks, exclamation point, quotation marks, apostrophe, comma, colon, semicolon,) in sentences
Identifying the need for capital letters and punctuation marks in printed text

LANGUAGE EXPRESSION

Identifying the correct forms of verbs, adverbs, adjectives, and pronouns
Identifying the subject of a sentence
Combining sentences
Identifying redundant sentences
Identifying the correct sentence to complete a paragraph
Sequencing sentences within a paragraph
Identifying run-on sentences
Recognizing double negatives
Identifying incorrectly used words or phrases
Identifying the predicate of a sentence
Identifying correctly formed sentences
Identifying run-on sentences
Identifying sentences that do not fit in a paragraph
Choosing the right paragraph for a given purpose

SPELLING

Identifying correctly spelled words
Identifying incorrectly spelled words

STUDY SKILLS

Taking notes
Understanding a chart
Understanding the use of reference methods
Choosing an appropriate topic
Understanding a table of contents
Alphabetizing words
Using a map
Completing an application
Using a thesaurus
Identifying reference sources
Identifying a search topic

Math

COMPUTATION

Adding whole numbers, integers, decimals, and fractions
Subtracting whole numbers, decimals, and fractions
Multiplying whole numbers, integers, decimals, and fractions
Dividing whole numbers, integers, decimals, and fractions

CONCEPTS

Using expanded notation
Comparing and ordering whole numbers and integers
Finding multiples
Associating numerals and number words
Understanding place value
Understanding number sentences
Rounding
Identifying fractional parts
Comparing and ordering fractions and decimals
Reducing fractions
Converting among decimals, fractions, and percents
Finding square roots
Using exponents and exponential notation
Factoring numbers and finding the greatest common factor
Recognizing prime and composite numbers
Recognizing numeric patterns
Using operational symbols and properties
Estimating
Understanding decimal place value
Recognizing equivalent fractions and reciprocals
Identifying the lowest common denominator
Renaming fractions and decimals
Using a number line with fractions and decimals

APPLICATIONS

Understanding congruence and transformations
Finding perimeter, area, and volume
Understanding points, lines, segments and angles, and their characteristics
Understanding time concepts
Reading a thermometer
Understanding bar, line, and circle graphs
Solving oral and written word problems
Understanding probability, averages, and combinations
Formulating simple number sentences
Understanding inequalities
Recognizing plane and solid figures and their characteristics
Recognizing value of money and money notation
Using standard and metric units of measurement
Estimating weight and size
Understanding tables and charts
Identifying information needed to solve a problem
Understanding ratio and proportion
Using a coordinate graph
Solving simple equations

Strategies

Listening carefully
Following group directions
Adjusting to a structured setting
Utilizing test formats
Maintaining a silent, sustained effort
Locating questions and answer choices
Managing time effectively
Following oral directions
Considering every answer choice
Noting the lettering of answer choices
Recalling word meanings
Taking the best guess when unsure of the answer
Skipping difficult items and returning to them later
Identifying the best test-taking strategy
Working methodically
Comparing answer choices
Eliminating answer choices
Rereading questions
Referring to a passage to find the correct answer
Using Logic
Recalling the elements of a correctly formed sentence
Locating the correct answer
Identifying and using key words, figures, and numbers
Recalling the elements of a correctly formed paragraph
Following written directions
Taking the best quess
Substituting answer choices
Marking the right answer as soon as it is found
Understanding unusual item formats
Following complex directions
Trying out answer choices
Using context to find the answer
Inferring word meaning from sentence context
Converting problems to a workable format
Staying with the first answer
Previewing items
Responding to items according to difficulty
Finding the answer without computing
Analyzing questions
Identifying and using key words to find the answer
Skimming a passage
Referring to a passage to answer questions
Indicating that the correct answer is not given
Subvocalizing answer choices
Indicating that an item has no mistakes
Reasoning from facts and evidence
Avoiding overanalysis of answer choices
Referring to a reference source
Checking answers by the opposite operation
Performing the correct operation
Reworking a problem
Computing carefully
Using answer choices as a clue to finding the right answer
Checking answers

Table of Contents
Reading

Unit 1 Vocabulary

Unit 2 Reading Comprehension

Unit 3 Test Practice

Lesson 1 Synonyms

Examples

Directions: Read each item. Choose the word that means the same or about the same as the underlined word.

A **negotiate a deal**	B **To alternate goals is to —**
A cancel	**F** switch
B investigate	**G** achieve
C arrange	**H** reinforce
D question	**J** ignore

Read each question and the answer choices carefully. Make sure the space you darken in the answer rows matches the question on which you are working.

Practice

1 **discontinue the newspaper**

A cancel
B buy
C enjoy
D lose

2 **great impact**

F inspection
G friendship
H investment
J influence

3 **generate support**

A afford
B create
C appreciate
D avoid

4 **endure hardships**

F reject
G reduce
H tolerate
J increase

5 **To reside nearby is to —**

A build
B visit
C move
D live

6 **A terrible stench —**

F odor
G roar
H sound
J accident

7 **Great turmoil —**

A concern
B disorder
C mountain
D calm

8 **Trivial payments are —**

F huge
G quick
H small
J slow

STOP

ANSWER ROWS A Ⓐ Ⓑ Ⓒ Ⓓ 1 Ⓐ Ⓑ Ⓒ Ⓓ 3 Ⓐ Ⓑ Ⓒ Ⓓ 5 Ⓐ Ⓑ Ⓒ Ⓓ 7 Ⓐ Ⓑ Ⓒ Ⓓ
B Ⓕ Ⓖ Ⓗ Ⓙ 2 Ⓕ Ⓖ Ⓗ Ⓙ 4 Ⓕ Ⓖ Ⓗ Ⓙ 6 Ⓕ Ⓖ Ⓗ Ⓙ 8 Ⓕ Ⓖ Ⓗ Ⓙ

Examples

Directions: Read each item. Choose the answer that means the same or about the same as the underlined word.

A Scorn their help

A ask for
B reject with contempt
C accept with joy
D worry about

B Toshi is a competent worker.

To be competent is to be —

F inadequate
G busy
H capable
J quiet

If you aren't sure which answer is correct, take your best guess.

Practice

1 Avoid misfortune

A good luck
B a large amount of money
C a small amount of money
D bad luck

2 Do something manually

F by computer
G by hand
H by machine
J by command

3 Cherish a memory

A hold dear
B think badly of
C recall
D forget

4 We set up partitions in the room.

F video equipment
G rows of chairs
H dividing walls
J exhibition booths

5 One component hasn't arrived yet.

Component means —

A visitor
B team
C part
D competitor

6 The large horse was docile.

Docile means —

F energetic
G easy to manage
H hard to ride
J aggressive

7 The schedule you are proposing seems feasible.

Feasible means —

A impossible
B difficult
C enjoyable
D reasonable

ANSWER ROWS A Ⓐ Ⓑ Ⓒ Ⓓ 1 Ⓐ Ⓑ Ⓒ Ⓓ 3 Ⓐ Ⓑ Ⓒ Ⓓ 5 Ⓐ Ⓑ Ⓒ Ⓓ 7 Ⓐ Ⓑ Ⓒ Ⓓ
B Ⓕ Ⓖ Ⓗ Ⓙ 2 Ⓕ Ⓖ Ⓗ Ⓙ 4 Ⓕ Ⓖ Ⓗ Ⓙ 6 Ⓕ Ⓖ Ⓗ Ⓙ

Examples

Directions: Read each item. Choose the answer that means the opposite of the underlined word.

A **luscious fruit**

A sweet and juicy
B ready to eat
C tasteless and dry
D pretty to look at

B **a voluntary action**

F required
G sudden
H friendly
J angry

Skip difficult items and come back to them later. If you are still not sure of the right answer, eliminate choices you know are wrong and then take your best guess from the remaining answers.

Practice

1 **gallant knights**

A brave
B cowardly
C armed
D elegant

2 **bisect something**

F put together
G cut in half
H discover
J replace

3 **genuine leather**

A beautiful
B inexpensive
C real
D fake

4 **reveal the truth**

F suspect
G doubt
H keep hidden
J make known

5 **become belligerent**

A angry
B warlike
C competitive
D peaceful

6 **was prohibited**

F forbidden
G difficult
H allowed
J simple

7 **appear unkempt**

A neat
B lazy
C messy
D tired

8 **feel malice**

F concern
G kindness
H satisfied
J anger

STOP

ANSWER ROWS
A Ⓐ Ⓑ Ⓒ Ⓓ 1 Ⓐ Ⓑ Ⓒ Ⓓ 3 Ⓐ Ⓑ Ⓒ Ⓓ 5 Ⓐ Ⓑ Ⓒ Ⓓ 7 Ⓐ Ⓑ Ⓒ Ⓓ
B Ⓕ Ⓖ Ⓗ Ⓙ 2 Ⓕ Ⓖ Ⓗ Ⓙ 4 Ⓕ Ⓖ Ⓗ Ⓙ 6 Ⓕ Ⓖ Ⓗ Ⓙ 8 Ⓕ Ⓖ Ⓗ Ⓙ

Lesson 4 Multi-Meaning Words

Examples

Directions: Read each item. Choose the answer you think is correct.

A **Can you page Dr. Henderson?**

In which sentence does the word page mean the same thing as in the sentence above?

A Which page are you reading?

B The page held the knight's lance.

C I like to page through catalogs.

D Page me when you need a ride home.

B **The _______ was locked at five o'clock.**

Sandy was _______ at second base.

F safe
G door
H out
J chest

Tips

Skim the items. Answer the easiest items first. Then go back and do the more difficult items.

Use context to find the best answer.

Practice

1 **A command is wrong in this software.**

In which sentence does the word command mean the same thing as in the sentence above?

A The king will command your presence.

B Each command tells the computer to do a different thing.

C The general is in command here.

D She will command respect everywhere.

2 **Close the flap, then tape the box.**

In which sentence does the word flap mean the same thing as in the sentence above?

F The flap with the address should be on the outside.

G The huge bird began to flap its wings.

H Her story made quite a flap.

J The shutter began to flap against the house when the wind picked up.

3 **The bell will _______ at noon.**

Gloria lost her _______ in the kitchen.

A sound
B glove
C pen
D ring

4 **The runner began to _______ .**

That _______ is still in good shape.

F sweat
G car
H tire
J turn

5 **This is a very _______ problem.**

The apartment _______ has a pool.

A complex
B difficult
C building
D simple

STOP

ANSWER ROWS A Ⓐ Ⓑ Ⓒ Ⓓ 1 Ⓐ Ⓑ Ⓒ Ⓓ 3 Ⓐ Ⓑ Ⓒ Ⓓ 5 Ⓐ Ⓑ Ⓒ Ⓓ
B Ⓕ Ⓖ Ⓗ Ⓙ 2 Ⓕ Ⓖ Ⓗ Ⓙ 4 Ⓕ Ⓖ Ⓗ Ⓙ

Examples

Directions: Read the paragraph. Find the word below the paragraph that fits best in each blank.

Buying a new car is more ___(A)___ than you might think. You have to ___(B)___ which car you want and then shop for the best price. Most people then have to borrow money from a bank to pay for the new car.

A **A** partial
B involved
C unlikely
D meaningful

B **F** deny
G socialize
H furnish
J determine

Skim the paragraph. Use its meaning to find the right answer. If necessary, try substituting each answer choice in the blank.

Practice

The trucker was ___(1)___ of the accident ahead by a call on her radio. Markie began to ___(2)___ , and as she approached the scene, she saw that it looked pretty bad. Several cars had already stopped at the wreck, so she ___(3)___ that the injured passengers were being helped. Markie pulled on to the ___(4)___ of the road about one hundred yards ahead of the accident, put her flashers on, and set ___(5)___ flares along the road. She grabbed her first-aid kit from the truck and ___(6)___ up to the wreck.

1 **A** alarmed
B informed
C suspicious
D involved

2 **F** decelerate
G refrain
H extinguish
J rescind

3 **A** denied
B resented
C concluded
D compounded

4 **F** intersection
G instinct
H proximity
J shoulder

5 **A** caution
B inhibited
C isolated
D incidental

6 **F** bantered
G unweighted
H bolted
J swindled

STOP

ANSWER ROWS
A Ⓐ Ⓑ Ⓒ Ⓓ 1 Ⓐ Ⓑ Ⓒ Ⓓ 3 Ⓐ Ⓑ Ⓒ Ⓓ 5 Ⓐ Ⓑ Ⓒ Ⓓ
B Ⓕ Ⓖ Ⓗ Ⓙ 2 Ⓕ Ⓖ Ⓗ Ⓙ 4 Ⓕ Ⓖ Ⓗ Ⓙ 6 Ⓕ Ⓖ Ⓗ Ⓙ

Examples

Directions: Read each question. Fill in the circle for the answer you think is correct.

A Which of these words probably comes from the Old Icelandic word *gapa* meaning *a mouth that is opened wide*?

A gain
B gourd
C gape
D grate

B Raymond was ________ when he learned his bike was missing.

Which of these words means Raymond was bothered very much?

F angry
G distraught
H confused
J relaxed

Stay with the first answer choice. Change it only if you are sure it is wrong and another answer is better.

Practice

1 Which of these words probably comes from the Middle English word *muflein* meaning *wrapped up*?

A muffled
B mottled
C mounted
D molted

2 Which of these words probably comes from the Latin word *quaerere* meaning *to seek*?

F quaint
G quest
H quell
J quince

3 Which of these words probably comes from the Middle English word *couchen* meaning *to lie down*?

A cloud
B crowd
C catch
D crouch

4 The judges tried to make an ________ decision in the science contest.

Which of these words means the decision was fair?

F influential
G irresponsible
H offensive
J impartial

5 Gina felt ________ after staying up late to watch the eclipse.

Which of these words means Gina didn't have much energy?

A sluggish
B fictitious
C ambitious
D hopeless

STOP

ANSWER ROWS A Ⓐ Ⓑ Ⓒ Ⓓ 1 Ⓐ Ⓑ Ⓒ Ⓓ 3 Ⓐ Ⓑ Ⓒ Ⓓ 5 Ⓐ Ⓑ Ⓒ Ⓓ
B Ⓕ Ⓖ Ⓗ Ⓙ 2 Ⓕ Ⓖ Ⓗ Ⓙ 4 Ⓕ Ⓖ Ⓗ Ⓙ

E1 be obliged to attend

A asked
B happy
C unhappy
D required

E2 Which of these probably comes from the Middle English word *faltre* meaning *to be uncertain*?

F falter
G flatten
H father
J folder

For Numbers 1–8, find the word or words that mean the same or almost the same as the underlined word.

1 a fast tempo

A song
B dance
C pace
D car

2 a tract of land

F region
G deed
H purchase
J sale

3 massive rocks

A small
B huge
C beautiful
D ancient

4 plot a revolution

F end
G join
H lose
J plan

5 A tyrant is —

A a fair leader
B an unjust ruler
C a police officer
D an enemy

6 A long reign is a —

F period of rule
G strike
H time of famine
G relationship

7 An unusual specimen is a —

A jungle animal
B event
C sound
D scientific sample

8 Crucial evidence is —

F useless
G medical
H important
J hidden

GO

ANSWER ROWS E1 Ⓐ Ⓑ Ⓒ Ⓓ 1 Ⓐ Ⓑ Ⓒ Ⓓ 3 Ⓐ Ⓑ Ⓒ Ⓓ 5 Ⓐ Ⓑ Ⓒ Ⓓ 7 Ⓐ Ⓑ Ⓒ Ⓓ
E2 Ⓕ Ⓖ Ⓗ Ⓙ 2 Ⓕ Ⓖ Ⓗ Ⓙ 4 Ⓕ Ⓖ Ⓗ Ⓙ 6 Ⓕ Ⓖ Ⓗ Ⓙ 8 Ⓕ Ⓖ Ⓗ Ⓙ

9 **Felicia made an impartial decision.**

Impartial means —

A hasty
B emotional
C fair
D biased

10 **Did you inquire about the cost?**

To inquire is to —

F ask
G talk
H argue
J bargain

11 **Abdul wrote his notes on the margin of the paper.**

Margin means —

A middle
B back
C front
D edge

12 **Did Paula regret going to the meeting?**

To regret is to feel —

F sorry about
G good about
H undecided about
J concerned about

13 **The company's new slogan is exciting.**

A slogan is a —

A product
B saying
C building
D plan

For Numbers 14–19, find the word that means the opposite of the underlined word.

14 **alert sentry**

F attentive
G inattentive
H frightened
J lonely

15 **inaccurate statement**

A long
B wrong
C correct
D hopeful

16 **versatile tool**

F expensive
G having many uses
H inexpensive
J having only one use

17 **should encounter**

A avoid
B attract
C attribute
D isolate

18 **erratic flight**

F swift
G incredible
H straight
J minimal

19 **intense feelings**

A empty
B weak
C strong
D irate

GO

ANSWER ROWS 9 Ⓐ Ⓑ Ⓒ Ⓓ 11 Ⓐ Ⓑ Ⓒ Ⓓ 13 Ⓐ Ⓑ Ⓒ Ⓓ 15 Ⓐ Ⓑ Ⓒ Ⓓ 17 Ⓐ Ⓑ Ⓒ Ⓓ 19 Ⓐ Ⓑ Ⓒ Ⓓ
10 Ⓕ Ⓖ Ⓗ Ⓙ 12 Ⓕ Ⓖ Ⓗ Ⓙ 14 Ⓕ Ⓖ Ⓗ Ⓙ 16 Ⓕ Ⓖ Ⓗ Ⓙ 18 Ⓕ Ⓖ Ⓗ Ⓙ

For Numbers 20–23, choose the word that correctly completes <u>both</u> sentences.

20 **We heard a ________ sound from the room above us.**

It was so hot I was sure I would ________ while we stood in line.

F faint
G quiet
H collapse
J dim

21 **The Johnsons are ________ to the Murrays who live next door to us.**

When Karen ________ her story, she presented all the details.

A associated
B recited
C disclosed
D related

22 **The knight wore a coat of ________ to protect him in battle.**

We can ________ the package today and hope it arrives on time.

F mail
G ship
H leather
J send

23 **You will have to complete this form to ________ for the job.**

Be careful when you ________ the medicine to the burned area.

A interview
B rub
C apply
D compete

24 **The singers did a <u>fine</u> job.**

In which sentence does the word <u>fine</u> mean the same thing as in the sentence above?

F We enjoyed a <u>fine</u> dinner at a small restaurant.

G The <u>fine</u> for speeding is $50.

H The <u>fine</u> sand blew into the tent.

J There are many <u>fine</u> details in this painting.

25 **The <u>title</u> of this story doesn't match what it is about.**

In which sentence does the word <u>title</u> mean the same thing as in the sentence above?

A There seems to be some confusion about the <u>title</u> to the house.

B I forget the <u>title</u>, but the movie was about a survivor of a shipwreck.

C His <u>title</u> was the Duke of York.

D She held the tennis <u>title</u> for seven years.

26 **Will she be able to <u>lead</u> the team?**

In which sentence does the word <u>lead</u> mean the same thing as in the sentence above?

F The horse's <u>lead</u> was dragging on the ground.

G The best way to <u>lead</u> is by example.

H The <u>lead</u> singer thanked the others in his group.

J Our <u>lead</u> was down to two runs.

GO

ANSWER ROWS 20 Ⓕ Ⓖ Ⓗ Ⓙ 22 Ⓕ Ⓖ Ⓗ Ⓙ 24 Ⓕ Ⓖ Ⓗ Ⓙ 26 Ⓕ Ⓖ Ⓗ Ⓙ
21 Ⓐ Ⓑ Ⓒ Ⓓ 23 Ⓐ Ⓑ Ⓒ Ⓓ 25 Ⓐ Ⓑ Ⓒ Ⓓ

27 Which of these words probably comes from the Scandinavian word *bangla* meaning *to work ineffectively*?

A bugle
B bundle
C bridle
D bungle

28 Which of these words probably comes from the Middle English word *desolatus* meaning *forsaken*?

F deploy
G deny
H desolate
J disintegrate

29 We were able to ________ the cold because we had the right clothes.

Which of these words means we were able to put up with the cold?

A tedious
B satiate
C tolerate
D impend

30 The surface of the statue had been ________ by the weather.

Which of these words means the surface of the statue had been eaten away?

F corroded
G corroborated
H deflected
J harried

Read the paragraph. Find the word below the paragraph that fits best in each numbered blank.

Margita __(31)__ thought that her brother's idea to open a lemonade stand was __(32)__ . She went along with the idea because she wanted to __(33)__ him. Sancho was only twelve, but he had big ideas about going into business. They obtained a license from the town clerk, built a pushcart, and parked their cart near the courthouse. By the end of the summer, Margita had __(34)__ her position completely. She and Sancho had earned more than $5,000.

31 A moderately
B incessantly
C initially
D desperately

32 F adroit
G absurd
H dependable
J optimistic

33 A berate
B encourage
C dismay
D insinuate

34 F solidified
G partaken
H deteriorated
J reversed

581

STOP

ANSWER ROWS 27 Ⓐ Ⓑ Ⓒ Ⓓ 29 Ⓐ Ⓑ Ⓒ Ⓓ 31 Ⓐ Ⓑ Ⓒ Ⓓ 33 Ⓐ Ⓑ Ⓒ Ⓓ
28 Ⓕ Ⓖ Ⓗ Ⓙ 30 Ⓕ Ⓖ Ⓗ Ⓙ 32 Ⓕ Ⓖ Ⓗ Ⓙ 34 Ⓕ Ⓖ Ⓗ Ⓙ NUMBER RIGHT ______

Lesson 8 Critical Reading

Example

Directions: Read each item. Choose the answer you think is correct. Mark the space for your answer.

The ad in the paper was for a "driver's helper." Judy didn't know what that was, but she decided to apply. To her surprise, she got the job, and discovered it was to work on an ice truck. She rode with the driver as he made his deliveries and helped him unload the ice and fill up customers' freezers.

A Which of these is a fact from the story?

- **A** The job sounds like fin.
- **B** Papers are the best place to find jobs.
- **C** Loading ice is hard work.
- **D** Judy got the job.

Read the question, look at the answer choices, then read the question again. Choose the answer you think is right, then compare it to the question again.

Practice

Read this passage. Then do Numbers 1–2.

He was a failure, at least as far as the people of Spain were concerned. He hadn't found the Cities of Gold, nor had he returned with great treasure. Francisco Coronado, had, however, explored much of the New World, and had brought the Spanish culture to a region that would eventually become the American Southwestern states.

1 Which of these is a fact expressed in the passage?

- **A** Because he had not found treasure, Coronado was a failure.
- **B** The Spanish culture is best suited for warm climates like the Southwest.
- **C** Coronado explored a region that would become part of America.
- **D** Coronado was the most successful of the Spanish explorers.

2 This passage would most likely be found in —

- **F** a fiction story.
- **G** a travel brochure.
- **H** an adventure story.
- **J** a biography.

For Number 3, choose the best answer to the question.

3 Which of these probably came from a science fiction story?

- **A** The children of the pioneers who had been born in space had an unusual trait.
- **B** The distances between stars are so great as to be unimaginable.
- **C** "Madam," the waiter whispered, "the fly is doing the backstroke."
- **D** Like the other buildings in the town, the restaurant had quite a history.

STOP

ANSWER ROWS A Ⓐ Ⓑ Ⓒ Ⓓ 2 Ⓕ Ⓖ Ⓗ Ⓙ

1 Ⓐ Ⓑ Ⓒ Ⓓ 3 Ⓐ Ⓑ Ⓒ Ⓓ

Example

Directions: Read each passage. Find the best answer to the questions that follow the passage.

Clyde and Bonnie met their friends at the Harlow Creek bridge. They had planned a picnic for Labor Day, but before the fun began, they had a job to do. They had decided to spend two hours picking up litter from around the bridge and the picnic area before they had their own picnic. They figured it was a small price to pay to enjoy a clean park.

A After they finish their work, the young people will probably feel —

- **A** tired and dejected.
- **B** tired and satisfied.
- **C** dejected and annoyed.
- **D** annoyed and tired.

Look for key words in the question. If you can find the same key words in the story, you will find the right answer nearby.

Practice

Read the letter below. Use it to answer the questions on the following page.

134 Fifth Street
Contentment, Texas 75444
June 15, 1996

Dear Jerry,

My family and I would like you to visit us for two weeks, starting July 3. My dad can pick you up at the airport, and he will take you back for the return trip. Since your family moved to Michigan last year, all your friends here miss you and are eager to see you again.

The annual Fourth of July town picnic, parade, and fireworks show will be spectacular, as usual. The theme this year is "The Champions of Contentment." Our class has a float that will feature the people who have won awards during the year. The band will march and play, and there will be horses and clowns. We are even having a pet beauty contest. Won't that be great?

After things settle down from that, we can go fishing in the abandoned rock quarry at the edge of town. It has been stocked with rainbow trout. Mother has promised to cook what we catch, but we have to clean the fish ourselves.

We will go to my grandfather's farm for a day or two and help him stack his hay in the barn. It will be hard work, but we can ride his horses in the hills when we are finished.

On July 11, the YMCA swim classes will hold a demonstration. I will finish my lifeguard course this summer. Of course, you'll want to be there when I "rescue" someone and then get my medal and certificate. I'll have to go to classes for a few mornings, so you will be forced to play pool, lift weights, or do something else at the Y while I am in swim classes. I am sure you won't mind that!

All of us are looking forward to your visit, and we have lots of things planned. Rest up before you come, because we will be too busy to rest much while you are here. Please let us know as soon as you can when you will arrive!

Your friend,
Joe

1 How often is the town's celebration held?

A Once a month

B Once a year

C Once every five years

D This is the first one

2 Which of these is most likely to happen next?

F Joe will hear from Jerry.

G Joe will visit his grandfather.

H Jerry will catch the next plane to Texas.

J Joe will get his lifeguard certificate.

3 In this letter, the word "rescue" in quotation marks means that —

A Joe will really save someone's life.

B the ceremony will have to wait until Joe rescues someone.

C the class will only talk about rescuing people.

D Joe will not actually save a person but will pretend to.

4 Where will the boys ride horses?

F at the quarry.

G near the YMCA.

H in the hills.

J the letter doesn't say.

5 Joe's letter suggests that he and Jerry both like —

A watching television and movies best.

B reading books and magazines.

C going to picnics and parties.

D doing active things.

6 What kind of letter is this?

F Letter of complaint

G Business letter

H Friendly letter

J Letter to the editor

7 In this letter, the phrase "forced to play pool or lift weights" means that —

A Jerry will actually enjoy doing these things.

B Joe hopes Jerry won't mind doing these things because they are not fun.

C the two boys won't be spending much time together.

D there are some things Jerry will do even if he doesn't like them.

GO

ANSWER ROWS A Ⓐ Ⓑ Ⓒ Ⓓ 2 Ⓕ Ⓖ Ⓗ Ⓙ 4 Ⓕ Ⓖ Ⓗ Ⓙ 6 Ⓕ Ⓖ Ⓗ Ⓙ

1 Ⓐ Ⓑ Ⓒ Ⓓ 3 Ⓐ Ⓑ Ⓒ Ⓓ 5 Ⓐ Ⓑ Ⓒ Ⓓ 7 Ⓐ Ⓑ Ⓒ Ⓓ

Glaciers

In some very cold regions of the earth, the snow never melts. As more snow falls, the accumulated mass of the snowfield becomes heavy, and the weight compacts the lower level of snow to ice. Over time, glaciers form. They are masses of snow and ice that glide along the ground. These huge ice masses exist where the annual snowfall is so great it doesn't melt, such as the polar regions and in very high mountains. Glacial ice now covers about 10 percent of the earth's land area.

Snow is fluffy when it falls, but when it accumulates without melting, it becomes granular and eventually compacts into solid ice. The solid glaciers move at a speed that depends on the glacier's weight and the steepness of the slope. In steep mountains, they can move 60 feet per day. In addition, the lower levels move more than the top, and great rifts or cracks form, making glacier exploration hazardous.

There are two kinds of glaciers: valley glaciers and ice sheets. A third kind, piedmont glaciers, is a combination of the other two. Valley glaciers follow the high valleys of mountains such as the Rockies, the Cascades, or the Alps. Rocks on the underside scrape the valleys and make them wider, deeper, and U-shaped. The glacier continues moving to the warmer lowlands, where part of it melts.

An ice sheet is a broad layer of ice that spreads outward in all directions. It is usually slower moving than valley glaciers because of the flatter terrain on which it forms. A continental glacier is an ice sheet that covers most of a continent. Greenland and Antarctica are largely covered by continental glaciers. Sometimes two valley glaciers merge at a low level and fan out over a large area to form a piedmont glacier, which looks much like an ice sheet.

Pieces of a glacier at the edge of the ocean can break off and become icebergs. These huge floating chunks of ice have sunk many ships. In 1912, when the *Titanic* struck an iceberg in the Atlantic Ocean, more than 1500 lives were lost.

Glaciers shaped our land masses through erosion by gouging out and moving rocks and dirt. They also create deposits as they transport debris and drop it in new places. In the Rocky Mountains of Colorado, many of the spectacular peaks were formed by valley glaciers. This is also true of Yosemite Falls in California. The fiords and inlet harbors of Norway and Greenland were carved out by glacial sculpture. The lakes that dot the northern part of the United States were formed by the melting ends of glaciers. Glaciers are responsible for underground reservoirs of water and for mineral-rich soil in some areas.

Climate changes that have accompanied glaciers have even affected human beings' development and their migrations on the planet. During cold weather, when glaciers grew, humans moved to warmer areas. When the glaciers receded, people were able to move back and settle in northern areas.

8 **There is enough information in this article to show that —**

F glaciers existed long ago but are not on earth now.

G piedmont glaciers and ice sheets do not move.

H icebergs formed by glaciers can be very dangerous.

J the speed of glaciers depends on how much snow there is.

9 **The web shows some important ideas in the article.**

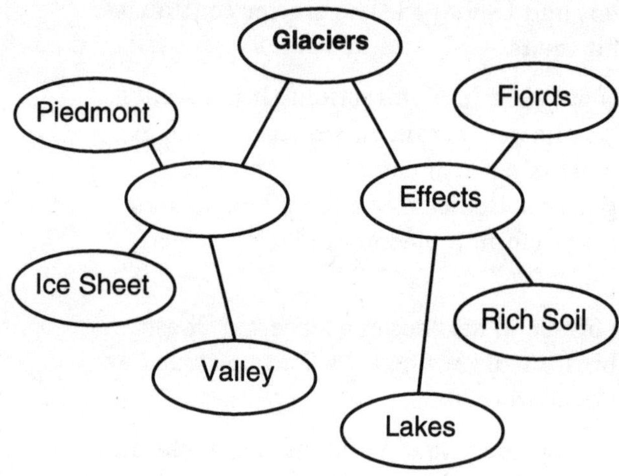

Which of these belongs in the empty space?

A Types

B Icebergs

C Glacial sculpture

D Snow to ice

10 **A piedmont glacier is —**

F always near an ocean.

G more slow moving than either a valley glacier or an ice sheet.

H a continental glacier.

J formed when two valley glaciers come together.

11 **The principal reason that glaciers form is because —**

A the temperature of the earth is lower than before.

B snow falls faster than it melts.

C snow melts and then refreezes in mountain valleys.

D icebergs accumulate near the coastline of polar regions.

12 **This article was written in order to —**

F express an opinion.

G describe a problem.

H compare two ideas.

J present facts.

13 **The climate changes that accompanied the glaciers—**

A caused many animal species to become extinct.

B affected humans' development and migrations.

C increased the number of icebergs.

D formed most of the mountain ranges.

ANSWER ROWS 8 Ⓕ Ⓖ Ⓗ Ⓙ 10 Ⓕ Ⓖ Ⓗ Ⓙ 12 Ⓕ Ⓖ Ⓗ Ⓙ

9 Ⓐ Ⓑ Ⓒ Ⓓ 11 Ⓐ Ⓑ Ⓒ Ⓓ 13 Ⓐ Ⓑ Ⓒ Ⓓ

Example

Directions: Read each passage. Find the best answer to eachquestion that follows the passage.

Many people who feed birds dislike one of our feathered friends, the jay. It is large, aggressive, and noisy, often chasing other birds away from a feeder. If a group of jays comes to a feeder, they can often empty it in minutes searching for the food they like best.	**A** **The author of this story —** **A** enjoys watching jays. **B** describes jays in negative terms. **C** feels jays are good feeder visitors. **D** enjoys taking photos of birds.

Skim the passage, then look at the questions. Answer the easiest questions first. Then do the more difficult questions.

Practice

What makes a hero?

Much has been said and written recently about heroes, chiefly because many people think we have too few of them. There are many different kinds of heroes, but they all seem to have two things in common. First, heroes, by their actions, reveal the great possibilities of human nature. Second, heroes can also stand the test of time, and their accomplishments will not be easily forgotten. Because of these characteristics, we need to choose our heroes carefully.

Olympic track star Jackie Joyner-Kersee, who many people believe is a hero, warns young people to be careful of making heroes of athletes. She hopes that if someone tries to imitate her, it will be because she accomplished her goals by working hard. Joyner-Kersee says that a hero should be someone who has made a difference in another person's life.

Poet Maya Angelou believes that a hero inspires people to treat others well and to be concerned about the greater good. A hero should display courtesy, courage, patience, and strength all the time. A hero should inspire others to follow their concerns with actions that improve the world, even if only in small ways.

Author Daniel Boorstin suggests that, "*Celebrities* are people who make news, but heroes are people who make history." Thus, if a person truly deserves to be called a hero, he or she will not be soon forgotten.

We all need heroes. We need to be able to look up to people who have been there, done that, and succeeded. Many times the greatest heroes are the people we deal with daily—relatives, friends, and neighbors—who have kept going when it would have been easier to give up. The parent who puts her or his family ahead of a potential athletic career, the grandparent who chooses to stay and work instead of seeking fortune, the teacher who might have made more money at another career but chose to help others—all of these people can be classified as heroes. A hero quietly and steadily sets a good example, an example that beckons others to follow it.

1 A good title for this passage is —

A "Sports Heroes"

B "There Are No More Heroes"

C "Heroes, Who Needs Them?"

D "Everyday Heroes"

2 In the selection, heroes are defined as all of these except —

F people who have made a difference in someone's life.

G people who have made a fortune at their careers.

H people who have kept going and not given up.

J people who make history and not just news.

3 There is enough information in this story to show that —

A different people have different definitions of who is a hero.

B we have fewer heroes today than we did in the past.

C it is rare when a typical person has a chance to become a hero.

D young people today really don't need heroes anymore.

4 Which words would best describe a hero?

F ...two things in common...

G ...stand the test of time...

H ...made more money...

J ...people who make news...

5 Why do people need heroes?

A To show how to make news and bring great fame

B Because most people don't know how to do the right thing

C To set a good example for them follow

D Because the world is a very different place than it was before

6 The writer probably includes the first sentence to —

F show that sports figures are heroes.

G establish the time frame for the passage.

H prepare the reader for what is to come.

J introduce the people in the passage.

7 In this passage *celebrities* are —

A people who make news.

B everyday heroes.

C athletes to be imitated.

D people who make history.

GO

ANSWER ROWS A Ⓐ Ⓑ Ⓒ Ⓓ 2 Ⓕ Ⓖ Ⓗ Ⓙ 4 Ⓕ Ⓖ Ⓗ Ⓙ 6 Ⓕ Ⓖ Ⓗ Ⓙ

1 Ⓐ Ⓑ Ⓒ Ⓓ 3 Ⓐ Ⓑ Ⓒ Ⓓ 5 Ⓐ Ⓑ Ⓒ Ⓓ 7 Ⓐ Ⓑ Ⓒ Ⓓ

Are horses our best friends?

In movies about the Old West, the cowboy often loved his horse more than he loved any human being. The two were inseparable, and the man depended on his strong companion every day. Today, machines do much of the work on a ranch, but cowboys still depend on their steeds. Many other people today use horses for recreation or keep them as pets.

The early horse, called eohippus, was about the size of a fox and lived fifty million years ago. Over the years, this little relative of the horse grew and became strong. Between ten and five thousand years ago, humans learned to tame and ride horses, and they became an important part of our history.

Genghis Khan and his warriors from Mongolia used horses to control much of Asia and Europe. Arabs developed one of the finest breeds in the world and loved their horses so much that they let them sleep in their tents. The Spanish explorers brought horses to the Americas, and when they escaped and multiplied, horses changed the lifestyles of many Native Americans forever. These Spanish horses, called mustangs, allowed Plains Indians to hunt buffalo more efficiently. They learned to ride horses with unmatched skill, and the Comanches and Apaches were said to ride as if they and the horse were one.

The mustangs also served Western settlers and cattlemen well, and both the U.S. Cavalry and Pony Express used them. They were known for their speed and endurance, and were able to withstand the harsh weather of the deserts, plains, and mountains. The mustang, with its love of freedom, has come to be a *symbol* of the American West.

The quarter horse, which was bred from the mustang, was America's first racing horse. Anyone who rides on rough mountain trails will appreciate the strength and surefootedness of the quarter horse. These beautiful animals have great stamina and speed, but are bred to run only short distances.

Thoroughbreds are the principal racers in America today, and were imported from England more than a century ago. All thoroughbreds are descendants of Arabian horses taken to England in the 1700s. Thoroughbreds are not as strong as quarter horses, but they can run faster for longer distances.

Quarter horses, thoroughbreds, Arabians, and other specialized breeds of horses are popular around the world. Even though they don't serve people in the way they did a hundred years ago, they are still used for work, for competition, and for pleasure riding. And as anyone who owns a horse will tell you, they are lovable animals that can easily find their way into your heart.

GO

8 Which words tell how much some people loved their horses?

F ...they and the horse were one...

G ...they let them sleep in their tents...

H ...use horses for recreation...

J ...its love of freedom...

9 The boxes show some of the main ideas in this passage.

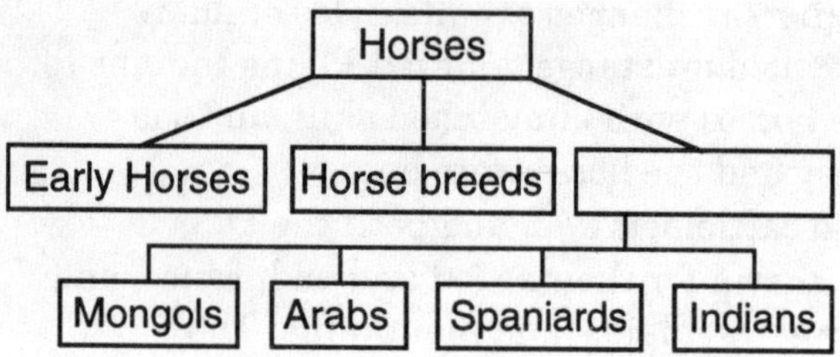

Which of these belongs in the empty box?

A How horses were used

B Racing horses

C Riding horses

D People who used horses

10 Before Spanish explorers arrived in the Americas —

F horses were there.

G American horses were the size of a fox.

H Native Americans rode buffalos.

J cowboys used horses.

11 In the passage, the word *symbol* means —

A a mathematics sign.

B a thing that stands for something else.

C a picture of a horse.

D how people learned to ride horses.

12 The lifestyles of the American Indians changed when horses were brought to the New World because —

F the horses were a major source of food.

G they worshipped the horses.

H they could travel and hunt better.

J Apaches and Comanches became allies.

13 Which of these is an *opinion* stated in the passage?

A Horses are lovable.

B Quarter horses are fast for short distances.

C Mongols used horses.

D Arabian horses came to America from England.

14 This passage can best be described as —

F an editorial.

G an adventure.

H a review.

J a description.

GO

ANSWER ROWS 8 Ⓕ Ⓖ Ⓗ Ⓙ 10 Ⓕ Ⓖ Ⓗ Ⓙ 12 Ⓕ Ⓖ Ⓗ Ⓙ 14 Ⓕ Ⓖ Ⓗ Ⓙ
9 Ⓐ Ⓑ Ⓒ Ⓓ 11 Ⓐ Ⓑ Ⓒ Ⓓ 13 Ⓐ Ⓑ Ⓒ Ⓓ

Animal Attraction

Almost every major city in the world shares one attraction, a zoo. From the Philadelphia Zoological Garden, America's oldest zoo, to the one in Sydney, Australia, which most people reach by ferry, zoos are loved by tourists and residents alike.

Humans have kept animals for their enjoyment and entertainment from prehistoric times. The ancient Egyptians, Greeks, and Romans kept small zoos, but the origin of the zoo as we know it today took place during the Renaissance in sixteenth century Europe. These zoos were termed "menageries" because they were an attempt to bring together at least one of each type of animal. By the eighteenth century, there were major zoos in Vienna, Austria, Paris, France, Madrid, Spain, and London, England.

Over the past several hundred years, zoos have changed considerably. At first, they were no better than prisons for animals, with small cages and barely acceptable food. In the last fifty or so years, however, zoos have provided animals with larger and more natural habitats, better food, and opportunities for recreation and socialization. Zoos also moved from being purely entertainment to serving as research and education centers. These changes have improved life for the animals in the zoos, have helped us preserve animals in the wild, and have made visiting a zoo more enjoyable for both children and adults.

The idea that a zoo should be a menagerie is also changing. In some places, the zoo has focused on animals from a particular habitat, such as the Arizona-Sonora Desert Museum in Tucson or Ghost Ranch in northern New Mexico. In others, the emphasis is providing an "up close and personal" experience by allowing visitors to drive through areas where animals range freely in an open habitat.

Almost all zoos are owned by nonprofit organizations or municipalities such as cities or counties. They are supported by admission fees, the sale of food or merchandise in the zoo, taxes, or gifts from charitable foundations. In the United States, Canada, and most European nations, zoos belong to a professional association that conducts regular inspections to see that the animals are receiving appropriate treatment.

Many people are surprised to learn that the majority of the employees in a zoo are responsible for administration, maintaining grounds, taking tickets, selling food and merchandise, and other routine functions. The two "glamour" jobs are curator and zookeeper, and there are relatively few of these positions available in any zoo. A curator is responsible for acquiring animals, designing exhibits, supervising animal care, and performing related tasks. A zookeeper is the person visitors see bathing the elephants, feeding the lions, or making sure the rhinoceros has a stout rubbing post. In addition to these two positions, most zoos have at least one veterinarian, some technicians, and perhaps an animal researcher or two.

A modern zoo requires as much administration as a small city. Visitors see only a small part of what is involved in running a zoo. A great deal of effort must be expended to maintain the health and well-being of the animals, protect keepers who work with the animals, and create an environment that is stimulating for the animals and entertaining for visitors. All this effort seems to be paying off, however, for zoos are popular attractions year-round, and it is a rare person indeed who doesn't enjoy spending a day at a zoo.

15 **A menagerie would have —**

A many examples of the same animal.

B examples of many different animals.

C animals in a natural setting.

D animals in cramped cages.

16 **What is a major difference between modern zoos and those of a hundred years ago?**

F Animals are treated better today.

G Animals are treated worse today.

H Cages were larger a hundred years ago.

J Most zoos are in large cities today.

17 **In the third paragraph, what does the word "socialization" mean?**

A To exercise

B To eat natural foods

C To spend time together in natural groups

D To learn more about keepers and people who visit a zoo

18 **What is a "glamour" job?**

F One that requires the worker to be attractive

G One that seems like fun and everyone is familiar with

H One that involves a lot of behind-the-scenes work

J One that pays well

19 **Who ensures that zoos do a good job caring for their animals?**

A A curator

B A zookeeper

C A charitable organization

D A professional association

20 **Where would a passage like this be most likely to appear?**

F In a popular magazine

G On the front page of a newspaper

H In a science book

J On an advertisement for a city zoo

21 **According to this passage —**

A zoos were developed only in the last century.

B people have been fascinated by animals for thousands of years.

C the first zoo in the world is in Philadelphia.

D the best zoos were built during the Renaissance.

22 **What is this passage mostly about?**

F Managing zoos

G The history of zoos

H Animals

J Zoos

STOP

ANSWER ROWS 15 Ⓐ Ⓑ Ⓒ Ⓓ 17 Ⓐ Ⓑ Ⓒ Ⓓ 19 Ⓐ Ⓑ Ⓒ Ⓓ 21 Ⓐ Ⓑ Ⓒ Ⓓ

16 Ⓕ Ⓖ Ⓗ Ⓙ 18 Ⓕ Ⓖ Ⓗ Ⓙ 20 Ⓕ Ⓖ Ⓗ Ⓙ 22 Ⓕ Ⓖ Ⓗ Ⓙ

E1

The first attempts at human flight were made with a strange-looking device called an ornithopter. This odd aircraft uses the flapping movement of a pair of wings. You can buy a miniature ornithopter at a toy or hobby store, but no ornithopter large enough to carry a human has been invented yet.

Ornithopters were probably invented before planes because —

A planes are expensive.

B people were smaller.

C people tried to imitate birds.

D planes require fuel.

Read the title to the story and then the story. Read each question and choose the answer you think is best. Mark the space for your answer.

Ruler of the Jungle: Animated Repeat

Ruler of the Jungle, the newest Tiger adventure, is finally coming to theaters. Moviegoers have been eagerly awaiting the new animated movie for months. The first of the series, *Tiger Versus Trouble*, was a huge success, attracting millions of viewers. The sequel was also well received, with Terrance rescuing his friends, defeating the bad guys, and generally fighting evil and doing good. Audiences will not find the newest Tiger exploit so entertaining, however.

The scenery is still breathtakingly beautiful, and the music is rich and forceful, but the action is dull. The scenes seem to be a repeat of Terrance's earlier adventures. The action scenes seem so familiar, the viewer might wonder if the animators have tried to re-use some frames from the earlier movies.

Megamovie Company's latest production, like the previous two, is a technical marvel, blending photographic beauty with cartoon animation. *Ruler* will, no doubt, win awards for bringing together the real and the imaginary with such art. The music score is flawless; it will probably be a best-selling album.

The weakest part of the movie is the plot, which was the best part of the two earlier productions. Terrance again finds himself in trouble as he unwittingly stumbles into problems. He uses his intelligence, his strength, and his friends' assistance to overcome adversity and to help the good guys win. The problem with the story line is that it is too much like the other versions. Terrance does not have any really new adventures; they are all re-hashes of his old exploits. The only new addition is his love interest in Chloe, the lovely female tiger.

Small children will probably not notice the repetition, and students or adults who appreciate art and music will perhaps not care, but moviegoers who eagerly anticipated another good story will not find it in *Ruler of the Jungle*.

Natalie Nelson

1 **This passage can best be described as—**

A a review.

B an advertisement.

C an interview.

D a biography.

2 **According to Natalie Nelson, what is the poorest part of the movie?**

F The scenery and artwork

G The music

H The triumph of good over evil

J The lack of new adventures

3 **Which word is used to describe the writer's opinion of the action in *Ruler of the Jungle*?**

A Re-hash

B Exploits

C Animated

D Anticipated

4 **Which character appears in *Ruler of the Jungle* but not in the two previous tiger movies?**

F Terrance

G Terrance's friends

H The evil Dr. Snake

J Chloe

5 **Which company produced *Ruler of the Jungle*?**

A Technical Marvel

B Moviegoers

C Megamovie Company

D Tiger Adventure

6 ***Ruler of the Jungle* is intended for —**

F only young people.

G children, students, and adults.

H people who like adventure.

J animators.

7 **From the passage, you can conclude that Terrance is —**

A a person who rules the animals of the jungle fairly.

B a real tiger who survived as a cub in the jungle.

C an animated character who gets into different adventures.

D the producer of the three movies mentioned in the review.

GO

ANSWER ROWS E1 Ⓐ Ⓑ Ⓒ Ⓓ 2 Ⓕ Ⓖ Ⓗ Ⓙ 4 Ⓕ Ⓖ Ⓗ Ⓙ 6 Ⓕ Ⓖ Ⓗ Ⓙ

1 Ⓐ Ⓑ Ⓒ Ⓓ 3 Ⓐ Ⓑ Ⓒ Ⓓ 5 Ⓐ Ⓑ Ⓒ Ⓓ 7 Ⓐ Ⓑ Ⓒ Ⓓ

In this essay, a young man today tries to describe what it must have been like for his grandmother to come to America many years ago.

¶1 The year was 1914. In a few months, Archduke Francis Ferdinand, the heir to the Austrian throne, would be assassinated in Sarajevo. Woodrow Wilson was President of the United States, and a recent invention, the flying machine, was all the rage. Moving pictures were silent, and Edgar Rice Burroughs created a character for the ages, Tarzan of the Apes.

¶2 None of this, however, mattered to Mariana Potalivo, a fifteen-year old girl standing in a train station in the small Italian town. She and her brother, Nicholas, were taking the first step on a journey that would end almost halfway around the world in the most wonderful country she had ever heard of, America. Mariana was frightened of what lay ahead, but she was also excited. Besides, she had no choice. She had been promised in marriage to someone she had never even met, a young man from a nearby village who had already made the journey to America and who had found a most precious treasure, a job.

¶3 The small town of Compobasso was a very poor farming community in a poor country. Had she stayed in Compobasso, Mariana would have married a local boy, raised a family in the same house as his parents, and most likely never have traveled farther than Pescara, a city on the Adriatic coast. Her husband would have tried his best to scrabble out a living from the rocky soil, and her children would have done the same, as her family had done for over a thousand years.

¶4 The train ride across Italy to Naples was difficult. Although Francisco, her husband-to-be, had paid for Mariana's ticket on the ship, her parents had spent almost every cent they had on passage for her brother. Nicholas was only nine years old, but he was supposed to serve as her protector on the journey. The family had barely enough money left for two third-class train tickets to Naples. The two children sat on a hard bench for almost two days with dozens of other people, many of whom carried all their earthly possessions and who were making the same journey as Mariana and Nicholas. In addition, the third-class cars held farmers bringing their goods to market, from baskets of fruits and vegetables to chickens, goats, and pigs.

¶5 The children carried very few possessions themselves, some clothes, a photograph or two, and letters that would introduce them to people in America. Most of what they brought was food: cheese, dried fruit, bread, and sausage. They had no idea if anything would be available to eat on the train or the ship, and even if it was, they had only a few pennies to pay for it. Hour after hour they sat on the bench, swaying with the train, barely speaking, trying not to think of the family and friends they were leaving, perhaps forever. Both Mariana and Nicholas knew that going to America would open up a whole new life for them, but they were sad to be leaving the only life they had ever known.

¶6 When the train reached Naples early in the morning, they were tired and sore from the trip. They had no time to complain, however, because their ship would be leaving that afternoon. The children began the long walk from the railroad station to the dock, and even though they had never been to Naples before, had no difficulty finding the way. Hundreds of other people were doing exactly the same thing. All Mariana and Nicholas had to do was follow the crowd.

¶7 At the dock, Mariana and Nicholas stared at the ship, as did most of the other people in the crowd. It was the hugest thing they had ever seen, larger even than the church in Pescara. They slowly made their way up the gangplank and handed the steward their tickets. As they did, the realization of what was happening hit them. Once the ship left the dock, they would never set foot in Italy again, never sit in the town square on a warm summer evening and sing the old songs, never see their family again.

8 In paragraph 4, what is the meaning of the word "passage"?

F The trip to Naples

G A brief story

H The food the children carried

J The trip across the ocean

9 Why does the writer begin with a description of world affairs in 1914?

A World events would play an important part in the story.

B They help the reader understand the time period in which the story is set.

C They caused Mariana and her brother to leave their village.

D The children were interested in what was happening.

10 How does the writer feel about his grandmother?

F He admires her for undertaking such a difficult journey.

G He feels she gave up too much by leaving her village.

H He wishes she had been more aware of world affairs.

J He wishes she had stayed in her village in Italy.

11 In paragraph 3, what is the Adriatic?

A A small town

B A region of Italy

C A body of water

D A large city on the coast

12 How did Mariana feel about marrying someone she had never met?

F Unhappy and angry about having to leave her village

G Happy to have the opportunity to take a trip on a boat

H Disappointed because her brother had to go with her

J Willing to accept it because it was a tradition

13 In paragraph 2, why is a job called a "precious treasure"?

A The job paid very well.

B Not many people in the village had jobs.

C The job was in America.

D Jobs were easier to find in Italy than in America.

14 Around 1914, it appears as if—

F many other people were leaving Italy for America.

G only a few people were leaving Italy for America.

H the trip from Italy to America was easy and inexpensive.

J farming in Italy was a good way to earn a living.

GO

ANSWER ROWS 8 Ⓕ Ⓖ Ⓗ Ⓙ 10 Ⓕ Ⓖ Ⓗ Ⓙ 12 Ⓕ Ⓖ Ⓗ Ⓙ 14 Ⓕ Ⓖ Ⓗ Ⓙ

9 Ⓐ Ⓑ Ⓒ Ⓓ 11 Ⓐ Ⓑ Ⓒ Ⓓ 13 Ⓐ Ⓑ Ⓒ Ⓓ

How did skiing change from necessity to sport?

Skiing today is a sport enjoyed by millions of Americans. More than a hundred years ago, however, people living in the West used skis for transportation, not recreation. The first Colorado skiers, for example, were miners looking for gold and silver in the 1860s. In the deep snows of winter, skis were the only way these miners could get around. Ministers, mail carriers, and even teachers were other early skiers in the Rocky Mountains.

Skiing was brought to America by settlers from Norway and other northern European countries. Their skis were long, wooden boards that looked very different from modern skis. And instead of two poles, early skiers used just one long pole to push themselves along. In addition to introducing Americans to skiing, European immigrants were responsible for founding many of America's ski resorts. The first Colorado ski resort opened in 1930, although other resorts in the East were started before that time.

In the early days of recreational skiing, people actually walked to the top of a mountain before they could ski down. Inventors soon solved that problem by creating various mechanical devices that could carry people up a mountain. This development helped skiing become more popular because it was so much easier to do. Another development that popularized skiing was a group of soldiers who trained for World War II in Colorado. Their heroics during the war influenced many people to take up the sport.

As more people learned to ski, resorts began to sponsor winter carnivals that included competitions. Steamboat Springs, Colorado, has had a festival every year since 1914, and almost every ski resort has a festival of one kind or another. The Winter Olympics also focused a lot of attention on skiing, encouraging many Americans to take up the sport.

Vail, Colorado, has a ski museum that pays tribute to early American skiers. There you can learn about people who have been *inducted* into the Skiing Hall of Fame, like John Lewis Dyer, a minister who went around the mining camps in western Colorado on 11-foot handmade skis. You can also see the huge backpacks mail carriers used to deliver their letters and packages, see how equipment and skiing styles changed, and learn how skiing went from a necessity to a popular sport.

15 In the skiing museum, you would be most likely to find —

A pictures of the first Summer Olympics held in 1896.

B the latest ski fashions.

C ski boots that people wore in the 1940s.

D the names of the people who qualified for the next Olympics.

16 Mechanical devices to carry skiers up a mountain were invented soon after—

F the first downhill ski trails opened.

G skis were invented.

H skiing was used for transportation.

J the ski museum opened in Colorado.

17 After reading this passage, you should be able to —

A describe how Europeans invented skiing.

B explain how skiing became a sport.

C name the first ski resort in Colorado.

D name the first miner who used skis.

18 This story is *mainly* about —

F traveling by foot in the mountains of the American West.

G a sport brought to America by European immigrants.

H how modern technology changed a popular sport.

J how a sport developed from an activity that was a necessity.

19 In this passage, the word *inducted* means —

A made a member of.

B invited to speak at.

C visited often.

D helped to develop.

20 You can tell from this passage that —

F skis are longer today than they were in the past.

G gold and silver are found where there is a lot of snow.

H Steamboat Springs was the first ski resort in Colorado.

J people in Europe were skiing before Americans.

21 Skiing in America began in—

A the West.

B the East.

C areas where there was an Army base.

D the California mountains.

22 According to the article, skiing probably has become popular because of all these events except—

F Army skiers in World War II.

G the Winter Olympics.

H advertisements by ski manufacturers.

J the invention of the ski lift.

GO

ANSWER ROWS 15 Ⓐ Ⓑ Ⓒ Ⓓ 17 Ⓐ Ⓑ Ⓒ Ⓓ 19 Ⓐ Ⓑ Ⓒ Ⓓ 21 Ⓐ Ⓑ Ⓒ Ⓓ

16 Ⓕ Ⓖ Ⓗ Ⓙ 18 Ⓕ Ⓖ Ⓗ Ⓙ 20 Ⓕ Ⓖ Ⓗ Ⓙ 22 Ⓕ Ⓖ Ⓗ Ⓙ

Grace Darling

The Darling family lived an isolated existence because the father was a lighthouse keeper on a rugged coastline in England. His job was to keep the beacon light burning so that ships would not pass too close to shore and be torn apart on the rocks. Mr. Darling worried that his lovely daughter, Grace, would miss out on too much of life if she stayed at the lighthouse, but he could not bear to be separated from his family. The loneliness he would have had to endure was not so bad as being kept apart from his loved ones. So the Darlings lived peacefully in the tall tower on the rocky shore, and Grace did her schoolwork under the direction of her mother. She fished, sailed, and explored with her father.

One night, after Mr. Darling had made sure the beacon was shining brightly across the ocean, a thunderstorm came up. Such storms were the only thing Grace did not like about living at the lighthouse. Sometimes it seemed that the wind would tear the building apart and scatter its boards and bricks across the sea. This night was worse than usual: the wind raged and howled, the lightning flashed, and the thunder rumbled and cracked. Grace and her parents were about to go down the circular stairs to their snug basement when she looked out the windows just as brilliant lightning lit up the entire sky.

"Father, look! There is a ship out there!" she cried.

"It will be all right, my dear," her father answered. "The light will warn them to steer clear of the rocks. Let's go below."

When the lightning flashed again, Mr. Darling watched in horror as the ship broke apart. With the next flash, the Darlings could see several survivors who had clung to the hull and were stuck on the rocks, holding on for dear life.

"Let's go out and rescue them," begged Grace.

"We can't go out in this storm," her father answered. "We will perish ourselves."

At last the storm seemed to lessen some, though it was still fierce; Mr. Darling finally relented. Grace insisted on going with him in their small boat. They rowed mightily against the raging waves and managed to reach the people. They fought their way back to the lighthouse. Grace and her father saved twelve lives that night. Mr. Darling gave Grace the credit because of her persistent pleading.

23 Why did the lighthouse beacon not protect the ship from the rocks?

A The sailors did not see it.

B It was not lit in time to help them.

C The storm blew the sailors into the rocks.

D The sailors ignored its warning.

24 Which strategy would *best* help the reader understand this story?

F Picturing what the Darlings' snug basement looked like

G Thinking about what fierce power storms can have

H Imagining what Grace and her father did in the boat

J Thinking about Grace's relationship with her father

25 Why did Mr. Darling say his daughter was responsible for the rescue?

A She insisted that they go out.

B She was too young to understand the danger.

C Rescue was not part of his job.

D She was a better rower than he was.

26 In the second paragraph, Grace appears to be —

F extremely brave.

G dutiful.

H observant.

J somewhat frightened.

27 In the story, Grace showed that she was all of these *except* —

A persistent.

B clever.

C sympathetic.

D brave.

28 The *main* idea of this story is the importance of —

F looking out the windows at the right time.

G being willing to help others when they are in need.

H taking care of family members first.

J knowing how to swim.

29 The basement of the lighthouse is —

A safer than the rest of it.

B large and beautiful.

C where the beacon is kept.

D damp and cold.

GO

ANSWER ROWS 23 Ⓐ Ⓑ Ⓒ Ⓓ 25 Ⓐ Ⓑ Ⓒ Ⓓ 27 Ⓐ Ⓑ Ⓒ Ⓓ 29 Ⓐ Ⓑ Ⓒ Ⓓ

24 Ⓕ Ⓖ Ⓗ Ⓙ 26 Ⓕ Ⓖ Ⓗ Ⓙ 28 Ⓕ Ⓖ Ⓗ Ⓙ

For Numbers 30 through 33, choose the best answer to the question.

An accident on the interstate this morning slowed rush hour traffic to a crawl. A truck loaded with bricks went out of control and overturned near Grand Avenue. This is the same section of road that caused the death of two motorists last month. It's time the state did something to improve the situation.

30 This passage would most likely be found in —

- **F** a magazine article about bricks.
- **G** an encyclopedia entry about trucks.
- **H** a newspaper article about an accident.
- **J** a review of an upcoming book.

31 Which of these sentences expresses a fact stated in the passage above?

- **A** The state has done a poor job of taking care of the road.
- **B** A truck loaded with bricks went out of control on the interstate.
- **C** Traffic is usually heaviest during the morning rush hour.
- **D** The section of interstate near Grand Avenue is the most dangerous.

32 Which of these statements makes use of a metaphor?

- **F** The clouds blocked the sun, causing the temperature to drop.
- **G** To Regina, the opposing team seemed much larger than her own.
- **H** The crowd was a river, sweeping Gene through the stadium gates.
- **J** The fish was so big we needed a second boat to haul it in.

33 Mary's heart sank when she heard her test score. It was good, but she wasn't sure it was high enough to earn her an A for the semester.

Which of these best explains the meaning of the phrase "Mary's heart sank"?

- **A** She was very disappointed.
- **B** She was very excited.
- **C** Suddenly she couldn't breathe well.
- **D** The test was easier than she had thought.

ANSWER ROWS 30 Ⓕ Ⓖ Ⓗ Ⓙ 32 Ⓕ Ⓖ Ⓗ Ⓙ
31 Ⓐ Ⓑ Ⓒ Ⓓ 33 Ⓐ Ⓑ Ⓒ Ⓓ

NUMBER RIGHT ______

Name and Answer Sheet

To the Student:

These tests will give you a chance to put the tips you have learned to work.

A few last reminders...

- Be sure you understand all the directions before you begin each test. You may ask the teacher questions about the directions if you do not understand them.
- Work as quickly as you can during each test.
- When you change an answer, be sure to erase your first mark completely.
- You can guess at an answer or skip difficult items and go back to them later.
- Use the tips you have learned whenever you can.
- It is OK to be a little nervous. You may even do better.

Now that you have completed the lessons in this book, you are on your way to scoring high!

STUDENT'S NAME

LAST | FIRST | MI

(A) (B) (C) (D) (E) (F) (G) (H) (I) (J) (K) (L) (M) (N) (O) (P) (Q) (R) (S) (T) (U) (V) (W) (X) (Y) (Z)

SCHOOL

TEACHER

FEMALE ◯ MALE ◯

BIRTH DATE

MONTH	DAY		YEAR	
JAN ◯	(0)	(0)		(0)
FEB ◯	(1)	(1)		(1)
MAR ◯	(2)	(2)		(2)
APR ◯	(3)	(3)		(3)
MAY ◯		(4)		(4)
JUN ◯		(5)	(5)	(5)
JUL ◯		(6)	(6)	(6)
AUG ◯		(7)	(7)	(7)
SEP ◯		(8)	(8)	(8)
OCT ◯		(9)	(9)	(9)
NOV ◯				
DEC ◯				

GRADE

(7) (8) (9)

Fourth Edition Book 8

Scoring High

in

Reading

PART 1 VOCABULARY

E1 Ⓐ Ⓑ Ⓒ Ⓓ	6 Ⓕ Ⓖ Ⓗ Ⓙ	13 Ⓐ Ⓑ Ⓒ Ⓓ	20 Ⓕ Ⓖ Ⓗ Ⓙ	27 Ⓐ Ⓑ Ⓒ Ⓓ	31 Ⓐ Ⓑ Ⓒ Ⓓ
E2 Ⓕ Ⓖ Ⓗ Ⓙ	7 Ⓐ Ⓑ Ⓒ Ⓓ	14 Ⓕ Ⓖ Ⓗ Ⓙ	21 Ⓐ Ⓑ Ⓒ Ⓓ	28 Ⓕ Ⓖ Ⓗ Ⓙ	32 Ⓕ Ⓖ Ⓗ Ⓙ
1 Ⓐ Ⓑ Ⓒ Ⓓ	8 Ⓕ Ⓖ Ⓗ Ⓙ	15 Ⓐ Ⓑ Ⓒ Ⓓ	22 Ⓕ Ⓖ Ⓗ Ⓙ	29 Ⓐ Ⓑ Ⓒ Ⓓ	33 Ⓐ Ⓑ Ⓒ Ⓓ
2 Ⓕ Ⓖ Ⓗ Ⓙ	9 Ⓐ Ⓑ Ⓒ Ⓓ	16 Ⓕ Ⓖ Ⓗ Ⓙ	23 Ⓐ Ⓑ Ⓒ Ⓓ	30 Ⓕ Ⓖ Ⓗ Ⓙ	34 Ⓕ Ⓖ Ⓗ Ⓙ
3 Ⓐ Ⓑ Ⓒ Ⓓ	10 Ⓕ Ⓖ Ⓗ Ⓙ	17 Ⓐ Ⓑ Ⓒ Ⓓ	24 Ⓕ Ⓖ Ⓗ Ⓙ		
4 Ⓕ Ⓖ Ⓗ Ⓙ	11 Ⓐ Ⓑ Ⓒ Ⓓ	18 Ⓕ Ⓖ Ⓗ Ⓙ	25 Ⓐ Ⓑ Ⓒ Ⓓ		
5 Ⓐ Ⓑ Ⓒ Ⓓ	12 Ⓕ Ⓖ Ⓗ Ⓙ	19 Ⓐ Ⓑ Ⓒ Ⓓ	26 Ⓕ Ⓖ Ⓗ Ⓙ		

PART 2 READING COMPREHENSION

E1 Ⓐ Ⓑ Ⓒ Ⓓ	6 Ⓕ Ⓖ Ⓗ Ⓙ	12 Ⓕ Ⓖ Ⓗ Ⓙ	18 Ⓕ Ⓖ Ⓗ Ⓙ	24 Ⓕ Ⓖ Ⓗ Ⓙ	30 Ⓕ Ⓖ Ⓗ Ⓙ
1 Ⓐ Ⓑ Ⓒ Ⓓ	7 Ⓐ Ⓑ Ⓒ Ⓓ	13 Ⓐ Ⓑ Ⓒ Ⓓ	19 Ⓐ Ⓑ Ⓒ Ⓓ	25 Ⓐ Ⓑ Ⓒ Ⓓ	31 Ⓐ Ⓑ Ⓒ Ⓓ
2 Ⓕ Ⓖ Ⓗ Ⓙ	8 Ⓕ Ⓖ Ⓗ Ⓙ	14 Ⓕ Ⓖ Ⓗ Ⓙ	20 Ⓕ Ⓖ Ⓗ Ⓙ	26 Ⓕ Ⓖ Ⓗ Ⓙ	32 Ⓕ Ⓖ Ⓗ Ⓙ
3 Ⓐ Ⓑ Ⓒ Ⓓ	9 Ⓐ Ⓑ Ⓒ Ⓓ	15 Ⓐ Ⓑ Ⓒ Ⓓ	21 Ⓐ Ⓑ Ⓒ Ⓓ	27 Ⓐ Ⓑ Ⓒ Ⓓ	33 Ⓐ Ⓑ Ⓒ Ⓓ
4 Ⓕ Ⓖ Ⓗ Ⓙ	10 Ⓕ Ⓖ Ⓗ Ⓙ	16 Ⓕ Ⓖ Ⓗ Ⓙ	22 Ⓕ Ⓖ Ⓗ Ⓙ	28 Ⓕ Ⓖ Ⓗ Ⓙ	34 Ⓕ Ⓖ Ⓗ Ⓙ
5 Ⓐ Ⓑ Ⓒ Ⓓ	11 Ⓐ Ⓑ Ⓒ Ⓓ	17 Ⓐ Ⓑ Ⓒ Ⓓ	23 Ⓐ Ⓑ Ⓒ Ⓓ	29 Ⓐ Ⓑ Ⓒ Ⓓ	35 Ⓐ Ⓑ Ⓒ Ⓓ

UNIT 3 TEST PRACTICE

Part 1 Vocabulary

E1 sudden transition **A** activity **B** decision **C** attack **D** change	**E2 Which of these probably comes from the Latin word *malus* meaning *pole*?** **F** malice **G** must **H** mast **J** malt

For Numbers 1–8, find the word or words that mean the same or almost the same as the underlined word.

1 nice attire

A foolish
B rapid
C dress
D painstaking

2 naturally expand

F attack
G grow
H weaken
J shrink

3 dwell nearby

A surround
B drink
C live
D chase

4 sensational story

F exaggerated
G dogmatic
H representative
J vigorous

5 Famine means about the same as —

A period of drought
B time of hunger
C great harvest
D rush to escape

6 Simmer means about the same as —

F cool
G boil quickly
H spill
J cook slowly

7 To capsize is to —

A turn over
B slow down
C soak
D speed up

8 If something is frivolous it is —

F cheap
G important
H unnecessary
J expensive

GO

9 A sudden motion scared the bird.

Motion means —

A movement
B sound
C wind
D storm

10 The stray calf wandered into a neighbor's yard.

Stray means —

F young
G happy
H frisky
J wandering

11 It started out as a dismal day.

If something is dismal it is —

A gloomy
B beautiful
C gorgeous
D busy

12 A horde of insects was in the garden.

Horde means —

F small group
G nest
H large group
J family

13 The objective was not very clear.

Objective means —

A agreement
B reason
C goal
D function

For Numbers 14–19, find the word that means the opposite of the underlined word.

14 candid answer

F direct
G offensive
H hostile
J dishonest

15 will merge

A separate
B associate
C harden
D flow

16 entice birds

F attract
G ignore
H repel
J detract

17 persuade his friends

A convince
B discourage
C determine
D avoid

18 a huge windfall

F unexpected good luck
G expected result
H harsh criticism
J sad news

19 commotion nearby

A loud group
B working professionals
C school students
D quiet activity

For Numbers 20–23, choose the word that correctly completes both sentences.

20 She came up with a _______ solution.

The _______ I am reading has some interesting characters.

- **F** great
- **G** novel
- **H** book
- **J** surprising

21 This wall feels like it is _______ .

What was that loud _______ ?

- **A** stable
- **B** noise
- **C** strong
- **D** sound

22 A large navy ________ is located near my aunt's home.

We waited for our friends at the ________ of the mountain.

- **F** yard
- **G** base
- **H** bottom
- **J** dock

23 We may have to _______ to taking the train instead of driving.

The _______ had two swimming pools.

- **A** change
- **B** hotel
- **C** resort
- **D** agree

24 **A scrap of paper fell from his desk.**

In which sentence does the word scrap mean the same thing as in the sentence above?

- **F** We'll have to scrap that idea.
- **G** Scrap metal can be recycled and used again.
- **H** Each scrap of cloth in the quilt held a memory for the family.
- **J** The children began to scrap about who would sit in the front seat.

25 **The express train gets there at 9:00.**

In which sentence does the word express mean the same thing as in the sentence above?

- **A** It is sometimes hard to express yourself.
- **B** Leanna wanted to express the problem using an algebraic formula.
- **C** We received an express order to finish this job today.
- **D** Express shipping costs more but is worth the extra expense.

26 **The corn was ground with stone tools.**

In which sentence does the word ground mean the same thing as in the sentence above?

- **F** The ground was soaked by heavy rain.
- **G** Ground coffee loses its flavor faster than coffee beans.
- **H** The leading candidate lost ground to her nearest competition.
- **J** One of the wires in an electric circuit is called a ground.

GO

27 Which of these words probably comes from the Anglo-French word *taune* meaning *yellowish-brown*?

A tawny
B town
C tread
D tore

28 Which of these words probably comes from the Latin word *refugere* meaning *to flee*?

F deploy
G refugee
H desolate
J disintegrate

29 A ________ arose concerning the location of the new road.

Which of these words means an argument developed over the road?

A conclusion
B fellowship
C mobilization
D dispute

30 The mayor paid ________ visits to students in the school system.

Which of these words means the mayor visited occasionally?

F constant
G periodic
H enjoyable
J sudden

Read the paragraph. Find the word below the paragraph that fits best in each numbered blank.

The bicycle race had grown from a ___(31)___ to an international event. Thousands of riders now competed, not for money, but for the challenge. The race was only thirty miles long, not an ___(32)___ distance for a bicycle race, but it climbed four mountains that were each over ten thousand feet high. Only half of the racers who start the race ___(33)___ finish it. Those who do finish get only a shirt for all their efforts, and the ___(34)___ of being among just a handful of riders who are considered masters of the mountains.

31 A corrupt
B lenient
C friendly
D local

32 F acceptable
G inordinate
H elaborate
J ostentatious

33 A affirmatively
B unusually
C eventually
D seemingly

34 F satisfaction
G tribulation
H insecurity
J antagonist

STOP

E1

Don wasn't at all sure he wanted to ride the tram. It was the size of a large van and was suspended from three cables that stretched from the base of a mountain to the top, a distance of over two miles. It was supported by four towers, and at some points was over 400 feet above the ground. The tram had never had an accident, but Don was still frightened.

The tram in this story —

A is two miles above the ground.

B runs on four cables.

C has a good safety record.

D is the size of a large bus.

Here is a story about a very close call with lightning. Read the story and then do Numbers 1 through 8 on page 38.

The storm started out like the others that summer, and there had been many of them. Clouds began to develop around three o'clock, they covered the sky completely by seven, and within half an hour, the rain came down in torrents. A little thunder and lightning added drama to the event, and then it all ended.

Jasmine stood by a window watching the rain fall when a bolt of lightning hit the house. At the same instant, a terrific crash of thunder shook everything. She jumped back from the window and clutched her chest. Jasmine had a hard time catching her breath and her heart was pounding like crazy.

"Are you all right, Jasmine?" Mr. Harrison rushed to her side with a worried look on his face.

"I'm okay, Dad. Boy, was that ever close. Did you see where it hit the house?"

"It looks like the lightning hit the television antenna. I wonder if anything was damaged. Run into the kitchen and try the phone. I'll turn the television on."

Jasmine ran into the kitchen and picked up the phone. There was a dial tone, so she hung up and ran back into the family room.

"The telephone still works, Dad. How's the television?"

"It works, but the color is way off. It will probably have to be repaired. Let's take a look outside. The storm is pretty much gone."

They walked around the house looking for signs of damage. There weren't any until they came to the television antenna. The antenna itself seemed to be fine, but the wire going into the house was blackened.

"Bingo, a direct hit. Let's check to see what happened inside."

The two of them walked back into the house and checked where the television antenna came in. Jasmine noticed that the antenna wire was beside the line to the second phone. She walked over to the table and picked it up. There was no dial tone.

"Dad, there's no dial tone on this phone. I'll bet the lightning jumped from the television wire to the telephone line and damaged the phone. What shall we do?"

"The phone company has a 24-hour service number. Why don't you give them a call and let them know what happened? If they want to set up a service appointment, I can stay home any morning this week. Your mother and brothers are going to be in for a surprise when they get home."

GO

1 **This story suggests that the summer has been very —**

A stormy.

B dry.

C hot.

D uneventful.

2 **How did Jasmine discover that one of the phones didn't work?**

F Noticing the burned wire

G Calling the number

H Asking the service operator

J Listening for a dial tone

3 **What leads the reader to believe that Mr. Harrison has great confidence in Jasmine's ability?**

A He accepts Jasmine's judgment about how she feels.

B He takes Jasmine outside to inspect the house.

C He gives Jasmine the responsibility of calling the telephone service center.

D He allows Jasmine to tell her mother and brothers what happened.

4 **From this story, you can conclude that —**

F lightning is not likely to damage a television.

G lightning can strike a house and not injure the people inside.

H lightning occurs mainly at night or in the early evening.

J televisions are built better than phones.

5 **In this story, a hard rain is called —**

A a rush.

B a bolt.

C a drama.

D a torrent.

6 **Choose the sentence that tells what the passage is mostly about.**

F A girl and her father are in the house when lightning strikes it.

G Two people repair the damage done by a lightning strike.

H When lightning strikes a house, the two people in it panic.

J A lightning strike damages most of the electrical circuits in a house.

7 **When Jasmine's father says "Bingo," it indicates that —**

A the lightning strike caused damage but it wasn't serious.

B the place where the lightning hit was on fire.

C the phones in the house had escaped damage from the lightning.

D he has found the place where the lightning struck.

8 **In the beginning of the story, the author creates a sense of —**

F tragedy.

G anger.

H excitement.

J relief.

What would you have done?

For years, Jeremy had looked forward to being old enough to participate in the youth livestock show. His father had raised animals when he was a youngster, and Jeremy's two older sisters had won championships. Their trophies were all proudly displayed in the glass-front case in the dining room. Jeremy was sure that this year his would be added to the case. His prize pig, Cookie, "was a winner if he ever saw one," Jeremy's dad had said several times.

Jeremy had read dozens of articles furnished by his teacher. He had carefully mixed the food and vitamins that were recommended for a pig. His mother had driven him to a veterinarian's office twenty miles away to get a special vitamin supplement that would produce the healthy skin that Cookie needed to win. Jeremy walked Cookie for exercise and taught her to follow him around.

Mr. Henson and Jeremy had built a special pen, and Jeremy taught Cookie to push the automatic waterer with her nose to get a drink whenever she wanted it. Jeremy was convinced that pigs were the smartest animals.

Two weeks before the big show, Cookie was all ready. Everyone was proud and excited. Then something unexpected happened: Cookie got sick. The veterinarian came, but no one was sure exactly what caused the illness. She got better quickly, however, and was her old self after just a few days. Everyone in the family breathed a sigh of relief.

There was, however, one problem. Cookie had lost a lot of weight from the illness. She gained some of it back, but she was still several pounds too light and would be disqualified at the weigh-in. Jeremy was so disappointed that he was on the verge of tears because there was nothing he could do. Then his friend, Tim, said he had heard of some people who showed pigs and made them drink a lot of water so they would gain a few pounds. He said it would not hurt Cookie at all and it would be Jeremy's only chance to win.

Tim described what they would do to make Cookie drink the water. The more Tim talked, the worse Jeremy felt. He thought of how Cookie would feel after drinking all that water.

Jeremy looked at Tim and then looked at Cookie. He walked over to his pig, picked up her rope, and headed back to her pen. As he walked away, he heard Tim saying, "What's the matter, man? Don't you care anything about winning?"

"Not if it means hurting Cookie," Jeremy said. "She means too much to me. My little pig is more important than any old prize."

GO

9 The message of this story is that —

A people should not get too attached to their pets.

B some people are just not cut out to be winners.

C it is sometimes difficult to make the right choice.

D listening to friends is usually the right thing to do.

10 There is enough information in this story to show that —

F Jeremy did his best to prepare Cookie for the competition.

G Tim had a better attitude about winning than Jeremy.

H Jeremy's teacher should have been paying closer attention to the boys.

J Jeremy was too concerned about winning, like the rest of his family.

11 Why did Cookie lose weight?

A Jeremy fed her the wrong things.

B She didn't get enough water.

C She ate too much.

D She got sick.

12 Jeremy did all of these things to make Cookie a champion pig except —

F read dozens of articles from his teacher.

G run with her on a treadmill.

H walk Cookie for exercise.

J get a special vitamin for healthy skin.

13 The veterinarian —

A suggested that Jeremy make Cookie drink more water.

B did not know what caused Cookie's illness.

C had treated Jeremy's sisters' show animals.

D was also a judge in the youth livestock show.

14 This story is organized according to —

F a main idea and supporting information.

G an opening conclusion and examples.

H an unusual set of comparisons.

J a problem and a solution.

15 To be disqualified is to be —

A forced to enter a competition.

B invited to enter a competition.

C eliminated from a competition.

D disappointed by a competition.

16 In this story, the reader learns that —

F to be shown, pigs had to weigh a certain amount.

G Jeremy's family had put a lot of pressure on him to win.

H raising a show pig means you can't have other pets.

J pigs are smarter than almost any other animal.

A No-Guilt Treat

Most people like homemade ice cream in the summertime, but it can be loaded with fat and calories. Here is a treat that is easy to make and that may burn up more calories than it provides. The recipe is for orange sherbet, but you can vary the fruit flavor by using different kinds of soft drink.

You will need the following:

Three large clean coffee cans
Three small clean coffee cans
Duct tape or other strong tape
Crushed ice
Ice cream salt or rock salt
One can of sweetened condensed milk
One can of crushed pineapple, with juice
One two-liter bottle of orange soft drink
Several friends or family members

Preparation method:
Mix the condensed milk, pineapple, and soft drink. Pour the mixture into a smaller coffee can, leaving a space of at least one-fourth of the volume for expansion as the sherbet freezes. Put the plastic lid on, and tape it firmly with duct tape. Be sure to go around the can several times to get a good seal so that no liquid from the outer can will get in. Set the small coffee can in the center of a large can. Fill the space between the cans with crushed ice and a generous amount of rock salt. The rock salt will help the ice freeze the sherbet mix more quickly. Shake the can to settle the ice and add more ice and salt. The ice and salt mix should be packed firmly. Put on the plastic lid and carefully tape it in place. Be sure the tape makes several continuous loops across the top and bottom of each can. Repeat the process with the remainder of the mixture and the other two cans.

The people who expect to enjoy the sherbet should toss, kick, throw, and roll the cans around for 30 to 45 minutes. The more activity there is, the better the sherbet will be. After a few minutes of agitation, frost will begin to form on the outside can. When this happens, you know that the freezing is taking place.

When you think the sherbet has had time to freeze, open the outer can, pour out the water, add more ice and salt, and wait as long as you can stand it. This step will ripen and firm the sherbet. Then get the bowls and spoons and enjoy your no-guilt treat!

17 Agitating the can consists of all of the following *except* —

A rolling the can.

B tossing the can.

C setting the can down.

D kicking the can.

18 You could also make this recipe with —

F an electric ice cream freezer.

G one large plastic bucket and ice.

H an ice cube tray and freezer.

J two paper bags of different size.

19 If you wanted to make ice cream instead of sherbet, which part of the instructions would you have to change?

A Use ordinary table salt and ice cubes instead of crushed ice and rock salt.

B Use strawberry soda instead of orange.

C Nothing needs to be changed.

D Use an ice cream recipe or mix instead of the one given.

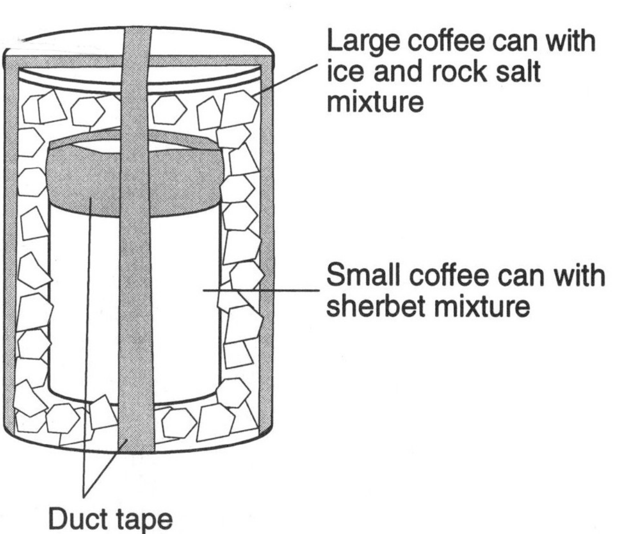

20 This recipe is good for a family picnic because —

F it requires group participation and is good to eat.

G leftovers can be stored in the freezer or an ice chest.

H it does not have many ingredients.

J several people can be served.

21 The phrase "as long as you can stand it" was put in the recipe to suggest that —

A the longer the sherbet ripens, the better it will taste.

B the cold sherbet will make everyone around it cold.

C people will have a hard time waiting for the sherbet to be ready.

D it will take a long time for the sherbet to ripen.

22 The rock salt —

F flavors the sherbet.

G keeps the cans from making noise.

H prevents spoilage.

J makes the ice work faster.

23 Another good name for this recipe would be —

A "Almost Ice Cream."

B "Can-can Sherbet."

C "An Interesting Dessert."

D "Good and Cold."

Read the passage and questions on the next page. Choose the answer that is better than the others.

If you ever wanted to write a book about little-known Americans who have made significant contributions to the country, your subjects would include people like Grace Hopper, a computer scientist, Charles Drew, the inventor of the blood bank, or Luis Alvarez, one of the creators of the guidance system that allows planes to land in difficult weather. Your book would also include an obscure character who, in his time, was larger than life, John Charles Frémont.

Born in Savannah, Georgia, in 1813, Frémont was known as "the Pathfinder" because of his explorations of the American West. He was appointed to the Army Topographic Corps and joined the Nicollet expedition to map the region between the upper Mississippi and Missouri Rivers. In 1842, he was given his own expedition to survey the Oregon Trail. His success led to a second expedition, the exploration of much of the West that was still uncharted territory. His hardships and deprivations made news around the country, and for a time, he was perhaps the most famous person in America.

To understand how difficult exploration was for Frémont and his men, consider this: there was not a single road through the Rocky or Sierra Mountains. Frémont's expedition was often traveling in winter at elevations above 10,000 feet with limited supplies of food and clothing. They had no accurate maps, yet they successfully traversed an area that is about one-third the size of the forty-eight contiguous states.

When he returned East, much of the information gathered by Frémont was considered to be ridiculous, yet it was true. He verified the existence of the Salt Lake in Utah and described a Great Basin between the Rockies and the Sierra mountains. He found the best pass through the mountains, and proved false the idea that there was a great river that flowed due west from the Rockies to the Pacific Ocean.

At the conclusion of his second expedition, Frémont moved to California, a land he had come to love on his journey. He was one of the moving forces behind the attempt to gain independence for California from Spain, which finally occurred in 1848. Frémont contributed in many ways to the development of California, and was one of its first senators to the U.S. Congress. When gold was discovered in California, Frémont was among the many who became rich overnight. As history has proven, this was the high point of his life.

Because of his popularity among the general public and his strong stand against slavery, Frémont was chosen to run for President by the newly formed Republican party. He was defeated by James Buchanan and returned to California. When the Civil War broke out, he fought for the Union, holding the rank of major general. He was not an effective general, which, combined with his strong opinions, caused him to leave the army.

After the war, Frémont's fortunes continued to slide. He mismanaged his land holdings and made poor investments, losing most of his fortune. He was appointed as governor of the Arizona Territory from 1878 to 1883, after which he again returned to California. He died in 1890 while on a visit to New York City.

Throughout his life, John Charles Frémont was a controversial figure. He constantly sought the support of political figures for personal advancement and married the daughter of the powerful senator, Thomas Hart Benton. During his expeditions, he often ignored direct orders, yet seemingly followed "secret" orders given from above. His men were extremely loyal to him, even though he put them in constant danger and many died. He was an instigator of the California rebellion that brought the region under U.S. control, but seemed to be doing it for personal gain. In the army, Frémont was found guilty of disobedience and unacceptable conduct, but he received a Presidential pardon. Despite these controversies, no one can dispute the fact that Frémont's courage and determination opened up the West and hastened America's rise to greatness.

GO

24 What was the purpose of the Army Topographic Corps?

F To seek independence for California

G To build roads through the Rockies

H To explore and make maps

J To build towns in the West

25 In the first paragraph, what does the word "obscure" mean?

A Little-known

B Famous

C Successful

D Highly regarded

26 What does it mean to say Frémont was a "moving force" behind the attempt to gain independence for California?

F He moved to California because it would soon be independent.

G He was one of the people who wanted independence, but did not want to fight for it.

H He was one of the people who was not sure about independence.

J He was one of the people who worked hard for independence.

27 When Frémont first arrived in California —

A it was a Spanish possession.

B it had recently gained independence.

C it was an American state.

D gold had just been discovered.

28 What is this passage mainly about?

F The exploration of the American West

G What it takes to run for President

H A little-known American hero

J How politics can cause the fall of a hero

29 Why were Frémont's men loyal even though he put them in danger?

A He respected them and they knew the importance of their job.

B They feared him and the President.

C They were interested in getting rich.

D They didn't mind traveling through the mountains in the winter.

30 Why would the President have granted Frémont a pardon?

F Frémont was working under secret orders from another country.

G There was little evidence to prove Frémont was a troublemaker.

H Frémont promised to help California become independent.

J Despite his problems, Frémont had accomplished a great deal.

31 Why does the author believe that the discovery of gold in California was the high point of Frémont's life?

A He had more money then than he ever would again.

B From that point onward, most of what he tried ended in failure.

C Being rich is more important than running for President.

D He accomplished nothing before and nothing afterward.

GO

For Numbers 32 through 35, choose the best answer to the question.

32 The detective walked into the dining room and noticed a strange odor. It was not unpleasant, nor was it strong. She couldn't identify the odor, but she knew she had smelled it before.

This passage was probably taken from —

F a mystery.

G a comedy.

H a science story.

J an historical novel.

33 The top of the cliff was twenty yards away. Woodie looked over the face of the cliff and spotted a dozen handholds. He reached deep within himself, grasped the nearest handhold, and made his way toward the top.

Which of these best explains the meaning of the phrase "reached deep within himself?"

A Fought off fear

B Considered how he would climb up

C Looked for a way down

D Relied on his last reserves of energy

Read this passage. Then do Numbers 34 and 35.

The cliffs near Centralia are actually made of volcanic rock that is about 2 million years old. The view from the top is spectacular, and the cave near the crest is the favorite spot for tourists. The walk up is long and tiring but worth the effort.

34 This passage would most likely be found in —

F a report on volcanoes.

G a travel brochure.

H an encyclopedia entry about cliffs.

J a newspaper article about walking.

35 Which of these is a fact expressed in the passage?

A The walk up is long and tiring but worth the effort.

B The cave is the favorite spot for tourists.

C The cliffs are made of volcanic rock about 2 million years old.

D The view from the top is spectacular.

STOP

Table of Contents

Language

Lesson 1 Punctuation

Examples

Directions: Mark the space for the punctuation mark that is needed in the sentence. Mark the space for "None" if no more punctuation marks are needed.

A Pete how did you finish your dinner so quickly?

A , **B** ; **C** : **D** None

B The judges chose three finalists: Tonya, Albert, and Leticia.

F ? **G** " **H** . **J** None

Read the sentence. First check the end punctuation, then check for missing punctuation inside the sentence.

If you are not sure which answer choice is correct, look at the answer choices. Ask yourself: "Are any of these punctuation marks needed in the sentence?"

Practice

1 "Grab that rope" yelled the deck hand.

A . **B** ! **C** , **D** None

2 This house, I should add, is selling for less than it cost when it was built.

F : **G** " **H** , **J** None

3 The officer asked, "Is there some way I can help?

A " **B** , **C** . **D** None

4 The contents of the package pleased everyone homemade cookies, fruit, and brownies.

F , **G** ; **H** : **J** None

5 No the telephone is not for you.

A ; **B** , **C** : **D** None

6 "Let's get started before the crowd arrives," suggested Bandar

F . **G** , **H** ! **J** None

GO

ANSWER ROWS
A Ⓐ Ⓑ Ⓒ Ⓓ 1 Ⓐ Ⓑ Ⓒ Ⓓ 3 Ⓐ Ⓑ Ⓒ Ⓓ 5 Ⓐ Ⓑ Ⓒ Ⓓ
B Ⓕ Ⓖ Ⓗ Ⓙ 2 Ⓕ Ⓖ Ⓗ Ⓙ 4 Ⓕ Ⓖ Ⓗ Ⓙ 6 Ⓕ Ⓖ Ⓗ Ⓙ

For Numbers 7–13, read each answer. Fill in the space for the choice that has a punctuation error. If there is no mistake, fill in the fourth answer space.

7 **A** Several things had been knocked
B to the floor by the quake a pot,
C a bag of groceries, and a chair.
D *(No mistakes)*

8 **F** Trees, shrubs, and, wildflowers
G grew on the hillside because
H of the water provided by the spring.
J *(No mistakes)*

9 **A** Although the house is
B on a busy street, it is quiet because
C of a well-placed wall.
D *(No mistakes)*

10 **F** Central High School
G Aldan, IL 62988
H March 23 1995,
J *(No mistakes)*

11 **A** Randford University
B Median, IL 60513
C Dear Dean Fortney
D *(No mistakes)*

12 **F** Please send me a copy of your catalog.
G of summer courses. I am a high school
H student and would like to take a course.
J *(No mistakes)*

13 **A** I look forward to receiving the catalog.
B Sincerely,
C *Wotan Pawlski*
D *(No mistakes)*

For Numbers 14–17, read each sentence with a blank. Choose the word or words that fit best in the blank and show the correct punctuation.

14 Remember to bring your _______ you will not be admitted to the reception.

F invitation; or
G invitation, or
H invitation or,
J invitation or

15 The _______ face was covered with dust and sweat.

A riders
B rider's
C riders'
D riders's

16 After you type this _______ I will make the copies we need for the meeting.

F report Jacob
G report, Jacob:
H report, Jacob,
J report, Jacob

17 _______ wondered Adrian, looking at the ruins in the valley.

A "Why do you think they left?"
B "Why do you think they left."
C "Why do you think they left,"
D "Why do you think they left"

ANSWER ROWS
7 Ⓐ Ⓑ Ⓒ Ⓓ 10 Ⓕ Ⓖ Ⓗ Ⓙ 13 Ⓐ Ⓑ Ⓒ Ⓓ 16 Ⓕ Ⓖ Ⓗ Ⓙ
8 Ⓕ Ⓖ Ⓗ Ⓙ 11 Ⓐ Ⓑ Ⓒ Ⓓ 14 Ⓕ Ⓖ Ⓗ Ⓙ 17 Ⓐ Ⓑ Ⓒ Ⓓ
9 Ⓐ Ⓑ Ⓒ Ⓓ 12 Ⓕ Ⓖ Ⓗ Ⓙ 15 Ⓐ Ⓑ Ⓒ Ⓓ

Examples

Directions: Mark the space for the answer that shows correct punctuation and capitalization. Mark the space for "Correct as it is" if the underlined part is correct.

A
- **A** All of us wi'll have to help.
- **B** Dont' carry more boxes than you can handle easily.
- **C** This shouldn't be too heavy for you.
- **D** We have'nt finished, but we can stop now for a break.

B If necessary, we can mail it to you.
- **F** necessary. We
- **G** necessary we,
- **H** necessary: we
- **J** Correct as it is

Remember, you are looking for the answer that shows correct capitalization and punctuation.

Skip difficult items and come back to them later.

Practice

1
- **A** Our house was built in 1990; theirs was built in 1994.
- **B** Joe walked with Linda; As far as the playground.
- **C** Most of the trees in this neighborhood, were planted between 1970 and 1980.
- **D** One of the nicest things about living here is: the park.

2
- **F** On this trip my Father visited Texas.
- **G** One of the hardest parts of a vacation, is getting to the Airport on time.
- **H** While waiting in the airport, Ken was able to call his parents.
- **J** After the plane took off, another plane, took its place at the Gate.

3
- **A** "Do you know where we can buy some poster board." wondered George.
- **B** "A craft store is on Palmer street," suggested Sally.
- **C** Lou Ella commented "we can't take the bus there."
- **D** "Is that the only craft store in town?" asked Carl.

4 "Your room is on the fifth floor," said the clerk, "And the pool is on the roof."
- **F** clerk "and
- **G** clerk, "and
- **H** clerk; "and
- **J** Correct as it is

5 The stores construction was delayed because of a trucking strike.
- **A** stores'
- **B** stores's
- **C** store's
- **D** Correct as it is

6 The ball and your shoes are in the closet.
- **F** ball, and
- **G** ball and,
- **H** ball, and,
- **J** Correct as it is

GO

ANSWER ROWS A Ⓐ Ⓑ Ⓒ Ⓓ 1 Ⓐ Ⓑ Ⓒ Ⓓ 3 Ⓐ Ⓑ Ⓒ Ⓓ 5 Ⓐ Ⓑ Ⓒ Ⓓ
B Ⓕ Ⓖ Ⓗ Ⓙ 2 Ⓕ Ⓖ Ⓗ Ⓙ 4 Ⓕ Ⓖ Ⓗ Ⓙ 6 Ⓕ Ⓖ Ⓗ Ⓙ

One of the newest ways of keeping a house warm is radiant
(7) heating; coils of plastic tubing are built into the floor or slab of the
(8) house. When it becomes necessary to heat the house hot water is
forced through the tubing. The floor becomes warm, and because
(9) heat rises, so does the air in the rest of the house. It is an efficient
(10) heating system. That is becoming more and more popular.

7 A heating, coils
B heating. Coils
C heating: Coils
D Correct as it is

8 F house, hot
G house. Hot
H House. Hot
J Correct as it is

9 A the house, it
B the House, it
C the house; it
D Correct as it is

10 F system, that
G system; that
H system that
J Correct as it is

January 18, 1995

(11) Kimmon Travel Co,
1314 Branford Avenue
Solex, ID 83109
(12) Dear Mrs. Willis:
(13) Thank you for sending us *A Guide to the Idaho mountains.* It
(14) arrived yesterday but our tickets did not. Could you please give us
a call and let us know when to expect them?

Sincerely yours,
Jane Gibbons

11 A Kimmon Travel Co
B Kimmon Travel Co.
C Kimmon travel co.
D Correct as it is

12 F Dear Mrs. Willis,
G Dear Mrs Willis:
H Dear Mrs. Willis;
J Correct as it is

13 A *Idaho Mountains.*
B *idaho mountains.*
C *Idaho Mountains?*
D Correct as it is

14 F yesterday; but
G yesterday; but,
H yesterday, but
J Correct as it is

GO

ANSWER ROWS 7 Ⓐ Ⓑ Ⓒ Ⓓ 9 Ⓐ Ⓑ Ⓒ Ⓓ 11 Ⓐ Ⓑ Ⓒ Ⓓ 13 Ⓐ Ⓑ Ⓒ Ⓓ
8 Ⓕ Ⓖ Ⓗ Ⓙ 10 Ⓕ Ⓖ Ⓗ Ⓙ 12 Ⓕ Ⓖ Ⓗ Ⓙ 14 Ⓕ Ⓖ Ⓗ Ⓙ

For Numbers 15 and 16, read the sentence with a blank. Mark the space beside the answer choice that fits best in the blank and has correct capitalization and punctuation.

15 The dog is ________ went for a long hike with us.

A sleeping, She
B sleeping; she
C sleeping: She
D sleeping she

16 The other night my family had dinner at ________

F an Indian restaurant.
G an indian restaurant.
H an Indian Restaurant.
J an Indian, restaurant.

Lydia wrote this report about the history of technology. Read the report and use it to do Numbers 17–20.

When they talk about technological advances, most people think about Telephones and Satellites. They forget that every civilization had its own kind of advances. Ancient humans, for example, discovered fire, the wheel, and agriculture. These discoveries don't sound very hi-tech: but they laid the foundation for the advanced civilizations of Africa, Europe, and the americas

(1) (2) (3) (4)

17 **In sentence 1, Telephones and Satellites is best written —**

A telephone's and satellite's
B telephones' and satellites'
C telephones and satellites
D As it is

18 **In sentence 3, humans, for example, is best written —**

F humans for example
G humans. For example
H humans for example,
J As it is

19 **In sentence 4, hi-tech: but is best written —**

A hi-tech, but
B hi-tech. But
C hi-tech; But
D As it is

20 **In sentence 4, the americas is best written —**

F the America's.
G the Americas.
H the Americas'.
J As it is

STOP

ANSWER ROWS 15 Ⓐ Ⓑ Ⓒ Ⓓ 17 Ⓐ Ⓑ Ⓒ Ⓓ 19 Ⓐ Ⓑ Ⓒ Ⓓ
16 Ⓕ Ⓖ Ⓗ Ⓙ 18 Ⓕ Ⓖ Ⓗ Ⓙ 20 Ⓕ Ⓖ Ⓗ Ⓙ

E1

"We're number one!" shouted the fans as the clock ran out.

A , **B** ; **C** : **D** None

1 You will have your choice of several trips the museum, the space center, or the university.

A : **B** ; **C** , **D** None

2 Ned your report about agriculture was the best you have ever written.

F ! **G** ; **H** , **J** None

3 The news weather, and sports can be heard on the radio each hour.

A : **B** , **C** ; **D** None

4 The interstate is clogged with traffic; the surface roads are almost empty.

F ; **G** , **H** : **J** None

For Numbers 5–7, read each answer. Fill in the space for the choice that has a punctuation error. If there is no mistake, fill in the fourth answer space.

5 **A** "I didn't do it," argued Nancy.
B "I was at the library from
C noon until five o'clock."
D *(No mistakes)*

6 **F** My brother writes a column;
G for our local newspaper.
H It's about sports in schools.
J *(No mistakes)*

7 **A** It was becoming clear that
B wed' taken the wrong trail
C and were heading away from the lake.
D *(No mistakes)*

For Numbers 8 and 9, read each sentence with a blank. Choose the word or words that fit best in the blank and show the correct punctuation.

8 Kevin, _______ found the puppy wandering around the school.

F not Sharon,
G not Sharon
H not Sharon:
J not, Sharon

9 The kitchen is too _______ let's eat on the back porch.

A hot
B hot,
C hot:
D hot;

GO

ANSWER ROWS E1 Ⓐ Ⓑ Ⓒ Ⓓ 2 Ⓕ Ⓖ Ⓗ Ⓙ 4 Ⓕ Ⓖ Ⓗ Ⓙ 6 Ⓕ Ⓖ Ⓗ Ⓙ 8 Ⓕ Ⓖ Ⓗ Ⓙ
1 Ⓐ Ⓑ Ⓒ Ⓓ 3 Ⓐ Ⓑ Ⓒ Ⓓ 5 Ⓐ Ⓑ Ⓒ Ⓓ 7 Ⓐ Ⓑ Ⓒ Ⓓ 9 Ⓐ Ⓑ Ⓒ Ⓓ

For Numbers 10–13, read each group of words. Find the sentence that is written correctly and shows the correct capitalization and punctuation.

10 F "It's so good to see you," said Donna to her old friend Kent.

G "This is my first class reunion, commented Lena."

H Abbie suggested "we should try to get together more often."

J Amos, said, "I can't believe so many people showed up"

11 A Clocks, and watches are on sale this weekend at sanborns department store.

B Harold's designs, is one of the newest stores in the mall.

C Stamps, boxes, and wrapping paper are available at the Joyce's Gift Shop.

D The school store sells pens paper and other school supplies.

12 F We had a funny experience in a small town, in new York.

G Matlock, the town next to ours, has a music festival each summer.

H Many people are discovering, the attractions in their own States.

J Large cities like Chicago and san Francisco, have many summer events.

13 A Nellie, tried to fix the leaky faucet in the bathroom.

B If you see, Lloyd, let him know I am looking for him.

C It's your turn Brandon

D Pancho, did you call me?

For Numbers 14–17, read the sentence with a blank. Mark the space beside the answer choice that fits best in the blank and has correct capitalization and punctuation.

14 The _______ because it is near the ocean, has lots of rain.

F northwest
G northwest,
H Northwest;
J Northwest,

15 The Pet Emporium is at _______ , right beside the gas station.

A 23 Randolph St.
B 23 Randolph st.
C 23 randolph st.
D 23 randolph st

16 The Grand Canyon, which is in Arizona, is one of our most popular _______ .

F National Parks
G National parks
H national parks
J national Parks

17 _______ suggested Susanna.

A "Let's walk to the park,"
B "Lets walk to the park,"
C "let's walk to the park,"
D "Let's walk to the Park,"

GO

ANSWER ROWS
10 Ⓕ Ⓖ Ⓗ Ⓙ 12 Ⓕ Ⓖ Ⓗ Ⓙ 14 Ⓕ Ⓖ Ⓗ Ⓙ 16 Ⓕ Ⓖ Ⓗ Ⓙ
11 Ⓐ Ⓑ Ⓒ Ⓓ 13 Ⓐ Ⓑ Ⓒ Ⓓ 15 Ⓐ Ⓑ Ⓒ Ⓓ 17 Ⓐ Ⓑ Ⓒ Ⓓ

For Numbers 18–21, look at the underlined part of each sentence. Find the answer choice that shows the correct capitalization and punctuation for the underlined part.

18 Linda announced "The winner of the contest is Millie Anderson."

- **F** announced, "the
- **G** announced, "The
- **H** announced ",The
- **J** Correct as it is

19 If you want to know my opinion, I think she did the right thing.

- **A** opinion I
- **B** opinion: I
- **C** opinion? I
- **D** Correct as it is

20 The gym closes at noon on Saturday, the library is open until six o'clock.

- **F** saturday. The
- **G** Saturday: the
- **H** Saturday; the
- **J** Correct as it is

21 The computer is new but the printer is three years old.

- **A** new, but
- **B** new. But
- **C** new; but
- **D** Correct as it is

For Numbers 22–25, read the passage. Find the answer choice that shows the correct capitalization and punctuation for the underlined part.

(22) "Are you sure this is the right color?" asked Mrs. Georgio. She
(23) looked at the walls the painter's had already completed and then
at the fabric sample. The client for whom she was working was
(24) very picky and Mrs. Georgio did not want to offend him. Her
design business was successful because Mrs. Georgio paid close
(25) attention to details. If the paint was not correct, doctor Martin
would certainly notice.

22
- **F** color," asked
- **G** color," Asked
- **H** color asked,"
- **J** Correct as it is

23
- **A** painters had
- **B** painters' had
- **C** painters, had
- **D** Correct as it is

24
- **F** picky; and
- **G** picky. And
- **H** picky, and
- **J** Correct as it is

25
- **A** correct Doctor
- **B** correct, Doctor
- **C** correct. Doctor
- **D** Correct as it is

GO

ANSWER ROWS 18 Ⓕ Ⓖ Ⓗ Ⓙ 20 Ⓕ Ⓖ Ⓗ Ⓙ 22 Ⓕ Ⓖ Ⓗ Ⓙ 24 Ⓕ Ⓖ Ⓗ Ⓙ
19 Ⓐ Ⓑ Ⓒ Ⓓ 21 Ⓐ Ⓑ Ⓒ Ⓓ 23 Ⓐ Ⓑ Ⓒ Ⓓ 25 Ⓐ Ⓑ Ⓒ Ⓓ

This is more of Lydia's report about technology. Read the report and use it to do Numbers 26–29.

(1) Technology has always built upon itself, fire, for example, was discovered accidentally, probably as the result of a lightning-started brush fire. (2) Once humans learned to use fire and make it themselves, they were able to create metals from ore. (3) With metals such as bronze and iron, humans could make better tools: utensils, and weapons. (4) Fire technology, in other words, led to metal technology.

(5) Another thing that technology does is improve life. (6) Fire creates light, so humans could stay up later at night. (7) They could also stay warmer in cold weather and even move into areas that were too cold before. (8) Primitive humans ability to live in northern Europe and Asia was the result of the discovery of fire.

26 In sentence 1, itself, fire, is best written —

F itself: fire,
G itself fire
H itself. Fire,
J As it is

27 In sentence 3, tools: utensils, is best written —

A tools utensils
B tools utensils,
C tools, utensils,
D As it is

28 In sentence 8, humans ability is best written —

F human's ability
G humans' ability
H humans, ability
J As it is

29 In sentence 8, northern Europe is best written —

A northern Europe,
B Northern Europe
C Northern Europe,
D As it is

STOP

ANSWER ROWS 26 Ⓕ Ⓖ Ⓗ Ⓙ 27 Ⓐ Ⓑ Ⓒ Ⓓ 28 Ⓕ Ⓖ Ⓗ Ⓙ 29 Ⓐ Ⓑ Ⓒ Ⓓ NUMBER RIGHT ______

Lesson 4 Usage

Examples

Directions: Read the directions for each section. Fill in the circle for the answer you think is correct.

A The coat _______ you bought last year still looks brand new.

A that
B this
C who
D when

B
F The maps you gave Ben and I will help us plan our trip.
G Me and him are taking the train today.
H Karen saw Matt and I, but we didn't see her.
J She and I are going to the movies tomorrow afternoon.

If you are not sure which answer choice is correct, eliminate answers you know are wrong and then take your best guess.

It might help to say each answer choice to yourself. If an item has a blank, try each answer choice in the blank and say the completed sentence to yourself.

Practice

For Numbers 1–3, choose the word or phrase that best completes the sentence.

1 Richard let _______ into the house.

A myself
B his
C himself
D we

2 The farmer _______ the crops already.

F will plant
G has planted
H plants
J have planted

3 This game is _______ than the other one.

A more challenging
B most challenging
C challenging
D challenged

For Numbers 4–6, choose the answer that is a complete and correctly written sentence.

4
F The rivers in our state is cleaner because of a new law.
G Planting trees or shrubs help to hold the soil along rivers.
H The birds beside the road don't seems to mind the traffic.
J The stars seem especially bright tonight.

5
A Haven't you got no pencil or paper?
B She couldn't find your phone number.
C I didn't have no idea where you lived.
D Lee hadn't never been to your house.

6
F Kim is the one who found the keys.
G Who's hat is under the kitchen table?
H The pen what you are looking for is here.
J A shopper which was here yesterday forgot her umbrella.

GO

ANSWER ROWS
A Ⓐ Ⓑ Ⓒ Ⓓ   1 Ⓐ Ⓑ Ⓒ Ⓓ   3 Ⓐ Ⓑ Ⓒ Ⓓ   5 Ⓐ Ⓑ Ⓒ Ⓓ
B Ⓕ Ⓖ Ⓗ Ⓙ   2 Ⓕ Ⓖ Ⓗ Ⓙ   4 Ⓕ Ⓖ Ⓗ Ⓙ   6 Ⓕ Ⓖ Ⓗ Ⓙ

For Numbers 7–12, read each answer choice. Fill in the space for the choice that has a usage error. If there is no mistake, fill in the fourth answer space.

7 A The most exciting thing that
B happened to us was a flat tire. A
C movie star stopped to help us!
D *(No mistakes)*

8 F The job we did was acceptable,
G but we coulda done even better
H if we had been given more time.
J *(No mistakes)*

9 A The walkathon was great, but
B by the time we were finished,
C we were really wore out.
D *(No mistakes)*

10 F The fishes you saw were salmon.
G They return from the ocean each
H year and spawn in this creek.
J *(No mistakes)*

11 A I don't know about the rest of
B you, but I am certain that
C Denine and me will be ready.
D *(No mistakes)*

12 F The most likely person to be
G chosen is Ishmael. He has been training
H the longest and were in great shape.
J *(No mistakes)*

For Numbers 13 and 14, choose the best way to write the underlined part of each sentence. If the underlined part is correct, fill in the fourth answer space.

13 However it is cold, the sun is shining and it feels warmer than it really is.

A Yet
B Although
C Despite
D *(No change)*

14 The traffic was heavy next week because a convention will be in town.

F will be heavy
G were heavy
H is heavy
J *(No change)*

For Numbers 15 and 16, choose the answer that is a complete and correctly written sentence.

15 A With his tail wagging, Bill threw the stick to the eager dog.
B While taking a test, a bird flew into our classroom and out again.
C Before buying the bicycle, the clerk told me it was on sale.
D Just before she left, Adona reminded us to close the windows.

16 F The newest store in the mall, which is a nature shop.
G You can borrow this book, remembering to return it in a week.
H On our way here, we saw a flock of geese land in a field.
J Pull the shades down, with the sun coming in through the window.

GO

ANSWER ROWS 7 Ⓐ Ⓑ Ⓒ Ⓓ 9 Ⓐ Ⓑ Ⓒ Ⓓ 11 Ⓐ Ⓑ Ⓒ Ⓓ 13 Ⓐ Ⓑ Ⓒ Ⓓ 15 Ⓐ Ⓑ Ⓒ Ⓓ
8 Ⓕ Ⓖ Ⓗ Ⓙ 10 Ⓕ Ⓖ Ⓗ Ⓙ 12 Ⓕ Ⓖ Ⓗ Ⓙ 14 Ⓕ Ⓖ Ⓗ Ⓙ 16 Ⓕ Ⓖ Ⓗ Ⓙ

Here is more of the report Lydia wrote about technology. Read the report and use it to do Numbers 17–20.

Technology often has its beginning in nature. (1) Fire, which was mentioned earlier, is one example. (2) Another is the basket. (3) Primitive humans probably using the nests of large birds as the first baskets. (4) They soon learned to weave their own baskets by imitating the structure of a nest. (5) Eventually, as finer materials such as grasses were used, humans learned to weave cloth. (6)

Some of the technologies discovered by primitive humans remain a mystery today. (7) Scientists still don't know, for example, that the pyramids were built. (8) Huge stones weighing many tons had to be lifted over a hundred feet. (9) This would be a difficult feat even today, but Egyptians they were able to do it more than 4,000 years ago. (10)

17 **In sentence 2, earlier is best written —**

A early
B earliest
C more early
D As it is

18 **In sentence 4, using the nests is best written —**

F use the nests
G used the nests
H uses the nests
J As it is

19 **In sentence 8, that the pyramids is best written —**

A which the pyramids
B like the pyramids
C how the pyramids
D As it is

20 **In sentence 10, Egyptians they were is best written —**

F Egyptians were
G Egyptians was
H Egyptians they was
J As it is

ANSWER ROWS 17 Ⓐ Ⓑ Ⓒ Ⓓ 18 Ⓕ Ⓖ Ⓗ Ⓙ 19 Ⓐ Ⓑ Ⓒ Ⓓ 20 Ⓕ Ⓖ Ⓗ Ⓙ

Examples

Directions: Read the directions for each section. Fill in the circle for the answer you think is correct.

A The bank gave a radio to new customers.
A (bank) B (gave) C (radio) D (customers)

B A wide river blocked the traveler's progress.
F (wide) G (river) H (blocked) J (traveler's)

C It is snowing.
The snow is not falling hard.

A It is snowing, and not hard.
B Although not hard, it is snowing.
C It is not snowing, but hard.
D It is snowing, but not hard.

Stay with your first answer choice. You should change an answer only if you are sure the one you chose is wrong.

Remember, the subject comes before the verb in most sentences.

Practice

For Numbers 1–3, find the underlined part that is the simple subject of the sentence.

1 The officer stopped the truck for a safety inspection.
A (officer) B (stopped) C (truck) D (safety)

2 The two regional winners are from Illinois and Wisconsin.
F (two) G (regional) H (winners) J (Illinois)

3 After lunch, the students remained in the cafeteria for a movie about nutrition.
A (lunch) B (students) C (remained) D (cafeteria)

For Numbers 4–6, find the underlined part that is the simple predicate (verb) of the sentence.

4 A deep puddle formed under the bridge.
F (deep) G (puddle) H (formed) J (bridge)

5 Visitors enter the museum through a pair of huge doors.
A (Visitors) B (enter) C (museum) D (pair)

6 With the saddle off, the horse raced around the field faster than before.
F (With) G (saddle) H (horse) J (raced)

GO

ANSWER ROWS A Ⓐ Ⓑ Ⓒ Ⓓ C Ⓐ Ⓑ Ⓒ Ⓓ 2 Ⓕ Ⓖ Ⓗ Ⓙ 4 Ⓕ Ⓖ Ⓗ Ⓙ 6 Ⓕ Ⓖ Ⓗ Ⓙ
B Ⓕ Ⓖ Ⓗ Ⓙ 1 Ⓐ Ⓑ Ⓒ Ⓓ 3 Ⓐ Ⓑ Ⓒ Ⓓ 5 Ⓐ Ⓑ Ⓒ Ⓓ

For Numbers 7–9, choose the answer that best combines the underlined sentences.

7 Tickets for this concert are free.

You must order tickets ahead of time.

- **A** You must order tickets ahead of time, and tickets for this concert are free.
- **B** Tickets for this concert are free, despite you must order them ahead of time.
- **C** Tickets for this concert are free; you must, however, order them ahead of time.
- **D** You must order tickets ahead of time, or tickets for this concert are free.

8 The radio station is having a contest for student announcers.

We visited the radio station last week.

- **F** The radio station, which we visited last week, is having a contest for student announcers.
- **G** Because we visited the radio station last week, it is having a contest for student announcers.
- **H** The radio station, that we visited last week, and is having a contest for student announcers.
- **J** A contest for student announcers, which is by the radio station that we visited last week.

9 A deer stepped into the road.

The car swerved to avoid it.

The car narrowly missed the deer.

- **A** A deer stepped into the road, and a car swerved to avoid it, and the car narrowly missed the deer.
- **B** Swerving to avoid it, the deer stepped into the road and was narrowly missed by the car.
- **C** The car, which narrowly missed the deer, had swerved to avoid it, as the deer stepped into the road.
- **D** The car swerved to avoid a deer that stepped into the road, narrowly missing it.

For Numbers 10 and 11, choose the best way of expressing the idea.

10
- **F** Having just built a house, the volunteers stepped back, filled with pride, and admired it.
- **G** Filled with pride, the volunteers stepped back and admired the house they had just built.
- **H** The volunteers were filled with pride, stepping back to admire the house they had just built.
- **J** The house they had just built filled the volunteers with pride, so they stepped back and admired it.

11
- **A** Calling the box office, Catherine wasn't sure what time the movie started.
- **B** Catherine wasn't sure what time the movie started, so she called the box office.
- **C** Because she called the box office, Catherine wasn't sure what time the movie started.
- **D** Although she wasn't sure what time the movie started, Catherine called the box office.

GO

Lydia's report about technology continues here. Use it to do Numbers 12–15.

(1) Many forms of technology were used for a different purpose before their most powerful application was discovered. **(2)** The button, for example. **(3)** It was used as an ornament before someone discovered that a button and a hole could fasten clothing quite well. **(4)** Another example is the wheel. **(5)** For centuries, it was used horizontally to make pottery. **(6)** Someone eventually turned a wheel on its side and changed history in an instant. **(7)** A third example is writing it was invented to record business transactions long before anyone thought to use it to record spoken words.

12 Which of these is a run-on?

- **F** 1
- **G** 4
- **H** 6
- **J** 7

13 How can sentences 5 and 6 best be combined without changing their meaning?

- **A** For centuries, it was used horizontally to make pottery until someone eventually turned a wheel on its side and changed history in an instant.
- **B** It eventually turned on its side and changed history in an instant, before having been used to make pottery.
- **C** Having been used to make pottery for centuries, the wheel was turned on its side, eventually changing history.
- **D** History was changed in an instant after centuries of using a wheel to make pottery, someone eventually turned it on its side.

14 How is sentence 1 best written?

- **F** Many forms of technology, which were used for one purpose, before their most powerful application was discovered.
- **G** Before their most powerful application was discovered, many forms of technology they were used for one purpose.
- **H** Before their most powerful application, it was discovered, many forms of technology were used for a different purpose.
- **J** As it is

15 Which group of words is *not* a complete sentence?

- **A** 2
- **B** 3
- **C** 4
- **D** 5

STOP

ANSWER ROWS 12 Ⓕ Ⓖ Ⓗ Ⓙ 13 Ⓐ Ⓑ Ⓒ Ⓓ 14 Ⓕ Ⓖ Ⓗ Ⓙ 15 Ⓐ Ⓑ Ⓒ Ⓓ

Example

Directions: Read the directions for each section. Fill in the circle for the answer you think is correct.

Read the paragraph below. Find the best topic sentence for the paragraph.

A ______________. She had painted for more than sixty years, but had shown her work to no one other than her husband. A friend had discovered her paintings accidentally and insisted that Mrs. McClellan show them. At the age of seventy-eight, she was having her first art show.

A Art is often a very private thing.

B It was one of the proudest moments of Mrs. McClellan's life.

C Talent emerges in some people very late in life.

D Mrs. McClellan had always lived what she considered to be a normal life.

Remember, a paragraph should focus on one idea. The correct answer is the one that fits best with the rest of the paragraph.

If you are sure you know which answer choice is correct, mark your answer and move on to the next item.

Practice

Read the paragraph below. Find the best topic sentence for the paragraph.

1 ______________. She would prove to be one of the longest-lived sovereigns in the history of the world. Under Victoria's rule, the British empire spread around the globe, making it the world's first superpower.

A In 1837, Queen Victoria assumed the throne of England.

B England has had some remarkable rulers, from Henry VIII to Victoria.

C The Victorian Period was named after a queen of England.

D A queen is often, but not always, simply a figurehead.

Find the answer choice that best develops the topic sentence below.

2 Mountain biking is fast becoming a national craze.

F The sport started in Colorado or California, depending on your source of information. A mountain bike may cost more than one thousand dollars.

G Many ski areas offer mountain biking in the summer. You take a chair up and ride down.

H Millions of people around the country enjoy mountain biking everywhere from New York's Central Park to California's Sierra Mountains. Consumers seem to love these go-anywhere bikes with fat tires, a sturdy frame, and twenty-one gears.

J A mountain bike looks clunkier than a touring bike. The sturdy frame and knobby tires, however, make a mountain bike an all-terrain vehicle. Even with twenty-one gears, it is still hard work pedaling up a steep hill.

GO

ANSWER ROW **A** Ⓐ Ⓑ Ⓒ Ⓓ **1** Ⓐ Ⓑ Ⓒ Ⓓ **2** Ⓕ Ⓖ Ⓗ Ⓙ

For Numbers 3 and 4, read the paragraph. Find the sentence that does not belong in the paragraph.

3 1. Plants grow in the most unusual places. 2. Everyone, for example, has probably seen a determined weed poking through an asphalt street. 3. More observant people might have noticed an occasional berry bush growing in the crotch of a tree. 4. Home gardeners grow plants in their own backyards.

A Sentence 1

B Sentence 2

C Sentence 3

D Sentence 4

4 1. A Small Craft Advisory is a warning issued by the National Weather Service. 2. The National Weather Service is an agency of the federal government. 3. It may include winds from 18 to 33 knots. 4. In addition, dangerous waves may form, posing a hazard to small boats.

F Sentence 1

G Sentence 2

H Sentence 3

J Sentence 4

For Numbers 5 and 6, read the paragraph. Find the sentence that best fits the blank in the paragraph.

5 For many people, the beginning of spring is marked by the opening of trout season. ______________. There they huddle shoulder to shoulder with other fishing enthusiasts. Most of the anglers never catch a fish, but they still enjoy celebrating the end of winter with their comrades.

A In some states, however, it is legal to fish for trout all year long.

B Fishing for trout has a long history and has been the subject of many books.

C The most popular varieties of trout are brook, brown, and rainbow.

D On this long-awaited day, anglers arise long before dawn and head to their favorite stream.

6 Learning a language other than English is becoming more important. In today's global marketplace, anyone who speaks more than one language is at an advantage. ______________. In addition, they will be more likely to advance and be offered opportunities for international travel.

F Job seekers have an easier time finding work if they know a second language.

G Languages that use the Latin alphabet are usually easier to learn.

H More languages are taught in schools today than twenty years ago.

J Home-study courses are one way that people learn a second language.

GO

ANSWER ROWS 3 Ⓐ Ⓑ Ⓒ Ⓓ 4 Ⓕ Ⓖ Ⓗ Ⓙ 5 Ⓐ Ⓑ Ⓒ Ⓓ 6 Ⓕ Ⓖ Ⓗ Ⓙ

For Numbers 7–9, use the paragraph below to answer the questions.

[1]The sun, which is a star, is at the center of the solar system. [2]Nine planets, including the earth, revolve around the sun. [3]The planets also rotate on their own axes. [4]Between the planets Mars and Jupiter are smaller bodies called asteroids that may be the remains of a planet that disintegrated in the distant past. [5]Comets occasionally pass through the solar system but are not considered part of it.

7 **Choose the best opening sentence to add to this paragraph.**

A A planet and a star are different in many ways.
B Our galaxy contains many millions of stars.
C The earth is the third planet from the sun.
D The earth is part of a cluster of objects called the solar system.

8 **Which sentence should be left out of this paragraph?**

F Sentence 1
G Sentence 2
H Sentence 3
J Sentence 4

9 **Where is the best place for sentence 5?**

A Where it is now
B Between sentences 1 and 2
C Between sentences 2 and 3
D Before sentence 1

10 **Which of the following would be most appropriate at the beginning of a report on the Boston Tea Party?**

F Because of their association with Great Britain, colonists in America drank a lot of tea. It was a great inconvenience when the British gave the East India Company a monopoly on tea importation and allowed them to control the price.

G On December 16, 1773, a group of patriots in Boston climbed aboard several ships in the harbor and threw bales of tea overboard. This seemingly insignificant act proved to be one of the earliest skirmishes in the Revolutionary War.

H The Boston Tea Party established Massachusetts as a center of resistance against British rule. It led to the Coercive Acts of 1774, which were intended to penalize Massachusetts and the city of Boston for harboring revolutionaries.

J The Revolutionary War between Britain and her colonies did not happen all at once. For more than ten years before shots were fired at Lexington and Concord, minor skirmishes took place all over the colonies, especially in the colony of Massachusetts.

GO

Here is more of Lydia's report about technology. Use the story to do Numbers 11–14.

(1) People in previous centuries were not as uninformed as we might think. **(2)** A calculating machine, the forerunner of the computers that help scientists design and guide rockets, was created by Charles Babbage in 1823. **(3)** Consider the rockets that are sent into space almost daily. **(4)** The basis of this technology is the invention of gunpowder by the Chinese around 1000 A.D. **(5)** The telescopes we use to observe rockets in flight owe their development to Dutch opticians around 1600 A.D. **(6)** These and countless other developments were the building blocks of the technologies we use every day.

11 Which sentence could be added before sentence 1?

A Technology ranges in size from the smallest computer chip to the largest rocket.
B Some of today's most advanced technologies had their roots hundreds of years ago.
C Different civilizations developed different technologies.
D Very few areas of life have been unaffected by technology.

12 Which sentence is *not* in the correct place?

F 1
G 2
H 3
J 4

13 What supporting information could be added before sentence 6?

A Eye glasses and telescopes are based on similar technology.
B Their gunpowder was made of charcoal, sulfur, and potassium nitrate.
C The two kinds of telescopes are those that use lenses and those that use mirrors.
D The telescope itself was invented in 1608 by the Dutch scientist Johann Lippershey.

14 Which sentence does *not* belong in the story?

F 1
G 3
H 5
J 6

STOP

ANSWER ROWS 11 Ⓐ Ⓑ Ⓒ Ⓓ 12 Ⓕ Ⓖ Ⓗ Ⓙ 13 Ⓐ Ⓑ Ⓒ Ⓓ 14 Ⓕ Ⓖ Ⓗ Ⓙ

E1

Find the underlined part that is the simple predicate (verb) of the sentence.

An excited crowd of supporters awaited the return of the governor.
A B C D

For Number 1, choose the word or phrase that best completes the sentence.

1 _______ will arrive at the party a little late because we must pick up Alonso.

A I and her

B I and she

C She and I

D She and me

For Number 2, choose the answer that is a complete and correctly written sentence.

2 **F** The grass is growing more slower because there has been so little rain.

G Our new lawn mower is quietest than the old one.

H The lid to the gas can was on more tighter so I couldn't loosen it.

J A loose bolt rattled whenever the lawn mower was started.

For Numbers 3–5, read each answer choice. Fill in the space for the choice that has a usage error. If there is no mistake, fill in the fourth answer space.

3 **A** We had to paint the walls
B twicte since the first coat
C didn't cover very well.
D *(No mistakes)*

4 **F** The price of gasoline is high
G because both the state and federal
H governments tax it so much.
J *(No mistakes)*

5 **A** We wanted to go riding yesterday, but
B catching the horses were a lot
C harder than we thought it would be.
D *(No mistakes)*

For Number 6, find the underlined part that is the simple subject of the sentence.

6 This afternoon the principal will visit our classroom for an hour.
F G H J

For Number 7, find the underlined part that is the simple predicate (verb) of the sentence.

7 Lewis and his sister climbed the stairs to their apartment on the fifth floor.
A B C D

GO

ANSWER ROWS E1 Ⓐ Ⓑ Ⓒ Ⓓ 2 Ⓕ Ⓖ Ⓗ Ⓙ 4 Ⓕ Ⓖ Ⓗ Ⓙ 6 Ⓕ Ⓖ Ⓗ Ⓙ
1 Ⓐ Ⓑ Ⓒ Ⓓ 3 Ⓐ Ⓑ Ⓒ Ⓓ 5 Ⓐ Ⓑ Ⓒ Ⓓ 7 Ⓐ Ⓑ Ⓒ Ⓓ

For Numbers 8–10, choose the answer that best combines the underlined sentences.

8 Almost everyone rode the roller coaster.

Ellen didn't because of her injured hand.

F Ellen didn't ride the roller coaster, and almost everyone else did, because of her injured hand.

G Almost everyone rode the roller coaster except Ellen, who didn't because of her injured hand.

H Almost everyone, except Ellen because of her injured hand, rode the roller coaster.

J Ellen, who didn't ride the roller coaster because of her injured hand, and everyone else did.

9 Your sister was here earlier.

Your sister left this package for you.

A Your sister, who was here earlier, left this package for you.

B Because she was here earlier, your sister left this package for you.

C Your sister left this package for you and was here earlier.

D Although she was here earlier, she left this package for you.

10 The library is on the first floor.

The library is at the end of the hall.

The computer center is in the library.

F The library, which is on the first floor, is at the end of the hall, and the computer center is in it.

G The computer center, which is in the library, and the library is on the first floor at the end of the hall.

H The library, although it is at the end of the hall, is on the first floor, and the computer center is in it.

J The computer center is in the library, which is on the first floor at the end of the hall.

For Numbers 11 and 12, choose the best way of expressing the idea.

11 A The kind of bicycle you want is not in the store, although they have them.
B The store has bicycles, although not the kind you want.
C The store, which has bicycles, although not the kind you want.
D Although not the kind of bicycle you want, the store has them.

12 F Because they were in the distance, the pioneers would have to cross the huge mountains.
G Huge mountains were in the distance, although the pioneers would have to cross them.
H In the distance were the huge mountains that the pioneers would have to cross.
J Huge mountains, in the distance, and the pioneers would have to cross them.

GO

ANSWER ROWS 8 Ⓕ Ⓖ Ⓗ Ⓙ 9 Ⓐ Ⓑ Ⓒ Ⓓ 10 Ⓕ Ⓖ Ⓗ Ⓙ 11 Ⓐ Ⓑ Ⓒ Ⓓ 12 Ⓕ Ⓖ Ⓗ Ⓙ

Read the paragraph below. Find the best topic sentence for the paragraph.

13 _______________ . The most common way is when the earth's crust shifts, causing the surface to buckle upward. A less common way of forming mountains is through volcanic action. Both types of mountains are found in the United States.

- **A** Mountains are formed in one of two ways.
- **B** Volcanoes are among the most powerful forces of nature.
- **C** The earth is not as stable as you might think.
- **D** Humans were not around when most of the earth's mountains were formed.

Find the answer choice that best develops the topic sentence.

14 In some homes, it is necessary to install a water softening appliance.

- **F** In large cities, homes receive their water from a central source like a lake or reservoir. In more rural areas, homes have their own wells.
- **G** Water often contains minerals that make the water "hard." The amount of dissolved minerals varies from place to place.
- **H** It is usually connected to the water supply where it enters the house. Pipes carrying water must be buried far enough underground so they don't freeze.
- **J** The purpose of this appliance is to remove dissolved minerals from the water supply. These minerals are not harmful, but they prevent soap from forming a good lather.

Read the paragraph below. Find the sentence that does not belong in the paragraph.

15 1. Both the sun and moon exert a strong influence over the earth. 2. This influence is most obvious in large bodies of water. 3. The oceans are the largest bodies of water. 4. The gravitational attraction of the sun and moon cause the tides, which are bulges in these bodies of water.

- **A** Sentence 1
- **B** Sentence 2
- **C** Sentence 3
- **D** Sentence 4

Read the paragraph below. Find the sentence that best fits the blank in the paragraph.

16 Farming in the United States is undergoing a radical change. _______________. The size of these farms, however, is increasing. In addition, fewer farms are owned by families and more are owned by large businesses.

- **F** Larger farms are usually more profitable than smaller farms.
- **G** The number of working farms is decreasing each year.
- **H** This is not the first time in history such a change has taken place.
- **J** Soybeans are one of the most profitable and useful crops.

GO

ANSWER ROW 13 Ⓐ Ⓑ Ⓒ Ⓓ 14 Ⓕ Ⓖ Ⓗ Ⓙ 15 Ⓐ Ⓑ Ⓒ Ⓓ 16 Ⓕ Ⓖ Ⓗ Ⓙ

Below is the conclusion of Lydia's report about the history of technology. Read the conclusion and use it to do Numbers 17–20.

(1) The pace of technological advances faster throughout history. (2) This means that the time between advancements <u>has got small</u>. (3) The potter's wheel, for example, was invented about 3500 B.C. (4) It took more than a thousand years for the wheel to be turned over and used for vehicles. (5) Electricity was first produced by Alessandro Volta in 1800. (6) In less than a hundred years, electric lights, motors, and other devices had been created. (7) In other words, technological advances are occurring more rapidly today than in the past. (8) This trend is expected to continue in the future. (9) Considering the rapid acceleration of technological advancements, who knows what the world of tomorrow will be like.

17 In sentence 2, <u>has got small</u> is best written —

A has gotten smallest
B gets smallest
C has gotten smaller
D As it is

18 How is sentence 4 best written?

F More than a thousand years passed; however the wheel was turned over and used for vehicles.
G The wheel was not used for vehicles, until more than a thousand years.
H More than a thousand years, it took, for the wheel to be turned over and used for vehicles.
J As it is

19 Which of these sentences would best follow sentence 6?

A Within another twenty years, electricity was being used for hundreds of purposes.
B Today, electrical appliances are found in every home.
C Electricity was far from the last great discovery.
D After electricity was created, other advancements soon took place.

20 Which group of words is <u>not</u> a complete sentence?

F 1
G 4
H 6
J 7

ANSWER ROWS 17 Ⓐ Ⓑ Ⓒ Ⓓ 18 Ⓕ Ⓖ Ⓗ Ⓙ 19 Ⓐ Ⓑ Ⓒ Ⓓ 20 Ⓕ Ⓖ Ⓗ Ⓙ NUMBER RIGHT ______

Examples

Directions: Follow the directions for each section. Choose the answer you think is correct.

A What time will be ________ for you? **A** convenent **B** convienient **C** convenint **D** convenient	**B** **F** benefit show **G** surfase area **H** correctly multiply **J** sticky residue

Read the directions carefully. Be sure you know if you should look for the correctly spelled word or the incorrectly spelled word.

Remember, words that look familiar are usually spelled right. Words that look strange are usually spelled wrong.

Practice

For Numbers 1–5, find the word that is spelled correctly and fits best in the blank.

1 The bell caused a ________ of activity.

A flurry
B flurrie
C flury
D flurrey

2 Were you able to ________ the controls?

F mannipulate
G manipulait
H manipulate
J menipulate

3 Annie made a ________ argument.

A pursuasive
B persuasive
C perswasive
D purswasive

4 The discovery proved to be ________ .

F significent
G significant
H significint
J signifigant

5 ________ art can be hard to understand.

A Abstrak
B Abstrect
C Abstract
D Abbstract

For Numbers 6–8, read the phrases. Choose the phrase in which the underlined word is not spelled correctly.

6 **F** cautious approach
G friendly quarrel
H bisect an angle
J loud disturbence

7 **A** daily routene
B clever detective
C amusement park
D inspire confidence

8 **F** minor annoyance
G optimistic attitude
H mild symptum
J impressive showing

GO

ANSWER ROWS **A** Ⓐ Ⓑ Ⓒ Ⓓ **1** Ⓐ Ⓑ Ⓒ Ⓓ **3** Ⓐ Ⓑ Ⓒ Ⓓ **5** Ⓐ Ⓑ Ⓒ Ⓓ **7** Ⓐ Ⓑ Ⓒ Ⓓ
B Ⓕ Ⓖ Ⓗ Ⓙ **2** Ⓕ Ⓖ Ⓗ Ⓙ **4** Ⓕ Ⓖ Ⓗ Ⓙ **6** Ⓕ Ⓖ Ⓗ Ⓙ **8** Ⓕ Ⓖ Ⓗ Ⓙ

For Numbers 9–11, read each answer. Fill in the space for the choice that has a spelling error. If there is no mistake, fill in the last answer space.

9
A hectic
B overlap
C novise
D prominent
E *(No mistakes)*

10
F encoureged
G insulted
H peasant
J tributaries
K *(No mistakes)*

11
A methodical
B wrinkle
C baffled
D departure
E *(No mistakes)*

For Numbers 12–14, read each phrase. One of the underlined words is not spelled correctly for the way it is used in the phrase. Fill in the space for the word that is not spelled correctly.

12
F invading horde
G scent of roses
H dinner role
J sharp angle

13
A nominations for president
B sharp all
C stir soup
D wrap a package

14
F vague answer
G hungry calf
H bread horses
J orange grove

For Numbers 15–18, find the underlined part that is misspelled. If all the words are spelled correctly, mark the space under No mistake.

15 Your conduckt (A) during the emergency (B) was heroic (C). No mistake (D).

16 The signature (F) on the document (G) is authentec (H). No mistake (J).

17 Try to avoid repetitious (A) ideas when you compose (B) your article (C). No mistake (D).

18 My mother had to lengthin (F) the gown (G) because I had grown (H) so rapidly. No mistake (J).

ANSWER ROWS 9 Ⓐ Ⓑ Ⓒ Ⓓ Ⓔ 11 Ⓐ Ⓑ Ⓒ Ⓓ Ⓔ 13 Ⓐ Ⓑ Ⓒ Ⓓ Ⓔ 15 Ⓐ Ⓑ Ⓒ Ⓓ Ⓔ 17 Ⓐ Ⓑ Ⓒ Ⓓ Ⓔ
10 Ⓕ Ⓖ Ⓗ Ⓙ Ⓚ 12 Ⓕ Ⓖ Ⓗ Ⓙ Ⓚ 14 Ⓕ Ⓖ Ⓗ Ⓙ Ⓚ 16 Ⓕ Ⓖ Ⓗ Ⓙ Ⓚ 18 Ⓕ Ⓖ Ⓗ Ⓙ Ⓚ

E1

New kitchen ________ are expensive.

A apliances
B aplliances
C applianses
D appliances

E2

F feel refreshed
G entertain friends
H clear indacation
J hazardous area

For Numbers 1–6, find the word that is spelled correctly and fits best in the blank.

1 ________ is the mark of a good athlete.

A Consistency
B Consistincy
C Consistancy
D Consistencey

2 What is the ________ of that elevator?

F capasity
G capacity
H capacitie
J capasitey

3 A gas furnace is very ________ .

A ifficient
B effecient
C effecent
D efficient

4 Terry ________ the charcoal.

F ignighted
G ignitted
H igknighted
J ignited

5 The auto mechanic seemed very ________ .

A compitint
B competent
C compitent
D competint

6 The town was ________ by the storm.

F devistated
G devastitated
H devastated
J devastatated

For Numbers 7–10, read the phrases. Choose the phrase in which the underlined word is not spelled correctly.

7 **A** seem arrogent
B probable cause
C good salary
D hasty decision

8 **F** we concurr
G assist them
H slight fracture
J hesitate briefly

9 **A** feel obliged
B narrow margin
C saluted sharply
D gas guage

10 **F** repel insects
G attentive audience
H show integerity
J prosperous decade

GO

ANSWER ROWS E1 Ⓐ Ⓑ Ⓒ Ⓓ 2 Ⓕ Ⓖ Ⓗ Ⓙ 5 Ⓐ Ⓑ Ⓒ Ⓓ 8 Ⓕ Ⓖ Ⓗ Ⓙ
E2 Ⓕ Ⓖ Ⓗ Ⓙ 3 Ⓐ Ⓑ Ⓒ Ⓓ 6 Ⓕ Ⓖ Ⓗ Ⓙ 9 Ⓐ Ⓑ Ⓒ Ⓓ
1 Ⓐ Ⓑ Ⓒ Ⓓ 4 Ⓕ Ⓖ Ⓗ Ⓙ 7 Ⓐ Ⓑ Ⓒ Ⓓ 10 Ⓕ Ⓖ Ⓗ Ⓙ

For Numbers 11–13, read each answer. Fill in the space for the choice that has a spelling error. If there is no mistake, fill in the last answer space.

11 **A** aggressive
B fertilize
C delighted
D mancion
E *(No mistakes)*

12 **F** circumstance
G inaccurate
H revarence
J encounter
K *(No mistakes)*

13 **A** tantalyze
B familiar
C misfortune
D astounding
E *(No mistakes)*

For Numbers 14–16, read each phrase. One of the underlined words is not spelled correctly for the way it is used in the phrase. Fill in the space for the word that is not spelled correctly.

14 **F** petty complaint
G fishing lure
H slender tree
J pore showing

15 **A** vocal group
B large tract
C steal beams
D seem bored

16 **F** mountain peek
G be certain
H crisp lettuce
J rapidly pursue

For Numbers 17–20, find the underlined part that is misspelled. If all the words are spelled correctly, mark the space under No mistake.

17 Shortsited people waste their time and other resources. No mistake.
A B C D

18 Several of the contributers to the paper were from the debating club. No mistake.
F G H J

19 We registered for an excersion into the redwood forest. No mistake.
A B C D

20 The decision was rendered by an impartial judge. No mistake.
F G H J

STOP

ANSWER ROWS 11 Ⓐ Ⓑ Ⓒ Ⓓ Ⓔ 14 Ⓕ Ⓖ Ⓗ Ⓙ Ⓚ 17 Ⓐ Ⓑ Ⓒ Ⓓ Ⓔ 19 Ⓐ Ⓑ Ⓒ Ⓓ Ⓔ
12 Ⓕ Ⓖ Ⓗ Ⓙ Ⓚ 15 Ⓐ Ⓑ Ⓒ Ⓓ Ⓔ 18 Ⓕ Ⓖ Ⓗ Ⓙ Ⓚ 20 Ⓕ Ⓖ Ⓗ Ⓙ Ⓚ
13 Ⓐ Ⓑ Ⓒ Ⓓ Ⓔ 16 Ⓕ Ⓖ Ⓗ Ⓙ Ⓚ

NUMBER RIGHT ______

Example **Directions:** Follow the directions for each section. Choose the answer you think is correct.

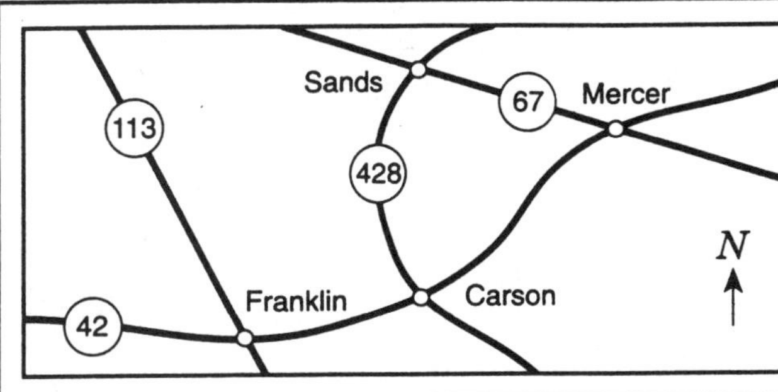

A Look at the map on the left. What direction would you go to travel from Sands to Carson?

A North
B South
C East
D West

If you are not sure which answer choice is correct, try this strategy. Read the question, look at the illustration if there is one, and then look at the answer choices. If necessary, read the question again. Then try to find the right answer.

Practice

Use this table comparing cordless telephones to answer Numbers 1 and 2.

CORDLESS TELEPHONES

MODELS	FEATURES					
	Channels	Noise Filter	Replaceable Battery	Memory Dial	Redial	Switchable Tone/Pulse
Anderson	10	•		10	•	•
Danson	2	•	•		•	•
Granville	6		•	10	•	•
Kingsley	10			6	•	•
Orson	6	•		10	•	•
Ranyo	10		•	6	•	•
Sotay	2	•			•	•
TransBand	10	•	•	10	•	•

1 How many phones have noise filters?

A 2
B 3
C 5
D 8

2 Which phone has the most features?

F TransBand
G Anderson
H Ranyo
J Granville

GO

ANSWER ROWS **A** Ⓐ Ⓑ Ⓒ Ⓓ **1** Ⓐ Ⓑ Ⓒ Ⓓ **2** Ⓕ Ⓖ Ⓗ Ⓙ

This application form is for students to complete if they want a summer job. Use the form to do Numbers 3–5.

APPLICATION

1. Name ______________________
2. Address ______________________
3. City/State/Zip ______________________
4. Telephone ______________________
5. Desired Position ______________________
6. Desired Salary ______________________
7. Experience ______________________

____

____

____

8. References (List three. Provide each person's name and a daytime phone number.)

____

____

____

3 Suppose you were interested in a job as an assistant gardener. On which line would you write this job?

A Line 1 **C** Line 5
B Line 2 **D** Line 6

4 What should you write on line 8?

F the names of people who know what kind of job you can do
G the names of your family members
H the names of the people with whom you want to work
J the names of your classmates

5 Where would you show that you had worked part-time for a year at a garden center?

A Line 5
B Line 6
C Line 7
D Line 8

Read each question below. Mark the space for the answer you think is correct.

6 Suppose you wanted to use an exact quote by Karen Blixen about Africa. Which of these methods would you use?

F Include the name of her book in the bibliography.
G Use quotation marks and include her name in the glossary.
H Include her name in the table of contents and index.
J Use quotation marks and indicate where you got the quote.

7 For which reason would you use a thesaurus?

A to find a synonym for a common word you feel you have overused
B to find the definition of a word whose meaning you are unsure of
C to find the pronunciation of a word you are not sure how to say
D to find a word that rhymes with a word you have already used

8 Pete wants to write a story about everyday life in the American West during the 1800s. Which of these would provide the best picture of everyday life then?

F a description of what happens when a large gold strike is discovered
G a description of how Rachel, a 12-year old girl, spends her days
H a description of how a young man escaped from a gang of robbers
J a description of how a family survived being lost in the desert

ANSWER ROWS 3 Ⓐ Ⓑ Ⓒ Ⓓ 5 Ⓐ Ⓑ Ⓒ Ⓓ 7 Ⓐ Ⓑ Ⓒ Ⓓ
4 Ⓕ Ⓖ Ⓗ Ⓙ 6 Ⓕ Ⓖ Ⓗ Ⓙ 8 Ⓕ Ⓖ Ⓗ Ⓙ

E1

In a textbook, where would you find the year that the book was published?

A the index
B the bibliography
C the back of the title page
D the table of contents

E2

Which of these would you most likely find in the index of a science book?

F solar power, 227-256
G Technology Publishing, Dallas
H Jupiter: the largest of the planets
J Chapter 23, Fiber Optics

Study the magazine table of contents below. Use it to do Numbers 1–4.

Boating Today

Cover: Sailing under Philadelphia's Ben Franklin Bridge
Photography by Nelson Hunter

2 **From the Editor:** Boating Safety on Crowded Waters

3 **Letters to the Editor**

6 **City Waters**
Boating adventures in five large cities
by Kate Warnock

10 **Rivers to the Sea**
Navigating small boats in tricky currents
by Will Marley

17 **In-season Maintenance**
Keeping your craft in tip-top shape while you enjoy it
by Kip and Mary Teeter

20 **Canyons of Blue**
Utah's Lake Powell is hard to reach but worth the effort
by Ida Gonzales

27 **Update:** Is the new law in Texas working?
by Jean Shields

32 **End of Issue**
Things they never told you when you bought your boat
by Karen Anderson

1 On which page would you find letters written from readers to the editor of the magazine?

A Page 1
B Page 2
C Page 3
D Page 27

2 On which page does an article begin that relates to the picture on the cover of the magazine?

F Page 6
G Page 10
H Page 17
J Page 32

3 Which of these might be found on page 23?

A a road map showing how to get to Chicago
B a discussion of a new product to protect a boat's hull
C a list of places where boating is hazardous
D a road map showing how to get to Lake Powell

4 Who wrote about a hard-to-reach lake?

F Karen Anderson
G Will Marley
H Nelson Hunter
J Ida Gonzales

GO

ANSWER ROWS E1 Ⓐ Ⓑ Ⓒ Ⓓ E2 Ⓕ Ⓖ Ⓗ Ⓙ 1 Ⓐ Ⓑ Ⓒ Ⓓ 2 Ⓕ Ⓖ Ⓗ Ⓙ 3 Ⓐ Ⓑ Ⓒ Ⓓ 4 Ⓕ Ⓖ Ⓗ Ⓙ

The map below shows an imaginary continent named Natara and a nearby island, Orad Island. Use the map to answer Numbers 5–8.

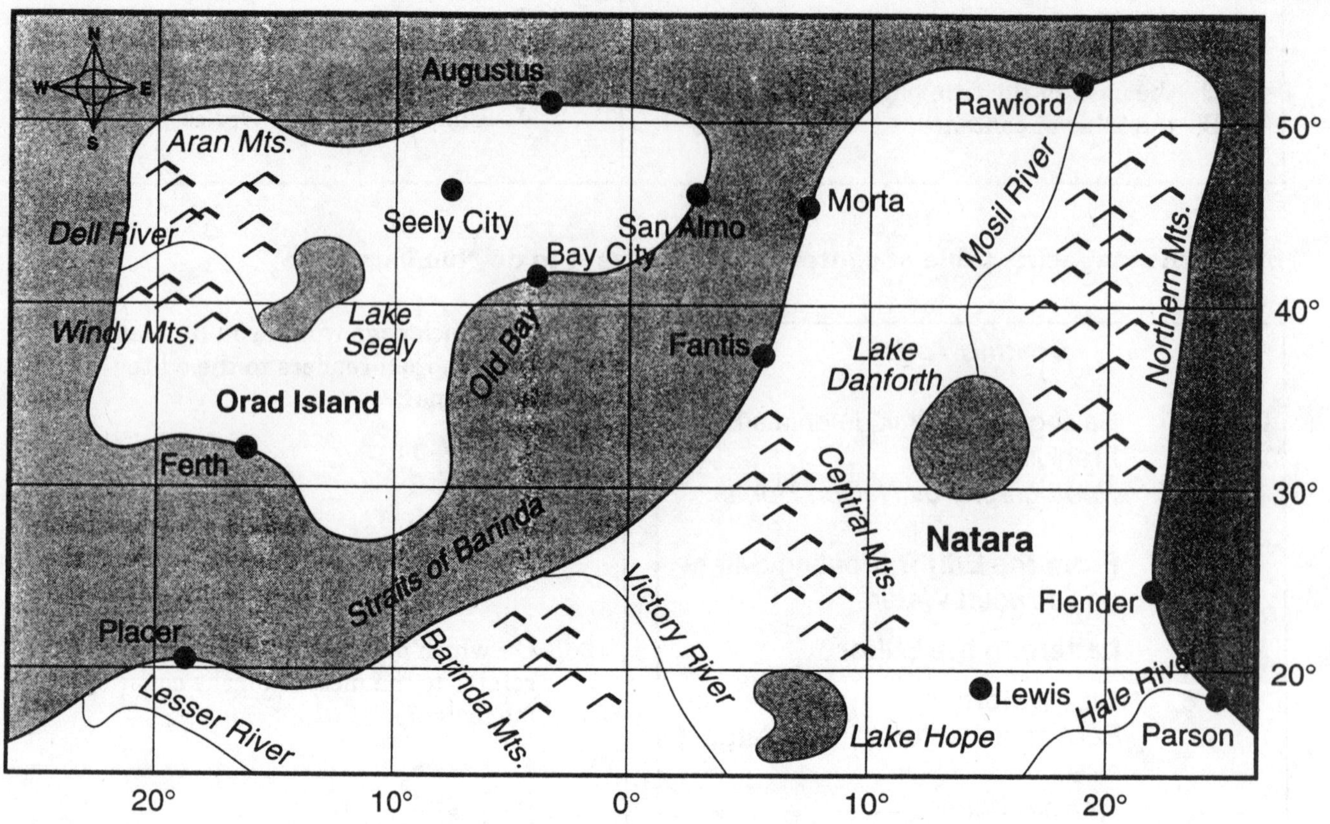

5 Which city is at 53° N, 18° E?

A Augustus
B Flender
C Ferth
D Rawford

6 Where is the Dell River?

F east of Lake Seely
G between the Aran and Windy Mountains
H south of the Central Mountains
J between the Central Mountains and Victory River

7 Which city on Orad Island is closest to Morta?

A San Almo
B Bay City
C Augustus
D Fantis

8 Which city is on the east coast of Natara and not on a river?

F Parson
G Fantis
H Flender
J Placer

GO

ANSWER ROWS 5 Ⓐ Ⓑ Ⓒ Ⓓ 7 Ⓐ Ⓑ Ⓒ Ⓓ
6 Ⓕ Ⓖ Ⓗ Ⓙ 8 Ⓕ Ⓖ Ⓗ Ⓙ

In order to use reference materials, you must choose a word or phrase with which to search. For Numbers 9–11, select the best word or phrase to answer the question.

9 Which key term should you use to find information about the depth and area of the Atlantic Ocean?

A Ocean
B Atlantic Ocean
C Depth and Area
D World Oceans

10 Wind is caused by unequal heating of the earth's surface. Which term should you use to find more information about one of the most severe forms of wind, the tornado?

F Wind
G Heating
H Severe
J Tornado

11 Which key term should you use to find information about the advantages and disadvantages of using planes, trains, or trucks to transport manufactured products?

A Plane
B Train
C Transportation
D Manufactured Products

For Numbers 12–14, choose the word that would appear first if the words were arranged in alphabetical order.

12 **F** subacute
G subalpine
H subculture
J subbing

13 **A** consort
B conspire
C console
D conspiracy

14 **F** mastic
G masthead
H mastoid
J mastodon

For Numbers 15 and 16, choose the important phrase that should be included in research notes on city planning.

15 A well-designed city should allow residents to live, work, and play easily, while at the same time it should be safe and attractive.

A cities should be well-designed to allow residents
B cities should be convenient for residents, safe, attractive
C residents allowed to live, work, play in city
D well-designed by residents for convenient cities

16 Parks should be placed so they are convenient and inviting, with both open spaces for play and secluded areas where residents can escape the hubbub of the city.

F convenient and inviting parks with open and secluded spaces
G parks for residents in secluded areas or open spaces
H inviting residents to open spaces or secluded areas
J residents can escape to open spaces in a park

ANSWER ROWS 9 Ⓐ Ⓑ Ⓒ Ⓓ 11 Ⓐ Ⓑ Ⓒ Ⓓ 13 Ⓐ Ⓑ Ⓒ Ⓓ 15 Ⓐ Ⓑ Ⓒ Ⓓ
10 Ⓕ Ⓖ Ⓗ Ⓙ 12 Ⓕ Ⓖ Ⓗ Ⓙ 14 Ⓕ Ⓖ Ⓗ Ⓙ 16 Ⓕ Ⓖ Ⓗ Ⓙ

NUMBER RIGHT ______

To the Student:

These tests will give you a chance to put the tips you have learned to work.

A few last reminders...

- Be sure you understand all the directions before you begin each test. You may ask the teacher questions about the directions if you do not understand them.
- Work as quickly as you can during each test.
- When you change an answer, be sure to erase your first mark completely.
- You can guess at an answer or skip difficult items and go back to them later.
- Use the tips you have learned whenever you can.
- It is OK to be a little nervous. You may even do better.

Now that you have completed the lessons in this book, you are on your way to scoring high!

STUDENT'S NAME

LAST | FIRST | MI

○ A B C D E F G H I J K L M N O P Q R S T U V W X Y Z

SCHOOL

TEACHER

FEMALE ○ MALE ○

BIRTHDATE

MONTH	DAY		YEAR	
JAN ○	0	0		0
FEB ○	1	1		1
MAR ○	2	2		2
APR ○	3	3		3
MAY ○		4		4
JUN ○		5	5	5
JUL ○		6	6	6
AUG ○		7	7	7
SEP ○		8	8	8
OCT ○		9	9	9
NOV ○				
DEC ○				

GRADE

⑦ ⑧ ⑨

Third Edition Book 8

Scoring High

in

Language

PART 1 LANGUAGE MECHANICS

E1 Ⓐ Ⓑ Ⓒ Ⓓ	4 Ⓕ Ⓖ Ⓗ Ⓙ	8 Ⓕ Ⓖ Ⓗ Ⓙ	12 Ⓕ Ⓖ Ⓗ Ⓙ	16 Ⓕ Ⓖ Ⓗ Ⓙ	19 Ⓐ Ⓑ Ⓒ Ⓓ
1 Ⓐ Ⓑ Ⓒ Ⓓ	5 Ⓐ Ⓑ Ⓒ Ⓓ	9 Ⓐ Ⓑ Ⓒ Ⓓ	13 Ⓐ Ⓑ Ⓒ Ⓓ	17 Ⓐ Ⓑ Ⓒ Ⓓ	20 Ⓕ Ⓖ Ⓗ Ⓙ
2 Ⓕ Ⓖ Ⓗ Ⓙ	6 Ⓕ Ⓖ Ⓗ Ⓙ	10 Ⓕ Ⓖ Ⓗ Ⓙ	14 Ⓕ Ⓖ Ⓗ Ⓙ	18 Ⓕ Ⓖ Ⓗ Ⓙ	21 Ⓐ Ⓑ Ⓒ Ⓓ
3 Ⓐ Ⓑ Ⓒ Ⓓ	7 Ⓐ Ⓑ Ⓒ Ⓓ	11 Ⓐ Ⓑ Ⓒ Ⓓ	15 Ⓐ Ⓑ Ⓒ Ⓓ		

PART 2 LANGUAGE EXPRESSION

E1 Ⓐ Ⓑ Ⓒ Ⓓ	4 Ⓕ Ⓖ Ⓗ Ⓙ	8 Ⓕ Ⓖ Ⓗ Ⓙ	12 Ⓕ Ⓖ Ⓗ Ⓙ	15 Ⓐ Ⓑ Ⓒ Ⓓ	18 Ⓕ Ⓖ Ⓗ Ⓙ
1 Ⓐ Ⓑ Ⓒ Ⓓ	5 Ⓐ Ⓑ Ⓒ Ⓓ	9 Ⓐ Ⓑ Ⓒ Ⓓ	13 Ⓐ Ⓑ Ⓒ Ⓓ	16 Ⓕ Ⓖ Ⓗ Ⓙ	19 Ⓐ Ⓑ Ⓒ Ⓓ
2 Ⓕ Ⓖ Ⓗ Ⓙ	6 Ⓕ Ⓖ Ⓗ Ⓙ	10 Ⓕ Ⓖ Ⓗ Ⓙ	14 Ⓕ Ⓖ Ⓗ Ⓙ	17 Ⓐ Ⓑ Ⓒ Ⓓ	20 Ⓕ Ⓖ Ⓗ Ⓙ
3 Ⓐ Ⓑ Ⓒ Ⓓ	7 Ⓐ Ⓑ Ⓒ Ⓓ	11 Ⓐ Ⓑ Ⓒ Ⓓ			

PART 3 SPELLING

E1 Ⓐ Ⓑ Ⓒ Ⓓ Ⓔ	3 Ⓐ Ⓑ Ⓒ Ⓓ Ⓔ	7 Ⓐ Ⓑ Ⓒ Ⓓ Ⓔ	11 Ⓐ Ⓑ Ⓒ Ⓓ Ⓔ	15 Ⓐ Ⓑ Ⓒ Ⓓ Ⓔ	19 Ⓐ Ⓑ Ⓒ Ⓓ Ⓔ
E2 Ⓕ Ⓖ Ⓗ Ⓙ Ⓚ	4 Ⓕ Ⓖ Ⓗ Ⓙ Ⓚ	8 Ⓕ Ⓖ Ⓗ Ⓙ Ⓚ	12 Ⓕ Ⓖ Ⓗ Ⓙ Ⓚ	16 Ⓕ Ⓖ Ⓗ Ⓙ Ⓚ	20 Ⓕ Ⓖ Ⓗ Ⓙ Ⓚ
1 Ⓐ Ⓑ Ⓒ Ⓓ Ⓔ	5 Ⓐ Ⓑ Ⓒ Ⓓ Ⓔ	9 Ⓐ Ⓑ Ⓒ Ⓓ Ⓔ	13 Ⓐ Ⓑ Ⓒ Ⓓ Ⓔ	17 Ⓐ Ⓑ Ⓒ Ⓓ Ⓔ	
2 Ⓕ Ⓖ Ⓗ Ⓙ Ⓚ	6 Ⓕ Ⓖ Ⓗ Ⓙ Ⓚ	10 Ⓕ Ⓖ Ⓗ Ⓙ Ⓚ	14 Ⓕ Ⓖ Ⓗ Ⓙ Ⓚ	18 Ⓕ Ⓖ Ⓗ Ⓙ Ⓚ	

PART 4 STUDY SKILLS

E1 Ⓐ Ⓑ Ⓒ Ⓓ	3 Ⓐ Ⓑ Ⓒ Ⓓ	6 Ⓕ Ⓖ Ⓗ Ⓙ	9 Ⓐ Ⓑ Ⓒ Ⓓ
1 Ⓐ Ⓑ Ⓒ Ⓓ	4 Ⓕ Ⓖ Ⓗ Ⓙ	7 Ⓐ Ⓑ Ⓒ Ⓓ	10 Ⓕ Ⓖ Ⓗ Ⓙ
2 Ⓕ Ⓖ Ⓗ Ⓙ	5 Ⓐ Ⓑ Ⓒ Ⓓ	8 Ⓕ Ⓖ Ⓗ Ⓙ	11 Ⓐ Ⓑ Ⓒ Ⓓ

E1

Did the dog bark when you came in

A . **B** ! **C** ? **D** None

1 Finally you should remember to wear a hat and use sun screen.

A : **B** ; **C** , **D** None

2 The gymnasium was packed with the following fans students, parents, and teachers.

F ; **G** : **H** . **J** None

3 "You can wash the windows with vinegar," suggested Norm.

A : **B** , **C** ; **D** None

4 Russel my cousin, has lived in Michigan for a long time.

F , **G** ? **H** : **J** None

For Numbers 5–7, read each answer. Fill in the space for the choice that has a punctuation error. If there is no mistake, fill in the fourth answer space.

5 **A** Sharona got dressed, washed
B her face, and brushed her teeth before
C coming downstairs for breakfast.
D *(No mistakes)*

6 **F** "It's no use, Ted muttered."
G "No matter what we try, we
H still can't get this car started."
J *(No mistakes)*

7 **A** When I tried to call the
B number you gave me I
C got a busy signal again and again.
D *(No mistakes)*

For Numbers 8 and 9, read each sentence with a blank. Choose the word or words that fit best in the blank and show the correct punctuation.

8 The item you ordered will be delivered by ________ shipping will be free.

F Tuesday. Or
G Tuesday: or
H Tuesday, or
J Tuesday or,

9 The ________ science projects were set up in the auditorium.

A children's
B childrens
C childrens's
D childrens'

For Numbers 10–12, read each answer. Fill in the space for the choice that has a capitalization error. If there is no mistake, fill in the fourth answer space.

10 F One of the most important
G aspects of commerce is selling U.S.
H goods and services to other Countries.
J *(No mistakes)*

11 A People who own a house or apartment
B must spend a lot of time maintaining
C and improving their property.
D *(No mistakes)*

12 F My Uncle, Toby Hazlett,
G is a teacher who is running
H for office in our county.
J *(No mistakes)*

For Number 13, read each group of sentences. Find the one that is written correctly and shows the correct capitalization and punctuation.

13 A Teresa thought for a minute. "I have a suggestion. Lets spend Saturday morning cleaning up the park. Have you seen how much trash is there?

B "I don't know," answered Chang. "That's a big job, and it will take us all morning. I'm not sure I want to volunteer that much time."

C "We have all used the Park a zillion times" Argued Pedro. "It's only one Saturday morning, and we'll have fun. We can have a picnic after."

D Tonie smiled and added, Come on, Chang. You'd just sleep in on Saturday. Meet us at eight oclock at the park. I'll bring my mother's brownies."

For Numbers 14–16, read the sentence with a blank. Mark the space beside the answer choice that fits best in the blank and has correct capitalization and punctuation.

14 The manager of our team, ________ makes sure the equipment is ready for our games.

F Lori Gallagher
G Lori Gallagher:
H Lori Gallagher;
J Lori Gallagher,

15 The highest peak in our county is ________ it is more than 3000 meters high.

A mt. Sorrel:
B Mt. Sorrel;
C Mt. Sorrel
D Mt Sorrel,

16 The carnival will open on ________ I can't go until Friday.

F Tuesday but
G Tuesday. But
H Tuesday, but
J Tuesday: but

Choose the correct answer for Number 17.

17 Which is the correct way to begin a business letter?

A Dear Madam:
B Dear Madam
C Dear Madam;
D Dear madam,

Frances is spending the summer with her cousins. This letter is to her parents. Read her letter and use it to do Numbers 18–21.

July 4, 1995

Dear Mom and Dad,

I miss you! but not as much as before. How is that big old dog of mine? Is he wondering where I am? Give him a hug for me.
(1) (2) (3) (4)

Aunt Rita and Uncle Bill took us to Minneapolis and st. Paul last week. We went shopping, had dinner, and then went to a baseball game. Watching the game was great; the Twins, however, didn't win. Marcie was really bummed. I can't believe she's such a fan.
(5) (6) (7) (8)

I'm reading a book called angle of repose. Uncle Bill said it was the best book ever written. You know how he exaggerates. He's almost right, though. It is the best book I've ever read.
(9) (10) (11) (12) (13)

18 In sentence 1, you! but is best written —

F you, but
G you. But
H you but,
J As it is

19 In sentence 5, and st. Paul is best written —

A and St. Paul,
B and St. Paul
C and, St. Paul
D As it is

20 In sentence 7, great; the is best written —

F great the
G great: the
H great. the
J As it is

21 In sentence 9, angle of repose is best written —

A Angle of Repose
B *angle of repose*
C *Angle of Repose*
D As it is

STOP

E1

Find the underlined part that is the simple predicate (verb) of the sentence.

At last, the weary explorers reached the lake for which they were looking.

A: last — B: weary — C: explorers — D: reached

For Number 1, choose the word or phrase that best completes the sentence.

1 The newspaper ________ a list of students who made the honor roll.

- **A** publishing
- **B** were published
- **C** have published
- **D** has published

For Number 2, choose the answer that is a complete and correctly written sentence.

2 **F** We will all meet this afternoon, at the park beside the school.

- **G** If you would like we can meet at your house at two o'clock.
- **H** Unless you hurry, you will never catch up with Chad and Maria.
- **J** No we will not be able to bring our dogs to the park.

For Numbers 3–5, read each answer choice. Fill in the space for the choice that has a usage error. If there is no mistake, fill in the fourth answer space.

3 **A** At the banquet tomorrow night,
B Lenore will except the award she
C received for her volunteer service.
D *(No mistakes)*

4 **F** An exceptionally large package
G arrived for Sal. He has no idea
H what it is or who sent it.
J *(No mistakes)*

5 **A** Before I left for school this morning,
B I should of walked the dog. Now
C my father will have to do it.
D *(No mistakes)*

For Number 6, find the underlined part that is the simple subject of the sentence.

6 Even with the bad weather, the crowd was much larger than we expected.

F: Even — G: weather — H: crowd — J: larger

For Number 7, find the underlined part that is the simple predicate (verb) of the sentence.

7 Tornadoes occur more often in the United States than in any other country.

A: Tornadoes — B: occur — C: often — D: country

For Numbers 8–10, choose the answer that best combines the underlined sentences.

8 You can go to the baseball game.

Come home right after it is over.

F You can go, to the baseball game, although you should come home right after it is over.

G You can go to the baseball game, but come home right after it is over.

H Come home right after the game is over, but you can go to it.

J Coming home right after the baseball game, although you can go to it.

9 Let's take a walk after dinner.

Let's walk to the creek.

A Let's take a walk to the creek after dinner.

B After dinner, let's take a walk, and take it to the creek.

C Let's take a walk after dinner, a walk to the creek.

D After dinner, let's take a walk, which is to the creek.

10 Kisha is Mac's sister.

Kisha went to Purdue University.

Purdue University is in Indiana.

F Kisha is Mac's sister, and she went to Purdue University, which is in Indiana.

G Purdue University, which is in Indiana, is where Kisha went, who is Mac's sister.

H Kisha, who is Mac's sister, went to Indiana, where Purdue University is.

J Mac's sister Kisha went to Purdue University, which is in Indiana.

For Numbers 11 and 12, choose the best way of expressing the idea.

11 A Although you go to the store, please pick up the things I've written on this list.
B While you go to the store, and please pick up the things I've written on this list.
C When you go to the store, please pick up the things I've written on this list.
D On this list are written things you should pick up, please, when you go to the store.

12 F I really can't, Horace, believe you want to go to school this summer.
G This summer, I really can't believe you want to go to school, Horace.
H Horace, I really can't believe you want to go to school this summer.
J Really, Horace, this summer I can't believe you want to go to school.

Read the paragraph below. Find the best topic sentence for the paragraph.

13 _______________. Some businesses manufacture products such as automobiles, toys, or clothing. Others provide services, such as banking, entertainment, and retail shopping. A few businesses such as telephone companies offer both products and services.

A Businesses usually fall into one of two categories.

B One of the benefits of living in the United States is the ability to start a business.

C Large and small companies have different ways of succeeding.

D Successful businesses know what their customers want.

Find the answer choice that best develops the topic sentence.

14 Brenda was looking forward to her trip to the ocean.

F She and her family would fly to Florida. They would spend a week there visiting her aunt and uncle.

G She had heard all about the ocean from her friend, Steven. He had recently moved from Delaware to Kentucky.

H Like many other young people who live in Kentucky, she had never seen the ocean. She couldn't imagine what that much water must look like.

J She had lived in Kentucky her whole life. She enjoyed water sports like swimming, fishing, and boating.

Read the paragraph below. Find the sentence that does not belong in the paragraph.

15 1. Many people believe that the person known as "Calamity Jane" was a fictional character. 2. She was, however, a very real person named Martha Jane Canary. 3. She lived from 1852 to 1903 and was known as an expert with both horses and a six-shooter. 4. The Old West was the home for many interesting characters.

A Sentence 1

B Sentence 2

C Sentence 3

D Sentence 4

Read the paragraph below. Find the sentence that best fits the blank in the paragraph.

16 An automobile engine works on a simple principle. _______________. An electrical spark ignites the mixture of gasoline and air. When the mixture explodes, it forces the piston out of the cylinder so it turns a shaft.

F Automobile engines have four, six, or eight cylinders.

G Gasoline and air are mixed in a cylinder with a piston.

H The engine is connected to a series of gears called the transmission.

J Gasoline is a substance that is easily ignited.

Below is more of the letter Frances wrote to her parents. Read the letter and use it to do Numbers 17–20.

Every Tuesday morning, all of us go to a camp
(1)
for disabled children. They have a horseback riding
(2)
program there, and we are volunteers. I'm learning
(3)
a lot about horses. Did you know that a horse has a
(4)
blind spot right in front of its face? Because a
(5)
horse's eyes are located on the side of its head,

it <u>can't hardly see</u> what is in front of its nose.

The blind spot, caused by the location of the
(6)
horse's eyes, makes the horse turn its head to see.

I'm amazed to see how well so many of the
(7)
children can ride. One little girl can't walk and
(8)
uses a wheel chair. When she gets on a horse,
(9)
although she rides like a champion. She is only
(10)
eight years old and wants to go to the Olympics

some day. Isn't that great?
(11)

17 Which sentence could be added after sentence 2?

- **A** There are many different kinds of camps in Minnesota.
- **B** As I am sure you remember, I don't know very much about horses.
- **C** Most of the children at the camp are from Minnesota.
- **D** Aunt Rita and Uncle Bill have done it for several years now.

18 Which sentence needlessly repeats an idea?

- **F** 2
- **G** 3
- **H** 6
- **J** 8

19 How is sentence 9 best written?

- **A** When she gets on a horse, but she rides like a champion
- **B** When she gets on a horse, however, she rides like a champion.
- **C** She rides like a champion, however, and she gets on a horse.
- **D** As it is

20 In sentence 5, <u>can't hardly see</u> is best written —

- **F** can't see
- **G** can't see hardly
- **H** can't not see
- **J** As it is

STOP

E1

_______ the town will take three hours.

A Evacuating
B Evacuting
C Evuacuating
D Evaccuating

E2

F write a narrative
G arid land
H protest the decision
J sparcely populated

For Numbers 1–6, find the word that is spelled correctly and fits best in the blank.

1 The deer seemed to _______ from nowhere.

A materilize
B materialize
C materealize
D materialise

2 The _______ asked us to take a seat.

F receptionest
G receptionast
H receptionist
J reciptionist

3 Shannon is a _______ performer.

A versatile
B versatil
C versateil
D versatal

4 The workers _______ a good contract.

F negotiated
G negotiatted
H nigotiated
J nigotiatted

5 We decided to _______ the paper.

A discontenue
B discontinnue
C disconttinue
D discontinue

6 The weather was hot but _______ .

F tolirable
G tolerable
H toleribe
J tollerable

For Numbers 7–10, read the phrases. Choose the phrase in which the underlined word is not spelled correctly.

7 A become lengthy
B perceptive comment
C spontanious applause
D biased against

8 F achieve prosperaty
G minor incident
H deep cavern
J enjoyable situation

9 A possible conflict
B nicely decorated
C seem inactive
D enirgetic response

10 F neatly organized
G edible fruit
H influentual official
J use a protractor

For Numbers 11–13, read each answer. Fill in the space for the choice that has a spelling error. If there is no mistake, fill in the last answer space.

11 A strategy
B appearance
C gallant
D convincing
E *(No mistakes)*

12 F candid
G modern
H despense
J reveal
K *(No mistakes)*

13 A certafied
B tyrant
C disintegrate
D informal
E *(No mistakes)*

For Numbers 14–16, read each phrase. One of the underlined words is not spelled correctly for the way it is used in the phrase. Fill in the space for the word that is not spelled correctly.

14 F school motto
G sow a shirt
H assure them
J new title

15 A staid alert
B recent issue
C too complex
D wander around

16 F design specialist
G clever plot
H skim milk
J lion's main

For Numbers 17–20, find the underlined part that is misspelled. If all the words are spelled correctly, mark the space under No mistake.

17 Harry's opinion (A) went contrarie (B) to that of the majority (C). No mistake (D).

18 Native Americans learned to cultavate (F) arid (G) regions (H) of the American West. No mistake (J).

19 The cargo (A) was rapidly unloaded (B) from the freigter (C). No mistake (D).

20 A legendery (F) soccer player addressed (G) an audience (H) of young players. No mistake (J).

STOP

E1

On the map on the left, if you were at 2nd and Central, which direction should you go to get to the library?

A Southwest
B Southeast
C Northwest
D Northeast

Study this outline for a report about computer manufacturing. Use it to answer Numbers 1–4.

COMPUTER MANUFACTURING

I. Materials
   A. External parts
      1. Cases
      2. Cables
      3. Connectors
   B. Internal parts
      1. Electronics
      2. Power supply
      3. Disk drives
II. ____________
   A. Inspect parts
   B. Assemble parts
   C. Test finished parts
      1. Visual inspection
      2. Run test program
      3. ____________
III. Warehouse
   A. Package computers
      1. Label accurately
   B. Box and ship
   C. Store safely
IV. Sales
   A. Find new customers
      1. Sell existing products
      2. Develop new product ideas
   B. Follow-up old customers
      1. Check satisfaction
      2. Determine future needs
V. Service
   A. Gain new contracts
      1. Contact clients
      2. Make presentations
   B. Provide service
      1. Troubleshooting
      2. System analysis
      3. Preventive maintenance

1 Line II of the outline is blank. Which of these fits best in the blank?

A Manufacturing
B Pricing
C History of computers
D Advertising

2 Suppose you wanted to add a new heading labeled VI to the outline? Which of these would be most appropriate?

F Computer Chips
G Special Packaging
H Robotic Assembly
J Research and Development

3 Line II.C.3 of the outline is blank. Which of these fits best in the blank?

A Assemble keyboard
B Test in heat and cold
C Ship to customers
D Create new designs

4 How could part III of the outline be improved?

F Add "Visit customers" as part III.D.
G Remove "Box and ship" from the outline
H Make "Store safely" part B and "Box and ship" part C.
J Move "Store safely" from part III to part V.

GO

Use this card from a library card catalog to do Numbers 5–8.

622.4

S **Saunders, Judy**
Assistive Dogs for Physically Challenged Adults / Judy Saunders. Edited by Philip Case and Jean Willis. Illustrations and photographs by Fritz Barnum. Denver: Mountain View Publishing Company, 1994.
256 p.; col. illus.; 24 cm

1. Assistive dogs 2. Guide dogs 3. Physically challenged II. Case, Philip III. Title

5 Fritz Barnum is the name of the—

A author
B publisher
C person who provided the illustrations and photographs
D person who trained the assistive dogs for the book

6 Which number would be most helpful in finding this book in the library?

F 622.4
G 256
H 24
J 1994

7 In which section of the card catalog would this card be found?

A Title
B Subject
C Publisher
D Author

8 Which of these books would most likely have been written by the same author?

F *The History of Dogs*
G *Dog Diseases*
H *Training Guide Dogs for the Blind*
J *Living Spaces for Challenged Persons*

This is an index from a book about Italy during the Renaissance. Use the index to do Numbers 9–11.

INDEX

Page numbers in **bold** type refer to illustrations.

Arno River, water displays on, 19, 282; in flood, 223, 279-280; palaces on, **315**
Bank, Medici, branches of, 34; and the government, 55; decline of, 158-173
Charles V, Holy Roman Emperor, succeeds Emperor Maximilian, 234; takes Milan, 238; marches on Rome, 241, 243-246
Clothes, of 14th century Florence, 21; of 15th century Florence, 22-24; ceremonial attire, **73**; of Roman women, 116-117; of national militia, **211**; uniforms of pages, 268-269
Festivals, pageants, 111; tournaments, **116**; weddings, 280-281
Florence, in 15th century, 19-21; government, 26-28; trade, 33; pageants and festivities, 111, 118-119; wedding customs, 117-118; flood and famine in, 223
Michelangelo Buonarroti (1475-1564), history, 165; his tomb, **312**; his early work, 322; his great works, 389-397
Milan, government of, 27; Florence and, 42, 79-80; Venice and Naples declare war on, 84; Spain and, 219
Savonarola, Girolamo (1452-1498), 178-182; his power in Florence, 191; attitudes toward, 192-193

9 Which page would contain a picture of clothes worn by the national militia?

A 21 **C** 73
B 23 **D** 211

10 Which page would contain a description of the government of Florence?

F 19 **H** 111
G 27 **J** 117

11 Which page would contain information about the relationship of Florence and Milan?

A 24 **C** 78
B 42 **D** 80

STOP

Table of Contents
Math

Lesson 1 Numeration

Example

Directions: Read and work each problem. Find the correct answer. Mark the space for your choice.

A Which of these numbers comes between 95 and 115?

A 150
B 105
C 94
D 149

B In which of these problems can the dividend be evenly divided by the divisor?

F 116 ÷ 9
G 114 ÷ 8
H 118 ÷ 8
J 117 ÷ 9

Read each question carefully. Look for key words and numbers that will help you find the answers.

Look at each answer choice before you choose the one you think is correct.

Practice

1 To which value does Arrow A point?

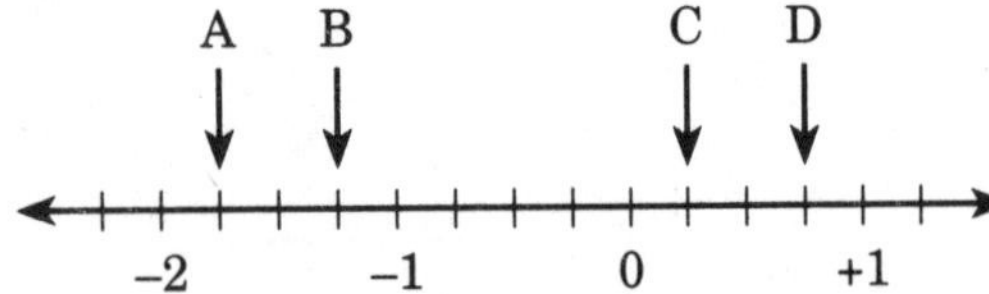

A $1\frac{1}{2}$
B $-1\frac{3}{4}$
C $-1\frac{1}{4}$
D $-2\frac{1}{4}$

2 What number should replace the ☐ to make the following a true statement?

483,916 = ☐ + 80,000 + 3000 + 900 + 10 + 6

F 400,000
G 4,000,000
H 4
J 40,000

3 Another way to write 3^5 is —

A 3 + 5
B 3 x 5
C 5 x 5 x 5
D 3 x 3 x 3 x 3 x 3

4 What number is 10,000 more than 23,971,056?

F 23,961,056
G 23,972,056
H 23,981,056
J 24,081,056

5 What is the greatest common factor of 39 and 143?

A 104
B 13
C 9
D 81

GO

ANSWER ROWS
A Ⓐ ● Ⓒ Ⓓ   1 Ⓐ Ⓑ Ⓒ Ⓓ   3 Ⓐ Ⓑ Ⓒ Ⓓ   5 Ⓐ Ⓑ Ⓒ Ⓓ
B Ⓕ Ⓖ Ⓗ Ⓙ   2 Ⓕ Ⓖ Ⓗ Ⓙ   4 Ⓕ Ⓖ Ⓗ Ⓙ

6 Which of the number sentences below is <u>false</u>?

F $-5 < 0$

G $-5 > -8$

H $4 < -1$

J $-6 > -10$

7 What is the value of the expression in the box?

$$(5 + 3)^2 \div 4$$

A 16

B 2

C 8

D 11

8 One value of $\sqrt{27}$ is between —

F 6 and 7

G 20 and 30

H 2 and 7

J 5 and 6

9 What is the <u>least</u> number that is evenly divisible by 16 and 24?

A 384

B 48

C 64

D 8

10 What is the prime factorization of 75?

F 3 x 25

G 1 x 75

H 3 x 5 x 5

J 3 x 3 x 5

11 $5.09 \times 10^4 =$

A 50,900

B 509

C 5,090,000

D 509,104

12 Which number is between −7 and 5?

F 6

G 9

H −9

J −2

13 Which group of integers is in order from greatest to least?

A 0, 4, 8, 12, 19

B 5, 2, 0, −2, −7

C −6, −2, 0, 19, 14

D −2, 0, 5, 9, 18

14 If 5 motorcycles are as long as 3 cars, what is the smallest number of motorcycles and cars that would be the same length?

F 3 motorcycles and 5 cars

G 50 motorcycles and 30 cars

H 15 motorcycles and 9 cars

J 1 motorcycle and 1 car

15 For the school picture, the students wanted to arrange themselves into lines of 12 each. There weren't enough students, so one line had just 7 students. Which of these could be the number of students?

A 48

B 91

C 120

D 70

STOP

ANSWER ROWS 6 Ⓕ Ⓖ Ⓗ Ⓙ 8 Ⓕ Ⓖ Ⓗ Ⓙ 10 Ⓕ Ⓖ Ⓗ Ⓙ 12 Ⓕ Ⓖ Ⓗ Ⓙ 14 Ⓕ Ⓖ Ⓗ Ⓙ
7 Ⓐ Ⓑ Ⓒ Ⓓ 9 Ⓐ Ⓑ Ⓒ Ⓓ 11 Ⓐ Ⓑ Ⓒ Ⓓ 13 Ⓐ Ⓑ Ⓒ Ⓓ 15 Ⓐ Ⓑ Ⓒ Ⓓ

Example

Directions: Read and work each problem. Find the correct answer. Mark the space for your choice.

A Six hundred twenty thousand =

1) 60,200
2) 600,200
3) 1620
4) 620,000

B What is 0.28 rounded to the nearest tenth?

1) 0.3
2) 0.1
3) 3.1
4) 0.03

Be sure the answer space you fill in is the same number or letter as the answer you think is correct.

Key words, numbers, pictures, and figures will help you find the answers.

Practice

1 Which of these is a prime number?

1) 39
2) 75
3) 57
4) 29

2 How much would the value of 825,910 be decreased by replacing the 8 with a 7?

1) 10,000
2) 100,000
3) 1000
4) 1

3 What number goes in the box to make the equation true?

$$3\frac{1}{9} - 1\frac{\square}{9} = 1\frac{2}{9}$$

1) 8
2) 1
3) 13
4) 9

4 Which is the best estimate of $17.88 \times 52\frac{1}{9}$?

1) 15 x 50
2) 20 x 50
3) 15 x 55
4) 20 x 60

5 Look at the number pattern below. What numbers are missing from the pattern?

3
4 4
7 4 7
14 8 8 14
28 16 15 16 28
— 32 30 30 32 —

1) 32 and 48
2) 42 and 42
3) 56 and 56
4) 56 and 32

GO

ANSWER ROWS A ① ② ③ ④ 1 ① ② ③ ④ 3 ① ② ③ ④ 5 ① ② ③ ④
B ① ② ③ ④ 2 ① ② ③ ④ 4 ① ② ③ ④

6 Using the digits 3, 1, 6, 9, and 8 in two 5-digit numbers, what are the largest and the smallest numbers you can write?

1) 98,163 and 13,986

2) 98,136 and 13,896

3) 98,361 and 13,698

4) 98,631 and 13,689

7 What is 3,287,469 rounded to the nearest ten thousand?

1) 3,280,000

2) 3,010,000

3) 3,290,000

4) 310,000

8 Which of these is <u>not</u> equivalent to 8 x (9 – 2)?

1) (8 x 9) – (8 x 2)

2) 72 – 16

3) (8 x 9) – 2

4) (9 – 2) x 8

9 Look at the number pattern below. One number is missing from the pattern. Which number sentence could be used to find the missing number?

1, 3, 5, 9, 15, ___ , 41, 57

1) (15 + 9) + 1

2) (41 – 15) + 1

3) (5 + 9) + 10

4) (57 – 41) + 15

10 How many 2-letter codes can be made from the letters C-A-N if the letters can be repeated in the code? (For example, CC)

1) 12

2) 9

3) 27

4) 6

11 The squares below contain numbers that are related to each other according to the same rule. What number is missing from the third square?

3	6
18	2

4	20
60	5

2	?
42	7

1) 14

2) 9

3) 16

4) 21

12 For a school trip, 56 students went to a museum. All but 11 of the students paid $5.00 to see the video about volcanoes. Which number sentence shows how much the students paid in all to see the video?

1) (56 + 11) x 5

2) (56 – 11) x 5

3) (56 x 5) – 11

4) (56 – 11) + 5

13 Which of these is <u>not</u> equal to the others?

1) 65%

2) $\frac{65}{100}$

3) 0.065

4) 6 ÷ 5

STOP

ANSWER ROWS 6 ①②③④ 8 ①②③④ 10 ①②③④ 12 ①②③④
7 ①②③④ 9 ①②③④ 11 ①②③④ 13 ①②③④

Lesson 3 Fractions and Decimals

Example

Directions: Read and work each problem. Find the correct answer. Mark the space for your choice.

A 1.05 =

A $\frac{10}{15}$
B $\frac{15}{10}$
C $\frac{100}{105}$
D $\frac{105}{100}$

B Which of these is greater than the others?

F two and four tenths
G nine tenths
H one and nine tenths
J two and nine hundredths

Pay close attention to the numbers in the problem and in the answer choices. If you misread even one number, you will probably choose the wrong answer.

If a problem is too difficult, skip it and come back to it later, if you have time.

Practice

1 Which decimal gives the best estimate of the amount of the circle below that is shaded?

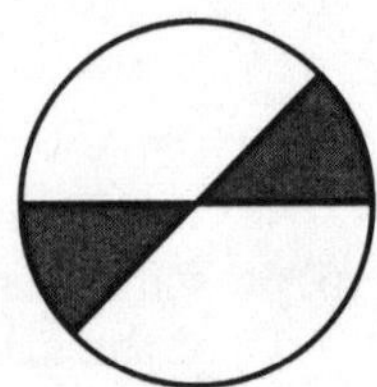

A 0.125
B 0.40
C 0.25
D 0.625

2 Which of these is less than $\frac{4}{9}$?

F $\frac{1}{3}$
G $\frac{1}{2}$
H $\frac{3}{4}$
J $\frac{5}{8}$

3 What is the reciprocal of $\frac{3}{8}$?

A $\frac{8}{3}$
B $\frac{1}{3}$
C $\frac{1}{8}$
D $\frac{5}{8}$

4 How would you write 27% as a fraction?

F $\frac{2}{7}$
G $\frac{27}{100}$
H $\frac{.27}{100}$
J $\frac{17}{10}$

5 Which of these is another name for six and fifteen thousandths?

A 6.15
B 6.00015
C 6015
D 6.015

GO

ANSWER ROWS A Ⓐ Ⓑ Ⓒ Ⓓ 1 Ⓐ Ⓑ Ⓒ Ⓓ 3 Ⓐ Ⓑ Ⓒ Ⓓ 5 Ⓐ Ⓑ Ⓒ Ⓓ
B Ⓕ Ⓖ Ⓗ Ⓙ 2 Ⓕ Ⓖ Ⓗ Ⓙ 4 Ⓕ Ⓖ Ⓗ Ⓙ

6 Which of these is the simplest name for $\frac{18}{72}$?

F $\frac{2}{8}$

G $\frac{4}{35}$

H $\frac{1}{4}$

J $\frac{1}{7}$

7 What is another name for $2\frac{2}{9}$?

A $\frac{29}{2}$

B $\frac{11}{9}$

C $\frac{22}{9}$

D $\frac{20}{9}$

8 What is the least common denominator for $\frac{2}{9}$, $\frac{1}{5}$, and $\frac{4}{15}$?

F 45

G 25

H 27

J 90

9 What is 0.074 expressed as a percent?

A 74%

B 7.4%

C 0.74%

D 0.074 %

10 In this number line, P points closest to —

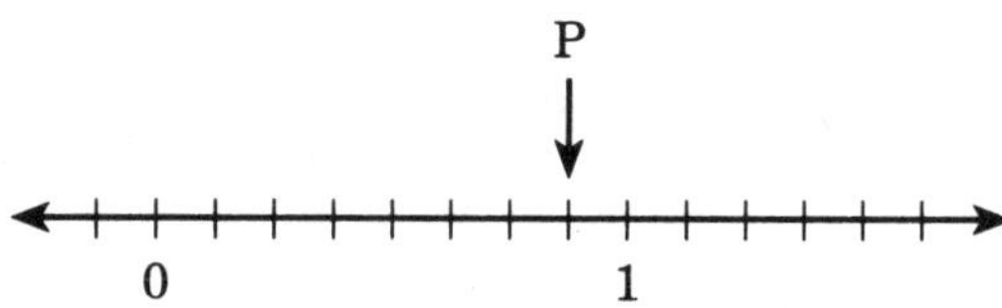

F 1.12

G 0.85

H 0.6

J 1.6

11 $\frac{3}{16} = \frac{9}{\square}$ $\square =$

A 48

B 32

C 4

D 3

12 A fisherman wants to buy the lightest sinker he can to hold his bait on the bottom of the lake. Which of these should he buy?

F $\frac{2}{3}$ ounce

G $\frac{3}{16}$ ounce

H $\frac{1}{4}$ ounce

J $\frac{4}{9}$ ounce

13 Which of these is twenty-three hundredths?

A 2300

B 23.001

C 0.0023

D 0.23

14 Suppose you wanted to write the numeral 54.085 but forgot the decimal point. How would this change the value of the numeral?

F It would make it 1000 times smaller.

G It would make it 1000 times greater.

H It would make it 100 times greater.

J It would not change the value.

15 How would you write 0.5% as a decimal?

A 5.00

B 0.05

C 0.005

D 0.5

STOP

ANSWER ROWS 6 Ⓕ Ⓖ Ⓗ Ⓙ 8 Ⓕ Ⓖ Ⓗ Ⓙ 10 Ⓕ Ⓖ Ⓗ Ⓙ 12 Ⓕ Ⓖ Ⓗ Ⓙ 14 Ⓕ Ⓖ Ⓗ Ⓙ
7 Ⓐ Ⓑ Ⓒ Ⓓ 9 Ⓐ Ⓑ Ⓒ Ⓓ 11 Ⓐ Ⓑ Ⓒ Ⓓ 13 Ⓐ Ⓑ Ⓒ Ⓓ 15 Ⓐ Ⓑ Ⓒ Ⓓ

E1

If you estimate by rounding to whole numbers, what is 4.8 plus 3.21?

A 5 + 3

B 4 + 3

C 4 + 4

D 3 + 3

E2

What is the greatest common factor of 12, 42, and 54?

F 3

G 7

H 6

J 9

1 The absolute value of −41 is —

A $\frac{1}{41}$

B 41

C $\sqrt{41}$

D 41^2

2 6 x 7 − 9 =

F 31

G −12

H 12

J −21

3 Which of these fractions is closest to 0 ?

A $\frac{2}{5}$

B $\frac{1}{12}$

C $\frac{1}{2}$

D $\frac{3}{8}$

4 Which of these is another way to write 4.8 million?

F 48,000,000

G 4,008,000

H 4,080,000

J 4,800,000

5 $5^3 - 50 =$

A 75

B −25

C 3

D 25

6 Which point is at $1\frac{3}{8}$ on this number line?

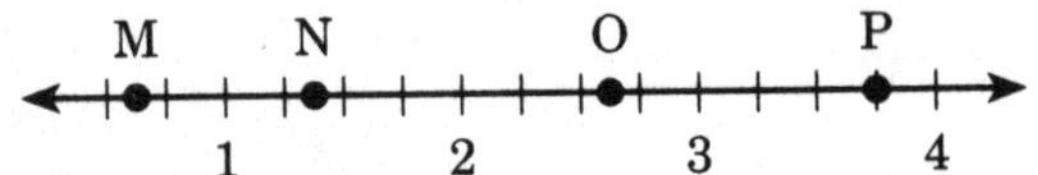

F M

G N

H O

J P

7 What number completes the number sentence shown below?

8 x □ = 40 x 60

A 50

B 40

C 300

D 500

GO

ANSWER ROWS E1 Ⓐ Ⓑ Ⓒ Ⓓ 1 Ⓐ Ⓑ Ⓒ Ⓓ 3 Ⓐ Ⓑ Ⓒ Ⓓ 5 Ⓐ Ⓑ Ⓒ Ⓓ 7 Ⓐ Ⓑ Ⓒ Ⓓ
E2 Ⓕ Ⓖ Ⓗ Ⓙ 2 Ⓕ Ⓖ Ⓗ Ⓙ 4 Ⓕ Ⓖ Ⓗ Ⓙ 6 Ⓕ Ⓖ Ⓗ Ⓙ

8 Which of these is another way to write 300 + 0.01 + 0.007 ?

F 301.007

G 300.017

H 317

J 300.17

9 Which of these is <u>not</u> equal in value to the others?

A $\frac{6}{100}$

B 6%

C 0.006

D $100\overline{)6}$

10 Which of these percentages gives the best estimate for the amount of the circle that is shaded?

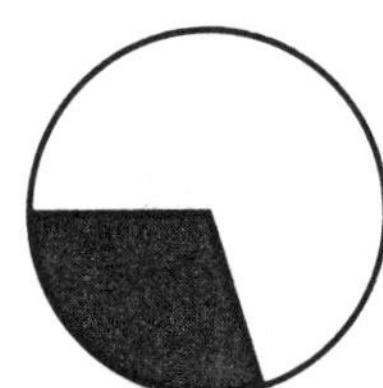

F 25%

G 15%

H 20%

J 30%

11 The newspaper said that about 1300 cars cross a bridge each day. Today, the actual number of cars that crossed the bridge was 1260. To what place value was the actual number rounded to get 1300?

A to the hundreds place

B to the tens place

C to the thousands place

D to the ones place

12 In the numeral 274,958, the 4 means —

F 40 thousand

G 4 hundred

H 4 hundred thousands

J 4 thousand

13 Which of these is between 0.045 and 0.07?

A 0.052

B 0.042

C 0.083

D 0.029

14 Which of these is a composite number?

F 7

G 5

H 91

J 29

15

$$\begin{array}{r} -9 \\ +6 \\ \hline \end{array}$$

A +3

B −3

C +15

D −15

16 What is the smallest number that can be divided evenly by 7 and 28?

F 14

G 112

H 56

J 36

ANSWER ROWS

8	Ⓕ Ⓖ Ⓗ Ⓙ	11	Ⓐ Ⓑ Ⓒ Ⓓ	14	Ⓕ Ⓖ Ⓗ Ⓙ
9	Ⓐ Ⓑ Ⓒ Ⓓ	12	Ⓕ Ⓖ Ⓗ Ⓙ	15	Ⓐ Ⓑ Ⓒ Ⓓ
10	Ⓕ Ⓖ Ⓗ Ⓙ	13	Ⓐ Ⓑ Ⓒ Ⓓ	16	Ⓕ Ⓖ Ⓗ Ⓙ

NUMBER RIGHT______

Lesson 5 Addition

Example

Directions: Mark the space for the correct answer to each addition problem. Choose "None of these" if the right answer is not given.

A

$$\begin{array}{r} 812 \\ +\ 139 \\ \hline \end{array}$$

A 1051
B 942
C 852
D 941
E None of these

B

$6 + {}^{-}1 =$

F −8
G 5
H 7
J −5
K None of these

If the answer you find is not one of the answer choices, rework the problem on scratch paper.

If you rework a problem and still find that the right answer is not given, mark the space for "None of these."

Practice

1

$$\begin{array}{r} 4982 \\ 9 \\ 274 \\ +\ 5613 \\ \hline \end{array}$$

A 10,877
B 10,878
C 9878
D 9877
E None of these

2

$12 + {}^{-}8 =$

F 20
G −4
H −20
J 4
K None of these

3

$\frac{1}{4} + \frac{2}{3} + \frac{3}{8} =$

A $1\frac{5}{24}$
B $\frac{6}{15}$
C $1\frac{7}{24}$
D $\frac{6}{24}$
E None of these

4

$\frac{21}{100} + \frac{7}{10} =$

F 0.91
G 0.28
H 1.48
J 0.721
K None of these

5

$0.723 + 0.028 =$

A 0.931
B 0.7258
C 0.951
D 0.741
E None of these

6

$65.37 + 0.882 =$

F 66.252
G 650.252
H 65.919
J 605.919
K None of these

7

$$\begin{array}{r} 866 \\ +\ 59 \\ \hline \end{array}$$

A 813
B 825
C 925
D 815
E None of these

8

$47 + 0.8 =$

F 470.8
G 47.8
H 47.08
J 407.08
K None of these

GO

ANSWER ROWS
A Ⓐ Ⓑ Ⓒ Ⓓ Ⓔ 1 Ⓐ Ⓑ Ⓒ Ⓓ Ⓔ 3 Ⓐ Ⓑ Ⓒ Ⓓ Ⓔ 5 Ⓐ Ⓑ Ⓒ Ⓓ Ⓔ 7 Ⓐ Ⓑ Ⓒ Ⓓ Ⓔ
B Ⓕ Ⓖ Ⓗ Ⓙ Ⓚ 2 Ⓕ Ⓖ Ⓗ Ⓙ Ⓚ 4 Ⓕ Ⓖ Ⓗ Ⓙ Ⓚ 6 Ⓕ Ⓖ Ⓗ Ⓙ Ⓚ 8 Ⓕ Ⓖ Ⓗ Ⓙ Ⓚ

9

$$\begin{array}{r} 5\frac{1}{8} \\ +\ 2\frac{2}{5} \\ \hline \end{array}$$

A $3\frac{1}{5}$
B 8
C $7\frac{21}{40}$
D $8\frac{3}{13}$
E None of these

10

$$\begin{array}{r} 5.627 \\ +\ .228 \\ \hline \end{array}$$

F 5.201
G 5.855
H 5.845
J 5.835
K None of these

11

$\frac{1}{2} + \frac{4}{5} =$

A $\frac{9}{10}$
B 1
C $1\frac{1}{5}$
D $\frac{5}{7}$
E None of these

12

4592.88 + 5.5 =

F 4598.38
G 45,925.38
H 45,926.38
J 4597.38
K None of these

13 18.6 + 0.072 + 4.79 =

A 22.462
B 22.672
C 23.751
D 23.462
E None of these

14

825.916 + 23.57 =

F 849.586
G 850.486
H 849.486
J 84.9486
K None of these

15

$$\begin{array}{r} 9\frac{5}{9} \\ +\ \frac{5}{6} \\ \hline \end{array}$$

A $9\frac{1}{3}$
B $9\frac{10}{36}$
C $10\frac{7}{9}$
D $10\frac{7}{18}$
E None of these

16

$$\begin{array}{r} .92 \\ .76 \\ +\ .21 \\ \hline \end{array}$$

F 10.89
G 1[illegible]
H [illegible].9
J 189
K None of these

17

$5\frac{4}{10} + 3\frac{5}{10} = \square$

A $8\frac{9}{10}$
B $8\frac{9}{20}$
C $9\frac{1}{10}$
D 9
E None of these

18 $6 + {}^{-}9 + {}^{-}3 =$

F $^{-}6$
G 18
H 0
J 6
K None of these

STOP

ANSWER ROWS
9 Ⓐ Ⓑ Ⓒ Ⓓ Ⓔ 11 Ⓐ Ⓑ Ⓒ Ⓓ Ⓔ 13 Ⓐ Ⓑ Ⓒ Ⓓ Ⓔ 15 Ⓐ Ⓑ Ⓒ Ⓓ Ⓔ 17 Ⓐ Ⓑ Ⓒ Ⓓ Ⓔ
10 Ⓕ Ⓖ Ⓗ Ⓙ Ⓚ 12 Ⓕ Ⓖ Ⓗ Ⓙ Ⓚ 14 Ⓕ Ⓖ Ⓗ Ⓙ Ⓚ 16 Ⓕ Ⓖ Ⓗ Ⓙ Ⓚ 18 Ⓕ Ⓖ Ⓗ Ⓙ Ⓚ

Example

Directions: Mark the space for the correct answer to each subtraction problem. Choose "NG" if the right answer is not given.

A $4 - {}^{-}2 = \square$	**A** 2 **B** 8 **C** 6 **D** −2 **E** NG	**B** $105 - 0.5$	**F** 100 **G** 105.5 **H** 103.5 **J** 65 **K** NG

If the right answer is not given, mark the space for "NG." This means "not given."

When you are not sure of an answer, check it by adding.

Practice

1 $559 - 89$

A 570
B 539
C 439
D 470
E NG

2 $36.8 - 4.1 =$

F 31.13
G 32.79
H 32.7
J 40.9
K NG

3 $40 - .64 = \square$

A 39.46
B 40.64
C 40.36
D 24
E NG

4 $4175 - 2856$

F 1319
G 2721
H 2319
J 7031
K NG

5 $54.6 - 0.87$

A 54.27
B 53.73
C 53.63
D 54.73
E NG

6 $6 - {}^{-}8 =$

F 2
G −2
H −14
J 14
K NG

7 $20.01 - 0.09 =$

A 19.92
B 19.11
C 20.01
D 20.11
E NG

8 $9.847 - 4.216$

F 4.631
G 5.631
H 5.629
J 4.629
K NG

GO

ANSWER ROWS
A Ⓐ Ⓑ Ⓒ Ⓓ Ⓔ 1 Ⓐ Ⓑ Ⓒ Ⓓ Ⓔ 3 Ⓐ Ⓑ Ⓒ Ⓓ Ⓔ 5 Ⓐ Ⓑ Ⓒ Ⓓ Ⓔ 7 Ⓐ Ⓑ Ⓒ Ⓓ Ⓔ
B Ⓕ Ⓖ Ⓗ Ⓙ Ⓚ 2 Ⓕ Ⓖ Ⓗ Ⓙ Ⓚ 4 Ⓕ Ⓖ Ⓗ Ⓙ Ⓚ 6 Ⓕ Ⓖ Ⓗ Ⓙ Ⓚ 8 Ⓕ Ⓖ Ⓗ Ⓙ Ⓚ

9

$$\begin{array}{r} 8\frac{7}{8} \\ -\ 1\frac{1}{4} \\ \hline \end{array}$$

A $7\frac{1}{7}$
B 10
C $8\frac{5}{8}$
D 11
E NG

10

$\frac{10}{19} - \frac{6}{19} = \square$

F 4
G $\frac{4}{19}$
H $\frac{14}{19}$
J $\frac{1}{3}$
K NG

11

$$\begin{array}{r} \frac{7}{13} \\ -\ \frac{4}{13} \\ \hline \end{array}$$

A $\frac{11}{13}$
B $\frac{3}{26}$
C $\frac{3}{13}$
D $\frac{11}{26}$
E NG

12

$6\frac{1}{4} - \frac{3}{4} =$

F $5\frac{1}{2}$
G $6\frac{1}{4}$
H $6\frac{1}{2}$
J $5\frac{3}{4}$
K NG

13

$7.3 - 0.3 =$

A 6.27
B 3.3
C 4.3
D 7
E NG

14

$-4 - 8 =$

F 12
G −12
H 4
J −4
K NG

15

$$\begin{array}{r} 47.46 \\ -\ 0.57 \\ \hline \end{array}$$

A 47.12
B 46.98
C 46.89
D 47.99
E NG

16

$4867.2 - 12 =$

F 4866
G 4867.18
H 4867.12
J 4855.2
K NG

17

$23.045 - .274 =$

A 23.231
B 22.671
C 22.679
D 23.771
E NG

18

$$\begin{array}{r} 762 \\ -\ 0.052 \\ \hline \end{array}$$

F 761.948
G 761.48
H 762.958
J 761.958
K NG

19

$-18 - 5 =$

A 13
B −13
C 23
D −23
E NG

STOP

ANSWER ROWS
9 Ⓐ Ⓑ Ⓒ Ⓓ Ⓔ 12 Ⓕ Ⓖ Ⓗ Ⓙ Ⓚ 15 Ⓐ Ⓑ Ⓒ Ⓓ Ⓔ 18 Ⓕ Ⓖ Ⓗ Ⓙ Ⓚ
10 Ⓕ Ⓖ Ⓗ Ⓙ Ⓚ 13 Ⓐ Ⓑ Ⓒ Ⓓ Ⓔ 16 Ⓕ Ⓖ Ⓗ Ⓙ Ⓚ 19 Ⓐ Ⓑ Ⓒ Ⓓ Ⓔ
11 Ⓐ Ⓑ Ⓒ Ⓓ Ⓔ 14 Ⓕ Ⓖ Ⓗ Ⓙ Ⓚ 17 Ⓐ Ⓑ Ⓒ Ⓓ Ⓔ

Example

Directions: Mark the space for the correct answer to each multiplication problem. Choose "NH" if the right answer is not given.

A $3.6 \times .2$	**A** 72 **B** 7.2 **C** 0.72 **D** 6.2 **E** NH	**B** $-2 \times 14 =$	**F** 29 **G** −29 **H** 16 **J** −16 **K** NH

If the right answer is not given, mark the space for "NH." This means "not here."

Take your best guess when you are unsure of the answer. If you can eliminate answer choices before guessing, you will improve your chances of choosing the correct answer.

Practice

1 6.01×7.92

A 47.5992
B 13.93
C 42.92
D 47.4992
E NH

2 $(2 + 4)3^2 =$

F 26
G 18
H 38
J 54
K NH

3 0.2×0.9

A 0.11
B 11
C 0.19
D 19
E NH

4 10% of □ = 15

F 0.15
G 150
H 15
J 1.5
K NH

5 $8 \times \frac{7}{8} =$

A $8\frac{1}{8}$
B $\frac{56}{8}$
C 7
D $\frac{7}{64}$
E NH

6 498×22

F 10,956
G 10,222
H 9956
J 9922
K NH

7 $330 \times .01 =$

A 33
B 3.03
C 0.303
D 3.3
E NH

8 $20{,}409 \times 6001$

F 12,474,409
G 122,474,409
H 122,474,009
J 12,475,409
K NH

GO

ANSWER ROWS
A Ⓐ Ⓑ Ⓒ Ⓓ Ⓔ 1 Ⓐ Ⓑ Ⓒ Ⓓ Ⓔ 3 Ⓐ Ⓑ Ⓒ Ⓓ Ⓔ 5 Ⓐ Ⓑ Ⓒ Ⓓ Ⓔ 7 Ⓐ Ⓑ Ⓒ Ⓓ Ⓔ
B Ⓕ Ⓖ Ⓗ Ⓙ Ⓚ 2 Ⓕ Ⓖ Ⓗ Ⓙ Ⓚ 4 Ⓕ Ⓖ Ⓗ Ⓙ Ⓚ 6 Ⓕ Ⓖ Ⓗ Ⓙ Ⓚ 8 Ⓕ Ⓖ Ⓗ Ⓙ Ⓚ

9

$5\frac{2}{3} \times 9 =$

A $45\frac{2}{3}$
B $\frac{18}{27}$
C 51
D $48\frac{1}{3}$
E NG

10

$\frac{5}{12} \times \frac{3}{8} =$

F $5\frac{1}{96}$
G 8
H $\frac{15}{91}$
J $\frac{5}{32}$
K NG

11

$16 \times \frac{3}{4} =$

A 12
B $4\frac{1}{4}$
C $\frac{3}{64}$
D $12\frac{1}{4}$
E NG

12

$\frac{4}{9} \times \frac{1}{2} =$

F $\frac{5}{18}$
G $\frac{2}{9}$
H $9\frac{1}{2}$
J $\frac{2}{18}$
K NG

13

$13 + 2 \times 4 =$

A 20
B 60
C 19
D 64
E NG

14

$5 \times {}^{-}8 \times 2 =$

F 80
G 50
H −50
J −80
K NG

15

$$\begin{array}{r} .402 \\ \times\ .705 \\ \hline \end{array}$$

A 28.3401
B 0.28341
C 2.831
D 28.341
E NG

16

10% of 18 =

F 108
G 0.108
H 1.8
J 0.18
K NG

17

$0.41 \times 0.15 =$

A 0.0615
B 41.15
C 0.415
D 61.5
E NG

18

$$\begin{array}{r} 3085 \\ \times\ 206 \\ \hline \end{array}$$

F 635,501
G 635,410
H 605,510
J 63,551
K NG

19 24 is what percent of 96?

A 36%
B 30%
C 24%
D 25%
E NG

STOP

ANSWER ROWS
9 Ⓐ Ⓑ Ⓒ Ⓓ Ⓔ 12 Ⓕ Ⓖ Ⓗ Ⓙ Ⓚ 15 Ⓐ Ⓑ Ⓒ Ⓓ Ⓔ 18 Ⓕ Ⓖ Ⓗ Ⓙ Ⓚ
10 Ⓕ Ⓖ Ⓗ Ⓙ Ⓚ 13 Ⓐ Ⓑ Ⓒ Ⓓ Ⓔ 16 Ⓕ Ⓖ Ⓗ Ⓙ Ⓚ 19 Ⓐ Ⓑ Ⓒ Ⓓ Ⓔ
11 Ⓐ Ⓑ Ⓒ Ⓓ Ⓔ 14 Ⓕ Ⓖ Ⓗ Ⓙ Ⓚ 17 Ⓐ Ⓑ Ⓒ Ⓓ Ⓔ

Lesson 8 Division

Example

Directions: Mark the space for the correct answer to each division problem. Choose "N" if the right answer is not given.

A

$4\overline{)38}$

1) 8
2) 8.5
3) 9
4) N

B

$\frac{1}{8} \div \frac{1}{2} =$

1) $\frac{1}{4}$
2) $1\frac{1}{4}$
3) $\frac{1}{16}$
4) N

Pay close attention when you are dividing decimals or fractions. It is easy to make a mistake by misplacing the decimal point or forgetting to invert fractions.

If the right answer is not given, mark the space for "N." This means the answer is not given.

Practice

1

$-54 \div 6 =$

1) 48
2) −9
3) 9
4) N

2

$7\overline{)1.435}$

1) 2.05
2) 2.5
3) 0.205
4) N

3

$\frac{1}{7} \div \frac{5}{7} =$

1) $\frac{1}{5}$
2) $1\frac{2}{7}$
3) $\frac{5}{49}$
4) N

4

$4.29 \div 10 =$

1) 0.0429
2) 10.429
3) 42.9
4) N

5

$84 \div 12 = \square$

1) 8
2) 7
3) 8 R4
4) N

6

$40\overline{)2497}$

1) 63
2) 63 R4
3) 62 R17
4) N

7

$.35\overline{).105}$

1) 30
2) 0.3
3) 0.035
4) N

8

$225\overline{)189}$

1) 0.84
2) 84
3) 8.04
4) N

ANSWER ROWS

A ①②③④ 1 ①②③④ 3 ①②③④ 5 ①②③④ 7 ①②③④

B ①②③④ 2 ①②③④ 4 ①②③④ 6 ①②③④ 8 ①②③④

9

$347 \div 100 =$

1) 3.47
2) 103.47
3) 34.7
4) N

10

$6\overline{)7818}$

1) 133
2) 1298
3) 1303
4) N

11

$54 \div 2\frac{1}{4} =$

1) $27\frac{1}{4}$
2) 24
3) $24\frac{1}{4}$
4) N

12

$4\frac{1}{8} \div 3\frac{2}{3} =$

1) $\frac{8}{9}$
2) $1\frac{1}{8}$
3) $1\frac{1}{3}$
4) N

13

$\frac{19 + (48 \div 6)}{3} =$

1) 43
2) 27
3) 9
4) N

14

$\frac{5}{14} \div \frac{2}{7} =$

1) $1\frac{1}{4}$
2) $2\frac{1}{7}$
3) $\frac{10}{98}$
4) N

15

$^-63 \div {}^-9 =$

1) $^-7$
2) $^-9$
3) 6
4) N

16

$40.8 \div 0.6 =$

1) 68
2) 240.8
3) 680
4) N

17

$\frac{-56}{-14} =$

1) -6
2) 16
3) 4
4) N

18

$0.002 \div 500 =$

1) 40
2) 0.4
3) 4
4) N

19

$167.238 \div 6.52 =$

1) 26.65
2) 275.65
3) 25.65
4) N

20 Estimate the answer for this item.

$9357 \div 216\frac{9}{10}$ is closest to

1) 500
2) 50
3) 4000
4) N

STOP

ANSWER ROWS 9 ① ② ③ ④ 12 ① ② ③ ④ 15 ① ② ③ ④ 18 ① ② ③ ④
10 ① ② ③ ④ 13 ① ② ③ ④ 16 ① ② ③ ④ 19 ① ② ③ ④
11 ① ② ③ ④ 14 ① ② ③ ④ 17 ① ② ③ ④ 20 ① ② ③ ④

E1

200) 300

A 1500
B 150
C 67
D 230
E None of these

E2

0.8 ÷ .25 =

F 3.2
G 20
H 0.2
J 0.55
K None of these

1

956.4 – 83.88 =

A 873.48
B 873.52
C 872.53
D 872.52
E None of these

2

28
49
70
+ 53

F 200
G 210
H 190
J 180
K None of these

3

816
x 495

A 393,920
B 32,392
C 40,392
D 403,930
E None of these

4

24 x 0.672 =

F 24.672
G 16.128
H 162.8
J 161.28
K None of these

5

$\frac{3}{5} \div 12 =$

A 20
B $2\frac{1}{5}$
C $2\frac{1}{12}$
D $\frac{1}{20}$
E None of these

6

4 + ⁻8 + ⁻6 =

F 18
G −18
H 10
J −2
K None of these

7

0.7) 5.964

A 0.82
B 8.52
C 52.57
D 0.0852
E None of these

8

2 x ⁻6 x 3 =

F −36
G 416
H 18
J 56
K None of these

9

25007
– 8469

A 16,532
B 17,462
C 17,538
D 16,538
E None of these

10 (15 – 6) (4 + 5) =

F 81
G 150
H 41
J 189
K None of these

GO

ANSWER ROWS
E1 Ⓐ Ⓑ Ⓒ Ⓓ Ⓔ 2 Ⓕ Ⓖ Ⓗ Ⓙ Ⓚ 5 Ⓐ Ⓑ Ⓒ Ⓓ Ⓔ 8 Ⓕ Ⓖ Ⓗ Ⓙ Ⓚ
E2 Ⓕ Ⓖ Ⓗ Ⓙ Ⓚ 3 Ⓐ Ⓑ Ⓒ Ⓓ Ⓔ 6 Ⓕ Ⓖ Ⓗ Ⓙ Ⓚ 9 Ⓐ Ⓑ Ⓒ Ⓓ Ⓔ
1 Ⓐ Ⓑ Ⓒ Ⓓ Ⓔ 4 Ⓕ Ⓖ Ⓗ Ⓙ Ⓚ 7 Ⓐ Ⓑ Ⓒ Ⓓ Ⓔ 10 Ⓕ Ⓖ Ⓗ Ⓙ Ⓚ

11

$$\begin{array}{r} \frac{1}{4} \\ \frac{1}{18} \\ + \frac{1}{3} \\ \hline \end{array}$$

A $\frac{23}{36}$
B 1
C $1\frac{1}{6}$
D $\frac{2}{3}$
E None of these

12

5 is what % of 40?

F 25
G 12.5
H 10
J 30.5
K None of these

13

$90 - {}^{-}30 =$

A 3
B −30
C −60
D 30
E None of these

14

50 is what percent of 2000?

F 25%
G 30%
H 300%
J 2.5%
K None of these

15

$5.39 - .6 =$

A 5.33
B 4.79
C 4.69
D 0.61
E None of these

16

$$\frac{(25-9)+20}{4}$$

F 21
G 11
H 9
J 24
K None of these

17

$4^2 \div (2+6) =$

A 0.5
B 1
C 8
D 4
E None of these

18

$(60 + 24) \div 12 =$

F 62
G 7
H 29
J 8
K None of these

19

$$\begin{array}{r} 36.85 \\ \times \quad 20 \\ \hline \end{array}$$

A 720.85
B 7370
C 56.85
D 737
E None of these

20

$150 \div {}^{-}30 =$

F −5
G 50
H 120
J −20
K None of these

21

$$\begin{array}{r} 18\frac{4}{15} \\ - 10\frac{3}{5} \\ \hline \end{array}$$

A $6\frac{3}{4}$
B $5\frac{3}{8}$
C 6
D $7\frac{2}{3}$
E None of these

22

$\frac{2}{3} \times 27 =$

F 16
G 9
H 18
J 6
K None of these

STOP

ANSWER ROWS
11 Ⓐ Ⓑ Ⓒ Ⓓ Ⓔ 14 Ⓕ Ⓖ Ⓗ Ⓙ Ⓚ 17 Ⓐ Ⓑ Ⓒ Ⓓ Ⓔ 20 Ⓕ Ⓖ Ⓗ Ⓙ Ⓚ
12 Ⓕ Ⓖ Ⓗ Ⓙ Ⓚ 15 Ⓐ Ⓑ Ⓒ Ⓓ Ⓔ 18 Ⓕ Ⓖ Ⓗ Ⓙ Ⓚ 21 Ⓐ Ⓑ Ⓒ Ⓓ Ⓔ
13 Ⓐ Ⓑ Ⓒ Ⓓ Ⓔ 16 Ⓕ Ⓖ Ⓗ Ⓙ Ⓚ 19 Ⓐ Ⓑ Ⓒ Ⓓ Ⓔ 22 Ⓕ Ⓖ Ⓗ Ⓙ Ⓚ

NUMBER RIGHT______

Lesson 10 Geometry

Example

Directions: Find the correct answer to each geometry problem. Mark the space for your choice.

A The triangle on the right has two angles that measure 90° and 50°. What is the measure of the third angle?

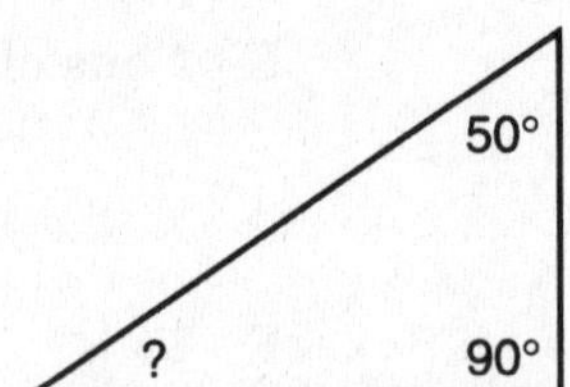

A 220°

B 50°

C 30°

D 40°

Read the question carefully and think about what you are supposed to do. Then look for key words, numbers, and figures before you choose an answer.

Practice

1 The map below shows the distances between six cities in Central County. Suppose you wanted to go from City 4 to City 1. What is the shortest distance you must travel?

Central County

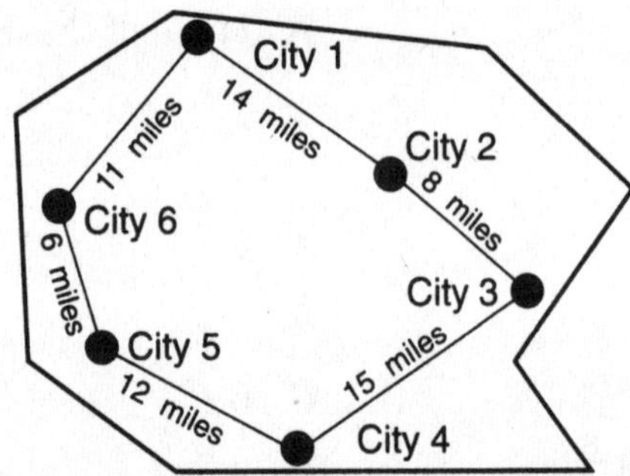

A 37 miles

B 27 miles

C 17 miles

D 29 miles

2 What is the volume of a freezer that is 6 feet high, 4 feet wide, and 3 feet deep?

F 72 cu ft

G 27 cu ft

H 13 cu ft

J 62 cu ft

3 Which number sentence shows how to find the area of a lawn that is 12 yd by 18 yd?

A Area = (2 x 12 yd) + (2 x 18 yd)

B Area = 12 yd + 18 yd

C Area = 12 yd x 18 yd

D 90 square meters

4 Which of these is an obtuse angle?

F 90°

G 120°

H 12°

J 0°

GO

ANSWER ROWS A Ⓐ Ⓑ Ⓒ Ⓓ 1 Ⓐ Ⓑ Ⓒ Ⓓ 2 Ⓕ Ⓖ Ⓗ Ⓙ 3 Ⓐ Ⓑ Ⓒ Ⓓ 4 Ⓕ Ⓖ Ⓗ Ⓙ

5 The two cubes below are identical in size. What shape would be formed if you joined the cubes together end to end?

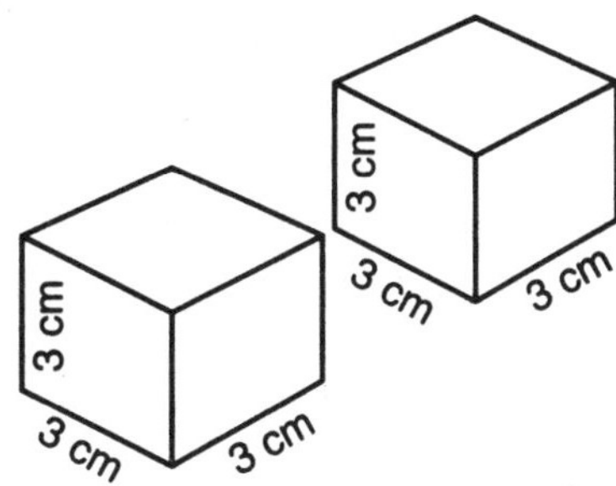

A a rectangular prism with dimensions 3 cm by 3 cm by 9 cm

B a cube with dimensions 6 cm by 6 cm by 6 cm

C a rectangular prism with dimensions 3 cm by 3 cm by 6 cm

D a cube with dimensions 9 cm by 9 cm by 9 cm

6 In the picture below, Figure A and Figure B are congruent. What is the perimeter of Figure A?

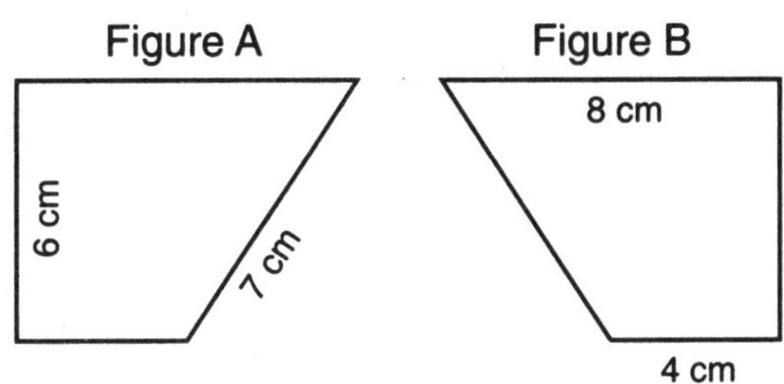

F 25 cm

G 13 cm

H 42 cm

J It can't be found.

7 Which of these statements is true?

A A right angle is 100°.

B Perpendicular lines never intersect.

C Parallel lines form a 90° angle.

D Two rays make up an angle.

8 What is the best estimate of the measure of angle FLJ in the figure below?

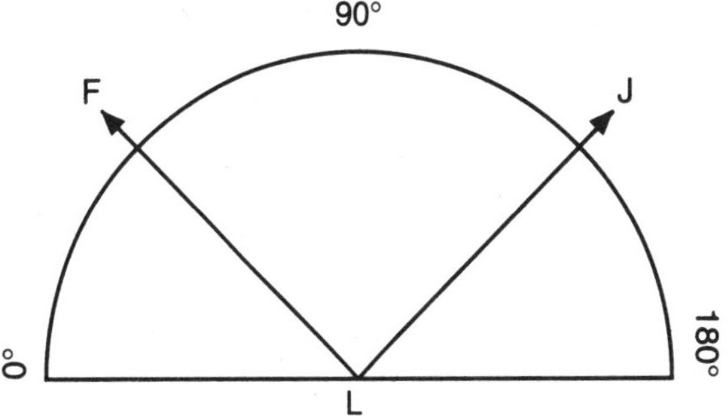

F 45°

G 90°

H 135°

J 180°

9 In the figure below, all the angles are right angles. What is the area of the figure?

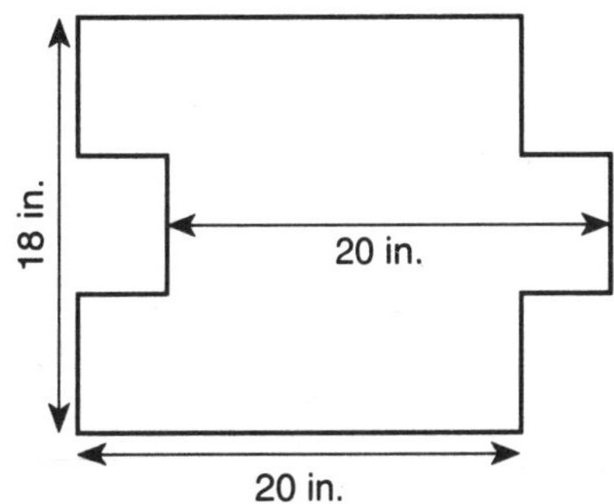

A 58 sq. in.

B 360 sq. in.

C 7200 sq. in.

D 340 sq. in.

10 In triangle ABC, just two of the angles are equal. What kind of triangle is it?

F a right triangle

G an equilateral triangle

H an isosceles triangle

J a parallel triangle

ANSWER ROWS 5 Ⓐ Ⓑ Ⓒ Ⓓ 6 Ⓕ Ⓖ Ⓗ Ⓙ 7 Ⓐ Ⓑ Ⓒ Ⓓ 8 Ⓕ Ⓖ Ⓗ Ⓙ 9 Ⓐ Ⓑ Ⓒ Ⓓ 10 Ⓕ Ⓖ Ⓗ Ⓙ

11 What is the volume of the rectangular prism shown below?

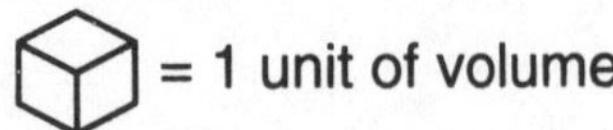

A 14 units

B 60 units

C 63 units

D 90 units

12 The radius of the circle below is —

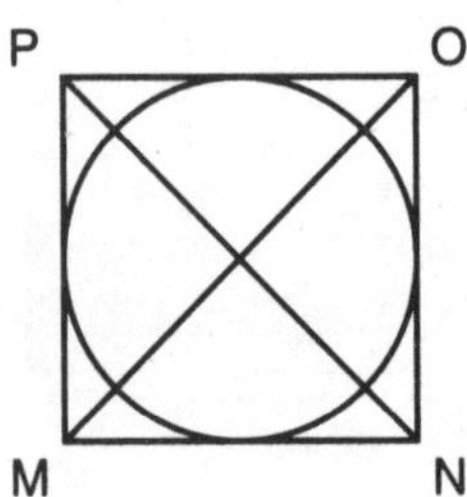

F the same as $\overline{PN}$

G half of $\overline{OM}$

H half of $\overline{MN}$

J the same as $\overline{ON}$

13 What is the area of a piece of cardboard that is 15 inches long and 12 inches wide?

A 180 square inches

B 27 square inches

C 54 square inches

D 270 square inches

14 A family is building a fence in their yard. The fence will be the same shape as the yard, but will be 1 foot inside each edge of the yard. How long will the fence be?

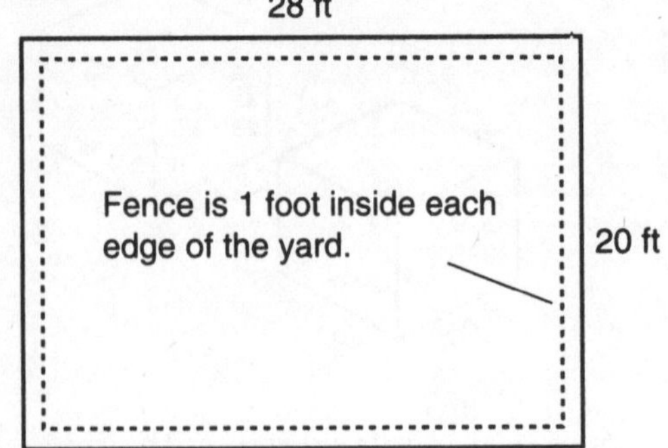

F 96 ft

G 88 ft

H 92 ft

J 95 ft

15 Look at Shape A. Suppose you rotated the shape one-half turn clockwise. What would the shape look like?

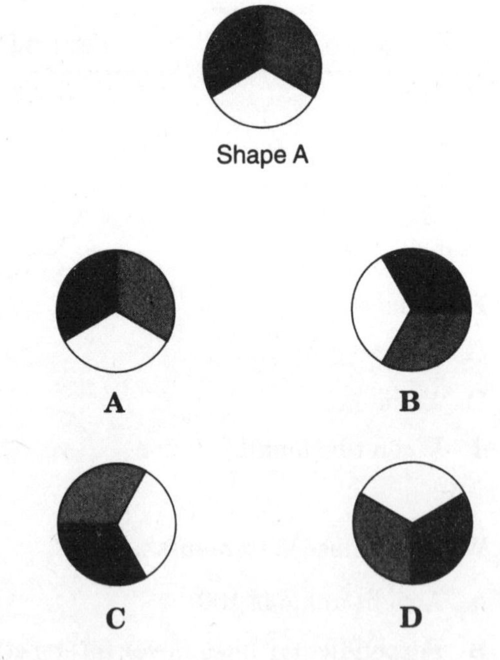

GO

ANSWER ROWS 11 Ⓐ Ⓑ Ⓒ Ⓓ 13 Ⓐ Ⓑ Ⓒ Ⓓ 15 Ⓐ Ⓑ Ⓒ Ⓓ
12 Ⓕ Ⓖ Ⓗ Ⓙ 14 Ⓕ Ⓖ Ⓗ Ⓙ

16 How many of the shaded shapes will it take to cover the grid shown below?

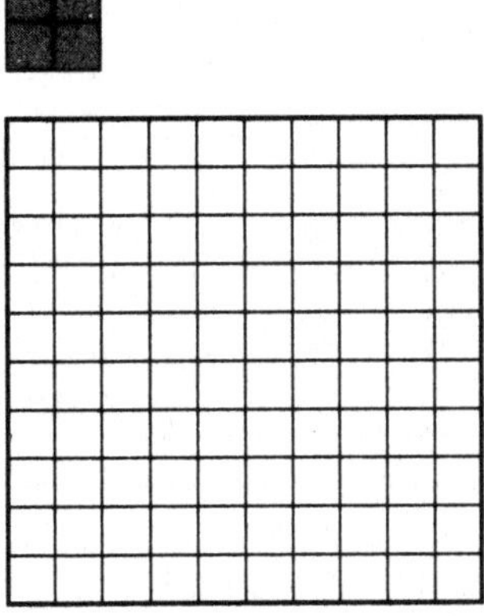

F 100

G 40

H 25

J 20

17 Molly and Rudy both have square yards. The sides of Rudy's yard are half as long as the sides of Molly's yard. Which of these statements is true about their yards?

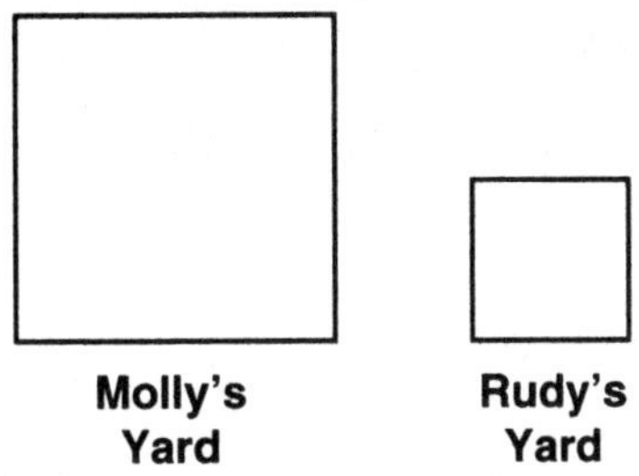

A The area of Rudy's yard is $\frac{1}{2}$ the area of Molly's yard.

B The area of Rudy's yard is $\frac{1}{4}$ the area of Molly's yard.

C The area of Rudy's yard is $\frac{1}{8}$ the area of Molly's yard.

D The area of Rudy's yard is $\frac{3}{4}$ the area of Molly's yard.

18 Look at this rectangular prism. Which plane is parallel to ADCB?

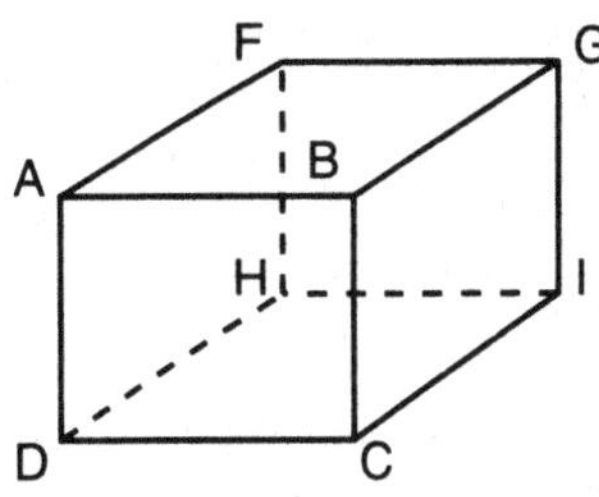

F FHIG

G ABFG

H DHIC

J AHIB

19 The two figures below are similar. What is the perimeter of the smaller figure?

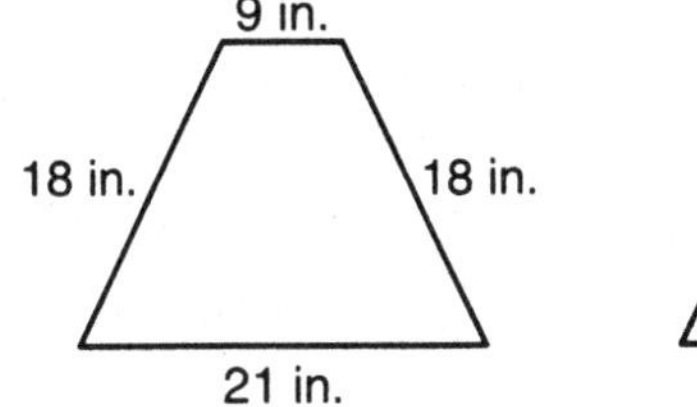

A 66 in.

B 33 in.

C 28 in.

D 22 in.

20 Which of these statements would prove that the triangle below is equilateral?

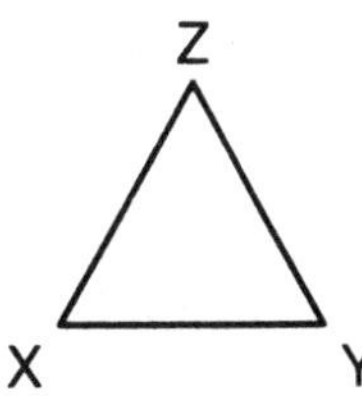

F XY = XZ + YZ

G Angle YXZ = 90°

H Angle YZX = 60°

J XY = (XZ + YZ) ÷ 3

STOP

ANSWER ROWS 16 Ⓕ Ⓖ Ⓗ Ⓙ 18 Ⓕ Ⓖ Ⓗ Ⓙ 20 Ⓕ Ⓖ Ⓗ Ⓙ
17 Ⓐ Ⓑ Ⓒ Ⓓ 19 Ⓐ Ⓑ Ⓒ Ⓓ

Example

Directions: Find the correct answer to each measurement problem. Mark the space for your choice.

A About how many centimeters long is $\overline{XZ}$?

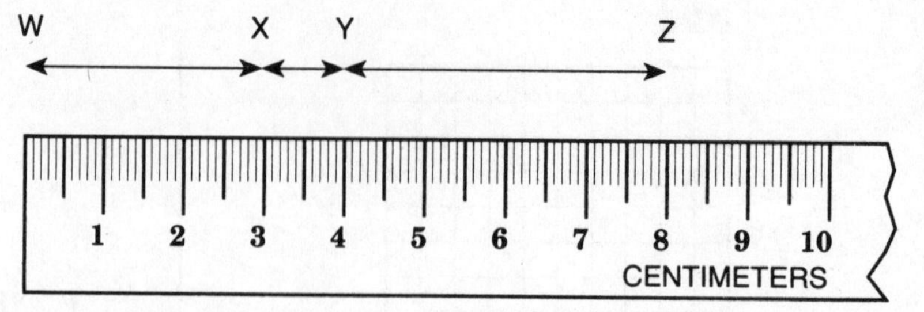

A 4 centimeters

B 8 centimeters

C 5 centimeters

D 10 centimeters

If you are confused by a problem, read it again. If you are still confused, skip the problem and come back to it later.

For some problems, you will have to work on scratch paper. Be sure to transfer numbers accurately and compute carefully.

Practice

1 Suppose you had 10 coins in your pocket totaling $.54. Which of the following statements is true about the coins?

A Some of the coins are nickels.

B None of the coins are pennies.

C Two of the coins are quarters.

D Five of the coins are dimes.

2 A bottle holds 4 liters of water. If you drink 1500 milliliters of water, how much will be left in the jar? (1 liter = 1000 milliliters)

F 3500 milliliters

G 5500 milliliters

H 2500 milliliters

J 4850 milliliters

3 Whic' of these is the greatest volume?

A 18 pints

B 12 quarts

C 2 gallons

D 30 cups

4 Charlie flew from Texas to California. When he arrived, he called his friend Maxine in New York. Charlie made the call at 8:00 P.M. California time. In New York, it was 3 hours later. What time was it in New York when Maxine received the call?

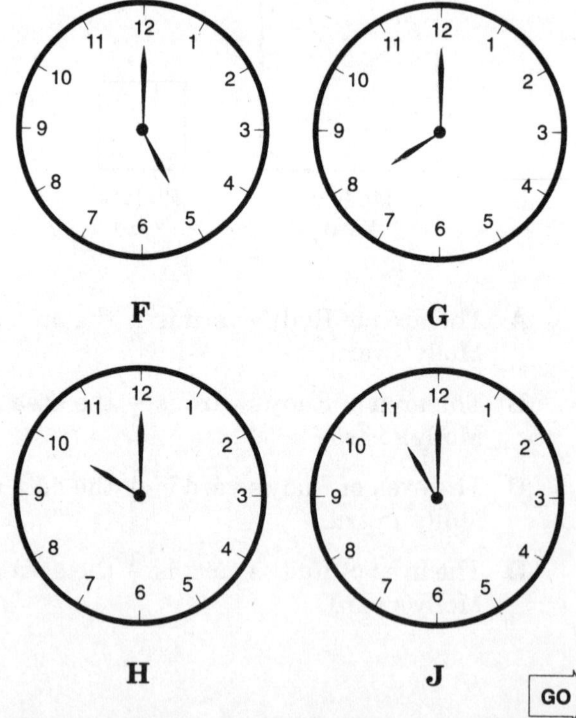

GO

5 A bus was scheduled to leave the station at 2:25 P.M. Because of a rain storm, the bus was delayed for 2 hours and 50 minutes. What time did the bus leave the station?

A 4:15 P.M.

B 4:25 P.M.

C 5:15 P.M.

D 5:25 P.M.

6 A worker had a roll of tape that was 12 yards long. She cut 5 feet of tape from the roll. How much tape was left on the roll?

F 10 yards

G 7 yards

H 9 yards and 2 feet

J 10 yards and 1 foot

7 How many inches are in 8 feet?

A 96

B 80

C 84

D 98

8 An unsharpened pencil is about how long?

F 16 inches

G 1 foot

H 1 inch

J 6 inches

9 The Harmon family heats their house with a coal burning stove. When the coal is delivered by truck, the weight of the coal is probably given in —

A pounds

B tons

C ounces

D gallons

10 Which of these might be 4 yards wide by 8 yards long?

F a small closet in a bedroom

G a kitchen table

H a one-car garage

J a bed

11 The height of a mountain would probably be given in —

A meters

B miles

C inches

D centimeters

12 What fraction of a yard is 30 inches?

F $\frac{5}{2}$

G $\frac{5}{6}$

H $\frac{3}{4}$

J $\frac{3}{10}$

13 The scale on the drawing of a house shows that 2 centimeters = 1 meter. What would the real dimensions of the living room be if it was 8 centimeters by 12 centimeters on the drawing?

A 8 meters by 12 meters

B 16 meters by 24 meters

C 6 meters by 10 meters

D 4 meters by 6 meters

14 3967 milliliters is equal to —

F 0.03967 meters

G 39.67 meters

H 3.967 meters

J 3000.967 meters

STOP

ANSWER ROWS 5 Ⓐ Ⓑ Ⓒ Ⓓ 7 Ⓐ Ⓑ Ⓒ Ⓓ 9 Ⓐ Ⓑ Ⓒ Ⓓ 11 Ⓐ Ⓑ Ⓒ Ⓓ 13 Ⓐ Ⓑ Ⓒ Ⓓ
6 Ⓕ Ⓖ Ⓗ Ⓙ 8 Ⓕ Ⓖ Ⓗ Ⓙ 10 Ⓕ Ⓖ Ⓗ Ⓙ 12 Ⓕ Ⓖ Ⓗ Ⓙ 14 Ⓕ Ⓖ Ⓗ Ⓙ

Example

Directions: Find the correct answer to each problem. Mark the space for your choice.

A A lake is normally 24 feet deep. Which number sentence shows the depth after a storm makes the lake 2 feet deeper?

1) 24 − 2 = □
2) 24 + 2 = □
3) 24 x 2 = □
4) 24 ÷ 2 = □

B Sandra bought 20 baskets for $2.00 each and sold them for $5.00 each. How much did she make all together?

1) $100
2) $40
3) $23
4) Not Given

Choose "Not Given" only if you are sure the right answer is not one of the choices.

Read each problem carefully. Look for key words, numbers, and figures in each problem. If you must work on scratch paper, be sure you perform the correct operation.

Practice

1 There are 25 students in a class. Sixty percent of them are girls. Each girl volunteers 45 minutes a week in the library. Which number sentence shows how much time they volunteer all together in 4 weeks?

1) [(25 x 60) x 45] x 4 = □
2) (25 x .6) + (45 x 4) = □
3) [(25 x .6) + 45] x 4 = □
4) [(25 x .6) x 45] x 4 = □

2 The bus ride from Alonzo's house to school is 7 miles. The ride home is only 4 miles because the driver uses a different route. Alonzo rides the bus 5 days each week and goes to school for 38 weeks each year. Which of these shows how far Alonzo travels by school bus each year?

1) (7 + 4) x (5 + 38) = □
2) (7 + 4) x (5 x 38) = □
3) (7 x 4) x (5 x 38) = □
4) (7 x 4) + (5 x 38) = □

3 Regular gasoline costs $1.39 a gallon and high performance gasoline costs $1.59 a gallon. Molly's car gets 30 miles per gallon of gas and her gas tank holds 15 gallons. Which of these questions can not be answered using only the information given?

1) How much will it cost Molly to drive back and forth to the mall?
2) How much will it cost Molly to fill up her gas tank?
3) How far can Molly drive if her tank is filled?
4) How much does it cost Molly to drive one mile using regular gas?

4 Skis normally sell for $300. They are on sale for $270. What percentage discount is this off the regular price?

1) 30%
2) 10%
3) 27%
4) 11.1%

GO

ANSWER ROWS A ①②③④ 1 ①②③④ 3 ①②③④
B ①②③④ 2 ①②③④ 4 ①②③④

The graph below shows the prices of five different cars. Use the graph to answer questions 5, 6, and 7.

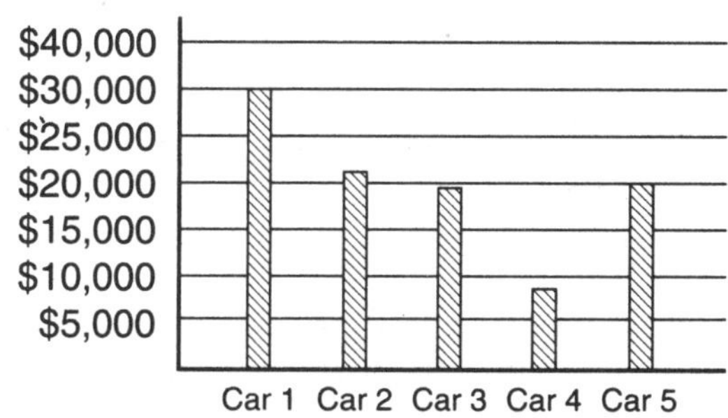

5 Which of these is closest to the average price of the five cars?

1) $15,000

2) $17,000

3) $23,000

4) $20,000

6 Car 1 is on sale for 15% off the regular price. How much would the car cost if you bought it on sale?

1) $15,000

2) $25,500

3) $28,500

4) Not Given

7 Nadine wants to buy Car 5. She already owns a car, and the dealer will pay her $3000 for it. In the state where Nadine lives, there is a 5% sales tax. What is the total price Nadine must pay for her car?

1) $17,850

2) $18,000

3) $17,000

4) $21,000

8 Donna, Len, and their friends are spending Saturday downtown shopping, going to the movies, and having dinner. They got on the subway at 9:15 and arrived at City Hall station at 10:05. How long did the subway ride take?

1) 60 minutes

2) 1 hour and 5 minutes

3) 55 minutes

4) Not Given

9 Donna and Len had $35 to spend on gifts for their parents. They had earned the money recycling aluminum cans. Donna earned $5 more than Len. How much did Len earn?

1) $20.00

2) $30.00

3) $15.00

4) $10.00

10 At lunch, Donna ordered a sandwich and soft drink for $3.50 and Len ordered pizza and milk for $4.50. Their friends ordered meals that totaled $22.00. The group decided to give the waiter a tip of 15%. What was the total cost of the meal, including the tip?

1) $31.50

2) $34.50

3) $45.00

4) Not Given

11 The mall in the Plaza Building has 56 stores. Donna and Len shopped in $\frac{2}{7}$ of them. In how many stores did they shop?

1) 8

2) 28

3) 16

4) 18

GO

ANSWER ROWS 5 ① ② ③ ④ 7 ① ② ③ ④ 9 ① ② ③ ④ 11 ① ② ③ ④
6 ① ② ③ ④ 8 ① ② ③ ④ 10 ① ② ③ ④

The chart below shows the nightly rates at a campground. Use the chart to answer questions 12 through 14.

CAMPGROUND RATES

	10' x 20'	20' x 40'
Without Electricity	$7.00	$10.00
ith Electricity	$9.00	$12.00

rom September to May, rates are reduced by $3.00 per night.

12 How much would it cost to stay 5 nights at a 10' x 20' camp site without electricity?

1) $50.00
2) $36.00
3) $45.00
4) Not Given

13 When the Armenta family went camping, they planned to stay 10 nights at a small site without electricity. After 2 nights, they moved to a large site with electricity. They stayed at this site for the rest of their vacation. How much did they spend in all for their stay at the campground?

1) $110.00
2) $100.00
3) $64.00
4) $86.00

14 What percentage would you save on the cost of a large camp site with electricity if you stayed at the campground in October rather than in July?

1) 30%
2) 33%
3) 25%
4) Not Given

15 The Carbondale school has 685 students and 32 teachers. One day, 134 students and 5 teachers were absent because of the flu. How many students and teachers in all were present at school that day?

1) 583
2) 578
3) 139
4) Not Given

16 A softball player gets a hit 4 out of every 15 times she comes to bat. She batted 45 times last season. How many hits did she get?

1) 34
2) 7
3) 11
4) Not Given

17 A carpenter is building a door for a closet. The opening of the closet is 7 feet tall and 30 inches wide. The wood the carpenter will use is 8 inches wide. What other information does he need to determine how many pieces of wood to buy?

1) the cost of the pieces of wood
2) the thickness of the pieces of wood
3) the length of the pieces of wood
4) the diagonal dimension of the opening

18 Tony and Deena are inventing a board game. They want to use a six-side block with one of the vowels (A, E, I, O, and U) on each face. The letter A will be used twice. If they roll the block 30 times, how many times will the letter E probably come up?

1) 5 times
2) 6 times
3) 10 times
4) Not Given

GO

ANSWER ROWS 12 ①②③④ 14 ①②③④ 16 ①②③④ 18 ①②③④
13 ①②③④ 15 ①②③④ 17 ①②③④

The graph below shows the number of acres farmed in two different counties over a four-year period. Use the graph to answer questions 19 through 21.

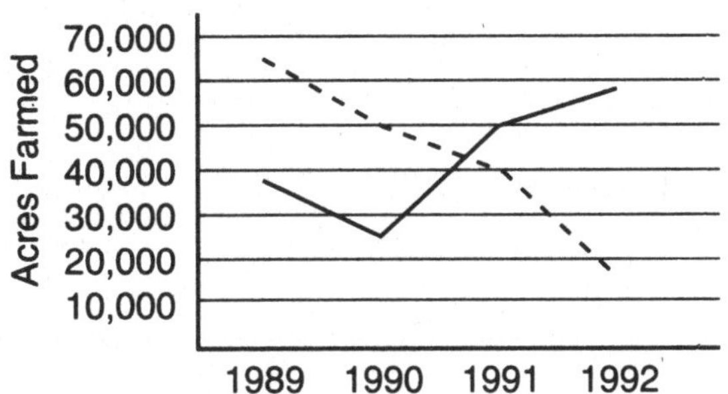

County A - - - - -

County B ———

19 Which of these might describe what is happening in County A as shown by the information on the graph?

1) Houses are being torn down so the land can be used for farming.
2) Farm land is being sold so it can be used to build houses.
3) The price of farm land is decreasing.
4) The cost of houses is decreasing.

20 In 1990, the amount of land used for farming in County B was half of what it was in 1960. About how many acres of County B were used for farming in 1960?

1) 50,000 acres
2) 12,500 acres
3) 60,000 acres
4) 25,000 acres

21 From 1989 to 1990, the amount of land farmed in County A decreased by —

1) about 75%
2) exactly 20%
3) more than 30%
4) about 25%

Read this passage and look at the chart. Then do numbers 22 through 24.

Roberto is the editor of the school paper. There are 800 students in the school. The paper is 4 pages long, and he wants to print 1000 copies.

PRINTING RATES			
	2 pages	4 pages	8 pages
250 copies	$50.00	$100.00	$160.00
500 copies	$80.00	$140.00	$260.00

22 According to the chart, how much will it probably cost to print the school paper?

1) $140.00
2) $280.00
3) $260.00
4) $400.00

23 The price per page can be found by calculating the total number of pages printed and dividing it into the cost of printing. What is the lowest price per page shown on the chart?

1) 6.5 cents per page
2) 2.6 cents per page
3) 7 cents per page
4) 10 cents per page.

24 The extra copies Roberto is printing are for parents, teachers, and students' friends. If the school paper is published 4 times each year, about how much does it cost to print these extra copies?

1) $208.00
2) $224.00
3) $390.00
4) $600.00

ANSWER ROWS 19 ① ② ③ ④ 21 ① ② ③ ④ 23 ① ② ③ ④
20 ① ② ③ ④ 22 ① ② ③ ④ 24 ① ② ③ ④

Example

Directions: Find the correct answer to each measurement problem. Mark the space for your choice.

A What is the value of y in the number sentence $4y + 3 = 19$?

A 4

B 16

C 22

D 5

B 20 more than Z is 62. Which equation shows this problem?

F 62 + 20 = Z

G Z – 20 = 62

H Z + 20 = 62

J 62 + Z = 20

If you are sure you know which answer is correct, just mark the space for your answer and move on to the next problem.

Before you choose an answer, ask yourself, "Does this answer make sense?"

Practice

1 Which equation is represented by the line on this graph?

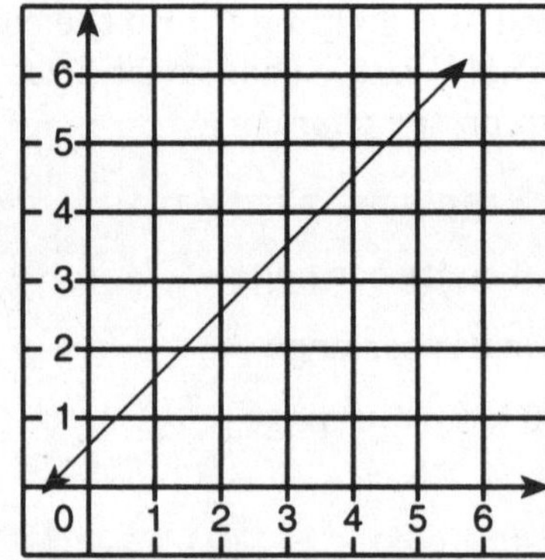

A y = x + 5

B y = x + 0.5

C y = x – 0.5

D y = 0.5 x

2 What is a subset of the solution set for this inequality?

$$24 \div z > 3$$

F {1, 2, 3, 4, 6, 8, 12}

G {12, 36, 48}

H {2, 3, 7, 8}

J {2, 3, 4, 6}

3 8m – 13 = 27 m =

A 5

B 2

C 14

D 40

4 If $z = 9$, then $3z + 7 =$

F 27

G 20

H 34

J 4

GO

ANSWER ROWS A Ⓐ Ⓑ Ⓒ Ⓓ 1 Ⓐ Ⓑ Ⓒ Ⓓ 3 Ⓐ Ⓑ Ⓒ Ⓓ

B Ⓕ Ⓖ Ⓗ Ⓙ 2 Ⓕ Ⓖ Ⓗ Ⓙ 4 Ⓕ Ⓖ Ⓗ Ⓙ

5 For which of these equations would $a = 5$ when $b = 9$?

A $2a + b = 19$

B $2a - b = 19$

C $b - a = 19$

D $2ab = 19$

6 What will be the coordinates of point A if you move triangle ABC three units to the right?

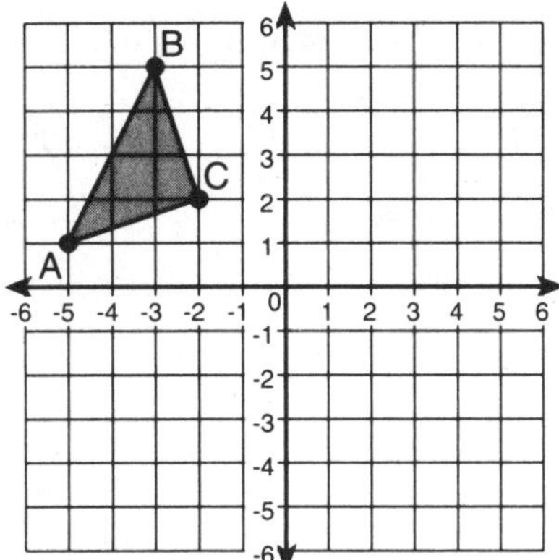

F (2, 1)

G (−2, 1)

H (3, 1)

J (−2, −1)

7 Samantha works for a construction company. Her job is to estimate the cost to build houses. One of the equations she uses is C = A x $60, where A is the area in square feet of the house and $60 is the average cost of construction per square foot. What do you think the C in the equation stands for?

A The company's estimate of the number of rooms in the house

B The cost per room of the house

C The product of the length and the width of the house

D The company's cost to build a house

8 If $5 < a$ and $a < b$, what should replace the $\square$ in the expression $b \square 5$?

F $<$

G $=$

H $>$

J $-$

9 What number must be subtracted from 8 to get a number x that is less than −2?

A a number greater than −2

B a number less than 10

C a number greater than 10

D a number between −2 and 8

10 What should replace n in the equation shown below?

$$\frac{5}{2} \times \frac{2}{n} = 1$$

F 1

G 15

H 2

J 5

11 Suppose that a and b are positive numbers and that $a < b$. What is always true about the ratio $(a \times 2) \div (b \times 2)$?

A The ratio is less than one.

B The ratio is more than one.

C The ratio is equal to one.

D The ratio is a negative number.

12 If $4y + 0 = 28$, then $y =$

F 32

G 7

H 24

J 6

ANSWER ROWS 5 Ⓐ Ⓑ Ⓒ Ⓓ 7 Ⓐ Ⓑ Ⓒ Ⓓ 9 Ⓐ Ⓑ Ⓒ Ⓓ 11 Ⓐ Ⓑ Ⓒ Ⓓ
6 Ⓕ Ⓖ Ⓗ Ⓙ 8 Ⓕ Ⓖ Ⓗ Ⓙ 10 Ⓕ Ⓖ Ⓗ Ⓙ 12 Ⓕ Ⓖ Ⓗ Ⓙ

E1

Gina bought 4 rolls of film. One roll can take 36 pictures. If Gina takes an average of 12 pictures a week, how long will the film last?

A (4 x 36) x 12 = ☐

B (4 ÷ 36) ÷ 12 = ☐

C (4 + 36) x 12 = ☐

D (4 x 36) ÷ 12 = ☐

E2

What is the area of a park with dimensions 48 yards by 100 yards?

F 4800 square yards

G 480 square yards

H 296 square yards

J 48,100 square yards

1 Rex studies an average of 2 hours each weekday night and 4 hours on the weekend. How long does he study each week?

A (5 x 2) + 4 = ☐

B (7 x 2) + 4 = ☐

C (5 x 4) + 2 = ☐

D 5 x (2 + 4) = ☐

2 When Caryl checked her savings account, she found she had $438.95. A week later, she withdrew $50 for the class trip. The following week, she put $65 in the bank she received for her birthday. How much money did she then have in the bank?

F $438.95 – ($50 + $65) = ☐

G $438.95 + ($50 + $65) = ☐

H $438.95 + $50 + $65 = ☐

J $438.95 – $50 + $65 = ☐

3 There are 36 inches in a yard and 1760 yards in a mile. Which of these would you use to find out how many inches were in half a mile?

A (1760 ÷ 0.5) x 36 = ☐

B (1760 x 0.5) x 36 = ☐

C 1760 x 36 = ☐ x 0.5

D (☐ x 0.5) x 36 = 1760

4 Which of these is about 150°?

F **G**

H **J**

5 What is the area of the *unshaded* portion of the figure below?

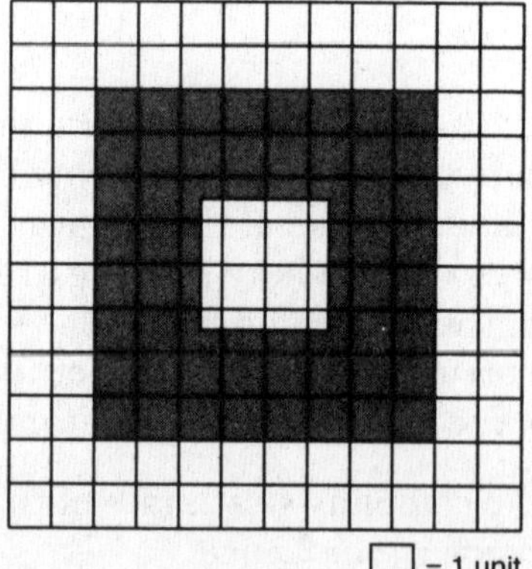

A 64 units

B 144 units

C 89 units

D 80 units

GO

The chart below shows the population, average income, and altitude (feet above sea level) of five different cities. Use the chart to answer numbers 6 through 8.

	Pop.	Average Income	Altitude (in feet)
Marshall	5190	$12,384	203
West Bend	10,905	$14,920	5590
Wingate	13,937	$19,375	2167
Bedford	6881	$11,934	4328
Harding	7933	$16,732	1642

6 Which of these is the approximate ratio of the average income in West Bend compared to that in Wingate?

F $\frac{5}{4}$

G $\frac{3}{4}$

H $\frac{1}{4}$

J $\frac{1}{2}$

7 If you went from Marshall to Bedford, how much would the altitude increase?

A 4125 feet

B 4531 feet

C 5387 feet

D 3125 feet

8 Which of these is the best estimate of the average population of the five towns?

F 14,000

G 6500

H 10,500

J 9000

9 What fraction of 5 pounds is 10 ounces?

A $\frac{1}{2}$

B $\frac{1}{5}$

C $\frac{1}{8}$

D $\frac{5}{16}$

10 Which of these is the greatest volume?

F 2500 milliliters

G 250 liters

H 250 milliliters

J 2.5 kiloliters

11 Which of these statements is true about points M and N?

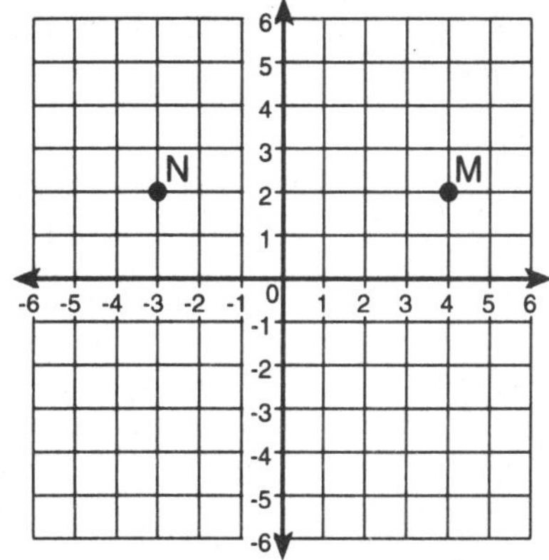

A They have the same x-coordinate.

B They have the same y-coordinate.

C They have the same x and y-coordinates.

D They both have negative x and negative y-coordinates.

12 What is the selling price of a pair of shoes if the merchant buys them for $18 and wants to sell them for 100% more?

F $35.00

G $9.00

H $118.00

J Not Given

GO

ANSWER ROWS 6 Ⓕ Ⓖ Ⓗ Ⓙ 8 Ⓕ Ⓖ Ⓗ Ⓙ 10 Ⓕ Ⓖ Ⓗ Ⓙ 12 Ⓕ Ⓖ Ⓗ Ⓙ
7 Ⓐ Ⓑ Ⓒ Ⓓ 9 Ⓐ Ⓑ Ⓒ Ⓓ 11 Ⓐ Ⓑ Ⓒ Ⓓ

13 Louise was shipping a present to her brother. The box was 15 inches long, 12 inches wide, and 3 inches high. She taped the box using the pattern shown below so the ends of the tape don't overlap. How much tape did she use?

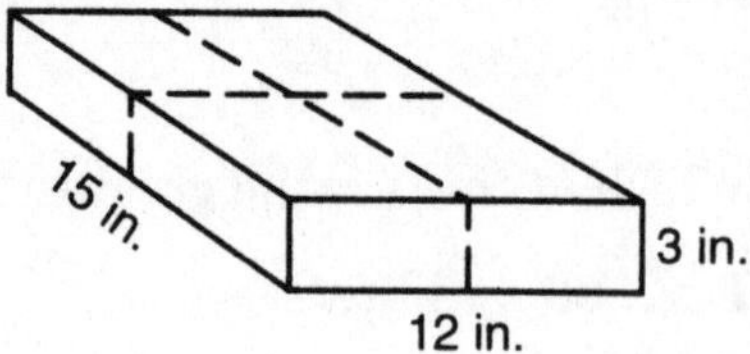

A 60 in.

B 30 in.

C 33 in.

D Not Given

14 If a = 5 and b = 4, what is the value of the expression below?

$$\frac{(4a + b)}{6} =$$

F 4

G 1.5

H 24

J Not Given

15 Doris looked at the thermometer one morning and saw it read –5°F. She knows that ice begins to melt at 32°F. Doris is going ice skating, but wants to stop before the ice begins to melt. How much must the temperature rise before Doris will have to stop skating?

A –27°F

B 27°F

C –39°F

D 37°F

16 A truck driver makes four trips a week. The distances of the trips are 1268 miles, 783 miles, 593 miles, and 1502 miles. What is the average distance he drives?

F 1136 miles

G 1136.5 miles

H 1036.5 miles

J Not Given

17 A jeweler bought 2 meters of gold chain. He used 70 centimeters for a necklace and 20 centimeters for a bracelet. How much gold chain did he have left?

A 1100 centimeters

B 1.1 meters

C 0.9 meters

D Not Given

18 What is the perimeter of the shaded shape inside the square below?

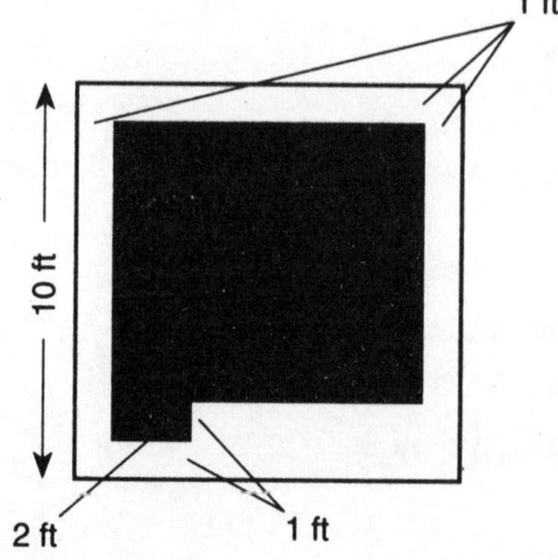

F 40 ft

G 32 ft

H 31 ft

J 36 ft

GO

19 Which statement is true about the figure shown below?

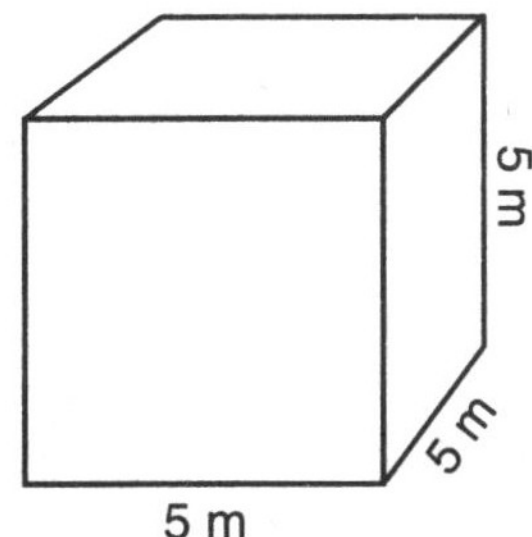

A The volume is 225 cubic meters.

B The area of each face of the cube is 15 square meters.

C The surface area is 150 square meters.

D The figure has a total of 5 faces.

20 For a school project, Ervin counted the number and kind of nuts in a can of mixed nuts. He found that there were 21 cashews, 6 Brazil nuts, 14 pecans, and 79 peanuts. If you shook the can of nuts and poured just one out, what are the odds it would be a Brazil nut?

F 6 out of 100

G 1 out of 20

H 6 out of 79

J 1 out of 60

21 How long is the rectangle shown below?

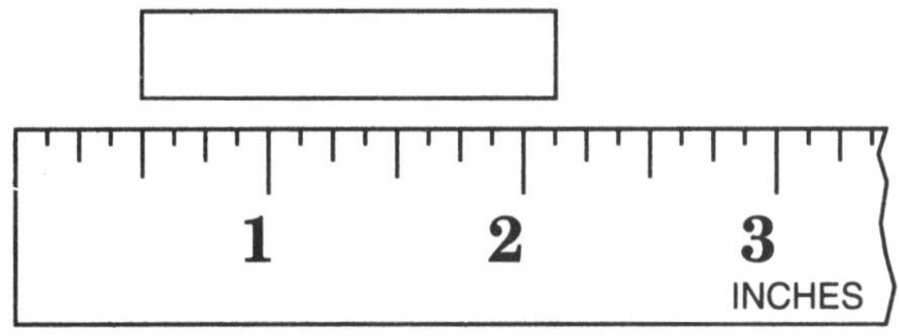

A $2\frac{1}{8}$ inches

B $2\frac{1}{2}$ inches

C $1\frac{1}{2}$ inches

D $1\frac{5}{8}$ inches

22 How much interest would you earn in 2 years on $500 in a savings account that paid 4.5% simple interest per year?

F $45.00

G $50.00

H $9.00

J $55.00

23 The Venn diagram below show[illegible] how many students in a class have a d[illegible] a cat, or a dog and a cat. How many [illegible]e students have a cat as a pet?

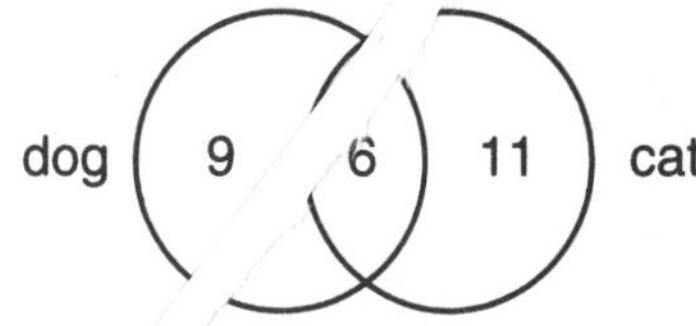

A 11

B 5

C [illegible]

D 17

24 Four friends spent the day rock climbing. The first one to begin climbing was Carmina and the last one was Washington. Cynthia began climbing 2 minutes before Washington, and Wyatt began climbing 4 minutes after Carmina. Washington started his climb 10 minutes after Carmina. Which of these statements about the group is true?

F The order in which they began climbing was Carmina first, then Cynthia, Wyatt, and Washington.

G Wyatt began climbing eight minutes before Washington.

H Four minutes passed from when Wyatt began climbing to when Cynthia began.

J Cynthia and Wyatt began climbing at the same time.

STOP

ANSWER ROWS 19 Ⓐ Ⓑ Ⓒ Ⓓ 21 Ⓐ Ⓑ Ⓒ Ⓓ 23 Ⓐ Ⓑ Ⓒ Ⓓ
20 Ⓕ Ⓖ Ⓗ Ⓙ 22 Ⓕ Ⓖ Ⓗ Ⓙ 24 Ⓕ Ⓖ Ⓗ Ⓙ

NUMBER RIGHT______

To the Student:

These tests will give you a chance to put the tips you have learned to work.

A few last reminders…

- Be sure you understand all the directions before you begin each test. You may ask the teacher questions about the directions if you do not understand them.
- Work as quickly as you can during each test.
- When you change an answer, be sure to erase your first mark completely.
- You can guess at an answer or skip difficult items and go back to them later.
- Use the tips you have learned whenever you can.
- It is OK to be a little nervous. You may even do better

Now that you have completed the lessons in this book, you are on your way to scoring high!

PART 1 CONCEPTS

E1 Ⓐ Ⓑ Ⓒ Ⓓ
E2 Ⓕ Ⓖ Ⓗ Ⓙ

1 Ⓐ Ⓑ Ⓒ Ⓓ
2 Ⓕ Ⓖ Ⓗ Ⓙ
3 Ⓐ Ⓑ Ⓒ Ⓓ
4 Ⓕ Ⓖ Ⓗ Ⓙ
5 Ⓐ Ⓑ Ⓒ Ⓓ
6 Ⓕ Ⓖ Ⓗ Ⓙ
7 Ⓐ Ⓑ Ⓒ Ⓓ
8 Ⓕ Ⓖ Ⓗ Ⓙ
9 Ⓐ Ⓑ Ⓒ Ⓓ
10 Ⓕ Ⓖ Ⓗ Ⓙ
11 Ⓐ Ⓑ Ⓒ Ⓓ
12 Ⓕ Ⓖ Ⓗ Ⓙ
13 Ⓐ Ⓑ Ⓒ Ⓓ
14 Ⓕ Ⓖ Ⓗ Ⓙ
15 Ⓐ Ⓑ Ⓒ Ⓓ
16 Ⓕ Ⓖ Ⓗ Ⓙ
17 Ⓐ Ⓑ Ⓒ Ⓓ
18 Ⓕ Ⓖ Ⓗ Ⓙ
19 Ⓐ Ⓑ Ⓒ Ⓓ
20 Ⓕ Ⓖ Ⓗ Ⓙ
21 Ⓐ Ⓑ Ⓒ Ⓓ
22 Ⓕ Ⓖ Ⓗ Ⓙ
23 Ⓐ Ⓑ Ⓒ Ⓓ
24 Ⓕ Ⓖ Ⓗ Ⓙ
25 Ⓐ Ⓑ Ⓒ Ⓓ
26 Ⓕ Ⓖ Ⓗ Ⓙ

PART 2 COMPUTATION

E1 Ⓐ Ⓑ Ⓒ Ⓓ Ⓔ
E2 Ⓕ Ⓖ Ⓗ Ⓙ Ⓚ

1 Ⓐ Ⓑ Ⓒ Ⓓ Ⓔ
2 Ⓕ Ⓖ Ⓗ Ⓙ Ⓚ
3 Ⓐ Ⓑ Ⓒ Ⓓ Ⓔ
4 Ⓕ Ⓖ Ⓗ Ⓙ Ⓚ
5 Ⓐ Ⓑ Ⓒ Ⓓ Ⓔ
6 Ⓕ Ⓖ Ⓗ Ⓙ Ⓚ
7 Ⓐ Ⓑ Ⓒ Ⓓ Ⓔ
8 Ⓕ Ⓖ Ⓗ Ⓙ Ⓚ
9 Ⓐ Ⓑ Ⓒ Ⓓ Ⓔ
10 Ⓕ Ⓖ Ⓗ Ⓙ Ⓚ
11 Ⓐ Ⓑ Ⓒ Ⓓ Ⓔ
12 Ⓕ Ⓖ Ⓗ Ⓙ Ⓚ
13 Ⓐ Ⓑ Ⓒ Ⓓ Ⓔ
14 Ⓕ Ⓖ Ⓗ Ⓙ Ⓚ
15 Ⓐ Ⓑ Ⓒ Ⓓ Ⓔ
16 Ⓕ Ⓖ Ⓗ Ⓙ Ⓚ
17 Ⓐ Ⓑ Ⓒ Ⓓ Ⓔ
18 Ⓕ Ⓖ Ⓗ Ⓙ Ⓚ
19 Ⓐ Ⓑ Ⓒ Ⓓ Ⓔ
20 Ⓕ Ⓖ Ⓗ Ⓙ Ⓚ
21 Ⓐ Ⓑ Ⓒ Ⓓ Ⓔ
22 Ⓕ Ⓖ Ⓗ Ⓙ Ⓚ

PART 3 APPLICATIONS

E1 Ⓐ Ⓑ Ⓒ Ⓓ
E2 Ⓕ Ⓖ Ⓗ Ⓙ

1 Ⓐ Ⓑ Ⓒ Ⓓ
2 Ⓕ Ⓖ Ⓗ Ⓙ
3 Ⓐ Ⓑ Ⓒ Ⓓ
4 Ⓕ Ⓖ Ⓗ Ⓙ
5 Ⓐ Ⓑ Ⓒ Ⓓ
6 Ⓕ Ⓖ Ⓗ Ⓙ
7 Ⓐ Ⓑ Ⓒ Ⓓ
8 Ⓕ Ⓖ Ⓗ Ⓙ
9 Ⓐ Ⓑ Ⓒ Ⓓ
10 Ⓕ Ⓖ Ⓗ Ⓙ
11 Ⓐ Ⓑ Ⓒ Ⓓ
12 Ⓕ Ⓖ Ⓗ Ⓙ
13 Ⓐ Ⓑ Ⓒ Ⓓ
14 Ⓕ Ⓖ Ⓗ Ⓙ
15 Ⓐ Ⓑ Ⓒ Ⓓ
16 Ⓕ Ⓖ Ⓗ Ⓙ
17 Ⓐ Ⓑ Ⓒ Ⓓ
18 Ⓕ Ⓖ Ⓗ Ⓙ
19 Ⓐ Ⓑ Ⓒ Ⓓ
20 Ⓕ Ⓖ Ⓗ Ⓙ
21 Ⓐ Ⓑ Ⓒ Ⓓ
22 Ⓕ Ⓖ Ⓗ Ⓙ
23 Ⓐ Ⓑ Ⓒ Ⓓ
24 Ⓕ Ⓖ Ⓗ Ⓙ
25 Ⓐ Ⓑ Ⓒ Ⓓ
26 Ⓕ Ⓖ Ⓗ Ⓙ
27 Ⓐ Ⓑ Ⓒ Ⓓ
28 Ⓕ Ⓖ Ⓗ Ⓙ
29 Ⓐ Ⓑ Ⓒ Ⓓ

Part 1 Concepts

E1	E2
Which of these decimals is equal to $\frac{7}{8}$? **A** 0.875 **B** 0.78 **C** 0.87 **D** 0.0875	What is the smallest number that can be divided evenly by 9 and 27? **F** 108 **G** 3 **H** 54 **J** 72

1 $\sqrt{121}$

A 12

B 11

C 21

D 19

2 The distance from Denver to Craig is 199 miles. From Craig to Grand junction is 153 miles. Which numbers would you use to estimate the distance from Denver to Grand Junction by going through Craig?

F 200 and 150

G 200 and 100

H 200 and 200

J 100 and 250

3 In the circle below, the shaded portion represents the percentage of students who passed a fitness test. What percentage did not pass the test?

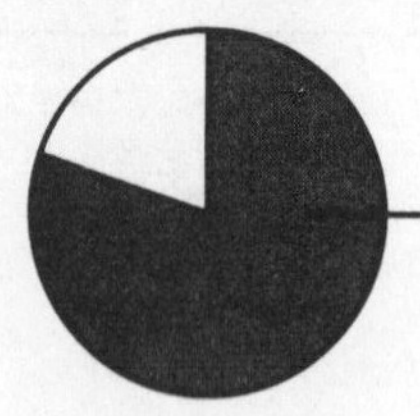

A 80%

B 30%

C 10%

D 20%

4 Which of these is another way to write 9.1005?

F (9 x 1) + (1 x 0.1) + (5 x 0.01)

G (9 x 0.1) + (1 x 0.1) + (5 x 0.0001)

H (9 x 1) + (1 x 0.1) + (5 x 0.0001)

J (9 x 1) + (1 x 0.001) + (5 x 0.0001)

5 Which of these number sentences can be used to find the number that is missing from the pattern below?

1, 5, 13, 29, ___, 125

A (13 + 29) = 42

B (29 x 2) + 3 = 61

C (125 ÷ 5) x 2 = 50

D (125 – 29) ÷ 2 = 48

6 Which arrow points most closely to $-1\frac{1}{8}$?

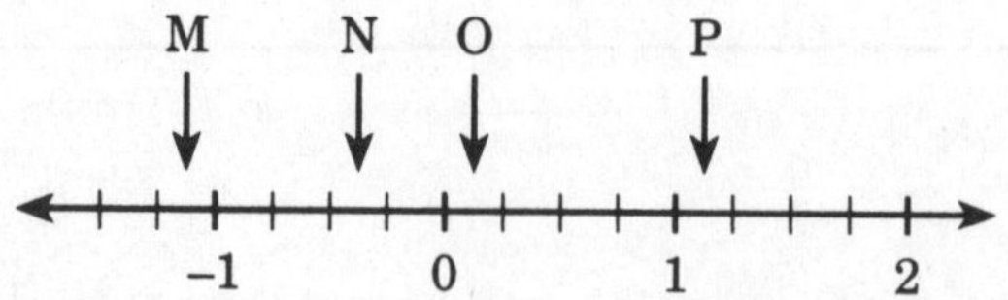

F N

G P

H M

J O

GO

7 $\frac{7}{12} = \frac{21}{\square}$

A 26

B 17

C 36

D 15

8 Which of these is 5,672,871 rounded to the nearest hundred thousand?

F 5,600,000

G 5,670,000

H 5,673,000

J 5,700,000

9 Which number sentence is <u>false</u>?

A −4 > 3

B −4 > −13

C 5 > −2

D 2 > 0

10 What number completes the number sentence below?

$$9 \times \square = 18 \times 30$$

F 2

G 60

H 15

J 3

11 How much would the value of 459,086 be decreased by replacing the 5 with a 4?

A 10,000

B 1000

C 100,000

D 100

12 What is the reciprocal of $\frac{2}{5}$?

F $\frac{5}{2}$

G 2.5

H 1

J

13 $3.91 \times 10^3 =$

A 0.391

B 391

C 39,001

D 3910

14 Which group of integers is in order from least to greatest?

F −5, 3, 0, −2 3

G 7, −5, 0, 1, 8

H −3, −2, 0, 5, 9

J 3, 4, −7, 8, −9

15 Paul went to the Post Office and found that stamps came in packages of 8 and envelopes came in packages of 6. What is the least number of each Paul can buy to have the same number of stamps and envelopes?

A 48

B 24

C 18

D 96

16 Emma stacked boxes of soap on a shelf so that there were 6 boxes in each stack. She had 3 boxes left over. Which of these coulc be the total number of boxes?

F 66

G 53

H 39

J 41

17 Which of these is not equal in value to the others?

A $\sqrt{64}$

B $\frac{48}{6}$

C $(11 - 7) \times 2$

D $1 + 3 \times 2$

18 Which of these is greater than the others?

F two and three eighths

G twenty-three hundredths

H two and eight hundredths

J two thirds

19 $6^4 =$

A $6 + 6 + 6 + 6$

B $6 \times 6 \times 6 \times 6$

C 6×4

D $4 \times 4 \times 4 \times 4 \times 4 \times 4 \times 4$

20 Nine hundred twelve thousand, fifty =

F 91,250

G 912

H 912,050

J 901,250

21 What is the value of the expression in the box below?

$$(10 - 4)^2 \div 12$$

A 7

B 3

C 0.5

D 4

22 Which is the best estimate of $4.89 \times 23\frac{8}{9}$?

F 4×24

G 5×24

H 4×23

J 5×23

23 How would you write 43% as a fraction?

A $\frac{4}{3}$

B $\frac{3}{4}$

C $\frac{40}{30}$

D $\frac{43}{100}$

24 Which gives the prime factors of 84?

F $3 \times 2 \times 2 \times 7$

G 12×7

H $3 \times 4 \times 7$

J $3 \times 2 \times 4 + 3$

25 What should replace the □ in the number sentence below?

$$35 \times \square = 0.035$$

A 10^3

B 10^{-4}

C 10^{-3}

D 10^0

26 While reading a book about science, Veronica came upon a formula that used "the absolute value of 100." Which of these is the absolute value of 100?

F 10

G 100

H 100^2

J -100

STOP

Part 2 Computation

E1

$-5 + 7 =$

A 3
B -3
C -2
D 12
E None of these

E2

$\frac{2}{3} \times 27 =$

F 54
G 18
H 9
J 16
K None of these

1

$14 - {}^{-}3 =$

A 11
B -17
C -11
D 16
E None of these

2

$4 \times (7 + 3) =$

F 31
G 40
H 30
J 19
K None of these

3

$32.7 - 17 =$

A 32.67
B 31.3
C 15.7
D 31
E None of these

4

$2^3 \div (12 - 8) =$

F 5 R3
G 5.75
H 4
J 2
K None of these

5

$\frac{5}{8} \times \frac{2}{5} =$

A $\frac{1}{4}$
B $\frac{1}{5}$
C $\frac{1}{40}$
D $\frac{1}{8}$
E None of these

6

$$\begin{array}{r} 278 \\ -\ 41 \\ \hline \end{array}$$

F 273
G 319
H 264
J 137
K None of these

7

$0.6\overline{)216}$

A 360
B 36
C 3.06
D 30.6
E None of these

8

$$\begin{array}{r} .516 \\ \times\ .625 \\ \hline \end{array}$$

F 32.35
G 0.3225
H 33.25
J 0.3335
K None of these

9

$$\begin{array}{r} \frac{9}{14} \\ -\ \frac{7}{14} \\ \hline \end{array}$$

A $\frac{2}{7}$
B 2
C $\frac{1}{7}$
D $\frac{2}{9}$
E None of these

10

$[51 - (15 \times 2)] \div 3 =$

F 47.5
G 41
H 10 R2
J 7
K None of these

GO

11 $\frac{5}{12} \div \frac{5}{6} =$

A $\frac{5}{12}$
B 2
C $\frac{1}{2}$
D $1\frac{2}{5}$
E None of these

12 65 is 20% of what number?

F 85
G 13
H 335
J 235
K None of these

13 $(20 - 11)(8 + 9) =$

A 26
B 163
C 9
D 153
E None of these

14 $\frac{-72}{-18}$

F 4
G 0.25
H −4
J 0.4
K None of these

15 $\frac{31}{40} + \frac{29}{40}$

A $1\frac{19}{40}$
B $1\frac{1}{2}$
C $2\frac{1}{10}$
D 2
E None of these

16 $4\frac{1}{5} \times \frac{4}{7} = \square$

F $4\frac{7}{20}$
G $4\frac{5}{12}$
H $7\frac{1}{2}$
J $2\frac{2}{5}$
K None of these

17 $\frac{(43 + 2) - 10}{5} =$

A 43
B 9
C 7
D −90
E None of these

18 $-23 - 8 =$

F −31
G 15
H −15
J 31
K None of these

19 $\frac{4}{100} \times \frac{3}{10} =$

A 12
B 0.12
C 0.012
D 1.2
E None of these

20 $505.7148 \div 8.395 =$

F 6.24
G 62.24
H 62.2425
J 60.024
K None of these

21 $9\frac{3}{4} + 10\frac{5}{8} =$

A $21\frac{3}{4}$
B $20\frac{3}{8}$
C 20
D $19\frac{3}{8}$
E None of these

22 $18.9 + 0.037 + 4.62 =$

F 22.999
G 23.999
H 23.89
J 23.557
K None of these

STOP

E1

On a camping trip, 4 students shared a tent with 1 teacher. How many students and teachers were there if they needed 22 tents?

A $(4 + 1) \times 22 = \square$

B $(4 \times 1) \times 22 = \square$

C $(4 + 1) \div 22 = \square$

D $(4 + 1) + 22 = \square$

E2

Joseph had 2 gallons of paint. He used 3 quarts to paint his closet. How much paint did he have left?

F 7 quarts

G 1 gallon and 2 quarts

H 5 pints

J Not Given

1 There are 8 windows in a house. Each window has 2 panes of glass. If it takes 3 minutes to clean one pane, how long will it take to clean all the windows?

A $3 \times 2 \div 8 = \square$

B $(3 + 2) \div 8 = \square$

C $3 \div 2 \div 8 = \square$

D $3 \times 2 \times 8 = \square$

2 Leon has $250.00 in his bank account. The account earns 4% interest a year. How much money will he have in his savings account at the end of a year?

F $\$250 \times .04 = \square$

G $\$250 + (\$250 \times .04) = \square$

H $\$250 \times (\$250 \times .04) = \square$

J $\$250 + \$250 + .04 = \square$

3 The gas tank in a car holds 20 gallons. It is now $\frac{1}{4}$ full. If gas costs $1.25 a gallon, how much will it cost to fill the tank?

A $20 \times \frac{1}{4} + \$1.25 = \square$

B $20 \div (\frac{3}{4} \times \$1.25) = \square$

C $\$1.25 \times (20 \times \frac{3}{4}) = \square$

D $\$1.25 \times \frac{1}{4} \times 20 = \square$

4 What is the median of the following set of numbers?

{3, 2, 2, 3, 2, 6}

F 2

G 6

H 3

J 4

5 What is the figure below called?

A an angle

B a line

C a ray

D a line segment

6 137 milliliters is the same as —

F 0.0137 liters

G 1.37 liters

H 0.137 liters

J 1370 liters

7 If $3x - 14 = 40$, then $x =$

A 15

B 8

C 18

D 12

GO

8 In the figure below, which pair of angles is complementary?

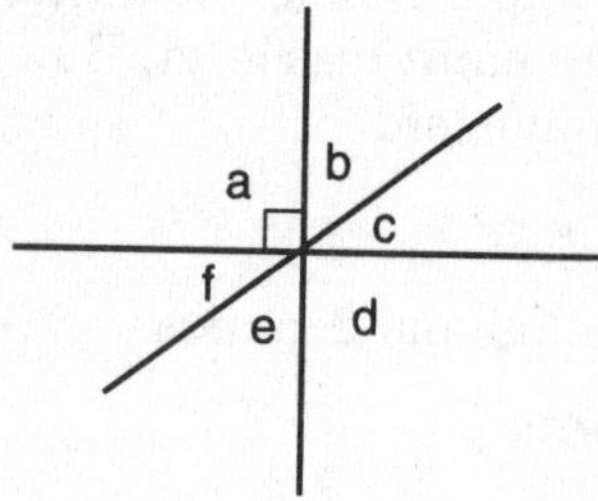

F a and b

G a and f

H b and d

J b and c

9 Suppose you had 15 coins that totaled $2.00. None of them are pennies and none are half-dollars. Which of these might you have?

A 10 dimes and 5 quarters

B 4 nickels, 5 dimes, and 4 quarters

C 5 nickels, 5 dimes, and 5 quarters

D 5 nickels, 4 dimes, and 6 quarters

10 Two out of five people who shop at a supermarket pay by check. If 175 people shop at the supermarket, how many of them pay by check?

F 70

G 150

H 140

J 35

11 What number must be added to 7 to get a number x that is less than -5 but greater than -10?

A a number greater than 16

B a number between -17 and -12

C a number between 0 and -9

D a number less than -17

The graph below shows the amount of money five students saved in two years. Use the graph to answer questions 12 through 14.

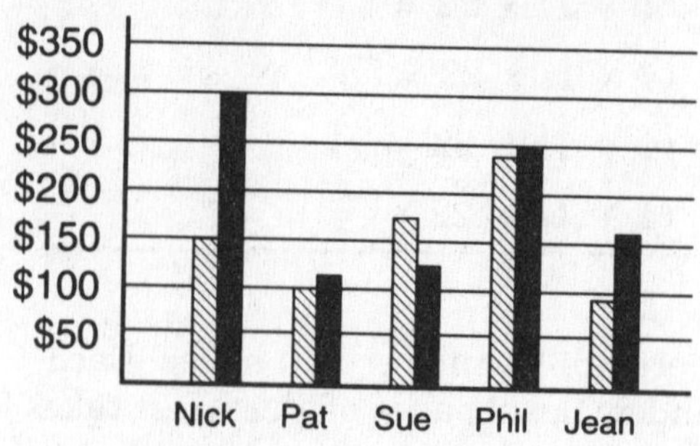

12 Which student's savings doubled from 1991 to 1992?

F Pat

G Jean

H Sue

J Not Given

13 Even though Pat didn't deposit any money in 1992, the amount of money she had in her account increased because of the interest she earned. About what rate of interest did she receive on her money?

A 30%

B 10%

C 3%

D 105%

14 Based on the graph, which student might have deposited $50 in January of 1992 and withdrawn $100 in April?

F Jean

G Nick

H Sue

J Phil

GO

15 The two figures below are congruent. Which is a pair of corresponding sides?

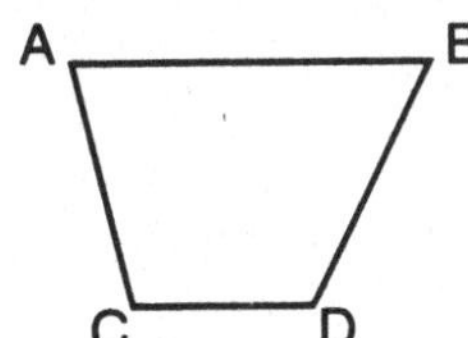

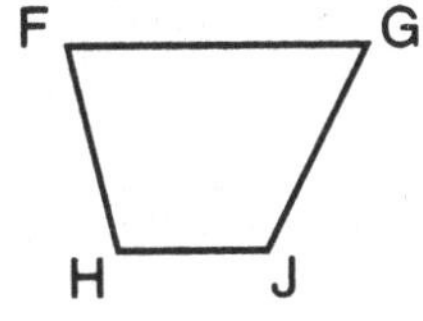

A AB and CD

B CD and HJ

C AC and GJ

D FG and FH

Read this passage, then answer questions 16 and 17.

The Monroes are building a fence around their yard. The yard is 52 feet wide and 64 feet long. The fence will be 5 feet high and will be made with boards that are 6 inches wide. There will be one gate in the fence, and it will be 4 feet wide.

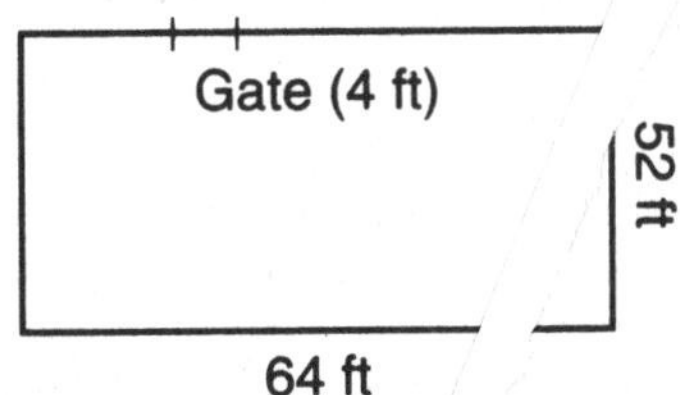

16 What is the total length of fence they must build, not counting the gate?

F 228 feet

G 16,640 feet

H 3328 feet

J 236 feet

17 The gate will be made out of the same kind of wood as the fence. How many boards will the Monroes need to build the gate? The boards are 10 feet long.

A 5

B 8

C 10

D 4

18 What will be the coordinates of point B if you move triangle ABC four units down?

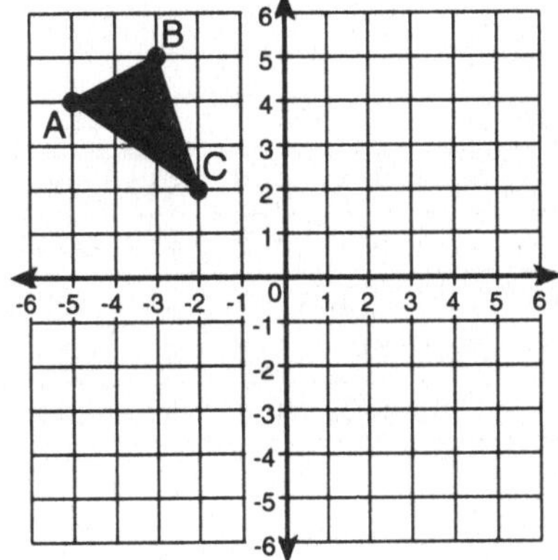

F (−7, 1)

G (−3, 5)

H (−3, 1)

J (−3, −5)

19 What fraction of 2 gallons is 10 pints?

A $\frac{1}{20}$

B $\frac{5}{8}$

C $\frac{5}{16}$

D $\frac{1}{5}$

20 For which of these equations would $a = 3$ when $b = 7$?

F $2a = b$

G $ab = 10$

H $2a + b = 15$

J $a^2 = b + 2$

21 If 5 workers can build 2 cars in an 8-hour shift, how long will it take 15 workers to build 36 cars?

A 48 hours

B 54 hours

C 6 hours

D 18 hours

The chart below shows the area, price, and down payment for different houses. Use the graph to answer questions 22 through 25.

	Area	Price	Down Payment
First Choice	1700 sq. ft.	$102,000	$12,000
Family	2000 sq. ft.	$120,000	$14,000
Haven	2500 sq. ft.	$150,000	$16,000
Executive	3000 sq. ft.	$210,000	$25,000
Royal	4000 sq. ft.	$280,000	$30,000

22 What is the price per square foot of the Haven model?

F $80 per square foot

G $50 per square foot

H $25 per square foot

J Not Given

23 What is the difference between the most and least expensive homes?

A $178,000

B $68,000

C $168,000

D $182,000

24 How much larger is the Executive model than the Haven model?

F 10%

G 20%

H 25%

J 30%

25 If you had $18,000 and wanted to buy the Royal home, how much more would you need to make the down payment?

A $12,000

B $30,000

C $22,000

D $8000

26 In the triangle below, angle MNO is a right angle. If angle MON equals 30°, what is the measure of angle NMO?

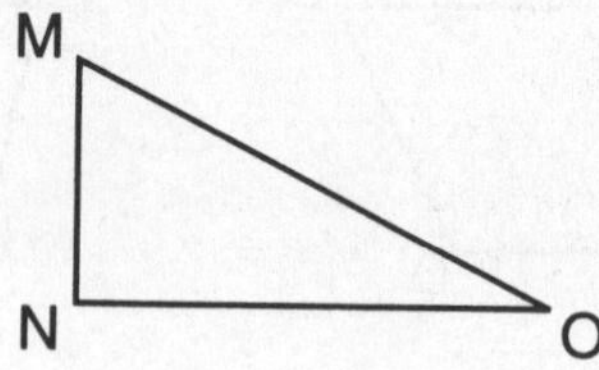

F 40°

G 45°

H 60°

J 70°

27 Woody wants to send 6 gifts to his family in Indiana. Each gift weighs $2\frac{1}{4}$ pounds. How much do the gifts weigh all together?

A $12\frac{1}{4}$

B $13\frac{1}{2}$

C $12\frac{1}{2}$

D $13\frac{1}{4}$

28 At a family reunion in the Southwest, there were 42 people from Colorado, 28 from New Mexico, 17 from Utah, and 3 from Arizona. If you began speaking to one of the people without knowing where the person was from, what are the chances the person would be from Colorado?

F 7 out of 15

G 21 out of 50

H 6 out of 15

J 21 out of 40

29 A standard paperback book is about —

A 10 in. by 12 in.

B 2 in. by 4 in.

C 8 in. by 16 in.

D 4 in. by 7 in.

STOP

Answer Keys

Reading
Unit 1,
Vocabulary
Lesson 1
A C
B F
1 A
2 J
3 B
4 H
5 D
6 F
7 B
8 H
Lesson 2
A D
B H
1 D
2 G
3 A
4 H
5 C
6 G
7 D
Lesson 3
A C
B F
1 B
2 F
3 D
4 H
5 D
6 H
7 A
8 G
Lesson 4
A D
B F
1 B
2 F
3 D
4 H
5 A
Lesson 5
A B
B J
1 B
2 F
3 C
4 J
5 A
6 H
Lesson 6
A C
B G
1 A
2 G
3 D
4 J
5 A
Lesson 7
E1 D
E2 F
1 C
2 F
3 B
4 J
5 B
6 F
7 D
8 H
9 C
10 F
11 D
12 F
13 B
14 G
15 C
16 J
17 A
18 H
19 B
20 F
21 D
22 F
23 C
24 F
25 B
26 G
27 D
28 H
29 C
30 F
31 C
32 G
33 B
34 J
Unit 2, Reading
Comprehension
Lesson 8
A D
1 C
2 J
3 A
Lesson 9
A B
1 B
2 F
3 D
4 H
5 D
6 H
7 A
8 H
9 A
10 J
11 B
12 J
13 B
Lesson 10
A B
1 D
2 G
3 A
4 G
5 C
6 H
7 A
8 G
9 D
10 F
11 B
12 H
13 A
14 J
15 B
16 F
17 C
18 G
19 D
20 F
21 B
22 J
Lesson 11
E1 C
1 A
2 J
3 A
4 J
5 C
6 G
7 C
8 J
9 B
10 F
11 C
12 J
13 B
14 F
15 C
16 F
17 B
18 J
19 A
20 J
21 B
22 H
23 C
24 H
25 A
26 J
27 B
28 G
29 A
30 H
31 B
32 H
33 A
Unit 3, Test Practice
Part 1
E1 D
E2 H
1 C
2 G
3 C
4 F
5 B
6 J
7 A
8 H
9 A
10 J

11	A
12	H
13	C
14	J
15	A
16	H
17	B
18	G
19	D
20	G
21	D
22	G
23	C
24	H
25	D
26	G
27	A
28	G
29	D
30	G
31	D
32	G
33	C
34	F

Test Practice
Part 2

E1	C
1	A
2	J
3	C
4	G
5	D
6	F
7	D
8	H
9	C
10	F
11	D
12	G
13	B
14	J
15	C
16	F
17	C
18	F
19	D
20	F
21	C
22	J
23	B
24	H
25	A
26	J
27	A
28	H
29	A
30	J
31	B
32	F
33	D
34	G
35	C

Language
Unit 1, Language
Mechanics
Lesson 1

A	A
B	J
1	B
2	J
3	A
4	H
5	B
6	F
7	B
8	F
9	D
10	H
11	C
12	F
13	D
14	J
15	B
16	H
17	A

Lesson 2

A	C
B	J
1	A
2	H
3	D
4	G
5	C
6	J
7	B
8	F
9	D
10	H
11	B
12	J
13	A
14	H
15	B
16	F
17	C
18	J
19	A
20	G

Lesson 3

E1	D
1	A
2	H
3	B
4	J
5	D
6	F
7	B
8	F
9	D
10	F
11	C
12	G
13	D
14	J
15	A
16	H
17	A
18	G
19	D
20	H
21	A
22	J
23	A
24	H
25	B
26	H
27	C
28	G
29	D

Unit 2, Language
Expression
Lesson 4

A	A
B	J
1	C
2	G
3	A
4	J
5	B
6	F
7	D
8	G
9	C
10	F
11	C
12	H
13	B
14	F
15	D
16	H
17	D
18	G
19	C
20	F

Lesson 5

A	A
B	H
C	D
1	A
2	H
3	B
4	H
5	B
6	J
7	C
8	F
9	D
10	G
11	B
12	J
13	A
14	J
15	A

Lesson 6

A	D
1	C
2	F
3	C
4	F
5	B
6	J
7	C
8	G
9	D
10	F
11	B
12	J
13	A
14	H

Lesson 7

E1	C
1	B
2	F
3	D
4	H
5	B
6	F
7	C
8	H
9	B
10	J
11	B
12	F

13 A
14 J
15 B
16 H
17 B
18 J
19 C
20 F

Unit 3, Spelling
Lesson 8

A B
B H
1 B
2 H
3 D
4 G
5 A
6 G
7 D
8 F
9 A
10 K
11 D
12 H
13 B
14 H
15 A
16 J
17 B
18 G

Lesson 9

E1 D
E2 F
1 A
2 G
3 C
4 H
5 A
6 J
7 B
8 H
9 B
10 J
11 D
12 H
13 A
14 J
15 C
16 F
17 A
18 G
19 B
20 J

Unit 4, Study Skills
Lesson 10

A B
1 C
2 F
3 C
4 F
5 C
6 J
7 A
8 G

Lesson 11

E1 C
E2 F
1 C
2 F
3 D
4 J
5 D
6 G
7 A
8 H
9 B
10 J
11 C
12 F
13 C
14 G
15 B
16 F

Unit 5, Test Practice
Part 1

E1 C
1 C
2 G
3 D
4 F
5 D
6 F
7 B
8 H
9 A
10 H
11 D
12 F
13 B
14 J
15 B
16 H
17 A
18 F
19 B
20 J
21 C

Test Practice
Part 2

E1 D
1 D
2 G
3 B
4 J
5 B
6 H
7 B
8 G
9 A
10 J
11 C
12 H
13 A
14 H
15 D
16 G
17 D
18 H
19 B
20 F

Test Practice
Part 3

E1 A
E2 J
1 B
2 H
3 A
4 F
5 D
6 G
7 C
8 F
9 [illegible]
10 [illegible]
11 E
12 H
13 A
14 G
15 A
16 J
17 B
18 F
19 C
20 F

Test Practice
Part 4

E1 D
1 A
2 J
3 B
4 H
5 C
6 F
7 D
8 H
9 D
10 G
11 D

Math
Unit 1, Concepts
Lesson 1

A B
B J
1 B
2 F
3 D
4 H
5 B
6 H
7 A
8 J
9 B
10 H
11 A
12 J
13 B
14 [illegible]
15 [illegible]

Lesson 2

A 4
B 1
1 4
2 2
3 1
4 2
5 3
6 4
7 3
8 3
9 1
10 2
11 1
12 2
13 3

Lesson 3

A D
B F
1 C
2 F
3 A
4 G
5 D
6 H

7 D
8 F
9 B
10 G
11 A
12 G
13 D
14 G
15 C

Lesson 4

E1 A
E2 H
1 B
2 F
3 B
4 J
5 A
6 G
7 C
8 G
9 C
10 J
11 A
12 J
13 A
14 H
15 B
16 H

Unit 2, Computation

Lesson 5

A E
B G
1 B
2 J
3 C
4 F
5 E
6 F
7 C
8 G
9 C
10 G
11 E
12 F
13 D
14 H
15 D
16 G
17 A
18 F

Lesson 6

A C
B J
1 D
2 H
3 E
4 F
5 B
6 J
7 A
8 G
9 E
10 G
11 C
12 F
13 D
14 G
15 C
16 J
17 E
18 F
19 D

Lesson 7

A C
B K
1 A
2 J
3 E
4 G
5 C
6 F
7 D
8 G
9 C
10 J
11 A
12 G
13 E
14 J
15 B
16 H
17 A
18 K
19 D

Lesson 8

A 4
B 1
1 2
2 3
3 1
4 4
5 2
6 3
7 2
8 1
9 1
10 3
11 2
12 2
13 3
14 1
15 4
16 1
17 3
18 4
19 3
20 2

Lesson 9

E1 E
E2 F
1 D
2 F
3 E
4 G
5 D
6 K
7 B
8 F
9 D
10 F
11 A
12 G
13 E
14 J
15 B
16 H
17 E
18 G
19 D
20 F
21 D
22 H

Unit 3, Applications

Lesson 10

A D
1 D
2 F
3 C
4 G
5 C
6 F
7 D
8 G
9 B
10 H
11 D
12 H
13 A
14 G
15 D
16 H
17 B
18 F
19 D
20 H

Lesson 11

A C
1 A
2 H
3 B
4 J
5 C
6 J
7 A
8 J
9 B
10 H
11 A
12 G
13 D
14 H

Lesson 12

A 2
B 4
1 4
2 2
3 1
4 2
5 4
6 2
7 1
8 4
9 3
10 2
11 3
12 4
13 1
14 3
15 2
16 4
17 3
18 1
19 2
20 1
21 4
22 2
23 1
24 2

Lesson 13	
A	A
B	H
1	B
2	J
3	A
4	H
5	A
6	G
7	D
8	H
9	C
10	J
11	A
12	G
Lesson 14	
E1	D
E2	F
1	A
2	J
3	B
4	J
5	C
6	G
7	A
8	J
9	C
10	J
11	B
12	J
13	D
14	F
15	D
16	H
17	B
18	G
19	C
20	G
21	D
22	F
23	D
24	H
Unit 4, Test Practice	
Part 1	
E1	A
E2	H
1	B
2	F
3	D
4	H
5	B
6	H
7	C
8	J
9	A
10	G
11	A
12	F
13	D
14	H
15	B
16	H
17	D
18	F
19	B
20	H
21	B
22	G
23	D
24	F
25	C
26	G
Test Practice	
Part 2	
E1	E
E2	G
1	E
2	G
3	C
4	J
5	A
6	K
7	A
8	G
9	C
10	J
11	C
12	K
13	D
14	F
15	B
16	J
17	C
18	F
19	C
20	K
21	B
22	J
Test Practice	
Part 3	
E1	A
E2	J
1	D
2	G
3	C
4	F
5	D
6	H
7	C
8	J
9	C
10	F
11	B
12	J
13	B
14	H
15	B
16	F
17	D
18	H
19	B
20	J
21	A
22	J
23	A
24	G
25	A
26	H
27	B
28	F
29	D

Reading Progress Chart

Circle your score for each lesson. Connect your scores to see how well you are doing.

Unit 1	Lesson 1	8, 7, 6, 5, 4, 3, 2, 1
	Lesson 2	7, 6, 5, 4, 3, 2, 1
	Lesson 3	8, 7, 6, 5, 4, 3, 2, 1
	Lesson 4	5, 4, 3, 2, 1
	Lesson 5	6, 5, 4, 3, 2, 1
	Lesson 6	5, 4, 3, 2, 1
	Lesson 7	34, 33, 32, 31, 30, 29, 28, 27, 26, 25, 24, 23, 22, 21, 20, 19, 18, 17, 16, 15, 14, 13, 12, 11, 10, 9, 8, 7, 6, 5, 4, 3, 2, 1
Unit 2	Lesson 8	3, 2, 1
	Lesson 9	13, 12, 11, 10, 9, 8, 7, 6, 5, 4, 3, 2, 1
	Lesson 10	22, 21, 20, 19, 18, 17, 16, 15, 14, 13, 12, 11, 10, 9, 8, 7, 6, 5, 4, 3, 2, 1
	Lesson 11	33, 32, 31, 30, 29, 28, 27, 26, 25, 24, 23, 22, 21, 20, 19, 18, 17, 16, 15, 14, 13, 12, 11, 10, 9, 8, 7, 6, 5, 4, 3, 2, 1

Language Progress Chart

Circle your score for each lesson. Connect your scores to see how well you are doing.

Unit 1 Lesson 1	Lesson 2	Lesson 3	Unit 2 Lesson 4	Lesson 5	Lesson 6	Lesson 7	Unit 3 Lesson 8	Lesson 9	Unit 4 Lesson 10	Lesson 11
17	20	29	20	15	14	20	18	20	8	16
16	19	28	19	14	13	19	17	19	7	15
15	18	27	18	13	12	18	16	18	6	14
14	17	26	17	12	11	17	15	17	5	13
13	16	25	16	11	10	16	14	16	4	12
12	15	24	15	10	9	15	13	15	3	11
11	14	23	14	9	8	14	12	14	2	10
10	13	22	13	8	7	13	11	13	1	9
9	12	21	12	7	6	12	10	12		8
8	11	20	11	6	5	11	9	11		7
7	10	19	10	5	4	10	8	10		6
6	9	18	9	4	3	9	7	9		5
5	8	17	8	3	2	8	6	8		4
4	7	16	7	2	1	7	5	7		3
3	6	15	6	1		6	4	6		2
2	5	14	5			5	3	5		1
1	4	13	4			4	2	4		
	3	12	3			3	1	3		
	2	11	2			2		2		
	1	10	1			1		1		
		9								
		8								
		7								
		6								
		5								
		4								
		3								
		2								
		1								

Math Progress Chart

Circle your score for each lesson. Connect your scores to see how well you are doing.

Unit 1 Lesson 1	Lesson 2	Lesson 3	Lesson 4	Unit 2 Lesson 5	Lesson 6	Lesson 7	Lesson 8	Lesson 9	Unit 3 Lesson 10	Lesson 11	Lesson 12	Lesson 13	Lesson 14
											24		24
											23		23
								22			22		22
								21			21		21
							20	20	20		20		20
					19	19	19	19	19		19		19
				18	18	18	18	18	18		18		18
				17	17	17	17	17	17		17		17
			16	16	16	16	16	16	16		16		16
15		15	15	15	15	15	15	15	15		15		15
14		14	14	14	14	14	14	14	14	14	14		14
13	13	13	13	13	13	13	13	13	13	13	13		13
12	12	12	12	12	12	12	12	12	12	12	12	12	12
11	11	11	11	11	11	11	11	11	11	11	11	11	11
10	10	10	10	10	10	10	10	10	10	10	10	10	10
9	9	9	9	9	9	9	9	9	9	9	9	9	9
8	8	8	8	8	8	8	8	8	8	8	8	8	8
7	7	7	7	7	7	7	7	7	7	7	7	7	7
6	6	6	6	6	6	6	6	6	6	6	6	6	6
5	5	5	5	5	5	5	5	5	5	5	5	5	5
4	4	4	4	4	4	4	4	4	4	4	4	4	4
3	3	3	3	3	3	3	3	3	3	3	3	3	3
2	2	2	2	2	2	2	2	2	2	2	2	2	2
1	1	1	1	1	1	1	1	1	1	1	1	1	1

Additional Post Test Answers

Comprehension – Answer Key

COMPREHENSION PUZZLE

Complete each of these sentences. Put one letter in each box. Then follow the directions at the bottom of this page. (Reviewing the skills on page 1 or the outside back cover will help you find the right words.)

1. You can use the ______ to help you find the meaning of an unknown word. — CONTEXT
2. Details in a story add up to the ______. — MAIN IDEA
3. To ______ an outcome is to tell how you think a story will end. — PREDICT
4. A ______ is a person in a story. — CHARACTER
5. A cause leads to an ______. — EFFECT
6. When the meaning is not stated directly, you must make an ______. — INFERENCE
7. The order in which events occur is their ______. — SEQUENCE
8. To draw a ______ is to figure something out. — CONCLUSION

Write the circled letters in order here. If you did the page correctly you'll end up with the word for what you've been practicing as you read the selections in this book.

COMPREHENSION

Vocabulary – Answer Key

Unit 1

A.
1. succotash
2. converge
3. realist
4. cohesion
5. regarded
6. familiarize
7. fractional
8. marathon
9. abnormal
10. scribes
11. abdicated
12. collage

B.
1. d
2. e
3. f
4. j
5. h
6. g
7. b
8. i
9. a
10. l
11. c
12. k

C.
1. b
2. a
3. b
4. a
5. b

D.
1. camellia
2. propel
3. customary
4. rationalize
5. suite
6. intricate
7. controversy
8. adorn
9. impression
10. boycott
11. clique

Unit 2

A.
1. casual
2. continuous
3. clause
4. agitated
5. preceded
6. manner
7. latter
8. taut
9. inferred
10. instantaneous
11. misshape

B.
1. g
2. f
3. a
4. h
5. c
6. b
7. d
8. e

C.
1. pessimism
2. adopt
3. insipid
4. negligence
5. impulsive
6. adapt
7. proclaimed
8. leisurely
9. lamented
10. resilient

D.
1. effect
2. dessert
3. modest
4. disinterested
5. council
6. hordes
7. personal
8. jested
9. harmonious
10. hostility
11. inhabits

Unit 3

1. D
2. E
3. C
4. H
5. B
6. F
7. D
8. F
9. A
10. G

Vocabulary Puzzle

1. wetland
2. bound base
3. borrowed
4. superpower
5. context
6. passive
7. optimism
8. major
9. uninterested
10. homograph
11. theorize

When I use a word, it means just what I choose it to mean—neither more nor less.

Grammar– Answer Key

PARTS OF SPEECH
Lesson 23

1. deer's
2. scarves'
3. brothers'-in-law
4. She
5. Her
6. Many
7. her
8. Which
9. went, have/has gone, had gone
10. sat, have/has sat, had sat
11. is flying, were flying
12. are winning, was winning
13. The cold loudly fiercly that wintry
14. Later white quietly the frozen
15. growing shining
16. dampened
17. to garden
18. Gardening relaxing
19. *adj*
20. *av*
21. *prep*
22. *conj*
23. *pro*
24. *n* (infinitive)
25. *adj.*
26. *n* (gerund)
27. *n*
28. *conj*
29. *adv*
30. *lv*

SENTENCE STRUCTURE
Lesson 34

1. churches have
2. statues sit
3. Have you seen
4. (You) look
5. vegetable
6. delicious
7. leafy
8. is chard
9. salads flavor
10. of that hedge (adjective)
11. below the upper branches (adverb)
12. F
13. R
14. S
15. The Chinese had printed books
16. books became common
17. more people learned how to read
18. Would the world be different
19. fight
20. squeezes

FINAL TEST

1. B
2. G
3. D
4. E
5. D
6. E
7. A
8. F
9. A
10. G
11. D
12. E
13. A
14. E
15. C
16. G
17. A
18. F
19. C
20. F

ACTIVITIES

A. 1. predicate adjective
2. adjective
3. action verbs
4. noun
5. predicate adjective
(Note that the sentence is inverted; The borograves were all mimsy)
6. noun
7. conjunction
8. noun (if raths is seen as a verb); adjective (if raths is seen as a noun)

B. *Answers may vary. Following are some examples.*
1. Chris has finished the job on time.
2. Chris is on the job again.
3. Chris has been on the job on time.
4. Chris has been talking to himself again.
5. Chris found talking to himself was boring.
6. Chris found talking books in the closet.
7. Chris has finished dancing in the closet.

Capitalization & Punctuation – Answer Key

CAPITALIZATION
Lesson 7

A. *Students should have capitalized the following words:*

1. Aztec Indian Mexico

2. Pacific Ocean Gulf of Mexico

3. Aztec Tenochtitlan

4. Lake Texcoco

5. Spaniards Mexico

6. February Hernando Cortes Aztec

7. Tenochtitlan November

8. Montezuma Aztec

9. Aztecs June Spaniards

10. May Cortes August Aztec

B. *Students should have circled the following words:*

11. Europe

12. Asia Africa Americas

13. Sir Edmund P. Hillary New Zealand

14. May Mount Everest Himalaya Range

15. Sierra Club of North America

C. *Students should have written these sentences, using capital letters as shown:*

16. Edna St. Vincent Millay was an American poet.

17. She was born in Rockland, Maine, in 1892.

18. She was graduated from Vassar College in 1917.

19. In 1920, she published a book entitled *A Few Figs from Thistles.*

20. Another book, *Conversations at Midnight,* contains poems about World War II.

PUNCTUATION
Lesson 20

A. *Students should have added end marks as shown:*

1. Ducks have webbed feet, don't they?

2. Loons also have webbed feet.

3. Look! What a beautiful loon!

B. *Students should have punctuated the following name and address as shown:*

4. Mr. P. D. Ferndale

5. 9 E. Forest Ave.

6. Chicago, IL

C. *Students should have punctuated the following letter as shown:*

7. April 16, 1985

8. Dear Mr. Ferndale:

9. Enclosed is my check for two tickets to the 8:30 P. M. Pink Mink concert.

10. Yours truly,

D. *Students should have punctuated the following sentences as shown:*

11. The Liberty Bell, America's most famous bell, is in Philadelphia, Pennsylvania.

12. On July 8, 1776, it rang for the first time, and it was rung every July 8 until 1835.

13. As it rang, the bell cracked.

14. The crack hasn't ever been repaired.

15. However, the bell has been struck on on a few special occasions since.

16. The inscription on it says, "Proclaim liberty throughout the land unto all the inhabitants thereof."

17. It has been known by these three names: the Old State Bell, the Bell of the Revolution, and Old Independence.

18. In fact, it wasn't called the Liberty Bell until 1839.

19. The bell is made of iron, tin, and copper.

20. Kevin, have you read The Liberty Bell, a book about this bell?

Capitalization & Punctuation – Answer Key

FINAL TEST

1. D	**6.** G	**11.** C	**16.** F
2. G	**7.** A	**12.** E	**17.** A
3. A	**8.** H	**13.** B	**18.** F
4. E	**9.** C	**14.** E	**19.** D
5. B	**10.** E	**15.** A	**20.** G

ACTIVITIES

Answers will vary. Check that students have used capital letters and punctuation marks correctly. Punctuation marks are shown or noted.

Suggested Extension: *Have each student make a photocopy of his or her completed page to create a class yearbook. If possible, have each student could make enough copies for the entire class, allowing each student to have his or her own yearbook.*

Yearbook · 198_

A record of (apostrophe needed) ______ class at ______
teacher's name — name of school

Paste your photo here.

Background Information

Name: ______
first — middle — last

Birthdate: (commas needed) ______
day — month — date — year

Time of Birth: (colon needed) ______ A. M. *or* P. M.
hour — minute — before or after noon

Place of Birth: (comma needed) ______ , ______
city — state

Personal Interests

- The three television programs I enjoy most are ______ , ______ , and ______ .
- My favorite book, ______ , was written by ______ .
- The place I would most like to visit is ______ , and the person I would most like to meet is ______ .

Predictions

- If I become famous, my picture will be on the cover of (underline needed) ______ ; the accompanying story will tell how I ______ .
- If I meet a classmate twenty years from now, he or she will probably say, " ______ ."
- I will celebrate New Year's Day in the year 2000 by ______ .

Standard Usage – Answer Key

VERBS
Lesson 11

1. make
2. makes
3. prints
4. is
5. are
6. has
7. is
8. has
9. are
10. Do
11. paid
12. bought
13. came
14. brought
15. did
16. became
17. cut
18. known
19. made
20. written

PRONOUNS/WORD CHOICE
Lesson 20

1. It
2. their
3. themselves
4. its
5. her
6. they
7. You and I
8. them
9. beautiful
10. beautifully
11. well
12. good
13. stronger
14. better
15. most easily
16. an
17. ever
18. anything
19. Whose
20. accepted

FINAL TEST

1. A
2. H
3. D
4. E
5. D
6. G
7. D
8. G
9. B
10. E
11. C
12. H
13. B
14. G
15. A
16. G
17. D
18. F
19. B
20. G

ACTIVITIES

Riddle Look at this group of words. As you study it, can you find why it's unusual? In fact, it is so uncommon that your probability of finding a group similar to it is about a million to two. Why is it so unusual?

It (1) doesn't (2) have (3) any (4) of the (5) most commonly (6) written (7) letter, (8) which (9) is *e*. (10)